The
Heavens
Are Weeping

Geo. R. Browder

THE
HEAVENS
ARE WEEPING

The Diaries
of George Richard Browder
1852–1886

Edited by Richard L. Troutman

ZONDERVAN PUBLISHING HOUSE • GRAND RAPIDS, MICHIGAN

To the memory of my college history teacher
Dr. Frieda A. Gillette,
and to the thousands of young men and women
whom I have had the high privilege
of teaching during the past twenty-nine years.

THE HEAVENS ARE WEEPING
Copyright © 1987 by Richard L. Troutman

Judith Markham Books are published by
The Zondervan Corporation
1415 Lake Drive, S.E.
Grand Rapids, MI 49506

Library of Congress Cataloging in Publication Data

Browder, George Richard, 1827–1886.
The heavens are weeping.

"A Judith Markham book."
1. Browder, George Richard, 1827–1886—Diaries.
2. United States—History—Civil War, 1861–1865—Personal narratives.
3. Kentucky—History—Civil War, 1861–1865—Personal narratives.
4. Methodist Church—Kentucky—Clergy—Diaries.
5. Kentucky—Biography. I. Troutman, Richard L. II. Title.
E601.B875   1987   973.7'82   87-6269
ISBN 0-310-43810-1

Printed in the United States of America

87 88 89 90 91 92 / DC / 10 9 8 7 6 5 4 3 2 1

Contents

Illustrations

Preface

Only rarely in life does the apparently insignificant become unforgettable. Such a moment occurred in my life one morning in October 1974 when Susan Riley, a freshman from Olmstead in Logan County, Kentucky, came up to me after an American history class and said, with a touch of shyness mixed with pride, "Dr. T., would you like to see my great-great-grandfather's diaries?" I told her I'd be delighted. A few days later, after discussing the matter with her father, David, and her paternal aunt, Elizabeth, Susan brought me two of the journals.

The first thing that caught my eye about the diaries was their timeworn condition. They had obviously been read and reread many times by Browder's descendants. It wasn't long before I understood why.

With candor and literary beauty, George Dick (as he is affectionately remembered) described his daily existence, not just the dramatic moments (a brush with death in a carriage accident, a camp meeting interrupted by drunkards, a fire in his stable, the death of his beloved slave girl), but the mundane (selling watermelons, catching frogs, gathering apples, waging war on potato bugs, reading to his children and slaves, and just plain "piddling about"). Susan Riley had introduced me to a remarkably rich and compelling document written by an intelligent and perceptive person.

My adventure with George Richard Browder had begun.

*   *   *

George Dick began keeping a journal in 1846, the year he accepted his first appointment as a Methodist preacher, and with the exception of two or three lapses, he continued to make almost daily entries until shortly before his death in 1886. Regrettably, eight volumes are lost, five before 1852, and those covering parts of 1861–62, 1871–72, and 1879–80. Nevertheless, fifteen handwritten copybooks, containing more than 2300 pages, remain as an eloquent witness to an exciting era.

It is little short of a miracle that any of the diaries have come down to us. George Dick willed them to his wife, Lizzie, who in turn passed them along to their youngest son, Wallace. Time and indifference took their toll. Sometime during the 1920s Wallace sold his father's farm, and after a short stay in Alabama, he returned to Olmstead to live with his brother-in-law, C. W. Roach, whose farm lay about a half mile from George Dick's. Some of the diaries may have disappeared during these moves. Those that survived wound up in the loft of a small weather-beaten frame storage shed on the Roach place. There, during the 1930s, Susan Riley's uncle Walker, then a teenager, discovered the neglected volumes and took them home to his mother, the late Helen Roach Riley, a granddaughter of George Dick. Since that time the journals have been in good hands. Mrs. Riley's deep attachment to them passed on to her daughter, Elizabeth, who for the past eighteen years has been a faithful guardian of George Dick's "great treasure."

The Browder diaries vividly illustrate once again that history is more than the biographies of famous statesmen and generals. It also consists of countless men and women who, in the words of English historian A. L. Rowse, "have left no name, but who . . . make the material of history, just as a coral-reef is built up out of the lives of millions of small marine creatures." Unfortunately, history's little people seldom leave any record to remind us of their "reef-building," a fact that makes George Dick's legacy all the more noteworthy. As a result of his disciplined efforts, we can enjoy an intimate, often moving, glimpse into an age vastly different from our own. Moreover, the Browder diaries enhance our understanding of that age, for in providing us with a window into his small world, by describing ordinary flesh-and-blood people living through real events and crises, George Dick has illuminated the larger landscape of nineteenth-century America. Although the Civil War section of the diaries may not be unique, it is certainly the most extensive account written by a noncombatant whose family was caught up in the horror of that conflict.

In addition to their obvious historical value, the diaries reward the reader with all of the pleasures inherent in a firsthand account. Most obvious, perhaps, is the feeling that one is actually present with George Dick, participating in his daily activities and sharing his emotions. Indeed, there are occasions when one has the sense of capturing his thoughts the moment they are experienced, as for example one evening when he recorded: "Here sits good Lizzie – writing to her sister – there black *Mary* nods over her knitting – little Helen, sweet thing! is sleeping in the cradle. *Isaac* is singing in the kitchen & taking all together I think we are a happy family." One also delights in George Dick's expressions of surprise and shock in response to events that have just occurred: "Just as I came down my wife opened the door & saw two negroes armed & in federal uniform standing by the door, one of whom immediately leveled his gun at her!" But most of all the reader finds pleasure in George Dick's treatment of commonplace matters that take on fresh meaning when expressed in uniquely personal terms. The following are typical examples: travel ("A miserable ride, over *deep* mud, just a little frozen on top. Such a constant pull, through mud and slush, for nearly a whole day, I have seldom had"); hard times ("The companies I insured my life in, for my wife & children, all broke & my money thrown away!"); forgetfulness ("I went ten miles beyond Russellville before I discovered that I was a week ahead of my appointment. I felt blank & cheap"); taxes ("This very cold day Logan county votes & assures a tax, which I fear will grind us all our lives & oppress our children after us"); Christmas ("Such a hubbub among the children! Santa claus put candy in my sack! Oh Ive got a jews harp! See my little cat! heres my handkerchief! Ive got firecrackers! look at the cakes!"); visitors ("I delight to see my friends . . . , but there are times when it is a great luxury to have the house to ourselves"); middle age ("I believe this is the first night in 20 years that we have spent at home without a child in the house. It is lonely"); water supply ("Aunt Betsy has returned making her visit much shorter at Tom's than she intended because a frog fell in the cistern & she will not drink the water"); debt ("If my hogs had not died with cholera, my finances would have been easier but as it is now I am in debt and troubled at the thought"); introspection ("This is the last day of 1877. . . . I feel serious. I look back over the year & see errors – short-comings – failures. I am sorry. I am ashamed. I am penitent"); parenting ("I feel much concern about my children. Some of them I fear are becoming very worldly & wayward & self-willed"); and, of course, the weather ("The very moon beams seem hot and we get in the shade – out of the moonshine to get a cool breath. The wind that comes feels like it was blowing out of a furnace").

Another appealing feature of the Browder diaries is the realization that the extant volumes include nearly all of George Dick's adult life. The oldest surviving journal picks up the story when he is twenty-six years old, recently married, and the father of a year-old daughter. In the entries that follow, with the exceptions noted above, George Dick offers us the rare privilege of participating in his private thoughts and daily activities for the next thirty-four years. We trace his children from birth to young adulthood; we meet his neighbors and share in the social intercourse of a small rural community; we follow his career as a Methodist preacher, limited initially by debilitating illnesses and then blossoming into years of fruitful service; we note the excitement with which his farmer's heart greets each returning spring; we observe his growing apprehension over the direction of national events and watch in disbelief as the familiar patterns of his life are disrupted by civil conflict; we relive his encounters with nature's fiercest blows – droughts, floods, tornadoes, and blizzards; and we travel with him by horseback and buggy and later by railroad and steamboat to preach thousands of sermons and to preside at hundreds of love feasts. Herein lies the enduring value of George Dick's labor, namely, the life and reality with which he endows an era that embraces one of history's most dramatic moments.

In determining the published form of the Browder diaries, I have tried to let George Dick tell his story with as little editorial interference as possible. Footnotes have been used only when necessary; the great bulk of them occur in connection with the Civil War narrative. George Dick's writing style was typical of the times: a generous use of abbreviations and ampersands, short dashes in the place of commas and periods, possessives without apostrophes, and the omission of periods after abbreviations. With two exceptions I have allowed these to stand as they appear in the original manuscript. For the sake of readability, I have placed a period at the end of each sentence. With respect to abbreviations, I have expanded them only when the meaning is not obvious. For example, most readers probably would not recognize "hgd" as an abbreviation for hogshead, or "Hag" for the Old Testament book of Haggai. Peculiarities such as placing the $ sign after the monetary amount or using no $ sign at all, or writing o'clock as Oclock have been left unchanged. Fortunately, George Dick was a good speller (even though he did not fare well in spelling contests); on those rare occasions when a misspelled word occurs, I have corrected it.

I have provided a number of helps that I trust will increase the reader's enjoyment of the diaries. These include an introduction that places George Dick in historical perspective; a brief chronology of his life; a listing of his relatives and their relationship to him; maps that locate many of the places in Kentucky mentioned in the diaries; a who's who section, containing biographical sketches of many of the people in Browder's life; and a glossary. The latter includes definitions of the terms George Dick used quite often, terms that were, almost without exception, peculiar to his farming activities or to the organization and practices of the Methodist Church. An asterisk (*) following a term the first time it occurs in the text indicates that the term is included in the glossary. Finally, since it is not always clear from the context whether the people referred to by George Dick are white or black, the names of all blacks are italicized. Such a distinction is important to the reader's understanding of race relations in nineteenth-century Kentucky.

One of my most challenging editorial tasks was to compress the 2000-page typewritten copy of the diaries into the limits of the present volume. Approximately two thirds of the narrative had to be pruned. The decision on some deletions came easily. One can readily understand that in describing his daily activities over such a long period of time, George Dick included much that strikes the reader as repetitious and flat. Consequently, a great many entries relating to the weather, visits to and from relatives and neighbors, a seemingly endless variety of farming operations (such as plowing, planting, harvesting, mending fences, putting up ice, hauling out manure, shearing sheep, killing hogs, and stripping tobacco), and George Dick's comings and goings as a preacher and presiding elder in the Methodist Episcopal Church, South, have been excluded. At the same time I recognize that life is made up largely of the commonplace, and I therefore have included a sufficient number of references to Browder's roles as husband, father, son, neighbor, farmer, and preacher to give a sense of reality to his life. In my decisions as to what to omit and what to retain, I have been guided by the desire to produce not only a volume in which the narrative flows smoothly but one that faithfully mirrors the life and times of a man named George Dick.

Acknowledgments

As I reflect on the thirteen years since that October day in 1974 when I first learned of the Browder diaries, I am keenly aware of how much I am indebted to the people who have made possible the publication of this volume. I wish to thank Susan Riley Walker, her father David, and her aunt, Elizabeth Riley, for entrusting the diaries to my care and for granting me permission to edit and publish them. I owe a special thanks to Elizabeth Riley for sharing her considerable knowledge of the people and places of nineteenth-century Logan County and for helping me unravel the Browder and Walker family genealogies.

I also gratefully acknowledge the support I have received from Western Kentucky University, including a Faculty Research Grant in 1974 which underwrote the expense of reducing the diaries to typewritten form. The University also granted me sabbatical leaves during the fall semester 1978 and the summer of 1982.

My heartfelt thanks also to the secretaries in the History Department at Western Kentucky University who were equal to all of the typing burdens laid upon them, including *three* complete drafts of the diaries – in the days before they had access to word processors and computers! These unsung heroes are: Carolyn Phillips, Earlene Chelf, Marcia Stahl, Jane Brown Wilson, Becky Pleasant, Mary McKenzie, Lecia Mayhew Priddy, Ruth Cornelius, Thelma Carter, Chandra Carter, and Trena Burchett. I am especially thankful to Jane Brown Wilson for her thoughtful Christmas gift to me in 1978 – photographs of the surviving structures of the Browder era, some of which are included in this volume.

I am grateful to all the people who so graciously responded to my requests for information in the course of my research. These include a number of my colleagues in library services at Western Kentucky University: Nancy Baird, Penny Harrison, Riley Handy, Pat Hodges, Helen Knight, Connie Mills, Virginia Pearson, Adolfina Simpson, Nancy Solley, and Susan Knight Tucker. Help also came from Margaret Bailey, Rena Milliken, and Cathy Taylor Williams of Russellville, Kentucky; Ursala Beach and Carolyn Miles of Clarksville, Tennessee; Nancy Bradford and Richard A. Weiss, Kentucky Wesleyan Library, Owensboro, Kentucky; Helen English, George Dick's granddaughter, Monroe, North Carolina; Brad Gernand, Western History Collections Library, University of Oklahoma; the late Elizabeth Gleaves and Sarah Gleaves (the great-granddaughter and great-great-granddaughter of George Dick, respectively); Shelia Brown Heflin, Owensboro Public Library, Owensboro, Kentucky; Margie Helm; Drucilla Jones and Darlene Keown of

Bowling Green, Kentucky; Mary Henney and Rosalyn Lewis, United Methodist Publishing House, Nashville, Tennessee; Kenneth Lile, a Methodist preacher of Greenville, Kentucky, whose knowledge of Kentucky Methodism was very helpful; Julia Mason of Owensboro, Kentucky; Cheryl Paterson, Vanderbilt University Archives; Claribel Philips of Hawesville, Kentucky; Doris Reed of Georgetown, Kentucky; Sandra Roff, New York Historical Society; Jimmy Shemwell, Latham Funeral Home, Elkton, Kentucky, who one afternoon in the fall of 1984 walked from his place of employment to the Elkton Cemetery to check out a date on a tombstone for me; and the late Robert B. Stewart, George Dick's great-grandson, Montgomery, Alabama.

Several professors in Cherry Hall on the campus of Western Kentucky University read the introduction and offered helpful suggestions. My sincere appreciation to Mary Ellen Miller and Janet Schwarzkopf of the English Department, and to Charles J. Bussey, Carlton Jackson, Frederick I. Murphy, and especially, Lowell H. Harrison of the History Department. Dr. Harrison's three pages of single-spaced, handwritten comments were typical of the thorough reading he has given to many a colleague's manuscript over the years.

And how can I forget my dear friend Dr. Margaret Howe of Western Kentucky University's Department of Philosophy and Religion! After I had received rejection notices from over a dozen publishers, Margaret, who was fascinated by the diaries after having read a portion of them, took the initiative in August 1981 and sent selected excerpts along with a strong endorsement to Zondervan Publishers. That was the beginning of a happy association with some of the choicest people in the publishing business. I am deeply grateful for the warm and friendly relationship I have enjoyed with the following highly competent individuals: Stan Gundry, Cheryl Forbes, Carol Holquist, Rachel Hostetter, Jonathan Petersen, and especially Judith Markham and Bob Hudson who have worked most closely with me in the preparation of the manuscript.

Finally, I wish to thank my family — my wife, Merle; my son, Mark; and daughters, Annie and Betsy — for their support and encouragement during the long years I have been working on the diaries. Betsy's enthusiasm for my undertaking has been especially appreciated. She was barely five months old when I first heard about the diaries, and over the years she has grown up thinking George Dick was a member of the family. I'll always remember how she disarmed me one morning at breakfast about four years ago when out of the blue she said, "Daddy, aren't diaries supposed to be sort of personal?" "Yes," I replied, to which Betsy responded, "Then why are you publishing them?"

RICHARD L. TROUTMAN
Western Kentucky University
Bowling Green, Kentucky
March 14, 1987

Introduction

On a cool, cloudy June day in 1884, George Richard Browder sat at his walnut desk working on a sermon, nothing new for a man who had spent nearly forty years in the ministry. But this day's effort was special. As he gathered his thoughts for a message on family training, memories of his own childhood filled his mind. George Dick was moved as he remembered the efforts of his stepmother to teach him the catechism, his father's morning and evening songs in family worship, the visits his family made to the neighbors, where they talked and sang and prayed until bedtime, and the "old time" Methodist preachers who came frequently to his home and slept in the room overhead. Once again he and his father rode to church together on old Fan, and then later he rode by himself on a mule with a sheepskin saddle and a blind bridle.

Among George Dick's fondest recollections were the camp meetings he and his family attended each fall. Two meetings in particular made lasting impressions on him. One was at his home church, Bethlehem, in 1831, when he was only four years old. As he placed a silver dollar given to him by his father into the missionary hat, one of the preachers laid his hand on his head and said, "Lord, bless the little boy and make him a missionary."

That prayer was answered seven years later. George Dick recalled that at nearby Ash Spring camp meeting, he made a decision that firmly set the direction of his life. During a morning service, while old Uncle John Moore was preaching, he was "strangely moved to weeping and sorrow" and was led by his stepmother to the altar, where he cried out for God to save him. Thinking that he "would sink into Hell & deserved such a fate & giving up in despair I looked to Jesus as the *only* hope & trusting him I felt the thrill of a new creation & life from the dead rushing through my young heart."

That George Dick should find himself kneeling in the straw at Ash Spring was not unexpected. His spiritual heritage had brought him to that moment. His paternal great-great-grandfather, Richard, was one of the earliest members of the Methodist Church in Dinwiddie County, Virginia. It was there that George Dick's father, Robert (1804–90), was born and where his parents, David and Mary Cousins Browder, carefully nurtured him and his five older brothers and sisters in their spiritual development. Consequently, when Robert and his oldest brother, Richard (1789–1878), left Virginia in 1820 for the fertile soil of south-central Kentucky, they took with them not only their dreams for a better life but their deep personal faith in God as well. Settling first in Green County, where Robert taught school for several years, they pushed westward in 1825 to Olmstead (then Hogan's Station) in southern Logan County. Robert and Richard were joined by their sister, Jane, who with her husband, the Rev. Caleb Bell, had emigrated in 1822 to near Elkton in Todd County, which joined Logan to the west. The Browders were part of a great westward surge in the years after the War of 1812.

In 1828 at least three other Browders and their families located in Logan County. Robert and Richard welcomed their brother, William (d. 1845); their sister, Ann W. (d. 1847) and her husband, the Rev. John P. Moore (1786–1842), whose sermon at Ash Spring led to George Dick's conversion; and their paternal uncle, Littleberry (1755–1848), who, as a layman, had already achieved a reputation as a leader in the Methodist movement in Virginia.

The three Browder brothers settled on adjoining farms to the west and north of Olmstead. There they prospered, became slaveowners, and in the 1830s, replaced their simple frame houses with more imposing brick structures, two of which still stand. The Browders were interested in more than raising corn and tobacco. When they arrived in Olmstead, they found a small struggling Methodist Society made up of a dozen or so people, including a few blacks. Their earnestness and zeal on behalf of the church contributed greatly to the survival and growth of Methodism in southern Logan County.

The godly example George Dick inherited from the Browder side of his family was reinforced by the spiritual legacy from his mother, Helen Sarah Walker (1806–27). Unlike Robert Browder, Helen was a first-generation Kentuckian. Her father, David (1760–1820), second cousin to George Wythe, a signer of the Declaration of Independence, was a Revolutionary War veteran who served under General Lafayette and witnessed the British surrender at Yorktown in 1781. In the early 1790s he and his younger brother, George, left their native Virginia for the beautiful Bluegrass region of central Kentucky. After settling briefly near Danville in Boyle County, David moved on to nearby Fayette County. Described as "a plain, unobtrusive farmer" with "superior intellectual powers," he took an active part in local politics, serving as clerk of the county and circuit courts and, from 1793 to 1796, as a member of the Kentucky House of Representatives. During these years he also married Mary Barbour (1778–1815) of Garrard County, who would bear him eight children. About 1800 David, accompanied by his wife and three small children, was on the move again, this time to southern Logan County, where his sister, Helen Walker Call, and her family had also settled. Except for a tour of duty as a major in the army during the War of 1812, David spent the next seventeen years improving his 3000-acre farm, which lay a short distance from Olmstead to the northeast. After the death of his wife in 1815, six days after childbirth, he again sought public office and in 1816 successfully campaigned for election to the U.S. House of Representatives. Reelected two years later, he served in Congress until his death in 1820, achieving a reputation as an outspoken champion of Jeffersonian Democracy.

Helen Walker's father was only one of several close relatives who achieved an outstanding record of public service. Her cousin David Walker (1806–79), born and raised in Logan County, moved to Arkansas, where he became Chief Justice of the State Supreme Court. He also presided over the Convention of

1861, which passed the secession ordinance severing Arkansas' connection with the Union. Another cousin, Richard K. Call (1792–1862), served for six years as governor of Florida Territory (1836–39 and 1841–44). His older brother Jacob (d. 1826) had represented Indiana in the U.S. Congress during 1824–25.

In addition to her father, three other members of Helen's immediate family entered public life. Her oldest brother, Col. James Volney Walker (1799–1854), served in both houses of the Kentucky legislature. Because of his record of public service and his reputation as a kind neighbor, the little village of Volney, one mile north of Olmstead, was named in his honor. One of his sons, James D. Walker (1830–1906), represented Arkansas in the U.S. Senate from 1879 to 1885. Helen Walker's two younger brothers, George Keith Walker (1809–66) and David Shelby Walker (1815–91), held important offices in Florida politics. President Jackson appointed George as secretary for the Florida Territory, and David was governor of the state from 1865 to 1867. In view of the Walker family's accomplishments, it is little wonder that in later years George Dick should be referred to as having been born "of sound family stock."

BROWDER'S LIFE: AN OVERVIEW

The farm on which Robert Browder settled in January 1825 was located about a mile to the west of David Walker's residence. It was not long before nineteen-year-old Helen caught his eye and he soon found himself riding frequently down Old Volney Road to visit her. After a brief courtship, they were married on December 30, 1825. Robert took his bride to live in his simple frame house with one room below and one above. There, thirteen months later, on January 11, 1827, George Dick was born.

The year that had begun so happily for the young couple ended in sadness. Death was an ever-present reality in ante-bellum Kentucky, and seven months after George Dick's birth, his mother died. Although he was too young to remember her, the young boy grew up very conscious of his heritage and throughout his life maintained close ties with his Walker relatives.

The impact of Helen Browder's death on her family was softened somewhat by Robert's good fortune in his second marriage. Sarah L. Gilmer of Christian County, the daughter of a Methodist preacher, became his wife on December 25, 1828. Although Sarah bore Robert ten children, none was loved more than George Dick. And none was more carefully trained in the basic tenets of the Christian faith. Sarah not only taught him the catechism but, more importantly, set before him the example of her holy life. It was altogether appropriate that she should have been the one to lead George Dick to the altar at the Ash Spring camp meeting in 1838.

George Dick's childhood was similar to that of other boys growing up in rural south-central Kentucky in the 1830s. By his own account he remembered playing in the barn, wading in the Whippoorwill Creek, and rolling in the snow. He set snares, baited traps, fed sheep, and rounded up calves with "black George," one of his father's slaves. He roasted potatoes at the barn at night while his father "fired" tobacco, and he helped to build the new house by carrying brick from the kiln set up in the yard. Often arising before daybreak, he rode horseback with a bag of corn or wheat to be ground into flour at Donley's Mill on Elk Fork or Poor's Mill on Whippoorwill Creek. When he was old enough, he helped his father with plowing, sowing corn, and setting out tobacco plants.

Work and play alternated with generous doses of book learning. Robert Browder could afford to send his son to one of the small private schools in the Olmstead community. George Dick's first teacher was his uncle, Robert Hutchings, whose school was located at Old Bethlehem Church in Olmstead, not far from the Browder farm. He also attended school at Volney, less than a mile to the northwest of his home, where he was a pupil of William (Billy) Washington, a distant relative of the first president. The usual struggles with his studies and trials with his teachers filled the young boy's school days. Years later he could still recall the pain of an occasional whipping and the disappointment of frequently having to stay in at play time.

George Dick's education included several years away at school. He spent some time with his stepmother's parents, the Gilmers, who lived near Hopkinsville in Christian County, two counties to the west, and with his maternal aunt, Frances Walker Gwynn, in Oldham County, far to the northeast. More important, however, were the years he spent during the 1840s at the Male Academy in Clarksville, Tennessee, just across the state line. With its strong emphasis on Greek, Latin, and mathematics, the academy not only introduced George Dick to the glories of ancient Greece and Rome but also exposed him to models of literary expression that, when combined with the familiar prose of the King James Bible, inspired him to write with clarity, beauty, and power.

It was probably during those years at the academy that George Dick yielded to an inner compulsion to preach the gospel. There is nothing to indicate that the young man experienced any serious doubts in arriving at such a commitment. Just as his spiritual heritage had prepared the way for his conversion at Ash Spring, so his religious training and environment led him naturally into a life of service to the church. In 1846, when he was nineteen, the quarterly conference of Logan Circuit licensed him to preach; and in October of the same year, the Louisville Conference of the newly organized Methodist Episcopal Church, South, admitted him on trial. His first appointment was to the Hopkinsville Circuit as a junior preacher under the watchful eye of A. H. Redford, preacher in charge. During the next four years he successfully completed the requirements for the ministry as set forth by the church. Bishop William Capers of South Carolina ordained him as deacon in October 1848; two years later Bishop James O. Andrew of Georgia, whose controversial ownership of slaves split the Methodist Church in 1845, ordained him as elder.

During his years of preparation for the ministry, George Dick continued to enjoy a relationship with a young lady he had met during his school days in Clarksville. Ann Elizabeth Warfield (1830–97) was the oldest daughter of a well-to-do merchant and farmer, George H. Warfield, who had migrated to Clarksville from Ann Arundel County, Maryland, in 1835. Just how Lizzie and George Dick met is not known. But the fact that the Clarksville Female

Academy, which Lizzie probably attended, was located only three blocks from the Male Academy suggests some interesting possibilities. At any rate, on September 5, 1850, after a courtship of several years, and just before George Dick's ordination as elder, he and Lizzie were married. It was a happy union. Every anniversary was an occasion for George Dick to extol Lizzie's charms and to confide in his journal his love and affection for her.

Newly married and newly ordained, George Dick looked forward to the 1850s with great anticipation. His heart and mind were prepared for the rigorous demands of the ministry. Unfortunately, his body was not. A sore throat, which caused him considerable suffering, prevented him from accepting a regular appointment during the entire decade. The problem may have stemmed in part from his style of preaching during his early ministry. By his own admission, his first efforts were characterized by an "ardor and vehemence" that resulted in "tear & wear" on his throat. This does not mean that Browder ceased to preach during the 1850s. On the contrary, he did so as often as his throat allowed. Because of his kind and compassionate nature, he was in considerable demand at funerals. It is said that he probably preached more funeral sermons during the 1850s than any other man in Kentucky.

Other matters also occupied George Dick's time during these years. He was a popular speaker for causes that lay close to his heart: temperance, education, and the Sunday school movement. He gave considerable attention to his 143-acre farm (a gift from his father in 1853), which adjoined his father's land to the south along Whippoorwill Creek. For a brief period beginning in January 1857, he also tried his hand at teaching. In less than two months, a pain in his chest and another bout with a sore throat forced him to abandon the effort. Finally, his growing family required more and more of his time. Five of his eight children were born during the 1850s: Helen Susan (1851), Robert Walter (1853), Hanson Warfield (1855), George Richard (1857), and Sarah Virginia (1858).

George Dick's physical problems continued to unsettle his life during the 1860s. In the first year of the new decade, he was feeling well enough to ask the Louisville Conference to make him "effective" once more, that is, assign him to a regular appointment. Unfortunately, his health soon failed, and again he had to give up the full-time ministry. This was the beginning of a discouraging cycle of hope and disappointment that lasted for the next ten years. In 1862 the Louisville Conference sought to ease his return to full-time work by naming William Alexander to assist him on the Logan Circuit. That year went well as did the next two spent on the Hadensville Circuit. But within a few months after his appointment to the Russellville Circuit in 1865, a series of illnesses including nausea, "torpidity" of the liver, boils, and cholera forced him to retire once more. Undaunted, George Dick was back again in 1866 and for the next three years ministered faithfully to the Elkton and Allensville circuits. During the spring and summer of 1869, however, a prolonged series of chills accompanied by nausea laid him low. He exclaimed, "These sick spells are wearing me away very fast, I suffer dreadfully." In September he withdrew once again from full-time preaching.

Distressing as they were, the illnesses that sapped George Dick's energies and tested his resolve to preach the gospel were not the only trials he faced during these years. In late 1860 he was overwhelmed by the loss of his little daughter, Sarah Virginia. The distraught father recorded in his family Bible that his beloved Ginnie "died on the 21st day of Nov 1860, aged two years & two days. She suffered much, but her death was easy & calm."

Ginnie's death was the greatest personal tragedy in George Dick's life. But it was only the beginning of a long night of sadness for the Browders. In the same month that Ginnie died, events at the national level were already spinning out of control toward secession and the separation of the Union. The Browder family was among those caught up in the horrors of the Civil War when it burst upon the inhabitants of south-central Kentucky in September 1861. With a heavy heart, George Dick recorded in his journal the movements of Union and Confederate troops through the region, the terror inspired by marauding bands of guerrillas, the bitterness resulting from the war that set neighbor against neighbor, and the rumors, suspense, deprivations, and disruptions that were a part of everyday life. And always in the background were the slaves, growing ever more restless.

During these traumatic years George Dick was always certain of one refuge from the storms that beat upon his life: his home and family. "Glad to be home and to find all well" was a common entry in his journal after having been away for several days riding the circuit. The warm memories of his family during the 1860s prompted him in 1879 to write an anonymous article entitled "The Top Drawer" for publication in a church periodical. A copy of the article, now faded and watermarked, still survives on one of the dog-eared pages of a scrapbook in which Browder pasted a great many clippings during the 1860s, 1870s, and 1880s. He referred to his "cozy little home in the country, with a rich little farm" that enabled him to provide comfortably for his family of eight. Two more children had been born in the years after Ginnie's death: Luther (1861) and Wallace (1865).

In the article George Dick described the activities of his family on a cold, windy December evening in 1865 as they awaited his return from an appointment some twenty miles distant. Wood blazed brightly in the fireplace, and because Lizzie was afraid of lamps and oils, long candles lighted the living room. After a time of study and play, the children asked Lizzie to show them their "banks" in which Lizzie kept each child's valuables – their awards, presents, and little earnings. Helen prized her locket and gold pencil holder; Robert, the gold dollar he received for good behavior; Hanson, a premium for the most high grades; and George, his French harp. Inevitably the conversation turned to the difficult times through which the family had just passed. The children remembered that one winter shoes were so hard to get that they had to go barefoot until nearly Christmas. Robert and Hanson were glad they could contribute five dollars, half of the proceeds from their potato crop, to the relief of southern sufferers after the war. And they were all proud of their father's efforts in canvassing the neighborhood for clothes and money in the same cause. Finally, the children asked to see the contents of their mother's "bank." As they gathered at her knee, Lizzie removed the articles. One was a twenty-dollar gold piece, which her father had given to her for the purchase of a piece of furniture; it would come in handy in view of George Dick's small salary. The items that attracted the most interest, however, were little bundles of locks cut from the children's hair when they were babes. One by one the children identified their locks until one remained, unclaimed, a beautiful ringlet of dark hair tied up with a pink ribbon. The tears flowed once more in that moment of remembering. When everything was carefully packed away and returned to the top drawer, Lizzie led her family in singing, "I want to be an angel and with the angels stand." Soon the children heard footsteps on the porch, the door opened, and there stood their father, shaking the snow from his hat and coat. As he joined his family by the fireplace and talked over the advantages and disadvantages of the itinerant life, George Dick concluded that "the sweets far outweigh the bitter."

In the early 1870s Browder's improving health enabled him to return to the itinerant ranks, to the life he loved so well. Although concern for his health was never far from his thoughts ("I bought a small book [journal] because I may not live to fill a large one."), he managed to carry out virtually all of his responsibilities during the last sixteen years of his life. Moreover, his trained mind, his spiritual gifts, and his zeal for the ministry brought him increasingly to the attention of the church leadership. George Dick's success in raising money, for example, led in 1874 to his appointment as agent for two colleges sponsored by the Louisville Conference of the Methodist Church – Logan Female College in Russellville and Warren College in Bowling Green. He was not happy about the assignment, but he entered upon the work with a spirit that was characteristic of the man: "I did not seek it nor desire it but will do the best I can in it."

George Dick labored faithfully and patiently for two years under a severe handicap. An economic slump triggered by the Panic of 1873 held the country in its grip for the rest of the decade. "The times are hard – people have no money," he exclaimed. And what fund raiser could not identify with his painful observation: "Those that can help are not willing & those that are willing are not able." Nevertheless, the board of directors was pleased with his work and in 1876 granted him a month's vacation, which enabled him to take Lizzie and two of his sons, Robert and George, to the Centennial Exposition in Philadelphia. The trip, which also included stops in Cleveland, Niagara Falls, New York, Baltimore, and Washington, was the adventure of a lifetime, not only for the Browders but for seventeen of their Olmstead neighbors, most of whom probably had not ventured far from south-central Kentucky before.

The Centennial excursion turned out to be George Dick's last vacation. Three weeks after his return, his appointment as one of the presiding elders of the Louisville Conference ushered in the final and most productive phase of his life. It was an office for which he seems to have been admirably suited. A colleague once observed that while Browder was "good on a circuit [and] fair in a station, he excelled as presiding elder." For the next ten years he served the following districts: Bowling Green (1876–80), Russellville (1880–84), and Owensboro (1884–86). As presiding elder, he assumed responsibility for the preachers who ministered in the district to which he was assigned. Not only did he advise the bishop in appointing the preachers at the annual conference, but he worked closely with each one in a regular schedule of visitation as required by the Methodist system of quarterly conferences. He took advantage of these meetings to encourage, to exhort, to counsel, and occasionally, to admonish. Because George Dick believed strongly that the presiding elder's influence should be felt in his district, he frequently assisted his preachers in their protracted meetings as his time and energies allowed.

On two occasions Browder's routine as presiding elder yielded to responsibilities conferred on him by the Louisville Conference. In 1882 he was elected as a delegate to the general conference of the Methodist Episcopal Church, South. On the first day of the conference, which met in Nashville, Tennessee, George Dick was assigned to the Committee on Boundaries. He was obviously pleased when the committee elected him as its chairman, "much to my surprise, as we were all strangers to each other." Two years later he was honored again as a clerical delegate to the Centenary Conference of the Methodist Church, which met at Mount Vernon Place Church, Baltimore, in December 1884. George Dick and Lizzie marveled at the church with its "cushioned & silver marked pews and grand galleries & gas lights & parlors," the crowds who jammed into the 1600-seat sanctuary, and the high quality of the speeches. "Blessed be God," Browder exclaimed, "that my eyes behold this assembly."

The trips to Nashville and Baltimore were only brief interludes in the exhausting final decade of Browder's life. His work as presiding elder required considerably more time on the road, much of it on horseback. Several times, despite frail health, he recorded rides of thirty-five to forty miles in one day. Furthermore, he was absent from home for longer periods of time. During one stretch he was home only one day in three weeks; on another occasion he lamented having been away for eleven days. Such demands on his time took their toll on both George Dick and Lizzie. He left reluctantly on one trip in 1879, noting that "my dear wife has been left alone until she feels it keenly & this morning was not able to suppress the tears that told her grief. I would have been glad of any good excuse to stay at home."

True to his vows, Browder rarely looked for such excuses. The same sense of devotion to God and dedication to the church that had led him into the ministry characterized his labors up to his final illness. Indeed, in his last years he undoubtedly shortened his days as he pushed himself beyond his strength. George Dick believed in sowing bountifully.

THE NATIONAL SCENE

As Browder lived out his life in relative obscurity, he manifested a keen interest in events unfolding beyond south-central Kentucky, an interest growing out of genuinely patriotic impulses. When he was born in 1827, America was young, scarcely fifty years old, and still growing. The acquisition of Louisiana (1803) and Florida (1819) had more than doubled the size of the United States. And a vast, sparsely populated wilderness stretching westward to the Pacific lay just beyond, waiting to be taken.

An optimistic mood pervaded the land during the decades after the War of 1812. Americans believed that they had created, in the words of future President James K. Polk, the "most admirable and wisest system of well-regulated self-government ever devised by human minds." Coupled with this abiding faith in the superiority of their institutions was the conviction that a kindly providence guided the nation's destiny and had entrusted to it the dual mission of spreading civil liberty and Christianity to all of North America and beyond. If Americans did not share a common past, they nevertheless found unity in their aspirations for the future.

Paradoxically, the same Americans who exulted in their rising strength and divinely appointed status viewed with increasing concern the emergence of a divisive sectionalism. To a large extent nature itself had decreed that the American people should be divided. The semitropical climate of the southern states contributed significantly to a way of life that differed from the states of the North. Among these differences, none was more remarkable than the presence of millions of black slaves concentrated in the southern part of the nation. Almost without exception sectional differences, whether economic, political, social, or cultural, were attributable to the fact that human bondage flourished in one section of the Republic and not in the other.

Before the 1840s sectional tensions had flared into the open only rarely. The most memorable confrontation occurred in 1819 and 1820, when Missouri, a part of the Louisiana Territory, applied for admission to the Union as a slave state. Missouri's application aroused controversy not only because its admission would upset the balance between slave and free states but because the determination of its status would have important implications for the spread of slavery into the federal territories. In the famous Missouri Compromise, Congress admitted Missouri as a slave state and Maine as a free state, thus preserving the balance between the sections. More importantly, in an effort to prevent further conflict, Congress prohibited slavery in the rest of the Louisiana Territory north of 36° 30' north latitude.

The decision did not come easily. For a brief moment suppressed feelings were vented in an angry debate that left both sides bruised and shaken. Thomas Jefferson, in retirement at Monticello, observed that the bitter exchange "like a fire-bell in the night, awakened and filled me with terror." John Quincy Adams, whose political star was rising, referred to it as the "title page to a great tragic volume."

Although the Missouri Compromise temporarily put to rest the explosive issue of slavery expansion, sectional tensions continued. Free and slave states sparred over such issues as the protective tariff, national land policy, and the annexation of Texas. More ominous was the appearance of an aggressive antislavery movement in the North. Before the 1830s slavery was not a major issue, and organized efforts at the national level to abolish it attracted few followers. Although most Americans could not fail to see the contradiction between the practice of human bondage and their ideals of liberty as expressed in the nation's creeds, it was generally acknowledged that since slavery depended almost entirely on state laws, there was little that could be done about the problem. Consequently, most early opponents of slavery advocated shipping emancipated blacks to Africa or appealed to slaveowners to treat their slaves more humanely. As William Ellery Channing, a leading Unitarian clergyman from New England, told southerners: "We consider slavery your calamity, not your crime. We will share with you the burden of putting an end to it."

During the 1830s and 1840s, however, a new generation of antislavery leaders emerged who did not share Channing's compassionate understanding of the South's dilemma. Reformers such as the provocative William Lloyd Garrison, who uncompromisingly demanded the immediate abolition of slavery, and the more influential Theodore Dwight Weld, who advocated its gradual extinction, managed to keep the cruelties and barbarities of slavery before the public eye year after year. By means of lectures, pamphlets, the organization of local, state, and national antislavery societies, and in some cases, petitions to Congress, these abolitionists sought to convince both northerners and southerners that America should no longer tolerate such a monstrous evil.

Southerners resented this rising crescendo of condemnation. By the 1830s slavery had won wide acceptance as the keystone in the arch of southern civilization. Writers and politicians extolled the virtues of their "peculiar institution," asserting that slavery, by freeing the master class from the drudgery of manual labor and allowing it time to engage in intellectual pursuits, would enable the South to create a civilization rivaling those of ancient Greece and Rome. John C. Calhoun, the South's most famous spokesman and defender, went so far as to proclaim slavery "a positive good." "We see it [slavery] now in its true light," he said, "and regard it as the most safe and stable basis for free institutions in the world."

Although the great majority of Americans, North and South, did not identify themselves with either abolitionists or proslavery zealots, events played into the hands of the extremists on both sides. Abolitionist attacks, not only on slavery but on the southern way of life, made it easier for the fanatical defenders of slavery to attract moderate southerners to their support. At the same time, southern efforts to capture runaway slaves and to thwart the First Amendment by effectively tabling antislavery petitions to Congress, drove northern moderates into the arms of the abolitionists.

The antislavery movement gathered momentum at a time when the South was growing increasingly apprehensive about its future within the Union. Simply stated, the heart of the problem was this: southerners were convinced that the very survival of their civilization depended on the expansion of slavery. Among other things this meant carving new slave states out of the American wilderness to preserve the sectional balance. Nature, however, was unkind to the South. Geographic conditions changed at about the ninety-fifth meridian, and slavery was not thought to be profitable in the regions west of that line. Pioneers moving into this area would in all likelihood establish free labor communities. Southern leaders were alarmed, therefore, at the prospect of more and more free states emerging from the western territories; they believed that the resulting shrinkage in the slave power in Congress would ultimately lead to a national assault on slavery.

Although southerners expected the inevitable, they sought desperately to avoid it. At every opportunity southerners championed their right to take their slaves into the federal territories. Consequently, the question of slavery in the territories became the most explosive political issue in the United States in the fifteen years preceding the Civil War. The opening round in the struggle came as a result of the Mexican War (1846–48), in which the United States wrested from Mexico virtually all of what is now the American Southwest. Since the Missouri Compromise had applied only to the Louisiana Territory, the question of slavery expansion surfaced once more. Indeed, the Mexican War had scarcely begun when a proposal to exclude slavery from any territory to be acquired from Mexico was introduced in the House of Representatives. This so-called Wilmot Proviso touched off another bitter controversy between North and South. Moving to the brink of secession, the South finally agreed to the Compromise of 1850, which included a set of proposals formulated by Henry Clay of Kentucky, who sought to resolve a number of differences between the two sections. Among other things Congress admitted California as a free state, abolished the slave trade in the District of Columbia, and approved a law intended to be more effective in returning runaway slaves to their masters. On the all-important territorial question, Congress in effect applied the principle of popular sovereignty to the rest of the Mexican Cession, which was divided into two territories, Utah and New Mexico. This meant that in each territory the people themselves, acting through their territorial legislatures, would decide on the question of slavery, thus removing the issue from the emotionally charged halls of Congress.

By and large, the great majority of Americans, North and South, accepted the Compromise with a sigh of relief. Extremism had been rejected, and although troublesome problems remained, a national crisis had been averted. Stephen A. Douglas of Illinois, who played a major role in pushing the Compromise proposals through the U.S. Senate, expressed the sentiments of most Americans when he declared in late 1850: "I have determined never to make another speech on the slavery question. Let us cease agitating, stop the debate, and drop the subject." This attitude prevailed through the presidential election of 1852 as candidates of both major parties, Democrats and Whigs, campaigned on platforms endorsing the Compromise. It was a quiet, colorless election. In a far-off corner of Logan County, Kentucky, George Dick voted for the losing Whig candidate, Winfield Scott, recording that he "never saw as little excitement at a presidential election."

The fragile truce ushered in by the Compromise of 1850 was shattered in 1854, when Congress, under the leadership of Senator Douglas, passed the ill-fated Kansas-Nebraska Act. Emerging out of a terribly complex series of political maneuverings, this measure repealed the Missouri Compromise and applied the principle of popular sovereignty to the unorganized portion of the Louisiana Territory, a region closed to slavery for over thirty years. Although southerners were jubilant at the possibility of adding new slave territory, the North was aroused as never before. Abolitionists and moderate northerners alike were appalled at the repeal of the Missouri Compromise and raised a chorus of angry protest. The question of slavery in the territories, which most northerners thought had been settled forever, was now suddenly reopened.

The controversy swirling around the Kansas-Nebraska Act set in motion a number of forces leading ultimately to secession and civil war. Among those forces was a political realignment in the North that resulted in the creation of the Republican party. Holding firmly to the position that slavery must be kept out of the federal territories, the new party sprang up spontaneously all over the North. Although not an abolitionist party, it was, nevertheless, the long-dreaded sectional party, with the potential of winning a national election without capturing a single vote from the slave states. It was an alarming prospect for the South.

The years after the Kansas-Nebraska Act were filled with a sense of crisis as a series of spectacular episodes brought the nation to the brink of war. Violence flared not only in Kansas during 1855−56 as proslavery and antislavery settlers contended for control of the territory but even in the halls of Congress, where emotions reached a fever pitch. In the election of 1856, the South held its breath as the Republicans, in their very first try, narrowly missed winning the presidency. The Supreme Court, in the famous Dred Scott case, stirred further controversy and emboldened the South with its decision in 1857 that since slaves were property, slaveowners had a constitutional right to take them anywhere they pleased, including the territories. The following year, a series of debates in Illinois between the upstart Abraham Lincoln and the veteran Stephen A. Douglas captured national attention and kept alive the issue of slavery in the territories. Finally in 1859 John Brown brought the troubled decade to a frightening climax when he launched his raid on the federal arsenal at Harpers Ferry, in the mountains of northern Virginia. Brown's abortive attempt to rally the slaves, arm them, and send them forth in a sort of private war against slavery sent a shock wave of horror through the South. Widespread rumors of northern plots to foment slave uprisings and of abolitionist conspiracies to poison all whites created an atmosphere of panic. More and more southerners, especially in the Deep South, talked about leaving the Union.

Within a few months after John Brown's raid, at a time when the nation could ill afford another crisis, Americans found themselves caught up in the excitement of another presidential campaign. The election of 1860 turned out to be a national tragedy. Even before the major parties met in the spring of that year to nominate their candidates, the Alabama legislature expressed the sentiment of many in the Deep South when it passed a resolution advocating secession if the Republicans triumphed in November. Alabama's fears were realized. The Republicans, with Abraham Lincoln, a native Kentuckian, as their standardbearer, carried every northern state and scored a smashing victory in the electoral college.

Clement Eaton, an eminent historian of the Old South, referred to Lincoln's election as the "detonator" of secession. After nearly a decade of crisis, many southerners were convinced that their destiny lay outside the Union. Without waiting to see what Lincoln would do, seven Deep South states seceded and, during the first week of February 1861, formed the Confederate States of

America with Jefferson Davis, also a native Kentuckian, as their president. Lincoln moved cautiously after his inauguration one month later. He did not attempt to recover federal property seized by the Confederates, but he did make an effort to send provisions to the small garrison of federal troops holding Fort Sumter, located on an island in the Charleston, South Carolina, harbor. Interpreting this as a hostile act, the Confederates opened fire from their shore batteries, and after a withering bombardment the fort surrendered on April 14, 1861.

The North bristled with indignation upon hearing of the attack on Fort Sumter. Lincoln immediately issued a call for 75,000 volunteers to put down the rebellion and declared a naval blockade of the South. The president's actions precipitated another round of secession, this time among the slave states of the Upper South. Virginia, North Carolina, Arkansas, and Tennessee refused to acquiesce to Lincoln's policy of coercion and joined the Confederacy. The nation was swept along on a wave of emotion unmatched in its history. Paradoxically, at the same time, there was a deep sense of relief on both sides. The tension of the secession crisis had been broken, and after years of compromise and controversy, the war that many had feared but not really expected had come.

THE KENTUCKY SCENE

The political storms that thundered across the American landscape during the 1850s were not confined to the national arena. Emotions ran high within the states as well, especially those located along the border separating North and South. In no state was the drift toward secession and civil war viewed with greater alarm than in Kentucky. The Bluegrass State was situated on the frontier of two cultures. It was southern in its folkways and agrarian values but similar to the North in its economic diversity. If Kentucky's surplus mules, corn, hemp, whisky, and slaves followed traditional trails and waterways to the South, the recent introduction of the railroad resulted in a significant increase in the state's commercial relations with the states along her northern border.

Although Kentucky's pre-war status defies easy definition, the state did share one important link with the South – human bondage. Slavery came to the region with the earliest settlers. As early as 1775 at least one slave was among those killed in an Indian attack on Daniel Boone's party as they blazed the Wilderness Road from Cumberland Gap to Boonesborough. Hundreds of others soon followed in the company of westward-moving pioneers, most of whom came from the slave states of Virginia, North Carolina, and Maryland.

Kentucky's slave population grew rapidly after the American Revolution, increasing from approximately 12,000 in 1790 to over 40,000, nearly a quarter of the total population, by 1800. The number of slaves actually increased at a faster rate than the white population until 1830; after that, the *proportion* of slaves to whites began to decline. This was due in part to the decreased demand for slaves to clear the fields and to build the houses, barns, and fences that were required in the initial period of settlement. Another important factor was the rapid expansion of the cotton kingdom into Alabama and Mississippi, which not only attracted a considerable number of Kentucky planters and their bondsmen but also provided a profitable market for the state's surplus slaves. Consequently, although Kentucky slaves numbered over 225,000 in 1860, they constituted only one fifth of the total population.

The distribution of slaves throughout the state and the size of individual slaveholdings were important facets of Kentucky's "peculiar institution." Slaves were concentrated in several distinctive areas: the Bluegrass region in the north-central part of the state, Henderson and Oldham counties on the Ohio River, and a strip of south-central Kentucky embracing Trigg, Christian, Todd, Logan, and Warren counties. Few slaves were found in the mountainous region of eastern Kentucky. Statewide the great majority of whites owned no slaves at all. The federal census reveals that on the eve of the Civil War only one family in four held slaves. Furthermore, modest-sized holdings were the rule. Only seven Kentuckians owned over 100 slaves. Nearly 90 percent of the slaveholders held fewer than 20 slaves; over 20 percent held only one.

In the early years of the state's development, most Kentuckians gave little thought to the social and moral issues raised by slavery. A few denominations, especially the Presbyterians, Baptists, and Methodists, voiced some opposition to the practice throughout the antebellum period, and during the 1820s and 1830s, the American Colonization Society's efforts to ship emancipated blacks back to Africa attracted considerable support in the state. But for the most part, slavery was accepted as a familiar element in a way of life inherited from the slave states along the Atlantic seaboard.

During the 1840s, however, things changed. Kentucky, as a part of the slave South, was included in the bitter attack launched by antislavery spokesmen as their crusade gathered momentum. Indeed, the Bluegrass State soon became the focus of that onslaught. Thomas D. Clark, the distinguished historian of Kentucky, observed that during the 1840s "every abolitionist in the land had his eye on the Kentuckians." The opposition came both from without and within. In 1839 Theodore Dwight Weld published his influential tract *American Slavery As It Is*. During the years he was associated with Lane Theological Seminary, located just across the Ohio River in Cincinnati, Weld gathered hundreds of items on slavery in Kentucky. His volume was filled with slave dealer advertisements, descriptions of families torn apart by the auction block, and accounts of atrocities committed against slaves. With sales of over 100,000 the first year, Weld's book became an important source of abolitionist propaganda.

If Kentuckians resented the unfavorable publicity generated by Weld's exposé, they were outraged by the antislavery campaign conducted by their very own Cassius M. Clay, one of the most boisterous figures in the state's history. Clay, the son of a wealthy slaveholder of pioneer stock, had decided early in life that he did not like slavery, an attitude confirmed during his attendance at Yale University, where he came under the influence of William Lloyd Garrison. In 1845 he founded in Lexington, in the heartland of Kentucky slavery, a weekly antislavery newspaper called *The True American* in which he advocated gradual emancipation through legal means. Never a tactful person, Clay offended many, and in anticipation of trouble, he fortified his office with two four-pounder cannons, rifles, shotguns, Mexican lances, and a keg of black powder. Two months of *The True American* was all that the angry Lexingtonians could take. One day when Clay was at home ill, a group of sixty men surged into his office, boxed up his equipment and shipped it off to Cincinnati, where the fiery crusader continued his publication.

The mounting attack on slavery in Kentucky served only to stiffen opposition to emancipation. Convinced that slavery was a state issue, Kentuckians deeply resented outside interference in their affairs. Furthermore, the question of what to do with the blacks if slavery were ended greatly troubled them. For these and other reasons, although the overwhelming majority of Kentuckians had no vested interest in slavery, they nevertheless continued to support the system. At no time was this more clearly illustrated than in the bitterly fought election of 1849. Not a single antislavery candidate was elected.

If Kentucky's commitment to southern folkways was an important factor in the decision to perpetuate slavery, her heritage of loyalty to the Union held the state steady during the tumultuous decade preceding the Civil War. Kentucky, after all, was the home of Henry Clay, one of the political giants of his time, who for over forty years had used his considerable personal charm and political influence to heighten America's sense of nationhood and to lessen sectional animosities. His state overwhelmingly supported him in his efforts to promote national harmony. At no time was this more ably demonstrated than during the crisis of 1850. As Clay struggled in the Senate to win support for his compromise proposals, Kentucky sent a block of native marble as its contribution to the Washington Monument with these words chiseled into it: "Under the auspices of Heaven and the precepts of Washington, Kentucky will be the last to give up the Union." When Clay died in 1852, his mantle fell upon John J. Crittenden, who, as Kentucky's senior U.S. senator, labored valiantly, though unsuccessfully, to effect a reconciliation between the sections during the winter of 1860–61. A letter to Crittenden from one of his constituents in February 1860 indicated that Clay's legacy was still intact: "The great, sound, conservative heart of the commonwealth are [sic] for the Union, the Constitution – the whole flag, every stripe & every star in its place."

Kentucky's tradition of devotion to the Union was reflected in the results of the presidential election of 1860. Two native sons were among the contenders – Abraham Lincoln, Republican, and John C. Breckinridge, Southern Democrat. Nevertheless, the Constitutional Union party candidate, John Bell of Tennessee, whose platform was simply the preservation of the Union, carried the state with a plurality of 13,000 votes.

In the frantic early months of 1861, Kentucky's status loomed large in the thoughts of both Union and Confederate leaders. After the secession of the Upper South, Kentucky was the most important of the four remaining border slave states, which also included Maryland, Delaware, and Missouri. President Lincoln understood this when he declared, "I hope to have God on my side, but I must have Kentucky." But Lincoln also knew that he had to be patient in dealing with the state. Kentuckians were in no mood to be pushed in any direction. To some extent Kentucky's inner paralysis stemmed from Governor

Beriah Magoffin's Confederate sympathies and a badly divided state legislature. More important, however, was the realization that a tilt to either side would bring to Kentucky its own nightmare of civil war. Consequently, in May 1861 the legislature adopted a resolution of "strict neutrality," a decision that sent thousands of hot young bloods out of the state to join Confederate and Union fighting units elsewhere.

Kentucky's official declaration of neutrality could not conceal the strong current of Unionism running within the state. Some indication of that strength may be gauged by the results of the statewide elections held during the summer of 1861. In the congressional elections in June, the Unionists won nine of the ten seats. State elections held in early August yielded lopsided Unionist majorities in both houses of the legislature. Encouraged by these results, Lincoln authorized the establishment of Camp Dick Robinson in Garrard County for the purpose of stepping up the recruitment of Kentuckians for the Union army. Confederates, meanwhile, conducted similar efforts from Camp Boone, Tennessee, just across the state line from Guthrie in south-central Kentucky. Citizens of the commonwealth watched in disbelief as the rush of events pushed them inexorably into the maelstrom of civil conflict.

They did not have long to wait. On September 4, 1861, Confederate forces shattered Kentucky's neutrality when they marched northward from Tennessee to seize the Mississippi River town of Columbus in the western corner of the state. In a countermove the next day, Union troops commanded by Ulysses S. Grant occupied Paducah, about forty miles to the northeast. Both sides understood the strategic importance of the river systems located in this region. The Mississippi, Tennessee, and Cumberland waterways led into the very heartland of the South. Kentucky, therefore, became the key to Confederate success in the West. In recognition of that fact, President Jefferson Davis on September 10 assigned Albert Sidney Johnston, a native Kentuckian and one of the South's ablest and most highly respected generals, the formidable task of winning the state for the Confederacy.

General Johnston faced insuperable difficulties: lack of supplies, inadequate systems of communication and transportation, a largely inexperienced and incompetent staff of officers, and an army only half the size of the enemy to defend a 400-mile straggling Confederate line that stretched across the length of southern Kentucky and on westward to Indian Territory. Shortly after assuming command at Nashville, Johnston ordered troops northward to occupy Bowling Green, which soon became a major Confederate stronghold. In the absence of any major clash with Union forces during the fall of 1861, he spent much of his time fortifying key positions and training raw recruits, most of whom were non-Kentuckians. Volunteers from the surrounding area rallied to the Confederate cause in smaller numbers than expected.

Johnston's advance into south-central Kentucky gave heart to the Confederates in the state who wished to establish formal ties with the Confederate States of America. Two meetings at Russellville in Logan County during October and November 1861, the latter attended by 115 delegates from 68 counties, resulted in the creation of the Provisional government of Kentucky with Bowling Green as its designated capital. In December the Confederate government officially admitted Kentucky into its ranks. At best it was a tenuous relationship. The fledgling state government's existence depended on the continued support of Johnston's army. When that protection broke down two months later, Confederate Kentucky virtually ceased to exist.

General Johnston's decision to evacuate his 28,000 troops from south-central Kentucky in February 1862 resulted from reverses in both the eastern and western sectors of his Kentucky line of defense. It was General Grant who dealt the most telling blow. In a brilliant maneuver he simply skirted the entrenched Confederate forces at Columbus and quickly reduced the more strategically located Forts Henry and Donelson on the Tennessee and Cumberland rivers. With his position untenable, Johnston withdrew from Kentucky and, with Grant in pursuit, retreated all the way to northern Mississippi. There the Confederate general rallied his forces and, in a desperate attempt to regain the initiative, recrossed the Tennessee line in early April 1862 to attack Grant's army at Shiloh. The two-day battle cost the South and Kentucky dearly. Among the casualties were General Johnston himself and over 1400 brave Kentucky soldiers, Union and Confederate, including George W. Johnson, the Confederate governor of Kentucky, who died as a private.

Despite these setbacks the Confederate desire for Kentucky remained irresistible. Whatever doubts southern leaders may have had about Kentucky's longing to be rescued from Union control were swept aside in July 1862, when John Hunt Morgan, that charismatic cavalryman from Lexington, Kentucky, galloped northward out of Tennessee with nearly 900 men and for over three weeks frightened Unionists and disrupted communications in central Kentucky.

Morgan generated intense excitement during his raid, but the expected surge of Kentuckians into the Confederate army never materialized. Nevertheless, he prepared the way for another major southern effort to bring Kentucky under Confederate control. In mid-August General Kirby Smith marched northward from Knoxville, Tennessee, through Cumberland Gap and closed in on the Bluegrass region with 12,000 men. Two weeks later the main Confederate force of 28,000 men under General Braxton Bragg moved westward out of Chattanooga and invaded through south-central Kentucky. Poor planning, inadequate communications, and incompetent leadership doomed an effort that appeared to have bright prospects for success. After the bloody and inconclusive battle of Perryville in central Kentucky on October 8, 1862, the Confederate armies retreated southward for the second time in eight months. Although Kentucky continued to be the scene of minor actions during the rest of the war, most notably three more raids by the gallant Morgan from 1862 to 1864, the Confederates never again posed a serious threat to the state.

During the months that great armies marched across Kentucky's rolling countryside, her citizens faced a host of internal problems spawned by the conflict. Guerrilla activity was among the most vexing. Heartless scoundrels, many of them deserters or draft evaders, robbed, pillaged, and murdered. Almost every neighborhood had its Tom Morrow, a former schoolmate of George Dick, who harassed southern Logan County. During the last two years of the war, such lawlessness threatened the very foundation of Kentucky's social and political order. Federal authorities resorted to stern measures in attempting to deal with the problem, especially as it related to guerrillas suspected of Confederate leanings. On June 1, 1862, Brigadier General Jeremiah T. Boyle, commander of the Kentucky department, ordered that "when damage shall be done to the person or property of *loyal* citizens by marauding bands of guerrillas, the disloyal of the neighborhood will *be held responsible, and a military commission appointed to assess damages and enforce compensation."* George Dick's father, Robert, and other Confederate sympathizers in the Olmstead community were among those who felt the sting of Boyle's directive. Boyle's successor, General Stephen Burbridge, a thirty-three-year-old farmer from Logan County, went even further. In 1864 he issued his famous Order No. 59, in which he threatened to arrest Confederate sympathizers within a five-mile radius of where a guerrilla crime had been committed, and in the event a Union man was murdered, four guerrilla prisoners of war would be shot in public. In executing his policy of retaliation, Burbridge displayed much zeal and little tact, and he was not always careful to distinguish between guerrilla prisoners of war and legitimate Confederate captives. A howl of protest across the state finally led to his removal in February 1865. The *Louisville Journal* exulted: "Maj. Gen. John M. Palmer of Illinois has been appointed to command in Kentucky. Thank God and President Lincoln."

Disloyalty was another problem that plagued Kentuckians. Suspicions surfaced easily in a state from which approximately 30,000 men poured into southern armies. From 1861 to 1862 the Unionist-dominated legislature took steps to discourage Confederate activities. Teachers, ministers, jurors, and all public officials were required to take loyalty oaths. The legislature also expelled disloyal members, set stiff penalties for Kentuckians who enlisted in the Confederate army, and established fines of up to $100 for those who displayed the Confederate flag. State attempts to control disloyalty were supplemented by the activities of federal agents. Union military officers interfered in the electoral process by removing the names of undesirable candidates from ballots and openly intimidating voters. Lincoln himself declared martial law and suspended the writ of habeas corpus during the local elections of August 1864. Efforts to restrain the enemies of the war in Kentucky included outrageous acts committed against private citizens by the unpaid volunteers who made up the Home Guard, a second militia created by the legislature in 1861 to undertake a close surveillance of Confederate sympathizers at the county level. Under the guise of suppressing treasonous activities and protecting Unionists, some units of the Home Guard became little more than armed bands determined to run local affairs to suit themselves.

As Kentuckians grappled with problems created by guerrillas and disloyalty, events soon forced upon them another issue of major importance, namely, the future of slavery in the state. When the war began, Lincoln made clear that his objective was to preserve the Union and not to free the slaves. Privately he was not opposed to emancipation, but he resisted efforts to associate the federal government with such a move because he did not want to divide the nation further. The president preferred that individual states take the initiative. With that in mind, Lincoln in March 1862 called upon the four loyal border slave states to adopt a program of gradual emancipation that included compensation for slaveowners and colonization of the freed men and women. Kentucky officials vehemently rejected Lincoln's appeal as did the leaders in the other border states. Rebuffed by the states yet convinced that emancipation was necessary both as a wartime measure and as a means of winning the support of the European liberals, Lincoln in September 1862 made public his Emancipation Proclamation, which committed the federal government to freeing the slaves. The proclamation, which went into effect on January 1, 1863, applied only to those states or parts of states in rebellion. Although it did not immediately threaten slavery in the Bluegrass State, Kentuckians understood its implications, and the governor and legislature loudly condemned Lincoln's action.

That protest was mild, however, when compared with the full-throated outcries attending the recruitment of black soldiers in Kentucky. When the employment of blacks in the military service was advanced by some federal officials early in the war, the suggestion was rejected. Northern public opinion was not prepared to accept the idea of using black troops to save the Union. Mounting white casualty figures created great pressure for change, however, and in May 1863 the federal government organized the Bureau of Colored Troops to supervise the enlistment of blacks. Lincoln, keenly aware of the sensibilities of white Kentuckians on the race issue, suggested as a first step that only free blacks be enrolled in the state, but even that proposal aroused such opposition that he had to abandon the effort temporarily. Meanwhile, considerable numbers of Kentucky slaves were fleeing from their masters and volunteering for service in the Union army. George Dick noted on July 18, 1863, that his hired slave, Henry, was missing and probably "aiming for some of the Yankee camps." Henry took Browder's favorite saddle horse, Mack, with him.

The Union's need for manpower finally broke down Lincoln's reluctance to alienate his native state. In February 1864 he ordered the enrollment of all adult male blacks. Slaves were included in the directive with a promise of freedom to all who entered military service. The president's decision sent shock waves throughout Kentucky. For a brief moment the state bordered on anarchy as respected army officers and leading political figures with sound Unionist records bitterly denounced Lincoln and, in some cases, advocated the use of force to prevent black enrollments. Governor Thomas Bramlette was among those who flirted with sedition, but he finally issued a proclamation urging calm after having been persuaded to back away from an open confrontation with the president. After a brief flurry of anti-Negro violence, white Kentuckians grudgingly acquiesced to black enrollments. George Dick expressed the feeling of most whites when in August 1864 he saw several companies of black soldiers for the first time and exclaimed: "The sight was very revolting to me."

The Union army played a major role in bringing slavery to an end in Kentucky. Nearly 30,000 blacks, along with their wives and children, broke their fetters through enlistment, and many more earned their freedom as a result of employment in army work gangs. When General John M. Palmer assumed his position as military commander of the state in early 1865, he encouraged thousands of slaves to flee across the Ohio River to freedom under the protection of his famous "Palmer's Passes." As a result of the army's efforts, slavery was seriously weakened in Kentucky, and little remained to be done in October 1865 when the Thirteenth Amendment finally ended human bondage in America.

The Civil War cost Kentucky more than her slaves. Of the approximately 90,000 whites and blacks who served in the Union army and the approximately 30,000 whites who entered Confederate ranks, an estimated one-third lost their lives to battle wounds and disease. Thousands of others were maimed for life and joined thousands more who carried both the physical and emotional scars of conflict. These grisly statistics can only begin to suggest the traumatic impact of the war on the Bluegrass State. Furthermore, hatreds emerging from the struggle produced deep cleavages in Kentucky society and laid the groundwork for generations of violence. As John Fox, Jr., expressed it in his novel *The Little Shepherd From Kingdom Come,* the legacy of bitterness "add[ed] the last horror to the . . . great war and prolong[ed] that horror for nearly half a century after its close." Kentuckians had paid a high price indeed to keep "every stripe & every star in its place."

THE LOCAL SCENE

While the long shadow of the war touched virtually every community in the state, south-central Kentucky, because of its location, had been especially vulnerable. Situated on the main route of two Confederate invasions and occupied during most of the war by either Confederate or Union forces, the region experienced nearly four years of unrelenting crisis. Although George Dick's beloved Logan County lay just to the west of the main invasion routes, it was nevertheless the scene of the numerous minor skirmishes and raids, especially during the early months of the conflict. On one occasion in September 1862, Browder climbed a tree in his front yard to view retreating Confederate soldiers, including his half-brother Frank, passing southward along the Clarksville Road with several hundred Union troops in hot pursuit. Three months later he observed thousands of men in Union blue streaming southward "with banners & bayonets gleaming in the sunlight."

When the Confederate threat to Kentucky subsided after 1862, the citizens of Logan County endured the nightmare of guerrilla terrorism and the trauma of prolonged Union military occupation. Marmaduke Beckwith Morton, who later served for many years as managing editor of the *Nashville Banner,* recalled that as a boy growing up on a farm near Russellville during the Civil War he was awakened each morning by the boom of the "sunrise gun"; the most familiar music was that of army bugles sounding "boots and saddles." Almost every day the sound of cannon could be heard from Bowling Green on one side to Russellville and Clarksville, Tennessee, on the other. War and battles, guerrillas, and runaway slaves were all the talk. One day as his family was sitting down to lunch, several hundred Yankee soldiers appeared, ordered something to eat, and then rode through the farm, emptying the corn cribs, driving away horses and cattle, and "helping themselves to provender, leaving gates open, swearing, and abusing the 'd—d sesesh' [secessionists]." Morton also remembered that a wooden horse was erected on the square in Russellville, on which "refractory" Confederate sympathizers were forced to ride.

In a way Logan County was a microcosm of both the state and nation, mirroring the deep divisions within American society. Approximately 1000 of her native sons served in the Confederate army; another 500 augmented Union ranks. Logan's North-South split personality, like that of the nation, resulted primarily from geographical factors. North of Russellville the land is hilly and the soil often thin and rocky. South Logan, by contrast, is level and possesses some of the richest farmland in Kentucky, much of the soil measuring fifty to sixty feet deep over limestone. When the early settlers from Virginia and the Carolinas began moving into the county in the 1780s and 1790s, men of limited means settled on modest holdings in the less desirable north, owned few or no slaves, and for the most part remained loyal to the Union. The more affluent, meanwhile, established themselves on the fertile soil to the south, produced crops of tobacco, corn, and wheat with slave labor, and overwhelmingly supported the Confederacy. With their greater wealth and formal education, the families who settled in south Logan not only dominated the political life of the county but produced leaders of state and national stature as well. In the years before the Civil War, Russellville, with a population of approximately 1200, could boast of four governors and four chief justices of Kentucky, six governors of other states, five congressmen, six United States senators, and two federal cabinet officers.

Logan's proud achievements could hardly have been anticipated by those familiar with its early history. The region attracted not only farmers, merchants, and lawyers but considerable numbers of criminals fleeing justice back East – murderers, horse thieves, highway robbers, and counterfeiters. The area soon became known as "Rogue's Harbor." Peter Cartwright, the famous Methodist circuit rider who moved to Logan County in 1793, observed that "although there was law, yet it could not be executed, and it was a desperate state of society."

Civilizing influences in the early nineteenth century eventually tamed Logan's lawlessness. Certainly religion played an important part. During the 1790s the Presbyterians, Baptists, and Methodists had established small societies in the Red River area south of Russellville, but it was not until the outbreak of the Great Revival of 1800 that Christianity exerted a significant impact on the inhabitants of south-central Kentucky. God's chief instrument in bringing about this remarkable awakening was James McGready, a Presbyterian minister from North Carolina, who in 1796 arrived in Logan County to take charge of the Red River Presbyterian Church. By the end of 1797, he had organized two more churches on the Gasper and Muddy rivers. To these three small groups, McGready preached the importance of a conversion experience and a personal witness of the Holy Spirit. Revival stirrings were evident as early as 1797, but in June 1800, as McGready described it, the awakening "exceeded all that my eyes ever beheld on earth." Beginning at Red River, where "multitudes were struck down under conviction," the revival spread quickly to the Gasper and Muddy river congregations, where great crowds assembled "to see a strange work," some traveling distances of forty, fifty, even one hundred miles. Twenty to thirty families came to the Gasper River meeting in wagons with their provisions and camped near the churchyard, thus establishing Logan County as the birthplace of the camp meeting in America. Before long Kentucky and then the entire South were ablaze with the revival fires of one of the greatest religious movements in the nation's history.

The Great Revival did more than satisfy the spiritual hunger of isolated and unchurched frontiersmen. It also played an important part in raising the moral tone of their communities. As one student of frontier religion put it, "The fact seems indisputable that the camp meeting caused many to lead a more socially desirable existence." In Logan County a growing emphasis on education was one evidence of that desire to improve society. Indeed, churches and schools enjoyed a close relationship in the early nineteenth century. Although classes at first were usually held in homes, some church buildings also served as schools. And more often than not, the teachers were ministers. In 1798 James McGready became "the first teacher of the language" in Russellville; in the same year Lewis Moore, a Baptist minister at the Head of Muddy River, began teaching both the black and white children of his neighborhood; and in 1806 Valentine Cook, a Methodist preacher, settled at Muddy River and built a small house in which to preach and teach.

With little public support for education until the twentieth century, local neighborhoods, if they had any schools at all, had to rely primarily on their own resources. After considerable discussion someone would donate a small plot of land upon which a log schoolhouse was built. This crude little structure usually contained a plain dirt floor, backless benches or seats hewn out of logs, oiled paper to cover window openings, and a large log-burning fireplace. In the towns the early schoolhouses were likely to be less primitive. Russellville, for example, could boast of Newton Academy, founded in 1798, which was a brick building with two rooms below, two above, and a hallway on each floor. Financial support for these early schools came from parents, who paid from fifty cents to a dollar per month for each child. By the 1840s a few improvements were discernible, including a split-log floor, a table for the teacher, and a few textbooks in grammar and arithmetic.

Teachers labored under severe handicaps. It was difficult, for example, to teach writing and arithmetic without blackboards and few slates. Tables located under the windows enabled the pupils to practice their lessons with quill pens dipped in ink made from oak galls, pokeberry juice, and iron rust. In the absence of books, much of the teaching was conducted by word of mouth with considerable attention to the mastery of words. For this reason spelling was an important part of the curriculum, and spelling bees became popular diversions for school children and adults alike.

George Dick's neighborhood was blessed with schools from an early date. As early as 1816 William F. Gaines taught at Old Volney, a short distance to the north on the Russellville-Clarksville Road. Volney Institute had some distinguished teachers, among them James H. Fuqua, who later became state superintendent of public instruction. By 1818 another school was operating in a little grove where Olmstead now stands. In a "near new log house" the Reverend Thomas Smith taught both boys and girls the "more advanced branches of learning," including elementary grammar, geography "with the use of maps," and arithmetic "beyond the rule of three." Smith apparently followed a teacher known as "the eccentric Dr. Thurston," who never drank water but always brought with him a jug of "Blackjack tea." During the 1860s the Volney and Olmstead schools gave way to the Browder Institute, located about a mile west of Olmstead, on land donated by Richard Browder, George Dick's uncle. With James H. Fuqua as principal, the new school attracted a considerable number of boys and girls, perhaps too many. George Dick stopped by the school during the fall of 1869, and upon observing that only two or three out of eighty students had copy books and were learning to write, he lamented: "It is a shame that teachers are either so crowded or so neglectful."

George Dick's visit to Browder Institute was typical of the interest in education shared by many parents, who, in return for their tuition payments, expected good performances from both their children and the teachers. For this reason the annual "exhibition," usually in early June, was the high point in the school year. On these occasions the oral examinations, recitations, and orations of the students provided an opportunity for the entire community to evaluate the quality of the year's work.

Educational opportunities beyond the elementary grades also existed for those citizens of south-central Kentucky who could afford them. A number of academies, emphasizing a classical education centering on Latin, Greek, and mathematics, flourished in the larger towns in the region and across the border in nearby Tennessee. Russellville alone could point to the establishment of at least four schools offering high-school level work before 1838. And in 1856 the town witnessed the founding of two reputable colleges: Bethel College, a Baptist school for men, and its counterpart, Russellville Collegiate Institute, which was taken over in 1860 by the Louisville Conference of the Methodist Church and renamed Logan Female College. Each school employed a staff of six well-qualified teachers and enrolled approximately 150 students.

As Logan Countians struggled to provide educational opportunities for their children, they also grappled with other problems arising from their time and place. It is difficult for Americans living in the second half of the twentieth century to imagine what it was like to live without electricity, indoor plumbing, and the internal combustion engine. Steam engines had revolutionized the iron and steel and textile industries of the Northeast, but few Americans were freed from the burden of backbreaking labor and the drudgery of doing things by hand. This was especially true of farmers. Corn, for example, was planted by hand, cultivated by hand, harvested by hand, and shucked by hand. One last time-consuming step was required to transform the corn into meal. A small boy generally rode horseback astride a sack of corn several miles to the nearest water mill. There the corn was ground, a portion of it retained by the miller, and a sack of meal placed on the horse for the return trip. The young lad's reward came that evening, when he sat down to a supper of hog meat, milk, and hotcakes or eggbread made from the freshly milled corn meal.

The trip to the mill and back could take the better part of a day, a fact that points up another problem faced not only by Kentuckians but by most Americans before the Civil War, namely, the problem of distance. There simply was no way to move quickly from one place to another, and unless one lived near a navigable stream or a railroad, there were few travel options available. One could walk, ride a horse, or ride in a horse-drawn carriage, wagon, or sleigh. Mules sometimes took the place of horses.

Animals presented a continual challenge to travelers. In 1853 George Dick nearly broke his leg when his horse fell; in 1874 he barely escaped serious injury when he was thrown from his buggy and landed under the wheels; and in 1885, as he tried to mount a borrowed horse, the animal wheeled around so violently that he fell off into the street, bruising his hip and leg. Occasionally, frightened animals could become uncontrollable. In 1854 George Dick's wife, Lizzie, and his stepmother barely escaped with their lives when a team of runaway horses with a wagon careened through the streets of Russellville and narrowly missed crashing into their buggy. George Dick's cousin was badly crippled in 1872, when a mule ran away with her buggy. The most traumatic experience of all occurred in October of the same year, after an evening worship service at Stevenson's Chapel, near Russellville. Horses pulling a wagon filled with women and children took fright and ran out of control into the woods. Panic ensued as men, women, and children raced through the darkness, calling out to each other in a frantic effort to account for missing loved ones. One woman was seriously injured.

Safe travel depended not only on trustworthy animals but on good roads. Weather conditions, therefore, were a constant concern for travelers as they ventured out on the unpaved roads of Logan County. Winter and spring rains could transform such roads into quagmires, quickly sapping the energy of both man and beast. During summer dry spells the mud turned to dust. Snow-covered roads created other problems as George Dick learned in 1881, when the sleigh in which he was riding overturned three times. ("I set sleigh-riding down as a humbug.") Traveling at night without lights could also be risky, especially during a new moon or cloudy weather. On one such night in 1863, in "a darkness that might almost be felt," George Dick and his companions frequently lost the road, their horses running into trees and fences.

In 1825 a new era in transportation opened up for Logan Countians. On January 2 the first stagecoach rolled into Russellville and, with a blast from the stage horn, pulled up in front of the only tavern in town, where it elicited wonder and admiration from the people who gathered around. In the driver's seat was an amazing eighteen-year-old named Rolla Rohrer, who the year before had carried mail on horseback between Russellville and Nashville, covering the fifty miles in seven hours with several changes of horses. Soon Russellville was linked by stagecoach to Hopkinsville to the west, Bowling Green to the northeast, and Nashville to the south. These impressive vehicles, normally pulled by two horses, could accommodate up to a dozen passengers inside and two more on top. In addition, they also carried laundry, bread baskets, coops of poultry, flour, and grain. The body of the coach swung on heavy rawhide springs, which produced a rocking sensation. During the winter months a generous layer of straw on the floor of the unheated coach afforded some relief from the cold. Stagecoaches rumbled along from five to seven miles per hour with frequent changes of horses. On his run from Nashville to Hopkinsville, by way of Russellville, Rohrer changed horses seven times during the eighty-five-mile trip. Old Volney, about a mile from George Dick's home, was a regular stagecoach stop where horses were exchanged.

Until 1860 stagecoaches provided Logan County with its only means of public transportation. Then a new and formidable competitor appeared – the railroad. Although railroad advocates had been active since the 1830s in Kentucky, especially in the Bluegrass region, they made little headway until the 1850s. As early as 1830 work began on a railroad to connect Lexington with Louisville. By 1834 the section from Lexington to Frankfort, the state capital, was completed, but construction on the Louisville to Frankfort route faltered and was not finished until 1852.

Even before the last spike was driven in the Lexington, Frankfort, and Louisville Road, a movement was afoot that would bring the iron horse to Logan County. In the late 1840s the idea of a railroad through western Kentucky linking Louisville to the southern market generated considerable excitement in the region along the Louisville and Nashville turnpike, regarded by many as the most logical route. In 1850 both Kentucky and Tennessee granted charters for the construction of the Louisville and Nashville Railroad. Since neither the federal nor the state governments provided any assistance for the project, the L & N had to depend on local support to provide the estimated $5,000,000 needed to build the road. Construction began in 1853, but financial problems delayed completion until 1859. Fortunately for George Dick's neighborhood, the L & N undertaking gave impetus to the construction of a branch line to run from Memphis eastward through Clarksville, Tennessee, and then northeastward through Logan County to connect with the main line at Memphis Junction, just south of Bowling Green. George Dick's father, Robert, played an important part in raising Logan County's subscription of $300,000 for the project. The first train ran from Bowling Green to Clarksville on September 24, 1860. Although George Dick's journal lay neglected during this time, he undoubtedly witnessed this historic event, since several hundred feet of the railroad track ran along the eastern border of his farm. Nearby Hogan's Station was renamed Olmstead in honor of the popular foreman who had supervised the building of the L & N through southern Logan County.

The railroad was the nineteenth century's answer to the problem of distance. For the residents of the Olmstead community, it meant that the trip to Bowling Green, approximately forty miles away, required slightly more than an hour, instead of seven to eight hours by stagecoach. Even far-off places were now within comparatively easy reach. When George Dick returned from southern Illinois after a visit in 1872, he marveled that he could eat supper in Ashby and breakfast at home the next morning after an overnight trip of 223 miles. "Surely," he exclaimed, "railroads are great institutions." Four years later it took only two days by train for George Dick and Lizzie to travel from Washington, D.C., to Olmstead when they returned from their Centennial vacation. Without the railroad the trip would have become an exhausting journey of over two weeks.

The L & N did more than speed up the movement of people and freight. It also accelerated the flow of information from the outside world. Earlier in the nineteenth century, Logan Countians had kept abreast of events primarily through the reports of travelers and the efforts of Russellville printers, who from an early date had published newspapers for the surrounding area, first the *Mirror* (1806–10), then the *Weekly Messenger* (1810–36), and finally the *Russellville Herald* (1836–79), a paper to which George Dick was a faithful subscriber and an occasional contributor. Since these early newspapers were published only once a week and relied heavily on news items that had already appeared in papers in other parts of the country, their coverage of national events could easily be out of date by two to three weeks or more. The railroad changed all that, for every depot possessed the amazing telegraph, which could bring the news of great events to formerly remote areas within a matter of hours. The telegraph at Olmstead Depot, just a half mile from George Dick's farm, arrived just in time to allow that community to follow closely the events of the tumultuous decade that lay ahead: political crises, the movements of armies, and the results of great battles.

Although Logan Countians on the eve of the Civil War could point to their achievements in education, transportation, and communication as evidence of their progress toward a more settled society, there were some important ways in which their living conditions had changed but little since pioneer days. This was true with respect to the uncertainty of life itself. Today it is not unusual for one to approach middle age without having suffered the loss of a single close relative. In the nineteenth century such cases were rare; death was a frequent reminder of one's mortality.

Medical care as it exists today, with licensed physicians, professional nurses, hospitals, and reputable drugs, simply was unknown in Kentucky before the twentieth century, and it was much the same for the rest of the country. The medical profession was not lucrative and enjoyed little prestige; consequently, it attracted few qualified men. Some were barely literate. Kentucky required no formal training of physicians until 1874 and no licenses to practice medicine until the twentieth century. Age-old remedies dominated medical treatment. Common practices, all designed to remove from the patient the poisons responsible for this illness, included blistering (applying hot cups to raise blisters in which the alleged poisons collected and from which they were drained), bleeding (drawing blood from the patient to the point of fainting), and the use of calomel (a purgative that had the unfortunate side effect of rotting one's teeth and bones). Few pain killers were available. The most common were whisky and laudanum, the latter a mixture of alcohol and morphine. Aspirin was not introduced until the twentieth century. With few drugs available physicians frequently concocted their own pills, potions, and salves.

Patent medicines were also popular. Among those advertised regularly in the *Russellville Herald* were Hurley's Stomach Bitters, Coe's Cough Balsam, Brile's Universal Fever Pills, Bull's Worm Destroyer, Dr. Seabrook's Elixir of Pyrophosate of Iron and Calisaya, and Lyon's Periodical Drops ("The Great Female Remedy for Irregularities"). Occasionally, as a public service the *Herald* shared a remedy with its readers. The following cure for diphtheria, "highly recommended by physicians, the press, and people who have used it," appeared in October 1867:

Nitrate of potash	one	drachma	(powdered)
Alum	one	"	"
Table Salt	two	"	"
Black Pepper	one	"	"
Yellow Puccoon Root	one	"	"

After combining the above ingredients with boiling water and apple vinegar, readers were directed to use the resulting portion as a gargle, "swallowing a little."

In a view of the primitive state of medicine during the nineteenth century, it is perhaps no exaggeration to say that from beginning to end, life was a veritable struggle for survival. Childbirth was an agonizing ordeal taking place at home with female relatives and friends attending; doctors normally were summoned only if complications developed. Breach births invariably resulted in death to both mother and child. Childhood was another critical period. Many infants died during the first year as victims of cholera infantum, or diarrhea, resulting from contaminated milk or water. Diseases such as mumps, measles, scarlet fever, smallpox, whooping cough, and diphtheria appeared with distressing regularity. Diphtheria alone took a frightful toll. George Dick recorded on January 8, 1876, that he met a "Bro & Sister Gray" in Trenton, Kentucky, "returning from the burial of her oldest daughter − 14 years old . . . the third they have buried in 8 days." Six weeks later on a return visit, he wrote the following heartrending entry: "Poor Sister Gray looks very sad & sorrowful after the death of *all* five of her children with Diphtheria."

Adults lived with similar uncertainties. Dysentery ("bloody flux") and typhoid fever, which nearly took George Dick's life in 1856, were endemic during the summer months. Tuberculosis ("consumption") and smallpox also claimed many lives. Although vaccination and inoculation for the latter were known, they were rarely practiced. Epidemics of Asiatic cholera struck periodically, sometimes with devastating force. The disease left Russellville "a Great House of Mourning" during the summer of 1835. So many died and so many fled the village that the task of burying the victims was carried out only with the greatest difficulty. Cholera ravaged Kentucky again from 1849 to 1854, in 1866, and in 1873. When George Dick learned during June 1873 that the disease was raging in Memphis and would undoubtedly make its way to Kentucky, he observed with a note of resignation: "We ought to be prudent, use disinfectants and trust in God for safety." In that statement he summed up perhaps the best defense available against any disease during his lifetime.

Despite the grim realities of their existence, Kentuckians found numerous ways to enjoy life and to relieve the drudgery and isolation so characteristic of rural living during the nineteenth century. They were especially fond of large outdoor gatherings such as agricultural fairs, racecourses, political meetings, barbecues, and, most of all, county court day. James Lane Allen, a popular nineteenth-century Kentucky author, once described court day as "the centre of the Kentuckian's public social life, the arena of his passions and amusements, the rallying point of his political discussions, the market-place of his business transactions, a civil unit of his institutional history." On the same Monday each month (in Logan County it was the fourth Monday), the roads leading to the square around the courthouse of the county seat were clogged with carriages, buggies, horsemen, pedestrians, and droves of livestock, all pouring in from the surrounding country and neighboring hills. It was "as though by some vast suction system the town had with one exercise of force drawn all of the country life into itself." The whole family participated in this monthly holiday. Court day was a time for buying, selling, swapping, bartering, sharing local news, exchanging political opinions, and exhibiting livestock. It was an occasion made to order for politicians, itinerant vendors of patent medicines, and wandering musicians, who with their voices and fiddles entertained the crowds with "Gentle Annie," "Sweet Alice," "Ben Bolt," and other popular ballads of the day. Less happily, the first court day of the new year was also the time when slaves were hired out for the year or sometimes put up for sale on the block in front of the courthouse.

The annual county fair, normally held at the county seat, provided another important social outlet for Kentuckians. The first fair in Kentucky was held in Lexington as early as 1816, but it was not until the 1830s that fairs became popular in a number of counties, including Logan. After 1838, when twenty-five county organizations sponsored fairs, the movement waned only to revive again during the 1850s. Robert Browder, George Dick's father, played an important part in the resurgence of interest in Logan County. By the 1850s the fair had become more than an exhibition of blooded stock, the latest inventions, and superior vegetables; it was a festival for the entire family to enjoy. People poured into town, filling hotels and private homes to overflowing. Enterprising merchants awaited them with a generous supply of goods imported from northern manufacturers.

Almost everything raised on the farms and grown in the fields and gardens could be found at the fair as well as home manufactures and mechanical devices. Entries for which premiums were awarded included livestock, vegetables, fruits, grains, flowers, farm machinery, beds, carriages, hams, and chewing tobacco. George Dick thoroughly enjoyed the three-day fair held in Russellville in 1854, especially the buggy horse contest in which the driving was "spirited & expert." On the last day he took five pounds of his choice tobacco, but admitted rather sheepishly that it was "only 3d best in a show of three entries."

Entertainers, human and animal, also brightened the lives of south-central Kentuckians. In 1823 the Russellville Thespian Society scheduled four evenings of drama during the year. The featured plays, which included *Speed the Plough* and *She Stoops to Conquer,* were always followed by "a celebrated farce" such as *The Irishman in London* or *Love-à-la-Mode.* The following year area residents had a unique opportunity to see a "large and learned" elephant, billed as "the most sagacious animal in the world" and "one of the Greatest Curiosities ever offered to the public." Among other attractions during these early years were Siamese Twins, D. D. Bicknell's Puppet Show, Doctor Rose the Juggler, and an occasional circus.

By the late 1850s and after the Civil War, a considerable variety of performing groups were appearing in Bowling Green, Russellville, and other nearby towns. These included concerts by the Peak Family and the Empire Minstrels; plays by McFarland's Theatre, E. T. Stetson's Theatre, and the Cincinnati Dramatic Company; shows by the Bailey Troups, B. W. Ringer, and the Gaity Theatrical Company; and performances by such disparate entertainers as traveling Indians, a Chinese juggler, fighting bears, a four-legged baby, and Meredith Holland, "the Great Supernatural Calculator," who allegedly could solve "the most complex and abstruse mathematical problems."

Nothing, however, could generate excitement like the circus. Among those that scheduled appearances in south-central Kentucky were Spalding and Rogers; Bailey and Company; P. T. Barnum; and Maginley, Carroll and Company. It was a great day when the advance guard of the circus drove into Russellville and plastered the livery stable with posters of lions, tigers, and bareback riders. Some days later the circus lumbered into town, much to the delight of the populace, who gazed at the fat woman and the living skeleton in the sideshow and consumed generous amounts of popcorn, peanuts, ginger cakes, red lemonade, and striped stick candy. A parade featuring the circus band with its loud, brassy music frequently preceded the performances.

The Maginley, Carroll and Company's circus entertained large crowds at afternoon and evening exhibitions after its arrival in Russellville by special railway train in October 1867. Among the featured attractions were Madame Carroll, "Premiere Dame du Cirque"; Madamoiselle Tinkham, "the beautiful French Equilibriet'; the Belmont Brothers, gymnasts and acrobats ("The Hanlon Brothers are tame in comparison"); Professor William Cobb's trained dogs, goats, and monkeys; William Naylor, "champion bareback rider of America"; Sam Reinhart, "the Great Grotesque Clown and champion Leaper"; and the Cornet and Stringed Band "that can challenge the World." Two days later the *Russellville Herald* noted approvingly that Maginley's Circus was "an old fashioned circus, and the performances in the ring were free from everything rowdy or vulgar."

Kentucky country folks also found enjoyment in a number of activities associated with nineteenth-century rural living. These included husking bees, quilting parties, dances, shooting matches, cock fights, fishing, and hunting. Husking bees were especially popular, normally occurring late in the fall, when the harvest was done and frost had signaled the approach of winter. Neighboring families, including their slaves, came together for an afternoon and evening of work, feasting, and entertainment. The husking began early in the afternoon with whites and blacks gathered two and three deep around a huge pile of corn, which was divided roughly in half. The huskers, divided into two teams captained by black songsters, competed to see which would be the first to shuck through the center of the pile. The singing of the blacks was plaintive and melodious with the songsters' improvised lyrics alternating with an answering chorus. When the last ear of corn was shucked and thrown into the crib, the workers gave a shout that might have been heard for miles.

The huskers vied not only with each other but with the women of the neighborhood, who carried on a quilting bee in the "big room" of the farmhouse. It was a race to see if the corn pile or the quilt would be finished first. When the competition ended, a feast prepared by the servants was spread on the dining room table. As the old folks sat down to eat, the sound of the fiddle in the big room attracted the young people, who danced and feasted until daybreak.

THE RELIGIOUS SCENE

Although outdoor gatherings and traveling entertainers provided important diversions for nineteenth-century Kentuckians, nothing compared with the church as a socializing force among a scattered, frequently isolated rural population. Indeed, the church had a great deal to offer. For those who had only recently emigrated to the Bluegrass State, the familiarity of old customs and beliefs was a powerful antidote for loneliness and homesickness. The church satisfied the need for a sense of community as congregations, sharing similar beliefs and goals, came together for worship and fellowship. Identifying with a particular church carried with it some practical benefits also. Church members cared for each other during times of sickness and hardship and willingly assisted each other in such projects as building cabins or raising barns. One recent scholar, in summarizing the impact of religion on the lives of Kentuckians, concluded that "couples met, courted, married, lived by, and died within the physical and spiritual confines of their church."

Kentucky's religious foundations were laid during the late eighteenth century, when pioneers began to pour into the region from Atlantic seaboard colonies. As early as 1775 Roman Catholics from Maryland settled in Harrodsburg and secured a foothold in the face of overwhelming Protestant advantages. By the early 1780s the Baptists, Methodists, and Presbyterians had all established churches in the Bluegrass Region of north-central Kentucky. The Episcopalians, handicapped by their pro-British image and internal problems, were not successful in planting a church until the 1790s. Although all of these groups were important in creating the rich mosaic of Kentucky's religious culture, it was the Baptists and Methodists who were most successful in winning the hearts of the western settlers.

The growth of Methodism was especially noteworthy. By 1844, just sixty years after the famous Christmas Conference in Baltimore, when they severed their English connections, American Methodists had become the largest Protestant body in the United States with over 1,068,000 members. Their accomplishment was remarkable when viewed against the backdrop of the

1790s. Weakened by schism and struggling against a spiritual malaise that affected the entire country, the Methodists were unlikely candidates for such a lofty status among the nation's churches. Then came the Great Revival of 1800 and its marvelous creation, the camp meeting. Although a number of denominations adopted the camp meeting and benefited from it, none embraced it with more enthusiasm than the Methodists, and none garnered a greater harvest of souls. Between 1796 and 1804 the church grew from 56,664 to 115,411. As Francis Asbury, America's first Methodist bishop, witnessed the numbers flocking into his church, he exulted that "camp meetings have done this: glory to the Great I Am." By 1812 approximately 400 Methodist camp meetings were being held each year. In that same year the Western Conference of the Church enjoyed a fifty percent increase in membership.

Other factors, most of them peculiar to Methodism, also help to explain the success of the movement. Certainly the frontier-minded leadership of Bishop Asbury was important. When he arrived in America in 1771, he observed that some of the Methodist leaders did not have a passion for the wilderness, to which he responded, "I think I shall show them the way." And so he did. By the time the faithful bishop died in 1816, he had crossed the Appalachian Mountains sixty-two times and had traveled over 250,000 miles on horseback, much of it on roads or trails that beggared description. "My horse trots stiff," he once confided to his journal, "and no wonder when I have ridden him an average of 5,000 miles a year for five years successively."

Methodist theology was another feature that appealed to a nation caught up in a rising tide of egalitarian impulses after the War of 1812. In contrast to the Calvinists, who preached a limited atonement, the Methodists believed that when Jesus died on the cross, he paid for the sins of the entire human race and that salvation was potentially available to all. How individuals responded to God's free gift depended upon the exercise of their free will. "So then every one of us must give an account of himself to God," was a favorite Methodist text. Those who chose to accept God's redeeming grace inherited eternal life; those who resisted were condemned to eternal punishment. The doctrines of free grace, free will, and individual responsibility harmonized well with America's emerging democratic spirit.

The Methodists also enjoyed the advantages of a unique scheme of organization. Individual congregations, called classes, were linked together in circuits and visited by a preacher on horseback every six to eight weeks. Circuits were grouped together into districts under the vigilant eye of a presiding elder. The districts in turn comprised the annual conferences presided over by a bishop. Representatives of the latter bodies met every four years in a general conference of the entire church.

The circuit system, which originated in England with John Wesley, the founder of Methodism, was well suited to the American environment. Many frontier communities either had too few Methodists to justify a stationed preacher or were too poor to support one. The Church responded by marking out circuits, often 400 to 500 miles in circumference, and putting riders on them. When a preacher finished his circuit, he simply started all over again. In his absence the spiritual oversight of each congregation was often entrusted to the care of a lay member called the class leader. The circuit system created a superbly mobile force that enabled the Methodists to keep pace with America's westward-moving population.

Circuit riders were the "wheel horses" of the Methodist way. Equipped with a horse, a saddle and bags, a Bible, a hymn book, an umbrella, an overcoat, and sometimes a change of clothes, these remarkable men roughed it along the trails, challenged the dangers of the wilderness, and labored with courage and zeal for the sake of the gospel. Because they were undaunted by bad weather, their example in the face of blizzards or cloudbursts led to a folk saying: "There is nothing out today but crows and Methodist preachers." Circuit riders spent a good part of their lives poor, hungry, cold, wet, and saddlesore. They put up wherever they could, usually in a one-room cabin overrun with children, frequently fifteen to twenty, "for Providence is bountiful on the frontier in this matter." After a meal of corn bread and pork and after having led the family in evening devotions, Methodist preachers frequently spent the night sleeping in front of the fireplace on a flea-infested rug. They were equally accommodating in the matter of divine worship, adjusting readily to holding meetings in rude log cabins, barns, roadside taverns, or out-of-doors under the spreading branches of maples and beeches. They were indeed "native timber, with the bark on."

The work of the circuit rider was supplemented not only by the class leader but also by the faithful efforts of lay or local preachers. Whenever a young man of exemplary character manifested a gift for public speaking, he was encouraged by the class leader and the circuit rider to preach at every opportunity. When the presiding elder came around to hold "quarterly conference," the young man was then recommended for a "local preacher's license." Frequently local preachers were graduated to the itinerant ministry; that is, they were subject to appointment by the annual conference. Many, however, preferred to remain at home, pursuing secular vocations and preaching in their own or nearby neighborhoods as opportunities arose. In the absence of the circuit rider, local preachers often assumed responsibility for officiating at baptisms, marriages, and funerals. They also rendered invaluable service in conducting the Sunday class meetings and assisting in revivals.

Local preachers who were caught up in the westward movement played an important role in carrying Methodism to the frontier. In the words of A. H. Redford, an early historian of Kentucky Methodism and a close friend of George Dick, they went "not only as pioneer settlers, but as pioneers of their faith." Indeed, the first Methodist classes in the West were organized by lay preachers who later transferred them into the pastoral care of the circuit rider. The work of Francis Clark in Kentucky provides a good example. In 1783 he emigrated from Virginia to the vicinity of Danville in Mercer County, where he immediately organized a Methodist society. As a result of his efforts and the labors of other local preachers, there were soon enough Methodists in Kentucky to justify the creation of a Kentucky circuit, to which Bishop Asbury assigned James Haw and Benjamin Ogden. In 1786 they held their first services in the home of Thomas and Mary Stevenson at Kenton's Station in Mason County.

By the 1790s Methodism had spread to virtually all of the settled parts of Kentucky. It apparently reached southern Logan County about 1794, when a society was organized in the Red River region. At about the same time, Richard Bibb, a local preacher from Virginia built Bibb's Chapel, perhaps the first Methodist church building in the county, on his land six miles east of Russellville. Methodism, "much despised, and watched with a jealous eye," grew slowly in these early years compared with the Baptists and the Cumberland Presbyterians. (The latter group split off from the Presbyterian Church after the Revival of 1800 primarily because of differences over predestination, an educated ministry, and the use of revivalistic techniques.) Nevertheless, between 1806 and 1810 several more struggling Methodist societies emerged in such places as Russellville, Cook's Chapel (three miles northeast of Russellville on Muddy River), Kennerly's Chapel (nine miles north of Russellville), and Pleasant Run (eight miles southeast of Russellville).

Methodism established a foothold in the Olmstead neighborhood in 1815, when John J. Mackall, a layman, organized a class in his home consisting of himself, his wife, his mother, and an old black woman. By the time George Dick's father, Robert, arrived in 1825, the congregation had grown to fourteen, including four blacks. S. P. V. Gillispie, the traveling preacher who served this small society, was assigned to a circuit that embraced parts of Logan and Todd counties in Kentucky and portions of Robertson and Sumner counties in northern Tennessee; consequently, he held preaching services at the Mackall home only once every four weeks. There were seldom any Sunday services. In 1827 the group succeeded, "after many difficulties," in erecting a house of worship. Bethlehem Church, later referred to as Old Bethlehem, was a wooden structure built on land donated by Mackall and stood across the road from the present Olmstead school. Robert Browder and his brother, Richard, followed closely the construction of Old Bethlehem and undoubtedly gave enthusiastic support to the effort. At the end of 1827, Robert could look back over a year that had been eventful indeed – the building of a new church, the birth of George Dick, and the death of his dear wife, Helen.

About the time of Old Bethlehem's completion, the little congregation was strengthened by an influx of Methodist families from Virginia. Among them were the Hutchings, Moores, Sydnors, and Youngs, all destined to figure prominently in George Dick's life. None, however, made a more important contribution to the cause of Methodism in southern Logan County than George Dick's great uncle, Littleberry Browder, who arrived from Virginia in 1828. Uncle Berry, as everyone called him, was already advanced in years when he moved to Kentucky, but no one could match his zeal for the church. He immediately took charge of the Bethlehem congregation as class leader, visiting the sick, holding prayer meetings in private homes, and exhorting on Sundays. He had a reputation for being powerful in prayer. One contemporary observed that in revivals Uncle Berry rarely led in prayer without someone's conversion before his prayer was ended.

Soon after Uncle Berry's arrival, the first camp meeting ever conducted in the vicinity was held at Old Bethlehem. It continued for two weeks "with unabated interest" and resulted in over eighty "powerful" conversions. The congregation now began to flourish, and soon Old Bethlehem could no longer accommodate the crowds who sought to worship there. A new and larger brick church, also called Bethlehem, was erected about a mile to the west at the junction of the Clarksville and Olmstead roads. Bethlehem's growth and spiritual vigor undoubtedly played an important part in shaping George Dick's life as he advanced from childhood into his teenage years. Consequently, when he entered the ministry at the age of nineteen, he drew strength and assurance not only from the positive Christian atmosphere generated at home by his godly parents but from the example of the vibrant, close-knit fellowship of believers in Olmstead.

The church to which George Dick committed himself in 1846 possessed no such confidence. Only two years after it had emerged as the nation's largest religious body, the Methodist Church lay fragmented, joining the Presbyterians and Baptists as a victim of the controversy over slavery. In its formative years, American Methodism reflected the staunchly antislavery views of John Wesley. The Annual Conference of 1780, for example, expressed disapproval of slavery as "contrary to the laws of God, man, and nature," and four years later in Baltimore at the organizing conference of the Methodist Episcopal Church, the delegates adopted some rules of discipline for members who traded in slaves and preachers who owned them. In the decades that followed, however, cotton culture, with its slave-labor system, spread rapidly throughout the South and Old Southwest, and the church, in an effort to extend its membership in the region, not only made concessions to slaveholders but accepted a position that permitted southern members and clergy to control the denomination. By 1843 over 26,000 Methodists, including 1200 preachers, owned nearly 210,000 slaves. It was a potentially dangerous situation for the church, for as Professor Sydney Ahlstrom observed, "the church's unity depended . . . on the strict enforcement of silence or neutrality on the slavery question."

A half century of "silence or neutrality" ended during the 1830s as an increasing number of northern Methodists became actively involved in the antislavery crusade. When their efforts at the General Conferences of 1836 and 1840 failed to bring the church to a position favorable to their views, the splintering began. By 1841 the Wesleyan Methodist Church in Michigan had emerged, followed a year later by the Methodist Wesleyan Connection in New York. Everyone knew that the General Conference of 1844, which met in New York City, would be a difficult one. As it turned out, a potentially stormy session escalated into a major crisis over the case of a slaveholding bishop from Georgia. James O. Andrew, as a result of his two marriages, had inherited some slaves after his election as bishop in 1832. Though ignored for years, his ambivalent status by 1844 had become highly controversial. After more than a week of heated debate, the antislavery-dominated convention voted 111 to 69 to approve a resolution requesting Bishop Andrew to "desist from the exercise of his office so long as this impediment remains." It was too much for the southern delegates, who were now convinced that a division of the church was necessary. When a plan of separation was brought before the conference, it produced little debate and received near unanimous support from both northern and southern delegates. The plan provided for two general conferences, the right of the clergy to choose their affiliation, a mutual respect for state boundaries in the matter of church extension, and an equitable division of the publishing house and other properties. And so it was that sixteen years before the nation divided, an institution important to national unity moved inexorably toward its own dissolution. When the conference adjourned on June 10, a united Methodist Church did not meet again for nearly a century.

On the morning after adjournment, the southern delegates issued a call for a convention to meet in Louisville the following spring for the purpose of devising a way "to free the minority of the South from the oppressive jurisdiction of the majority in the North." In response to that announcement, nearly one hundred delegates from the thirteen southern annual conferences gathered at old Fourth Street Church in May 1845. By a vote of 94 to 3, they separated from the Methodist Episcopal Church and proceeded to organize the Methodist Episcopal Church, South. Bishop Andrew gladly accepted the invitation to become one of the two bishops in the southern church.

When the separation occurred, eighteen-year-old George Dick was only a year from beginning his first appointment as a junior preacher on the Hopkinsville Circuit. He undoubtedly was saddened by the disruption of his church, but at the same time he endorsed the decision of the Louisville convention as an honorable course of action. It was an understandable position for a young man who had grown up in an environment in which slaveholding was deeply rooted and accepted as an integral part of one's existence. Besides, he had other things to think about. The burden of preparing himself spiritually for the work of the ministry into which he was about to enter lay heavily upon him. His youth and inexperience quite naturally troubled him. And in this regard one of his journal entries indicates that he found considerable encouragement in St. Paul's admonition to Timothy: "Let no man despise thy youth; but be thou an example of the believers in work, in conversation, in charity, in spirit, in faith, in purity."

Browder's Kinfolk

Although the relationship of George Dick to most of the people who move across the pages of his journal is reasonably clear, sorting out his relatives poses some special problems. As an aid to the reader, I have prepared the following select list of personalities and indicated their ties to George Dick. Since the Sydnors played such an important part in Browder's life, I have included them in the listing as well; actually they were distantly related to him.

Bell, Caleb – husband of Jane Browder, George Dick's paternal aunt

Browder, Almeda – paternal aunt; wife of Robert Hutchings; mother of Dr. George H. and David B. Hutchings

Browder, Amanda Small – wife of Richard C. Browder, George Dick's paternal cousin

Browder, Annie – half-sister; wife of Dr. Daniel Bailey

Browder, Bowling – no known relationship; possibly son of Henry Browder

Browder, David – paternal cousin; oldest son of Richard Browder

Browder, David P. – half-brother; husband of Florence Bailey Browder

Browder, Elizabeth Anderson – first wife of Richard Browder, George Dick's paternal uncle

Browder, Emma Jones – sister-in-law; wife of William M. Browder

Browder, Fannie – daughter of William R. Browder, George Dick's paternal cousin; second wife of Dr. Daniel Bailey

Browder, Florence Bailey – sister-in-law; wife of David P. Browder

Browder, Francis G. (Frank) – half-brother

Browder, George R. – third son

Browder, Ginnie Warfield – wife of Thomas E. Browder; younger sister of George Dick's wife Lizzie

Browder, Hanson W. – second son; husband of Jenny Martin Browder

Browder, Helen P. Jones – first wife of William R. Browder, George Dick's paternal cousin

Browder, Helen S. – daughter and oldest child; wife of Charles W. Roach

Browder, Henry – no known relationship

Browder, James W. (Jimmy) – half-brother; husband of Margaret Walker Browder

Browder, Jenny Martin – daughter-in-law; wife of Hanson W. Browder

Browder, John N. – half-brother

Browder, Lizzie (Ann Elizabeth) Warfield – wife

Browder, Luther W. – fourth son

Browder, Martha H. – paternal cousin; daughter of William C. Browder; wife of Dr. J. S. Baker

Browder, Mary E. – paternal cousin; daughter of William C. Browder; wife of William B. Hughes

Browder, Mary M. – half-sister; wife of Thomas B. Sydnor

Browder, Mattie G. – daughter of Richard C. Browder, George Dick's paternal cousin; wife of Joseph J. Bell

Browder, Richard (Dick) – paternal uncle; married twice: (1) Elizabeth Anderson and (2) Susan Boyer

Browder, Richard C. (Dick) – paternal cousin; son of William C. Browder; husband of Amanda Small Browder

Browder, Robert – father; married twice: (1) Helen Sarah Walker and (2) Sarah Gilmer

Browder, Robert W. – oldest son

Browder, Sarah Boyer (Sallie) – second wife of Richard Browder, George Dick's paternal uncle

Browder, Sarah Gilmer – stepmother; wife of Robert Browder

Browder, Sarah Hazelwood (Sallie) – wife of William C. Browder, George Dick's paternal uncle

Browder, Thomas E. – paternal cousin; son of Richard Browder

Browder, Wallace W. – son and youngest child

Browder, Wilbur F. – second cousin; son of David Browder

Browder, William C. – paternal uncle; husband of Sarah Hazelwood Browder

Browder, William M. – half-brother; husband of Emma Jones Browder

Browder, William R. (Billy) – paternal cousin; son of Richard Browder; married twice: (1) Helen P. Jones and (2) Mary E. Sydnor

Browder, Willie Brock – second cousin; son of Richard C. Browder

Call, Wilkinson – second cousin of George Dick's mother Helen; U.S. Senator from Florida

Duncan, Courtenay Walker – cousin of George Dick's mother Helen; wife of Erastus B. Duncan

Hutchings, David B. – paternal cousin; youngest son of Almeda Browder Hutchings; husband of Martha Small Hutchings

Hutchings, Dr. George H. – paternal cousin; oldest son of Almeda Browder Hutchings; husband of Minerva Baker Hutchings

Hutchings, Minerva Baker – wife of Dr. George H. Hutchings, George Dick's paternal cousin

Moore, Ann Browder – paternal aunt; wife of John P. Moore

Moore, David B. – paternal cousin; oldest child of Ann Browder Moore; husband of Mary White Moore

Moore, George Nick – paternal cousin; youngest child of Ann Browder Moore; husband of Mary Gatewood Moore

Moore, John P. – husband of Ann Browder Moore, George Dick's paternal aunt

Roach, Charles W. – son-in-law; husband of Helen S. Browder

Sydnor, Catherine H. – wife of David B. Sydnor; mother of Thomas B. and Washington A. (Wash) Sydnor

Sydnor, David B. – husband of Catherine H. Sydnor; father of Thomas B. and Washington A. (Wash) Sydnor

Sydnor, David E. – second son of David B. Sydnor; married three times: (1) Piety Greenfield, (2) Frances Cornelius, and (3) Betty Hughes Thurston

Sydnor, Ellen Spillman – wife of Washington A. (Wash) Sydnor

Sydnor, Mary E. – daughter of David B. Sydnor; second wife of William R. Browder

Sydnor, Thomas B. – third son of David B. Sydnor; husband of Mary M. Browder

Sydnor, Washington A. (Wash) – oldest child of David and Catherine Sydnor; husband of Ellen Spillman Sydnor

Walker, David S. – maternal uncle; son of David and Mary Barbour Walker

Walker, Helen S. – George Dick's mother; daughter of David and Mary Barbour Walker

Walker, James D. – maternal cousin; son of James Volney Walker; U.S. Senator from Arkansas

Walker, James V. – maternal uncle; son of David and Mary Barbour Walker; husband of Susan McLean Walker

Walker, Rose – maternal cousin; daughter of James V. Walker

Walker, Susan McLean – wife of James Volney Walker, George Dick's maternal uncle

Warfield, Alexander G. (Alick) – youngest half-brother of George Dick's wife Lizzie; son of George H. and Elizabeth Johnson Warfield

Warfield, Amanda – half-sister of George Dick's wife Lizzie; daughter of George H. and Elizabeth Johnson Warfield

Warfield, Charles – paternal uncle of George Dick's wife Lizzie; husband of Mary Warfield; brother of Betsy Warfield Waters

Warfield, Dora Pollard – wife of George W. Warfield; sister-in-law of George Dick's wife Lizzie

Warfield, George H. – father of George Dick's wife Lizzie; married twice: (1) Susan Waters and (2) Elizabeth Johnson

Warfield, George W. – son of George H. and Susan Waters Warfield; brother of George Dick's wife Lizzie; husband of Dora Pollard Warfield

Warfield, James H. – son of George H. and Susan Waters Warfield; oldest brother of George Dick's wife Lizzie

Warfield, Susan Virginia (Ginnie) – daughter of George H. and Susan Waters Warfield; younger sister of George Dick's wife Lizzie; wife of Thomas E. Browder

Waters, Betsy Warfield – paternal aunt of George Dick's wife Lizzie; wife of Walter Waters; sister of Charles Warfield

Waters, Walter – husband of Betsy Warfield Waters, paternal aunt of George Dick's wife, Lizzie

Browder: A Brief Chronology

1827, January 11 – Birth
1846 – Licensed to preach
1848 – Ordained deacon
1850, September 5 – Marriage to Ann Elizabeth Warfield
1850 – Ordained elder
1850–60 – Superannuated
1851, August 5 – Birth of daughter Helen Susan
1853, April 23 – Birth of son Robert Walter
1855, January 21 – Birth of son Hanson Warfield
1857, June 17 – Birth of son George Richard
1858, November 19 – Birth of daughter Sarah Virginia (Ginnie)
1860, November 21 – Death of Ginnie
1860–61 – Preacher at Russellville Station
1861, April 6 – Birth of son Luther Wools
1861–1863 – Preacher on Logan Circuit
1863–65 – Preacher at Hadensville
1865, October 12 – Birth of son Wallace Warfield
1865–66 – Preacher on Russellville Circuit
1866–68 – Preacher on Elkton Circuit
1868 – Preacher at Allensville
1869–72 – Superannuated
1870, May 20 – Birth of daughter Lizzie Warfield
1870, September 17 – Death of Lizzie Warfield
1872–74 – Preacher on Allensville Circuit
1874–76 – Agent for Logan Female College and Warren College
1876–80 – Presiding Elder Bowling Green District
1880–84 – Presiding Elder Russellville District
1882 – Delegate to General Conference (Nashville)
1884–86 – Presiding Elder Owensboro District
1884 – Delegate to Centenary Conference of Methodist Church (Baltimore)
1886, September 3 – Death

Volume I

1852–1854

"Lizzie"
Ann Elizabeth Warfield Browder

"I do not feel worthy of such a treasure."

August 5, 1852 — This is little Helens birthday — a year old — she is very small — but pretty & sprightly. She is a great source of pleasure — interest & hope to us. She is company & amusement — & although her afflictions — colic, whooping cough, tooth fever biles have caused her to be troublesome — yet her bright eyes — constant smiles — prattling voice & playful ways more than compensate for our watchfulness & care. A few times we thought proper to punish her for displaying bad temper — and although her size would deny the rationality & propriety of our course — yet the result showed that she was capable of restraining her temper & a slight whipping always had the desired effect. It is very painful to us to chastise a sweet darling child — pleasant & loving — but the book of Wisdom teaches to use the rod of correction. I have full confidence in her mothers ability to govern & control her & pray God that we may both be spared to educate & train our dear babe to his glory & her temporal & eternal good. We have concluded to give her a piece of money each birthday to be kept until she is old enough to apply it to some good use of her own choosing.

August 6 — Lizzie was just getting ready to go to fathers [Robert Browder] when Helen was suddenly attacked with excruciating nausea, stupor & coldness — she looked & felt like a corpse but continued to breathe. We applied camphor — warm bath & mustard plaster to her wrists & ankles & sent Geo Nick [Moore] for Dr [George H.] Hutchings who soon came & gave an emetic which relieved the innocent sufferer.

August 7 — Tomorrow I have an appointment at Bethlehem [Church]. I am not prepared — religiously, intellectually, nor physically — to preach. Lord, prepare me by thy spirit!

August 8 — Up early — read some scripture — part of Wesley's sermon on the Narrow way — went to Sunday school. Walked through the woods — praying and thinking. At 11 preached Matt. 7:13–14 with some liberty.*

August 18 — I had a conversation with Dr Nick Thomas an Infidel author on the subject of religion. He was respectful & polite. I was kind & candid — told him his book was dangerous — his faith ruinous. If he was right I was safe. If I was right he was lost.

August 20 — After dinner went to fathers & heard that Bro Gilbert had cholera — ran over & found him almost dead — reduced — greatly — vomiting & purging copiously — cramped almost to death — & suffering most intense pain — more than I can describe. The Dr had failed to relieve him — father applied a large poultice of mush & red pepper to the stomach & bowels & rubbed the extremities with sp[iri]ts of Turpentine until the cramp was relieved. Dr Hutchings was called in & found him sinking — almost collapsed — suffering pain — almost blind & deaf — cold as death — drenched with perspiration — and complaining insufferable heat & suffocation. Nearly all night Dr & I watched by his bed — & natural pulse & beat restored. When in the worst pain he shouted glory — said he could see the Glory land — & was willing & waiting to go home. Who would exchange religion like this for ought else beneath the sun? When I come to die give me Jesus.

August 23 — Lizzie & I started down to her fathers [near Clarksville, Tennessee]. Roads muddy — stopped all night at uncle Charles [Warfield].

August 24 — Reached father W[arfield]s to dinner — was delayed on the way by breaking of a trace. Neighbor McCulloch was kind enough to lend us his buggie — but it was old & ugly, yet I am thankful for the loan.

August 25 — [Olmstead] Took Mc's buggie home — spend the night with father. I feel lost to be at home without Lizzie & Helen.

August 30 — I started home [from Bell's Chapel] & the weather being immensely hot we rode through Elkton in our shirt sleeves. I saw Gould just starting to [Annual] Conference* in Louisville. Poor Gould as usual is in a difficulty. He has been tried for falsehood but cleared & now he is charged with it again — together with many improper & foolish things. I find the prevailing sentiment to be that he is unqualified for usefulness as an itinerant preacher* & ought to be located.* The poor fellow is almost crazy & detained me several hours — urging me to go to Conference & defend him.

September 2 — Little George Warfield & I hitched up my young Maria & Tupper to aunt Sally's carriage & set out for daddy W[arfield]s [to pick up Lizzie and Helen]. The dear little gal was delighted to see me & began to laugh & chatter — "papa perty — papa perty."

September 4 — We all packed up & started, after dinner, to uncle [Charles] Waters — found all well & feasting on watermelons.

September 5 — Two years ago to day — I was married. Two years of peace — contentment & love — I have spent with her whose heart was mine in the happy days of childhood. May we long live to bless each other! We dined at uncle Charles [Warfield's] — and came back to uncle Waters tonight. In coming down the very steep hill in front of the house — the breast strops broke & the carriage dashed down upon the horses. My young mare which had worked so admirably — became frightened & her efforts to get away from the wheel that was pressing her down — broke out the tongue. I had taken the precaution to make Lizzie & the children get out or we might have been killed. The strops were nearly worn out & it seems almost miraculous that we all escaped unhurt after risking our lives so many times. I am quite unwell tonight — & feel some uneasiness about getting home with a broken carriage & horses that have been scared — but Tupper was not alarmed — & I think would not have run if the whole carriage had rushed against him.

September 6 – We patched up the carriage & started to church. The horses seemed perfectly gentle & we got on safely. A Bro Willis from Red River circuit* preached an appropriate sermon with good effect – we had several mourners* & a real shouting time.

September 7 – We came home & found that but little of consequence had been done while we were gone. Our servants[1] are as good as others – but all of them do better when they have an "overseer."

September 8 – I made an engagement with Thornton Smith to sell a load of Watermelons for me – I have an unusual success in raising them.

September 10 – I went to town[2] on some business of the Sons of Temperance.[3] I was amused on the way at some wagoners who were making great pretension to telling the age of horses & no two of them agreed to the age of any one horse out of almost a dozen. One of them describing a larger mule he had seen – said he was seventeen hands & ten inches high! not knowing that four inches make a hand.

September 11 – Father made a railroad speech at Gordonsville.

September 17 – I took my wagon & drove down to Bevears Mill – after the corn which was left there more than two months ago – & had to exchange it for meal. I do not like the signs much – & what I saw to day convinces me that a man will gain by *seeing* his grain measured at that mill.

September 20 – Rainy. Read the papers – fixed a hearth in our room which has needed repairing for a year.

September 24 – Washed out my gun – ready for pigeons & Hawks. We are expecting delegates to the Baptist Association,[4] to be held at Union – embracing next Sunday.

September 26 – A beautiful, bright sabbath. Lizzie went with us to church – an immense assembly was present thronging house – shed & grove – an array of buggies – barouches – carriages – wagons &c were dotted through the woods –

1. It is not known how many slaves George Dick owned. His name does not appear in the Slave Schedules of the U. S. Census for 1850. Entries for December 2, 1852, and February 5, 1852, indicate that he had perhaps three slaves – Mary, Isaac, and Ann.
2. "Town" to George Dick was Russellville.
3. The Order of the Sons of Temperance was organized in New York City in 1842. The fundamental principle of the movement was total abstinence. *Harper's Encyclopedia of United States History* (10 Vols., New York, 1905), VIII, 251.
4. A Baptist association consisted of a group of churches from a particular region organized for the purpose of providing fellowship among the local churches and carrying on evangelistic work. Robert G. Torbet, *A History of the Baptists* (Philadelphia, 1950), 72.

and every variety of dress — fancy & fashion was displayed. But of all the thousands who were there, comparatively few were attentive hearers of the word. Pendleton — Nixon & Baker & a man named Curtis were set forward as the heaviest metal of the denomination. Pendleton preached a sensible sermon & Curtis delivered a good missionary address — but made some erroneous statements as to the relative numerical strength of the church. Baker I did not hear — lacking confidence.

September 27 — Went to church again — heard bro Holland — a good plain preacher. The association is lukewarm on the subject of missions — and some of the brethren tried to arouse them by reference to the noble deeds of the methodists. The meeting closed to day & the friends have gone home. They have some respectable preachers — but no course of study prescribed for their young men & no annual examination of character — consequently many of their regular ministers live in comparative ignorance. It is alittle remarkable that every man of note among them had been engaged in controversy with some Methodist preacher — & all fully & fairly vanquished — public opinion being judge.

October 1 — Worked hard all day hauling in my tobacco.

October 4 — Went to see poor John Young who was much worse — & not entirely satisfied about his conversion. I talked — read & prayed for him — he seemed encouraged & said he was happy. Returning from Allensville I went to Ashspring to make some arrangements for a campmeeting & just as I was returning home John Nick [Browder] met me in a great hurry informing me that John was dying & wanted to see me. I went in a gallop but found him dead. He had a clear & powerful evidence of his future happiness & died in triumph. I assisted in preparing him for the grave — & came home in the night.

October 12 — Took the hands & went to work preparing camps at Ashspring — fear the weather will be cold — but look for a good meeting — find it a troublesome job. My fine gray mare Bell refused to work — stood on her hind feet — pulled back — lay down — hurt herself jumping over the other horse — yet was not frighted in the least — she is perfectly gentle. I had her whipped most severely — but she would not pull until I got another horse to move the wagon. I succeeded in making her work.

October 13 — I went again to work on the camps — my gray mare worked much more tractably. I am losing time from sowing wheat — & spending labor & money for the campmeeting but I hope all will be well. We all seem inclined to look for a revival — Lord send it!

October 15 — Packing & moving in — got to the ground just before dark — took Lizzie & and all the girls in the wagon.

October 16 – Quite a crowd is at the camp ground. I have been appointed to preach tomorrow morning at 11 oclock.

October 17 – I felt that it was almost impossible for me to preach. A strong wind was facing the pulpit – my voice was weak & throat sore – just as I was starting to the stand I saw Bro J. H. Bristow our California missionary. He was a God-sent man to me & preached us a clear – eloquent & powerful sermon with thrilling effect – after which he lifted a collection for the mission & raised 70 dollars. An immense crowd was present & 500$ could have been given easily if the people had only been liberal. Some drunken wretches got into a fight at the Spring & some desperadoes with whiskey & arms walked insultingly about the encampment. Oh for a law that would reach 10 rumsellers in every form. Our young men organized themselves into a night & day police & whipped several negroes for selling whiskey – well done! but better if they could have punished the white scoundrels who bought from them.

October 18 – At 11 oclock I preached with some liberty – 1st Pet. 4.18. A large audience listened attentively & a deep, earnest, serious, solemn impression prevailed. I was almost overcome with fatigue.

October 19 – Still the work revives. My old friend Wm Finley of Russellville a Protestant Methodist[5] – preached at 11. In appearance he is ugly – perhaps 4 ft 10 inches high – deep shrunken eyes – big mouth – low forehead – high cheeks & a real runt – lean & slender almost idiotic in appearance yet he preached to the utter amazement of a perfectly enraptured audience. His arguments were clear & lucid – his language bold correct & strong – his imagery sublime – beautiful & appropriate – his gestures impressive & graceful & his voice clear & shrill as a bugle & full – melodious & soft as the notes of Eolian harp – his intonation & emphasis almost a model of perfection – in short he is the most perfect "singe cat" I ever saw. The effect of his sermon was overpowering – the hardest sinners wept & the christians broke out in shouts of joyful triumph. There is an amazing paradox between his talent & his looks. He sets phrenology at defiance and physiognomy has deceived its notaries.

October 21 – Meeting closed. Sad time! We will never all meet again. I delivered the valedictory address – I hope with good effect. I hope our campmeeting may do good – about 30 have professed conversion.

October 24 – Lizzie & I went to Church. We dined with Dr. Hutchings & after dinner Dr. Duval preached a scattered, broken – incoherent upside down sermon on temperance – & contrary to my expectation – several of the old &

---

5. Dissatisfaction with the polity of the Methodist Episcopal Church led to the formation of the Methodist Protestant Church in 1830. The latter insisted upon lay representation in the conferences of the church and elimination of bishops and presiding elders. Matthew Simpson, ed., *Encyclopedia of Methodism* (Philadelphia, 1882), 602.

sober citizens sent in their petitions to join the sons of Temperance. Hurrah for the Dr! Hurrah for the sons!

October 31 — I set out for Russellville — to hear Dr Green preach the dedication sermon in new Methodist church. Found in Russellville that neither Green nor Erwin had come — so the dedication was indefinitely postponed. [Thomas] Bottomley prevailed on me to preach the first sermon in the new church — which I did from 1st John — 3.2 but had not perfect liberty — in showing the true condition of regeneration. I am told that Calvinists & Campbellites* were offended. I was invited with the other preachers to dine with judge Broadnax — who took me to task about my sermon. He gave us an excellent cold dinner, of which I ate heartily. He is the most intolerable boaster I ever heard — thinks no one has a table equal to his — brags on every thing he has — & talks a great deal about religion. He lacks charity — yet is proverbial for his liberality to benevolent causes. He was remarkably polite to a negro woman who waits on the table calling her "Miss Ann" "My dear" &c. I reached home after dark — with a sore throat.

November 2 — Went to election — at Ashspring — voted for Scott & Graham — for president & vice president of United States — voted for them because they favor Western improvements — & the Compromise.[6] I never saw as little excitement at a presidential election.

November 4 — Up before day — fixed my gate — hauled a load of corn, marked some pigs, got hogs out of corn field — hauled a very heavy load of pumpkins — had some trouble with Bell — went to Mr Gaines & got a load of brickbats for my cellar wall — took Helen & her nurse in the wagon — got home at dark — ate supper & cut up a large mess of pumpkins to cook & now am tired. Little Helen is the busiest creature I know — walks & talks & sings & sleeps & plays like she knew what life is for. A sweet little cherub is she.

November 6 — Early breakfast. I was amused at little Helen. When at prayers — she sat voluntarily in her little chair & looked about as demurely as a matron — & when we knelt, she got on the floor & laid her head in her chair. She is one of the most affectionate babes I ever saw — mild and confiding in her disposition, kind, obedient, & sprightly. She understands almost everything we tell her.

November 28 — Just as we were about starting to church — *Mary* let Helen burn her hand badly on the stove & then told a falsehood for which I gave her a little whipping. Helen seemed in such pain that I thought best not to leave her & did not get to church until after preaching.

---

6. General Winfield Scott and William Alexander Graham were the nominees for the Whig Party. The Democrats, with Franklin Pierce and William R. King as their standard bearers, won the election. The compromise referred to is the Compromise of 1850, which at the time appeared to resolve the major differences between North and South.

November 29 — A day spent in hard labor — hauling corn.

December 1 — A blithe & beautiful day — but like human hopes it shines but to hasten away — for soon the frost — & snow & storms will hide the blue sky — & lock up the rippling rill while man & beast will go shivering along the way. I hope to be comfortable — for my good father sent his wagon & hands to help & we have stored away many a barrel of rich yellow corn — & I have oats & fodder for my stock — & for ourselves we have wheat & corn & meat — & apples & nuts & plenty of vegetables — & when old Boreas howls & Jack Frost tinkles in the windows — & raps at the door — I hope we will have a hot fire — good temper — cheerful hearts — clear consciences — loaded tables & warm beds.

December 2 — Still hoarding up the corn — hogs almost fat — crib full & more in the field. How thankful I ought to be. I am thankful — although I have labored diligently & feel very sore & tired — yet I am happy & contented. Here sits good Lizzie — writing to her sister — there black *Mary* nods over her knitting — little Helen, sweet thing! is sleeping in the cradle. *Isaac* is singing in the kitchen & taking all together I think we are a happy family.

December 3 — Very rainy & damp. Last night I felt almost like suffocating with my throat. Today I am not well — but spent some time in picking over my apples. After dinner went to Volney & had some sport — weighing a hog — to satisfy a number of guessers — who rated him some at 50 & others at 100 lbs — he weighed 92. Time not very profitably spent — but I learned to sell pigs by weight not by guess.

December 8 — Worked diligently hauling & scattering manure.

December 14 — Helped about the hogs — scraping — cleaning &c — got done in good time. We killed 45 with father's. I put up ten.

December 16 — Lizzie in a great hurry about her lard & sausages. All greasy & dirty. I will be glad when hog-killing week is past.

December 17 — My fine mare Maria got frightened by crossing a trace chain & kicked & ran around — until she broke the gear & then stopped — seeming as quiet as if nothing had happened. I was once in great danger of being crippled — as the trunk on which I was riding fell nearly off & I was near the mares heels.

December 19 — Lizzie & I went to spend an hour with mother.[7] I question whether such visits are improper on the sabbath — when confined to the sick or religious families.

---

7. That is, his stepmother, Sarah Gilmer Browder.

December 25 – Hail Christmas! Children & servants all up – & kitchen – passage – rooms – & stairs ringing with "Christmas gift." Stockings & socks were quickly searched – & all the youngsters found that Santaclaus had dealt out cake & candy – Almonds, butternuts, fire crackers &c in liberal share to each – and all with hearty good will ate cakes & nuts & told tales – & laughed like Christmas would last forever.

December 26 – I hurried to Joe Waters – by request to preach the funeral of his wife who died yesterday evening – after a severe illness. I was too late not being properly notified. We buried a good friend & neighbor at the Old Bethlehem graveyard – where scores of saints are sleeping ready to hail the resurrection triumph – & burst into immortal life & glory.

December 31 – Such a stormy night! The clouds have hurried past & the wind turning cold & icy – howls & careens around the house – stealing under the window & feeling around our ears & noses. I slept but little & all night – the moaning, streaming, wailing, howling wind roared over the hills bending, breaking, freezing the leafless limbs of the forest oak. A fine time for meditation! The year [18]52 was dying – & with it died many illustrious men of earth[8] – & I was spared! My family had all survived save one harmless African infant. We may not *all* live through another year – so we must watch & pray.

January 5, 1853 – Went out to look for a plough boy.[9]

January 6 – Went to town to see a boy I heard of yesterday & hired him from Mr E. R. Sumpter. He is a small boy untrained to the farm yet cost me 55.00. His masters words were smoother than oil – but I learned afterward that he was a tyrant over his slaves. He made me believe he was *most humane.*

January 11 – My 26th Birth day! Time flies! When I was a little boy I expected to be wealthy & famous at this age. When I began to preach I expected to be eminently useful & distinguished by this time. When I got more experienced I expected to be holy – sanctified before this age – and now – I am nothing but poor George Dick with a sore throat & impaired constitution, having a heart too faithless & corrupt – to be numbered among those who are deeply pious – yet I trust in God's mercy & hope to be saved. Oh for grace to call in all my wandering thoughts & spend this year more to Gods glory than I did the last!

January 23 – Went home with Col Walk[er]s negro man *Jim* who ran away from his master one week ago to avoid a slight flagellation for lying & disobedience. He staid out until he was tired – then came here – professing to

---

8. Daniel Webster and Henry Clay both died during the year.
9. Some slave owners made a practice of hiring out their slaves to the highest bidders. Normally this was done on the first of January in the county seat. J. Winston Coleman, *Slavery Times in Kentucky* (Chapel Hill, 1940), 123 ff.

be almost starved & wanted me to go with him home. I left him & his master in an interesting conversation – called at Dr Hutchings to get some physic for black *Mary* who has been unwell for several days.

January 25 – Staid in house & read an agricultural paper. After dinner tried to burn a plant bed[10] but failed.

January 31 – I went to Mason's mill to see about my plank – stopped on the way & saw poor Mrs Page who was left a poverty stricken widow with 5 small children – she is living in an old school house dependent on public charity for her bread. I talked with her & promised her some corn & clothing for the children for which she seemed thankful.

February 5 – Snowing, & hailing nearly all day. Last night our poor old cow died – leaving a fine calf which Lizzie is trying to raise by hand. I cut down a tree to get some wood – *Isaac* & *Ann* both laid up sick.

February 6 – Cold – ground white – trees & houses full of sleet – spent some time doctoring a sick cow – read some – made children read. Black *Alick*[11] asked me "to read about the good man." I read him part of Sermon on Mt. & explained.

February 14 – Uncle James [Volney] Walker sent for me this morning to see him on business. I found him quite sick. He wanted me to have a strip of land surveyed between my line & his which he intended to give me as a present. Mr Carr offered me 20$ pr acre for it. I feel very thankful for the present & would cheerfully pay a fair price for the land, but uncle J will take nothing & says he is not positively sure that the land is not as much mine as his. It is a valuable gift.

February 15 – Uncle James is very sick & low spirited. I tried to point him to Christ. Poor man – he is not prepared for death. May God in mercy save him. He made me a deed to the land & seemed quite concerned about his soul. I sung and prayed with him. He says his trust is all in God.

February 16 – I visited uncle J. again – think he is some better. His black man *Lewis* is very ill & recovery doubtful – seems conscious of his state – yet feels happy at the thought of death – prays for his master & speaks confidently of a home in Heaven. The freedom & wealth of his master would be a poor exchange for the peace & comfort of this poor African slave!

---

10. Tobacco farmers sow their seed in a plant bed from which the young plants are transplanted to the field. In preparation for sowing, the farmers try to destroy the weed seeds in the ground by setting fire to the wood and brush piled on top of the bed.

11. Alick was the boy hired by George Dick on January 6.

February 21 — I staid all night expecting *Lewis* to die before day — but he is now getting well — so is the Col[onel].

February 22 — In the night little Helen was attacked with something like croup. We were alarmed — applied sp[iri]ts of Turpentine to her throat & gave her onion syrup.

February 28 — I went to Russellville — did some business & came home — rode fast — my mare got sick on the way. I bled her in the mouth.[12]

March 5 — I went to Red Oak Grove to attend the trial of *Edmond Newton* a local preacher* — (colored) charged with immorality, viz adultery.[13] Bros Gooch — Williams & I entered into investigation of *Newton's* case — but had no testimony sufficient to acquit or condemn him so we adjourned to meet at Bethlehem Sat[urday] before 4th Sun[day] in April. *Newton* came home with me.

March 6 — I went to class meeting* — small attendance — meeting more dull than common. I have serious & well grounded fears that the interest of class meetings is declining slowly & surely in this part of the country. Would it were different!

March 9 — Spent PM building a turkey house for Lizzie. *Isaac* & *Alick* cut & hauled the polls. If Lizzie fails to raise a good flock we shall not get pay for our labor. A day's work for all hands.

March 10 — Busy all day putting up & fixing the turkey house. It is a tedious job to me.

March 28 — This day the children & servants claim as holiday & we follow the fashion.[14] David Morton came to see me in great distress of mind to have a conversation on the relative duties of the minister. He was solemnly impressed with the conviction that he ought to visit Col Walker [Uncle James] & talk with him on the subject of religion — so after going some miles past his house he returned, staid all night with Walker, praying with him morning & night, but

---

12. George Dick resorted to a practice that was rather common at this time. It was believed that bleeding an animal removed impurities in the blood. In this case, he probably cut one of the sublingual veins under the tongue. Interview with Dr. Kenneth F. Deputy, Veterinarian, Bowling Green, Kentucky, May 18, 1979.

13. When a local preacher was accused of immorality, he was tried by a committee of his peers. If found guilty, he was expelled with the right to appeal to the next Quarterly or District Conference, the decision of which was final. Simpson, *Encyclopedia of Methodism*, 215.

14. George Dick was apparently following the practice of many slaveowners in allowing holidays as an incentive to his slaves. The holidays most often observed were Good Friday, July 4th, "laying-by" time (after harvest time), and Christmas. Coleman, *Slavery Times in Kentucky*, 68.

found no opportunity of talking to him – he having company. Morton spoke a few words to him this morning & started to town, but on the way his mind was so filled & overpowered with the importance of faithfully warning the Col of the danger of delay in religion that he felt his eternal destiny was hanging on the performance of that duty – so he came back to consult with me. We talked and prayed over the matter. I do humbly trust his message may be delivered with good effect & lead my dear unconverted uncle to the Lamb of God that taketh away the sins of the world.

March 30 – Plowed until dinner. Staid at the house reading later than common – went to the stable to get my horses & found stable on fire – the door nearly burned up, the side post on fire in a brisk blaze & the wind blowing strongly. I succeed[ed] after a severe effort in breaking off the burning plank & getting water on the posts – by the timely aid of Lizzie, who came running with an apron of salt & *Ann* with a tub of water. A few minutes later & my stables & crib with my whole supply of corn would have been consumed. I could not regard other than a providential escape & I thank God for his goodness & care.

April 4 – I went out & helped load in my timbers & at night gave my hired boy *Alick* a light flogging for indolence & trifling. I hate the necessity for punishment.

April 14 – A company of us in buggies & carriages & on horse back – set out in great glee to attend the marriage of Dr J. S. Baker to my cousin Martha H Browder at Charles Warfields in Tenn[essee]. We had a long string of carriages, 7 in number & attracted attention. I performed the service after which cousin Mary favored us with a most sumptuous & elegant dinner. I came home early & found Lizzie & Helen glad to see me & glad to get the nice confectionaries I brought, but poor Lizzie paid dearly for hers for in a short time her teeth began to ache & the late hour of one rolled on before she got relief from the excruciating pain. I have had a very pleasant trip indeed but I am quite tired, my throat is sore & my poor horse Tupper seems almost dead.

April 15 – Lizzie still suffering with tooth ache & almost crazy from effect of morphine & laudanum taken in vain to relieve the pain.

April 16 – Late this evening Lizzies tooth which has ached nearly all day – became so painful that it was almost unsufferable. I do not think I ever saw anyone suffer as she did. She has fortitude more than ordinary women – but under the torture of the hour she cried like a child & seemed almost overcome. An application of hot tanzy & vinegar gave relief. It should be remembered. I have read & piddled about nearly all day. The trees are unfolding their leaves & the white & red blossoms are shedding their fragrance in the air.

April 21 – Was aroused before day, with the news that *Ann* was sick, sent for the Doctor who was not at home. I went for him again & when I returned in great haste found Lizzie, greatly alarmed. *Ann* had become the mother of a likely boy!

April 23 — Last night I spent an uneasy restless, sleepless night. My dear Lizzie was the subject of great suffering. I sent for mother & cousin Catherine Sydnor & Dr Hutchings who promptly came & this morning I found myself the father of a fine boy![15] well formed & sprightly in appearance. I feel truly thankful to Almighty God that Poor Lizzie has passed safely through this fiery ordeal — & is doing well — & I am thankful for a "manchild." My prayer is that God may make him a useful — holy man — humble & honorable. My sweet little Helen is now more than 20 months old, the most interesting child in all the land. I went to church this morning & heard Bro. Murrell preach, after which the committee appointed on *Ned Newton's* case met & he brought forward papers proving that the testimony did not sustain the charge. Lizzie is doing well.

April 25 — The little boy is quite sick & has very sore eyes. Lizzie is quite feeble.

June 1 — Warm & sultry after a cold back ward Spring — for the last month I have been working alittle on the farm & looking around for barn timbers. James Warfield was up [from Georgia] in May & we had a pleasant time — talking, hunting & fishing together. One morning I shot a wild turkey in the orchard — first I ever killed. My throat has been tolerably well. Aunt Almeda [Browder] staid several days with Lizzie & was very kind & attentive. Ginnie Warfield has been up a month — has lots of beaux & is a great help to her sister. I raised my barn May 27th — had 30 or 40 hands. Geo Iverson built it — $25.00 — after timbers were hewed. Bro Young has been through making temperance speeches & collecting Bible money. Has raised quite an excitement among the whiskey friends. Lizzies breast has suppurated two or three times & she has suffered extremely. The cut worms have eaten up my corn — & I furrowed out & replanted. I have been alittle unwell for a day or two — cannot stand the hot sun.

June 3 — To day I have been afraid to work in the sun — & have staid about the house since 10 oclock at which time I left the plow almost overcome with heat. After dinner I drew the water out of the well & had it cleaned. A heavy job. Very tired.

June 5 — Lizzie rode out for the first time since her sickness — carried the babe to spend the day at fathers.

June 20 — Temple Woolls came up & brought our new carriage for which I paid his father 180$. I took a ride to the shop — to have a tongue made.

---

15. George Dick's second child and first son was called Robert Walter.

June 23 — Cloudy, rainy — all packed up & would start — between 2 showers — crowded in & packed down with trunks & sachels — bonnets & bundles — we rolled away through the rain [to Mr. Warfield's], our new carriage leaking most unpleasantly.

June 27 — [Clarksville] In the evening a young Bro Morris tried to preach. He has a fine voice, sings finely & dresses well, but is the veriest clerical ignoramus in my knowledge. He has sense & zeal but will not study. Undertook to preach on the "gospel net" & became so entangled in the "meshes" that he sunk & soared, towered & tumbled, raved & ranted, to get through the brush but all in vain. He failed. Yet he seems to be a good young man. I gave him some plain honest advice & promised to board him gratuitously if he would stay with me & go to school.

June 30 — [Olmstead] Found *Ann* complaining & doing nothing as usual when I leave home — farm business getting on slowly. My prospect for a crop is rather dull. My corn is late & thin — my tobacco unpromising, about half a crop standing. Father & I went down to hear Golladay & Blakey — candidates for the Senate — one for prohibiting the sale of ardent spirits & the other — G. opposing it. Neither of them fully argued the question at issue.

July 4 — This day 77 years ago our fathers declared us free from English dominion — we remember the day with gratitude, & thousands of hearts to day are rejoicing.

July 8 — Worked hard in the oat harvest — finished time enough to go preaching. That same little Morris was there, selling books — preached little better than his "net sermon." We dined together at Uncle Dicks [Richard Browder]. Billy [William R. Browder] & I went to Volney to hear the candidates. Hawkins for — Burkes against the liquor law — none of them good speakers. Burkes made some monstrous — false assertions. I asked him some questions — he got offended. Little do I care for his contempt. He advocates the rights of the whisky traffic. I once heard him say — at W. T. Evans — March 21st 1852 — that if he ran for the legislature — he would run on the Maine liquor law.[16] I so reported to some of my friends, but he thinking the whisky side strongest, no doubt, changed his policy — & denied ever being in favor of the law — and at Union on the 30th ult. called me to account for circulating such a report. I told him I did so report — told him when & where he said it — that I was responsible for whatever I say — & if he denied it I would make oath that he said it.

---

16. In 1846 Maine passed the first state law banning the sale of alcohol except for medicinal and industrial purposes. In 1851 under the leadership of Neal Dow, the prohibitionist forces pushed through the "Maine law," which made illegal the manufacture as well as the sale of alcoholic beverages. Alice Felt Tyler, *Freedom's Ferment* (Minneapolis, 1944), 347.

July 15 – Started after my family [who had been visiting since June 23 at Mr. Warfields]. Stopped at Charles Warfields to dinner – found all well. Cousin Mary and I had an old fashioned, familiar confidential conversation. She told me about the unfortunate coldness & bad feeling between her & Aunt Betsy [Waters]. I feel very sorry that such is the case – but from the best light I have I see that both are at fault & molehills have grown to mountains & "ocean is into tempest wrought to waft a feather or to drown a fly." I fear the breach will still be wider & the peace of several families be disturbed. I trace the chief mischief to a tattling tongue – the duplicity of whose owner has secured & betrayed the confidence of both parties. This evening a gentle shower relieved the heat & laid the dust, but did not invigorate the crops. I found my dear wife & children well & overjoyed to see me as indeed I was to see them. Little Helen clung about my neck & kissed me – slapping my cheek with unutterable affection. I never saw an infant so devoted to a father. She sat up & played with me long after her usual bed time.

July 16 – Father [Warfield] & I went nearly to cross roads – to a railroad meeting expecting to see a large crowd & distinguished speakers, but found one or two inexperienced speakers – a respectable collection of people & the poorest show for a barbecue that ever I saw at a public dining. I am astonished to see so many large property holders so indifferent about an enterprise – the most important that has ever excited the public interest in this region. Stock taken to day not a tithe of what the occasion required.

July 19 – I left my loved ones & came home. A most floodlike rain has torn the land, bent the corn – filled the pools & drowned part of my tobacco.

July 22 – I went to town to the temperance convention. A very large, orderly procession marched to a beautiful grove where Mr. Charles Eginton – Editor of the "Era" – made a most impressive & elegant chaste address, pleasantly diversified with soft words & hard arguments, amusing anecdotes & pathetic appeals – sublime & solemn quotations – an impressive spirited declamation. The vast concourse of ladies & gentlemen – several thousands in number, paid good attention. I hope the effect accomplished good. Bro Young followed with rather a rough coarse harangue of *hard words & soft arguments,* doing neither justice to himself nor good to the cause. He is a fine lecturer, but has been harrassed & perplexed by abuse & interruption on the part of grog shop politicians, & whisky candidates until he has gotten into the spirit of abuse & asperity. Sorry for it. After dinner the crowd reassembled at the stand expecting to hear some of their great men of the order – when to my astonishment – I heard my own name called for an address. I was unprepared for the occasion, had never made a temperance speech in my life – so I was silent – but the crowd was not – the cry "Browder – Browder – a speech from Rev Mr Browder" – rung around the audience & I arose and made a few incoherent remarks solemnly appealing to *Christians* of all names to aid in the great work of abolishing the rum traffic. Those that heard were deeply attentive & seemed impressed. I felt in earnest & feel now that I did my duty & am glad of it. I have no popularity to sacrifice. I care not a groat for fame bought at the expense of conscience. I was duly applauded & my address was highly eulogized – but I did not expect it – in a spontaneous oration.

July 27 – After dinner I went over to see Sister Thomas a very poor widow whose step daughter is dying with consumption. She caught the cold of which she is now dying – while getting wood for fire last winter! Shame on her neighbors – me among them. If I & others had "remembered the poor" we would have known & relieved their wants. I made up some provisions for them & went to console & pray for the sick. I went to church & heard Maxwell preach a sermon so far superior to what I have heard lately that I call it sublime. I exhorted* & went around the congregation. We got 13 mourners & several others are deeply serious. Oh for a revival even at Bethlehem! My poor soul needs it.

July 29 – Went to Mr Warfields, found Lizzie & children well.

July 30 – After dinner came up to uncle Waters bringing Lizzie & the babies. I am sorry to find that aunt Betsy and Mary Warfield are [still] unfriendly in their feelings. Uncle Waters has suffered his clerk to sell goods on sabbath. Mary has made some remarks about it which have been reported to him and B[etsy], wounding their feelings and making an incurable breach I fear. Waters and wife have withdrawn from church and I fear will suffer by it. I used my influence to reconcile the parties & from all I can see both are at fault – the whole disturbance has come from a most trifling cause.

August 1 – After dinner I came to Uncle Charles and had a long talk about the difficulty – he exculpates his wife – blames his sister. I advised prayer and forgiveness and a friendly interview between all. Lizzie and I came home. I went to Ash Spring & voted for Ewing – con[gress] – Blakey – Sen[ate] – Hawkins – Leg[islature] – latter two temperance candidates – both defeated.

August 2 – Underwood Morrow came for me in haste to see Lizzie Gaines who was thought to be near death with flux. I ran through the fields & got there time enough to converse rationally with her. She said she had peace with God & wished to be immersed. Dr Hutchings said she could not get well after it. I told the family that I did not believe immersion essential to baptism – that if I did I had not been immersed & according to their views (Campbellites) my office was ineffectual – that I could not take the responsibility of cutting off all hope of life by doing what was neither essential to her baptism nor salvation – that if the Drs (Hickman & Hutchings) would take responsibility I would do it – after they saw no possible hope of her recovery. She began to fail – sink – die – requested me to immerse her – which I did in a large box – inconveniently & in great haste – she died soon afterward. I think she would certainly have died without the immersion but it possibly shortened her hours. I feel that I acted rightly under the circumstances. Baptism by affusion[17] seems more accordant with divine benevolence & wisdom.

August 8 – Attended to threshing my wheat – a small crop. John Nick [Browder] & I bought Hughes machine for 100$. We can soon save the money – in threshing our own crops & make something threshing for others.

August 13 – To day I was compelled to attend court as a witness in the Tandy Snyder suit – case did not come up.

August 18 – Case came up. I gave in my testimony for the first time before a court – was excited – but as clear in my views & recollections as I ever was – made my statements candidly – truly – impartially. Mr Washington Ewing tried to make me state things which I did not know. I gave him a suitable rebuke. I was closely questioned and cross-questioned. Several told me that the judges & lawyers said they had never seen as clear headed a witness in all their experience.

August 23 – Went to Ash Spring & voted Railroad tax.

September 24 – Having worked hard all week, I made ready after dinner to take Lizzie home intending to leave her [and the children at Mr. Warfield's] until I go to Conference at Owensboro.

September 28 – Hauled tobacco until dinner – then packed up & started for Conference – rode as far as Russellville where I put up with Bro M[armaduke] B. Morton. Sat up very late reading Don Quixote – think many people might be benefited by reading the exploits of the crazy old knight. The book is a splendid Burlesque.

September 29 – Got started time enough to fall in with a trio of young men going to Greenville. We had a pleasant trip – rested a few moments at Greenville – them came on to Carrollton – & put up at a tavern kept by a whisky selling C[umberland] Presbyterian* named Lovelace – was kindly entertained. In return for which I gave the gentleman a pointed lecture on the liquor traffic. He took it in silence.

September 30 – Got an early start – paid my bill – 75 cts. About four oclock I drove in sight of Owensborough – & was greatly surprized to see such a large & populous city-like place. It covers a large tract of country & is laid out on the magnificent scale of a city. After riding over several streets & not seeing a single preacher I stopped at the tavern quite tired & glad to rest. I went to the Conference room & found the preachers all glad to see me. Such howdyeing &

---

17. That is, by pouring.

pulling – shaking hands – smiling – bowing & greeting I have not met before for 2 longs years. I did not know the brethren loved me so well. I was perfectly delighted to be with them all once more. Bro Parsons gave me a hug & pulled me off to his room, would take no denial. I was appointed to lodge with him and Bro Holman at Mr Frank Halls. He & his wife who is a distant relative of the celebrated H[enry] Clay are Baptists. They entertain us on a magnificent plan – & the furniture about the house gives evidence either of wealth & pride or poverty & folly – splendid mahogany sideboard with marble slab – fine chandeliers – with marble base & prismatic glasses – silver pitchers – silver coffee & tea pot – silver spoons & spoon bowl – silver forks & ivory handled knives – with other trappings & paraphernalia of fashion & fortune. The lady is a great talker & quite an intelligent interesting woman – her husbands senior by about half a score of years. I find great interest excited in regard to the election of delegates to Gen[eral] Conf[erence].* Ambition even finds a home in the church of God – among the ministers of the sanctuary! Shame! ! Shame!!

October 1 – I went out & found a few of the brethren – chatted a little then went in to business. Parsons & Sehon had a little speech making – then the election. Stevenson – Parsons – Z Taylor – Lee & Redford were chosen – Sehon & Barnett reserves. My vote was Parsons – Stevenson – Bottomley – Lee – Redford. This evening Dr Jenkins lectured on the china mission – exhibited a hundred chinese gods – & a real chinaman named Nequa. He is a pleasant looking fellow – too dark for an american & too white for an Indian. He wears a large shirt – or dress – coming down below his knees – close stockings & shoes with a square toe – a little tuft of needlework at the end. The front part of his head is shaved & all the hair from the middle of the head backward is platted & hangs in a long rope almost down to his heels. He is a good natured fellow & speaks English very plainly – says he admires our dress very much & thinks our ladies very handsome. I talked to him with a great deal of interest. He told me of the custom of his country – in regard to marriage – that the husband never sees the wife until after the nuptials are celebrated. He is to be married when he goes home.

October 2 – Sunday morning. We had a delightful lovefeast* – Bishop* Capers conducting it.

October 3 – Sehon attacked Parsons on the Conf floor – charging him with writing personal articles and denying it. Parsons made an able defense – but it was Greek meet Greek. I hardly know which got the better of the fight – but I think if Sehon had been elected to Gen Conf – there would have been no charge on Parsons.

October 4 – This has been a day of hurry & bustle with the Conf – speechmaking & offering resolutions has been the order of the fore & afternoon sessions. Russellville was chosen as the seat of the next conference. At night the Methodist church was crowded to see the preachers receive their appointments.

General satisfaction was given – some of course grumbled – only a few. Sam Akin & David Morton sleep with me & we have a most pleasant night – only too much crowded.

October 5 – Having looked & found my horses – & bade farewell to the brethren – Dave Morton & I set out for home. We passed through Hartford & at night stopped at Solomon Chapmans where there was a wedding & a merry company. It was with difficulty that we could get to stay but were treated very hospitably. The good old lady suspected that we had heard of the wedding & came purposely! I told her we had heard – but had been informed that there would be no company. I proposed prayer with the family – after which we retired. In the night Dave Morton was attacked with night mare & cried out – murder! murder! help! help! Soon a young man with a candle came cautiously peeping up the stairs to see if there was foul play when a voice from below cautioned him not to go up or he would be shot. I explained the cause of alarm – & the young men below joined in a volley of laughter – & with frolic & song – they wasted the hours of the night. I was unwell & could not sleep – so I listened to the revelry of the young – & occasionally to the soft affectionate chat of the bride & bridegroom in an adjoining chamber.

October 6 – After taking breakfast in advance of the family – we paid the moderate bill of 50 cts each – & came on our way rejoicing – crossed Green river in a ferry boat & by hard & constant travelling reached Russellville by 4 ½ oclock PM – where we halted. I fed my horses & supped at Bro Mortons – then came on home – having rode nearly 50 miles. I am *tired – tired.*

October 7 – After breakfast I made some business arrangements and came down to father Warfields – found my dear wife & sweet little children in usual health – but poor little *Mary* is quite sick with a disease very like Typhoid fever.

October 10 – I came home leaving Lizzie & the children in consequence of *Marys* sickness. I saw Dr Hutchings & got his notions about *Marys* case.

October 11 – Wrote to Lizzie sending *Mary* some physic.

October 17 – I have been very busy – firing* my tob[acco] – was quite alarmed once – thought the whole barn was on fire – the sun was shining on it & gave it exactly the appearance of fire. I wrote to father who is absent at New York to the Worlds fair. Wash Sydnor spends the night with me. I find housekeeping without my dear Lizzie to be a tasteless & lonely business. I feel very uneasy in consequence of her silence. I fear *Mary* is worse.

October 18 – Went to the [post] office & got a letter from Lizzie. *Mary* is still very ill. My wife is a devoted one. Her letters – her looks – her conduct – and her kindness to me all speak the deep – fervent love and confidence of her unsullied heart. I do not feel worthy of such a treasure – but I do feel very thankful to Almighty God for making my lot so favorable and giving me such a woman to be the partner of my joys and sorrows and the mother of my children. May we long live to bless each other.

October 21 — It is a rainy day. I made some fires under my tobacco, then wrote a letter to Dr Beard giving him some caustic strokes on the subject of old bachelors — which dog life I am now leading because Lizzie is necessarily absent. An old bachelor! What charms can he find in a house unblest by womans care & no children to call him "papa" — no wife to caress him & drive away the blues! must sit at table with one chair & eat in silence like a dog! have no one to listen while he reads nor counsel him in the hour of need — no soft hand to smooth his hair, no loving tender words to cheer a lonely heart! no joy in family worship — no hope of consolation in the winter of life when the snow storms beat upon his solitary roof & the bleak winds moan in consonance with his feelings. Old bachelor indeed! A man who would live so by choice deserves to feel mean enough to steal acorns from a blind pig, & too ugly to eat a good dinner! He ought to sleep cold forever, eat gar broth & live in a cave! If I live & God permit I shall go to see Lizzie & Helen & Robert tomorrow & know a joy that a stingy dried up old bachelor has no right to share! Let him shiver & freeze & grope about the world like a blank in creation — a spot on the face of beauty — he deserves no better fate! He that findeth a wife findeth a good thing. I have one that is a *wife*.

October 22 — A rainy cold morning — about 10 oclock I ordered my horse & set out to see Lizzie & the babies — rode fast & found Lizzie & the children in usual health & poor little *Mary* very poor with a distressing cough. Little Helen & the boy were glad to see their papa & a day with them is worth a dozen days of gloomy bachelordom!

October 25 — I was compelled to leave Lizzie to attend to my affairs at home — when I got home about dark I saw my father safe & sound at home again! He is delighted with the trip to New York & thinks the time & money well spent. If I ever get able I think I shall take my little family on such a tour — let them see the elephant.[18]

October 26 — Rainy — worked a little on the farm — read books & papers & made the best of a bad bargain — a bachelors nest. At night Geo Nick [Moore] — Billy [William R. Browder] & Dick [Richard C. Browder] came over & staid with me & we had a merry time. They are in a great glee about their visit to the Worlds fair.

November 2 — I took a walk — with the gun — while in the silent woods my mind felt serious & thoughtful. I recollected the work of the ministry & the days of my

---

18. "See the elephant" was a common slang expression meaning to see the unusual.

usefulness & holiness & was sad to feel my heart so cold – so often filled with worldly thoughts & follies. I knelt in silent solemn prayer to God & was comforted & blessed.

November 10 – Pulled some corn – & knocked about the farm – dined at Sydnors & sat until bedtime at Mr Gaines. Saw a Miss Hill who lives in Ill[inois] & gives such descriptions of life in a free state as makes me fall out with slavery.

November 12 – I came down to Mr W[arfield]s through the rain – found Lizzie & all well – glad to see me. *Mary* is mending rapidly.

November 19 – [Olmstead] I did not sleep well – felt nervous from want of sleep & felt some strange symptoms of epilepsy which made me quite nervous & restless. I feel thankful to have Lizzie & the little ones here again.

November 27 – Went with Thos Sydnor to Red Oak Grove to preach but being behind the time we rode very fast & Bell fell with me & caught my leg on the side of a gulley & sprained it badly coming very near breaking the bone. Dr Duval was there & gave me some Laudanum. He preached a warm exhortation & gave the "ruffle shirted velvet mouthed oily tongued" preachers a considerable rebuke.

December 1 – Look out for snow & hail – sleet & freezing nights. I hope we will have as pleasant a winter as we had last. Thanks to a kind Providence – for corn & fruits – wheat & fat hogs – sheep & wood close at hand. I went to the creek & brought a load of sand & soon Capt Burchett came to fix up the hearths & backs & jams – while I drove away after a few bushels of lime. 1st of Dec last I was congratulating myself on the prospect for good living & peace. The same pleasing prospect is still ahead – a good & devoted wife – sprightly children – obedient servants & full garners – with a good library – good fires & candles ought to make any man of good health & habits happy through the long winter nights – we are quite pleased to night though huddled up in the little room with the new hearth full of sand & our room fire place cut out and torn to pieces.

December 2 – Up before the morning birds. I hurried away after sand & brick & went to hauling corn – while Burchett & *Isaac* worked on the chimney places. I stay at home delighted at the prospect for more comfortable fires & rot proof hearth boxes.

December 7 – I spent forenoon in glazing our windows & the afternoon in putting away for winter use a fine crop of cabbage & turnips.

December 20 – Up before day – getting ready to kill our hogs. I killed 13 – 163 lbs each. I have been very busy all day. Tonight my old friend W. A. Washington[19] stays with us – we had a chat of old times.

December 21 – Went to smith shop & to Volney – got some little notions for the children to keep up pleasant recollections of Christmas.

December 25 – Such a hubbub among the children! Santaclaus put candy in my sack! Oh look Ive got a jews harp! See my little cat! heres my handkerchief! Ive got fire crackers! Look at the cakes! & such things pleased the children & kept them in constant excitement & surprise – while a shout of Christmas gift rung out from a dozen little mouths – for mothers children & ours. I feel thankful to see another Christmas.

December 26 – Wash Sydnor & I went to town – got the money for my hogs. Negroes are hiring very high – men from 100. to 125. here – & at Iron works from 150. to 225. pr year.

December 27 – Lizzie and I came down to Uncle Waters. He has lately been in very melancholy mood & under some mental alienation took laudanum to kill himself – but fortunately received timely relief. He seems better now & glad to see us.

December 31 – Very cold – ground rough & frozen. The year [18]53 goes out in a blustering & chilly night.

January 1, 1854 – New Year comes in a storm. The overshadowing clouds disgorge themselves of the burden of snow & as the multitudes of large flakes & broken fleeces descend, the careening wind drives them on in curling wreaths & pallid sheets – heaping up banks of beauty here & sweeping the bare earth yonder, adorning the forest with spotless robes & spreading the earth with a carpet of white while the air is clogged & vision arrested by the falling storm. About ten oclock the snow had ceased & I galloped over to church – through a piercing & freezing *south wind* – but found no one there – came home determining to be a better man this year than I was last. The sins & follies, the idleness & uselessness that marked my career last year – should never be known again – so I think at the end of every year & yet sluggish nature slumbers on in her dullness & apathy. Good Lord deliver me!

January 2 – I went to town & did some business for father – hired a man *Ed Sands* for 115.00 & came home.

---

19. William A. Washington, distantly related to President George Washington, taught school at Volney Institute during the 1830s. George Dick was one of Washington's pupils and out of that relationship a life long friendship developed. Margaret Barnes Stratton, *Place Names of Logan County and Oft-Told Tales* (Russellville, 1950), 21 ff.

January 4 – The young folks have been storming & frolicking for the last week & a party to night has taken precedence of our prayermeeting & disappointed the few of us who went.

January 7 – I worked at the barn preparing some stalls for my cattle – just finished them in time to shelter the cows from a heavy snowstorm.

January 9 – I went over & got the hands to putting ice for father. I worked hard all day & feel tired tonight. Ice house 2-3ds full.

January 11 – Rainy & *very muddy*. Helped hang my barn doors – cut some windows in barn – stripped* alittle tob[acco] – busy all day & accomplished almost nothing – fit emblem and anniversary of my birthday. It seems to me that I have lived so long to but little purpose. My whole life has been as unprofitably spent as this day – doing little whereas I should have done much – & putting off until tomorrow often times what I ought to do to day – especially in a moral & literary sense.

January 13 – A messenger delivered a letter informing me of the total derangement of uncle Waters & requesting me to go down immediately. I broke the unwelcome news to Lizzie & after dinner I rode down – near 20 miles in less than four hours & stopped twice on route. Uncle W. knew me instantly & seemed glad to see me. Aunt Betsy was in great distress. He seems reduced to a deplorable idiocy, from which his mind frequently recovers – & he has a lucid hour followed again by fits of despondency & mental abstraction. His constant aim seems to be to take his own life & making constant efforts to escape the vigilance of his watching friends. I was awake with him all night. Poor man! I pity him in my heart – & pray for his recovery – but he certainly cannot live long without a change. His friends have sent to Nashville – to secure proper treatment in the Asylum – deeming it the only hope of his relief.

January 14 – I talked to uncle Waters at his request, in a lucid hour – about his soul & tried to direct him to the mercy of God. Some months ago he took two phials of laudanum but was saved by timely medical treatment. I think his recriminations on himself & his deep regret has induced this more fatal and distressing insanity.

January 19 – [Olmstead] Rainy & gloomy! Stripped tobacco all day. Mixed some medicines at night. Our cook is sick – several of us have colds. Helen is attacked with sore eyes. I am very sorry for she had such bright, sweet eyes that I hate to see them injured. She is now at a most interesting age. Talks about almost everything, recollects what we tell, knows a part of the childrens catechism & kneels down to repeat her prayers after her Papa.

January 25 – I spent the day in reading, writing & looking over my old Agricultural papers – taking notes of such things as I expect to do during the year. For some time Lizzie & I have talked of going to a free state. Our cook has been sick for a week & Lizzie has done most of her own work, & still she is willing to dispense with slavery. I feel sometimes seriously inclined to go — for the sake of my children.

January 26 — Rainy & gloomy. I played with the children — wrote an article for Prairie Farmer, worked alittle & spent a dark day with a glad heart.

January 27 — I have been milking the cows for the last few days & find that I succeed very well, could do that part of the work in a free state.

February 16 — Corn sold to day at Martin Hogans sale for $1.98 cts pr bl [barrel][20] — 12 months cr[edit] — land 18 & upward pr acre — 1.00 is the average price for corn — & land until lately had sold at 8 to 12 same quality.

February 27 — I went to town as a delegate to the Sons of Temperance convention. Few were present & but little interest was manifested. The design is to get out & pay a lecturer to go through the congressional district & advocate a prohibiting law. I oppose the move.

March 5 — A lovely sabbath. By appointment I went to Bethlehem & preached to the blacks.[21] A good congregation was present & they paid good attention & seemed edified. *Geo McLean* followed — in an earnest exhortation. He had some fine ideas though clothed in scanty & withered speech. He soon had a storm. One old black man *Bob Hindes* made himself particularly conspicuous by leaping, falling about — screaming & making strange gestures. I doubt the genuineness of his religious enthusiasm. Old *Free Dick* was there in his glory.

March 9 — Rain! rain!! rain!! Nearly all day the rain has pattered on the roof — some times in gentle showers — sometimes in torrents — and still it rains at bed time. The ponds are full — the branches are full, the creeks are full, the ground is flooded, the low lands over-flown — & still heavy & sullen thunder roars in the South west & the warm wind drives up the burdened clouds.

March 11 — Went with Lizzie to Allensville & learned that several mills & bridges on Red river, Whippoorwill & elk fork had washed away — damaging the country to the amount of many thousands of dollars. Ponds are larger & deeper than I ever saw them & every little mill is like a river.

---

20. Corn measured by the barrel usually referred to corn that had been husked but was still on the cob; a barrel of corn was the equivalent of slightly more than three bushels. Corn in its shelled state was generally measured by the bushel.

21. Indications are that in south-central Kentucky blacks and whites usually worshiped separately. George Dick makes several references to his preaching to blacks on Sunday afternoon. It is possible he may also have preached to them on Sunday mornings before the whites occupied the church building, which may have been the case in this instance.

March 19 – Lizzie & I walked up to cousin D Sydnors & spent the evening – a poor black man belonging to Mrs Hawkins called & begged me in mercy to buy him as he was about to be sold for debt. I am sorry for the unfortunate man & will buy him if I am in justice to all concerned.

March 21 – Tom Foster came over to sell me the man *Tony* – above mentioned.

April 6 – Our little *Mary* is complaining.

April 9 – We have sat up with *Mary* for several nights & nursed her like our own child. She has been delirious for some days & nights. Her father came up friday night. We sent for him. She did not know him only a minute at a time. We look for her to die every day. Poor *Mary* – she feels like one of our children. We have done all we can & she must die.

April 10 – I have done but little except help nurse *Mary* – who is still sinking.

April 11 – Tonight about 15 minutes after nine oclock *Mary* died without a struggle or a groan & her suffering ceased. Alas, alas that the cruel grave should hide forever – one who was so attached to us & whom we regarded more as a friend & a child than a servant. She was an amiable, trustful, trusty, kind hearted little girl who loved our children & loved us with with filial affection. The pecuniary loss we do not regard – but our social loss is great – & our affliction sad. Yet we are consoled by the remembrance of our uniform kindness & care over her – & our efforts to teach her to love & fear God. I do not know that she ever lay down to sleep without saying the Lords prayer which Lizzie had taught her. She was always tenderly treated & could she have lived would ever have felt as a child to us. But she is gone! Yet we hope to see little *Mary* again for she often spoke of Jesus & Heaven during her illness & seemed to trust in Christ. Her place in our family will never be fully supplied.

April 12 – We had a decent black coffin & sent poor *Mary* to be buried by the side of her little sister – on the green bluffs of Red river – where she played in childhood – & where her little playmates can visit her grave. I should have delighted in the hope that *Mary* would at least live until our dear babes were old enough to remember her kindness – but we submit with humble resignation to the divine will & say "the Lord giveth & the Lord taketh away & blessed be the name of the Lord."

Volume II
1854–1861

"Oh that I might be spared such a bereavement."

May 1, 1854 – Soon after *Mary's* death – our hired man *Edwin Sands* was taken with Measles & lost some time in his illness. Then *John Humphreys* whose misconduct – lying & dishonesty has caused me to threaten him with whipping, left & refused to return. His father sent a young brother *Jackson* in his place – but he was a poor substitute & my business fell in the rear.

A few weeks our little Helen was quite ill with measles & for several days we despaired of her life. I had never believed that the thought of giving an infant back to God would have caused me such grief. We besought the Lord & he restored out little sufferer to health. Robert also had it & was quite feeble indeed but suffered much but was not as ill as Helen. *Lucy,* a little servant[1] had the disease very slightly. I feel very thankful that all are over it & now convalescent.

May 25 – Stripping tobacco. Sent Ginnie Moore & Warfield to town to a party to keep them in a good humor. I doubt the propriety of Christians attending public parties.

June 3 – I went with Ginnie Moore to Allensville & after hearing [two] good temperance speeches & partaking of a fine dinner – I addressed the audience on the same subject with some liberty & seemingly fine effect – several agreed to join the sons of Temperance & a liquor seller (I am sorry it was a cousin) George Nick [Moore] agreed to lay aside the traffic & sell no more. This result was partly brought about by my speech & partly by the opportune interference of a miserable drunkard – who denounced me as a liar & disturbed the congregation while I was speaking, thus giving me a fine text of which I took advantage & expatiated on the evils of intemperance.

June 14 – Helped harvest fathers wheat. I am thankful for so fine a yield – mine will do well. I think his will make 20 bu per acre for 40 acres.

June 19 – Finished my wheat – hauled out manure.

June 20 – *Jackson Humphrey* refused to work – was insolent & impudent & I promised to chastise him by his fathers instruction. He ran off & staid several hours – came back & promised to remain. I overheard him tell the negroes that he would never come back. I demanded his reason & he said my wife was constantly quarreling with him – an outrageous lie! She has ever been as kind to him as a sister. I got a switch & would have whipped him had he not begged pardon & promised to do better. I sent him home.

June 21 – *Jack* did not return – but told neighbors that I was a bad man – abused my wife to my brother & talked most insolently. I felt fretted & thought I would have him whipped – but fear it will do no good. They have been badly raised.

---

1. Just when George Dick acquired his slave girl Lucy Ann is not known. In the Family Record section of his family Bible, he noted that she was born "about 1847."

June 26 – Coming back from Allensville I was called in at *Humphreys* to see a little child expected to die. I baptized him & the family seemed greatly distressed and grateful for my visit. I feel glad to visit & minister to the sick – especially the poor – & at their request went back in the evening.

June 27 – Lizzie & I gathered a few blackberries.

June 29 – Busy at plow. The weather is intensely hot & I suffer greatly. I assisted in the burial of *Mr Humphreys* little child and administered such consolation as I could – & as they introduced the subject I told them plainly of *Jacks* & *Johns* course and urged them to fly the rod betimes.

July 1 – Working on farm – but the heat is so intense that we go out by light or alittle after & plow till 7 – then come in & rest & breakfast. We have to stop the horses every half hour almost to let them get wind.

July 2 – Went to Sunday School – led Classmeeting – preached to a *crowd* of negroes with great liberty and power. Several old men were cut to the heart & the altar was crowded with mourners.

July 3 – Sat up until one oclock making the plan of a 4 of July Temperance speech – being invited to address the meeting at Adairville tomorrow.

July 4 – Anniversary of our Independence! I went to Henry Browders to breakfast & he and I went in his buggie to Adairville – 12 miles. There was an immense crowd. Dr. Evans – myself – Bro Bottomley – & Bro Cobe of Tennessee made speeches in the order mentioned. Many listened attentively & many others walked about laughing and talking. An old drunkard Cornelius Barker accused me of lying. The truth sometimes hurts even a drunkard.

July 8 – [Olmstead] Chasing the shining plowshare.

July 11 – I went by George Nick [Moore]s urgent request & married him to Mary L. Gatewood. I felt more like being at a funeral than a wedding. The girl is good enough – but Geo N seems more reckless & headlong in his business than I have ever known him & I fear he will utterly fail & come to poverty. Yet I hope & pray for a different result. He gave me 10.$ in gold – but I gave it back not being willing to take a cent from him.

July 12 – Miles Templeton came up tonight to tell us that his little brother Geo had died to day of flux.

July 13 – We dug the grave at old Bethlehem & a collection of sympathizing friends buried the poor little boy. I read the funeral service.

July 14 – I have been plowing my tobacco. It is very fine & promises a good crop. My oats & wheat pay handsomely for the land and labor. My tob[acco] bids fair to be worth three times as much as any crop I ever made & my corn is now improving & growing rapidly. I try every day to cultivate a spirit of gratitude to God the giver of all mercies. I trust in him for all things & although I am unworthy he has never forsaken me. I feel my liberality enlarging with the increase of my goods & this is my daily prayer. I am now tired & can rest with a conscience ungalled by any unrepented sin.

July 17 – Went to fathers to see Margaret Cooper & her little son Tommy who is quite sick with flux. Went to Bowling Poors to get some whisky. *Ann* was attacked with flux Sunday evening and was soon cured by tablespoonful doses of melted fresh butter & neutralizing mixture alternately given. At Poors I saw Berry Copeland a poor drunkard ruined in soul & body by the rumseller. I gave him a serious good exhortation.

July 19 – After doing a few jobs, we got ready & started at 3 oclock to Adam Winlocks [Russellville], to attend the temperance celebration tomorrow at Pleasant run. We suffered with the intense heat & the horses were so hot, that we were until dark reaching the place. Our little Robert was delighted with the ride & played & sung & laughed & jumped nearly all the way. Helen & black *Lucy* were delighted with the town.

July 20 – I arose rather feeble. Lizzie unfortunately left her dress at home & was mortified at the necessity of borrowing one. A vast multitude assembled at the place appointed. The procession was formed & a beautiful bible was presented by Miss Amanda Gilbert, in behalf of the Ladies to Pleasant Run Division S[ons of] T[emperance] in a most beautiful, elegant, impressive & appropriate address. A most beautiful silk banner with a verse of forcible & stirring poetry, wrought in elegant needlework – was then presented. A most animated & eloquent address [was given] by Sallie Winlock & received by John Burr. Taking all together I have seldom witnessed a more interesting & imposing scene. Bro Morrow a Baptist preacher then delivered a strong impressive lecture on the Bible & Temperance – after which we had a sumptuous dinner. I was too feeble to eat & felt almost overcome with the excessive & intolerable heat. At 2 oclock I was called to the stand & for an hour & a quarter or half – I tried to advocate earnestly the benevolent principles of our order. I had the almost undivided attention of the whole audience. I quit almost completely exhausted.

July 21 – We came home. I found little Tommy Cooper very ill with flux.

July 24 – Lizzie & I went to Allensville & I went with Geo Nick to H L Atkins to settle for his tob[acco] which was transferred to my acct – I being responsible for the payment of the bills.

July 25, 26 — About the farm — sitting up at night with Tommy Cooper, who I fear, will die!

July 27 — I went to town for Dr Curd to consult with Dr H[utchings] about Tommys case.

July 29 — We went to Quarterly meeting* at Bethlehem. Bro [Nathaniel] Lee was not in time & Asbury Ivey preached. He is now stationed* in New Orleans, but certainly has not improved. His subject was the analogy between the church & a virgin. He preached the truth yet said many things that would have appeared better in older men.

July 30 — A good lovefeast. Our meeting closed with no revival & many of us are greatly in need of a *quickening*. Lizzie went tonight to sit up with Rebecca Caldwell who is expected to die. I staid at home to keep the children — the 1st time I ever staid with them away from their mother.

July 31 — Worked all day & went to sit up with Tommy but what was my amazement & sorrow to see a messenger calling me to preach Effie Winlocks funeral! She looked as well as I ever saw her at the Celebration.

August 1 — Washington Sydnor & I set out early in Will Caldwells buggie & by 11 oclock were at the house of mourning. A large concourse was present & I preached to a distressed family with some liberty & power. Effie died on Pisgahs top in full view of Heaven. Wash & I returned home & found that little Tommy Cooper had died this evening. He was an uncommon child, remarkable for the brilliancy of his precocious intellect, the kindness of his heart, his filial love & obedience & the urbanity of his manners. Cruel seems the shaft that strikes down such a child — & heavy is the blow that severs all relations of parent to child! May Heaven enable my afflicted cousin & her kind husband to submit without a murmur! Oh that I may be spared such a bereavement. Yet I pray to suffer Gods will.

August 5 — Little Helen's birthday — 3 years old. The drought is still distressing & the heavens seem as brass. In some places the corn is completely parched & dry — like stalks in the dead of winter. The prospect is gloomy.

August 10 — Blessed morning! A gentle shower is falling — slowly & pleasantly — the first rain of any worth for 31 days! In many sections the crops are ruined & here they are greatly injured.

August 11 — Threshing wheat — attended church. Bro Bottomley preached — after which he told me to think of the propriety of my taking the management of the Russellville female College which is proposed to be built. He thought I ought to take charge of the school. I doubt my qualifications for so responsible a place even if it should ever be offered to me — which I do not expect.

August 12 – I took the wagon & went to Allensville for shingles to recover the kitchen – learned that Geo Nick had sold out his store & houses for a farm – got home found my Duerson filly very dangerously sick with distemper – & had a disagreeable task to make her submit to the proper remedies.

August 13 – I was under the necessity of shaving this morning, because my razor was not at home last night. Our poor little Helen was quite sick – but she got better & we went to church to hear Bro Gooch. I got sleepy & nodded in despite of my effort to keep awake. This sabbath day I fear has been almost lost to me. I have become too cold & formal in my religion & have lost much of my fire & zeal. Oh for a deep and genuine revival in my own poor soul & throughout our church.

August 14 – The men came over to thresh my wheat. We had a very hot sultry day – finished before night. I think I will have 150 bushels – which is worth 1.00 per bu. Another bright prospect for rain has failed – & farmers are calculating on hard times & poor stock.

August 15 – Hard at work in my tob[acco] which is a gloomy prospect compared to its appearance a month ago. The worms & suckers are abundant.

August 20 – We went to classmeeting & had a good time, dined at uncle Dick [Browder]s again by urgent request & the repeated promise of "peach pies" for dinner! Went in the afternoon to see aunt Susan Walker who is sick with flux.

August 22 – Went to see aunt Susan who is quite ill. I felt a great concern for her – & stopped to pray that she might recover – or if she die that her death might induce her husband & sons to repent.

August 23 – While we were at breakfast *Isaac* came in & said that aunt Susan was dying & wanted to see us! Sad news! It sounded to us like the knell of doom. Lizzie & I mounted our horse & galloped over. She was calm, perfectly rational – happy & confident of her acceptance with God. Her voice was strong & her eye clear, but her sinking pulse told the tale. She had made uncle James, Andrew & John promise to try to meet her in Heaven! The near neighbors all gathered in & waited to see the last of one who lived right – "did justice, walked humbly & loved mercy" – one who had no enemies. We stay all night with aunt S. She must die! alas! alas! alas! so good a one must die!!

August 24 – Aunt Susan gradually sunk & had a few spasms – about 20 before 12 oclock M. she simply ceased to breathe & her pulse stood still in death. She was conscious to the last – and perfectly resigned to God's will. She approached her grave like one who wraps the drapery of his couch about him & lies down to pleasant dreams. I went to order the coffin. Lizzie staid at home with the children & I with uncle James. Poor man – how he suffers! May God in mercy lead him to the knowledge of the truth & give him the comfort of the Holy Ghost!

August 25 – Came home to breakfast, & prepared to preach the funeral sermon. I preached with some liberty & power to a large & deeply affected audience – "I would not live alway." (Job 7:16) A large concourse followed the corpse to her long home in the old grave yard – where her mother, father & sister sleep.

August 26 – I went to mill after my corn & found that the miller Berry Copeland had ground & sold it & had nothing to repay me – so I got no meal except alittle.

August 28 – Went to the mill but could get neither corn nor meal. The creek scarcely runs & still the drought prevails.

August 29 – At work on the farm – hanging & cutting tob[acco]. *Humphreys* bad boys here helping me while the old man is covering the kitchen. They would not go to the house.

August 30 – *Humphreys* boys came over for me to hire them. I agreed to give them 25 cts each & kept them busy hauling in tob[acco].

September 1 – Went to Division [of the Sons of Temperance] at night after working through the day.

September 2 – I set out to Fairview where I am to preach tomorrow. This is a distressing drought – there is only one place to water horses in the road for 20 or 30 miles & the crops will be shorter than ever known.

September 3 – At an early hour the church was crowded – a large & comfortable new church built since I was here. I preached nearly one hour & a half on the 2nd verse 3d chap of I John – with considerable liberty & power & with good effect for the whole congregation seemed affected deeply. The people of this society, Bell's chapel, are anxious to have me on this circuit next year & I feel inclined to try to serve them for I preach nearly as much as many of the itinerants – and I believe I could be more successful if I were in the regular work.

September 4 – I came home through a very hot sun. I am thankful to find all well. Tonight we had a lot of tob[acco] cut & on the ground & a large lot of corn down & to our surprise we had a severe storm of wind & rain – for which I feel truly thankful.

September 5 – The fourth anniversary of our wedding! Four years of mingled joy & pain. I am more & more convinced that marriage is a divine institution for the promotion of human happiness. My wife has been a blessing to me – her counsels have been wise – her kindness unchanging – her love undying. She is frugal & industrious – modest & sensible – governs her children wisely & keeps her house in order. Much of my honor & usefulness as a citizen is the result of her labor. I joyfully hail this anniversary of our marriage & record my thanks to her for her kindness & my gratitude to God who gave her to me & here I enter a prayer that the good Lord may spare us both to raise our children & to bless each other in years to come. I also acknowledge with shame my too frequent neglect of her & regret that I ever gave her cause to shed a tear for my unintentional indifference. Her heart is tender & coldness or roughness in a loved one is like winter winds to vernal flowers.

September 7 — Busy firing tob[acco]. Worked unusually hard to keep the fires regular — suffered greatly with heat & smoke — but in leisure hours enjoyed a treat in reading Wash. Irvings Sketchbook. Got a letter from Adairville enclosing $5.00 for my temperance speech.

September 10 — We went to Ashspring [to camp meeting]. A large crowd was present. Bottomley preached a clear & powerful sermon. I exhorted & we had several mourners. At 3 Tucker preached — & I exhorted with such earnestness & zeal that my throat suffered from the effort — but I think God owned his word for many were cut to the heart.

September 12 — Dr. McCallen preached a most excellent sermon on "Godliness" but we had rather a dull meeting until the afternoon when a young lady professed religion in the woods & came shouting to the stand after which we had a general class-meeting & a season of great power & rejoicing. My own soul was relieved of a dull & doubting mood & I felt happy & rejoiced in hope of Glory.

September 13 — At night Tucker preached & we had a time of great power & deep solemnity. A number of young men were deeply convicted & one was happily converted. We left just before midnight feeling that the Lord was with us & the victory on our side.

September 16 — Meeting still continues day & night. Bottomley left on Tuesday — and Tucker & Ivey do most of the preaching. The work still goes on & souls are converted.

September 18 — Meeting at night. I was alone. My throat & lungs were sore — yet I preached with zeal & solemnity & good effect Prov[erbs] 29th & 1st. We had a crowd of mourners but no conversions. This has been the most remarkable meeting I ever saw — a deep feeling of solemnity & reverence pervaded the whole audience & not an instance of ill behavior has occurred. About forty whites & several blacks professed religion & some 26 or 7 joined the Methodist church.

September 21 — I went to [annual] conference [in Russellville] & was rejoiced to see the brethren once more. The preachers received me like a band of brothers. I love them. I love the work & if my poor throat could be cured I would be an itinerant Methodist preacher.

September 23 — I came to town on horseback & sent my horse home. I took lodging in the very kind pleasant family of Bro Jas Allison — close to the church & the conference. I have always been fortunate in getting good boarding houses at Conference. As I passed by the Baptist church I heard Bennet haranguing the people on the "version" & he took occasion to persuade Baptist parents not to send their children to Paido Baptist[2] schools. I was sorry to hear of such a spirit but glad of the honesty that expressed it & I must confess that I was proud of the contrast between the order of preaching at the two churches. At night we had a missionary meeting & 2 fine addresses — one from Dr Parsons — the other from Dr Sehon & a liberal collection was raised — say 3 to 400$. I proposed & succeeded in making old Mr Washington a life member of the Missionary Society.

September 24 — We had an interesting love feast & many of us felt comforted. At 11 oclock Bishop Soule preached a sound logical & impressive sermon to a deeply interested & large audience. I never expect to hear the venerable old prophet again.[3] At 3 Bishop Paine preached a most excellent evangelical heart searching — spirit stirring sermon — strong & good in doctrine — chaste & elegant in style & solemn & impressive in delivery. I doubt if any heard it without serious emotions. I was glad to notice several Baptist preachers in the gallery. I hope some of them have sense enough to feel if not candor enough to acknowledge that a bishop may be a good man & a christian minister.

September 25 — Lizzie & mother came to town & barely escaped with their lives from a team of horses running away with a wagon which came so near dashing against my carriage that the escape seemed almost a miracle. Bro Hughes of Ten[nessee] preached a most powerful & melting sermon — and at 3 Bro Scobee preached a tame — incoherent sermon. At night Dr Taylor the Methodist missionary in China addressed a crowded audience & gave an account of his labors & the origin and progress of the chinese rebellion. It was the most intensely, thrillingly interesting thing I ever heard. I could have listened all night sitting on the floor as I was. I felt that the hand of God was almost visibly manifested in his preservation in the midst of a great heathen empire. An account of his visit to the insurgent camp is worth all the novels of Scott & Bulwer & Dickens & a thousand others in my estimation. When he was at one time in the jaws of death — he said he felt that it was most important for those heathens to have the bible than for him to live. When he came to speak of the sacrifices to be made of a missionary life — my heart was greatly moved — & I felt willing to give up my own children for the work. We raised 136 to 7 dollars to help rebuild Taylors chapel which was riddled by the balls in a battle between a band of ruffians & the chinese soldiers.

---

2. That is, Baptists who practiced infant baptism.

3. Bishop Soule was tougher than George Dick imagined. In fact, he recorded in his family Bible that the bishop baptized his son Luther on October 22, 1861. Soule finally died in 1867 at the age of eighty-six.

September 26 – The business of the Conf progresses pleasantly. The preachers were all examined & approved – poor Creighton Gould applied for a restoration of his credentials which was refused. We have received 12 on probation. At 7 we met at the Methodist church to receive our appointments. Just as Bishop Paine arose to read the appointments – Bro S J Johnson arose & deliberately asked for a location to the amazement & regret of the whole conference. He did this because he thought he had been unnecessarily removed from Elkton to Bowling Green to accomode Bro English who desired the Elkton circuit & Johnson had expressed a determination not to go to Bowling Green. I am very sorry indeed for his course.

October 8 – I went to see my corn at Pages & on the way heard a lowing or moaning like a cow underground. I looked & saw nothing – heard the same sound again & at last saw a very fine cow several feet under ground. I gathered in the neighbors & after several hours hard work we got her out after dark – though so much bruised & hurt as not to be able to walk.

October 9 – We were generally surprized to see aunt Betsy & uncle Waters coming to see us at last with a view of attending the agricultural fair at Russellville.

October 11 – Uncle W & I went up to the fair & saw a fine array of quilts, needlework – Janes – linen and other domestic manufacturers of the ladies & wagon plows, cultivators, &c of the men. Quite a creditable show.

October 12 – At the fair again – a splendid exhibition. I never saw a finer lot of stock & the contest for buggie horses was a most exciting & brilliant occasion. The ring was very full & the driving was spirited & expert.

October 13 – This morning I stripped & took 5 lbs of my tobacco to the fair but was only 3d best in a show of three entries. I think my crop a moderate one. The fair closed with credit to all concerned. On our way home a ruffian & miser by the name of John Muir began a frolic with *Reuben* a slave of Mr Gaines & being offended struck *Reuben* which called forth a remark from W Gaines Jr at which Muir cursed & swore blasphemously that he was not afraid of any man & could whip any body. I mildly said "John I am afraid you dont fear God as you ought!" No, he replied with an oath – then blasphemously cursed God & all men & me especially. He was exceedingly enraged & followed close to the carriage villifying & cursing me in a horrid manner – telling how he could whip me "before hell could scorch a feather," cursing my kinspeople & friends & my church. I bore his abuse with calmness – looked upon him with a smile & made no reply. I was vexed but could not condescend to quarrel. I was with David Sydnor sen & jr & they advised silence. The younger David however was angry & would have resented the insult furiously had he not been restrained. I am sorry such an occurrence has befallen me – but glad I bore it patiently – being "persecuted for righteousness sake" in this instance. Yet I must confess that I

88

felt the movings of revenge & determined to resist unto blood if he struck me in malice. I hope he will never renew his attack as my forbearance may fail.

October 17 – Tom Browder & I set out to Bowling Green with my horse & Mr. Gaines' buggie in some tob[acco] buying business for father. At night we were met by Dr J S Scobee who would have us go to his house where we were kindly lodged & entertained & where I met with Bro H W South of our conf who is a member of the mysterious order of know nothings.[4]

October 18 – We went to town and worked hard weighing & moving 32 hgds [hogsheads] of tob[acco]. I met with an old friend of my father – Asa T Mitchell, a quaint – jocular – & kind old gentleman. He treated me with great kindness – fed my horse – gave us all our dinner & kept us all night & seemed to feel that he was enjoying a privilege in befriending the son of an old acquaintance. I am proud of my venerable father & thankful to God that I am the son of such a man. His good name has often made friends for me in a strange place & his fame is worth more than fortune.

October 19 – Set out for home – called in Russellville & came home after dark – tired & cold – but to my regret I was told R C Browder was likely to be disappointed in a parson to marry him to Amanda Small & requested me to go – so I rode down in a hurry several miles – was long too late – had my trouble for no profit. After riding 50 miles I feel tired & sleepy.

October 21 – Took Lizzie & mother to Allensville – & came home feeling that this week & this year have almost been thrown away by me. We have had a constant whirl of company – a crowd of comers & goers until I feel like retirement would be sweet. I must be more industrious – stay more at home & attend more to my own business.

October 26 – Hauling in corn at home – the land that brings 8 to 10 bls ordinarily now yields 3 to 5. I have never heard of so distressing & general a drought in America. Corn is worth 3.00 pr bl.

October 29 – Sunday. Many are disappointed who expected to see me immerse the misses Waters in Whippoorwill – for it was rainy and muddy. I went to the creek & read the service in a shower – then went down into the water & immersed Gabriella – Sarah S – and Martha A. Waters – the first of my

---

4. In 1849 a secret society called the Order of the Star-Spangled Banner was organized in New York City to exploit anti-alien sentiment caused by a rising tide of Irish and German immigration. The movement spread to other regions of the country where Roman Catholicism was viewed as a threat to the American way of life. Members of the secret lodges generally replied to questions about the politics of the order with the stock remark, "I know nothing." Hence, they came to be called the Know-Nothings. They organized politically in 1854 as the American Party and in 1856 ran former president Millard Fillmore as their presidential candidate.

experience in that line. I performed the work well – except with little Gabriella who lifted up her head & I put her under the second time. I do not object to immersion on my own account – but I think affusion much more scriptural – rational, decent & solemn.

November 6 – I went to town – inquired about the mysterious order of "Know Nothings" & was told that no society of that name was known in Russellville. I am in favor of their principles as far as I can learn them from the papers. I am opposed to foreign influence & Roman Catholic politics in our government.

November 10 – At night I heard that our cousin Genl Richd Call – ex territorial gov of Florida was at uncle James & I went over to see him. I found him to be a very intelligent & friendly old gentleman. He claimed no relationship with any of us & we honored him with the title Genl.

December 1 – Here comes winter! & to day is not very like him. His old gray locks – shivering bones & icy breath will frighten many poor mortals yet before he renews his youth in the person of his blooming daughter spring. Well let winter come! Thanks to a kind Providence – though the season has been dry in the extreme – I trust we shall have corn & wheat & meat enough & a few vegetables such as cabbage – potatoes – salsafy &c – & for my stock we have oats & a large lot of good stalk fodder & shucks & straw. There are no indigent poor in our neighborhood! & no real drunkard. We have good churches & schools – preachers & teachers – good houses & friends & can laugh in our hearts while old Boreas howls about us & tries to thrust his chilling fingers into our faces.

December 4 – Had a rare time yoking some little oxen. The little fellows made *forcible* objections to being deprived of their liberty. They raved & ranted lustily.

December 15 – Plowing with my subsoil plow. It works finely – pulverizing the soil 10 to 12 inches.

December 19 – Busy all day looking over & burning several hundred old letters that have been on hand for years on years. A tiresome job.

December 20 – I went down to see Frances & Nancy Kelly by request and finding them in straightened circumstances – & wishing to sell their only calf worth 2.50 or 3.00 – I gave them 5.00 & took it for their accommodation.

December 23 – I went to Squire Adam's & posted a stray horse which has staid about my farm for 6 weeks frequently breaking my fences & leading my stock into mischief. This is the night of our temperance party at Volney & I was expected to deliver an address but the night is rainy & I feel quite unwell & unprepared & having to preach tomorrow I stay at home & look over my books.

December 24 — I am troubled with a rising under my right arm.

December 25 — Hail another Christmas Day! With gratitude I greet thee — we have preaching at the church. I had some tob[acco] in fine order for bulking* & spent some time getting it down — then went to church.

December 26 — Went to Dr Williams sale — the high price of all articles sold contradicted the universal song of hard times. His land was bid off at 17.50 pr acre! the intrinsic value of which is not more than 10.00 pr acre.

December 27 — I started to church — & came back — the rising under my arm being too painful for me to attend church.

December 29 — Dr Evans came over to see me — attempted to lance the bile but failed.

December 30 — Still housed up — restless — sore — yet not repining. I pierced my rising with a lancet — but not deep enough to afford relief.

December 31 — Sabbath. I again used the lancet & succeeded in effectually opening the bile which so relieved me that I went to church & to my sorrow learned that Bro Moore was absent & I would be compelled to preach. Unprepared physically — intellectually and spiritually I went to the woods & earnestly besought Gods assistance. I felt some relief & after praying & singing — just before I was about commencing — to my joy Dr Evans entered the house & preached a sound evangelical sermon.

The old year has almost gone! & who has spent it as he expected when the year came in? I know not one. Most of my plans for the year have signally failed. *Disappointment* is marked on every day — week & month. It is ever this with earth — yet I do not — will not repine. I have much to lament & regret — & much to rejoice. I see no merit in me — all my strength is weakness — my light is darkness & my wisdom ignorance. I humbly trust in God through Jesus Christ — & hope to be saved. My prayers — purposes & plans are to be a better Christian next year than I have been this, & being a better Christian I will surely be a better everything — husband — father — master — all.

January 1, 1855 — Around the family altar I assembled my household & committed them to Gods care & Providence through this year. I asked for peace, plenty, health & happiness in our family & in our land. I went to town through the mud — a vast concourse was assembled. I met many old acquaintances — was disappointed in hiring *Ed Sands* the man I had last year. I hired a man named *Hiram* from Mr Townsend at 105 dollars pr year. Found old Mr Fairfax Washington & his son William here to spend the night. I read several of Washington Irvings sketches for the company.

January 2 – Had a disagreeable task working my young oxen – drove them to Dr Williams & brought my grindstone home. They ran off with me – got contrary & stood still – ran on the fence – in the woods &c. I tore my coat badly & gave my wife an extra task. Oxen are troublesome as well as valuable. Young Luckett came this morning & claimed the stray horse which was here. I gave him up – charging only 2.00 for keeping him two months.

January 3 – I went over to see uncle James. He wants his money & I am sorely troubled to get it. I have written to Russellville – Bowling Green – Hopkinsville & Clarksville & none of the banks are discounting – & those who owe us have sold no pork – nor tobacco & cannot pay me.

January 6 – Went to town with William my brother – tried the bank again but got no money. I feel sorely perplexed.

January 8 – Gloomy – cloudy – rainy – busy stripping tob[acco]. *Isaac* & I made a stalk & straw frame for our wagon – would have saved time by doing it 2 years ago. I find by a dear experience that a man saves by doing things at the right time – though the circumstances seem unfavorable.

January 15 – Wrote to M B Morton requesting him to aid me in getting some money for uncle James who seems anxious to see his treasure again.

January 17 – Went to town & got $1176 which I paid to uncle James greatly to his joy & my relief.

January 21 – Lizzie being unwell – Dr Hutchings spent the day with us & mother also. Toward night the wind blew a hurricane & the snow came whirling & drifting in blinding folds & just in this storm our second son was born! How thankful that this storm is past! I hope our son will not live in a tempest because he was born in a storm. Lizzie is doing well & I am thankful – she says our boy is to be called Hanson Warfield for her father.

January 22 – Bitter cold – I hauled fodder & straw for my cattle. Lizzie is doing very well & the babe is quiet – weighs eight pounds.

January 23 – Went to town – nearly half the people at Volney had business in town & no one would go so I had to serve them all. I was in a snow storm from the time I left until I returned. My business was to pay R W Courts – agent for Mrs. Sands $115 for hire of her man *Edwin*. I had Ten[nessee] state bank paper – but was compelled to sell it at a discount to please the avarice of a miser. I was also required to pay interest on the note after being told that the middle of Jan would be time enough. I care no more for money than just the worth of it – but avarice & extortion I detest. I found Lizzie as well as usual under the circumstances. I feel thankful to get home with my good wife & 3 children.

January 26 — This morning the ground is hard frozen — the wind is cold & sharp as a prairie "norther" & the thermometer must be below zero. I hauled some corn & fodder to my cattle. A load of straw fell off the wagon & threw me just at the horses heels — my bay mare took fright & ran against the fence turning over the wagon & hurting my horse Tupper — but doing no serious damage. I feel thankful for such an escape. Went to fathers after dinner & got my gun. Tried to shoot some of the hundreds of wild ducks that daily trespass in my corn field — but failed.

January 27 — After dinner went to fathers where I saw our new neighbors — Mr and Mrs Davenport — with whom I am well pleased.

December 31, 1856 — My journal has long lain neglected! Since last I wrote times & seasons & scenes & feelings & circumstances have wonderfully changed! During the long interval between this & my last date I have passed through some sore trials & grievous temptations but have been delivered out of them all — sometimes my mind was dark & doubtful & evil threatened to subdue the good that was in me. I have had perverse & wicked thoughts & have often well nigh fallen. I confess with sorrow much remissness in religious duty — yet I have tried to do some good & have preached sometimes with effect & hope for good fruit. During the year of 1855 I worked hard & raised a fine crop. The whole country was overladen with every thing which the husbandman planted. Scarce any farmer had houses enough to hold his corn & thousands of bushels multiplied were shocked up in the field long after the cribs were full. Wheat, oats, tobacco, potatoes, all were abundant & the oldest men remembered no such crops. But in the Month of Sept the scourge came, a bilious Typhoid fever & almost every family was like a hospital & numbers died — principally negroes. David Sydnor buried two likely women — *Amanda* & *Ellen* — sisters — in a few hours of each other. On the second Sab[bath] in Sep[tember] — while preaching Billy Millers funeral — I was taken sick & compelled to leave the church. I was hauled home in Bro Davenports carriage — next day sent for Doct & had a very severe spell — most of my friends thought I would die. Just as I began to recover my dear little Helen was taken sick & as my dearest & kindest of all wives was worn down until thrown into a fever herself. I got up several times in the night to wait on Helen. This caused a dangerous relapse & barely failed to cause my death. Never did a devoted wife more faithfully watch a suffering husband. She hovered around me day & night like an angel of mercy & by prompt administration of medicine aided very greatly in my recovery. One time all of us were sick in bed except poor old *Isaac.*

I then saw more than ever the value of good neighbors & I trust never to be so ungrateful as to forget the kind friends who ministered to our afflictions. About the 24th of Oct Mr Warfield sent his carriage & carried us down to his house. While down there, my poor little Helen had a dangerous & well nigh fatal attack of nervous fever & I watched her day & night fearing that each day would be her last. During her illness, I received a letter from my father telling me that mother was at the point of death. As soon as I could leave Helen I hasted home

& found my dear mother the very picture of death. I prayed faithfully & fervently for her recovery & for my dear child – to my joy they both recovered. We came home in December & all rejoiced together in our deliverance. During the year there have been four deaths in my fathers family – 1st *Rachel,* then old aunt *Sookey* – then poor Archer Bagwell whom my father raised from helpless orphanage to be a man respected & beloved by all who knew him & who came back sick from his home in La. & lingered several months among us before he died in great peace – & lastly poor old *Michens.* I have hope that all these were eternally saved.

In the early part of the year I was requested to take the Volney School, which I did. Assisted by Temple Woolls I taught two sessions for moderate wages but suffered much with my throat. I think I gave general satisfaction.

The crops this year have been moderately good, but in some sections almost entirely failed – nearly half the tob[acco] was frosted & the wheat badly injured by rust – prices wheat 1.00 pr bu – corn $1.50 pr bl – pork 4 to 5 ½ pr lb – tob 10, 12 to 13 dols pr 100 lbs. My crop will little more than pay hire and expenses – but with my school & some stock which I purchased in the Emporium Real Estate & Manufacturing company – I hope to make something for the support of my family. I went to Mound City in Nov & was pleased with the prospect.

This year I have had trouble with my negroes. Poor *Ann* always perverse, insolent, illnatured, behaved so badly, that I yielded to her wishes & her husband's request & sold her – offering him the privilege of going, which he declined – & in mercy to him & his little boy I kept them here intending to take good care of them & treat them kindly – but *Isaac* quarreled I think unjustly with *Ellen*[5] a very good woman and requested to be sold not wishing to stay with her. I promised to gratify him & having received a letter from the owner of his wife, requesting me to sell him *Isaac* to be with his wife – & *Isaac* being willing to go, I wrote to Mr. Villine to come & get him and *Peter.* This winter will be long remembered on account of the great excitement throughout the South in consequence of the discovering a plot among the negroes to murder their owners & escape to free states.[6] Several negroes have been hung at the iron works, some at Pembroke near Hopkinsville & some at Gallatin Ten[nessee]. Many people are buying guns & revolvers & threatening to shoot the poor negroes on very trifling pretexts. Some negroes – *Billy Smith* & *Peter Newton* were sent to jail from Volney charged with plotting to kill capt Hawkins & family. Many think that *Billy* will be hung. Several negro preachers have been implicated & there is a growing prejudice against them – their religious meetings will be broken up & their liberties otherwise restricted. Poor unfortunate creatures! to be deluded in to such a futile effort. In Nov Mr W[arfield] had a very dangerous attack of Pleurisy & pneumonia. On my arrival

5. In his family Bible, Browder notes that he bought Ellen and her two children (Dolly Ann and Robert Underwood) for $1300 in 1856. Ellen was born in 1832.

6. In late 1856 wild rumors of an all-embracing slave revolt gripped the South. Excitement was high near Russellville where a black, who worked in one of the ironworks across the state line in Tennessee, was whipped to death for refusing to tell what he knew about the alleged plot. Coleman, *Slavery Times in Kentucky,* 107–108.

from Emporium I found Lizzie there & staid several days — sitting up the greater part of every night & did not leave until he was much better. He gave Lizzie a present of 20.00 & promised her a sewing machine.

Our little Hanson, once too pale & puny to encourage the hope of raising him, is now the fattest child we have ever had. Helen & Robert are both growing fast. These items gathered by memory from the events of the year, I have here roughly recorded & as I look back on the past & think of its changes, I grow sad. The ground is now covered with sleet & snow — & cold & silent, the old year is dying. I am here alone, by my fire — a lovely, faithful wife & three dear children are asleep. I look to the coming year with doubt, fear and hope. Would to God I had been more faithful in redeeming my vows but alas! alas! this year as all before it bears tidings of my unfaithfulness and sinfulness. I have not time to indulge in reflections. I hope to live a more religious & happier man. Now the New Year is almost here. I will commend myself & all my interests to Divine Providence & retire to rest.

January 1, 1857 — Went to town through the snow & cold to hire a negro man — had to pay 140. for *Hiram,* clothe him & pay his doctor's bill.

January 5 — Our school [at Volney] commences this morning with rather dull prospects.

January 13 — Tried the confinement of school room. Try to be patient & urge the children to learn — many are not doing as well as they should.

January 18 — So cold, so cold we staid at home, not supposing that any one would venture out to church. What was our surprise when Geo N. [Moore] and his wife came driving up in a sleigh 6 or 7 miles.

January 21 — Another snow. Dismissed school at 12 oclock until Monday next — on account of cold weather & deep snow — deepest we have had for several years — 6 to 8 inches — in many places drifted up in the most beautiful and grotesque heaps — resembling drapery of the clouds.

January 26 — I went to school — some new scholars — have about 31 when they are all together.

March 24 — In Feb. I discontinued my school in consequence of pain in my breast — sore throat — inability to do justice to the school & the insufficiency of my remunerations — went to work on the farm — rode about & soon felt better — more calm & peaceful — more cheerful — more religious.

So far I feel that the change on our place since *Isaac & Ann* left, is greatly for the better. *Isaac* declined going with *Ann* & asked me to sell him & *Peter* to D. B. Hutchings which I did for $900. Our peace on the farm is uniform — we have no quarrels — no fighting & but little scolding — good servants & good masters live in peace. I have tried & prayed to do my duty by my servants &

often met with ingratitude, dissatisfaction, insolence & insult. Up to this 24 of March – we have had peace & happiness this year. *Ellen* is a good girl & has not received one cross word, but kindness & frequently presents – to which she has been unaccustomed. I am truly thankful for the change.

I have sown my cloverseed, meadowgrass & am now sowing oats – having prized* nearly all my tobacco which article is now selling in N.O. as high was $20.00 pr 100 lbs. Geo H. Warfield had ¼ his crop frosted & sold that at 5 cts pr lb & still made $100 pr acre on his crop. Lands are now ranging from 30 to 60. dols. pr acre here – which a few years since were worth 10. & negroes are selling $1000. for women – & 1200 to 1500 for men.

October 7 – Tom Browder & I attended the agricultural fair at Russellville. While there I saw Geo N. Moore & was pained to learn that he was still desponding – oppressed & hopelessly in debt – & that he was living unhappily with his family & was on his way to N. Orleans – leaving his property & his family at the mercy of his creditors. Alas! alas! How well he might have done had he listened to the counsel of his real friends! But now he is ruined. I prevailed on him to come home with me – & at his request bought his hogs & mules & became responsible for his debts to the amount of $750. by which I hope to secure the 172.00 for which I am security. I would rejoice to lose the money if it could be of any real value to him personally – but as other of his creditors are more able to lose than I there is no cause why I should pay a security debt when it can be avoided.

October 8 – Geo N. slept but little – seems sad & is miserable. I went to see his wife, got the mules & hogs & told his wife of his intention. She is quite sad & regrets too late the objections she has urged to his going to Illinois. I found him here when I returned, told him his wifes request to come home & her promise to go with him *anywhere* – & proposed to go with him home but he declined & preferred staying here.

October 9 – Dr Evans came here to breakfast yesterday morning & this morning W. G. Caldwell – both to see Geo Nick who sold Caldwell his crop & farming implements & after breakfast I rode with him out to the road – we parted in sadness & tears. He expected to meet with Evans & go to Illinois & get a place & he intended to stay there & Evans was to come back & take his wife & child out when he moves his own family. Oh how my heart sickens at seeing him who has always been as my own brother in this deplorable condition.

November 22, 1860 – After more than three years of foolish & lazy neglect I take up my journal again driven to it by a sad, sad providence. On the 17th day of June 1857 – a lovely son was born unto us whose name we called "George Richard." He is now a very likely & promising boy. On the 19th of Nov 1858 another little angel came to our house – & smiled on us. We called her "Sarah Virginia" in honor to my excellent stepmother & my wifes only full sister. After a few weeks – little Ginnie became very puny & we thought she would die. She seemed the very picture of death & all remedies failed to relieve her. Never was a child more vigilantly watched nor tenderly nursed – by a loving mother – but still she drooped & would not thrive. At length we took her to a campmeeting at Red Oak Grove in Oct 1859 – at which there was a gracious revival. At this meeting our little babe begun to improve & grow stouter & better until she was a rosy cheeked, lively little girl, healthy & cheerful. She had the most beautiful & brilliant dark hazel eyes – with long graceful lashes – & a full set of soft silky hair that often fell in careless ease over her fine forehead, or fluttered in the passing breeze. Her head was a model of intellectual development – & was generally admired – her forehead was remarkably fine & full – neither too low nor high – & nothing seemed to be lacking in its formation. Except a slightly curved nose her features were all unusually regular & singularly pretty. Her form was not too slender nor in any way disproportioned – & her hands and feet were of that well set and pretty kind that often led our visitors to say "she has such pretty little feet and hands." In personal appearance & physical development little Ginnie was all that we could ask unless it be objected that she was rather too small for her age.

But the chief beauties that endeared her to us, were those of her remarkably sprightly mind. Her mind & heart were farther in advance for her years than her bodily growth was behind. She was as lively as a lark & as happy & cheerful as a child could be. As soon as her health began to improve she began to talk & to walk – & while very many remarked spontaneously that she was the smallest child they ever saw walking, many more often spoke of her unusual vivacity & keen perception. Her mind was of the quick & sprightly order rather than deep & strong.

In her disposition she was shy of strangers but warm hearted & trusting to all that were kind to her. The first words she learned to say were "Papa & Mama" but she soon learned to say "mother" & no little cherub ever expressed more love & ardent attachment & winning grace in the soft & gentle tones with which she ever after said "Papa – mama – mother – or sissy." She used to say "Papa's baby" or "mama's baby" in a tone & manner that I trust will ring in our ears until we hear it again in the bright world where children live with their parents forever! When I went away to my appointments & came home she would run to meet me prattling as fast as she could – "Muver papa tummin," "Muver papa tummin" (Mother papa's coming) until she came to my very feet when she would reach up her little hands & say "up tum (Up come) papa" & kiss me in the most affectionate & confiding manner. When night came on she would sleep either with her mother or me as seemed best to us – but generally loved her mother better than me. When my protracted meetings came on & I was very little at home – she always after said she was "mamas baby" & could hardly be induced to say she was "papas" but if I said "Ginnie who do you love?" She would say "love papa." She generally played around us until we went to sleep & nearly always awoke as soon as we were up – & her merry voice & winning ways were the comfort & delight of her mother & little brothers & her sister from dawn till dark. If her mother went away on a visit & left her with black *Ellen* who was always kind & careful with her – little Ginnie would be so glad to see her on her return that she would frisk about & laugh & caper & say "howdy mother, howdy Lizzy" in ecstacy of delight. She loved her little brothers very dearly & was very fond of her nurse (*Lucy*) & in her liberal heart would give away part of whatever she had — & would often run into the kitchen to divide her biscuit with *Ellens* little *Ida*[7] & say "bite" & make *Ida* taste it first. She was the best child in politeness & in remembering advice that I ever knew. She *always* said "yes sir" or "no sir" to me & "no mam" or "yes mam" to her mother & if we gave her a little present it made our hearts leap with joy more than tongue can tell when she almost invariably *looked* gratitude with her beaming eyes & said with her little tongue "Sanky mam" for (thank ye mam). She was very fond of nuts & her brother Robert whose mind & disposition are much like her own delighted in bringing her a pocket full of hickory nuts as he came home from school. She used to meet him with an expectant look & say "Hicky Lobby, hicky." She could not say Robert but always called him Lobby & Hanson she called Hanny & Helen sometimes sissy & sometimes Helly & Little Georgey she called "Dorgey." It has often sent a thrill of unutterable pleasure through my heart to see Georgey take her hand & say "Come on Ginny" while she always said "Well" & away they would go hand in hand tripping along & talking together like little angels on the plains of light & when wearied with their play they would come in the house & lie on the floor or sit in their little chairs & often would come to my lap & say "Papa tell tale" & when I would begin "Once there was a little girl named Ginnie" she would laugh with a real glee. Sometimes she would try to sing "Happy day" but would repeat no other words of the song. Every body loved our little Ginnie & she was a general favorite with white and black. In person & in disposition she was all that fond parents could ask in a babe & in this hasty sketch which I am writing in the fulness of my sad heart — I omit much that I wish to remember of my dearly beloved little daughter.

At the last session of the Conference which met at Bowling Green on the 3d of Oct I was made "effective"[8] & by request of the church at Russellville appointed to that Station. Our first Quarterly meeting embraced the first Sat & Sun in Nov. I prevailed on my dear wife, who nearly always stays at home, to go with me on the cars to spend Friday night & Sat & Sab[bath] night in town. I wanted her to go & yet felt rather more than usual uneasiness about the children all of whom except Hanson we left at home — Helen staying with her grandmother.

On Monday evening when Lizzie returned the children were all well & little Ginnie with a heart brimming full of love & joy ran to meet her shouting "Mamma Lizzy Muver" to the great delight of her mothers loving heart. On Tuesday morning I returned home & my little angel met me at the door & kissed me apparently as well as usual. I went to the Presidential election and voted for

7. Mary Ida was born on January 3, 1860.

8. For ten years Browder's status in the Louisville Conference was classified as supernumerary, a designation applied to those itinerant ministers who, for reasons of poor health, were unable to hold a regular appointment. Simpson, *Encyclopedia of Methodism*, 843. By being made "effective," Browder meant that he was well enough to receive an appointment from the Annual Conference.

Bell & Everett, the Union candidates & came home. Little Ginny hung around me & I nursed her to sleep. She soon aroused up & called "papa." I took her on my lap & nursed her to sleep again. That night I was aroused from sleep by a messenger asking me to go preach the funeral of Dr John A. Hutcherson whom I had received into the church last May. The next day I went & on my return night overtook me at W. J. Evans where I was pleasantly entertained until next day. When I reached home Hanson met me at the gate & said "Papa – Ginnie like to died last night – she had a spasm." I found her pale & very sick lying on her mothers lap. She had had a distressing convulsion in the night & a burning fever – followed by a dreadful cough. The Dr prescribed medicine & we nursed her day & night until Saturday – when I thought she was alittle better, so I left on the evening train & filled my appointment in town on Sunday. On Monday morning Bro Winlock came early to my room & said my father had passed through on the early train to Bowling Green & left word that my child was worse. I hurried home & she was in the cradle with a burning fever which refused to yield to medical treatment – & that weakening cough obstinately held on. The only word she said that day was "Papa." On Thursday she seemed alittle improved, the fever was less & the cough was loose. The Dr removed the poultices from the chest & discontinued the cough mixture. That night she was worse.

My most excellent & accomplished cousin Courtenay N. Duncan with her pious husband & children came down on that evenings train & spent that night & several days with us & helped us nurse our dear little babe. On Friday evening we called in the friends to see her die – & called the children home from school – but she revived & that lively spirit held on to life. Congestion of the brain came on & suffering such as we never can describe followed after. Oh that fever – scorching, wasting fever! & that cruel cough – the dear little creature tossed her head from side to side & those bright beaming eyes set back with a ghastly gaze. It seemed to our grieving hearts when all hope of recovery was gone that death would have been relief. My wounded soul sought sustaining grace from God. I could not pray for her unconditional recovery. I felt a desire to submit to the will of the Lord & earnestly besought Him in sincerity of soul to do with us & our child as his infinite mercy directed, but I did sincerely pray that if her death was providential that it might be easy & calm & that it might result in good to our souls. On Saturday she was so ill that I did not go to town but my good cousin Duncan kindly filled my place. I almost hourly expected to see poor little Ginnie breathe her last but still she lived & suffered. We watched & nursed & gave her remedies day & night but still she slowly sank away & on Tuesday evening again we called the family together to see her die – but again the innate vitality of my dear child refused to yield to death & again she seemed to revive – the fever was nearly gone – the cough had almost ceased, the sinking pulse returned & some even dared to hope that she would recover. Delusive hope! She was surely passing away. Little George came frequently with earnest look & solemn tone to inquire "Papa will Ginnie die? I don't want Ginnie to die." Poor little fellow – while his sister was sick he clung about me & often asked "if Ginnie would die." I heard him talking to Robert – "Lobby will you go up to heaven & play with Ginnie" and with such touching & simple-hearted questions the dear boy brought tears to our eyes — & Helen in her eagerness to know what would be her sisters enjoyments said "Mother — Ginnie don't know any body in heaven." My sweet Helen! Your little sister will know as she is known.

Cousin Courtenay left us that day & we looked for Ginnies release every hour & felt grateful to see her breathe easy & cease her moans & wild tossings. Her mother & I aided by the kindest of neighbors nursed her in our arms or sat by her cradle every hour, both of us never leaving the room at the same time. On Wednesday we did not dream it was so near. My kind old father sat down by my dear child to close her eyes in death. Shorter & shorter grew her breathing — then a pause — another breath & my poor heart gave vent to its grief over the corpse of my sweet little Ginnie. She was dead & oh my soul — how desolate & forlorn wouldst thou be if there was no hope of a reunion in heaven! My dear Lizzie! how sad — how sorrowful — how disconsolate! The child of her love in death. When her eyes were closed I went away to ask Gods blessing on us in our grief & thank him for granting my babe an easy death. I have always thought I had a sympathetic heart. I have attended more funerals & buried more dead than most country ministers of my age. I have mingled my tears with the sorrows of others — & offered consolation to the bereaved — but I never knew before the dark sadness of a bereaved parents heart. I never entered into the sympathies of the disconsolate as I thought I had. Oh the bitter floods that roll over a parents heart when a lovely child lies dead & cold in his arms!

My father had a deep grave dug beside my own dear brothers & sisters. George Warfield went to town on the cars to get a coffin for my treasure. Mary & Almeda McCulloch & Sarah Sydnor & my own dear Brothers William & Frank & my sister Mary came to keep watch over the cold clay of our once active & lively child — while Lizzie & I disconsolate & sorrow stricken lay down to talk of our grief & rest our weary bodies. On Thursday morning I felt more cheerful. I never murmured against God — but I loved my babe with a deep strong deathless love. I cheerfully give her back to the God who gave her to me. Bro Woolls could not come to attend the funeral as he was not at home — so my cousin R[ichard] C. Browder read the burial service in a very solemn & impressive manner & my venerable uncle Richard prayed a most excellent & appropriate prayer. Then the sympathizing friends screwed down the lid of the great walnut coffin covered with black cloth & shut out our babe from our sight. They laid the box on Mr Duersons buggie & we followed with sad hearts to see our treasure buried in the cold — cold grave. Ah my child — your father loved you tenderly — gave you to God in holy baptism & hopes to see you again where death will never disturb our bliss. Bright little angel of God! Will you ever hover around the path of your parents here or kindly guide your sister & brothers in the way to that Heaven which you now inhabit? This cold night it rains & storms & sleets — but you feel it not. Blessed child! While we suffer here — your sorrows all are over. Could you speak to us would you not chide us for our grief? Would you not say "Weep not for me dear father & mother. I am happier than you could ever have made me"? Then farewell our angel babe. We'll dry our tears & seek you in your own bright home. May our merciful God direct us in the way. I much regret that we never had her likeness – but we have it in our hearts – & this night I weep – but I sorrow not without hope. Oh how sad. We never spent a night here before since Ginnie was born unless she was with us. But alas ours is the common grief of our ruined race.

November 23 – Every thing reminds us of our little Ginnie. At prayer time – her little chair is vacant by her mothers side. At table she does not come running to me saying, "eat, papa eat." Oh how sad & solemn now is the loud blast of the Locomotive's whistle! Whenever she heard the whistle or rumbling of the train, she would go to some one to be lifted up to see. She used to say "tars tummin, mamma tars tummin" (cars coming). It will be long before we forget her winning ways.

December 5 – On Saturday evening I prevailed on Lizzie to take Helen & little George & go with me to town. It was windy & cold but we were very anxious to get a likeness of our dear boy – lest we should lose him & have no image of him for our eyes as well as our hearts. He is a very sweet child – sprightly – obedient & loving – with a full round face & form – well developed head – fine full eyes – dark hazel – very bright & expressive – with flaxen hair – rather dark & upon the whole inclined to be corpulent but a very pretty child – too pretty in fact for a boy. He seems especially dear to us since the death of his little sister. He often comes to ask "Papa where is Ginnie? Mamma will Ginnie come back? is Ginnie in Heaven" & sometimes in his dreams he talks to his little sister & asks if she is coming. We waited at the depot sometime for the cars & little George got cold. He was pleased with town & at Bro Blakeys he soon felt at home.

Monday afternoon we tried 1st Mr Dale & then Mr Bryan & at last got an imperfect likeness of our dear little boy sitting on my lap. He seemed unwell & at night was very nervous & restless & had high fever.

Tuesday morning we wrapped Georgie up head & feet in a blanket & went to the cars. Rodney met us at our Depot with the buggie – ground covered with snow – & wind cold. Georgie being well covered kept warm – played with his toys & ran about the room but at night was sick & nervous again with high fever – & *Ellen* our faithful servant woman was very unwell with pain in her limbs – back & breast.

Wednesday morning sent for the Doctor.

December 7 – This morning found little Georgie still quite sick & at times absentminded & almost delirious – but has less fever. *Ellen* is still sick & hired *Horace* is also laid up. I hope they will all soon be well. My kind father sent *Delilah* over to help us.

I have read the Presidents message[9] – an able document – dread the

---

9. On December 3, 1860, President James Buchanan sent a message to Congress in which he placed the blame for the sectional crisis squarely on the northern antislavery agitators. He warned them that unless they left the slave states alone, disunion would be

prospect ahead of the country. The Union is certainly broken if not entirely ruined. Oh how I longed for my children to realize the bright visions of national grandeur – that but yesterday spread out to the gaze of our people.

December 8 – Saturday night at home! When was I here before Sat. night? Affliction keeps me. My poor little George still has fever – is still frequently delirious – & I see many symptoms very like his dear little sisters affliction – but less violent. He has a little French harp which he keeps by him all the time – calling for it immediately when he misses it. So my poor Ginnie did with her little China doll. She noticed that longer than anything else & when her little hands were stiff so that she could not hold it she would press it to her body with her little arms & keep it by her side. I cannot feel that Georgie will die. I try to give him to God.

December 10 – Early Sabbath morning I went to town & at 11 preached to a very large & attentive audience with some little liberty from Titus 2, 11–13. Found my poor little Georgie still very sick – more feeble than when I left. My wife thought he was worse yesterday. Father & mother were here. I hope the Lord will spare my dear boy or give us a double portion of his spirit to support us in our affliction.

December 12 – Georgie is better. Went on the evening train to town – expected David Morton to preach for me but he was absent. I preached rather an unconnected but earnest sermon on the 126th Psalm. Eleven penitents came forward for prayers & seven were happily converted. I have seldom witnessed such a time of power and glory. In & around the altar & away up in the gallery there was a general shout of praise to God.

December 13 – Up at 4 ½ oclock to get off on the train – got home before Lizzie was up – found Georgie still alittle improving. *Ellen* also alittle better.

December 14 – Georgie is mending.

January 1, 1861 – This year has come in with troubles & threatenings. South Carolina has dissolved her connection with the union & other cotton states are preparing to follow. A collision is expected between the seceders & the Government forces – which will precipitate the South into a Revolution & no man can foresee the end.

If God in his wisdom does not help us – I know not what will become of the country. Naturally I never saw a brighter or more pleasant 1st of Jan – but financially & politically it is dark – dark – dark. Business is stagnated – money not to be had – property worth nothing in bringing money – laborers

---

inevitable. At the same time the President counseled the South not to secede from "apprehensions of contingent dangers in the future." John Bassett Moore, ed., *The Works of James Buchanan* (12 vols., New York, 1960), XI, 7–9.

unemployed – & banks – manufacturers – public works &c suspended – bread & meat scarce & high – & civil war staring us in the face! I went to see Lizzie & the children at Mr W[arfield]s Christmas day – & went next day to see aunt Betsy who was very sick – went from there on the cars to home – spent night at fathers & next day hired *Horace* at $105 – against 120 last year – could have gotten a boy cheaper by waiting – negroes are 25 pr cent lower. For two years we have made very short crops & this year had to send to St Louis to buy corn @ 3.50 pr bl. delivered at home.

Last year was hard on us. The winter killed the wheat. In March when I was in the woods – getting timbers *Ellens* cabin caught fire & burned up & the smoke house & the henhouses with nearly all their contents. Our dwelling was saved with great exertion by kind neighbors who gathered in before I got the word.

Then in April the cut worms cut down our corn & kept it cut down until the 3d planting – then in May or early June when the wheat was nearly ripe a dreadful gale swept down the fences & broke the fruit trees – & the hail beat down the wheat & buried & bruised much of the corn so that it never recovered & the wheat yielded less than half or even 3d of a crop. Then came a withering dearth – with hot winds & cut off the hay crop & stinted the corn & burned the tobacco & left us with little for support – & then in Nov. death came into the fold & stole a lovely lamb [Ginnie] from my little flock.

This has been a year also of blessings. My friends have shown themselves – they aided in rebuilding my houses & sent meat – & gave logs & lumber & boards & nails & work until I hardly felt the loss by fire. I have made a better crop of tobacco than most of my neighbors & as good corn as others – & on my circuit – I was successful & we gathered many into the fold & I feel confident that I have the confidence & esteem of the brotherhood – so that in the whole I have had more joy than sorrow – more pleasure than pain – & feel now like renewing my covenant & trusting God with all my heart for the future.

On Friday the 4th in accordance with the president's proclamation we observed the day as a day of fasting & prayer & had a large concourse at our church – services were conducted by Bro Gardiner – who made some most appropriate remarks & many & fervent were the prayers offered for the blessing of heaven on our distracted country.

* * *

[**Editor's Note:** George Dick's journal for January 2, 1861–May 9, 1862 is missing. During this period he served in the two appointments assigned to him by the Louisville Conference of the Methodist Episcopal Church, South: Russellville Station (1860–61) and Logan Circuit (1861–62).]

Volume III
1862–1864

"Lying is more fashionable than truth."

May 10, 1862 — The beginning of a new volume of my journal is always rather exciting to me. I can but wonder what painful or pleasant events I may be called to note — what changes in our domestic ties I may have to record — what losses or trials or changes for better or worse may befall us. I am glad I have kept a record of the past — yet I do not know that my children will ever read it to see the labor I have undergone to leave them a history of my life & times, which I should esteem a great treasure if coming from my own father to me.

I enter upon this volume, doubting whether I shall live to write the last page — or if I should, it is most uncertain whether all around me now will be alive & still with me when these pages are all full. I will probably record here the time & place when & where great battles were fought & victories won in this second revolution that now sweeps over the entire South & shakes the nation from center to circumference. I shall probably record the close of this desolating war & the conquest of the Southern people, or possibly I may write in these pages the acknowledgment of Southern Independence. It is not improbable that these very pages may unfold to the memory of my children some of the most startling events known in all the history of our sin cursed world. This is certainly a day of darkness in our land — distress in the nation & discouragement in the church & none can tell whether I shall write here the great apostacy & general corruption that we dread — or whether God in his mercy shall remove these storm clouds. Oh that God would rebuke the sword that devours the land — turn away his wrath from us & lift upon us the light of his countenance! I fear much that for our pride, self confidence, infidelity, avarice & worldliness — pestilence will be added to war & gaunt famine tread the footsteps of both, until "all faces gather blackness" & the hearts of the strong men quail. I enter upon this volume individually in prosperous circumstances — surrounded by domestic peace — piety & tranquility. There is great lack of fervent devotion & inward purity in my own heart — but outwardly my circumstances are favorable. My wife & children are loving, affectionate, true and pure. My kindred are honorable and prosperous — my servants are loyal and obedient — my neighbors as kind & constant — respectful & forbearing as I could expect men to be in this wicked world. Other communities have been disturbed, their houses searched, their families insulted by ruthless mobs, their schools & churches broken up by partisan bitterness — but such is not the case with us. God grant that I may still so write at the close of this book!

There is abundance of provision in the land and at cheap prices. The confederates bought the wheat — corn and pork of the farmers at high figures — and now these commodities are cheap & tobacco is in great demand at fine prices. Large crops of wheat were sown & that now promises to produce bread enough — and large crops of corn have been planted & is coming up unusually well, while the pestilent cutworms that for two years back gave us a vast deal of trouble are now comparatively harmless, and we have the rarity of a fourth consecutive crop of peaches, apples & cherries. I have planted 45 or 50 acres of corn, have 20 acres of wheat & 8 or 10 of oats — a large crop of beans, potatoes, cabbages & other garden vegetables. The flies have injured my tobacco plants less than most of my neighbors — my children are doing well at school — &

behaving well at home – we have so far had less sickness than many others – and considering all these mercies & the remembrance that an overruling Providence has always supplied our wants & delivered us in times of trouble, I ought to enter thankfully & hopefully upon the task of writing another volume in Diary.

May 11 – I went to Pleasant Grove & preached to a small audience of attentive hearers on "Trusting in the Lord" Prov[erbs] 3. 5,6. Sister Evans told me that Mrs B. K. Tully told Mrs Brown that she once thought I was a good man, but *now* I had gotten to be such a *liar* she had lost confidence in me. This statement grows out of the bitterness of these war times & partisan vindictiveness. Some one may have told the woman that I lied. I have had no conversation with her, except to meet her a few moments on the highway, & pass the usual salutations, since the war began – & as to lying, in the fear of God I have kept clear of it. When I was a little boy – I broke my fathers grindstone accidentally, by striking it with a stick to make it roll like a hoop. He asked me who did it & I hesitated. He urged me to tell the truth & I should not be punished. I confessed & got his blessing. Another time I was in fault, & he asked me if I did the thing complained of & when I told him I did he prepared to whip me, when I reminded him of his promise not to whip me and he frankly forgave my fault. Since that time I have no recollection of telling a lie – except one time when a drunken man intended beating his wife, who was hid in my fathers house for shelter & protection, asked me if I knew where she was & I told him I did not. This falsehood I told, thinking it better to deceive him than get his wife abused, & I was afraid to tell him that I knew where she was & not inform him. It would have been better and more manly to have told him that I would not tell him. Mrs Tully is mistaken, I have faults & sins enough, but lying is not one of them. At 4 I preached to the congregation of negroes, Dan[iel] 12.13, with great liberty and uncommon effect. Two or three came forward for prayers & seemed earnestly seeking pardon – & many in the audience were deeply affected.

The cars[1] ran down & back in a great hurry this evening, & reported that the famous John [Hunt] Morgan had come up into Ky & captured two trains, & destroyed about 50 cars at Cave City almost to Green river! He took all the soldiers on board prisoner, & turned loose all private citizens.[2] His object was to recapture his brother & a number of his men who were captured at Lebanon

1. That is, railroad cars.
2. After participating in the Battle of Shiloh in early April 1862, Morgan trained a 325 man outfit for raids into Tennessee and Kentucky. On May 11 they struck at Cave City where they burned one train. While they were there, a southbound train steamed into town loaded with Federal soldiers and with wives of several of the officers. The ever gallant Morgan decided not to destroy the train because it would deprive the women of a place to rest while they were awaiting rescue. Instead, he invited the officer in charge and the ladies to join him at the Cave City Hotel for lunch. He then ordered the train and everyone on it back to Louisville. Edison H. Thomas, *John Hunt Morgan and His Raiders* (Lexington, Kentucky, 1975), 37 ff.

Ten[nessee], but they were detained at Nashville & he did not get them. This is a bold move, equal in daring & success to the exploits of the old Marion.[3] Morgan will be a man of note whether the rebellion succeeds or not.

May 13 — Had a task of catching & penning the little roguish pigs, that are rooting up my corn. Tom [Browder] came up from Clarksville & brought a letter from father, the first we have had since he left[4] — he has had a long & severe spell of Pneumonia. He reports the supply of provisions very scarce in the South, yet the people are resolved to achieve their independence or die. Bacon is 40 cents pr lb — flour 20.00 pr bl — molasses 1.00 pr gal. This is distressing — very distressing. God grant to give us speedy peace — & restore the prosperity of our land.

May 14 — I wrote to Bro [Joseph] Redford [in Louisville] to know if he could get my supply of goods & groceries for next winter, as the uncertainty of getting them if the war continues gives me some solicitude.

May 15 — I manured my tobacco plants — & passing through my cornfield, I found that the moles or cutworms had destroyed a great deal of it.

May 16 — I moved my bees this morning to the new stand I made for them. It is singular to see how confused they appear when they fly to the old place & find the hive gone. It spurs my own industry to see the ceaseless activity of these frugal and thrifty insects. I finished replanting the corn that was worst missing. It is now getting late for corn planting — & we are having a dry spell. The skies look clear & hard & the wind stubbornly hangs in the North. Prospect for short crops remind me of taking my little Robert — when very small — to look at my corn in a rented field at Boyds when the drought had ruined the crop. Looking at the bare stalks & dry withered blades, I asked Robert what we should do if we made no corn. He looked thoughtfully a moment — then announced, "I don't know sir — but I would not steal." Dear child! He has always been conscientious & honest — & remarkable for his veracity. He is now 9 years old & if he ever told me a falsehood, I do not know it. He has often confessed things that he might have expected a whipping for — rather than tell a lie. I pray for wisdom & patience to raise my children so that they would rather suffer than lie or steal. One morning this week I had the painful duty of whipping Hanson for telling a

---

3. George Dick is referring to Francis Marion whose exploits in South Carolina against the British during the American Revolution earned him the nickname "Swamp Fox."

4. We learn from later journal entries that George Dick's father, Robert, had gone to Montgomery, Alabama, to stay with relatives. He apparently left Kentucky to escape prosecution for his open support of the Confederate cause. He was a member of the Southern Conference, which met in Russellville, October 29–30, 1861, to discuss Kentucky's connection with the Union. For some reason, however, he opposed the move to summon another convention (which met in November) for the purpose of considering outright secession. *Tri-Weekly Kentucky Yeoman* (Frankfort, Kentucky), Vol. IX, No. 148 (November 19, 1861), 3.

story about some misconduct. Little Georgie is a cheerful pleasant child & generally truthful, but occasionally will deny things he has done.

May 20 – I went to the depot & got a letter from Redford agreeing to buy my goods. My bee hive turned out another swarm this morning & I had a long chase to settle them, & a job to get them down from a tall hickory tree at least a mile from home – got stung on my right eye. *Abram & Henry*⁵ suffered them to light all about their heads & faces, & were not stung.

May 21 – The bees we labored to save yesterday, divided to day & part of them peaceably seceded & went away.

May 23 – Today the constant rattling of the bell announced the appearance of a fourth swarm of bees, from one hive! We settled them on the mulberry tree & made a rough hive for them. We now have five – two weeks ago we had one! Our bees are busy bees.

May 26 – Cousin Helen [Browder] told me to day that the court at Louisville had indicted my father for aiding the southern cause. If such be the case I hope he will stay at Montgomery until this unfortunate war is ended. I am sure they cannot prove him guilty of any crime. The union was dissolved without the consent & against the remonstrance of Ky & he thought it right to use his influence to carry the state with the south. To days paper reports the defeat of Genl Bank's federal army by the rebel Genl Jackson, surnamed "Stone Wall" for his valor & firmness. He has driven Banks across the Potomac with heavy loss.⁶ This advantage of the rebels will embolden them without disheartening their foes. The position of the armies is such that a few weeks at most must decide the

---

5. George Dick recorded in his family Bible that he bought Abraham Warfield at W. W. Warfield's sale after the latter's death on January 19, 1861. He added, "I think we paid eleven hundred dollars for him. Abraham was then a young man." Henry was a hired slave.

6. In the spring of 1862 the Army of the Potomac under the command of Union Major General George B. McClellan tried a new advance on Richmond, Virginia, the Confederate capital. His successful move up the peninsula between the James and York Rivers brought the Federals to the outskirts of Richmond by the end of May. McClellan's plans were thwarted, however, by Major General Stonewall Jackson who, in a series of brilliant maneuvers, halted the advance of a Union army up the Shenandoah Valley under Major General Nathaniel Banks. Banks retreated across the Potomac River after he was decisively defeated by Jackson at the Battle of Winchester on May 25. Banks' defeat denied necessary reinforcements to McClellan's army, which now retreated to Harrison's Landing on the James River after a series of hard fights in late June with Confederate forces under General Robert E. Lee. Allan Nevins, *The War for the Union* (2 vols., New York, 1960), II, 1244 ff; E. B. Long, *The Civil War Day By Day: An Almanac 1861–1865* (New York, 1971), 216 ff. It is interesting to note that as remote as south-central Kentucky was, George Dick was informed through the *Louisville Daily Express* of military developments within twenty-four hours after they occurred. In addition, the telegraph located at the Olmstead railroad depot kept the residents of the area up-to-date on news from the outside world.

result of the present campaign. The Southerners, I do not think, can sustain themselves long in retreating farther South — & if their present armies are cut off & captured they cannot raise another — & the same is probably true of the federals. It is reported that a large rebel cavalry force is in the rear of the federal army interrupting their communications & capturing their detached squadrons & many fear a general guerilla warfare. Where our evils are to end God only knows. The public mind is so absorbed in war & its parties that people hardly find time to think of anything else. I have time & again tried to resolve to study the Bible & other good books more & quit reading the papers & seeking the war news, but some exciting intelligence would come on immediately & fill my mind with thoughts connected with the state of the country. I am now taking the Louisville daily Express, which is a new paper published by Overton & Stackhouse and gives more news from the South than any other I get. It claims to be a *news* paper, neutral in politics.

May 27 — Mr Orndorff just returned from the South reports the wheat & oat crops as having failed — but corn was promising. Extracts from the Memphis papers quote salt at .40 cts pr lb. = 20.00 per bushel, & coffee 2.50 pr pound, flour 20.00 pr bl. & flour in N Orleans is said to bring 50.00 per bl! The Southern people cannot long sustain these famine prices. They will either break through & drive back their invaders, or they will be overcome & driven into submission to the federal government. The whole country is almost holding its breath to hear of the impending conflict at Corinth, which will probably decide the fate of the Southern Confederacy.[7]

May 28 — A disease has attacked my pigs that were penned up, to prevent their rooting up my corn. Four of them have died in the last day & night. Hog cholera is killing hundreds in this & other neighborhoods.

May 29 — I went to town & bought saltpetre, sulphur & copperas to improve the health of my hogs. I called on Bro Rizers & Barnes families, had several kind solicitations to return to the station when Bro Littles time is out. They like him vastly as a preacher, but his health is delicate & he does not visit much.

May 30 — My little boys were up early playing with the marbles I bought them as a reward of their industry at school. I had the pleasure of putting a new bucket on the well in place of the old one that had worn out two bottoms of wood & one of leather — which last I put on for a few days use until the new one I bought in Clarksville could be sent up, but in the irregularity of military control of the railroad, it never came — so the old leather bottom has lasted nearly half a year — showing that a little economy & a little necessity can make expenses less.

7. Confederate General P. G. T. Beauregard had retreated to Corinth, Mississippi, after the Battle of Shiloh on April 6–7, 1862. By April 30, Union Major General Henry W. Halleck had assembled 100,000 men at Shiloh and began his move toward Corinth. It took him four weeks to cover the twenty mile distance. Outnumbered, on May 30 Beauregard withdrew southward to Tupelo. Long, *Civil War Day by Day,* 218.

Tom Frazer – a Union lawyer, just returned from Louisville says no man in this country has been indicted by the U.S. Court at Louisville. If this is true, then the rumor of my fathers indictment is false. I do not believe he can be convicted of any unconstitutional act. Three men in every five in this region have done the same things that he has – except meeting in the convention that called for another convention to inaugurate a provisional government. He opposed the whole procedure & would have nothing more to do with it. As to his Southern sympathies, there is no discount on them.

June 2 – I went to the depot & got 6 boxes of goods, 4 barrels of salt – a barrel of sugar & half barrel of Molasses, which last must have fallen among thieves as it is less than ⅔ full. We got a lot of heavy blankets, slightly damaged & some of them new – for 1.00 each, heavy Brogan shoes 1.40 – good wool hats 10.00 pr dozen – &c. All things considered I am satisfied with the bill.

June 3 – The papers report a dreadful battle near the Chickahominy river before Richmond, in which McLellan acknowledges a heavy loss of men, munitions & artillery on Saturday, but claims to have regained the lost ground on Monday.[8]

June 6 – I went to Volney Academy to hear the children speak at the close of the session. Most of them did very well & some of the dialogues were very amusing – how such an occasion recalls the scenes of my own boyhood!

June 8 – Had the largest congregation at Keysburg that has been there for some months – yet not so large as we used to have before the war. I did not have so much liberty in preaching on the cause & cure of our evils as I had last Sunday – Isa[iah] 64, 6. The paper this evening reports the surrender of Memphis to the federal fleet.[9] The prospect is dark for the Confederates. The coast is all lost – the whole Mississippi river except at Vicksburg is lost – Ky, Mo, Arkansas – Florida & most of Ten[n] for the present at least are lost – & the desperate effort to hold Va & Richmond must determine the weal or woe of the South. The rebels claim a great victory at the battle of the "seven pines" on the Chickahominy & the federal papers are almost acknowledging a defeat.[10] I leave all this great matter in the hands of God – it is too deep for me. I shall submit to his providence & not murmur.

8. George Dick is referring to the Battle of Seven Pines or Fair Oaks, which took place just east of Richmond on May 31–June 1, 1862. McClellan's Army of the Potomac was opposed by Confederate General Joseph E. Johnston who was severely wounded during the engagement and replaced by Robert E. Lee. The Confederates failed to dislodge McClellan. *Ibid.*

9. At 5:30 A.M. on June 8, 1862, Commodore Charles Davis with five Federal ironclads and four rams engaged Confederate Captain James E. Montgomery with eight inferior makeshift vessels. The battle for Memphis involved ramming on both sides and close quarter fighting. By 7:30 A.M. it was all over. Except for Vicksburg, Union forces now controlled the Mississippi River. *Ibid.,* 222–23.

10. The rebel claim was not justified. Union losses were reported at 790 dead and 3594 wounded, while the Confederates lost 980 dead and 4749 wounded. *Ibid.,* 220.

June 12 — For two or three days past I have been very busy at work on the farm & in the garden — have done more plowing than I have for two years past, & feel able to do it. This is also harvest week & the clatter of the reapers is borne around the neighborhood on the breeze. The crop is light & badly damaged by rust and smut.

June 14 — I went with my little boys according to promise, to the creek — fishing & bathing — had but little success fishing, but the little fellows enjoyed the bathing very much. I went down to Rileys & got two gallons of whisky, for medical purposes — my wife & her sister & their two black women both being in need of bitters. My little Robert objected to carrying a bag with a jug of whisky in it — says he does not like whisky. I encouraged his correct taste. I do not like to be seen with it myself although we are a temperate family. We keep alittle for medicine, but *never* use it as a beverage.

June 16 — A. H. Redford came down this evening and gave us a most interesting account of our late conference in Louisville. He is confident of the final acknowledgment of Southern Independence — he thinks the South western division of the federal army has lost 75,000 men since the Confederates evacuated Bowling Green — by death, desertion, wounds, & capture — & the eastern army under McLellan almost as many.

June 20 — Uncle Dick [Browder] & aunt Sally came over to see us on the especial account of a little stranger that came in here, in a very dependent & helpless condition, between midnight & day break on the morning of the 18th. They found the little lady in bed with Ginnie, & Tom [Browder] was looking at her occasionally with a great deal of interest & the old folks seemed pleased at the little grand daughter. This is the second of Ginnies children that has been born under our roof.

June 21 — The papers to day confirm the evacuation of Cumberland gap by the Confederate forces.[11] Bowling Browder came home a short time ago from Montgomery, Ala. He says my father was well & anxious to come home. He reports the Southern people as determined on independence at any price. The military commander of Ky is arresting a great many Southern men & numbers are running off to the army.[12] Congress seems crazy. They say they are striving

---

11. On March 28, 1862, Brigadier General George W. Morgan was given command of the Seventh Division of the Federal Army of Ohio. His main task was to capture Cumberland Gap. Morgan achieved his objective on June 18 when the Confederates withdrew in the face of Federal threats. *Ibid.,* 190, 228.

12. On June 1, 1862, Brigadier General Jerry T. Boyle was named U.S. military commandant of Kentucky with headquarters in Louisville. On June 9 he announced that all persons who joined the Confederate forces, gave them aid or assistance, or went behind their lines would have to take an oath of allegiance and give bonds with security for their future good conduct, or else be arrested and sent to the military prison in Louisville. Richard and Lewis Collins, *History of Kentucky* (2 vols., Covington, Kentucky, 1878), I, 102.

to restore the union & all the time pursuing such a course as to increase the alienation & deepen the rebellion. They have now excluded negroes from all existing territories & all hereafter to be acquired. Genl Hunter on the coast has organized a regiment of negroes for U.S. service – & declared emancipation to all slaves in the region occupied by federal arms. The president however has nullified this proclamation as a usurpation of power on Hunters part, but says he reserves to himself the right to do so.[13] Genl Butler at New Orleans threatens to consider & treat as common prostitutes all the women of N. Orleans who by word or look or gesture "insult the federal soldiers," as if he could compel a proud, defiant & chivalrous people to treat as friends, those whom they consider base enemies. Distinguished citizens are arrested & imprisoned, some in irons, without the right of habeas corpus or speedy trial – without warrant & in violation [of] state & federal constitutions.[14]

June 22 – At 4, I preached to a crowded congregation of negroes, the largest I have seen for years – on Dan[iel] 12. 13, on occasion of the death of old aunt *Ably Anderson* – old aunt *Lucy Browder* – & her son *Hal,* all colored people, the last of whom died in Mo. The colored people frequently get me to preach their funerals, but nine out of ten would prefer a negro preacher – however ignorant, to almost any white preacher – however trained or eloquent. *Ned Jones* of Hopkinsville exhorted after me. He is a fine speaker – one of the very best and I think a good, pious man. I helped buy him to preach to the negroes. He is an orator.

June 30 – Went to see Temple Woolls – found his father there just from Louisville. He reports the probability of all preachers being compelled to swear allegiance to the U.S. Govt. I afterward learned that this very morning Old Bro Stevenson & other citizens of Russellville had been arrested & sent off to the Provost Marshall! Dr Stevenson was chairman of the military board of Confederates for which he has been much abused by union men & villified, slandered & blackguarded by the Louisville Journal. I rather intimated to Bro Stevenson that a minister ought not to meddle too much with war matters, but I believe him to be a good man. I see in this evenings Journal that Bro. Sehon, Bro Baldwin, Dr Howell & other ministers of Nashville have been sent to the Nashville penitentiary for declining to take the oath of allegiance. Merciful God! Has it come to this in America. Ministers shut up in a felons prison, & yet no

---

13. On April 12, 1862, Major General David Hunter, Commander of the Department of the South, issued an order confiscating and freeing all slaves in and around Fort Pulaski, Georgia. President Lincoln later rescinded the order as going beyond the power of a military leader. Long, *Civil War Day By Day,* 199.

14. Major General Benjamin F. Butler took over military control of New Orleans on May 1, 1862. The citizens of that city never forgave him for what they considered his "bestial acts." Among the most infamous was Butler's Order 28 on May 15 in which he observed that his soldiers had been the victims of repeated insults from the women of New Orleans; he declared that in the future any "female" who "by word, gesture, or movement" insulted one of his men would be "treated as a woman of the town plying her trade." *Ibid.,* 206.

crime alleged against them, no law violated only for refusing to take an oath that could not be constitutionally imposed upon them – their friends, forbidden to visit, or to send them food! Can the blessing of Heaven rest upon such a government? Can Andrew Johnson crush the people with a tyrants hand and yet be owned of God?[15] I do not judge God's providences. He allowed Job to be persecuted – Jeremiah to be imprisoned – John to be banished, & other apostles lashed & stoned & imprisoned, yet out of all the Lord brought good results. So may it be with these brethren, that they may be blessed & God-honored in their persecution. I have never acknowledged allegiance to any other government than that of the U.S. & would prefer taking the oath to being imprisoned to the injury of my health & the distress of my family, yet I protest against the right of the state to impose any involuntary oath upon me. The constitution prescribes no oath to private citizens or persons not in the official employment of the Government. I think it almost certain that all the public men will be required to take [the] oath of allegiance, pledging their lives & fortunes to the support of the govt. & not to aid, counsel, or abet the Confederate State or any person or persons now or hereafter in rebellion against the govt. I do not know what to do. My father & sister [Mary] & brother [John] & his family are in the South, & by the Conscript law of the South, my brother must be in rebellion – & no oath or penalty shall keep me from relieving him or his family as far as I can when I see them in distress. My wifes brother [George Warfield] is also entitled to my sympathy & assistance as a brother & not as a soldier, should he ever get home again. I must be allowed to explain & interpret the oath I take or I cannot consider it a moral obligation. I have done nothing & do not expect to do anything disloyal to the government I live under, but as all my sympathies are with the South – considering them as only seeking their *just rights* – I cannot voluntarily swear without hesitation, evasion or equivocation, not to countenance even their armed rebellion against the mad schemes of an abolition fanaticism.

I think we will have dark days in Ky, & it will be long perhaps before the war is over, & I have made up my mind to suffer many things that are even painful to me. As fully as I know how, I have committed my all of temporal and eternal interest into the hand of God. I am waiting patiently for the developments of time. The papers report fighting at different points. At James Island near Charleston, the federals under Genl Benham were defeated & routed with terrible slaughter.[16] McLellan in his siege of Richmond acknowledges serious loss in heavy skirmishing, but claims to have advanced his line. Many writers seem confident of European intervention in behalf of the South – while the federals boast that with their great armies & powerful navies they can conquer the rebels & defy Europe at the same time. The rebel papers still claim

---

15. Andrew Johnson, the future president, was appointed by Lincoln as Union governor of his native Tennessee.

16. On June 16, 1862, Union Brigadier General H. W. Benham directed an assault from James Island near Charleston against a Confederate position at Secessionville, South Carolina. The effort failed miserably. Benham apparently disobeyed orders in launching the attack and eventually was relieved of his command. Long, *Civil War Day By Day,* 227.

to be able to meet & vanquish their foes & even threaten the invasion of the North. The army of Va. [has been] consolidated to drive Stonewall Jackson from the Shenandoah Valley.[17] Jackson will find different game in Genl Pope from Fremont & Banks each of whom he has routed in the last few weeks. Some Southern men are alarmed & are returning to the union, and many union men are disgusted with the abolitionism of Congress & are espousing the Southern cause. So there seems to be no prospect for peace. My brother William has just returned from Columbia Ten[nessee] — where he went to get the horse & buggie father left there. He was compelled to take the oath before he could get out of Nashville either going or coming. The papers report guerillas in Ky and there is indeed a prospect of troublous times before us.

July 1 — We have a rainy gloomy day & it is very congenial with the feelings of many in this country. This evening the papers reported a terrible battle of two or three days continuance before Richmond, with terrible slaughter on both sides & resulting in the defeat of the federals — & consequently the safety of Richmond for the present.[18] The Southern men are greatly elated & feel confident now that European nations will interpose to stop the war.

July 2 — I went down to the Allensville depot. The papers give no further particulars of the great battle near Richmond, but the federals claim a great victory & say they have achieved their object & gained the desired position — that the fall of the city is now certain, but as they always claim victories at first & afterward admit their disasters, the public mind is not prepared to credit reports until they gain further information.

July 4 — This is a sad day in America. It is our national sabbath, but it finds almost a million of our people in arms against each other. Rumors of battle & slaughter in different parts of the long lines come every day. On Thursday last the skirmishing around Richmond began — & the battles, awful, terrific, bloody & murderous, have raged with unprecedented fury at intervals for six days resulting in the utter defeat of the federals, the retreat of McLellans army & the reported capture of most of his siege guns & other many other cannon & firearms & a loss of 20,000 or more killed — wounded & missing. The rebels also lost immensely as their eager legions crowded on the federal batteries dealing out volleys of grape, cannister, solid shot & shell — a perfect harvest of death. The gunboats too at different times poured their broadsides of destruction on the flanking brigades of confederates as they pushed the federals down on James

---

17. Major General John Pope was brought east from the Mississippi Valley to take over command of a new Army of Virginia, which was formed primarily from units commanded by Major General John C. Fremont and Major General Nathaniel Banks. Fremont refused to serve under General Pope and resigned his post. *Ibid.*

18. On June 25, 1862, the battle for Richmond, sometimes called the Seven Days' Battle, began. Lee forced McClellan to withdraw. The engagement ended on July 1 when McClellan successfully repulsed Lee's attack at the Battle of Malvern Hill, just north of the James River. *Ibid., 230 ff.*

River seeking shelter under the guns of their union clad fleet. The federals claim a great advantage in position & say they have killed Stonewall Jackson & captured 2,000 troops & one or two rebel generals.[19] Our nation then will celebrate this day with heavy hearts – the waving plumes – the measured step & skillful evolutions of the soldiers & the peal of booming cannon will seem a cruel mockery, to the countless thousands, whose hearts & hearthstones are desolated by the ravages of this unholy war. When will it end? peace! peace! peace! Oh for peace! on any honorable terms.

July 6 – I went to Gunns School house. The benches were moved out into the grove as the throng could not half get into the house. I never saw such a crowd at the school house. I had published *by request* to preach on national calamities. I had liberty & the almost undivided attention of the large auditory, sitting around on benches, on the naked ground, in buggies, stumps &c, & standing against trees. I was too prostrated to preach to the negroes in the afternoon, but *Old Uncle Jack Irvin* exhorted for me, & there seemed some interest among the children of Ham. Two came forward for prayers. I reached home very tired.

July 7 – I went over to fathers to see Bro Bosley, just returned from the confederate army – having resigned his chaplaincy. He represents the confederates as confident of success. The tidings from Richmond are more & more calamitous to the Union. The rebels claim to have captured 8 generals, 12,000 soldiers, more than 100 officers, 80 or 90 cannon, all the siege train – & immense supplies of army stores – clothing, arms, &c. The federals papers write despondingly for the present but promise great things in the future & seem confident of European intervention, which they think will be in favor of the South. There is no telling what scenes of excitement, blood & terror are yet before us. The federals are still arresting Southern men & sending them off to the prisons & their movements widen the breach & deepen the enmity. The rebellion is more formidable than ever.

July 8 – Bro Bosley came over to see me. He is going up into Ky to see his family. I am almost confident that he will be arrested & imprisoned as he says he will not subscribe to the federal oath. F. M. Bristow told Ed Hughes that we would all have to take it. I hope I will not be required to violate my conscience – or compelled to suffer imprisonment for conscience sake.

July 10 – Temple Woolls came over this morning & told me that Bros J. S. Moore & R. Fisk had been arrested by the federals – & old Mr Gaines says that Tom Jeffries was allowed to choose between expatriation, imprisonment & taking the federal oath. I cannot decide in my own mind what to do. If the federal oath is as I have heard, I dont think I can conscientiously take it. If it is forced upon me – it will not be my act.

---

19. Union losses were estimated at 15,800 while the Confederates lost 20,000. *Ibid.,* 235. Stonewall Jackson was not killed during the Seven Days' Battle.

Uncle Dick [Browder] in his kindness sent a mule & boy to day to help ɪ. plow.

July 12 — As the cars did not get any communication with Louisville last night & a report was in circulation that John [Hunt] Morgan had seized the railroad, there was great anxiety to see the papers to day. A rumor is afloat that a large rebel force has come into Ky & threatens to drive out the federals. The paper reports that Morgan surrounded three companies of Pennsylvanians & killed or captured all but 10 or 12. It is said that he sent 4 men with a flag of truce demanding a surrender without fighting as he had 1500 men, but they killed his truce bearers & were killed in turn.[20] A messenger from the South brings authentic intelligence that the rebels captured 20,000 prisoners, 100 siege guns, $2,000,000. worth of army stores & killed & wounded 60,000 federals in the late fearful battles around Richmond — & suffered immense losses themselves. It is also said that 30 days will not pass until all the feds are driven out of Ten[n]. The papers report a terrible bombardment of Vicksburg Miss, and the ruin of the city but say the fleets cannot take the place.[21]

There has been a very remarkable smoke or haze darkening the air all day — causing considerable curiosity and speculation. It is much like Indian summer but more dense. My heart is sad over the evils that threaten us. I fear Ky will be again the dark & bloody ground. Guerilla bands are hovering over the state & enmity grows deeper & hatred intensifies as the federals increase their intolerance to Secessionists. The papers seem to calculate certainly on European intervention & a European war. Oh the desolations of our country! When will our calamities end? Sick of war & its woes I turn my eyes to the "Hill whence cometh my help" — and pray God to guide me & mine in peace & safety through the coming week as he has through this that is now passing out, as I sit here and write while all around me are in a Saturday nights slumber.

July 13 — The morning found the air still burdened with smoky vapor. I heard today that it was probable that I would be arrested by the federals under charge of presenting a flag to the rebels on Christmas day. I think a minister ought not to meddle with these matters too much & it was an oversight in me to present

20. After his brief invasion at Cave City, Morgan made his way to Chattanooga, Tennessee, where he gathered recruits and formed a new regiment of Second Kentucky Cavalry. His men were ordered to Knoxville in early June 1862 where they engaged in rigorous training. Morgan left Knoxville on July 4 with about 900 men on the way to his first Kentucky raid. George Dick's entry for July 12 could refer to Morgan's raid on Tompkinsville on July 9 where he captured 400 prisoners, but it seems more likely that he is referring to the raid on Lebanon on July 11 where he took 200 prisoners and turned back a Federal troop train. Thomas, *Morgan and His Raiders*, 33 ff.

21. The bombardment of Vicksburg began on July 3, 1862. It continued for several days as the Federals tried to decide how best to take the fortress perched on the Mississippi bluffs. Earlier, on June 25, about 3,000 troops under the command of Brigadier General Thomas Williams had arrived from Baton Rouge, Louisiana, and set to work digging a canal that would allow small vessels to bypass the Confederate batteries on the east side. Long, *Civil War Day By Day*, 228, 236–37.

t on the score of ministerial impropriety, but not the principle gave utterance to no treasonable sentiments.

; are exciting times. Every day brings stirring news. To day the paper reports the capture of Murfreesboro by Confederates under [Nathan Bedford] Forrest, together with two brigadier Genls & a regiment of soldiers. Morgan is said to be near Frankfort with a force estimated variously from 1600 to 2,000. Enlistments in the North are said to come in slowly & the papers speak out openly of prospective European intervention.

July 15 – I made these figures "15" just as I finished writing the above on the 14th & remembered feeling an impression that the 15th might bring something to report. This is now Tuesday 22nd & I have passed a week of excitement & anxiety such as I have not known for some time in reference to myself. I went out on the morning of the 15th to work in my tobacco, leaving my coat at the house. About 10 oclock, being tired, I walked up to see David Sydnor who was not well, & had only been there a few moments when my hired boy *Henry* came up in haste & said "Mars George, better keep yourself close, them soldiers is down yonder," & sure enough they were & not being willing to go to Camp Chase[22] or take Lincolns oath I escaped through the corn field to the woods where I lay concealed for several hours – then ventured cautiously up to George Duersons where T. B. S. [Thomas B. Sydnor] soon found me & informed me that the soldiers claimed to be in search of Bro Bosley – that they inquired for me at the house, then went to the field where my negroes were at work and gaining no information from them as to my whereabouts, swore they intended to have me. My dear wife sent my clothes & all the information she had & advised me to leave. Mr Duerson kindly furnished me a horse & saddle & "I retired in good order" down Whippoorwill & the Watermelon Road – & "changed the base of my operations" to Charles Warfields where I spent the night & the following day & night – then went on to my father in laws where I met a cordial welcome & an asylum. Went to town [Clarksville] next day but heard nothing from home. On Sunday I went home with Aunt Betsy, staid all night & resolved to come home cautiously & stay if I could. I dined on Monday at Charles Warfields, & at William Hughes learned that the soldiers denied being after me at all – that the soldiers were all gone from Russellville, & there was no risk in coming home, so I came on & was greeted with tears of joy & kisses of love by my dear wife & children. This morning one week ago I left home & to day I thank God for my safe return. From all the evidence I can get, I am disposed to believe that the soldiers had no warrant for my arrest & only threatened me to my negroes in a foolish, blustering spirit – being home guards & feeling grand with uniforms and sabres. One of them, Marcus Richards was a man whom I have befriended when he was needy, gave him work & paid him money, out of sympathy – and when times were hard & his family needed bacon & coffee I

---

22. Camp Chase was a military prison located at Columbia, Ohio.

prevailed on one of my merchant brethren of Russellville to order a hogshead of bacon & sack of coffee in his name, the profits of which would give Richards his supply without cost & without laying out a dollar. The railroad was seized however, before the plan could be consummated – but my kind intentions were the same. I used my influence to get his sister a school in a good neighborhood and succeeded. I endorsed a note for $95 for his brother Claudius & had it to pay with several years interest $115. He may or may not have come to arrest *me* – but I should prefer that he would not hang around my house.

"The Louisville Express" a neutral paper, whose editorials were short & never censured the government nor favored rebellion, & whose extracts were gathered almost exclusively from Northern papers – was to day suppressed, I suppose for the sole cause that it was patronized mainly by Southern Rights men. Alas for our boasted "free speech & free press." It is rumored by two men just passing Hadensville that the rebel Col Woodward was on the march to Hopkinsville. I fear these small bodies, called guerillas, coming in & scouring the country, & yet not in force enough to hold it, will do much to intensify the hatred between Northern & Southern men, beside the damage they do to the crops & property of the country. I dread guerilla warfare more than the shock of vast armies in battle array. Guerillas are never still – life, liberty & property are not safe an hour.

July 23 – I wrote this morning to my father, hoping Mr Glasscock could be able to send it through by some one passing. I walked through my fields to see my corn. It is very promising & will make a fine yield with one more good rain. There is prospect of plenty in the land, but the restless, excited state of the public mind & the evils we suffer destroys the pleasure that abundance ought to inspire. The federal congress has passed a law confiscating the property of rebels & freeing their slaves – and already the government is raising negro regiments to fight their masters! and the border slave states are solemnly entreated by the president (Lincoln) to abolish slavery in their borders as hope of ending the war.[23] The members of congress from the border states have agreed to lay the subject before their people & there is now probability of a most exciting canvass in Ky on this delicate question & the decision of the people will probably not be reached on either side without bloodshed & fearful scenes of carnage & strife. The people of Ky if left to themselves will not vote for compensated or any other emancipation – & the Southern armies will doubtless make a desperate

---

23. The move to abolish slavery had been gathering momentum in Congress, especially since January 1862. On March 6 Lincoln, in keeping with his preference for gradual, compensated emancipation, sent a message to Congress calling for financial aid to any state that would adopt such a course of action. Congress approved the proposal but no state responded to it. By April 11 Congress had voted to abolish slavery in the District of Columbia. Congress gave further impetus to the emancipation movement when it passed the Confiscation Act on July 17. By its terms the slaves of all those who supported the rebellion would be freed when they were brought under Union control. The same law gave the President the power to employ blacks in prosecuting the war. Five days later Lincoln presented his Emancipation Proclamation to his Cabinet. Long, *Civil War Day By Day*, 158, 179, 192, 199, 200, 241.

effort to gain & hold the state as important to them, while the Northern armies will sacrifice the prosperity of the state forever rather than allow the rebels to get it. The papers will be under the surveillance of whatever military power holds the state & the people cannot in either case have a fair and uncontrolled expression of their opinion of this vital question. I fear for the result, yet I trust in God to direct to the best issue. I found this evening that the rumor about the suppression of the Express was false. The paper still comes. The country is again flooded with exciting rumors. It is certain that a confederate force of 40 men are in or near Elkton − & it is said that a large force is at Hopkinsville & a large number, (4000) in the vicinity of Franklin. It is said that Col Bristow, Provost Marshall Hollinsworth & other prominent union men have become alarmed and left the country. These rumors I write to show my children if they read these pages, the excitements and rumors that attend a civil war.

July 25 − Tomorrow our quarterly meeting begins, yet we talk more of the war & its lying rumors than of the services of the sanctuary. Alas for these perilous times.

July 26 − We went all of us − white & colored − to attend the services taking provisions with us to Bethlehem. The finances of the circuit are greatly in arrears, but all things considered I cannot complain of short pay. Anticipating it from the first, I have felt it to be my duty to use all exertion I could at home to meet my liabilities & supply my family wants. I have filled nearly all my appointments & visited the sick − & from house to house as opportunity offered. I suppose the circuit will pay me 250. or more in money & this will clothe my household − and by God's blessing we will make bread & meat at home.

July 27 − We all went to the Sanctuary. On the way I talked seriously to my precious little daughter about her soul. She said she thought she was a sinner, & yet she trusted in the Lord Jesus, loved him − thought if she died she would be saved through faith in him & wished to join the church & live a Christian. We had a pleasant love feast and at the close when the opportunity offered, my dear child left her seat & walked into the altar to give Bro [James S.] Woolls her hand in uniting with the church. Oh what a thrill of rapture did that act bring upon my heart! I wept tears of joy on the neck of my child & welcomed her into the church, praying with all the earnestness of my soul that God would accept her through Christ, guide, counsel, defend & direct her pathway through lifes dubious journey. This is not a sudden impulse of a warm-hearted child. She has always been of a religious temperament − has always been constant in saying her prayers & of late has frequently returned alone to read her bible. One night more than a year ago, after she lay down she could not sleep, but sobbed & cried aloud. I went to her bed & talked tenderly to know the cause of her grief − & by divers questions found that she was in heaviness of heart because she thought she was a sinner. I directed her young & trusting heart to the Savior. She said she trusted him & felt that she was forgiven. One day soon after she learned to read, she brought me a beautiful story, she had found in her Sunday School Visitor about a poor old lady who wanted a new dress – & when a kind little girl had offered her one of all the different fabrics & materials at her command, costly & common – & none were acceptable – the old lady then told the child, that she wanted a "robe of righteousness, washed white & clean in the blood of Jesus." This beautiful allegory impressed Helens mind very deeply & she thought then that she was made one of the Lords children, & would wear a robe of righteousness. Her mother overheard her in conversation with little Lizzie Eli on the subject of religion, & when Lizzie said that she was too young – & loved to play & romp too well to join the church, Helen replied, "I think we ought both to have religion before now." These & divers other circumstances assure me that Gods good spirit has impressed the mind of this darling child of my heart. I have several times of late been much concerned about the early conversion of my children & have prayed fervently for that result. I yet trust that God will give me all my household – & enable me to lead my family in the way to heaven. We must teach Helen to remember the importance of her action on this 27th of July 1862.

Learning that W. G. Caldwell was not expected to live Lizzie & I went down to see him – found him in a stupor – blistered dreadfully from diseased brain – very nervous – & very low. I went back & nursed him through the night, but there was no time when he was in a condition to talk about his soul.

July 29 – Spent the day nursing poor Caldwell – who is still unconscious & I fear must die.

James Morrow & some of his men attempted to seize a horse today belonging to George Gray of Russellville, when Gray & some other Southern rights men resisted – & in the numerous shots that were fired, Burgher, a Lieut. in the Lincoln army was killed on the spot & James Morrow – recruiting officer of the army was wounded by five different shots, breaking his arm, shooting him twice through the body – one shot in the lungs and another in the shoulder. George Gray was wounded – and one of the others said to be shot in the hand. This awful affair will cause trouble in our land. Morrow had been overbearing & insulting to Southern rights men – & his own party expected him to be killed. The remark both of his father & brother on hearing of the affair was, "he brought it on himself." We cannot tell what horrors are before us – 400 Govt soldiers arrived at Russellville tonight – & there is much apprehension of evil.

July 30 – Lizzie & I went over to see Billy Caldwell as we heard he was dying! His wife is greatly distressed – having 3 helpless children left poor & dependent, besides her little step son. I assisted in laying him out and dressing him for the grave.

July 31 – I went over to see the corpse of poor Billy Caldwell sent off to Clarksville for interment. Martial law is established in Russellville & the hearse had difficulty in getting out. Wm Herndon who volunteered to go for the coffin yesterday was arrested & required to return this morning. Great excitement prevails in town & country people are afraid to go in. Great suspense, anxiety and alarm prevail – & it is now believed that the country will be declared under martial law & probably the militia called out. I feel that evil days are at hand, but I trust in God for guidance and protection to me and all mine. I am willing to do right.

I got a letter last night from some unknown friend in Louisville informing me that Bro Bosley had voluntarily gone to Louisville, and offered his oath & bond, both of which were rejected & he thrown into the military prison most likely to go to camp Chase. He said that Bro Redford had left the city for his *health* & advised not to return until his *health* was improved, that the government had found it necessary to arrest all persons *suspected* of *disloyalty* &c. The last papers report guerillas still infesting Ky & doing much damage in Tennessee.

The U.S. Govt has at last agreed to an exchange of prisoners & the work is progressing. The government of Ky has called the legislature together, to prepare for state defences & to consider the Presidents proposition to the border states. We may look for further excitements.

August 3 – Had rather a slim congregation – many being afraid to risk their horses at church in view of the federal seizures, and some thinking that I would not venture out – while some had left home on a visit for their own safety during these exciting times.

August 4 – This is election day – & never before did Ky vote under such circumstances. Southern rights candidates are threatened with arrest & imprisonment & they have withdrawn from the track. The *Louisville Journal* has had several inflammatory articles of late tending to create civil war of the greatest intensity among ourselves – saying that "tigers, lions, mad dogs, rattlesnakes, &c are less dangerous in a community than men who *sympathize* with the rebellion." That paper has preannounced a general uprising of Southern men on this day & if there fails to be massacre – blood shed, assassination – & mobs today, it will not be the result of any mild counsels of Geo. D. Prentice. It is believed that soldiers will be scouting the country to arrest & intimidate Southern men – so I did not go home until after night, when I heard that all was quiet in my neighborhood.

August 5 – I feel thankful that so far as heard from – the election passed off quietly. A small vote was polled. The Louisville Journal to day reports a call to draft 300,000 militia for immediate service – & a draft to fill up the deficiency in the other 300,000 after the 15th of Aug. If there is no mistake in this order we may anticipate the most horrible times ever witnessed on this continent. It is now stated that the President will not *arm* the negroes, but employ them as military laborers.

August 6 – I learned just at night that David Browder had arrived from Montgomery so I went down to uncle Dick [Browder]s to see him and was delighted to learn that my father was well & cheerful & pleasantly situated & entertaining strong hopes of getting home early in the coming fall. This latter I regard as very uncertain however much I desire it.

August 8 – I spent the afternoon at work in my hay of which I have a good yield. I also spent some time in driving off the pestilent potato bugs that destroy my late potatoes, in less time than the Yankees destroy the Southern confederacy. I was surprised to see a large train of soldiers going down towards Allensville.

August 11 – The excitement in the country is kept up by rumors more than actions. Mr. L. H. Ferguson was forcibly seized & carried off on Friday last by federals but came back on Sat. On Friday night uncle Dick Browders negroes reported Lincolnites at the stable after horses, so Billy B[rowder] & David Hutchings spent the night in the corn field. To day it is rumored that the federal troops at Hopkinsville have been captured. Alas for the times!

August 12 – I learned my brother Frank & Tim Jones had determined to leave the country to go to Montgomery Ala. & were already making arrangements. I went over to see my mother – Frank & Tim having dined with me. I felt sad to see two young boys, both of whom might do well at home, leaving to avoid a draft in a war they consider unrighteous. I advised them not to go to the army, but to go to my father where they might probably get into a good business & be useful to their country. Frank left about sun down and seemed to carry a sad heart with him. I trust God in great mercy will preserve his life & save his soul & so of Tim Jones who is a good & purehearted boy.

William [Browder] came home from town & reported Geo D. Blakey Provost Marshall with orders not to pass anyone who would not take the oath, & if any refused to swear, to send them through the federal lines into the South! Some report that they are to be sent off without money or clothes. A train loaded with soldiers went *up* the road in the night running cautiously, with a hand car in advance. I do not know what it means.

August 13 – Old Bro Baker came over & told me that Gallatin Ten[n] had been taken by the Confederates & it was supposed the train last night was loaded with sick & wounded soldiers.[24] My Bro William learned at Allensville, that 2000 prisoners were captured by the rebels but this is doubtless an exaggeration. Communication with Louisville is reported cut off by burning a bridge near Gallatin. Rumor reports the rebels at Calhoun & Rumsey on Green river – & Morgan at Glasgow. The troops from Russellville are said to be gone & Blakey's authority was brief. They may aid in driving out the rebels & then return. I have been busy working my tobacco. The worms are very destructive – sometimes 20 and even 30 on a plant.

---

24. On August 12, 1862, John Hunt Morgan captured a garrison of Union troops when he seized Gallatin. *Ibid.,* 250.

August 14 – I went to the depot where I heard that the rebels had burned the bridge over Red river near Charles Warfields, so cutting off railroad communication between Nashville & Louisville & probably interfering with Genl Buells operations in Ten[n]. A very large train of federal soldiers went down this evening. There is certainly some trouble on hand as Geo. D. Blakey, B. K. Tully & other prominent unionists are reported to have left in great haste. A federal soldier told old Mr Page that Morgan had captured 60 wagons & as many car loads of provisions at Gallatin.

August 15 – This morning I saw Mr Paine at the depot who reports from the Louisville Journal that Stonewall Jackson had defeated Genl Pope[25] – that McLellan had been driven back from Malvern hill[26] – that Independence Mo[27] & Baton Roug[e] La had been recaptured by the rebels[28] – the gun boat Arkansas had chased & damaged part of the federal fleet[29] & other terrible tales of the rebel daring & dash. So the country is full of excitement & rumor. Both parties feel restless & weary – each hating & fearing the other. Truly these are evil times. It is reported that Old Bro Stevenson had died in Camp Chase. I hope this rumor is not true. Some body has an awful account to render for this war and its horrors.

August 16 – The excitement in the country continues – trains of soldiers are constantly passing backward and forward in apparent confusion. Tonight we have the confirmed report of the capture of Baton Rouge – & the report of the recapture of Cumberland gap by the rebels with 7000 prisoners,[30] Stonewall Jackson's great triumph over Banks & other items of rebel prowess. Mr Paine

---

25. Pope's Army of Virginia advanced southward from Culpeper toward Orange Court House. Jackson's large army was poised south of Culpeper to attack one corps and then another of Pope's army, but Major General Nathaniel Banks got in the first blow at Cedar Mountain and drove deeply into Jackson's ranks. When Major General A. P. Hill launched a counterattack, Banks withdrew. *Ibid.,* 249–50.

26. McClellan had actually pulled back on July 2, 1862, from Malvern Hill to Harrison's Landing on the James River. On August 14 he began to move northward to Aquia Creek and Alexandria to support Pope against Lee who was threatening. *Ibid.,* 236, 251.

27. Independence was taken by the Confederates on August 11, 1862. *Ibid.,* 250.

28. On August 5, 1862, Confederate Major General John C. Breckinridge attacked Federal troops at Baton Rouge under the command of Brigadier General Thomas Williams. Although Williams was killed, the Confederates failed to take the city and withdrew a few miles north to fortify Port Hudson. The Federal troops did not evacuate Baton Rouge until August 21. *Ibid.,* 248.

29. The *Arkansas,* commanded by Commodore Isaac Brown, had fared well in an engagement with Union Admiral David Farragut's fleet at Vicksburg on July 15, 1862. The vessel then was ordered south to assist the Confederates in their effort to capture Baton Rouge. On August 6 it was attacked by a Union ironclad and four other vessels. During the battle the *Arkansas's* engines failed, and it was abandoned by its crew and blown up. *Ibid.,* 249.

30. Actually, Cumberland Gap continued to be held by Union forces until September 17, 1862, when a Confederate invasion of Kentucky forced Brigadier General George W. Morgan to withdraw. *Ibid.,* 268.

informs me that this T. J. Jackson is an old Presbyterian & was one of the leaders in the union prayer meetings that were so common two years ago. It said that he has prayer every night in his tent & goes out alone to secret prayer before every battle. I hope this account is true & may God hear his prayers for his injured & persecuted country.

August 17 — I went over to Bowling Poors & married his daughter Amelia to James A. Clark. John Keller, James Day & others told me that the northern soldiers on the cars asked Fergusons negroes why they did not get their guns & shoot down these rebels — that they would all be free in a few weeks! Such sentiments instilled into the minds of poor ignorant slaves might cause great wretchedness & destruction of life but will not aid in loyalizing those who rebel against an abolitionized government. The cars ran back in great haste last night with their loads of soldiers, being informed that a rebel force was before them — and sure enough — the Red river Railroad bridge which had been reported burned before but was only a little injured was last night burned down, the guard having left in alarm & it [is] said the Sulphur Fork bridge near Springfield was also burned — and so Nashville is cut off by blowing up the tunnel on the main road & burning the bridges on the Edgefield & Ky. Hopkinsville too has been captured by Woodwards and Johnsons Cavalry & two companies disarmed and patroled — and Morgan is said to be at Glasgow — so that we are in a state of excited suspense not knowing what to expect & not being much astonished at anything that occurs. I had a large congregation at Ashspring. I preached with zeal & liberty the "Danger of desiring to be rich." William Adams who I had heard would not hear me preach because I was Southern — was in his place to day & I was gratified to find his prejudice giving way.

The negroes are rather afraid of familiarity with Yankees since they heard that Forrest hung quite a number that were taken in arms at Murfreesborough & also at Gallatin. This policy seems severe — but the Southern people can never consent to treat negroes as prisoners of war & exchange for them with white prisoners.

August 19 — I heard at Allensville an account of the capture of Clarksville with 250 federal prisoners & a quantity of arms & army stores by the rebels under Woodward. Large trains of soldiers continue to pass up & down the railroad keeping the country in suspense & anxiety. The resignation of Gov Magoffin of Ky & Lieut Gov Fisk adds to the uneasiness of Kentuckians.[31]

---

31. Beriah Magoffin was elected governor in 1859. A strong states' righter, Magoffin found his position increasingly difficult after the election of 1861, which resulted in Unionist majorities controlling the Kentucky legislature. He finally agreed to resign if someone who shared his views could be found to replace him. Lieutenant Governor Linn Boyd had died and John F. Fisk, speaker of the house, was unacceptable to Magoffin. In a series of ingenious moves, Fisk resigned as speaker, Senator James F. Robinson was elected speaker, Magoffin resigned, Robinson became governor, and Fisk once more was elected as speaker. Lowell H. Harrison, *The Civil War in Kentucky* (Lexington, Kentucky, 1975), 81 ff.

August 21 – We got a letter from father of 3d of Aug. He was well – hopes to get home in 90 days.

August 22 – Crutcher, the Baptist preacher told me this morning of the hanging of a man in Russellville yesterday supposed to be one of Woodwards guerilas. Col Bristow revoked his order in bare time to cut him down before he expired. This is an awful state of things. War with its horrors increases. I heard this morning that my brother Frank & Tim Jones had joined Capt Dortch & been regularly sworn into the Confederate service. If they were determined to go to the army I would have preferred their going into a larger body but then they were liable at anytime to be detailed into small bodies. A bridge builder just returned from the lower neighborhoods reports that Morgan captured 200 men day before yesterday not far from Nashville. This Morgan is quite a dashing fellow. The cars passed this evening carrying a crowd of paroled soldiers. My bro. William came home from town with a wonderful tale that four or five horsemen dressed in blue pants & check shirts, claiming to be Morgan's men, had told him about the capture of the guard & burning of Elkfork bridge & killing 40 men – and being pursued by the federal cavalry while they were seeking by ways to Gallatin – which story all turns out to be a falsehood. Perhaps the fellows meant the Red river bridge & had, in their fright, magnified a few wounded men into the forty killed they spoke of. They were afterward captured and ascertained to be horse thieves.

August 24 – At 3 oclock this morning I was startled from my slumber by a messenger requesting me to go immediately and see Sam Hine's wife who was very ill & much alarmed. My horses were all out in the pasture but as soon as we could find one I went & found her in a nervous fit – thinking that she was dying & going straight to perdition. She has always been regarded an uncommonly pious girl & was quite efficient in the altar exercises of revival meetings. She said when I approached her bed, "Im most gone. Im lost – going straight to Hell. Im the meanest creature in the world – so wicked" & with such laments she refused to be consoled. She did not want me to sing & pray. I began to quote the promises – & urge confidence. I argued & reasoned – persuaded & entreated – but she was inconsolable. I sang "O Lord of Rest for thee I sigh," but she said "too late, too late." After some time she became more calm & asked me to sing. I began again. Her countenance grew bright & she said, "Oh Im so happy – so happy – bless God. Thank God – Im not deceived now. Im not afraid to die now" – and when I prayed she joined in & seemed full of confidence & joy. I think this is a hysteric spell. She has had a long attack of fever. I came home – then went to church & preached with liberty to a large audience on "The Kingdom of Christ." At 4 I went to the colored peoples meeting & *Duncan Hines* exhorted with power & several penitents came forward. I was glad on my return to learn that our little black *Dolly*[32] had professed religion at the meeting.

---

32. In his family Bible, George Dick records Dolly Ann as the daughter of his slave woman, Ellen. Dolly was born March 9, 1852.

My wife has catechized her often & taught her to read — by the help of my little Helen.

The country is still excited with rumors of battles. To day my neighbors Paine & Mills were arrested by the federals that are fortifying at Fergusons, but Paine was soon released. I do not know of Mills. Rumors of passengers through the country report Pope defeated by Stonewall Jackson again & recruits rapidly flying to the rebels at Clarksville.

August 26 — Benny Waters came by & told me that the soldiers had been to his fathers after the old gentleman who eluded them, & had arrested William Grinter & Elias Carr, and also pressed two of Mr Waters' horses — but had become alarmed at what they supposed to be the tracks of "rebels" and turned the horses loose while they hid in the woods. They (the feds) are evidently uneasy. Rumor reports 2,000 cavalry (rebel) at Clarksville & constantly pouring in. There are so many false rumors we know not when to believe.

August 28 — There is some hope now of more quiet in the country as Governor Robinson has issued an order prohibiting any arrests of citizens unless written charges & affidavit of the accuser are presented and the accuser brought to light. This will stop much low-lived reporting of persons for private & personal enmity. The Journal reports the capture of Genl Johnson by the rebel Morgan.[33] McLellan has succeeded in joining Pope with the loss of Artillery, men, horses &c — but the feds claim a victory. It is rumored now that Fort Donelson is retaken by the Confederates — but contradicted by federals.

August 29 — There is quite a sensation in the country to day caused by the federal soldiers seizing horses. They took five of Mr Paine's best horses — 2 of Nelson Waters — & went to divers other places where they did not get any. Tommy Sydnor had my brother Franks horse in exchange for his & they took him and one also from Mrs Barton leaving her afoot away from home. They took six of Fergusons best and have impressed a number through the county. The rebels are also impressing horses & it is really to be feared that there will not be stock enough left to raise the next crop. Can it be that the comet that hangs now nightly in the Northwest is a sign of further bloodshed & wretchedness. So far I have escaped molestation but my heart grows sick over the evils of my country.

August 31 — Early I set out to P[leasant] Run — found no one at church — appointment had not been published — message never reached them. Went to see Billy Winlock. He is greatly reduced — slowly & surely dying with consumption. Yet is willing to live or to die. Surely there is a power in grace — to enable a young man in the morning of life — blessed with friends — fortune — popularity — sprightliness, all that makes life desirable — willing to die.

---

33. Morgan at this time was operating in middle Tennessee. The Union commander in the area, Major General Don Carlos Buell, assembled all his available cavalry under Brigadier General R. W. Johnson and sent him after Morgan. When the two met between Gallatin and Hartsville, Tennessee, Morgan forced Johnson to surrender. Carl F. Holland, *Morgan and His Raiders* (New York, 1943), 87.

September 1 — Raining! Thank God for rain enough to cool the heated air & settle the stifling dust. Heard rumors of another great battle in Va and defeat of the federals. Country all excited. A large cavalry squadron 140 or 50 strong came by my house. They seized horses & mules as they went. When Lizzie, Helen & I got to Allensville on our way to M. N. Lasley's, where I was to marry George Willis to Mrs Willock, the cavalry had just left having taken a mule & four horses — giving no receipts. The country is all in a stir. Parties at the wedding were for hiding their horses, but none were disturbed there.

September 2 — Got home at night to learn that some body had stolen my fathers horse Bill — & William had gone away with some of the mules & other horses to a safer place. One of old Bro Andersons horses was also stolen & it is not known whether it was by a private felon or rebel or federal soldiers.

September 3 — There is great commotion over the terrible battles now raging in Virginia — in hearing of the Federal capital. Stonewall Jackson has gotten in Popes rear & captured guns & trains & also lost heavily & Lee & Ewell & in a word almost the entire rebel and federal armies — in all nearly 500,000 men — are hurled against each other in battle shock. The nation is holding its breath — both North & South are trembling for the result.[34] The papers report great consternation in the North & compare it to the Bull run defeat — but say the result is not known. The Kentucky Genl Nelson who was marching to the relief of Cumberland gap has been defeated — routed — ruined — wounded himself — his brigadiers captured or killed & his artillery, train and all captured by the rebels under Genl Kirby Smith.[35] Lexington & Frankfort are also occupied by rebel forces & the Legislature & archives of the state have been moved to Louisville. The rebels came up yesterday to Allensville & burned Elkfork bridge & camped for the night at the Rum Spring. Unionists seem more alarmed now than Secesh [secessionists]. The governor has ordered out all able bodied men but they do not go. The country is almost bare of young men — most of them having gone to one army or the other — numbers are flying from the federal draft & a majority of them go to the rebel army. It is reported that the infantry are evacuating Russellville & the cavalry will no doubt follow suit if Woodward still hovers around the country. It is hoped now that the horse seizing trade is almost ended by both parties.

---

34. George Dick is referring to the Second Battle of Bull Run, which began on August 26, 1862, and reached its climax on August 29–30. Pope, failing to get relief in time from McClellan, was beaten but not routed by Jackson and Lee. The number of troops involved was approximately 75,000 for the Union and 50,000 for the Confederates. Long, *Civil War Day By Day*, 255 ff.

35. Major General Kirby Smith had become increasingly unhappy with his defensive position in East Tennessee and since early July had expressed a desire to move against George Morgan's force at Cumberland Gap. On August 13, 1862, he began his invasion of Kentucky, moving quickly through the Cumberland Mountains. Barbourville fell on August 18. Smith, however, now found himself in hostile territory and his need for supplies led him to advance toward Lexington, Kentucky. At Richmond he encountered and defeated Union forces under the command of Major General William "Bull" Nelson. Harrison, *Civil War in Kentucky*, 40–41.

We were pained this evening to learn that the mule had run off with Catherine Sydnors buggie & crippled her very badly – breaking her right thigh & badly bruising her right hip. She was carried to David Small's and will have to be brought home on a lounge or litter.

September 4 – After dinner I went with Lizzie to see Nettie Woolls & Emma Givens both of whom are quite sick with fever. I saw the federal cavalry again seizing horses. It is a sad thing to contemplate the state of the country. They took James Cams horses, but released them when they learned that he was a union man. This distinction will bring about retaliation if the rebels ever get possession of the country again. Complaining does no good although it looks hard to see armed men riding about in our fields carrying off our horses & mules without pay, insulting our wives & daughters if they remonstrate – & imprisoning peaceable citizens contrary to the constitution & the law. Cousin Helen Browder I know will feel grieved to see a federal soldier charging about on poor old Jim, her buggie horse, they took today – some 15 or 17 years old.

September 5 – Twelve years ago this afternoon I first felt that I was a married man! My dear wife has ever been true & faithful – willing always to sacrifice herself to the well being & happiness of her husband & children. Her energy & perseverance are wonderful and in her feeble health & suffering frame she does more for the comfort of her family than almost any woman of my acquaintance. For some time past she has had a cough which gives me some uneasiness. I pray God to spare her to me & to her children & to his church.

In the evening I called to see cousin Catherine who has reached home dangerously if not fatally bruised & mangled, yet seems patient and resigned.

My neighbor McCulloch has for several days & nights been active in trying to hide his horses from the federals & while they were hid out the rebel scouts found them & impressed his favorite Fillmore into service in the Confederate army! He chafes & writhes under the disappointment. He is Southern but to lose a horse – "ah! theres the rub."

It is rumored that Major Mansfield is to be arrested for keeping a horse brought to him by a runaway negro belonging to Dr Beaumont. This Mansfield is the same fellow that went to Downing Bells in Christian county to arrest him & was resisted in his attempt to search the house by Mrs Bell who stood with a Bowie knife & forbade them to ascend the stairs where she had hid her money – her husband not being at home. She cut the guns & tried to stab the men with her knife & finally took Mansfields pistol from him & would have shot him with it, but he ordered her to be seized. She succeeded in protecting her house from search, one of the officers ordering the men not to injure so brave a woman on pain of getting up a meeting. Mrs Bell whom I knew when a little girl in the person of Mary Walker Meriwether, acted very boldly telling the Yankees that she was willing to be killed if they desired – that her murder would fill up rebel ranks & that was her desire. Mansfield I learn says that affair has sent 500 men into the Confederate army.

September 8 – On Sunday I went to Gunns School house and preached with unusual liberty on "Thy kingdom come." The congregation was very attentive, much more so than I expected in view of the fact that quite a sensation was produced just before preaching time, by the appearance of a small squad of rebel soldiers impressing horses. One of them (Benny Waters) sent for me to convey a message to his mother & I took occasion to reprove them for going to church on the sabbath for the purpose of impressment. One of them said, "Mr Browder Sunday is the day of the greatest battles." I said "Sunday is not the day for horse stealing." Said he "Do you consider this *stealing* horses when we take them & give receipt of full value?" I told him it was not exactly stealing but taking by force just as the federals were doing. They went away taking 3 horses & leaving their owners in good humor. I do not think it requires much *pressing* to get horses from Southern men for Southern soldiers. The country is still in a state of feverish excitement & it is the most difficult thing to get a true statement. There is a general distrust & an almost universal disposition to exaggerate or misrepresent. Lying is more fashionable than truth, and yet I think there are many good & truthful men still in the country.

The papers report another terrible battle in Virginia & the federals still falling back while the rebel cannon thunders in hearing of the National Capital. The great question is not how to take Richmond, but how to save Washington? Divers rumors confirm the passage of thousands of federal soldiers into Ky from the South & it is generally believed that Buell is retreating & evacuating Nashville to rescue Louisville & Cincinnati which are now threatened by the rebels under Genl Kirby Smith.

Lizzie is away sitting up tonight with cousin Catherine who is reported worse.

September 9 – Very busy all day cutting, hanging & housing tobacco. A letter from Tim Jones states that the federals retook Clarksville, throwing shells into their camp. Ed Small was slightly scratched on the side with a piece of bomb, Tim had his forehead marked with a splinter & my brother Frank lost his hat. So the poor boys have got a taste of war.

September 10 – I had a presentiment this morning that something exciting would happen to day. I went out to work & soon came back. I saw a great dust in the Clarksville road & climbed a tree to see the soldiers passing – supposing them to be federals, but heard afterward they were confederates and my poor bro Frank & Tim Jones – & other neighbor boys were with them. Soon a troop of federal cavalry several hundred strong went on in pursuit – & as 200 federals are before them there will probably be an engagement but up to this hour – 12 oclock M. I have heard nothing more.

September 11 – I went to Volney on business – saw uncle Dick Browder in great trouble looking for old Bro Anderson (a union man) to get him to go to town & try to get his black boy *John* & his mule released, whom the federals took away yesterday morning while pretending to pursue the rebels.

On Sunday the federals seized a negro man belonging to Joshua Parsons, put him on one of Dr Bibbs horses – strapped a gun on him & forced him away contrary to his request & the remonstrance of his mistress – and also carried off a negro man of Dr Orndorffs who was on a visit to his wife at Parsons.

My man *Abram* to day was in a very ill humor – & talked very insolently to me, threatening to leave & never return. I talked very positively but very reasonably to him & he acknowledged his fault & promised reformation, so I excused him – believing that he had been misled by some outside influence. Thousands upon thousands of poor negroes in the South have been decoyed away from good homes & plentiful fare, to suffer privation – poverty – shame & neglect they never knew or would have known with their masters.

September 13 – John Noel came in at night from near Nashville & reports the retreat of the federals & the suffering condition of the army & the city. The deplorable condition of hundreds of poor runaway & stolen slaves – sick & deserted to wander about Nashville & beg in vain for bread of people who cannot supply their own wants. Negro women are lying about the streets in federal uniforms in distress & in pregnancy!

The country is still flooded with the most exciting rumors. The results of this war are like a grand dramatic scene – each act making the next more exciting. All eyes turn now to Washington which is in great danger of capture by the rebels & the federal papers write despondingly. In Ky times are stirring. Large forces are pouring into Ky and battles on large scales seem pending.

September 14 – [After attending church at Pleasant Grove] I came home – hearing rumors as I came – such as the burning of Nashville – capture of Louisville – surrender of Washington &c – all of which are doubtless false.

I dined at uncle Dick's with Tom. War news of course was the main topic of conversation. I went to see cousin Catherine in her affliction.

September 16 – Bro Morrison our P[residing] E[lder]* spends the night with us, having been over into Ten[n.] to marry a couple, because a late law of Ky requires all ministers before solemnizing the rites of matrimony to file in the clerks office their solemn oath to support the constitution and laws of U S & Ky & not to give aid or encouragement to any person or persons in the confederate states nor to sympathize with the rebellion – and hence Southern sympathizers must either abstain from marrying persons to go to Ten[n.].

September 22 – Days of Darkness! As I was on my way to Pleasant Run a young man overtook me and told me that Presley Herndon had gone to Henry B. Tully's house in a threatening attitude & that Tully had shot him, & killed him! A grudge growing out of this war was doubtless the cause of this tragedy. I hardly ever hear a gun fire without feeling more or less anxiety & uneasiness.

On Sabbath morning I preached with liberty "Thy Kingdom Come" to a large audience considering the times. Many have expressed a desire for my return to the circuit and several gave me small presents of money amounting to

14 dols. I spent the night with John Finch and on Monday returned through Russellville – the first time that I had been there for several months. On my return I learned that the rebel soldiers had been to E W. Andersons to demand a pistol of John A Miller which pistol belongs to James Morrow of the federal army. He refused to give it up & was arrested by the soldiers. I saw them & interceded – entreating them not to take him away from his child which was very sick. They at first refused to yield but afterwards left him telling him they still held him responsible for the pistol. Before & after I secured his release I expostulated with him & urged him rather to deliver up a pistol which under these circumstances both rebels & federals had decided subject to seizure, than be carried off from his family – but he would not listen to my advice, yet thanked me for my interposition & said he appreciated my motive. I feel sorry to see such things. He is a clever man & sensible and thinks he is right – but federal officers seize all property belonging to confederates, that they find in the hands of private citizens & parties that conceal it are held responsible & it is no worse on him than others. This is clearly a case of a man who cuts off his nose to spite his face. The country is still full of rumors about other great battles in Va – both parties claim victories. Federals are scouring the country between Bowling Green and Russellville, taking off all flour from mills & bacon from private houses & desolation & starvation seem at hand. A young Bro Gunn (Tom) son of Rev W. Gunn of the Ky Conf told Shep. Campbell that he knew almost 100 chaplains in the federal army who had backslidden & become wicked. He says the army has been almost starved – reduced to two meals a day & one small cracker & a bit of meat being a meal. Frank & Tim dined here on Sunday. Sorry I did not see them.

September 23 – Louisville papers of 17, 18, 19 inst. have reached Russellville. They report more hard fighting in Maryland[36] – & say the rebels captured 8000 prisoners at Harpers Ferry.[37] The rumored engagement between Major J. S. Scobee Confed. & Col Netta (fed) near Owensboro resulting in the killing of Netta & capture of his force proves an exaggeration. Netta was killed & his stores captured but not his men, as Mason & Willis of Russellville, just returned from Owensboro, report. Our Conference is appointed to meet there next Wednesday, but I feel afraid to go where there is so much excitement & uncertainty of getting back in safety. I much fear the business of the Conference will suffer & injury result to the church. Several of our brethren are chaplains in the federal & confederate armies & Major Scobee was a P[residing] E[lder] when he put on his regimentals. "Let the dead bury their dead, but go thou & preach the kingdom of God" said Jesus to the man that asked leave to stay & bury his father. I think ministers should not take the sword. Sam Johnson

---

36. George Dick is referring to the Battle of Antietam on September 17, 1862. Lee, with 40,000 troops, faced McClellan with 75,000. After a savage battle, one of the bloodiest of the war, Lee withdrew across the Potomac on the night of September 18–19. Long, *Civil War Day By Day*, 267–68.

37. Harpers Ferry, West Virginia, fell to the Confederates under Stonewall Jackson's command on September 15, 1862. About 12,000 Union prisoners were taken. *Ibid.*, 266.

formerly a talented preacher of our Conf. is now a federal captain & report says that he swears just as other wicked soldiers. I hope such is not the case. Oh for grace to act discreetly myself, that I bring no reproach upon the cause of Christ. I was gratified this morning in talking to one of the most intense & determined union ladies of this country, (Mrs Isham Miller) to learn that she had never heard but one person complain of me in this time of war & that was on account of a prayer which he construed into a petition for Southern success! If I have thus far kept aloof from causes of complaint I feel thankful.

September 28 – Our little Luther[38] was very sick all day yesterday & last night. I went to Adairville & preached on the resurrection to a very attentive congregation to day – in a very dirty house – raised a collection for widows & orphans & worn out preachers – got 6.45. Bro White & others paid me about 35. quarterage – or rather they gave it as a special present, in view of fact that I got nothing at the 2nd Quarterly meeting.

September 29 – I decline going to Conference on account mainly of the excited & unsettled condition of the country between here & Owensboro. Persons just from there represent travelling as very unsafe. Jimmy Lewis came up this morning & reported Maj Scobee & Col Johnson with their forces at Keysburg. Scobee thinks we cannot get out of Owensboro without taking the oath and another person just from there reports a large federal force as having arrived there since the Scobee-Netta affair. My wife will be alone & my child is sick – my attention is needed at home so I shall not try to go. I am informed reliably that I am wanted both on this circuit & in the Russellville Station – either will suit me, but under the circumstances the circuit is most desirable.

October 1 – Alarm and confusion! *Abram* woke me this morning with the story that Dortch's cavalry of which Frank is a member, was attacked yesterday & terribly cut to pieces by the federals near Russellville! Anxious to know the result I hasted up to Volney & to Nelson Waters, & to fathers – at which last place I saw two of the escaped soldiers without guns or horses. They say they were completely surprised – & the pickets gave no alarm. I learned afterward that four were killed and a few captured. But few of the men were in camp, when they were surrounded by the 70th Indiana – 800 strong – & barely made their escape with the loss of many horses and guns. Most of the men escaped, Frank & Tim & other neighbor boys among them, for which I feel devoutly thankful although Frank lost his gun in the skedaddle. Four of the federals were also killed & three wounded as persons just from town report. This evening I saw some more soldiers looking up horses that had strayed off. This is a trying time. My mother took down the engraving of David slaying Goliath in the name of the Lord, & showed it to the soldiers who staid at her house last night, and urged them to trust in the God of David & seek help from him. This was to me an impressive scene.

---

38. Luther Wools, Browder's fourth son, was born April 6, 1861.

It is now certain that Buell & his vast army have reached Louisville & the confederates are in a worse condition possibly than most of their friends suspected.[39] It is also said that the rebel forces after desperate fighting, have withdrawn from Maryland. The papers report Mr Lincolns proclamation freeing all negroes in any of the states or parts of states not represented by a majority vote of the people in the next congress.[40] The matter is now fairly up – & we may look for stirring times, such as we never saw before. God direct & defend the right!

October 3 – Lizzie is suffering severely with pain in her neck and back. Dear little Luther has recovered from his illness. Hanson, Robert, & George are busy gathering nuts & helping about the tobacco. I am sowing wheat in the barn lot. I went to visit John Hogan who is quite sick. I did not propose praying with him, as I ought to have done. It is an evil day to the church when we visit the sick and dying to talk only of war & its woes.

On my return home I overtook Frank & Tim both well. They look alittle worse for their hard life. The federal soldiers came back to Russellville yesterday & carried off the boots & shoes, drugs and medicines out of some of the stores, also Rhea's printing press & some 20 or 25 negroes, belonging to citizens. The papers report confederate forces marching back into Maryland. I see no hope of any more peace & prosperity in this country unless the South can hold her territory free from Northern control. Mr Lincoln, it is said, has declared the whole U. S. under martial law[41] & called for 400,000 more troops. If these come, it will make the largest army the world has ever seen since the days of Xerxes. He has called in all 1,750,000. It will be only the arm of Omnipotence that can sustain the South against such fearful odds. This looks indeed like the great battle of Armageddon.

October 5 – I went to Red Oak and preached to a large audience on the "Kingdom of God" and at 3 oclock, by request of Mrs Dr Bailey and others of the family I preached the funeral of old Sister Kennedy a Cumberland Presbyterian sister, who died yesterday. Mrs Bailey & others of that family have been so ultra & abusive toward Southern people, that I felt some surprise at being called upon to officiate. As I came nearer home I heard that David Browder had reported that my father & sister would get home this evening. I could scarcely believe it yet felt a great anxiety & suspense until I got to the

---

39. Buell had moved northwest from middle Tennessee in early September 1862. His army reached Louisville on September 25 and began to prepare for an offensive against Generals Braxton Bragg and Kirby Smith whose Confederate forces occupied most of the Bluegrass region. Harrison, *Civil War in Kentucky,* 42, 46 ff.

40. On September 22, 1862, after the Battle of Antietam, Lincoln presented a preliminary draft of the Emancipation Proclamation to his Cabinet. He continued to urge Congressional approval of compensated emancipation. Long, *Civil War Day By Day,* 270.

41. Lincoln issued a proclamation on September 24, 1862, suspending the writ of habeas corpus and providing for the military trial of "all Rebels and Insurgents, their aiders and abettors within the United States." *Ibid.,* 270–71.

house & found that he had not arrived. David left him at Columbia [Tenn.] homeward bound! I feel thankful to learn that he is near, & hope I shall see him before many days although it is still uncertain whether he would be safe to *stay* at home.

October 6 – A day of joy! A day of sorrow! As I was going to James Bibbs to carry bags to put my wheat in, David Small halted me to tell me that my father had come! was at Allensville! but had been advised to turn back to C. M. Warfields as a strong federal force was said to have arrived at Russellville. While he & I were talking – William & his wife & mother came on going in haste to meet father – and I went on too, although I left my dear wife at home suffering with Neuralgia. This I much regretted, but fearing that some changing fortune might put it out of his power to come home I felt that duty called me to see him. It was a joyful meeting when mother & father & most of their children met together in safety after a long & painful & exciting separation of seven months and nineteen days! My sister Mary too was well & hearty & aunt Mary & cousin Amelia & black *Harriet* were all overjoyed to see Kentucky again!

I was sorry to learn that the confederate troops had captured & carried off old B. K. Tully & his son Henry, & Henry's brotherinlaw Joe Aingell – the last two being considered accomplices in the murder of Presley Herndon who is a confederate soldier. Tully gave himself to the sheriff – and I am sorry the soldiers took him although they plead that Mr Lincoln has declared the states all under martial law. It is generally supposed that Tully acted in self defence – & rough using of him will bring bitter retaliation on Southern men if the federals get the power. I am glad to see that my father does not come back with a bitter revengeful spirit as many of the union men did who left home when the rebels were here.[42]

October 7 – Came home & found Lizzie quite sick, suffering severely with Neuralgia & a rising in her mouth.

October 8 – Most of the Southern rights men above us left home tonight fearing the threatened vengeance of the federals for the arrest & removal of Aingell & the Tullys.

October 9 – Weevils in vast numbers are destroying the old wheat & corn. I am sending my wheat to mill to grind up as the only hope of saving it, and then I shall not feel that my bread is safe as soldiers are in the habit of seizing whatever they want.

Bro W. H. Morrison dined with us to day – just returned from Owensboro Conference. I feel relieved to hear that the session passed off harmoniously with but little excitement, politics being prudently kept out of the deliberations. I am appointed on the Logan circuit with Bro Wm Alexander to assist. This suits me

42. George Dick is referring to the period September 1861–February 1862 when Confederate troops occupied south-central Kentucky.

well & under the circumstances I think meets the approbation of all the church, & I pray for a useful & prosperous career. I feel willing to serve God's church with or without pay, but I do not *feel* the same *fervor* that I have in days past. Oh for wisdom to preach Christ faithfully without giving offense to any of the brethren. Some now have neglected the assembling of themselves together through the influence of these evil days — having no confidence in the piety of those who differ with them on the great national quarrel.

October 11 — Very cold & windy. I stay in to read, & nurse my sick wife & child. Dr came and gave her medicine.

October 15 — There is an alarming disposition in the minds of the boys to run away to the Southern army. Little Joel Grizzard, Americus Oakes, John Hite, Dick Hughes, Alick Murray & other boys from 15 to 17 years old have run away & enlisted and even smaller boys are full of the spirit of war and their very natures seem to delight in hating the Yankees. This is a great evil & betokens an alarming recklesness in the coming generations. There is great need of a firmer & more scriptural family government.

October 18 — To day the country is all astir again. Day before yesterday swarms of federals were pressing down toward Woodwards camp near Trenton, & yesterday morning the doleful peals of cannon jarred the stillness of the dawn. To day we heard that the camp had been evacuated & the federals fired on vacant air! It is rumored that many Southern men have been arrested & horses & negroes carried off. Uncle Dick [Browder] & cousin Dick Browder, D. B. Hutchings & others were ordered to send provisions to their camp at Whippoorwill.

October 19 — My family went with me to Ash Spring where I warned the people against the wiles of the devil. At night I spent some time in telling my children the story of "The Hebrew Children" and impressing their minds with the importance of an unswerving integrity.

October 20 — I have felt restless to day & told my wife that I felt as if something serious was going to happen. A NIGHT OF TERROR! I sat up reading after Lizzie went to bed, sick with Neuralgia. *Lucy* was still up. I was suddenly aroused from a deep slumber by the scream of my wife. Amazed I leaped out of bed & found her chair of clothes, which she had moved some distance back in a light blaze! She had caught her night clothes on fire in trying, in her alarm to put out the others. I threw her down & smothered the fire on her as best I could with my hands, but in so doing the bed clothes caught on fire — the lounge was already in a bright blaze — the cradle cover was blazing all about our darling little Luther & he soundly sleeping beneath the flame & smoke. I snatched him from the burning bed — & in God's gracious providence just at that instant two of Mr Paines black boys who were passing by, rushed in & dragged the burning clothes into the yard — & our faithful *Ellen* & *George* came in to our relief just in bare time to save us from a fearful conflagration & possibly us & our children from a horrid death. No part of the house had taken fire but the fumes of burning cotton-wool &c were stifling & it seems to me that a few moments more & all would have been lost.

My poor wife was dreadfully burned on both hands & suffered the most excruciating torture. I never saw her in such agony. I forgot the painful burns on my own hands in trying to relieve her. We applied lard & then flour & black *Henry* brought the doctor in great haste — but he could do little more than we had done.

I gratefully acknowledge God's good providence in our timely deliverance. If I had been away — my wife & probably my children would have almost certainly have perished in the flames, or if I had been a moment later waking or Paines boys a moment sooner in passing by, I cannot see how we could have escaped. Let those mock at Gods *special* providence who will, but as for me I will trust Him & if my children live to read this account, I hope they will acknowledge their Heavenly Father's hand in their preservation. Lizzie is sure that the chair of clothes was much nearer the fire than she left it, & it is likely *Lucy* drew it up to sit on & left it — or possibly the fire might have popped out & caught the calico.

October 21 — Lizzie has suffered greatly. She is helpless as a babe not being able to use either hand.

October 24 — For several days I have done but little besides nurse my suffering wife. She is very feeble and suffers intensely — has no appetite so I went this evening to town & bought some oysters which she greatly relishes. I got some late papers. The rebel Col Morgan is doing great damage to the federals capturing their trains — burning bridges &c & paroling many prisoners. Bragg is reported to have left Ky with thousands of recruits & immense supplies of beef cattle, provisions, mules, clothing &c & the federal papers speak discouragingly of Buells operations in Ky.[43] I want grace to preach the gospel under whatever Government may be over me.

October 25 — This is a wintry day. I stay in to read and nurse. The snow fell in real wintry masses & the ground was covered some inch or two all night.

October 28 — I went to Allensville, heard that Morgans men had been to Elkton & Russellville, & had burned Whippoorwill bridge & pressed all of Fergusons Woolen goods paying confederate money. Woodwards men also pressed goods at Allensville & gave receipts. This is a very demoralizing habit & one greatly to be regretted. They plead necessity. I think they intend leaving Kentucky.

---

43. On October 8, 1862, three divisions of Buell's army engaged Bragg's forces at Perryville. Bragg withdrew after heavy fighting. Because Buell failed to pursue the enemy effectively, he was relieved of his command on October 24. Harrison, *Civil War in Kentucky,* 55–56.

October 29 – Lizzie still suffers much but is slowly improving. My sister Mary stays with us & dresses her hands most tenderly and kindly.

An amusing thing occurred with Hawes Wood, a strong union man, a few days ago. Two soldiers in federal uniform fell in with him on the road & he congratulated them & declared his devotion to the federal government & his willingness to give up all his property to support it. One of the soldiers expressed his gratification at finding so sound & liberal a patriot & proposed to exchange his jaded horse for the fresh animal Mr Wood was riding. Hawes readily proposed to give up his horse & also to fatten the soldiers horse by the time he returned. So they exchanged animals & Wood afterward learned that he had been aiding one of John Morgan's scouts in disguise! and had given his fine horse to one of the hated rebels! This tale Dr Hutchings told me, he also being a Union man, and Wood has been sick ever since.

November 1 – To day my bro. Frank is with us. He has joined Morgans cavalry & will soon be out of the state.

November 3 – I went to Charles Warfield's to see my father, who still feels unsafe to come home. Always anxious for his childrens welfare he is devising a plan for William & me to do well by buying tobacco this winter if the Southern troops are again driven back to their former lines. I regard speculation as a very uncertain business & I shall not individually be involved in it in any way to diminish my ministerial character and usefulness.

Frank set out to Springfield this morning where Bro Penick reports 10 or 15,000 rebel cavalry to be concentrated.

November 10 – The papers are again filled with exciting reports of foreign intervention in our war, but all is uncertainty & this is emphatically the age of lying. We cannot rely upon any reports we hear.

November 11 – I have worked some to day repairing my stable, have been busy doing but little. Lizzie is threatened with Erysipelas in the right leg and suffers much.

November 14 – For a day or two I have been doing but little more than wait on Lizzie who suffers much with painful risings on her leg. She is now better. Federal soldiers are again in the country & Southerners feel restless. Frank & a few other soldiers are in the rear of their command & I fear will be captured. Nashville is again crowded with federals & Ky is about clear of rebels.

November 16 – Before daylight I started to Pleasant Run. I preached with zeal & liberty on the "Striving to enter into the straight gate." I came on home through a most welcome rain. I am troubled with a bile on my neck, one under my left arm and fear a very severe rising near the thumb joint in the palm of my right hand.

November 19 — For two or three days we have had moist weather & now it pours down. For almost four months we have had drought and water had become very scarce and wheat was dying in the dust. I still suffer with my hand & now write without the use of my thumb, taking the pen between the front & middle fingers.

November 28 — For the first time in several days I am able to write alittle. I have had a large rising under my left arm & now have one in the back of my neck. I am sick & feeble. On Saturday Tom Browder came up & on Monday took my dear wife and all the children except Helen down to Mr Warfields. She was not willing to leave me & refused to do so but I urged her to go that she might get some rest. Monday night Capt Sam F Johnson & James Morrow with their cavalry camped in fathers horse lot & fed on his provender but did no other damage. They arrested Nelson Waters & the next day took W. T. Evans, E. W. Gunn, W. & H. Bailey, old Bro Reeves & a number of other persons, some of whom they have paroled — some sworn & others sentenced to camp Chase. Truly these are perilous times. Tonight Bro Alexander & I are here alone. Mary staid & dressed my sores as long as she was needed — a kind sister.

December 2 — On Sunday Morning I received an order from Col Bruce to appear before his Headquarters in Russellville on the morning of the 31st of Nov to testify in the case on N. H. Waters. I wrote a very respectful letter to Col Bruce telling him that I was not able to go to town & knew nothing of the case to testify and asking him to excuse me. Bro Waters was released and I heard no more of the case. Bro W. T. Evans was still on trial & many fear he will be exiled.

I still suffer much with my biles but am better. Yesterday we killed 13 of our hogs weighing in all 2618 lbs and to day the boys are cutting out & *Ellen* is drying up the lard. I am not able to help & my dear Lizzie is not at home. How I pity unfortunate widowers. I feel as if I would be a ruined man if I were to lose my wife.

Federal soldiers are now scouring the country arresting all the leading Southern Rights men, requiring them to take the oath of loyalty or be exiled from their homes. They are also seizing provisions & giving receipts payable at the end of the war! I am expecting them to come to our quarterly meeting and arrest all the preachers there.

December 6 — I went to First Quarterly meeting at Red Oak. Bro. Tim Gilbert went with me to H. Cornelius's & was glad to learn that I had not been killed by the soldiers as reported in his neighborhood. I cannot imagine how such a story should be circulated.

December 9 — I got Cousin David [Sydnor]s carriage & went to uncle Waters after Lizzie & the children, was glad to find them well & find my father there to meet me. He seems rather gloomy but bears up well considering all his trials, hiding out from home to avoid *persecution for opinions sake* in a free country.

December 11 – Came home & at night went to prayermeeting. The papers report that Morgan attacked Hartsville on Sunday morning & Col Moore, acting Brigadier, was compelled to surrender.[44] Also that Morgan attacked Gallatin & was repulsed. Morgan captured almost the entire brigade at Hartsville – some 5 regiments.

December 13 – I went to see Mr Dewees, a very honest poor man who has been long sick, prayed & sung with him & sent him some pork & flour. There are many rumors afloat of the recapture of Fort Donelson by rebel troops & a rebel cavalry is reported at or near Hopkinsville.

December 14 – I went to Keysburg & preached to a small congregation on "Religious earnestness" Lu[ke] 13.23–30. I heard that the federals had taken David Hutchings out of his bed & carried him off but had released him. Saturday night six robbers dressed in federal uniform with swords & pistols entered the house of Rev F. C. Plasters of Keysburg & robbed him of $100. and his brotherinlaw Black of $360. in gold. They said they were Morgans men & would plunder every man that took the federal oath. They are doubtless an organized band of thieves & probably belong to no army.

December 15 – Was somewhat surprised to learn that my cousin Everet Meade was with Morgans cavalry & had spent a night with McGhee McLean when the army passed Keysburg. He reports his brother David as having been unjustly suspected of making way with some union men & was consequently arrested & sentenced to be hung! Surely David Meade has not been condemned to be hung! A good & true man, a preacher of the gospel – but there seems no end to the bitterness & hatred of these party opponents. One of my Gwynn cousins is also reported to have died or been killed in the army.

December 16 – Terrible slaughter in Va. The accounts indicate a failure on the part of the federals to drive the rebels from Fredericksburg.[45]

December 17 – My hired boy *Henry* was very insolent, insulting – & defiant this morning when I reproved him quite mildly for running about at night. He refused persistently to be corrected & my man *Abram* refused to give me any assistance. So I held on to *Henry* & talked reasonably to him until young David Sydnor came when I took the boy up stairs without resistance, tied his hands & would have whipped him severely, but he begged piteously, confessed his fault & promised never to do so again, said he would pray to the Lord for help to do

---

44. On December 7, 1862, Morgan with about 1400 men surprised and captured a Federal garrison at Hartsville, Tennessee. About 1800 of Colonel A. B. Moore's troops were taken prisoner. Long, *Civil War Day By Day*, 293–94.

45. Federal troops under Major General Ambrose E. Burnside advanced toward the positions defended by Robert E. Lee at Fredericksburg, Virginia, on December 13, 1862. Burnside failed to dislodge the Confederates. Union dead, wounded and missing were estimated at 12,600; the Confederates lost 5,300. *Ibid.*, 295–96.

better so I untied him & forgave him – as I hope to be forgiven. I am glad that the trial of this morning did not in the least make me angry. I was perfectly calm all the time. This trouble is the result of Lincolns war.

December 18 – Killing the rest of our hogs – 20 in number. I heard this morning that Federals in Mo. had killed my old friend James A. Boyer & destroyed his property! When will horrors end? There is now a large Federal force in Russellville & we may expect depredations & loss of stock & provisions. My quiet & orderly brother David Morton was arrested & required to take the oath & give $500 bond & I suppose the rest of us will fare no better.

December 19 – The papers are now full of accounts of the terrible slaughter of federals at Fredericksburg which the federal papers say was a "trap" set by Lee & Burnside foolishly went into it.

December 22 – Lizzie & I went to spend the day with aunt Sally & uncle Dick [Browder]. The old lady is sorely grieved & distressed at the murder of her only son James Boyer by a federal soldier at Arrow Rock, Mo. Her son had just gotten a pass to visit his mother when he was cut down by the hand of a felon. On our return home we met 8 or 10 suspicious looking men who were going in full speed for miles back. At night a troop of federal soldiers came down in pursuit of them as a gang of robbers!

December 23 – As Bro Beardsley of our Conf. wanted to go to Clarksville & thence to Murfreesboro to persuade a young rebel to come back to his mother who is in great distress about him, I took him down to Mr Warfields in the buggie. As I got nearly home I heard that a large crowd of federals were coming on to Clarksville & I barely got home in time to avoid meeting them on the road. While I write thousands of them are streaming on down the road with banners & bayonets gleaming in the sunlight of this warm balmy summerlike Christmas Eve.

December 25 – Hail Christmas morning! Would to God the scenes this day recalls would properly impress all human hearts! The children are joyful over the stockings full of candy & cake & the servants are glad of presents and holiday, but gloom and war overhang the nation. The approaching 1st of Jan is the day appointed & published by Mr Lincoln for the uprising & emancipation of the slaves in all disloyal states "not to be opposed but aided by the army in *any effort they may make to obtain their freedom*" and many fear an insurrection attended by the greatest cruelties & outrages – & many think the slaves will refuse to go to work after Christmas. Individually I do not fear anything of the kind here but feel uneasy about the country farther South where the helpless old men & women & children are all in the power of the negroes who can be excited & deluded by designing abolitionists, to the commission of great outrages. This policy of the president will create division in the army & probably be the cause [of] many resignations & desertions.

Seward Sec. of State & Chase of the Treasury have resigned & also other officers, but the president declines to accept. Burnsides great defeat at Fredericksburg with a reported loss of 20,000 men has caused a great commotion in federal ranks. The rebels are also annoying & injuring the federal armies in the South & great battles are expected at Vicksburg & near Nashville – also at Mobile & Charleston. The country is all excitement & sorrow & this is altogether the gloomiest Christmas this generation ever saw. Sickness, desertion, capture & death are wasting both armies and there is hardly a family North or South that does not this beautiful Christmas day moan the loss of some absent loved one. I feel like trying to be resigned to the dispensations of Providence. If this war results in the liberation of all the slaves & the improvement of their condition, my heart & tongue will say "Amen" & I shall think we of the South were wrong in our view that God designed them for bondsmen forever – and if the war results in the overthrow of abolitionism – the establishment of slavery in a quiet & peaceful government – I shall think that abolitionism warred against God's providence & was brought to confusion. "If this thing be of God we cannot overthrow it."

December 27 – Old Mr Wm Washington spends the day & night with us – a good man no doubt but *terribly* prejudiced against the South – can only see one side & would prefer the overthrow & ruin of the South to a peaceful division of the National territory.

December 30 – The country is again astir with rumors of invasion. The ubiquitous John Morgan is reported to have burned a large number of cars on the Louisville & Nashville RR & also four bridges & Kirby Smith is said to be at or near Glasgow & Genls Marshall & Floyd marching on Lexington. There is much surprise & great suspense. The time for negroes to resume their work has arrived & they go to it as cheerfully & readily as if there were no rumors of emancipation. The negroes seem to be settling down into the conviction that their true friends are their masters. The anxiety & uneasiness of many masters seems to be removed. The Christmas holidays have been unusually quiet & no disturbance has occurred – for which I am thankful to God our kind preserver.

I have sold my tobacco for 16 ½ cts per lb to be prized & delivered at Russellville or a nearer station if the cars come. The train came down last night and Sunday evening the first time for several months.

December 31 – Watch night! Never were so many out from home before on New Years eve as are out now – out watching with deadly enmity. The dying year has almost witnessed the destruction of our nations glory. It has seen the bloodiest & most terrible battles of modern times – and all the result of a mad fanaticism Abolitionism. It has seen almost 200,000 men dying on the field or in the hospitals, victims to each others wrath. It has seen schools & churches broken up & neighborhoods destroyed – large sections of our country desolated – cities & towns bombarded & burned – freedom of speech & of the press taken away – the writ of "habeas corpus" suspended & prisons crowded with thousands of citizens arrested & confined without due process of law & even denied a knowledge of the charges against them or their accusers – property of individuals seized for public use without remuneration or consent of the owners – many men shot down or hung for opinions sake – some in the presence of their families – and all this in the name of freedom! The one party destroying the constitution under the pretext of trying to save it, the other taking away the rights of the people in the name of trying to secure them.

The dying year has seen thousands of professed Christians turn away from Christ to drink & curse & swear and hundreds of ministers leaving their pulpits to take the sword! Alas this has been a year of sorrow to our land and deep gloom still enshrouds us and the coming year may witness an increase of our sorrows. It promises now to be a year big with destiny. In my own life through the year past have been many imperfections & improprieties that I look upon with sorrow & repentance. In the main I have tried to do right but have indulged in passions, tempers, desires and actions that are unbecoming in a Christian man & minister. I lament my follies & hope that God for Christ's sake has forgiven all that he has seen amiss in me. The night is clear, calm & beautiful! May it portend a year of peace!

January 1, 1863 – Up before day to read & meditate. Oh that God would give me a strong & persevering spirit to put all my good resolves into execution. I went to Allensville on business and attended prayermeeting at Bethlehem. Think there was a good religious feeling prevalent but the war & its rumors sap the life of the church. John Morgan is careening along the L & N RR from Green river to Muldraughs hill, has burned Salt River, Rolling fork & Bacon creek bridges – & the trestlework – captured about 6,000 prisoners & now holds Muldraughs hill & the vast tunnel at his mercy – & is supported by Kirby Smith with a strong force – & consequently the country is in great excitement.[46]

January 4 – For several days past a terrible battle has been raging around Murfreesborough Ten[n.] with dreadful carnage doubtless, on both sides.[47] The federals acknowledge enormous losses in officers & men. I suppose the rebels lost more. Intense anxiety to know the results pervades the public mind &

46. Six days after his marriage on December 14, 1862, to Martha Ready at Murfreesboro, Tennessee, Morgan set out for Kentucky on his famous Christmas raid. His purpose was to destroy the railroad connection between Louisville and Nashville. He decided to strike at Muldraugh's Hill, thirty-five miles south of Louisville, the site of two wooden trestles fifty feet long and eighty feet high. After burning both of them on December 28, Morgan returned to Tennessee. By February 1, 1863, however, trains were running once more from Louisville to Nashville. Thomas, *John Hunt Morgan and His Raiders,* 65 ff.

47. The Battle of Murfreesboro or Stone's River began on December 31, 1862, with Union Brigadier General William S. Rosecrans facing a Confederate army commanded by Braxton Bragg. After some hard fighting, the Confederates withdrew from Murfreesboro toward Tullahoma on January 3. Rosecrans occupied Murfreesboro on January 5. Union losses were estimated at 12,800, while the Confederates lost 10,800. Long, *Civil War Day By Day,* 302–303, 307.

conflicting rumors are in circulation. John Morgan is reported by some to be in Louisville! but this is probably untrue – but he has again ruined our railroad.

January 8 – Terrible scenes of blood & carnage desecrate the country around Murfreesboro. For seven or eight days we have heard rumors of battle & many have heard the thundering cannon even up to yesterday. The federal papers claim a dearbought victory & paroled prisoners & grapevine telegrams report the rebels as still holding Murfreesboro. The most intense & increasing anxiety to know the truth pervades the public. Vicksburg is reported captured[48] & of course the Miss[issippi] River & other federal successes as reported make the prospects of the South gloomy enough.

This morning while hanging up my pork a messenger came to inform me of the death of Little Maggie, daughter of Bro J. A. Lewis! She was one of the sweetest little blue-eyed fair complected babes I ever knew & oh so loving & affectionate! She was eating a piece of ice when she suddenly threw up her hands – ran in the house & fell dead! I preached a little on 15th Chapter of 1st Cor. & tried to console the bereaved parents but oh who can bear such a sorrow! Bro L. was not at home when she died & he seems almost heart broken. "My dear" said he to his weeping wife as she gazed upon the cold clay of her lovely babe, "this is only the dust, the babe's in Heaven – an angel, an angel." "Yes dear" replied the wife, "but *the dust is so precious*"!

January 9 – I went to Bethlehem & preached a short sermon on the "Parable of the Ten Virgins" to a small audience – mostly my relatives. The reported evacuation of Murfreesboro is confirmed & it is thought that Vicksburg has surrendered with 10,000 prisoners. The president has reissued his abolition proclamation but strangely excepts from its operation nearly all the territory held by the federal forces & so modifies as to dissuade slaves from murdering their owners! What is to come next is the great question & each day seems to increase the public anxiety & widen the breach between the North & South. It seems strange that Kentuckians who say they are not abolitionists should rejoice at federal victories under the plan & policy of the government – yet it is true that they do rejoice. The democratic press of the North which now represents a large majority of the people pronounces the war unconstitutional as conducted & charges abolitionists with bringing it on the country. They say a restoration of the union by arms is impossible while the abolitionists say they will not have the union & the constitution *as they were* & yet Kentuckians rejoice over abolition victories! Consistency is a jewel!

January 11 – This day I am 36 years old & by the mercy of God I am stouter than I was a few years ago. I can preach more & with less injury to my throat. I can see as clearly as ever but at times I use glasses on account of weak eyes. I have some dullness of hearing when I take cold, but generally hear plainly. To

---

48. Vicksburg did not fall to Union forces until July 4, 1863.

day I went to Pleasant Grove & preached in the morning on the works of Christ – John 10.37–38 & after dining at Harmon Baileys I preached to the colored people on the parable of the fruitless fig tree planted in the vineyard – reached home in the night.

January 12 – Sent for Dr Hutchings again to see my hired boy *Henry* who is quite sick with Pleura Pneumonia. I sent him to mill on Thursday & also to help Mr Dewees cut out his pork. He began to complain in the evening & the next day I called in the Dr. The boy is very sick & I feel some uneasiness about him. He is a wicked sinner not prepared to die but says he is praying.

The reported capture of Vicksburg was untrue. The confederates repulsed Genl Sherman with heavy loss – they say 5000.[49] Bragg has fallen back from Murfreesboro to Tullyhoma removing all his cannon & stores & thousands of prisoners. The slaughter on both sides is dreadful. I rejoice to hear that our neighbor boys with Morgan escaped safely from their perilous raid into Ky. Since the railroad was torn up & the supplies cut off, federal soldiers have been scouring all the country pressing beef cattle, salt pork, bacon & flour wherever they can find them principally if not exclusively from Southern Rights men giving receipts for quantity but stating no price. Many expect to suffer for even the necessaries of life before this year shall pass.

January 13 – Staying at home to nurse *Henry* & read & meditate. Hung up the balance of our pork to smoke – but think it most likely the soldiers will seize it.

January 15 – To my surprise all the ground this morning was covered deep in snow & still the fleeces fell all day & the night came on with the clouds still dark & the robe of winter deepening in the fields & forests! Alas for the poor & the unsheltered soldiers who shiver in this storm!

January 16 – Still snowing. The ground is covered to the depth of 12 or 15 inches & in places much deeper. We stay in & read & sing & pity the poor.

January 19 – I rehired the boy *Henry* from Bro W. for 75.00.

January 21 – Eight years ago this day our Hanson was born in a perfect hurricane of wind & snow & to day he has been busy all day helping his papa strip tobacco and has done a fine days work for a little boy just learning how to strip. He was very proud to find that his pile weighed 54 pounds and I guess he will long remember this as his eighth birthday job. Robert too was not idle & 63 pounds was his days work. Nothing delights a father more than to see his children learning to do right & seeking to prepare for life's journey. This has been a pleasant day to me as I sat at work encouraging my little boys & listening

49. Major General William Tecumseh Sherman led an army from Memphis to take Vicksburg. His advance was halted at the Battle of Chickasaw Bayou, just north of the city. Sherman's losses were estimated at 1800. Long, *Civil War Day By Day,* 300 ff.

to them prattle, spurring each other up & promising to work well & not be lazy boys & because Hanson was a good boy and willing to work, his mother gave him a chicken & some molasses pies for his birthday dinner.

January 25 — At Allensville I preached to several Cumberland Presbyterians, Campbellites & sinners & a few Methodists — had liberty & dealt faithfully with the dancing & frolicking Christians that were out — while I exhorted them to "Strive to enter the straight gate." At 3 I preached to negroes & whites on paying vows & went out to Gunns to spend the night — found him in a bitter & unforgiving spirit toward the federals who arrested him & afterward pressed his bacon. Bro G is a good man but loves money & hates Yankees — a man of fine sense & kind feelings toward his friends — might do much for the church but buries a valuable talent — preaches but little.

January 26 — Tom Browder was at my house. Rebels are said to be advancing again on Murfreesboro & Rosecrans retreating. Most of our boys passed safely through the terrible battles of Murfreesboro. Gabe Lewis one of my old pupils was wounded in the thigh. My wifes cousin, Henry Warfield was one of the nine only who kept up in his company all the time — & once when his regiment took a battery & were compelled to abandon it, he stood in the enemies fire until he had killed all the horses of the battery, thus rendering it useless to them. Henry is a brave boy & ran off to go to war in sheer hatred of Yankee wrongs & to avenge Southern injuries.

February 3 — Snowed last night — very cold to day — stay in & read. As much interested in the book of Genesis as when I first read it. The bible is the only light we have on our origin, our duty & our destiny.

February 7 — The papers report that the federal congress has passed the bill authorizing the enlistment of 150 regiments of negro soldiers to be officered by negroes & used in the war against the South! Union men denounce this measure as odious — monstrous — villainous — say Lincoln & the cabinet & congress ought to be hung — but they will not join with the South in resistance to such tyranny. It seems now that the war is to be brought into Ky, Ten[n.], & Mississippi & we look for greater horrors & outrages. The confederates hang or shoot all the negroes they find in uniform & say they will give all the officers captured since the issuing of Lincolns proclamation into the hands of the State authorities to be punished for exciting insurrection. The penalty is death & this may lead to cruel & bloody retaliation. Oh the horrors of these evil times.

February 13 — Busy all the week at work with my corn & tobacco. Hope to have 4000 lbs tob[acco] sold @ 16 ½ cts. To day I went to Red Oak. Few out, preached 32 Psalm. Went to Sister Lucketts to dinner. I think they are too extravagant for their income. *Pride* is one cause of our national ruin & all the scourge that war has brought seems to have failed to humble us. War, war, oh dreadful war! Who can tell its horrors? This nation is a doomed & ruined nation.

The money of the government is 60 pr ct below gold & it takes 125 presses two thirds of a day to print Greenbacks enough to pay the expenses one day![50] and now the assessor of the war tax is going about to the annoyance & disgust of nearly all our people. John H. Tully (Jack) is the assessor for this county & such is the opposition to the war tax that he will be long remembered with public contempt.

February 14 – Twelve months ago to day I was horrified by the booming thunder of boats & batteries at the fearful battle of Fort Donelson – and this morning before I was dressed a messenger came to call me to the bedside of my dying cousin, Sallie Benningfield. I found her gasping for breath & cold with the chill sweats of dissolution, but buoyant in spirit & confident of her speedy entrance into the New Jerusalem. Said she was a long time distressed at the idea of dying, but now was glad to die – said her little angel daughter Lou Alice was with her & she could see her. I have seldom seen so calm & serene a death. I feel glad rather than sorry. If she could be well – she has but little to make her life desirable to her – & in the present gloom of the country – the consuming fires of civil war & growing prospect of further revolution & black flags, there is but little inducement for anyone to live except to provide for helpless families.

February 15 – At 3 I preached Sally Benningfields funeral to a very large & deeply affected audience on the 6, 7, 8 verses in 25th Ch of Isaiah. Capt Morrow sent for me to sing & pray for his wife who is very ill & much afraid to die. She was once a member of the church as was her husband, but she became careless & worldly & joined in the dance – & he is wicked, profane & revengeful & has been a great terror to Southern men, but of late has been more conciliatory & kind & has in part redeemed his character. I sang & prayed with his wife & both seemed deeply moved & wept & prayed. I staid all night with my old friends, Peter & C. P. Shields who were as kind & cordial as if there was no party strife in the land. Thank God for such spirits.

February 22 – Very cold & disagreeable. The congregation at Bethlehem was small. The soldiers have been camping in the church & it was infested with lice quite to the annoyance of some of our church members. I preached Rom[ans] 5.1–7 but fear I labored to but little profit.

March 1 – I went to Red Oak & preached Ezek[iel] 37 on the Dry bones – at night preached to the negroes on the fountain opened – Zech[ariah] 13.1st – staid with Tommy Sydnor at Cyrus McCutchens – had a controversy with some young ladies about dancing.

---

50. The U.S. Congress financed the Civil War principally through loans and paper money issues. In 1862 it authorized the issuance of legal tender notes or "Greenbacks." By 1865 over $450 million worth were in circulation. The value of the Greenback currency fluctuated with the fortunes of the Union armies. By July 1864 a Greenback dollar had dropped to an all-time low of thirty-nine cents in gold. Richard B. Morris, ed., *Encyclopedia of American History* (New York, 1953), 240, 502.

March 7 – For two weeks I have been very busy. We have had only a few days fit for outdoor work. I have planted out some peach trees – sowed some clover seed – prized my tobacco &c. My crop will fall short by 1000 lbs of my calculation. Sent a hogshead to depot to day – it brings me upward of $300. One day last week I saw my dog Watch in dreadful fit with all the appearance of hydrophobia & I killed him instantly by knocking him on the head with an axe. This week has been one of quiet but I have not had much religious enjoyment. There have been several skirmishes in this region with squads of rebel soldiers in the last ten or 12 days. Shaker town depot was burned – and also one or two steam boats & a train of cars – & the federals pursuing the burning parties fired on some of their own men & killed several. The papers speak rather mysteriously of affairs at Vicksburg & I shall not be surprised at exciting news from that point.

Congress has passed the Conscription act compelling all able bodied men between the ages of 20 & 45 years to take up arms at the call of the war department with few classes excepted.[51] This will either produce revolution in the North or pour overwhelming & irresistible thousands & legions upon the Southern rebels. It will be the breaking up of thousands of happy homes & drive thousands of men into rebellion who would otherwise stay quietly at home. The clergy are not exempted but I for one feel fully resolved not to take up arms in either side. I am positively a *peace man*.

March 9 – Called to see sister Grubbs whose husband is in the army as chaplain. I saw there one of the Southern negroes who was carried away by the soldiers. He was sick in camp & Bro Grubbs carried him home to cure him & keep him until his master can get him. He says he was taken from Bell's factory & does not know his real master.

March 15 – Had a large congregation & unusual liberty at Pleasant Run – preached with zeal & unction on Isa[iah] 25. 6–8th. At 3 the colored people got happy over *Aaron Gilberts* conversion & shouted so I could not preach. *Aaron* is a faithful slave of Thos H. Gilbert and has been long years seeking religion & last week at home he was converted & seems as joyful in the Lord as any one I ever saw. I spent the night with Bro Gilbert.

March 16 – *Aaron* came home this morning rejoicing & giving glory to God. Such a conversion is refreshing in these times of spiritual dearth & wickedness. When I reached home I found to my surprise that my cousin Geo. N. Moore was in the country & at night he came to see me. I was glad to see him again. He looks well – and is a Justice of the Peace. He confirms the awful accounts we have had of murders & desolation in Missouri.

---

51. Lincoln signed the draft bill on March 3, 1863. The law provided exemptions for the physically and mentally unfit. Quotas were set for each Congressional district based on population and the number of men already in the service. A drafted man could either hire a substitute or buy an exemption for $300. Long, *Civil War Day By Day*, 325.

March 23 — I went with Lizzie to Nelson Waters to see George Nick & Bettie start to Mo. — went with them to the depot. I felt sad to part with Geo N. & Bettie. One of the great attractions of Heaven is that its society is permanent — parting in sadness is unknown.

This evening I was shocked to learn that my dear aunt Sallie — widow of my uncle William [Browder] was brought home a corpse! She had gone up to Taylor Co to see a sister die & the sister still lives & she is dead. Aunt Sallie was one of the most exemplary women I ever knew & was a devoted Christian. She was staying with her daughter Ermine whose husband has gone to war with Morgan.

March 24 — To day we buried our dear old aunt beside her sainted husband & children in confidence that they will make a family together in Glory.

March 26 — According to promise I set out to take Lizzie in a two horse wagon to see her uncle & aunt. We reached Charles Warfields to dinner & were gladly welcomed by all — especially my dear father who heard we were coming & came to meet us. I much fear he will yet be taken by the Yankees.

April 10 — [Olmstead] Went to Adairville not expecting any congregation & was not disappointed. The day was warm & my horse took thumps[52] & I had no good result from this days labor.

April 11 — Planted corn & went to Mr Boyds to get some myrtle from the grave of my dear old uncle & aunt Moore to put on the resting place of my dear little Ginnie.

April 17 — Preached at Red Oak — Lu[ke] 24.49. Bro Grubbs the federal chaplain came in to preaching — seemed friendly — said he was trying to be religious — talked about politics & the war. There is much indignation among southern men at Genl Burnside for issuing his order 38, threatening with death or exile all persons who write to their friends in the rebel army or feed or clothe them or express any sympathy with them &c.[53] Such tyranny will work its own punishment. The federals have made complete failures at Vicksburg & at Charleston with the loss of some of their best iron clad vessels of war. The country is in great suspense as to the issue of pending results — but I am glad to believe there is a better feeling growing up between the different parties. The Louisville Democrat, a leading paper in Ky comes out in opposition to the administration party and it is more than probable that a majority of Kentuckians will go with him. There is a growing hostility between democrats & republicans

---

52. That is, hiccups.

53. Ambrose Burnside, commander of the department that included Kentucky, issued Order No. 38 on April 13, 1863. He threatened death to "the carriers of secret mails and writers of letters sent by secret mails." He also ordered the arrest of anyone declaring sympathy for the Confederate cause "with a view to being tried as a traitor." Conviction would result in death or deportation into Confederate-held territory. Collins, *History of Kentucky*, I, 122.

at the North & in some places they are fighting each other – dispersing meetings – destroying Newspaper presses &c. Our government is uneasy in regard to the attitude of England & the rebel gunboats being built on the Mersey & Thames are causes of serious apprehension. The roads are now getting dry & hard & the armies will soon be in motion & tidings of blood & slaughter & woe will probably be soon heralded over the land.

April 18 – I went to see Dr [Jonathan] Bailey who was kind enough to try to get my father to return home. He had been to see Col Maxwell – commandant at Russellville & learned that my father would be required to take the oath & give bond – & this he is not willing to do. So I suppose he must await the further issues of the war. Dr B was quite friendly to me.

April 21 – Was just going to look for my father expecting to be absent several days when Mr Golladays messenger came requesting me to preach his son's funeral at 3 oclock. It rained so constantly during & after the funeral that I did not get away, more especially as Mr Golladay in his grief insisted that I should stay. I tried as a minister to do my duty.

April 22 – I went to John Gilmer's 30 miles distant stopping at depot to buy papers & at Mrs. Meriwethers to rest & read them – found that the federals were seizing all the good horses they could find & a great excitement in the country in consequence. Father had left for parts unknown, not wishing to get either himself or his horse in federal hands.

April 23 – I set out – & late in the afternoon after a long & weary ride found my father & his friend James Small way out in the woods with their horses while federal soldiers were seizing horses not far from them. I felt sad to see such a sight but glad it is no worse. Father was well & cheerful.

April 24 – I rode early & constantly to get to my appointment at Pleasant Grove – found more out at meeting than usual – preached on paying vows & was glad I made the effort to get there. Saw a troop of federal cavalry – think they are finding horses & mules with a view to pressing – got home & found some of them had been here & examined my stock – inquired closely for me – talked roughly but not insultingly to my wife who gave them full measure of the same kind. They manifested a great desire to talk with my negro man in preference to my wife about the horses – but she insisted on speaking herself.

April 25 – Trying to prepare a subject for aunt Sally's funeral sermon tomorrow at Bethlehem – find it difficult to collect & control my thoughts. My memory & application have both failed since the horrors of the war have so much excited the country.   •

April 26 – Had a large congregation and preached with liberty "Blessed are the dead that die in the Lord" Rev[elation] 14.13. Preached to the blacks at 4 oclock. "The great day of his wrath" Rev[elation] 4.17. The negroes seemed in a religious mood.

May 1 – This bright & beautiful May day is a sad one to me & our country. I got a note from my father requesting me to bring Mother to see him. He is sick & low spirited. There are prospects for army movements that will result in great bloodshed & it is sad to read federal accounts of their wanton destruction of property. Of course I feel the greatest anxiety for the welfare of my brothers in the South – but Genl Burnsides severe order No 38 threatens with death any who feed, clothe, conceal or write to their rebel friends *by secret mails* (& there are no other) or even express sympathy for them & their cause. "Treason, expressed or implied" is his language – & I see in the Enquirer of 28th where one man is sentenced to be hung this May day – who was captured at Ruggle's mill Bourbon Co Ky. accused of being a spy – & two others are sentenced to imprisonment for harboring confederates. I shall try to conform to the laws over me however much I detest them & those who enforce them. I never objected to any army protecting itself against spies – but it seems to be cruel & inhuman to hang – exile or imprison a man for writing to a son or brother in the rebel army. Went with my mother to C. M. Warfields where I saw my father looking feeble & dispirited. He has been staying in the woods for weeks to save his horse from federal seizure. He has been advised by many friends, Union and Southern to come home & take the federal oath – & give bond & is almost persuaded to do so if he can take the noncombatants oath. I think he ought to be at home and yet I fear the result. His own health and my mothers & the welfare of my younger brothers & sisters demand his attention at home, as well as his pecuniary interest.

May 2 – Late in the night Dick B[rowder] & young Small came to tell me that Col Bruce [commandant in Clarksville] had sent my father & Bro Small a pass into his lines to take the non-combatants oath – & I may now expect him at home.

May 4 – I went over to the depot & heard that my father & Mr Small had gone to Clarksville to avail themselves of Col Bruces terms. I hope it will give them protection but fear they will not be safe. I am at my wits end & do not know what to advise. The papers report Lee retreating before the powerful army of Hooker advancing on Richmond.

May 5 – At home at last! My father is at home! After a long absence of 469 days or 14 ½ months. He reached home this evening, seemingly cheerful & contented. He went to Col Bruce – was treated with great courtesy & respect – took the non-combatants oath & gave bond of 2000 to keep it faithfully – & got a safeguard – requesting all home guards & federal soldiers to protect him until he violates his oath. This is gratifying – very. Lizzie & I and the children spend the night with him – & I now hope he will be permitted to stay at home in peace.

May 7 – Father sent for me – had been advised to either go to Russellville & take the oath or get back into Bruces protection. I advised him to send a copy of his papers to the officers & see if they would protect him while he staid in Ten[n.] until he learned the decision. He did so.

May 8 – In the evening I learned through a note from Dr Bailey that the federals at Russellville would ratify Col Bruces action through *courtesy*. So I sent my father.

May 9 – Our 3d Quarterly meeting was held in Keysburg. There is much talk about the dreadful battle that has been raging around Fredricksburg. To days paper reports the discomfiture & retreat of the federal army across the Rappahannock with heavy loss – 10,000 killed, wounded & missing. Lees generalship & the rebel numbers & valor were too powerful for Hooker & "the finest army in the world." The rebels also lost immensely & great slaughter on both sides will possibly result in nothing decisive.[54] Alas for us!

May 10 – Bright & beautiful Sabbath! The village was full of federal soldiers, galloping about & looking for rebels. A group of soldiers came to church & were very orderly & attentive to preaching & I dealt faithfully with them about "paying their vows" – Psa[lm] 50.14.

May 11 – [Olmstead] My father has been to Russellville & reported & received protection on the Noncombatants oath.

May 14 – Much interested in "The two homes" a premium book Mr Woolls gave my daughter Helen for the best deportment in school during last session. I feel gratified that two of my children got premiums. Hansons book is the "Gorilla Hunters" – reward for the greatest improvement in the school – both readable books but Helens exemplifies most beautifully the superiority of virtue & economy over vice & extravagance.

May 15 – Papers to day report Genl Vandorn & T. J. Jackson both dead[55] – federal loss at Fredericksburg immense – say 20,000 killed & wounded. Lo the

---

54. By April 30, 1863, Union Brigadier General Joseph Hooker's Army of the Potomac had crossed the Potomac River upstream from Fredericksburg, Maryland, and set up camp at Chancellorsville. The next day the Battle of Chancellorsville began with Hooker's forces matched against Lee and Jackson. The battle lasted through May 4 and resulted in Hooker retreating across the Rappahannock River the next day. There were heavy casualties on both sides. Union losses were estimated at 17,287 while the Confederates lost 12,764. One of the Confederate casualties was Stonewall Jackson who was mistaken for the enemy and shot in the arm by one of his own men. Jackson died on May 10 of complications resulting from the amputation of his arm. Long, *Civil War Day By Day,* 344–48.

55. Major General Earl Van Dorn was assassinated at Spring Hill, Tennessee, on May 7, 1863, by a Dr. Peters who accused the general of having an affair with his wife. *Ibid.,* 350.

horrors of the war still crowd upon us. There is now a military order requiring all male citizens 21 years old & upward to report at Russellville & take the oath or be arrested & sent beyond the federal lines to remain until the close of the war under penalty of being shot if they return! This is a cruel & merciless order of Brig Genl Shackleford – a Cumberland Presbyterian Bro. & may give him trouble to enforce it. Who ever takes this oath under such duress is not acting of his own free will & accord. I do not know what I shall do. I am willing to do right & submit to the lawful authorities – but military men have no just right to control peaceable citizens.

May 17 – There is much excitement in the country & hundreds are flocking in to take the oath of allegiance[56] – grumbling as they go & yet swearing that they "do it of their own free will, without any mental reservation whatever." I do not see how I can conscientiously swear that I do "of my own free will" what if left to myself I should not do – & yet I must or be banished from my home & my property confiscated. Ought a Christian man to swear against his conscience to avoid suffering any more than to obtain any desired good? Is the duress sufficient to force a man so to swear or is the injunction of scripture "submit to the powers that be" a law of conscience requiring obedience to the civil or military power right or wrong! I confess that I am in some trouble about it & do not know what to do, but suppose I must submit to what I cannot avoid considering that the action is not mine – just as if I should compel my son or servant to break the sabbath, against his will. *I* should be the sabbath breaker & not he. If I were compelled to lose my hand or my head, I should of my free will give my hand to save my head – but of my *free* will would lose neither. My Hogan neighbors, arrested some weeks ago accused of harboring guerillas have been released on oath & bond. As good a man as Thos Gilbert is put under 5000 bond – accused of disloyalty! Almeda, daughter of K. C. Mason – deceased – arrested for writing to her brother in rebel army has been detained for a week or more in Russellville & now sent on to Genl Burnside for further orders. Some are wearing ball & chain & many crowded up in Russellville courthouse – charged with aiding rebellion. Oh Russellville! Little did thy people think of such scenes when they shouted & rejoiced over the entering forces of [General Simon Bolivar] Buckner from camps Boone & Burnett a year ago last September.

The federal loss at Fredericksburg is now estimated at 30,000 & rebel loss,

---

56. The text of the oath read as follows: "I do solemnly swear that I will bear true allegiance to the United States and support and sustain the Constitution and laws thereof; that I will maintain the *national sovereignty paramount to that of all state,* county, or Confederate powers; that I will discountenance, discourage and forever oppose secession, rebellion, and disintegration of the Federal union; that I disclaim and denounce all faith and fellowship with the so-called Confederate armies; and pledge my honor, my property, and my life to the sacred performance of this solemn oath of allegiance to the government of the United States of America." Beneath this oath was printed – "The penalty for a violation of this oath is *death."* Collins, *History of Kentucky,* I, 102.

papers say not less – & rebels claim 50,000 stands of arms & immense supplies, clothing &c. Jackson Miss[issippi] is reported captured by feds[57] – & other federal successes. These are times of peril & trial such as I never expected to witness. C. L. Vallandigham the great statesman and orator of Ohio is condemned to close confinement in Fort Lafayette during the war for publicly denouncing the policy of the administration & warning the people that they were in danger of a military despotism.[58] In Ky a man was arrested – taken to Louisville & imprisoned by military for speaking disrespectfully of the President! but was released. Spies & detectives are roaming the country in disguise listening for some disloyal utterance to report – & seeking by stratagem to get men to avow Southern sympathies that they may arrest them & require oath & bond – consequently men are suspicious of their servants, neighbors, & even kindred blood if they disagree in politics. Confidence is withheld – & general mistrust prevails. The papers boast of raiders burning houses – haystacks – & carrying off booty & negroes, as if they had done virtuous acts & rebels do likewise – except burning houses & taking negroes. Swearing – drunkenness & thriftless indolence are vastly increasing in the land. Altogether the picture is a gloomy one. This summer must witness an immensity of suffering – blood & death.

May 22 – Went to Keysburg – was halted by some little boys on stick horses & carrying switch sabres. They said they were Morgans cavalry & would require me to go to the school house & take the oath! Even the children are full of war manoeuvres. I had a small audience, preached on Pauls prayer – Eph[esians] 3.14–21. Felt sad about the state of the country & the oath we are bound to take.

May 24 – This is the great gathering day at Pleasant Grove – where all the young folks are apt to collect & dress out. It is vulgarly called "Showday." At 4 – the negroes had a fine time & I preached a short sermon – Rev[elation] 14.13.

May 25 – I dined with my father & others at Uncle Dick [Browder]s where Lizzie was gone when I got home. We decided to go to Russellville tomorrow to comply with "order No. 18" compelling us under penalty of banishment to go to

---

57. On May 7, 1863, Brigadier General Ulysses S. Grant began to move from the Grand Gulf area on the Mississippi River toward Jackson, Mississippi. On May 14, as advance columns of the Union army neared the city, Confederate General Joseph E. Johnston, in the face of overwhelming odds, withdrew to the north. Jackson was occupied by Grant's forces by midafternoon. Long, *Civil War Day By Day,* 350 ff.

58. On May 5, 1863, former Congressman Clement L. Vallandigham, leader of the Peace Democrats or Copperheads, was arrested in Dayton, Ohio, for his treasonable statements against the war. On May 19 Lincoln directed that he be sent beyond the military lines of the United States and not be allowed to return. Vallandigham found himself equally unwelcome in the Confederacy. President Jefferson Davis ordered him sent to Wilmington, North Carolina, where he was put under guard as an "alien enemy." On June 11 the Confederacy shipped him to Canada from which Vallandigham conducted an unsuccessful campaign by mail for the governorship of Ohio. *Ibid.,* 349, 355, 358, 361, 364, 421.

Russellville & take the oath of Allegiance — & to aid in putting down rebellion. If there be any evil in this oath let it be upon those who impose it upon us. It is not our act when forced upon us.

May 26 — Bro Alexander & I went to town and took the oath & as for me I shall give no one an opportunity to convict me of violating it. The dictates of humanity I cannot disregard. I never did & will not now encourage the rebellion but as a Christian I must be humane even if I have to feed an enemy when hungry. Most of my old friends in town seemed very glad to see me & treated me most cordially.

For several days past the papers have been rejoicing over great Federal victories & the capture of great numbers of prisoners & cannon & military stores & it is believed that Vicksburg has fallen or must fall & also the greater part of the rebel army. If this is true, it is a severe blow to the rebellion & they have probably lost more at Vicksburg than they gained at Fredericksburg. I feel like withdrawing my thoughts from all public matters & trying more to be an humble Christian & get safely out of this wicked world.

May 28 — I see from the papers now that Vicksburg is not taken but is besieged.[59] Rebel reports say "The federals attacked but were repulsed."

May 30 — For the first time this spring I went with the children to fish in the pond. This has been a busy quiet week and tomorrow being a 5th sab[bath] — I have no appointment. I need rest.

The bloody battles around Vicksburg for a week or two past, have as yet failed to capture the city as reported & the prospect now seems doubtful. Alas for our country — & the end is not yet. I was to day looking over an old letter, from my brother John — written in March last — giving a list of prices in Montgomery. Hams 1.25 pr lb — flour 75. [to] 80 dols. pr bl — butter 1.50 [to] 2.00 pr lb — chickens 1.25 & turkeys 5. [to] 7. each.

June 6 — Planted some corn — worked out cotton — read paper. Vicksburg holds out but there is a terrible suspense all over the country among all parties. The result is doubtful but the capture probable.

June 7 — At 3 I baptized Bro W. A. Campbell in the river — he kneeling in the water & I pouring the element on him with my hands at his request. So we "both went down into the water both I & he & I baptized him" but neither of us was immersed!

June 13 — This has been an unusually busy week. We have had fine rains & I have worked hard planting tobacco — have 20,000 hills set out and more ready. The corn is drooping — the corn lice or ant cattle are sucking the roots.

---

59. Grant made his first assault on Vicksburg on May 19, 1863. His troops were repulsed. A second assault on May 22 also failed. Grant then ordered a siege that lasted six weeks. *Ibid.,* 355, 356.

June 15 – Tom Browder is up & reports a man from the South as telling that Grant had been dreadfully defeated at Vicksburg. The federal papers have alluded to reports of disaster to their arms but say it is not confirmed. To days paper tells that the rebels are jubilant over cheerful news from Vicksburg. The whole country here & the greater part of Europe is looking with intense interest at the result of Grants siege. The suspense in this country has never been greater. We look upon the defeat of either party there as decisive. If Grants army is destroyed – the federals must evacuate Tenn & probably Ky – & if Vicksburg & Pembertons army are captured the Southern confederacy is probably ruined. Hence the general anxiety to know the result. May the God of providence direct to the right issue!

There are hundreds of negroes leaving their owners & going to the federals. I feel certain that my hired boy *Henry* has contemplated leaving. He has threatened several times to leave without any provocation. Yesterday morning he was so insolent & insulting to my wife that I took him this morning & tied him, intending to whip him severely if he had not begged forgiveness & promised to reform. I regretted the occurrence but thought I was doing right. I cannot say that I have confidence in him & shall not be surprised if he leaves at any time. Horse thieves are prowling through the country stealing all the best horses – going disguised, sometimes as federal & sometimes as Confederate soldiers.

June 17 – I have been to aid in burying Ed Small. He was murdered at Keysburg yesterday by a federal soldier. He and a few others had been in pursuit of the horse thieves & had recovered part of the horses & wounded one of the robbers. Returning through Keysburg they passed the federal scouts who commended their success & passing on opposite the house of Dr Marshall where I was on Sunday, they were halted by a solitary soldier, but in sight of the others. They obeyed the order & also dismounted & held up their hands as commanded but Ed Small being in feeble health became tired and brought his hands down on his head to rest his arms when he was instantly shot through by the ruffian – and died in half an hour, his associates not being allowed to help him into the house. The captain reprimanded him & said he regretted it! The parents seem deeply grieved & the whole community seem justly indignant at so wanton & reckless a murder. The fiend was notified that the men were quiet & peaceable citizens & had been in search of the horse thieves. He threatened to shoot the man who told him that they were not thieves and when a lady asked to see the man who had killed Mr Small he showed his face, told his name & residence & said he was not ashamed to show himself!

To day my little George R is six years old & a fine, lively boy he is – but too much petted by having long been the baby. He has never been to school & does not know all the letters – but has now a sprightly mind though he cannot sound the letter "r."

To days papers startle us with the news that the rebel Gen. Lee has crossed the Rappahannock in immense force – defeating portions of the national army – capturing cannon & supplies, compelling Hooker to burn tents &c & move for the defense of Washington — while the Southerners are invading Pennsylvania & Maryland & threatening Ohio. For a time Vicksburg seems overlooked while intense amazement is excited by the daring & skill of Genl Robt Lee.[60]

June 21 — Had a fine congregation at Ash Spring & preached with some liberty Psa[lm] 103. 8–14. Some federal soldiers came on a horse pressing expedition & disturbed the interest of the congregation in the subject. They examined horses but did not carry any away — at 3 ½ preached to an attentive crowd of negroes Lu[ke] 13.23–30 with considerable liberty.

Learn this morning my hired boy *Henry* attempted to outrage our servant girl *Dolly* causing great indignation & wrath in her parents, then dressed up & rode one of my mules away without my consent. I think he deserves severe chastisement. Mrs John Hogans *Abram* had a difficulty yesterday with Dick Marshall the overseer & this morning through some continuation of the affair William Gaines shot the negro in the neck. A drunken negro — *Dick,* belonging to uncle R[ichard] Browder was the cause of a number of negroes being driven off from the depot & hence our *Ellen* says this has been a bad day. I feel sad & depressed in spirit — yet have an abiding confidence that God's good providence will protect us.

June 23 — Heard to day that Miss Almeda Mason had been sentenced & sent off to the military prison on Johnson's I[sland] to be confined during the war — for the crime of yielding to the dictates of common humanity & writing a letter to her brother in the rebel army! Genl Burnsides infamous order 38 can be enforced against helpless women in Ky! I think Genl B. a heartless tyrant. Genl Lees great army is said to be threatening Baltimore & Washington — part of his troops are already in Maryland & Pennsylvania — & to days paper reports John Morgan in Ky with 5 or 6000 men.

June 24 — One of the most incessant rains I ever saw in June. I staid in reading Jessie Lees history of the Methodists. Surely the times of the first revolution were much like these — preachers imprisoned — required to take the oath — congregations meeting to talk of the news — people flying from their homes &c.

June 26 — Rain! rain — how it rains. *Ginnies* girl *Laura* was so impudent this morning as to get a slap on the jaw & then she was so angry & sulky that *Ginnie* gave her a whipping, and then she ran away in a hard rain & will probably stay away & get sick.

We began to cut wheat — some of which is sprouting in the chaff as it stands on the stalk! a thing I never saw before.

---

60. In mid-May 1863, after the Confederate victory at Chancellorsville, General Lee and President Davis agreed that the Army of Northern Virginia should launch an offensive campaign northward. Such an invasion might loosen Grant's grip on Vicksburg and a victory on Union soil might affect the North's will to continue the struggle. In early June, Lee shifted his army around General Hooker's western flank and moved into the Shenandoah Valley. By the end of the month the Army of Northern Virginia was in Pennsylvania. *Ibid.,* 362 ff.

June 27 — Raining. *Laura* came home — still sullen — got a whipping — makes us all unhappy.

June 29 — More rain. There is as much suspense in the country about war as ever. Lees bold move into Penn. confounds the federals and amazes everyone. The difficulty of enrolling the conscripts increases. Officers are frequently mobbed — sometimes shot — and the papers report organized & armed resistance. In the South too the same things are reported & it is thought that N. Carolina is tired of the confederacy.

July 3 — Not a soul at Ash Spring — I sung several hymns & went to dine at Bro Brakes. We had a hard rain this evening. The wet weather is ruining the wheat. The oldest men say they never saw such a spell of wet weather in summer.

July 4 — Looking over my old journals & wishing I were a better man. To day there is a grand union barbecue at Gordonsville — but the order of the day will be to abuse the Southern people & no good will probably result from the meeting.

July 6 — There is great suspense & anxiety in this country about the war. For several days communication with Louisville has been cut off & the grapevine reports a formidable invasion of Ky. and also a great battle between Lee & Meade, Hookers successor, in Pennsyl. with advantage to the federals.

July 7 — To day I tried W. T. Evans plan of robbing bees — set a new hive in the place of the old one, removed the old one some distance & smoked the bees away. We got a fine lot of honey but fear the bees will not do so well — killed a great many — put a large veil over my face & hat — & put on gloves so I did not get a sting from the thousands that flew buzzing around. We have another rain.

July 8 — Dispatches report Genl Lee defeated with the loss of Genl Long Street & Ewell killed & Genl Early with 20,000 men & 100 pieces of artillery captured![61] Genl Lee escaped with his cavalry! Also Vicksburg surrendered on the 4th of July![62] If all this be true Genl Meade has suddenly & unexpectedly become famous & the rebels will feel the bitterest chagrin & mortification. Every body is talking about the news, but people often deceived are slow to believe.

---

61. The Battle of Gettysburg lasted from July 1 to July 3, 1863, with Brigadier General George Meade commanding the Union forces. There were heavy casualties on both sides. The Union army's losses were estimated at 23,000 while the Confederates lost 20,000. Neither Major General James Longstreet nor Lieutenant General Richard S. Ewell was killed. *Ibid.*, 374–78.

62. For over a year Federal troops had attempted to take Vicksburg, but all land and sea assaults failed. Six weeks of siege broke the city's resistance. Confederate General Pemberton surrendered with 29,000 troops. *Ibid.*, 378–79.

July 10 – This has been a dark & dreary day but no rain – the air is burdened with a smoky vapor & yet it is clear. The papers confirm Lees defeat but with less loss than reported & also the surrender of Vicksburg with 20,000 men. Of course Southern sympathizers are sad. I have honestly differed with the views of the dominant party. I have never believed in the right of subjugation but have always been resolved to submit without murmuring to the Providence of God. I calmly & hopefully wait for the end.

July 11 – This is a dark dreary morning – *very*. For a day or two there has been an unusual fiery redness about the sun & many children & negroes affirm that it stood still an hour on the evening of the 9th. We took about 40 pounds of honey from our new swarm of bees – good rent they pay for a cheap house. John Morgan with his band have crossed into Ind. & are tearing up railroads.[63]

July 12 – The densest & longest continued fog – vapor or smoke that I ever knew. Since it began four days ago, it has constantly increased until this morning at 7 oclock large trees cannot be seen at any considerable distance. Robbers have been plundering villages & country stores in this county. W. D. Boyer claims to have been robbed of $5000 worth of goods on Thursday night & Keysburg & Adairville also have been robbed. These outrages in our midst are deplorable & alarming & we have no power to prevent it. Ed Small lost his life in pursuing them & citizens are afraid to resist – & yet rabid unionists charge the outrages on the citizens as aiders & abetters! I have heard nothing from any one but condemnation of such conduct. I heard with regret the assertion made that 19/20 of the people were rejoicing in their hearts at such occurrences. I know to the contrary our citizens are better people.

July 13 – Still this strange smoke enshrouds us. Old people are wondering at it and the superstitious are uneasy.

July 14 – Still smoky & occasionally sprinkling rain to day. I am unwell with a cold. Worked & read – applied caustic to wart in my nose that has caused me some uneasiness.

July 15 – Suffered all night with a sense of suffocation – could not breathe through the nose. To day I have been quite unwell, but this evening sowed some hungarian grass, buckwheat & turnips.

---

63. In the spring of 1863, Morgan approached Braxton Bragg with the idea of a raid into the states north of the Ohio River. Bragg gave approval only for another strike into Kentucky for the purpose of destroying Federal supplies and disrupting the L & N Railroad. Morgan disobeyed orders, however, and crossed the Ohio River at Brandenburg on July 9. On July 26, after Morgan and his men had exhausted themselves in raids through southern Indiana and Ohio, they were finally captured near Lisbon, Ohio, just sixty miles from Lake Erie. The raid covered 1100 miles. Morgan was imprisoned at Columbus, Ohio. Thomas, *John Hunt Morgan*, 75 ff.

July 16 — The papers to day report great excitement in the North & South. The rebels have lost Vicksburg & Port Hudson & consequently the Miss. river. Johnston is reported defeated & retreating before Sherman.[64] Lee is safe on the South side of the Potomac. John Morgan's cavalry are away out in Ohio & causing the greatest alarm. New York has been overrun with rioters resisting the draft & it had to be suspended.[65] Troubles thicken on every hand.

July 17 — I went to Gunn's School house — six persons out. Preached alittle — Gal[ations] 4.26th. Found Luther very sick on my return. Doctor had been sent for. My little daughter Helen & black *Dolly* in looking for eggs in the hayloft, found a pistol hidden by our hired *Henry*. I took an old pistol from him several weeks ago & forbade him to have one.

July 18 — Poor little Luther was very sick all night and we slept but little. This morning *Henry* was missing and my favorite saddle horse Mack! I suppose he is aiming for some of the Yankee camps.

July 19 — I preached on The Holy Spirit at Pleasant Run — John 16.13 with some liberty & unction. Bro. Winlock wants me to come back to the circuit. I stopped out of a hard rain & kept dry under a grapevine — found Luther alittle better but still very sick — fever not broken. My old horse Mack either slipped the bridle or was turned loose. He came home Saturday & *Henry* was seen at Wm Cornelius.

July 21 — Papers report the capture of Morgan & his men. As things now look on paper the Southern confederacy is about to wind up in defeat & failure. If God be not in the move to make a new nation the confederates will not stand and their affairs are now in that condition that they must see that only the God of armies can deliver them and if their success is in the future they must acknowledge Gods hand in it. The judge of all the earth will do right.

July 22 — Very busy topping tobacco & working cabbage — must now labor assiduously if I save my crop & pay my debts. It is *almost impossible* to hire help. For several days & nights the foxes which are often seen in our cave have been very destructive on our poultry & poor Helen is grieved at the loss of her fine flock of bantams.

---

64. On July 5, 1863, after the fall of Vicksburg, General Sherman turned toward Jackson, Mississippi. Johnston's army, in the face of superior numbers, finally evacuated the city to Sherman's troops on July 16. Long, *Civil War Day By Day,* 380 ff.

65. The first names in the new Federal draft were drawn in New York City on July 11, 1863. When drawing resumed on July 13, a mob gathered and a full scale riot broke out. The draft headquarters was stormed, houses were raided, and fires broke out in scattered sections of the city. Blacks and Federal officials became the primary victims of the mob. Firm army control, augmented by the return of troops from Gettysburg, finally brought the rioting to an end on July 16. It is estimated that a thousand people were killed and wounded with property losses amounting to over one million dollars. The draft was postponed until August 19. Less destructive riots broke out in Boston; Portsmouth, New Hampshire; Rutland, Vermont; Wooster, Ohio; and Troy, New York. *Ibid.,* 384.

July 23 — I feel some solicitude & anxiety about my future course. I want to travel & preach — & yet in these war times I cannot support my family on the pay of a preacher. I must devote part of my time to labor. If I am sent to a distant field of ministerial work, I cannot work any of importance on the farm. I would gladly devote my whole time to the ministry if the church would support my family — but this they will not do *now.* I do not feel at liberty to locate — nor do I feel willing to go to a distant appointment & cannot choose my own. I shall try to be guided by the indications of Providence. I am busy at work trying to get my home matters ready for Quarterly meeting.

July 24 — I went to Allensville & bought my little Robert a nice saddle which pleased him wonderfully. This day I observed as a day of fasting & prayer.

July 25 — Our Quarterly meeting assembled at Bethlehem — good congregation. Bro W. H. Morrison recently released from long confinement in Military prison *for opinions sake only* — preached a most excellent sermon.

July 26 — One of the best love feasts I have seen for years. Bro Morrison preached with liberty & unction. The communicants at the sacramental table were many & serious. Provisions on the ground for all & to spare.

July 27 — Bro Morrison preached with liberty & power — 8 or nine boys & girls, some small, others nearly grown, came forward for prayers & nearly all of them professed conversion. My own dear little Robert came of his own accord & wept & prayed with earnest penitence until he said God had forgiven his sins. He said "Papa I feel that I am in the hands of God. I feel like I had a few sins & Jesus has taken them away." I asked him, "Robert, how do you expect to get to Heaven?" He replied, "I expect to obey all of Jesus Christs orders." & the child seemed so earnest & intelligent on the subject that my wife & others as well as myself thought he understood the matter & was moved & renewed by the Holy Spirit. Oh for grace to raise my children for God's glory. I am much rejoiced to see my little Helen so actively engaged in the meeting with her associates. Blessed are they that seek God in early life! Robert came with my little brother Jimmy who also professed religion & several others & joined the church in his eleventh year as I did in my 12th. Just 12 months ago to a day Helen joined the church. She on the 27th of July [18]62, Robert same day — 1863.

July 28 — Bro W. H. Morrison preached a masterly sermon the "Wages of sin & gift of God" & again we had a crowd of mourners & one professed religion. Bro Fisk preached a clear & powerful sermon at 3, on 1st Pet. 4.13 & with good effect, but his delivery is very singular — & unnatural & injures the usefulness of a talented man. Ten mourners came up for prayers & three young ladies were converted.

July 29 — We had another fine congregation. Bro Fisk preached a very superior sermon. Bro J A Lewis preached with considerable success in the afternoon.

Several penitents – two professed religion. Bro Alexander, the Baptist preacher was with us in good spirit & Christian temper. I invited him to preach. The meeting deepens in interest & still penitents older than the first are crowding the altar. The revival is the only one we have had on this circuit for three years – & now that the public mind is full of war this work is wonderful.

July 30 – A rain last night stopped the wheat threshing & to day the congregation was large. Our Baptist brother Alexander preached a pointed – powerful sermon on "Go thy way." After noon I preached on thankfulness for conversion – Rom 6.17 – and while using Fletchers illustration of sudden & instantaneous conversion, by two men carrying burdens of sand – one losing his suddenly by breaking the cords & the other by the sand leaking out, Nettie Woolls was converted & made very happy in the love of God. Five professed to day.

July 31 – Bro Wm Alexander preached "Repent or perish" with great power & we had a wonderful time – quite a number – I think 7 professed conversion.

August 1 – To day the house was *full*, & we had a time of great rejoicing. Both Alexanders preached & it is generally thought that our Alick preached best – 8 or 10 professed conversion – thirty seven up to this time. This is in some respects the most remarkable meeting I ever saw. It seems to have come by surprise! and although we have had a long spiritual dearth – yet the members all rally around & sing & pray & talk to mourners & go out in the congregation after sinners, as if inspired by sudden & supernatural zeal – and Baptists, Presbyterians and Methodists blended in one common brotherhood vie with each other in the great work. Many of our Baptist friends have seen their children converted – 8 of the Smalls, one McCulloch &c among the Baptists & upward of 20 have joined our church. This Saturday night I had meeting for the negroes & black *George* exhorted & had a crowd of mourners and four professed religion, our *Lucy* & *Ginnies Laura* among them. I have greatly desired *Lucys* conversion as the only hope for her welfare in this world or the next.

August 2 – This morning I immersed Miss Ginnie Hogan & uncle Dick [Browder]s *Lucinda* in my pond and at 11 preached to the largest congregation I have preached to for years on the office & effect of the Holy Spirit. Bro Hester preached powerfully on repentance & a crowd of mourners and a number of conversions crowned the work. *Black George* had 20 or 30 mourners among the negroes & at night four more conversions which added to the whites make 54.

August 3 – Blessed be God – the revival goes on even in evil days. To day we had ten conversions most of them young men & women & still others crowd to fill up the altars. It is well for us, for politically we are sorely tried and to day Ky loses the right of free suffrage! Military officers sit to question men & refuse to allow all to vote who will not vote the administration ticket or take unconstitutional & illegal oaths.[66] I was required to swear that I had not directly nor indirectly aided the rebellion since April 11th 1862. Fortunately I have not aided & so I claimed the right to vote – but although the judges were members of my church & have known me from my childhood, they required me & other peace men to swear but allowed *war* men to vote without swearing. Isham Miller & Wm Adams were the judges. May God give me patience and charity. Amen. At some places they refused to open polls for Wickliff – Dem[ocrat] – peace man – & at Allensville old Bro. Wooldridge was arrested for refusing to say that he was glad Morgan was captured & hoped Charleston would fall. An election by bayonets! Oh! God pity us.

August 4 – I turn away sad & disgusted from political affairs. Our revival deepens & widens – older & harder sinners are crying for mercy & 9 or 10 souls professed religion. About 70 whites and a considerable number of colored people professed religion. I never saw all denominations work together so well before.

August 5 – Twelve years ago this day Helen, our first born was given to us & has up to this time been a child of comfort & hope to us. To day a troop of federal soldiers came by the church in pursuit of guerillas that captured a Capt & Lieut at Elkton & fired on the train above Clarksville yesterday. To day our meeting was not so interesting. Only two professed religion – both clear & powerful – Wm Murray & Eliza Rutherford.

August 6 – To day the meeting was more lively and four persons professed saving faith in Christ.

August 7 – Bro Settle preached well yesterday evening, as he did this morning but the meeting seemed to drag & faith & zeal seemed tired for the first time in the fourteen days. I exhorted with all my power & called all the young converts together to sing & pray & we caught the fire again & a general rejoicing came on. We had in the afternoon a speaking meeting & it cheered us to hear many young converts exhort their associates to seek the favor of God. Moore & Morrison returned.

August 8 – Bro Alexander preached a good sermon on the prodigal son – & in the evening Bro Foggy a Baptist preached an excellent sermon and we had some happy conversions – among them my neighbor Mrs Paine.

---

66. On July 31, 1863, General Burnside declared martial law in Kentucky "for the purpose only of protecting the rights of loyal citizens and the freedom of election." When he visited Lexington, Kentucky, on August 10, the General said "the disloyal had no right to approach the ballot box, and therefore had no right to complain of martial law." Collins, *History of Kentucky,* I, 127.

August 9 — This sabbath the largest crowd assembled at Bethlehem that I ever saw there. Dr Stevenson preached to a crowd of women in the house & Bro Hester to the white men & Bro Lewis to the negroes in the woods — and there was preaching at the three stands also in the afternoon. There must have been 1500 or 2000 persons at meeting and I never saw more orderly deportment. Great solemnity prevails. One old negro man 80 years old or more professed religion — *Lewis Browder*. Eighty two whites & about 30 blacks have professed religion & still the work goes on.

August 15 — Twenty two days our meeting has continued & 98 or 99 whites & 45 negroes have professed conversion & to day there are ten or 12 penitents at the altar. The congregation has been larger every day than the first.

One of the speaking meetings was intensely interesting. Frank Andersons little son, James Thomas, spoke with more thought, sense & calmness than any child I ever heard talk in a religious meeting. Years ago I pointed out that boy for a preacher. We appointed Thurs evening last for the close — as the interest seemed dying out. I exhorted and the power of God came on us & the altar was crowded with mourners & so here we are yet. When the brethren advised me to close the services with the first sabbath, a sister (Mrs Bibbs) came with tearful eyes and asked me to appoint meeting for the next day — and that next day the work of revival began and she has seen her two stepsons both converted to God & so a great mountain has been removed from her heart. Many have selected special persons to pray for & have seen them converted. One old man sixty years old professed to be reclaimed. My neighbors Mr & Mrs Paine — both gay & worldly — have professed religion & joined our church. I have often prayed for his conversion — thinking his influence injurious to our young people but I was not expecting his conversion now!

To day a number of my friends sent over to help me work out my tobacco which was getting injured. My father & Bro James Small have gone to Camp Chase at Columbus, Ohio to see their sons who were with Morgan in his raid into Indiana & were all captured. Genl Burnsides stringent order forbidding friends to visit or clothe them will probably prevent my father from seeing poor Frank who is now for the first time a prisoner of war. Federal papers report that Genl Morgans head has been shaved & other outrages & indignities practiced upon him in the Ohio *penitentiary*.

August 16 — The fourth consecutive sabbath we have spent at Bethlehem. Bro Foggy preached the imputed Righteousness of Christ & that the atonement was neither universal nor partial! I thought a man of his piety & talent might have preached a sermon more suited to the occasion & circumstances. Bro Lewis preached the closing sermon & we had a number of mourners & two little boys professed religion making one hundred & one whites & the colored people report 49 or 50 conversions. So ended one of the most remarkable meetings I ever attended. For 23 days together hundreds of people from all directions have attended church & I have seen or heard of no bad behavior. Since we began revivals have broken out at Stevensons chapel, Hermon & Briar patch. May we not look for better times!

August 19 – David [Browder] came over & brought the sad news that Bro George Adams' son Frank who was captured with Morgan had died at Camp Chase & Lizzie & I were requested to go down. We went to Charles Warfields.

August 20 – On the way to Bro Adams we met Mrs Dortch at the river. Her horse kicked out of harness in the middle of the river and I waded in to her assistance. She was in the act of getting out & would have drowned as she could not have stood up in the current. Two wagoners were crossing at the time but would not assist her. She expressed gratitude for my help.

Bro Adams family were in great grief yet rejoicing in the happy peaceful death of their dear Frank. He died in bright prospect of heaven – & although he had never been known to sing at home, he sang with clear full voice "Oh happy day when Jesus took my sins away." The scene was thrilling – a Christian dying in prison & exulting to the last in the glory of God. Bro Adams only found one federal officer who seemed to sympathize with his affliction & was willing to admit him to his son's prison.

August 21 – We came home through the dust & heat. My father returned from Camp Chase, having been better treated by federal officials than he expected. He was not admitted into the prison but saw Frank through the enclosure & communicated with him freely by writing & was allowed to supply his wants in part. The boys were mostly well & cheerful but poor Frank says "There is no God in Camp Chase." I fear he is backslidden. May the Lord reclaim him!

August 26 – Very busy in my tobacco as a matter of necessity – would much prefer being at church.

August 27 – What shall I do? To day the officer with a band of soldiers came & enrolled me as a conscript in the federal army! I have tried to submit myself to the laws & obey the constitution but my conscience will not allow me to fight & I cannot do it. I pray God to deliver me from the necessity. I do not feel able to pay the $300 exemption but will sacrifice property to do it rather than sin against my convictions of right. The apostles submitted to imprisonment & stripes because it was "Better to obey God than men." God help me.

August 30 – Very cold. Frost on the fence! Alick [William Alexander] & I went over to see Jesse Harper who has been long sick & much concerned about religion. He was overjoyed to see us. We read – sung & prayed and as we were singing "On Jordan's stormy banks" &c with the chorus "Glory be to God on high," his soul was converted & he shouted Gods praise aloud.

August 31 – [Harpers School House] A good morning meeting. Bro Pierce a federal chaplain came out. Pierce is said to be a man of good spirit & fine talent but is very affected. A little boy of George Kings – five or six years old said "Ma don't you think that preacher prays mighty proud? I don't like proud preachers." What a rebuke! I came home at night.

September 1 – Here is autumn – God be praised for fine crops. The country is full of fruits & blessings – & now revivals of religion are abounding in all directions.

September 2 – Good meetings, good behavior. Federal soldiers attend nearly all the time & seem serious. I urged them publicly & privately to seek religion & one poor fellow came forward for prayers.

September 3 – I preached 32nd Psalm with good effect. After dining at George Kings, Alexander & I went over to see Jesse Harper who was much worse – after singing & prayer he revived & sat up & asked to be baptized & I administered the ordinance. Alick preached well at night & we had 4 conversions – one old black man 60 years of age making 15 since the meeting commenced.

September 4 – I was so wearied that it was necessary for me to come home & rest.

September 5 – 13 years ago this beautiful day I was happily married to the woman of my choice & have cause to bless God more & more every year for so good & wise a wife. Long before I married I prayed for a good wife & I am fully satisfied with the answer.

September 6 – I went to Red Oak & preached to an attentive audience on "Hope," then went to Harpers School house & preached to a great crowd Isa[iah] 25.

September 8 – After morning service I came home – found all well. My business at home needs my attention but I cannot stay.

September 12 – The meeting tonight was one of the most joyful I ever witnessed. There was a general desire in the community for Dr R. M. Beauchamps conversion & tonight he was happily converted & joined the church. An electric shock would scarcely have thrilled the congregation more. First his sister & then his numerous friends & soon almost every christian united in a simultaneous shout of "Glory to God" "Bless the Lord" & for an hour or more there was a time of great power & rejoicing – & several souls were happily converted. Alick & I went to sister Parkers with the Dr & there we had another season of rhapture. His servants & his sisters seemed overwhelmed with joy & gratitude. The colored woman leaped up & shouted & tumbled about almost convulsed with ecstacy exclaiming with a loud voice "Why glory to God – Glory – my master has got religion!" Then she would embrace him in her arms & weep & say "Thank God, thank the Lord, my master has set out to meet old mistress in Heaven!" How I wish the misguided abolitionists who are honest could have witnessed the scene.

September 13 – At night Alick preached with less than usual liberty, yet so general is the awakening that 23 penitents – most of them grown, came for prayers & six of them were able to go away rejoicing in God's pardoning love & the hundreds that crowded the house seemed to feel the divine presence & power.

September 14 – Glad to get home & find all well. Lizzie was weary with waiting & sad at my long delay. I feel the effect of absence from home but now while God is troubling the waters I must go and urge poor sinners to plunge in & be healed of their maladies.

September 15 – The great revivals seem to absorb every other interest. We hear but little of war. The papers report still increasing federal successes & the rebels are greatly pressed & much discouraged. Unless Providence interposes by direct agency or European intervention, the rebellion must soon be crushed – & from the signs of the times a military power will take the place of our once liberal Republic. Free speech is suppressed, *habeas corpus* is gone – the press is under military censorship – the constitution is ignored, the ballot is under the bayonet – conscription forces us to fight – negroes are armed against their masters – confiscation & exile are common – & a tide of evil is overwhelming the land. The French have established a throne in Mexico in violation of our Monroe doctrine & a war with that power is imminent & the South will be driven to an alliance with that nation.[67] Bragg has given up Chattanooga & Buckner Knoxville[68] & still the conquering federals crowd on augmented by thousands of negro laborers & conscripted abolitionists. Sixty days will probably tell the story of the great revolution or else a war between the U.S. & France. My daily prayer is & has been "God defend the right." I think this is a prophetic period & God is in the movement.

September 16 – [Harpers School House] A good meeting last night – two conversions.

---

67. In late 1861 Britain, Spain and France sent a joint military expedition to Mexico for the purpose of collecting debts in default. Britain and Spain withdrew shortly, but France, under the leadership of Napoleon III, remained to pursue larger designs. The French army overthrew the Mexican government in 1863, set up a satellite state, and placed Ferdinand Maximilian of Austria on the throne in 1864. The North, absorbed in the Civil War, paid little attention to these developments. But as the war was pushed to a successful conclusion, American public opinion demanded that the French be expelled. It is doubtful that Secretary of State William H. Seward's protests had any measurable impact on the French. Nevertheless, they finally withdrew in the spring of 1867 leaving Maximilian to face a Mexican firing squad. Thomas A. Baily, *A Diplomatic History of the American People* (New York, 1964), 349 ff.

68. General Bragg withdrew from Chattanooga and retreated into Georgia when he realized that General Rosecrans' Army of the Cumberland was cutting in behind him. Federal troops entered the city on September 9, 1863. General Burnside had forced the Confederates out of Knoxville on September 2. Long, *Civil War Day By Day,* 403, 407.

September 17 — An approaching rain caused me to dismiss early, had the darkest ride to John Gilberts that I ever had anywhere — frequently lost the road & the horses were as blind as their riders — often striking trees & fences. A lady rode close by me & clung to my hand for guidance & I could not see the white covering on her head — nor any other object — it was "darkness that might almost be felt."

September 18 — Quite cold. I immersed old Mrs Herndon (70 years old) in Sister Parkers pond, then came home through town & took authority to solemnize the rites of matrimony under the law. The oath was not so objectionable as the one I had already been required to take.

September 19 — I suffered all night with toothache.

September 20 — Sunday. A large crowd. I was not able to preach, but Bro. Redmon was. I baptized a number of young men & women and administered the sacrament of the Lords supper. Bro Grinter preached at night & I baptized 34 or 35 negroes & administered the Lords Supper to almost 100 or possibly more. This was a day of bodily affliction to me but my soul has been comfortable. At night only two mourners came forward & both of them were comforted, so we closed the meeting with a clean altar.

September 21 — I suffer much with my jaw which continues to swell. Found all well at home except *Ginnie's* little *Addie* who is wasting away & does not improve. I fear they will lose her. A messenger had called for me to marry Dr Thurston & Bettie Hughes on Thursday evening at 6 oclock. I am also called to marry Milton Hardin & Bell Merritt at nine oclock A.M. the same day, 20 miles apart. I am much worn down with 8 weeks of constant & almost uninterrupted ministerial labor & need rest badly.

September 28 — Much confusion about getting to [Annual] Conference. Trains stopped — military have the railroad &c.

September 29 — Bros Alexander, Morrison, Petree, A. C. Johnson, Lewis & I got on the cars and at night got off stage at Glasgow and Alick & I were sent to lodge in the pleasant home of a Presbyterian family, Mrs Helm.

September 30 — Bishop Kavanaugh being detained at home by the illness of his wife, J. H. Linn D D was elected President by a large vote & N. H. Lee chosen Secretary. Bro Owen — former Sect. — was much mortified at the result & positively refused to act as assistant. He supposed that he was left out only because he was a unionist, but he received 10 or 12 votes by Southern preachers & Bro Lee one or more by unionists, so that there was no party vote. I was for Owen. A good spirit seemed to prevail among the brethren.

October 1 – J. H. Bristow Federal chaplain seemed kind and conciliatory toward his brethren & his meek Christian spirit won him much esteem. I am sorry that R. G. Gardiner another chaplain exhibited a different spirit – intimated more than once that all who sympathized with the South – were *traitors* &c – made free use of the word "treason" and was more than once called to account by Bro N. H. Lee. He brought several charges against Bro T. J. Moore who had been a rebel chaplain. It was much feared that he would mar the harmony & peace of the conference. Later in the session, however, he became more conciliatory.

October 2 – Just at the close of the prayer in the morning – the military entered the conference room & read an order for the arrest of any disloyal minister who might decline to take the oath of Allegiance to U.S. government & demanding that the flag should be raised as an evidence of loyalty. Dr Parsons first, then all of us individually & singly raised the little banner & Dr Linn made a beautiful & telling speech on the design of a flag as emblematic of the great principles of *"constitutional liberty"* declaring the loyalty of all good ministers to the constitution of our country. Bros E. M. Crow & Joel Peak were then personally questioned by the officer as to their loyalty and being satisfied he withdrew his troops & we proceeded to business.

Bro Gorin the banker took me with him to dinner where Bro Parsons told me of the discussion on Bristows resolution to reaffirm the 23d Article of our religion, which was unanimously voted for, all no doubt approving the doctrine of loyalty to the constituted authorities but many feeling that if they had disapproved, they would not have been safe to vote differently.

October 4 – At 3 I heard J. H. Bristow preach a powerful sermon to soldiers & citizens in the court house. If all chaplains would always preach as he did good results would follow. At night we had the Sacrament of the Lords supper after which the appointments were read out & the brethren generally received them cheerfully. Dr Nicholson had withdrawn from the church being notified by the P[residing] Elders that "in view of his peculiar habits he could not be acceptable in their districts." It is affirmed that he drinks ardent spirits to excess. What a pity! what a shame!!

October 5 – Dr Alexander & I were especially solicited to remain a week and aid in a protracted meeting but I felt as if duty called me home. I had a pleasant trip home & from Cave City to Bowling Green the conductor did not find Morton & me & we could not find him – so we paid no fare. Got home at night delighted to find wife & children well & such greetings as I receive from my dear ones would make a stoics heart leap for joy.

October 7 – I was surprised by an unexpected visit from Mr [George H.] Warfield – & equally so at its object. His boy *Simon* ran away to the federal army, was caught & returned. Again he ran away & having stolen many things at home was arrested & put in jail where he lay until he was humbled, sick & worn out. He begged his master earnestly to take him out, but he forbade his ever coming on his place again — but finally released him & gave him to me on his good promises. *Simon* reached here on Sunday morning 20th of Sep. & has been well satisfied & well-behaved ever since & for some time has been much concerned about religion at the altar for prayers. Last week the federal soldiers went to Mr Warfields & drove all his negro men & boys out of the field & started them off to work on the North Western Railroad, connecting Nashville with Paducah. He succeeded in getting five or six released, they still retaining four — *Ike Corney* — *Wesley, Horace* & *Plummer*. Mr Warfields wife is much distressed about *Plummer* her favorite and so he came up to take *Simon* back & try to exchange him for *Plummer*. *Simon* went away very reluctantly & I cannot feel that it is altogether right but although Mr Warfield had given him to me I made no objection as he thought proper to take him.

For some time the papers have been full of details of the terrible defeat of Rosecrans on Chickamauga creek beyond Chattanooga & it is now uncertain whether he will be able to supply his army if indeed he is not compelled to capitulate. Hence the hurry to complete the railroad. The rebel Wheeler has again been in the rear of the federal army & captured many prisoners, horses, wagons, medicines &c.[69] The next morning after our conference left Glasgow, the rebel Capt Hughes with 85 men dashed into the city, surprised & captured the entire garrison (about 300) except six men who ran away barefooted & bare headed & made their escape. The bank was robbed of all the state's money — some $9,000. During our conference several horses were stolen in the town, among them several horses of preachers, Bros Rodgers, Reed & Hays each losing a horse.

October 9 — Dear little *Addie* died this morning just after sunrise. Her troubles & sufferings are past. I went to town & got the coffin. There was much excitement about guerillas & a large stampede of negroes last night. Eight ran away from Dr Stevenson & several from judge Edwards, but this is now too common to excite surprise. *Mary Mildred, Mary* & *Ginnie McCulloch* & *Bettie Warfield* kept watch of little *Addie's* remains.

October 10 — We buried little *Addie* beside her little brothers grave where Christ will watch the sleeping dust, till he shall bid it rise.

October 11 — I started early to Bells Chapel — was in good time, preached with liberty & unction, "Awake thou that sleepest" &c. Old sister Thornhill shouted, old uncle Bell got happy — and there was a general good feeling. Some of the more ultra unionists had said they would not support a preacher with Southern

---

69. On September 19, 1863, Union and Confederate forces clashed at Chickamauga, about twelve miles south of Chattanooga. General Rosecrans' Union troops were routed on the second day of battle and retreated in confusion. Confederate General Bragg failed to pursue Rosecrans, however. Union losses were estimated at 16,000; the Confederates lost 18,000. Confederate cavalry under Major General Joseph Wheeler harassed Rosecrans' army from September 30 to October 17. Long, *Civil War Day By Day*, 410 ff, 415.

sympathies, but they rallied around me & invited me to their houses. By Gods grace I shall ignore politics & preach the gospel − & I hope for good times.

October 16 − [Olmstead] My father has returned from Louisville, bringing my new coat & pants. I felt shabby at Conference with my old ones & David Morton who has been proverbially careless about his dress was rigged up in fine style. He urged me to dress up & be more tidy in my appearance − said he had made a solemn vow to God to dress in a more genteel manner. I told him that such was my own resolve. I never bought more than one suit of *fine* clothes in my life.

October 22 − To day I have been busy sowing Rye & wheat & right in sight of my house, the robbers were plundering the merchants of Volney, Gaines & Miller. They had robbed Gordonsville, & it is said they shot a man who was trying to escape them. They took off 3 horses from the school house − 2 of them George Youngs − 1 Dick Campbells & also Dr Rists horse & Mr McCulloch's. They took Mrs Blackford's negro *John* & also one of Mrs Hawkins' but they escaped. It is rumored that they were overtaken & some of them shot at Dr Baileys. There were forty two of them well mounted & heavily armed, and citizens who resist or pursue them are threatened with death & houseburning. We are in peril & do not know what to do for safety. Soldiers in garrisoned towns are not able to protect us.

December 11 − For weeks I have been going on regularly to my appointments. 3d Sun. in Nov our Quarterly meeting met at Mt Hermon. Stewards* estimated my claim at 700$. Paid 10!

During the time my journal has been neglected, our country has been agitated with war news. Grant is reported to have defeated Bragg with great loss at Chattanooga[70] while Gen Lee has driven Meade back across the Rappahannock − Longstreet has failed to capture Burnside & is now retreating. Thousands of negroes are enlisting in the federal army & hundreds & thousands more are deserting their masters. Many are leaving this country & the money value of slaves is nought. Negroes are not sold and they are becoming indolent & selfwilled. Our Governor offers no protection to the right of property & the president is opposed to any peace that does not destroy slavery. Times now look like slavery is doomed. If such be the will of God I say Amen − but I cannot so understand the Bible.

To night Lizzie is watching with cousin Catherine [Sydnor] who seems to be approaching the end − suffering the most torturing pain (from gravel) yet trusting in the Lord & patient.

70. On October 23, 1863, General Grant arrived at Chattanooga to take command of the besieged Army of the Cumberland. By November 23 he was ready to take the offensive against General Bragg. The contest for Chattanooga reached a climax on November 25 with the Battle of Missionary Ridge in which the Confederate line was cut in several places. Bragg's army was forced back toward Chickamauga Creek. Union losses were estimated at 5800; the Confederates lost 6600. *Ibid.*, 423, 425, 436−38.

December 13 — Came home [from Bell's Chapel] & found that cousin Catherine had died.

December 15 — Was out in woods chopping when I received a note from aunt Betsy Waters informing me of the death of uncle Waters & requesting me to preach his funeral. Lizzie & I with Tom & Ginnie [Browder] went down & found her in great distress. His death was sudden & unexpected. In the morning he walked out to see his stock, took to vomiting about noon & died before bed time.

December 16 — Was very cold & rainy & but few came out. I preached "Precious in the sight of the Lord, &c" Psa[lm] 116/15th & we buried him in his own garden. Tom & Ginnie are going to live with aunt B. & have half of what is made after paying all expenses.

December 21 — Paid Mat Watkins 168 dollars for 100 borrowed 11 years ago & overlooked.

December 22 — Lizzie & I went to town, bought Christmas presents for children & servants. At night a band of robbers came into the country & took a horse from Dick Campbell — two from Nathan Penick & all the money they could find — took $200. at Bro Ivey's. George Hall fired at them & he thinks killed one. They shot at him & burned his house and all its contents. He reported his loss at $5000 & the military order that the Southern rights neighbors shall pay it.[71] The assessment is two or three times the worth of the property — but if it were only a part of the value it is unjust & oppressive to require people to pay it who knew nothing of the raid & had no connection with it. I would willingly help replace his loss — but not by force — not to be considered a party to the crime.

December 25 — What a noise! Children & negroes up long before day, catching Christmas gifts & looking after the doings of Santa Claus — rejoicing over stockings full of candies cakes & nuts. We went by invitation to dine at Dr H[utching]s with father, uncle Dick [Browder] & David H[utchings] & Stamper Baker with their families and partook of a fine Christmas dinner.

December 27 — Was rainy & I did not go to church. Read Paradise Lost & talked to the young people.

January 1, 1864 — Cold! So cold! I almost froze going to the depot. The cars were froze up — got to town by 11 Oclock. Several men frost bitten. I hired two boys — *Jeff* & *Bob* — both small, for 18% — Tom Jeffries taking the war risk. I hired several for others.

---

71. Among the instructions to provost marshals issued on June 9, 1862, by Major General Jerry T. Boyle, U.S. Commandant of Kentucky, was the following: "When damage shall be done to the person or property of *loyal* citizens by marauding bands of guerillas, the disloyal of the neighborhood will *be held responsible, and a military commission appointed to assess damages and enforce compensation.*" Collins, *History of Kentucky,* I, 102.

January 6 – Worked hard putting up ice.

January 11 – Thirty seven years ago to day I was born into this world of woe & sin. Much of my time has run to waste. I trust to God for mercy & free salvation.

January 12 – Temple Woolls & family here – his little boy Sydnor is very ill.

January 13 – Saw some soldiers scouring the country notifying innocent people to appear at Russellville & pay amounts assessed them to give George Hall $4,700 for $1500 destroyed by the robbers. Father was assessed 60 – D. B. Sydnor 72, uncle Dick [Browder] 78, Henry Browder 12, &c. I have not been notified as yet.

January 14 – We sat up with Temples baby – it died this morning at about 2 oclock lying on my wifes lap. I went to town & got the coffin. Saw Bro W. T. Evans, a good & true man, ordered into close confinement as a hostage for the man that burnt George Hall's house! How such injustice is to improve the public peace I cannot see. Who is to find, or surrender the robber while an innocent man lies in prison?

January 15 – We buried Temples babe beside my own dear little Ginnie.

January 18 – Bro T. J. Moore came to see me. Was a chaplain with Morgan – has lain long in prison & been badly treated. We will aid him in his pecuniary distress.

January 23 – Busy prizing tob[acco] for a day or two & other little jobs. I got $50. from Billy Browder by Ned Hughes for George Nick, who, having fled for safety from Mo. is living in a cabin in Ill[inois] & chopping wood for a living.

January 24 – Preached in evening to negroes on 2nd Titus – do not think they like close plain preaching on that scripture that requires obedience to masters.[72]

January 30 – Had a very muddy ride to Fairview to Mortons Quarterly meeting.

January 31 – A rainy Sabbath. Small audience. Redford & I stay at Bro Kenners in the house where Jeff Davis the Southern president is said to have been born.

February 12 – Lizzie & I went to town – shopping. I am more than ever convinced that my wife can do better trading than I can, gets better bargains.

---

72. Titus 2:9, 10 (King James Version) reads: "Exhort servants to be obedient unto their own masters, and to please them well in all things, . . . shewing all good fidelity."

February 18 – Our troubles are increasing in Ky. Congress is determined to enlist negroes among us, not satisfied with inducing them to run away & enlist. Mr Lincoln calls for a draft for 500,000 more men by 15th of March & we fear the result.[73] Negro soldiers are riding through the country just below us seizing other negroes & causing great alarm. Papers report great preparations by the rebels for invading Ky again – abandonment of the siege of Charleston, critical condition of federal forces in Knoxville &c. John Morgan has escaped from the penitentiary in Ohio & is now organizing a select force for cavalry dashes again. So here we are in uncertainty & painful suspense.

February 21 – There is much excitement over the telegraphic news that Mr Lincoln, tomorrow will issue a proclamation of universal emancipation to all the negroes in the U.S.[74]

February 27 – Went to see sister Sugg in her bereavement – her husband died from a wound in battle on Chickamauga. Spent night at Charles W[arfield]'s. Negro soldiers have driven off all his negro men but one – another one came back to day.

February 29 – Leap year! Cold & snowy & sleeting. I married John Snaden to Sue Weatherford & got a fee of $20. No Civil law being in force in Ten[n.] they came to Ky to marry at his fathers. When we got home we learned that a large number of negroes had run away – Fathers *Bob* & his hired boy *George* among them. All of Jackson McLeans & most of Mrs Hawkins, mostly *union* peoples negroes.

March 6 – [Hadensville] At 3 I preached I Pet[er] 2.7th to the negroes. Several mourners. They seem devotional at church but many have lost all confidence in their piety or sincerity. I came home at night because so many negroes are running away & stealing horses that my family feels safer when I am at home.

March 9 – There is much excitement now in the country about the military interference with negroes. They are being enrolled in our state and the people are not satisfied. Union men are secretly hoping for Southern success.

March 13 – [Bell's Chapel] Largest congregation I have yet had – preached "Devils Wiles" with great liberty. Staid at uncle Bell's – was edified in hearing

---

73. Lincoln's call for more troops was issued on February 1, 1864. Earlier on October 25, 1863, the President had exempted Kentucky from black enlistments as soldiers, but that exemption was now terminated. On February 5 the Kentucky legislature protested against the enlistment of Kentucky blacks and asked the President to remove black soldier camps from the state. Collins, *History of Kentucky,* I, 128, 130.

74. There was no basis for this rumor. President Lincoln had issued his Emancipation Proclamation on September 22, 1862, but it promised to free on January 1, 1863, only those slaves in states that were in rebellion against the United States. Universal emancipation did not come until the passage of the Thirteenth Amendment in 1865.

the old man talk of early Methodism. He is a holy good man — greatly opposed to parties & jewelry & had been a uncompromising union man. He & his party are now bitter against Lincoln.

March 14 — Sensation! Last night Caleb Bells only negro woman & her husband stole her masters mules & uncle Bells wagon & ran away to the Yankees. One of Bro Petrees & two of Reeves & others. Union men lose more in proportion than rebels or Southern rights men.

March 15 — I visited sister Temple & Bro Crouch, have now visited nearly all the families on my circuit. This week I have sold a good many books — Southern history of the war — Life of Stonewall Jackson — Army of the Cumberland. The negro enrolling has begun here & there is much indignation & excitement.[75]

March 26 — [Olmstead] Having been quite busy all the week, I went on Saturday as far as Bro Kimbroughs on my way to Salem. I left with a saddlebags full of books & sold them all. I find a ready sale for the Life of Jackson.[76]

March 27 — [Salem] Beautiful Sabbath! House full. I preached with some unction but the congregation seems very cold indeed. After dining with Finley Mitchell, I preached to the colored people at Salem, the first sermon they have had for a long — long time. Had a small congregation. There is a great prejudice among many of our people against negro meetings. I have tried to overcome it & have partially succeeded. At Bethlehem — Red Oak & Pleasant Grove — where large negro congregations have had regular preaching, fewer negroes have run away than from almost any other places.

April 8 — [Elkton] Congregation good — all things considered. There has been much prejudice in this town toward Southern preachers, & it is not all gone, yet I have seen no disrespect to me. Some do not go to church, who were once prompt to attend.

April 11 — Found all well at home. Robbers have been in again plundering & stealing.

75. On March 15, 1864, Kentucky Governor Thomas E. Bramlette asked the people to submit quietly to black enrollment and to "trust the American people to do us the justice which the present Congress may not do." On March 22, the Governor and others went to Washington to talk with President Lincoln about the problem. A compromise was reached by which the Governor agreed to black enrollments, but only after Kentucky failed to furnish her quota of white men. Quotas were not met, however, and on April 18 Brigadier General Stephen Burbridge, who became Commander of the District of Kentucky on February 15, 1864, issued General Order No. 34 for the enlistment of able bodied blacks in Kentucky. The blacks were to be sent to training camps outside the state. Collins, *History of Kentucky,* I, 130, 132, 133.

76. It was well that George Dick sold all of his books before May 14, 1864. On that date General Burbridge issued General Order No. 39 in which he prohibited the circulation of *The Life of Stonewall Jackson* and similar books. *Ibid.,* 133.

April 14 – Was taken with a severe chill.

April 15 – Great pain in my jaw kept me in bed.

April 16 – Still sick. Bro J. W. Lambuth, our missionary to China, came over to see me. He is a good man I think but seems to lack the necessary energy & adaptation to make a successful collector of missionary funds. I was too unwell to be very much interested in his company.

April 18 – At home. Can eat but alittle mush & milk & have but little strength.

April 19 – Rode out alittle.

April 20 – Called to see father. One of his servants *Delilah* started off to Paducah, was caught in Tenn & returned to him. The papers are full of reports of Forrests capturing & killing negro troops.[77] There is a decided lull in negro enlistments. They *seem* more contented. Large numbers are dying at Clarksville.

April 21 – The Spring is unusually backward. The woods look almost like winter. Pastures cannot grow. The air is cold & wind blows North & West nearly all the time. This season has disproved the old adage "An early Easter brings an early Spring."

April 23 – Ginnie & I with little Georgie went to aunt Betsy's. The old lady is quite lowspirited. Thieves & robbers have stolen her last horse, having taken seven. This robbing is alarmingly on the increase. Bands of soldiers, organized for protection to the country, steal away from their commands disguised as rebel guerillas and rob whatever they can. Last night a band of them stole several hundred dollars at Keysburg. When one of them was killed & another caught by citizens, they proved to be federal soldiers from Springfield. The papers are full of accounts of pillage & plunder in many parts of Ky.

Genl Grant, with the grandest army of the world is making one more movement against Richmond – & Lee with the flower & power of the rebel armies is waiting for him. Tremendous will be the shock.

April 25 – Soon after I went to bed a messenger called to me to go to see Dan Farris at Henry Browders. His middle finger had been shot off in one of the Va battles & his left hand and arm were paralysed from the effect. He had come back & taken the oath & was at work for Dr Baker driving oxen. To day he was taken with pain in the arm – which increased so fearfully that he raved like a madman – & went perfectly crazy with pain. In his delirium he was fighting his

---

77. George Dick is probably referring to Major General Nathan Bedford Forrest's attack on Fort Pillow, just north of Memphis, on April 12, 1864. The Fort was defended by 557 Union troops, including 262 blacks. Forrest sent 1500 men against them. According to Federal reports, over 200 men, especially blacks, were shot down after they had surrendered. Long, *Civil War Day By Day,* 484.

battles over, burying the dead, charging batteries, talking to his comrades, & cursing yankees, with the most awful oaths. Alternately praying & swearing. I staid all night with him but he was not in a condition to be benefited by religious services. He was sometimes amusing & sometimes shocking. I never felt so fully before the horrors & wickedness of war. When he thought he was burying the dead he was cursing & villifying yankees, urging the boys not to bury them deep, the buzzards would eat them − they would be nearer heaven than ever again − and all such horrible talk. It must be most revolting to refined sensibilities.

May 1 − [Hadensville] Bright, bland beautiful day. So like a Holy Sabbath. The report of soldiers out pressing horses turned many away from church. I preached Ex[odus] 2.9 with good effect and appointed a day for Sab[bath] school to meet − preached to a large crowd of negroes at 3 ½.

May 3 − [Olmstead] Prized tob[acco] till dinner. Went with Lizzie to Allensville. Bo[ugh]t coffee @ 50. cts pr lb, tea 2.25, molasses (common) 1.25 per gal, cheese .25 pr lb, domestic 50 cts pr yd & other articles in proportion. The expenses of living are double. Corn is 85 cts pr bu here and 1.30 pr bu farther up the country − wheat will be a failure to the extent of 1/2. I think mine will hardly make the seed sown. Tob[acco] is worth 20 cts pr lb here, and proportionately more in Louisville & N.Y. My man *Abram* made a large crop, about an acre which is worth more than $100 at home.

May 4 − Lizzie & I went to town trading, collected $500 advance on my tob[acco] − paid taxes, debts &c.

May 7 − Large congregation for Sat. at Bells Chapel. I preached Rom[ans] 6.17. Had good classmeeting & the church seemed much refreshed. The religious tone of this society seems improving. I staid with several friends at Greenfield's. He is very bitter against Lincoln & his party. There is a wonderful change in the party feeling in this country. The so called union party is now divided into Radical or abolition & conservative or constitutional.

May 9 − Stopped to pray with sister Puckett & at James Small's to read accounts of the terrible battles pending in Virginia between the fed[eral] Genl Grant & the rebel Genl Lee − each commanding the largest armies ever brought to the field in America.[78] The country is full of the most intense interest & anxiety, all concurring in the belief that this campaign will end the war − for weal or woe.

May 12 − At home. The papers are still full of battle rumors, the storm is breaking in vengeance − the sky is red with blood. Reports are confused & conflicting − both parties claiming victory. Oh the deep anxiety of the public.

---

78. Grant had now joined General Meade in preparation for a major effort against Lee. On May 3, he ordered Meade and the Army of the Potomac across the Rapidan River toward Richmond. Lee engaged Grant on May 5−6 in the Battle of the Wilderness, the first great battle of 1864. Union losses were estimated at over 17,000 out of 100,000; the Confederates lost approximately 7500 out of 60,000. *Ibid.,* 492 ff.

May 14 – The news comes in flaming with accounts of federal victories & rout & ruin to Lees army – but must be looked upon with allowance.[79]

May 25 – Busy on the farm.

May 29 – Bright sabbath! Large crowd at Hadensville. Crenshaw preached a fine sermon – raised missionary collection – got 27.30. In afternoon I preached to a smaller but attentive congregation – got upward of 60. subscribed & paid in.

Coming home I met a crowd of negroes some of whom told me of the burning of my negro cabin to day with all the clothing, furniture, money & other property of my poor negroes. Their testimony makes it an incendiary job – but who would be so base? This is the second loss of the kind they have sustained. I feel very sorry for them & will help them as far as I can.

May 30 – Went to town to report my collection & got supplies for my poor negroes. I was sent for at night to see James Carr die, aided in laying him out.

May 31 – Busy repairing fence destroyed by fire. Papers now excite the country with conjectures on the early capture of Richmond. Federal losses reported at 75,000 to 100,000 men. We here are overrun with robbers, who even in the broad day light halt & rob men on the high way. This county & Todd have both been full of them for a few days and a number of persons have been their victims. It is said that $2000 were stolen about Daysville – & at Trenton Dr Coleman was shot, because he would not give up his watch. This party were supposed to be federal soldiers, several companies of whom have been guilty of similar offenses.

June 1 – Our cousins, Minerva Hutchings, Carrie Walker, Ellen & Mary Sydnor kindly came over to day, to help Lizzie make up some more clothing for our poor negroes. Thank God for good friends.

June 4 – Went to Hadensville, held classmeeting, dined at Sister Salmon's, a nice & intelligent Baptist. She has a daughter, who is uncommonly intellectual, & a son an idiot. This latter took a great fancy to me & constantly clung to me.

June 6 – Got home early, went on train to see Mr Warfield – reported sick – glad to see me – called on his sick negroes.

---

79. On May 8 Grant and Lee faced each other once more at Spotsylvania Court House, the beginning of a series of battles that continued until May 21. Federal losses during this period were put at 17,500 out of 100,000. There are no reliable statistics for the Confederates. Lee, however, had not been routed. *Ibid.*, 496 ff. Continuing encounters between Grant and Lee finally culminated in the nine month siege of Petersburg, which was finally occupied on April 3, 1865. Six days later Lee surrendered at Appomattox Court House.

June 7 – Mr Warfield sent Lizzie a present of 100$. I came home in the morning & spent day superintending business. Negroes worked better than usual, seemed cheerful and obedient.

June 8 – A day of strange feelings! Found my plantation entirely deserted by negroes – not one left! *Abram, Bob, Jeff, George, & Ellen, Dolly Underwood, William, Ida, Nicholas, & Lucy* all gone! Took my wagon, old carriage, two horses & two mules. We felt lighter some how than usual, felt poorer, but freer, more dependent, yet more self-reliant. Lizzie got breakfast & I milked the cows. The children seemed gleeful & at family prayer we earnestly invoked Gods blessing, guidance and good providence in our new circumstances. William [Browder] & I with a number of others set out in search of our horses & wagons. Ten negroes left me – 3 from father – 8 from Nelson Waters – six from McCulloch, 3 from John Vick & others in a different neighborhood. We met part of the troop arrested and brought back – & had a vast deal of trouble & vexation in separating & deciding what to do with them. *George & Ellen* & all mine except *Jeff* and *Abe* escaped leaving their clothes & all their goods. We put the men under guard to send to Louisville & just as my wagon & carriage got in with the baggage, my brother William came with all the rest of our fugitives – looking warn, sad and confounded. They had been overtaken in a few miles of Clarksville. We whipped *Jeff & Bob & Lucy, & Ellen* made herself sick – quite sick – in the long tramp through heat, mud & rain, after they left the wagons. Poor unfortunate creatures, how I pity them, deceived & misled as they have been, yet listening to strangers rather than those who have raised & cared for them. They have been greatly abused in their minds. I should have been glad if they had gotten safe into Clarksville without my responsibility.

June 9 – We sent my *Abe*, who was very insolent & defiant to the man who arrested him – with fathers *Albert* & McCullochs *Rodney* – to Louisville to be hired out. Nelson Waters *Martha* was also very insolent & she was sent off. This was a sad day to me. Poor *Ellen* seems heartbroken & will not eat. She deeply regrets her folly & wishes *George* to come home & stay with her. The whole race have shown themselves so false & treacherous that few can confide in them atall, but *Ellen* has not lied to us nor stolen anything from us. Her poor children seem delighted to get back home & play with my children. I have acted in good faith with mine.

To night I went to marry George Adams & Harriet Sandifer about 5 miles distance. When I got back my dog kept a strange barking & would not be quieted. I tried to call him in the house & he would not come. I forced him in – he barked in the house and I turned him out. Soon I heard foot steps & a voice called the dog by name – Caesar. Some one went to the kitchen door & called to the negroes to open the door, said they would not hurt anyone. *Ellen* was frightened badly, as her groans indicated, yet she had the door opened! I went to get my gun – it was gone! The truth flashed upon me, the negroes had stolen it out. I gently called up the school boys, they had only one single shooting pistol. Just as I came down my wife opened the door & saw two negroes armed & in federal uniform standing by the door, one of whom immediately levelled his gun at her! She demanded who they were & what they wanted? They said "We are soldiers, come to get them people what was turned back." Lizzie replied "There are the people in the kitchen, they may go if they will, we did not bring them back & do not want them if they want to go with you." She told them that she had soldiers here who would be down in a minute. They swore they were ready for us & ordered the men to form a line. I saw some of them & heard the click of their guns. Just then I called out aloud, "Come on men with your guns & bring the pistols." At this they "fell back," talked awhile & retired, leaving us to watch through the remainder of the night.

At daylight I went out but could make no discoveries. *Ellen* said they swore they would take her back or burn up the premises. She says she begged them to go away – that she did not know any of them, but suspected that they were not soldiers. I learned that McCullochs *Boot,* a boy I used to hire, had found out through *Lucy* where my gun was – & taken it away. I was very angry at *Lucy* & when she denied any knowledge of the gun I cocked my pistol as though I would shoot & she told the same story that I had heard through another source. I ordered her to pack up & be ready to go on the cars to Louisville, but she wept, confessed her fault & begged to stay, so that I gave her another trial. Truly these are strange times. I can hardly realize the scenes we are passing through. I pray for God's guidance & protection.

June 15 – Another excitement! Last night a company of negroes claiming to be federal soldiers came here and demanded the surrender of my negro women! Said they had orders from Col Smith, but refused to show the order. I told them they were liars, that Col Smith had no authority in Ky. & did not send them, that as for *Ellen,* she was welcome to go if she was able to ride. I had intended sending her back as soon as I could, but I would not give up *Lucy* & the boys & would kill the first negro that broke into my house. They ordered me to open the door, threatened to "make me see hellfire if I did not" &c but I refused & told them to come in if they liked. They said a white man was with them and they were 35 in number, but they lied in both statements. I told them they were liars, cowards, & scoundrels, that their lives were in my hands. I could kill them if I wished, but did not want to shed blood. I then ordered them to stand & not leave, but they ran & soon were going full speed on the big road with *Ellen* & her 5 children on their way to Clarksville, although she has been too sick to eat or get out of bed since she was brought back. Pink Edwards & William Sadler [boarders] would have shot if I had let them. I did not feel that I would be morally justifiable in taking the life of a man under the circumstances. This was the ruling consideration. They are such treacherous & revengeful creatures, that our house may be burned at anytime. They threatened, if we fired on them, to burn the house & us in it.

After they left I examined & found my wagon gone. They said they brought a wagon with them. I looked for my horses to follow & recover the wagon, but could not find a horse – thought they were all gone, but found them in the morning.

June 16 – Have been feeble. Neighbors say I ought by all means to have killed some of those negroes – but I did not feel willing to have the remainder of my life embittered with the reflection that I had killed a fellow mortal.

The night before these fellows came to my house, a company of white thieves went to John Millers store & robbed him of several hundred dollars worth of goods. They promised to pay cash! Surely we have fallen upon evil times.

June 17 – Have been very busy plowing my corn. I think we are happier & less troubled without the negroes than with them. If *Jeff* & *Bob* stay & we keep well we can make a crop. *Lucy* seems anxious to get off with the Yankees.

June 20 – I am pleasantly surprised to find that my hogshead of *lug* tobacco in N.Y. had been sold for 27 cts lb – 1860 lbs netting me $458.15, after 44.00 charges. I now entertain good hope of getting clear of debt and having a sure title to a home for my dear wife and children.

June 21, 22 – Attending the examination of pupils at Prof Fuqua's School at Volney – am well pleased with the performances – classes have been well taught.

June 23 – Not well. Weather dry & hot. Negroes are running away, & others are coming back with doleful tales of disappointment, hunger & wretchedness. Papers give horrid accounts of slaughter & destruction of life and property, around Petersburg Va. & Marietta Georgia. Our Exhibition & concert were largely attended & excellent order prevailed. The performances were very fine. My little boys Robt & Hanson acquitted themselves finely & gained much applause.

Several horses were missing & a horse & buggie belonging to my cousin Mrs Tom Shaw could not be found until next day & then the sachel of clothes was gone. She came home with us in our wagon & the same night our *Lucy* ran off to the Yankees.

June 24 – My Dear Father & Mother, always kind sent *Cornelia* to help us. I feel assured that in some way God will provide for us. I think the loss of my negroes may prove a blessing to my children – active exertion may give them stronger constitutions & they will learn self reliance. God's will be done.

To night there is a grand fancy party at Dr H[utching]'s & the girls & boys appear in strange costumes.

July 1 – Took Lizzie, Helen, & Luther down to Mr. Warfields in the buggie.

July 4 – [Olmstead] Glorious day of Liberty. I worked, planting & hoeing tob[acco]. Grant must take Richmond. Oh for an end of this war! Terrible battles in Georgia & Virginia have not yet crushed the rebellion. One dollar in gold is now selling for 3 in U.S. notes & the tendency is upward. Goods of all classes advance in proportion.

July 6 – Lizzie came home. The passenger train got detached from the other cars – & just before the locomotive got into my fathers field, three pistol shots were fired, causing great alarm on the train, which speedily ran to Russellville & returned with an extra company of soldiers. Tom Morrow, a noted guerilla, was the only one in the neighborhood & he did the shooting but no one was hurt.

July 9 – Busy for several days working tob[acco] & saving oats. To day I went to Bell's chapel, had a very small audience. I spent the night with Bro Petree. He is now almost 80 & his wife 70, yet he is reduced to the necessity of driving cows, & doing the errands of a boy & his wife must wash & cook on account of their slaves escaping to the federal lines where they are harbored & taught insubordination to their owners. The old gentleman is very bitter against Lincoln, & wonders why in his extreme loyalty he could not sooner discern the intentions of the republican party.

July 12 – [Olmstead] Last night a band of thieves robbed George Herndon of his money, watch, & work horses, knocked him down & otherwise abused him. Surely we are in evil times. My father had carried a lot of provisions to the depot to send to my brother Frank at Chicago, but the agent had gotten orders to ship nothing to or for a rebel sympathizer & receive no freight! Yesterdays paper reports the rebels carrying things their own way in Maryland.

August 9 – I preached at Hermon on 3d Sat – & Sun evening went as far as Tom Clarks to attend Morton's meeting at Salubria. Monday evening went to George Clark's & was taken sick. Tuesday rode home through hot sun, barely able to be up. Took medicine, Dr came. I was very ill – bilious fever, tending to congestion of stomach & liver. I thought I was going to die. I was resigned & very happy – felt very unworthy, but had large views of the grace of God in Christ Jesus. My wife & children nursed me most tenderly – neighbors were very kind, the Dr was very attentive & by the grace of God I recovered. I suffered a great deal. My dear wife watched me night & day & almost made herself sick. Last Friday I ventured to town. For the first time I saw several companies of negro soldiers. The sight was very revolting to me & other Kentuckians.

August 13 – A few days ago my father and a few of his friends, W. T. Evans & James Small among them, set out for Louisville, Newyork & Chicago, to look after their tob[acco], their prisoner sons, & to stay until the great excitement in Ky about the arrests should subside. Very many prominent citizens of our state have been recently imprisoned by military order, without knowing the charges against them or who accused them.[80]

To day I was well enough (though suffering with a large rising under my left arm) to go to Bells chapel & preach with some liberty Gal[atians] 6.9.

---

80. President Lincoln was alarmed at the frequency of Confederate guerrilla raids into Kentucky. On July 5, 1864, he suspended the writ of habeas corpus and proclaimed martial law in the state. Collins, *History of Kentucky,* I, 135.

August 25 – For 13 days the meeting has continued being frequently disturbed by the presence of federal soldiers pressing horses (exclusively from Southern sympathizers) and the almost daily rains of the first week. 16 or 18 persons professed religion & almost as many joined our church. Bro W. H. Morrison our P[residing] E[lder] labored zealously & was rewarded by the conversion of both his boys. Bros Jordan Moore & Dr Phillips also labored efficiently. Bro J. C. Petree came in time to preach the closing sermon to day.

August 26 – Came home – found my dear wife much dispirited by my long delay. All well, thank God!

August 29 – A day of excitement in America. The great Democratic convention meets at Chicago resolved to defeat the Lincoln administration.

August 30 – On Friday night last, poor Joel Grubbs, an unfortunate man who had killed two men & had been a drunkard, but who was in many respects a clever men with a warm heart and generous impulses, was taken out of his house by federal soldiers & killed, not far from his home! There is much excitement & as this is the first case of the kind in our county, many fear a dreadful policy is inaugurated. Grubbs is the step-father of Billy Cloud who is said to be a guerilla & robber.

I received to day acct. of sales of my two hogshead of tob[acco], one at 45 cts the other at 53 cts pr lb in N.Y. both bringing the sum of $1722.65 added to my lug hgd [hogshead] – make upwards of $2200.00 in Green back for my little crop, leaving me $2000 clear – which will leave me free from debt if used as the law allows – as legal tender. I am thankful for the prospect. My wife will now have a home & by God's blessing we can live without our negroes. I consider myself fortunate & feel as if God's especial Providence directed my good fortune. Lizzie is at aunt Betsy's – her feeble health is a subject of sadness to me.

September 1 – Yesterday I preached in the afternoon on paying vows, & several penitents came forward – among them my dear little Hanson – weeping & praying & confessing himself a sinner. He seemed to understand the condition of salvation intellectually but I could not see that he was so earnestly engaged as I should like, yet he presently claimed that the Lord had forgiven him & made him happy & to day he insists on the same thing – and joined the church. I pray for the early conversion of my children & rejoice in every moment in that direction.

September 2 – I went to Russellville & received pay for my tob[acco] & paid off most of my debts. Many people were in town paying the amount assessed to them by the military, to indemnify union citizens for losses by rebels & guerillas. The best, & purest, most honorable, peaceable & quiet men in our country are by that act classed with horse thieves & house burners & made to pay for what they never did, and as a general rule the damages assessed have been three or four times as much as was sustained. It is supposed that the military get a large share of the booty. My father, uncle Dick & D. B. Sydnor paid each $100. on this last claim – L. H. Ferguson 500 & others in proportion. N. H. Waters, whose negroes house, provisions, & happiness are all destroyed in the war, was assessed $200. more and being unable to pay it has left the country.

September 5 – Returning home [from Aunt Betsy's] I met a squad of negro cavalry, or mounted infantry, pressing negroes, horses &c. They took the only man from Bro Smith notwithstanding his own & his wifes entreaties in view of his helplessness & the unwillingness of the negro to go with them. To day the federal draft was to begin & hundreds of young men are leaving for the South, and married men are looking for negro substitutes. I have had some little uneasiness myself, but am waiting.

Fourteen years ago this day I was married and the longer I live with my dear wife the more I love & esteem her. I see more of her excellencies & have daily cause to thank God for so good a gift. My home is lonely & cheerless without her – and I always feel safer & happier when she is with me. I left her with her sister & must keep house, without her for the present. To leave my family & be forced into the Lincoln army, I fear would destroy my soul & body. I pray God to deliver me.

September 6 – Went to William Gill's & to Allensville & paid him $320 on a note he holds against me. I am thankful to be almost free from debt, yet I dislike the idea of paying in depreciated currency. Gold & silver are enormously high. Their value is relatively increased, they will buy more horses, houses, land – stocks – bonds, merchandize than before – & it is a question whether the man who would exact gold or silver on *old* notes is not as unjust as the man who pays *old* notes with legal tender Greenbacks.

There is much talk about the reported fall of Atlanta Ga & the rout of the rebel army. There is a collision between the civil & military authorities in Ky. Governor Bramlette in a proclamation, forewarns & forbids the courts of Ky to obey a military order of Genl. Ewing.[81] What next.

September 9 – My wife & children came home. I was glad to see them well. Night before last, a base band of robbers stole John Millers goods, trampled some under their feet, took John Vick out & hung him alittle to make him give up his money – & some of them ravished two negro women, one at Vicks – the other at Millers. To day I went to town & deposited what money I had in the bank – not wishing to be robbed. For the first time I submitted to what Kentuckians call the humiliation of showing a military pass to negro pickets. The fellow took it *bottom upwards,* looked at it & gave it back to me.

---

81. On September 5 the Governor issued a proclamation forbidding compliance with Order No. 20, issued August 29 by Brigadier General Hugh Ewing. The Order required county courts to impose upon taxpayers a levy "sufficient to arm, mount and pay 50 men, to be raised in each county, and maintained until further orders." President Lincoln revoked the order. *Ibid.,* 140.

September 13 – Sold some bacon @ 20 cts pr lb & that is less than the market price – corn is six dollars pr bushel – and very scarce.

September 15 – I attended David Hutching's sale. Federals came there and took Wilson Page away with them.

September 16 – This evening the cars killed my fine calf for which I had been offered $30.

September 21 – As I sat in the field preparing skewers for my children to save tob[acco] leaves, a sad feeling & momentary presentiment of bad news came over me. I went to the house & was reading the Bible when Tom Sydnor & my brother Wm came & told me that I was *drafted! DRAFTED!* into the federal army. Shocking, crushing, horrifying intelligence! It casts a deep gloom over me & shadows like death settle down over my family. I am a man of peace. I cannot, I will not fight.

September 22 – I went to Bowling Green, to see about it. Too true, I am drafted. God have mercy! I cannot, will not gird on carnal weapons & go forth to stain my hands in the blood of battle, then return to minister at Gods altar. I am at a great loss what to do. I trust in Gods overruling Providence.

September 23 – I went to Russellville, having partially engaged a substitute. He did not come up. I was examined by a surgeon & declared unfit for duty. Tom Clark was in my condition & was exempted – this gave me hope. I telegraphed to Louisville for a substitute & several friends are at work here. Many seem interested for me & offer me money in any quantity.

September 24 – Went to Bowling Green to urge my plea of exemption for a rupture & hernia – could not be exempted. They were drafting Todd county & the excitement was intense. A soldier has promised me a substitute but failed. My good brother William left home on Thursday morning & has been gone ever since – but he got me a substitute! Such is the anxiety to procure them that 12 & 1500$ are offered, & every effort is made to overreach & dispossess those who bring them up. William & I took our man out at back end of the car, went *around* the crowd & got a room at a hotel until the arrangements could be made. The cars came before I got him enlisted & I had to leave William to do what he could for me. I was very uneasy & left with a heavy heart. Friends on the cars promised to help me – offered me money in abundance to get a substitute at any price. There is great distress in the land. I never saw such times before – hope I never shall again.

September 25 – Bro Morrison, overjoyed at escaping the draft, went with me to Salem & preached for me. I was sad, sad, sad. Came home very much oppressed & wondering what to do or where to go. Sad – sad – sad. I went out to pray – felt some comfort, committed my cause to God & promised to be more faithful if God would deliver me from this great calamity. I came in & was meditating, when *Jeff* came in & brought Williams note informing me that my substitute was accepted & I was free! Oh how my heart leaped with joy & gratitude! I laughed & cried & thanked God. No worldly care ever distressed me so – no worldly news ever gave me such relief.

Uncle Dick [Browder] offered me $400. & Dr Hutchings my union cousin, offered me a thousand dollars & said he would rather *give* me the amount than see me in the army. Friends from every quarter send me pledges of as much money as I needed & urged me to get a substitute at *any price*. I am thankful for such friends – at home, in Russellville, on my circuit, offers of money & expressions of sympathy come. I believe in Gods good providence.

September 26 – I feel like a new man. My friends greet me as if I had escaped from destruction. I worked a few hours, then went over to depot to meet my father who went to Bowling Green to help get my substitute.

September 27 – At work in my tobacco. The draft is all the talk. The distress is great, numbers of men are going to the rebel army, few beside negroes are going to the other. It is said that guerillas threaten the lives of all who put in negro substitutes. Robber outrages increase. Joab Smith, a quiet, harmless man, was taken out of his bed, a few nights ago & murdered in his own yard, near Keysburg. No man is safe.

This evening my man *Abram* returned from Louisville, professing a settled purpose to stay at home.

September 28 – Rainy & damp. At midnight I was called up to see a dying woman! six miles distance. The night was dark & cloudy, my horse was blind, my wife was sick, I was not well. Several men had been called out & killed, the negro that came was stranger. Lizzie was afraid for me to go & I first declined, but again remembered my vow & ordered my horse. I reached Coalman Lyne's in safety. Sarah Waters was still alive, had been greatly alarmed at the idea of death – wanted me to talk & sing & pray.

September 29 – Sang & prayed again. Sarah seemed comforted. I came home & found cousin Rose [Walker] here.

October 1 – Lizzie went with me to Hadensville. I preached to a small audience Rom[ans] 5.3,4,5. Spent the night at John Roachs. The family is in distress. Their son John is drafted. There are seasons of great trouble now passing over us. Every neighborhood is in distress. Some negroes are trying to buy substitutes.

October 2 – Lizzie & I spent the night with sister Mimms. One of her negroes is drafted & has quit work. So of others in the country & the excitement about the draft is much in the way of our meeting.

October 3 – Bro Alexander was with me & preached well but a company of federal soldiers rode right up to the door & stood for some time & so confused & disturbed the people that the sermon lost its effect. I brought Lizzie home.

October 7 – Last night guerillas robbed Daysville – captured Tom Blakey, Maj. of a negro regiment & would have shot him if he had not proved by Billy Grinter that he had resigned.

October 9 – [Bell's Chapel] Beautiful Sabbath, small audience. I preached on "Doing what Christ says" Lu[ke] 6.46. I need the sermon myself. Great excitement on account of rebel Genl Lyons attack upon Hopkinsville. The rumor dispersed a large negro gathering at the chapel in great haste. At all points on the circuit they ask for my return, this is gratifying – I wish to serve this people again.

October 15 – Bros Lewis, Alexander & I started to [Annual] Conf[erence] – was astonished at the crowd of travel.

October 16 – [Louisville] Went to 12th St to Bro. Brewers class. Alick & I received such demonstrations of love and affection as are rarely witnessed. Old friends hugged us to their bosoms, wept over us & blessed us in the name of the Lord. In the class, a man named Dolley, told me that he was convicted under my preaching 15 years ago & after long delay was brought to the Savior.[82] Bro Hall had been invited to preach & he did so with good effect. It was quite a coincidence that the three pastors who first served that church, viz myself Bro Alexander & Bro Hall, should all meet at one time at old 12th. I felt sad to see so few familiar faces. My old friends are dead or removed & I only recognized 12 or 15 in the congregation.

I was surprised at the vast improvement in the city. Localities once familiar to me, I could not recognize atall. At night Bish[op] Kavanaugh preached a good sermon at Walnut St.

October 17 – After tramping over the city on business we took the cars for Portland, thence crossed to New Albany & there spent the day waiting for the Golden Eagle. Walked over the city & was astonished at its size. The Eagle came on about sunset & we were delighted with her splendid fare & fine accommodations, as well as her gentlemanly officers. I never saw such fare on a boat before. Nearly every variety of fresh meats, fish & fowl, oyster, sardines, pickles, cakes, & confectionaries & tropical fruits in abundance.

October 18 – I arranged with the Capt. for Bish[op] Kavanaugh to preach at night – & he did it well. At 12 we reached Henderson – & lodged at the Hancock house paying 1.50 for a little sleep & a poor breakfast.

---

82. George Dick pastored the Twelfth Street Mission during 1848–49, his third year in the ministry. *Minutes of the Annual Conferences of the Methodist Episcopal Church South, for the Years 1845–1857* (n.p., n.d.), 165.

October 19 – Glad to see a full attendance of preachers. Bro Alexander & I boarded with my old friend Mrs Dr Glass, a sister of Hon. A. Dixon. I was agreeably surprised to witness the great improvement in the city – & rejoiced to receive the cordial greetings of the friends I knew and loved in other days. I see here many familiar faces, but I miss many who once loved me. They are gone to the church above – & some I learn have turned back to the "flesh pots of Egypt." Little boys & girls that used to sit on my lap 14 years ago, now are married & ask me out to dine & sup with them. So one generation pushes another to the tomb.

October 20 – Business progresses pleasantly. Good humor & love prevail. All the preachers think they have the best home. All the families try to excel others in kindness & attention to their preachers. I heard Gov Powell of U.S. Senate speak against Lincoln. He remembered me & seemed glad to see me, as I certainly was to see him. I never saw more harmony among the preachers. To day we had the memories of our deceased brethren & we had a melting time as we spoke of their labors of love & their triumphant deathbed scenes.

October 21 – I preached at 11 oclock with considerable liberty, Mal[achi] 3.16,17. I defended class meetings earnestly, & was surprised afterward to learn that an intelligent Presbyterian lady had pronounced it the best sermon she had heard during the Conf[erence].

October 22 – The conference progresses harmoniously. Rebel soldiers occupy the town, but they disturb no one. I saw 175, more or less, this morning on the street. The gun boat opened on them and they left.

October 24 – I have collected 22.50 for sister Randolph who was robbed a few nights ago of her cloak, dress, shoes, jewelry & gold, by a body of lawless wicked men, supposed to belong in Indiana. We finished the business of the Conference at night & after a long & interesting lecture, Bishop Kavanaugh read our appointments. The preachers with few exceptions were pleased, & I was delighted to be returned to Hadensville circuit.

Thus closed one of the most interesting Conferences I ever attended. No trials, no charges, some old cases were referred to the Presiding Elders. Bro T. J. Moore's character passed & he was sent to Fairview. Bro Artemas Brown withdrew, stating that his blood was all buckeye – that if the federal arms prevailed the M. E. Church South was disorganized & if the rebellion succeeded, there would be no room here for yankee preachers.

At the Missionary meeting Bros Brush & Linn indulged in the usual pleasantries on such occasions and some laughing ensued, whereupon Bro Cunningham very abruptly declared the meeting an irreligious one & called for singing & prayer as a means of reassuming a religious form. It was very abrupt & indecorous & he afterward saw his error & publicly begged pardon. With this exception our session was one of uninterrupted good feeling, & this occurrence was only momentary in its unpleasant consequences.

October 25 — Soon after breakfast, we learned that the Golden Eagle was at the wharf & Alick & I with a large number of other preachers took hasty leave of our kind friends & took passage for Louisville.

October 26 — The breaking of the "doctor"[83] detained the boat several hours & we did not get to Louisville until after night. Jimmy Lewis, Alick & I found comfortable quarters at cousin D. B. Hutchings.

October 27 — An immense crowd at the depot, made it impossible to get on the cars, and we had time to get up our goods. Col Fairleigh gave Jimmy Lewis a permit for himself & me & we bought cloaks, dresses, shoes &c at better terms than we could get them in Russellville. At 3 oclock the crowd still thronged the depot & we tried, earnestly but in vain to get on the cars. We took seats on the night train in box cars, such as cattle had occupied, but our hearts failed & we remained over night. I had a presentiment of danger on Muldraugh's hill, & felt that it was almost providential that David H[utchings] came down & advised us not to go. So we spent the night with him & he & I walked two miles, although I was very tired, to see Mrs Turners sick child. When we reached the house it was dead & bitter was the mothers grief. Just three years ago last Monday I preached her little Laura's funeral.

October 28 — By Davids management & help we got seats on the cars. At Bowling Green we learned that the night train had a collision on Muldraughs hill & one car was thrown off the track! I felt that we made a fortunate escape. I was very happy to get home & find my dear wife & children well. They greet me joyfully, as always they do.

November 8 — Very rainy — went to election — voted for McClellan — do not like him, but think he is better than Mr Lincoln. He was nominated by the peace men — & says he will restore the constitution. A small vote is cast, everybody feeling that Lincoln will be elected by force or fraud. This day, I think seals the fate of republican government in the U.S.[84]

November 12 — Negro Soldiers, just below us, pressing other negroes into service, caused a stampede in the neighborhood among the black men. My wife was not willing for me to leave today.

November 17 — A rebel prisoner, Capt Sam. W. English — 65th N.C. vol[unteers] — confined in block 9, Johnsons Island writes to me for clothes — sends a permit. I must send them.

---

83. The "doctor" was an independent steam pump with a working beam used on western river steamers.

84. George Dick's views on the election of 1864 were shared by most Kentuckians. Gen. McClellan, the Democratic nominee, lost the election to Lincoln but easily won Kentucky's vote by a margin of 64,546 to 27,797. Harrison, *Civil War in Kentucky*, 87.

November 19 – Went to Quarterly meeting, few out – church seems very dead.

November 20 – Spent the night with Bro Morrison at J. H. Hoozers [Hadensville] where the family & others in the community are much distressed by negro soldiers coming out from Clarksville and forcing all their negro men into service. The poor negroes were in great distress – went away weeping. They were made to stand in a line & orders given for all who were determined to go home to stand out – several stepped out, & one was knocked down & bayoneted & another was choked with a rope until his tongue hung out – others were afraid to step out, & so the oath was administered & they claimed as soldiers! Oh, the horrors & outrages of civil war & abolition power!

November 21 – Quarterly Conf[erence] met this morning at Jack Hoozers. They estimated my claim at 700. but had collected nothing. I came home. Very cold, freezing & snowing. Glad to find that my hogs were killed.

December 3 – I had class meeting at Hadensville, good time, had some religious comfort. One sister shouted aloud. Negroes returning from Clarksville are creating quite a sensation. I saw several coming back to their masters.

December 4 – I preached with some liberty on Dan[iel] 12.13 to a congregation apparently attentive, but really more interested in the exciting rumors that flood the country & the heavy cannonading near Nashville than in the sermon.

December 5 – Great excitement. Rebels are reported shelling Nashville & crossing Cumberland. Troops are moving in haste & horses are being gathered up in all directions by federals who tell us the rebels are coming. All is apprehension & suspense.

December 6 – Started by light [for home], to hide my poor blind horse & old Kate from the press gang. Went through the woods into their rear. Spent the day at D. E. Sydnors & Allensville – could painfully hear the booming cannon & imagine the horrors of the battle at Nashville. Rumors excite the public.

December 7 – John Vick wants me to take *Mary, Abrams* wife, & children & keep them until after the war. Our *Lucy* sends a request to come back to us. We consented.

December 12 – Came home [from Bell's Chapel], found Elkton in commotion. Hopkinsville is occupied by rebels & citizens & soldiers are flying. Merchants at Elkton had packed their goods on wagons to send off. All is excitement & suspense. Genl Hood's rebel army besieges & threatens Nashville & a change in powers is expected here.

December 13 – Great excitement in Russellville. McCooks fed[eral] brigade, estimated 5000 strong, passed through to attack Lyon at Hopkinsville. The men robbed the people on the route, of horses, bacon, fowl &c in the most reckless manner. Many strangers crowd into Russellville, flying from the rebel conscript.

December 22 – For several days the weather has been cold & disagreeable. Last Sat & Sun. continual rain kept me from Mt Hermon. Robbers have been through & plundered several houses. Hood is badly defeated & travelling southward. There is a general sadness & misgiving among Southern people.

Matrimony revives. I went though the cold & married John Nick Hoozer to Ann D. Edwards. The old people do not seem pleased. I see a painful increase of selfwill & wickedness in our land.

December 25 – Our dear children were getting up all through the night to see what Santaclaus had brought & were in great glee over candies nuts, & toys.

December 26 – Bought a few toys for my children to give them kind remembrances of home.

December 27 – Everybody seems quiet & calm, although the war rages & we look for increasing troubles. Lizzie & I went over to spend the day with father. The war & the troubles of the country weigh heavily on the old.

December 29 – I went to Russellville, Helen with me. My hired boys did not seem inclined to come back.

December 31 – Very cold, snow on ground. Nobody at Hadensville but a kind-hearted idiot, John Salmon. I spent night with his mother. We had a pleasant time & the old year dies, on a very cold night.

Volume IV
1865–1870

"Sometimes I have been sick & sometimes very busy."

January 1, 1865 — Hail another year! May peace return this year to our native land! I pray God, the horrors & miseries of last year may not be reinacted in this. The day is clear, cold & bright. A blessed Sabbath. I preached at Hadensville to a small audience, on sowing & reaping, then went down & spent the night with Bro Guthridge L. Randle. On the way I saw some federal soldiers riding about in Mr. Corneal's yard, pretending to be looking for a squad of rebels. They inquired of me where they could get a New Year's dinner!

I feel resolved to try to spend this year, more profitably than I did last year. I must be more industrous, both for the church & for my family. I have no help hired, but my man *Abram*, & if he is faithful I expect to give him ¼ of all the tob[acco] he makes. If we can have health, we can make a comfortable support.

January 2 — I spent the forenoon & dined with Bro John Snaden, then went to see Mr Warfield. He was well & gone to Clarksville to attend the burial of his wifes nephew William Munford, a very excellent & noble young man, who was acting Col. in Hoods rebel army, & was just in the act of cheering on his men, at the very cannons mouth, on the 30th of Nov. at Franklin Ten[n] when he fell shot in the head, & through both arms & both legs, with grapeshot. The family are in great distress. Mr Warfield got a letter from [his son] George who was captured, near Nashville on the 15th of Dec & carried to Camp Douglas where he is with my brother Frank. Poor boy! He has passed through hard times.

January 4 — I came home & went to work getting up my corn. Many negroes are leaving their masters & some are refusing to work. My man *Abe* solemnly vows that he will not leave me again. I have almost lost confidence in all of them.

January 11 — This is my 38th birthday! I weigh 164 lbs and am tolerably healthy. My throat is almost well & in the midst of evils, I am surrounded with mercies. I think I am gaining some grace & some knowledge but I feel very unworthy. I have a painful remembrance of many misdoings & shortcomings. I do not think I preach so well as I used to do & this is mostly my own fault, but I feel resolved to try to improve. I hauled corn to day & tried to hire a boy, but failed. For several weeks I have been reviewing Clarkes comments on Matt[hew] & find much new light.[1]

January 15 — [Mt. Hermon] Beautiful Sabbath, good congregation & excellent attention, after I requested a few young men to desist from talking. Hermon has a hard name for misbehavior, but it is generally said that I have the most orderly & attentive congregation, than any preacher has there.

---

1. George Dick is referring to Adam Clarke's *Commentary*. Clarke was born in Londonderry Co., Ireland, in 1760. As a young preacher in the Methodist society, he developed an interest in languages and eventually became a renowned scholar of Latin, Hebrew, and Oriental literature. He spent forty years in writing and publishing his commentary on the Bible. Simpson, *Encyclopedia of Methodism*, 225–26.

January 17 – [Olmstead] Today I cut trees & was tired. At night I was startled by a visit from Tom Smith in search of his brother Dick, who was running from the military. Dick had been deceived by his negro *Stephen's* telling him that he was not in the army, & so kept him at home until *Stephen* was arrested as a deserter, & Dick was charged with encouraging desertions, harboring deserters. He is very much alarmed & in great distress.

January 20 – Dick Smith & Presley Hines came over to breakfast, then Dick & Tom set out for Toronto, Can. having given me a power of attorney to check on his deposit in bank, as far as necessary for his use here.

January 22 – I took Robert in the buggie to Elkton, found the roads almost impassable. Had no congregation. Great mud holes just at the church door, key out of place, no wood, no sexton, not much interest any way. I felt discouraged.

January 25 – Very cold, Cousin David Sydnor spent day with me. We heard that guerillas robbed Daysville & Volney last night & stole John Vicks two mules, & Lafayette Rileys money. I fear we will have trouble. I feel thankful to have escaped thus far.

January 31 – I am taking Jaundice. I dread it.

February 3 – Staid in bed & sent for Dr Hutchings.

February 4 – Up alittle. Jaundice is a loathesome detestable disease. I have it very lightly, but cannot go to my appointment, at Hadensville.

February 16 – Not so lightly as I supposed. I have been in bed taking medicine for 8 or 10 days, suffering enormously and am still feeble & sluggish. My stomach & liver are both torpid & I have been quite as yellow as an ordinary field pumpkin. Could rub the yellow off my skin! In all my illness I did not feel that joy in religion that I have in other attacks, yet I felt resigned & not afraid to die.

My dear wife & children nursed me with the most assiduous care & little Helen frequently got up in the night to give medicine & make a fire. Our servants also – *Abram* & *Mary* – were attentive & kind & I have great cause to thank God for his goodness. For the first time in my life, medicines had no effect upon my system.

My poor Lizzie is worn down & sick & I feel uneasy about her. Robert, blessed child, is busy at work plowing well with two horses. Amanda Warfield came up last sabbath to go to school & Helen goes with her to Prof. J. H. Fuqua, while Hanson & George & Luther are busy with the lambs, & wood chopping & fire making & learning lessons from their mother who for a few weeks, has been busy teaching them at home. Little Georgie thinks he deserves credit for keeping smokes under the bacon & curing it up well & in good time – and so he does.

The public mind for several weeks past was much excited by hopes of peace, growing out of the visits of commissioners from Washington to Richmond & then others from Richmond to Washington; but the hope was delusive & the dark war cloud rolls on with deepening gloom & horror & the battles roar still saddens our hearts, and now there is much perturbation about another impending draft.

February 18 – I started to Mt Hermon. A band of guerillas crossed the road just ahead of me, under the lead of Tom Morrow, once my neighbor & school fellow, now one of the most desperately wicked men in all the land.

February 19 – A lovely sabbath, I had a good congregation & preached with some liberty Lu[ke] 24.50–3. The house was very dirty & I urged the people to a better treatment of Gods house.

April 3 – [Olmstead] Lizzie is sick with Neuralgia & suffers much. Cousin Rose [Walker] is with us. A stranger calling himself William Marks is here seeking employment. He reports that guerillas burned Cheathams mill where he was at work, & robbed him & others. I need a laborer, & take him on trial.

April 10 – Came through Elkton [after preaching at Bell's Chapel] where a considerable panic prevails on account of a raging epidemic, that kills all it attacks. None as yet have recovered, and none live longer than a few days. Brain fever. I got home at night.

We heard the booming of cannon, & the peal of musketry at the different military posts, in honor of the federal success. The rebellion is now fairly crushed. The great Southern cities have fallen into the hands of federals, & Richmond, the capital has been evacuated, & Genl Lees great army has surrendered to Genl Grant. Lee has won imperishable laurels as a great commander, but he lacked men & munitions to combat the powerful armies of the Union. I think peace will soon follow & slavery be abolished all over the land. If such be God's will I cheerfully acquiesce. I have looked to the results of this war as a providential settlement of the great slavery question, either in its establishment or its demolition. I think the northern states will yet be scourged, for unnecessary cruelties & oppression to the Southern people. There is a great grief in the South & great exultation in the north to night.

April 12 – Rain! wind! thunder! What a storm last night! The fences are washed away again & the streams are all flooded, the 3rd time in a few weeks. Cousin Rose says the Heavens are weeping over Lee's surrender!

April 17 – Startling news!! The public is greatly excited over the assassination of President Lincoln! At Fords Theatre on Friday night. The assassin brandished a dagger, & escaped, crying "Sic Semper Tyrannis." Sec Seward was assassinated in his own room about the same time & the country is in great consternation.[2]

April 18 – The assassination of Lincoln & Seward engross the public mind. Citizens are imprisoned & some shot in different places for apparent exultation. Several parties have been arrested, but the assassin is not found. Minute guns are firing at different military posts in token of the national distress. It is a very mysterious affair, the results of which are much to be feared. At noon we stopped work during the presidents funeral obsequies. This is a sad day to our country. The South is conquered & humiliated and the federal government is in deep sorrow in the midst of its great rejoicing.

April 20 – [Hadensville] I found Bro Hoozer (J. H.) in great distress about the willfulness of his daughter Martha in marrying Wm. Edwards, contrary to the wish of both parents. I used all my persuasive powers to reconcile the parties, showing her, how great was her obligation to her parents & showing the father, that he could not control her forcibly as she was 23 years of age. He at last yielded so far as to allow her to leave the house & go with Mr Edwards to James Hoozers where I married them, with peculiar feelings. I obtained a promise from the young man to abstain hence forth from drink.

April 22 – [Olmstead] This is our dear Roberts 12th birth day and he is truly a child of comfort to us. I do not think there is a better boy living than our Robert. He is a very exemplary Christian & as dutiful, affectionate, honorable & industrious as we could ask him to be. We never knew him to tell a falsehood on any occasion. Luther loves him most devotedly, and all the children look up to him.

Little Georgie was in ecstacies yesterday, over a very large turtle that he caught near the pond & to day we had a fine bowl of turtle soup.

April 26 – Went to depot to go to Russellville, having been awake most of the night with poor Luther who is very sick & nervous. The cars came nearly in sight & we heard them run off of the track & rapid firing immediately followed accompanied by sound of voices. A man running rapidly down the railroad, waving his handkerchief, soon relieved our suspense. It was young Wilkerson the road masters son who reported that Guerillas had thrown the cars off the track and captured the train, the guard being all scattered. He was greatly alarmed & reported women & childhood shot indiscriminately. I lent him my horse to ride to town, & then I set out to the scene of strife to give what assistance I could to the wounded, but they had all been removed before I got there. The train was not surrendered, but thrown off & damaged, & two of the guerillas, Tom Morrow & another, were reported shot. Two or three federal

---

2. On the same evening that Lincoln was assassinated, an attempt was also made on the life of Secretary of State William H. Seward. Although stabbed several times as he lay in bed recovering from a carriage accident, Seward survived the attack.

soldiers were badly wounded. It is a terrible piece of wickedness & the first thing of that kind I have seen. It is bringing war disagreeably near. Old Tom Morrows negro *Joe* says that the robbers pressed him to hold horses & he knows that Tom is badly hurt, near the head or neck.

May 1 – Hail May day! Heard from George & Frank. Coming home – paroled under Lees surrender.

May 19 – After a very busy week, plowing, replanting corn &c I went to see Mr Warfield about sending money to George, who is with Frank in Va, & both without money to travel on, & Govt agents will not transport them according to the terms of Lees surrender.

May 20 – We had a heavy rain, & as I got nearer home, I saw the flood increased until I was lost in amazement. The oldest men here have never seen the like. The dry branch is tearing away the railroad at a fearful rate, & Whippoorwill is higher than ever known before. My pond is running over both through the orchard & into the cave. The destruction to bridges, fences, mills & crops is incalculable. I did not get to my appointment at Mt Hermon.

May 26 – I went to town on horse back, the flood having damaged the railroad so as to stop all trains since last Sat. I was astonished to see water marks so high above my head that I could not reach it on horse back in places where I had never known water to stand before. Red River has swept away bridges, houses, mills & fences alarmingly, and Muddy River is reported 15 feet higher than ever before.

May 27 – I attended my 3d Quarterly meeting at Elkton. Few present. Finances far in arrears.

May 28 – We had a good love feast. At 3 I baptized 17 negroes & administered the Lords supper to a large crowd. I have not seen so many negroes together for a long time. White federal soldiers sat promiscuously among them & seemed to feel on terms of equality. A small company of colored troops are recruiting and taking in some.

A negro boy of James M. Graham, struck his master with an axe on Thursday or Friday, & came into town & enlisted in the negro company. The sheriff demanded him for civil law, & the Lieut. declined to give him up, without orders from higher Military officers. Quite a sensation exists in the community. A small negro boy in uniform on the street cursed and abused the whole town & the white people generally. A spirit of revenge is gaining ground.

May 29 – Mr Graham is dead, & the people begin to clamor for the blood of the negro who murdered him. Threats are rife on the street, & it is said that an anonymous letter persuaded the Lieut. that he had authority to deliver the culprit to the sheriff, so he gave him up & the citizens guarded him to the dungeon, while the negro troops beat a speedy departure from the town. I was glad to see them leaving.

June 1 – [Olmstead] To day our Gov. calls upon the people to fast & pray for the pardon of our sins, which he says "have culminated in the assassination of Abraham Lincoln." It is right to observe days of humiliation & prayer. We have greatly sinned before God & ought to be sorry, but I do not think the assassination of Mr Lincoln a national sin. I think the nation at large was opposed to such a procedure. Our nation has sinned in elevating wicked men to office, North & South. Mr Andrew Johnson – now President was too drunk to be inaugurated with decorum.[3] Many of our statesmen are corrupt, God-defying sinners, & I fear that many of those who call the people to pray for pardon are themselves blasphemous, and drunkards.

June 6 – The people are rather desponding, and altho the rebellion is crushed, we apprehend much trouble from our government officials about their negro policy. They either know nothing of negro character, or care nothing for the welfare of both white & black in the south. Genl Palmer who has charge of this department ignores the laws & constitution of our state & rules with military power. Even the ballot box is indirectly threatened, unless the state will vote with the radical part.

The indications in the Northern church lead me to fear that they will make an effort to disorganize the Southern church & claim all the church property. If such an attempt should be made, woe to the cause of Christ. Many men professing to fear God are yet striving to "sow discord among the brethren."

June 8 – While busy preparing a sermon for the annual commencement of Bro Mortons School [Logan Female College] in Russellville, I was called to go over to Dr Williamsons to bury one of the unfortunate refugees who left North Ga. on account of the war.

June 11 – I went to Russellville on horseback. Bro Morton had secured the services of Dr Joseph Cross for the annual sermon – as I had requested him to get a substitute if he could, but he acted rather shabbily in not informing me of the fact so I could have filled my own appointment. Dr C. preached an excellent evangelical sermon that had but little connection with the occasion and I was pleased & edified, but regretted very keenly that I had yielded to Mortons entreaties to neglect my appointment for his gratifications. Dr. Cross has just been released from the South where he has been a rebel chaplain. I was gratified to see Rev W. M. Grubbs a federal chaplain invite him to dine with his family. It showed a good spirit.

---

3. Johnson, apparently recovering from an attack of typhoid fever and in a weakened condition, had requested some whisky to bolster himself just before entering a warm Senate chamber to deliver a speech and take the oath of office. Consequently, he delivered a "rambling and strange harangue" which was received with mortification by his friends. He was no habitual drunkard. George F. Milton, *The Age of Hate* (New York, 1930), 145 ff.

June 13 – Busy making a frame for bean poles – and driving the reaper to cut fathers wheat.

June 16 – I took Helen in the buggie to Russellville to attend the examination & exhibition at the Female Academy. At night the crowd was immense – but bad boys in the gallery & timid girls on the stage made the exhibition rather uninteresting.

July 5 – Excessively hot – almost made myself sick putting up a horse rake for father. As I was working my tobacco a voice called out – "Do you want help?" Hanson who was with me cried out Uncle George! Uncle George! and there sure enough was George Warfield come at last! Then came Helen – running & jumping – & then came Lizzie – in full speed & we had a most joyful meeting. Dear boy – almost four years in the war – wounded & starved, worn out & often ragged, yet coming home pure & faithful & sound in mind & morals! Thank God. And dear Frank too – brave & daring, honorable & true – in many battles & skirmishes, long marches – & dangerous raids, long confinement in different prisons – often poorly clothed & barely fed atall – has come back looking well & cheerful – hailed with joy & love by father, mother, brothers & sisters – kindred & friends. Oh how we have all prayed to God for their preservation & how thankful we ought to be for their safe return!

July 18 – This morning Lizzie & I went to visit Mrs Isham Miller who has been sick a long time. She is a clever woman, but has abused terribly those who espoused the Southern cause & even absented herself for a long time from the church, because the preachers & people sympathized with the South – and I did not really know that she wished me to visit her, yet I would have gone if my time had not been so much occupied on my circuit & at home – if I had known how sick she continued. I have never willfully neglected the sick and have almost invariably been kindly treated, however bitter had been the political or religious prejudices of those I visit.

July 20 – Lizzie went with me to town. Divers persons told me that I was to be the next Presiding Elder of this District. It is a work I do not seek nor desire – would not take it as a matter of choice, would very much prefer a circuit. I should be afraid to rebel against the appointment if made.

There is some sensation in regard to Genl Palmers being interrupted by a negro woman in his radical speech. Dr Keene first & then Dr Evans was arrested, charged with inciting her to offer the indignity to the Military ruler of Ky, but when it was shown that the negro was crazy, they were released, and apologies made. Genl Palmer ought not to object to negro equality.

July 21 – Walked through my corn – pulled the first roasting ear – and spent the remainder of the day in reading. Since the war I have not read Newspapers a great deal.

September 1 — For several weeks I have been absent from home, nearly all the time. My Quarterly meeting at Hadensville embraced the 5th Sab[bath] in July & continued 9 days. We had plenty of preachers — Dr Joseph Cross, late chaplain in the confed. army preached some of the finest sermons ever preached by man — but comparatively few sinners repented — only six conversions reported. The congregations were said to be the largest & most orderly ever seen in that community.

On Monday 7th of Aug — the election was held in Ky. There was great excitement — illegal oaths — arrest & military interference, all failed to make Ky vote for the constitutional amendment.[4]

On Sat 12th of Aug. I commenced a meeting at Bells Chapel. We held on fourteen days. The congregations were large & attentive. Bro Cross was with us & preached wonderfully. He is the most eloquent man I ever heard, but has not the unction of some others. The interest was mainly among young men, some 10 or 15 of whom were mourners — mostly backsliders — rebel & federal soldiers side by side.

On Monday [August 28] I attended church at Bethlehem in the forenoon and at night, preached at Salem with some liberty & success — 12 or 14 mourners came forward & eight professed conversion. Next day preached again. Prov[erbs] 29.1st. Had new mourners. Next day preached Rev[elation] 2.24 — more mourners & one conversion. Came home at night very tired.

Thursday 31st of Aug. At three I preached on "Hope" with liberty & unction. The altar was crowded with mourners, among them my brother David & three other young men. Oh how sad to see the church backslidden so grievously. My own dear children say they are not backslidden. I talk to them frequently and freely.

September 2 — I began a meeting at Mt Hermon in connection with the C[umberland]. Presbyterians, Bro Gill their pastor, a good & great man assisting me.

September 3 — Congregation very large. I crowded the women together in spite of their hoops & so accommodated many with seats.

September 9 — I preached with good effect on Saving Hope. Conversions now number 18, & the interest increases.

---

4. The principal issues in the election were the ratification of the Thirteenth Amendment to abolish slavery throughout the United States and the effort of returned Confederate soldiers to regain civil and political rights. By a margin of two to one the Kentucky legislature rejected the amendment, despite the possibility of $100,000,000 in federal compensation to slaveowners. The legislature also repealed all of the wartime measures affecting the civil and political rights of Confederates and their sympathizers. Hambleton Tapp and James C. Klotter, *Kentucky: Decades of Discord 1865–1900* (Frankfort, Kentucky, 1977), 3, 13.

September 16 – For a day or two I have been very busy saving my tob[acco]. which up to this time I have almost entirely neglected. This evening I went to Mt Hermon, & heard Bro Hester preach. There are still several mourners, & I think 27 have professed conversion.

September 17 – Hail Sabbath of the Lord! I preached the concluding sermon to a large & listening audience on I John 3.2–3. I opened the doors of the church for Methodists & Cumberlands. We received 7, the Presbyterians 5. Some were already in the church & some will join Baptists. I am gratified to know that this people universally regret my departure. I think I could accomplish more here by the blessing of God than almost anywhere else during the next year. I think the *necessity* of changing pastors at least every two years is the error in our plan – & ought to be changed.

September 20 – Our Conference began its 20th Annual Session in Russellville. Most of the brethren were present – Bish[op] Kavanaugh presiding. Harmony prevails, & the preachers seem to love one another. Quite a sensation was raised in the conference by the proposition to appoint a committee on the state of the church. Many of us fearing trouble voted it down – being determined as far as possible to maintain perfect quiet.

September 21 – The conference is almost full and the crowd of spectators is immense. The case of C. B. Parsons attracts considerable attention. He was guilty of the gross impropriety of taking another mans wife into his bed room in the basement of the 12th St church in Louisville at nine oclock at night & remain with her alone for nearly an hour. Previous suspicions led to the *seeing* of this act by some of his official board who demanded an explanation. He wept & said he had been very foolish but not criminal – that he only invited the sister into his room "to eat sweet cakes & drink cider." He refused an investigation & went over to the church North. The papers published that "C. B. Parsons was driven from the church South by the disloyalty of its people." The members of 12th St church denied being disloyal and threatened to publish the circumstances of his leaving the church. He said "If they dare do it I will take away their church. I am a member of the loyal league."[5] So falls the great C. B. Parsons, once my intimate & admired friend.

September 22 – Russellville is crowded. The conference never attracted more attention at any place. Business progresses well but there is a great deal to do.

---

5. The Loyal League, usually called the Union League, originated in Philadelphia in 1862 as a patriotic society to enlist support for the Union cause. As the movement spread to the South, it became a vehicle for building a following among blacks who were encouraged to vote the Republican ticket. The League soon aroused considerable fear and criticism among Southerners. In the face of this opposition, which included attacks by the newly organized Ku Klux Klan, the League had disbanded across most of the South by late 1868. Glenn M. Linden, "Union League," in David C. Roller and Robert W. Twyman (eds.), *The Encyclopedia of Southern History* (Baton Rouge, 1979), 1261–62.

A. H. Redford made a long & stirring speech in favor of the church South and against the church, North. Much of which I thought was out of place. On returning to my boarding house I found myself sick, aching & feverish – rested very badly.

September 24 – Quite sick yet went out. Russellville has seldom been so full of people on Sunday. We had a glorious love feast – a season of joy. The Baptist & Methodist churches, occupied – the one by Dr. Sehon, the other by Bish[op] Kavanaugh, could not hold the people. So we got the Academy for Bob Holland, the Star boy of America. He is a wonderful young man. I never heard his equal for his age. But caressed, flattered, lionized, & lauded by people & press as he is, I fear he will be made vain. He seems now very meek & humble, but I am told that his pride is wounded if he is called equal even to Bascom, the prince of orators – as it is said he thinks himself *superior*. I came home at night sick.

September 25 – Just able to be out I took medicine & went to town. We voted almost unanimously on the resolutions in favor of abiding by the fortunes of the church South, whether prosperous or adverse. We appointed, for the first time, delegates to the General State Conventions of Baptist & Cumberland Presbyterian churches, to convey to them our expressions of good will & Christian charity – came home quite unwell.

September 26 – This is the last day of our Session. I think the whole community feels impressed that the Louisville Conference is a formidable body. Tonight is the great crisis – reading out the appointments. I was not well enough to stay, so Bro Morrison my P[residing] E[lder] told me I was to go to Russellville Station.

September 27 – I was greatly surprized to learn from Bro Alexander that to accommodate other brethren, I had been removed from Russellville Station & put on Russellville circuit which is quite inconvenient to me & unable to support me. This is not right. I do not in the least object to doing *my full share* of the hard work – but I object to being taken from where the *people wanted* me to be sent *where* they *do not* want me.

September 28 – Bro Woolls & wife spent the night with us. [He] is not pleased with my appointment. I do not grumble. The work is good enough & if the Lord will & my health permit I will work it faithfully.

October 12 – At supper time, an uninvited stranger, in great distress and destitution, without clothes, or shoes, or even hair on head and wailing piteously, came into our house. He was kindly received and his wants supplied. The children are all very much interested in him & my wife is so much pleased with him that she does all in her power to make him comfortable, even taking him on her arm to rest. Dr Hutchings and my mother were both here taking tea when he arrived, & they spoke favorably of his appearance. He makes himself quite at home and asks no questions. He speaks all the ancient & modern languages as fluently as his mother tongue, yet he has not told us his name nor destination nor the probable length of his stay. He is by no means a large gentleman, weighing only 9 ½ lbs in his clothes. He is quiet & contented and there is hope of usefulness & happiness in him. He is our 5th son! Our 7th child and his mother is doing well.[6] I thank God that it is so well and pray for grace & wisdom to guide us discreetly in raising our children.

October 20 – My good sister Emma has been with Lizzie several days & nights & my excellent mother, though old & infirm, was with her two nights & a day after her confinement. Lizzie is doing unusually well, but the babe is now troubled with Thrush.

October 26 – For two or three days I was very sick with fever, & the most terrible Nausea. I am sure sea sickness cannot be so bad. Dr Walton was with me Sat & Sun & treated me most kindly, but such was the state of my stomach that I could retain but little of his medicine. Nor could I talk to the friends who came to see me. I felt almost a stupid indifference about living or dying but felt sure that my peace was made with God.

October 29 – A Sabbath at home. I read & rested being up with baby last night. Cousin Rose Walker is with us and is a great help to Lizzie & Helen. I have suffered to day with tooth ache. Tonight I interested my children with the story of Daniel & his associates.

October 30 – I am still very feeble & my liver is very torpid. I am taking medicine 3 times per day, but do not get well. I hope to be able to go to my next appointment.

November 27 – Vain hope! next appointment day found me very sick again – and ever since I have been very feeble & frequently really ill.

December 1 – The most beautiful Autumn weather I remember to have seen has been our share for several months. My health is improving by the use of Sandfords Liver Invigorator. To day we killed our hogs, 15 weighing 3135 lbs or 215 lbs each. We have six others to sell!

I was never more surprised at company, than this evening when James Warfield & family arrived from Ark. They have seen hard times during the war, but have not seen as much of the actual horrors of war & battles as we have here.

December 2 – Very warm indeed, too warm for hogkilling. My father sent old *Ned* to cut & salt the meat. There was perhaps never a greater scarcity of Bacon & Lard in this country. There is hardly a family beside mine in the neighborhood

---

6. George Dick & Lizzie named their son Wallace Warfield.

that is not without these articles — mostly on account of the waste and stealing of the negroes. Robbing smoke houses is common & even stealing cows & live stock — particularly hogs & poultry.

December 4 — A much desired rain! Our poor cross, hired *Mary* has been in an ill humor for two or three days & to day is in bed. Several remarks lead to the belief that she is much more contrary than sick. Poor Negroes! I pity them in the delusion & ruin the yankee has forced upon them. If changing the status of the race be God's will I say Amen — but to my eyes certain ruin awaits the race under the new programme. Many of them remain with their masters. Many return & beg to be taken back as they were before — but the majority are restless — indolent, discontented, seeking constant changes — & not knowing what to do with their freedom. It is to be hoped that the experience of years will improve their condition. It is estimated that 1,000,000 have perished since the war — 25 pr ct!

January 1, 1866 — The old year has passed away! would we could blot out the wrongs & horrors it has witnessed. Oh for the pardon of all our individual & national sins.

Sat. before Christmas I went to McLeods station on the cars and walked across the hills to Duncan's shed to Quarterly meeting — found very few present — got the conference to take young Bro Chandler on the circuit until spring, hoping that my health would improve.

On Christmas morning as usual, the children were up early shouting "Christmas Gift" and eagerly examining the stockings full of candies, cakes, nuts, toys &c. that Good Santaclaus had provided.

Through the week there was quiet. The negroes were running about from house to house trying to make bargains for the years work.

A great many, both men & women applied to me. Our *Abram* vowed that he would not leave me — but his poor worthless wife is a great trouble to him. The young people have been having parties & Christmas trees — & there is altogether more cheer & hope than most people anticipated. Robert & Hanson are in ecstacies over a new knife & a new gun and feel great that they have each shot a bird — & Robert is proud to have killed a squirrel in the top of a tall tree — & when I shot two fine wild ducks at a long range — they thought the gun was grand.

Abram & *Mary* have gone — and we had a houseful of company Sunday unexpectedly. I have hired a man (Uncle Bells *Henry*) & his wife (*Kate Sydnor*) on reasonable terms & they move in to day. I hauled up their furniture Saturday. I pay *Henry* 150. & feed the family & clothe *Kate* — they pay their own doctor. Negro men are hiring 120. to 175. in different neighborhoods & women without children at 5. to 7. pr month — while women with two or three children work for food & raiment. Most of them in this neighborhood are hiring to their former owners, but many do not feel free unless they change homes. Many are roving about troubled to find employment and many others do not wish to work.

January 5 – James Warfield has been with me a few days trying to rent land. I killed my surplus hogs for him at 10 1/2 net. The six weighed 1600 lbs. He is waiting to hear from David H[utchings] about the rent of his Gaines farm.

January 6 – I went to Louisville for James, to see David. Rented the place.

January 9 – [Olmstead] My man *Abram* has not returned. I suppose he had found a home elsewhere. So be it.

January 19 – The warmest winter day I ever felt, I think. It was as warm as May, at night I could scarcely bear the cover on me.
    Merciful God! What a tornado! It seems to shake the very foundation of the earth. The storm fiend is howling most furiously. How the lightning glares and the thunder crashes! It seems every instant as if the house will be overturned as it quivers, and trembles in the beating blast. I leaped out of bed as the window panes were forced in, to try to save the house from burning as I feared the fire would be whirled all over the room. What shall we do? It waxes louder & fiercer – we hear the crash of falling limbs & lie horror stricken in the darkness, not knowing what to do. To stay in may be destruction, to run out is equally hazardous. So we run up stairs to see if the children are safe – & like St Paul once in the shipwreck we wish for the day.
    As soon as we could see I went out expecting to find the out buildings torn to pieces, but was thankful to see all standing except the carriage house, which was completely wrecked. Some of my neighbors did not fare so well. Dr Hutchings lost a barn. D. B. Sydnor a barn, stable & horse. George Duerson a barn and two mules. My father two barns, one very large & valuable & full of tobacco. Dr. Williamson a fine new barn full of tob[acco] and the roof & side of another. Many dwelling houses were damaged – & other out buildings destroyed while fruit trees & fences were blown in every direction. Nearly all the fencing in this neighborhood was blown down. This is altogether the most terrible and destructive storm that I ever was in and will be long remembered as the Night Storm. Before day it turned bitterly cold from such unseasonable heat & this morning the ground is covered with snow and the wind howls, freezing from the North West.

January 26 – Went with James to town to hire hands but did not get any.

February 7 – James had trouble with an insolent contraband & I went with him to see the boys Father, *Henry Bailey,* who directed James to correct him. George Duerson was present.

February 11 – Uncle Dick was very sick and I went down to see him – inflammation of the neck of the bladder. Dr thinks recovery very doubtful.

February 13 — Heard that the old negro *Henry Bailey* had been informed that he could make James pay for whipping his son and intended to arraign him & me before the Freedmens Bureau.[7] I was on my way to pay him for the months work his boy had done — though not worth much, for he is very trifling, but when I heard that he had threatened me with the Bureau I declined to see him for the present. There is some sensation about Small pox at Wash Sydnors. Old *Wesley* certainly had it & David [Sydnor]s wife & children have moved up to his fathers causing quite a panic there among the negroes.

February 14 — I went to town on business. I saw the agent of the Bureau who assured me that such a case as *Henry Baileys* could not result in any damage to the parties accused because he had consented to the whipping of his boy.

February 16 — Not well, went to see my dear old uncle who is very ill & I fear will die. He says he is willing & resigned to the Masters will, but would prefer living a few years — to arrange his temporal matters.

February 17 — Sick with cholera morbus all day.

February 18 — I hoped that this day would find me in my pulpit at Temples chapel, but here I am not well enough to go out. I have often failed to fill appointments this winter from my affliction.

February 19 — Able to ride to Allensville. Come by to see uncle Dick. He is slowly sinking — feels that he must die — talks of it calmly, blesses God for saving grace. Oh how I dread to see him die, who will fill his place in the church? For long years he has been one of the main pillars in the Temple here — & the last time I saw him at church, he was urging the brethren to repair the house of the Lord.

Poor *Wesley Sydnor* has died with Small pox & another negro has it at Marion Wooldridges. I fear it will spread all over the country.

February 21 — I often feel reproved by the conduct of my dear Robert who regularly reads his Bible whether the other children read or play. I feel much concern about my children. Some of them I fear are becoming very worldly & wayward & self-willed.

Poor old uncle Dick is worse to day. Oh if God would but spare him alittle longer to his family and church.

---

7. The Freedmen's Bureau was created by Congress in March 1865 as an emergency wartime relief agency to assist destitute whites as well as the newly freed blacks. Congress renewed the Bureau in 1866 with the provision that anyone charged with depriving a freedman of his civil rights was to be tried by a military tribunal or a Freedmen's Bureau agent in accordance with martial law. Although the legislation creating the Bureau originally applied only to the seceded states, Kentucky was soon included in its provisions by administrative order. Ross Webb, *Kentucky in the Reconstruction Era* (Lexington, Kentucky, 1979), 41, 43.

May 1 — For two months I have made no entry in my journal. Sometimes I have been sick & some times very busy. My health has very much improved & I have been able to preach several times & work considerably on the farm. I felt anxious to fill the work on the circuit but did not think that my health was sufficiently restored. My physicians, Presiding Elder & family all insisted that I was not able to do the work. So I asked to be relieved.

Yesterday morning we finished planting corn, have now planted forty acres. The pastures now are green, the woods are full of verdure & flowers, the corn is coming up beautifully & the oats are promising. Fruit trees are loaded with abundant crops & we have every indication of plenty in our land. Peace seems coming on. The president has declared the war at an end & a general amnesty is expected. President Johnson is gaining favor rapidly with conservative men, while the radicals & disorganizers are deserting him. He has vetoed two egregiously unconstitutional bills, the Freedmens bureau & the Civil Rights. The latter congress passed over his head by expelling a member & taking advantage of the illness of two others (Senators) in order to get the necessary majorities.[8] Rebels who hated Andy Johnson with a perfect hatred now endorse & support him.

May 3 — For several days I have been busy working on the farm. I regret I have had to stop my two sons Robert & Hanson from school.

Cousin David Sydnor has been very ill a long time & has suffered inexpressibly, but both he & uncle Dick are now able to walk about the house.

June 19 — Since I last wrote in my journal my health has been uncertain. I have worked some on the farm and preached some on the Sabbath. I preach funeral sermons far and near, & marry a number of couples. There are so many calls upon my time that I can do but little at home. I have a monthly appointment at Kimbrough's Academy [near Guthrie], a new & beautiful house in a neighborhood where there is no preaching and where the congregations are attentive. The third Sab. in May the house was full but I was taken sick with Cholera Morbus just as I was reading the morning lesson & compelled to leave the house, much to my regret & the disappointment of the congregation.

October 1 — During the months my journal has lain unopened, I have been variously engaged, but very much after the usual order, only I have worked rather more on the farm. My dear wife has been in bad health and I have been anxious to take her to her fathers for a long time, but a crowd of company & press of business and cares have prevented until last Friday when she & I with Georgie, Luther & Wallace got in the buggie and hurried away. I left before day next morning & waited long for the tardy train, but got home at last. We are keeping house without Lizzie, but I always feel badly when she is away. I can hardly realize how completely my happiness depends on her.

---

8. Congress also overrode Johnson's veto of the Freedmen's Bureau Bill.

Robert & Hanson have started with their sister to school. The precious children have worked most faithfully through the season and aided very greatly in raising the crop. They gathered & sold twenty or thirty dollars worth of peaches & would have sold a hundred or more if cholera had not broken up the trade. The crop was large & the late peaches good. Apples have fallen off until very few are left for winter. Potatoes & cabbage are tolerably good. Corn is plentiful here, but the scarcity elsewhere will make the price high. Hogs are scarce & in demand at high prices. I am fattening 35 at home & James Warfield is feeding 18 for me on the halves. Our servants so far have done well and I am thankful for the peace of the present year. Conference is coming on –

November 12 – I hardly knew what I was going to write when I left the above line unfinished in October. Conference [at Elizabethtown] came on and I attended. Bro Morrison & I were boarded at Mr Sam Thoma's by request. They are the wealthiest and most hospitable family in the town or county – and entertained us in a most lordly style. They are Presbyterian in their notions. I am some how or other nearly always boarded with Presbyterians and find them most excellent people. Conference business was most important & transacted in a Christian spirit. Bishop Dogget impressed the Conference and community most favorably. He is a master workman & breathes a pious spirit. The appointments were generally satisfactory to the preachers. I am appointed to Elkton Circuit by petition in place of Bro Fisk removed. I deeply regret his mortification at the change. I am sure he is a good & able man but the people do not appreciate him. If he knew the circumstances he would not have desired to return. I am glad that I had no agency in his removal. I go to that work most willingly & cheerfully but not by my own seeking. I trust I feel responsible for whatever influence God has given me among the people. It is truly gratifying to note the warm reception I meet at every point.

November 17 – Went to Quarterly meeting at Mt Hermon. Meeting better attended than usual. Quarterly conference seemed to consider the interest of the church spiritually and financially. They passed a resolution requesting me to raise collections in all the societies for the relief of the destitute brethren in the South – and seemed willing for me to say what my salary should be and they would pay it. I told them to pay me what they had promised to Bro Fisk and it would satisfy me. They accepted at once and made a satisfactory apportionment: 800.00.

December 2 – [Hadensville] Congregation rather small for so beautiful a day. I preached earnestly on the Rich man & Lazarus, then appointed Sam Taliferro, R. L. Smith, G. W. Hoozer, & D. S. Morrison a committee to raise corn &c for the destitute Preachers in the South.

December 25 – [Olmstead] Hail blessed Christmas. The children are up, rejoicing over stockings full of Christmas presents. The weather is sunny & bright, and Lizzie & I with the children went over to eat Christmas dinner with my father. This morning we went up to the school house and enjoyed the glee of the children getting presents from the Christmas tree.

January 1, 1867 – George Warfield & James Warfield with his family are here. James has failed to get a place in this neighborhood and is going to live with his wifes sister near Saundersville Ten[n]. I spend this day moving him over to the depot.

January 11 – This day I am forty years old. I am in moderate health, but not so stout as I have been. I can read as fine print as I ever could, but not so long at one time. I think I do not hear altogether so keenly as I once did. I have lost much of my energy & fire & am not nearly so talkative as formerly. I am greatly ashamed of my lethargy & want of intelligence. Instead of going forward & pressing eagerly on in my studies, I have halted by the way & do not preach as well nor as effectively I fear as I once did. I can only hope in the mercy of God & rejoice in the grace of Christ. My purpose is still steadfast to do good.

January 14 – I called to pray with old Bro. Petree [upon returning from Bell's Chapel], thence on to Elkton where I expected to aid in the organizing of a county Society for Southern Relief but found my father had already done the work, for which I am thankful. We are raising considerable supplies here for our starving friends in the South.

January 24 – I sent a check for the payment of my premium on Life Insurance policy of $2500. If I had my choice again I would prefer the Connecticut Mutual to the Globe, as I think they offer better terms.

February 19 – Some one sent Helen a novel by mail without a post mark – Amy Lawrence or the Free Masons daughter. I sketched myself to see if it was prudent for her to read. As a general thing I am opposed to romances. There is some good moral in this, that all the villainous characters met with sorrow & the good became happy.

February 21 – I suffer with a sore throat.

February 22 – Helen & I went to Russellville on the daylight train. The poor child had two teeth extracted, and bore it very well. I had considerable business to do, but suffered very much with my throat. Dr Grubbs recommended Chlorate of Potash as a wash.

March 4 – This day the new Congress goes into effect. Our state is not represented at present.[9] The Southern States are out, & the most extreme,

---

9. George Dick's observation about Kentucky's representation in Congress is puzzling. It was in July 1867 that the House of Representatives refused to admit Kentucky's congressmen, all of whom were Conservative Democrats elected overwhelmingly the

unjust, illiberal, & radical measures prevail in Congress. The president vetoes, but the party is powerful & carry measures over the veto. The future is dark.

March 5 – Wonderful. Notwithstanding the previous rain the snow this morning measures nine inches deep on a level surface. We have had bad luck with our lambs, having lost 8 of our 13 and our hogs are dying with cholera, nearly half of the shoats are dead, after being unusually well wintered & sheltered.

March 7 – Rode through snow, mud, & water to James Deeds [on the way to Bell's Chapel]. I lectured & catechized the children which I do more or less in every family.

March 8 – I found but few at chapel – had a pleasant class meeting. The creek rose so much that I came near getting wet on my way to uncle Bell's where I spent the night. There are few such men as uncle B. for piety, zeal, intelligence, industry, benevolence – & sprightliness of mind in the 78th year of life.

March 10 – Rain again. Another dumb Sabbath as bishop Asbury used to say on such days. I read Bible & Watsons sermons. Went home with Jordan Moore – spent some time in reading & religious conversation. Prayed & catechized the children – was delighted with the proficiency little Charley had made in the catechism I gave him two weeks ago. He has learned six chapters perfectly.

March 18 – I rode to Hadensville to see about shipping our supplies to the Southern preachers, found them still in hand & no prospect of early shipment as the roads are flooded & bridges broken South. I went down to Guthridge L. Randles. Mrs. R. was stricken down with Paralysis a few weeks ago. She is an old woman, unconverted and had expressed a great anxiety to see me. I found her in great grief of mind. She said she thought a few days ago that she was pardoned and accepted, but all that hope had left her. She thought she was mistaken. I sung & prayed earnestly, and I trust prayed with faith, and while we sang with spirit, Farewell, farewell to the parting soul – whose peace is made with Heaven, her soul seemed to trust in the Savior. She felt happy and expressed perfect willingness to die.

April 8 – Robert & I went to Father Warfields. We learned that the Quarterly meeting was protracted.

I went to town [Clarksville] with Mr W. Dined at Academy, saw many acquaintances. Amanda Warfield too was glad to see me. She was very serious about religion, & I talked to her on the subject. I was importuned & pressed to stay & preach, until I consented. I preached on Parable of Barren Figtree, very

preceding May. All but two of the congressmen eventually were seated between December 3, 1867, and January 10, 1868. E. Merton Coulter, *Civil War and Reconstruction in Kentucky* (Chapel Hill, 1926), 323.

earnestly — 17 came forward for prayers, & several claimed to be converted. Poor Amanda was deeply penitent & sorely distressed, but found no comfort. I spent the night with Bro Tarwater, by special request, & labored long & faithfully to produce a reconciliation, between him & Bro Hunter, who he & his wife think has neglected & injured him. I talked very kindly & plainly until past midnight. The sister wept freely, but could not see that Bro Hunter had not surely injured her husbands usefulness, & could not convince herself that it was unintentional. I think this whole trouble was first a trick of the devil, & might have been avoided if either Bro Hunter or Bro Tarwater had taken the Saviours advice & talked the matter over between themselves alone.

April 10 — Mr. Warfield desired me to stay & go back to Clarksville for Amanda's sake, so I rested & at night went back & preached with increased liberty on the parable of the wise & foolish virgins. The interest was perfect — several new mourners, & several conversions, as clear as I have seen for a long time. I was greatly encouraged at the conversion of Amanda Warfield. She seemed happy & full of comfort. Mr & Mrs Warfield greatly rejoiced at the tidings. Mr Warfield gave Robert a new hat, paid my stable bill, & gave me up a note I owed him, of 136.00 exclusive of interest — so I am abundantly paid, spiritually & temporally for my work of faith & labor of love.

April 15 — [Olmstead] Bro R. Scales of Ala[bama] staid with me. He is looking for supplies, as none that we collected for him has been forwarded. He says there is alarming destitution in his section of country.

April 28 — [Elkton] Raining nearly all day. dumb sabbath! At night went to Baptist church. Bro Massie preached Remember Lots wife. He showed, as he thought, that Christians sin often, sin always — "every step is marked with sin & stained with crime" — yet he can never apostatize or Fall from Christ. He will be brought back. He does not sin in spirit but only in the flesh. He interprets St Pauls carnal man in the 7th ch[apter] of Rom[an]s to be the inspired Apostle himself. He thinks every Christian is in uncertainty whether he be Christs or not. I have never heard the standard of Christian privilege set so low as he set it. It seems strange that he does not see in the 8th ch. that the converted man gets the victory over that "body of death."

May 12 — [Olmstead] Mr Sam Meriwether is building a new house in the yard for our hired hands — a framed or rather box house — 1 ½ stories.

June 10 — Attended Fuquas examination [at Browder Institute], children did well.

June 11 — Examination again. Very good. A fine rain at night set us to planting tobacco next day.

June 13 – Worked my potatoes & at night we all attended the exhibition which was very successful & creditable to teachers & pupils. Got to bed at one Oclock and arose after four to take train for District* [conference] meeting at Auburn. The session was pleasant. In the afternoon I opposed a resolution which I construed into a prohibition of Union Sunday Schools & was drawn into a earnest debate with T. J. Moore & J. S. Malone, A. S. Winlock taking grounds with me in favor of Union Schools in neighborhoods that could do better with union than denominational schools. The meeting voted with us very largely.

June 15 – The Conference adjourned & Bishop Doggett preached a masterly sermon – full of beauty, pathos & power. I came home to go to Mt Hermon tomorrow & here I am writing up my diary while wife & children are all asleep. I feel better & stronger spiritually, since I heard the bishops sermon – on last 2 ver[ses] in 1st ch[apter] of John.

July 1 – The seasons advance – but the crops are doing badly. Corn is small & from the excessive early rain has been badly cultivated. Very little tobacco planted by many farmers. I have only set about 3000 plants. Vegetables are late & unpromising. Oats low & suffering for rain. We have had no wetting rain for three weeks & crops begin to suffer, but God has blessed us with most beautiful weather for securing the harvest, & wheat is now ready for threshing & grinding. My dear Sons Robert, Hanson, and George have worked well all through the harvest & stood it like little men. In the main they are good & obedient children and are a great comfort to their parents.

July 2 – I went to the depot to get glass & putty for the new house windows. It is a very neat comfortable house, with a good room overhead, both floors tongued & grooved, two glass windows below & one above, & two good closets in the wall by the chimney. Our darkies seem to be well pleased with the change.

July 4 – Day once sacred in the annals of freedom. What strange sights do you behold this day in the Land of Washington & Patrick Henry? Military law superior to civil authority! News papers suppressed, courts overthrown, judges removed, citizens imprisoned, property confiscated, elections controlled by military authority. Negroes admitted to suffrage & their masters disfranchised. The Southern states held as conquered provinces & the public confidence destroyed! The good people ground down with oppressive taxation, & nine states not allowed representation in the national council! Verily the shouts of jubilation that once rung in these states, will be few or feigned to day.

The Maximilian dynasty in Mexico has failed in the defeat & capture of the invader, & the last papers report that he has been shot by order of the Liberals under Juares. Poor Mexico. Poor America.

August 5 – This is the sixteenth birth day of our only living daughter. She is now nearly grown. It seems almost yesterday that she was a cooing babe upon her mothers bosom. Her responsibility & ours is greatly increased. I trust that my dear wifes counsel & care & my own instructions & admonitions have not been lost on her. To day as we rode home from Hadensville alone, I talked very seriously & earnestly to her about the position in society she is about to assume, and the dangers & snares that beset the paths of youth. If she will heed the solemn warnings & lessons of this day I hope she will pass prudently & safely through the dangerous paths that reach from sixteen to 20 years of age. Gods word is the safe infallible guide for youth & age. I try to teach my children to read and reverence the word of the Lord.

During the past month I have filled all my appointments, except the 4th Sabbath morning at Elkton & afternoon at Providence, which rain caused me to disappoint. I preached at Hadensville 1st Sat & Sun with some liberty. Second Sabbath & Sat. I preached at Bells chapel. 3d Sunday & Sat at Mt Hermon. Sat 3 persons out, had prayermeeting. Sunday preached Psa[lm] 45th with fine effect – next day called to pray with Mat Lowery who has last week buried two children in the same grave – with whooping cough.

On the Tuesday previous I was called away to preach the funeral of Mrs Hildebrand, near Adairville – got home in the night very tired. Next day I was called away down in North Todd to preach the funeral of Philip Lawson a local preacher in the Todd circuit. On Thursday I preached the funeral sermon with quite an unction. I reached home just at night almost worn out & before I got off my horse, a messenger came for me to go to another funeral away over beyond Red Oak, the little child of a brother Eshew. I did not feel well enough to go in justice to myself & did not promise, yet I was sorry to decline.

April 14, 1868 – Three years ago this day, President Lincoln was assassinated. The excitement of that day is almost repeated now in the trial & impeachment of Andrew Johnson. He will almost surely be expelled for trying to preserve the constitution against radical schemers.[10] The country is in a deplorable state and growing worse. Clouds are darker & denser.

I am sorry I have so long neglected my diary as many important events have transpired and the influence of the political troubles has been sadly felt in the moral & spiritual growth of the church. Since my last entry, I have had better health than for some time previous.

Bishop Pierce reappointed me to the Elkton circuit, & I went on the first Sabbath to fill the first appointment at Hadensville. I was kindly greeted at all points & the brethren seem & say they are delighted with my return to the work.

I have had fine congregations & sometimes preached with liberty & unction, but we have succeeded very poorly in building up the church & my own poor heart has suffered frequently with coldness & the roots of the carnal mind. I feel & lament the plague of my own evil heart. As cares & responsibilities & vexations & bodily infirmities increase I found myself sometimes giving way to a peevishness & sometimes to a love of ease & selfindulgence that alarms & distresses me.

---

10. By a Senate vote of thirty-five to nineteen, one short of a two-thirds majority, Johnson narrowly survived the attempt to remove him from the presidency.

I have taken an additional policy of life insurance on the joint lives of Lizzie & myself for $2500, which I thought was a judicious & wise investment and a good provision for my wife if I should die, before our children are able to provide for themselves. I am conscientiously in favor of life insurance – & advise persons who need assurance to take a policy. I insured last with the Mississippi Valley Company.

On the 4th Sabbath in March, I preached the funeral sermon of my uncle Richard [Browder] & his widow, who died 20th of Feb – just seven weeks after his death – at Bethlehem. I felt the weight of my responsibility, & would have been glad for another to perform the task, but it was his request, that I should do it myself. "He was a faithful man & feared God above many."

May 5, 6, 7, 8 – Busy about home, receiving lumber for my house, replanting corn, shearing sheep, writing letters, visiting old & sick &c.

May 9 – After dinner I went to Bell's Chapel. In Elkton heard that aunt Polly Bell was very ill – not expected to live. I hurried to see her again – but she was dead! Died at 6 oclock – fully resigned & hopeful of heaven. Poor Uncle Bell, how I pity him trembling on the brink of the grave, almost 80 years old & weeping over the remains of his 3d companion!

May 10 – At 3 ½ preached aunt Pollys funeral sermon to a large & eagerly attentive audience. Text in 4th ch[apter] of 1st Thess[alonians] "Concerning them which are asleep." I spent night with Uncle Bell. Slept with him & tried to comfort him.

January 27, 1869 – A growing indifference about my journal, & much care of other matters & much absence from home have all conspired to make me neglect it. During the summer I had moderate health, filled my appointments regularly – & hope did some good. At Mt Hermon I held a protracted meeting at which about 30 persons professed conversion. A meeting at Bells chapel was less successful – about 4 conversions. At Elkton & Hadensville I labored hard but had no success.

My family was sick a great deal from August on until Christmas with chills & fever. We had seven cases of chills in one day. I sent Helen to school at the Logan Female College in Russellville & she seemed to be doing well, but took sick & we brought her home. She lost about six weeks time & went back to school but got sick again & I brought her home to stay. This I much regretted. Robert & Hanson worked in the crop until they took chills.

This last year was hard on my wife, the building on hand – workmen to board, hands to hire & many other things to look after & I most of the time away from home. Sam Meriwether & Moses Allen were the carpenters, F.M. Davenport the plasterer & Sam O. Peyton the painter. All of them did good work. We were late getting into the house & did not move in until about Christmas. I have paid many men in advance for work, and Sam Peyton is the only one that ever came promptly up & did the work according to agreement.

Our house is large, comfortable, convenient & neat, having four new rooms & two halls, six ward robes & a Book case and a two story portico to the New Building while the four old rooms are replastered & remodeled & made almost as good as new – & a commodious cellar under the dining room. The money paid out without counting our hauling, helping & boarding, was little less than $2,500.

Our crops of corn, wheat, oats, tobacco & peaches were all good – & if my hogs had not died with cholera, my finances would have been easier but as it is now, I am in debt & troubled at the thought.

Our last Conference was in Louisville. I had been asked for by Bro Brewer with whom I boarded when in 12th St Mission. It was a season of rejoicing with me to meet the friends I served & loved in the days of my youth. The rapid growth & improvement of the city since I lived here greatly surprised & pleased me. Bro A. G. Hughes from Auburn was my room mate. He had never seen a large city before & his great interest in everything increased my own pleasure. One of the most remarkable occurrences at the Conference was an invitation from the Jewish Rabbi to the Conference to go in a body & visit the New Synagogue or Temple, which we did. I never saw such magnificence elsewhere. It reminds me more of the description of Solomons Temple than aught else I ever saw. Tuesday night we received our appointments & I was glad to find myself sent to the Allensville circuit – composed of Allensville, Ash Spring, Bethlehem & Keysburg. The people at every point expressed great gratification at my appointment. I am now more convenient to my family than ever before. I feel thankful & resolved to labor faithfully in my Masters vineyard.

Aunt Betsy Waters spent a couple of months with us. She is quite old & infirm & thinks she will not live long. Her favorite girl *Margaret* left her to get married. I hardly saw a mother more distressed at separation from a daughter than aunt Betsy manifested at the departure of that negro girl. She raised her from a child – she was a good servant.

Last Sabbath I preached to a house full of persons at Hookers S[chool] H[ouse] on Mat[thew] 11.28. I stopped to see old mother Gill now 83 years old. I sung & prayed with her & she seemed greatly blessed. I find in her hands a note against me for 120 dollars now, which was given 12 years ago for $70. & forgotten in the heat of war & its confusion. Surely interest is a great moth. It eats while men sleep.

January 28 – I sowed a bed of tobacco seeds. I have hired *Henry Bell & George Hutchings,* negroes, to work my farm this year. I board them, & furnish tools, teams & land & give them a fourth of the corn, wheat, oats & tobacco.

January 29 – This day like ten days before it has been balmy & pleasant enough for Spring. It is pleasant without fire or coats. Many are sowing plant beds & plowing land. Some time ago I wrote to Thomas Jay Smith to borrow Two hundred dollars. This morning he sent me his check for money. I find it well to have friends. This necessity of borrowing comes of building too much house.

216

February 11 – This day my dear sister Mary was married to our nearest neighbor, Thomas B. Sydnor. I have seldom seen more numerous or heartfelt, congratulations. Mary & Tom are both very popular & the marriage is considered very suitable, the relations on both sides being pleased. Tommy & Mary are cousins of the second degree. He had a grand reception party, gotten up in the best style & largely attended. It was estimated that more than 3000 persons old & young, were present to enjoy the feast.

February 19 – There is considerable interest felt in this county at the prospect of voting $500,000 to aid in building the Owensboro & Russellville R. R. Most of us in this end of the county think the investment a bad one. I wrote two articles in the Russellville Herald against it – over signature of "One Voter."[11]

February 22 – Bro Morrison preached [at Quarterly Conference]. His voice continues hoarse & heavy. The same evil is growing upon me – I fear we will both soon be ineffective. My voice & lungs have been failing for a long time. I suffer *pain* & *weakness.*

February 27 – This very cold day Logan county votes & assures a tax, which I fear will grind us all our lives & oppress our children after us. I voted against the tax. I hope or rather desire that I may be mistaken in my apprehensions.

March 8 – We finished planting our early potatoes. Chesterfield Mason came in & being a shrewd trader he bought my beeves & sheep for ten or fifteen dollars less than I thought I would take for them.

March 12 – I went to Russellville on the cars – paid off most of my town debts with the proceeds of my beef & sheep sale. Helen has been in town two weeks completing her lessons in "Leather work" & not having finished, I could not bring her home.

March 23 – I went over this morning to attend the burial of poor old uncle *Billy,* an old family servant of my fathers, who suddenly fell dead in his room on Sunday night. He was very old & was rather a favorite. We feel sad at his death. I sung & prayed & made some appropriate remarks to the family & friends who were present.

March 25 – Very warm & raining. I had trouble driving home the cow I bought of W. B. Hughes. Milk cows are unusually scarce & very high. The one I bought is a poor scrawny heifer – young & small, price 25.00.

---

11. Despite George Dick's opposition, Logan County approved the $500,000 subscription. Hard times and corrupt management hampered the road's progress; by 1879 only 36 miles south of Owensboro had been constructed. During the 1880s the road, reorganized as the Owensboro & Nashville Railroad, finally reached Russellville. Maury Klein, *History of the Louisville & Nashville Railroad* (New York, 1972), 182 ff.

April 14 – I am troubled to raise money, to meet my note to the Security fire Insurance Co. I proposed to give them the old policy & take one of shorter time to correspond with the eighty dollars that I have paid them – but they would not allow the change. This causes me to fear their inability to meet losses. Yet they say they will sue if I do not pay up.

April 15 – John J. Hill – Life Insurance Agent of Miss. Valley Co. came down last night. I rode out with him to day & took a policy on Dr Blakey for $2000. Hill gives me an interest in his commissions for my labor & influence in favor of his company – which I give cheerfully & conscientiously – as I took a policy with him before I ever received or expected such an offer from him.

April 17 – Went to see Joe Gill. He took ten thousand dollars insurance – & yesterday D. E. Sydnor took five thousand. I have money enough this week to pay my debt to the Security Company.

April 20 – Went to town. Paid some of my debts & feel relieved.

April 25 – Blessed Sabbath! My congregations at Keysburg are getting larger. I do not know that I am accomplishing much good. My faith is not as strong as it should be, nor do I feel that consuming zeal at all times that once urged me on in my work. I have had of late more than usual worldly cares & I fear they have done me harm. Poor frail human nature!

April 28 – After looking at my tobacco plants – going to the depot – & visiting mother, I went with Lizzie down to her fathers.

April 29 – Mr Warfield & I rode over the place looking at his crops. It was interesting to me to ramble over the grounds that were so attractive to me in the days of my courtship – & it is still my joy that the pure hearted girl I then loved is my loving wife & wise counsellor now.

May 7 – [Olmstead] Sent off a hogshead of tobacco & worked some in my garden. I got a letter from Sister Napoleon B. Lewis requesting me to send $40 or $50 to her son John who is at Millersburg, preparing for the ministry. I would gladly send it if I could, but I am in debt & pressed greatly to meet my own engagements. I have never felt as great a financial pressure as now, but if I can borrow the money for her I will do it & feel that I do a righteous act.

May 8 – [Keysburg] After noon I went down to spend the night with Hon J. S. Golladay, who has always manifested considerable interest in my welfare & whose wife seems to appreciate my ministeral labors & visits very highly. I was cordially received & gladly & hospitably entertained. I prayed with them night & morning & did not forget my office & ministry. Mr Golladay is a wicked man, but better I think than the majority of politicians. He claimed the right to pay me ten dollars quarterage & said it was a just debt & not a present.

May 16 – Went to Allensville to commence a protracted meeting. The congregation was large. Bro J H. Hendrick, a C[umberland] P[resbyterian] minister, preached for us with energy & clearness.

May 19 – Our meeting increases in interest. One conversion, several penitents. Bro Luckett preached in the morning – Bro Hendrick at night.

May 23 – I was sick all this blessed Sabbath from the quinine & was not able to fill either of my appointments at Bethlehem or Keysburg. Bro Luckett is continuing the meeting at Allensville.

May 26 – I went to Allensville. Found some little discontent about the Old Presbyterians doing all the preaching while I was gone. I preached at night on paying vows & took charge of the meeting – there was an increase in the number of penitents & two or three professions.

May 31 – A four legged baby! This wonderful monstrosity was on exhibition in Allensville. I examined it curiously & was amazed at the sight. One head – & one stomach and body but two navels & two sets of bowels, & two pair of legs – with the general outline of two female children. The outer legs seem to be stout but the inner ones are not active – yet the form is almost perfect. Truly this is a wonderful deformity & will perhaps be as notorious as the Siamese twins. The father & mother named Corbin were with the children & seem very fond of it. Price of seeing – 25 cts.

June 1 – Summer day, but not summer weather. Our meeting continues.

June 5 – Glad to be at home with my family. It is a great trial to be away so much. My children need my attention.

June 6 – We had a morning prayer meeting. Before preaching I opened the doors of the church in behalf of the Old School Presbyterians & the Methodists – the Baptist ministers not being present & the Cumberland Presbyterians having no organization. Ten joined us & 6 or 7 the Presbyterian. I closed the meeting with reluctance, but think three weeks long enough at one place.

June 9 – Helen & I went to town in Aunt Betsys carriage. Helen is a good child, but I scolded her this day for buying an article of dress without asking me or getting her mothers consent. She knows I can not allow my children to run me in debt.

June 18 – We have much company. In the evening we went to Browder Institute to the exhibition. I suppose 1000 or 1200 people of all sorts & sizes were there. Many ruffians & rowdies, drinking & carousing, whistling – hissing – firing pistols & otherwise disturbing the exercises. These rascals all came from a distance. They do not belong in this vicinity. The great body of the audience behaved well & the scholars in the main performed their parts admirably. Some of the pieces were very fine. I was pleased with the performances of my sons who knew their pieces well & spoke loud & clear.

June 20 – The congregation at Ash Spring was larger than usual. Robert H. Youngs horse took fright, ran off & broke the buggie in pieces, running into Lafayette Rileys buggie & frightening his horse which stopped & kicked his buggie to pieces. It seems almost miraculous that no body was hurt. Mrs Riley had two children in the buggie with her.

June 27 – Very feeble & languid. I went to Bethlehem taking aunt Betsy Waters in the carriage. The congregation was large & I tried to preach for the first time in my life on the parable of the "Prodigal Son." I became very sick & was compelled to sit down requesting the congregation to sing. I tried after a little rest to finish the subject, but spoke with great labor without any great apparent effect and closed before finishing the subject. I was too sick to go to Keysburg.

June 30 – Thankful that up to 3 oclock P.M. I have escaped a chill without taking any medicine. Such is the irritable state of my stomach that I cannot safely take any nauseating medicines.

July 4 – Cloudy Sabbath. I took Georgie & Luther in the buggie to Allensville. Congregation unusually large. I preached with zeal on the subject of Missions & took up a collection & subscriptions of 35 or 6 dollars for mission work. I became very feeble, had a chill & could not go to Ash Spring.

July 6 – Very sick with a chill. These sick spells are wearing me away very fast. I suffer dreadfully yet I thank God for the hope of a world where the people "never say I am sick."

July 12 – Able to ride out alittle.

July 16 – Not so well to day – lay in bed. Aunt Betsy has returned making her visit much shorter at Tom [Browder]'s than she intended because a frog fell in the cistern & she will not drink the water. She feels more at home with Lizzie than any one else.

July 23 – Last Friday Helen & I went to down to see Mr Warfields family hoping that change of air & access to the sulphur springs would improve my health. George met us at the station & we were kindly welcomed but Saturday I felt a little puny, & Sunday I had another chill & another on Tuesday & was very sick Wednesday. I got up & came home quite feeble – & Thursday had another chill & suffered greatly. To day I am able to be up & read alittle & write a letter or so. I am using Smiths Tonic which has a great reputation as a chill cure – & hope to be relieved. I am greatly reduced & in very poor health – not able to preach atall.

220

July 24 – I lay in bed & am truly glad to write that I missed my chill. This is our Quarterly Meeting & I could not attend. Quarterly Conference met at my house & I read my reports. John W. Lewis came up to day to assist me on the circuit, which greatly relieves me.

July 31 – I trust I am improving. My strength is steadily increasing. To day I have been able to take considerable exercise, assist in salting the straw &c. We finished our wheat threshing at 12 – made about 300 bushels. Wheat very good. We had a large number of work hands to feed yesterday & to day. This is Saturday evening & I ought to be preparing a sermon, but feel unable to preach tomorrow with justice to my health.

August 2 – Election day. The laborers stopped work to go to town. I voted *against* the additional school tax – because the fund is insufficient to educate the children & is a bone of contention & source of strife.

August 7 – This afternoon the children & grown people have taken great interest in the eclipse of the sun – which was almost total – only a small part of the face of the sun being visible. Some of the fowls sought the roost & a few stars were very faintly discernable.

August 9 – Helen came home. Mr Warfield gave her a fine dress as a birth day present. I fear the growing pride & fondness for display of this day & time will ruin many precious souls.

I was grieved to day to learn that Dr Baker & D. B. Hutchings were both involved in debt, beyond their ability to pay – & many friends are likely to suffer heavily as securities. I would often have been involved in security debts but for my wifes caution & remonstrance. R[ichard] C. Browder says he would have been all right, financially, if he had listened to his wifes counsel. I hold that a man owes it to his family to be careful not to go security for speculators.

August 13 – This is the day appointed by our bishops for fasting & prayer. I appointed service at Bethlehem and not being strong enough to stand up & preach, I sat down & read Mr Wesleys excellent sermon on fasting – to the devout few – who assembled at the house of the Lord. Cousin Mary Browder, also sister Adams, her two daughters called to see us & Johnny Lewis spends the night with us. This summer has been a remarkable one for a crowd of visitors at every house of any note in the neighborhood. I delight to see my friends when I can make them comfortable, but there are times when it is a great luxury to have the house to ourselves.

August 14 – A new thing in our neighborhood occurred to day. A negro Barn Dance! This is almost an insult to the moral sense & sentiment of our community. The dance was on Wm Gaines' land. My workmen stopped business to attend the frolic.

August 17 — Aunt Betsy takes all hands to day to move her effects from Tom Browders over to my house — thinking her health demands the change as Ginnie is very delicate & has four small children & cannot nurse her in sickness, so well as my wife. Of course she is welcome to a home in my house — but the change is of her own choice with no influence of ours to induce it.

To day my cousin D. B. Hutchings, was sold out by the sheriff — for debt. Until recently he was thought to be wealthy & was trading like a man of large capital. He lives in the finest house in the country & supports a good style. He had been a very popular man & was unusually energetic. I fear he will suffer in reputation as well as finance. I greatly regret his misfortune as he was always a favorite cousin & very liberal to me. If I could help him I would — but a number of his best friends are involved with him & I fear will lose heavily, although he avers they shall not. This is another warning to young men to keep aloof from speculations & cling to legitimate industry.

August 30 — Called to see & pray with Bro Gill & Bro Rose — to both of whom I appealed for a missionary & conference donation. Bro R. made all his fortune by industry & *rigid economy* & does not see the religion of *giving*. He gave the price of one watermelon (1.00) to the worn out preachers, but not a cent to Missions. I reached home quite tired & feeling feeble — suffering with sore throat & deep cold.

September 1 — Still feeble — able to sit up & read & write alittle & walk out. I have serious fears that my health & strength are permanently impaired. I am in great uncertainty as to the propriety of taking an appointment from the Conference. I dread the idea of retiring from active service & yet I do not wish to take a work that I cannot fill.

September 4 — I lay in bed until after 9 oclock, then dressed & went to Allensville to our adjourned Quarterly meeting. The finances remain low. I got six hundred & 44 dollars for my years work and am satisfied. I furnished Bro Lewis a horse, saddle & saddlebags & paid him $25.00 for a months assistance.

September 9 — An immense throng crowded into Russellville to witness the laying of the corner stone of the new Logan Female College. Several hundred Free Masons were in attendance & performed the ceremonies of laying the corner stone with great precision. Dr Young (R.A.) & Bishop McTyeire made appropriate addresses. I have seldom seen a larger crowd — but the money subscribed did not atall correspond with the great multitude or the demands of the occasion — only a few hundred dollars being raised.

September 18 — Very early we all arose — had prayers & breakfast & Helen & I took leave of the dear ones at home & set out via Louisville to Owensboro, to attend the Conference. At Whippoorwill, Kate Oakes joined us. We expected to spend the Sabbath in the city & I had been announced in the city to preach at 12th St on Sabbath morning & night, but I found that I could not meet the class

I was appointed to aid in examining unless I pressed on, so we went immediately on board the Nightingale. The girls were delighted with the Ohio & the cities around the falls. The day was distressingly hot, but the night was delightful. The moon was bright & the girls spent much time on deck feasting their eyes on the beautiful river & its romantic scenery.

September 19 – A lovely Sabbath. I felt as if duty demanded that some of us preach to all that would hear. I asked the Captain & he gladly consented and made the arrangement. I expected surely some other brother would preach, but all refused & I followed my own conviction of duty & preached earnestly & with some liberty Phil[ippians] 2.12. "Work out your own Salvation" &c. The labor was great as it required great force of voice to be heard above the din of machinery & the puffing of escape pipes, but I succeeded, & hardly ever witnessed a more orderly & attentive audience.

The Captain sought an introduction (I did not know his name nor he mine). He told me his name was "Dolley." I said, "There was an old gentleman of that name at 12th St Louisville who was convicted and converted under my ministry."[12] He answered, "Yes sir, I am a son of that man." This little episode was delightfully interesting to me. The Captain treated me with great consideration during the trip. We landed at Owensboro at 8 oclock P.M. Sister Watkins came around & conducted us to her large & elegant house where we are to lodge during Conference.

September 20 – Several of the class absent. Committee – Dr S. W. Speer, H.M. Ford D. D. & myself – all present. Class seems well prepared for examination. At work all day with the class.

September 21 – Still at work with the class. All the essays were turned over to me to examine & report. This was considerable labor.

September 22 – Conference assembled. Bishop McTyeire was present. An unusually large number of brethren answered to the calling of the roll. I was appointed one of the Committee on Religious interest of Colored people & am also one of the "Joint board of Finance." At 2 oclock had to work again with our class. I have never seen so thorough an examination before since I have been in the Conference. Dr Speer is a very faithful examiner, but brings in many things that I think are irrelevent in the examination.

September 27 – The pleasantness of our session was interrupted to day by the preferring of charges against J. R. Bennett for fraud & falsehood. A Committee was appointed to try the case. At night they had a sad time in the committee, finding the charges all true.

---

12. See entry for October 16, 1864.

September 28 — A sad & solemn scene was enacted to day when the committee in Bennetts case reported his expulsion from the church. I never saw such a scene before & pray God I may never witness the like again. After some affecting & solemn remarks, Bishop M[cTyeire] called us to prayer & Dr Rivers prayed most powerfully & earnestly for the erring brother — & his parents & his wife (to whom he had been married only 2 weeks). Oh what a time of heart-searching & humiliation. Poor Bennett does not seem to realize his degradation & his bride is apparently equally insensible of his real condition. She is a sister of B. A. Cundiff, one of the Presiding Elders. Cundiffs wife seems to feel more than any of the connection the humiliation that has overtaken her husbands brotherinlaw.

This was a busy day — morning & afternoon — & at night we received our appointments. By advice of the Bishop & many other ministers, I consented to be a supernumerary* & rest from regular work — hoping to regain my health. The preachers were nearly all satisfied with their appointments. Always some few feel aggrieved & some complain. The 12th St Church at Louisville had sent a formal & official petition for my appointment to their station — & I suppose I would have been sent if I had been well. Bro E. W. Bottomley, the former pastor, was aggrieved & thought I had sought to supercede him — & he made this impression on the minds of some of the preachers. Nothing could be farther from the truth in the case — & I think I fully satisfied him & others that he was laboring under a wrong impression.

September 29 — At one Oclock we bade adieu to the very hospitable family of Dr Sam Watkins, & with a crowd of preachers, preachers wives & lay delegates we boarded the Steamer Palestine on our home ward voyage. We lay up a great part of the night on account of fog & reached Portland Thursday 30th Sep at 8 oclock P.M. We crowded into a street car — too many of us — & broke a wheel — & had to walk & carry baggage a considerable distance to the Spurrier house on 6th St near Main.

October 1 — The girls & I occupied the same room & slept soundly until breakfast was announced. We walked up Main St — went to Central market — went to Cave hill cemetery — the prettiest place I ever saw — went to see the Court house & H. Clays beautiful marble statue — went out on the R.R. Bridge & saw the grand falls — & the surrounding cities to our delight. Went into several large Book & Jewelry stores — into the art gallery & feasted our eyes on fine paintings — went up broad way & gazed at the grandeur of the lordly mansions that vie with each other there — went into the Jewish Synagogue & gazed with mute wonder at its magnificence — then returned to the hotel & took our baggage to Bro Brewers where we were kindly & gladly entertained.

October 2 — Up early — had prayers & breakfast & off to the train. A woman & man put their children on — were too late themselves — & the train dashed away — taking the screaming children & leaving the agonized mother & father behind. I begged to stop the train & put the children off — but the officers would not. They sent the children back by the Lebanon train. I asked the Conductor to telegraph back & let the mother know. He promised. At Russellville we had to get off & wait for the accommodation train as our Conductor would not stop at Olmstead.

Home Sweet home. Robert was waiting at the depot with the buggie. Lizzie though sick met us at the stile.

October 12 – I went to see Thos J. Smith, for my father to know if he could lend us twelve hundred dollars, to pay a security debt for D. B. Hutchings. Smith is an accommodating man & was glad to lend father the money. D. B. H. confidently affirms that he will repay the debt.

October 18 – I bought a turkey & a little butter for the dinner Lizzie intends giving her brother Georgie who is to be married to Dora Pollard on 20th inst. My father is greatly troubled about a $4000.00 protest from the Falls City bank in Louisville, drawn in favor of D.B. Hutchings. We saw D. B. H. this morning & he assures us that the draft is amply secured by collaterals. I went to Tom Smiths for the money, above mentioned & got his check for the 1200 dollars – William & I going his security. I stopped at the school house for a pen, ink & paper, found that out of 80 scholars from almost infancy up to manhood, only 2 or 3 had copy books or were learning to write at school. It is a shame that teachers are either so crowded or so neglectful.

October 20 – Busy hauling corn & sowing wheat until 12 oclock. Got ready & went with Robert & Hanson & Frank Browder to see George W. married. We rode fast – averaging 5 miles pr hour for 5 or six hours. Bro M G Alexander – the parson – was very much embarrassed. He pronounced on several occasions that he married them by authority of the Commonwealth of Kentucky – but he was in Tennessee. He required them to "serve honor & obey each other."

November 19 – Rainy & gloomy. I went over to see the result of R[ichard] C. Browders sale. The sheriff sold out all his perishable property to satisfy a debt of D. B. Hutchings, in Elkton Bank, on which Dick was security. His land is to be sold on Monday. No body seemed disposed to bid today & three thousand dollars worth or more of property went for 500 or 600. This will doubtless be redeemed.

December 24 – Busy to day hanging a gate & doing other little jobs. To night Helen has gone to her Grandpa Warfields. Robert & Hanson are at a candy pulling at D. B. Hutchings & I am writing up my journal, writing to James Warfield – talking to Georgie, Luther & Wallace about the birth, crucifixion, resurrection, ascension – & second coming of Christ. They seemed intensely interested. I hope good impressions were produced. Now as I am writing Lizzie is playing Santa claus & filling the expectant childrens stockings with crackers, cakes candy – nuts, toys &c. Oh God – grant that my children may now & always, love & obey Jesus whose birth we now celebrate.

December 25 – With all my brothers except John – & both my sister & brotherinlaw – we ate our Christmas dinner at Fathers according to annual custom. I scarce hope ever to see us all together again. Frank is preparing to leave for Ala. where he will raise cotton.

December 29 – Hanson & I hauled rails, Georgie plowed & Robert rode round making up a club for Parker Companys 1.00 store Boston.

January 3, 1870 – I went over to see my father. Frank & David left for Montgomery Ala last Thursday, 30th Dec. I gave Frank a mule, to be paid for if he gets able. I also gave him $27.00 in money, which is some relief to my father as well as to Frank. Father, Mother & I sat at table alone to day, being the same family that sat together, just 40 years ago.

January 5 – We sent *Henrys* plunder to the depot. Four years ago, he came here with one wagon load – & part of another. To day it takes four loads to move his ,ood. He & *Kate* have prospered with us – & we with them. I hope they may do well. *Sue* is now our cook & *Isham* & *Martha* our other servants.

January 6 – Hauling, straw &c. Sent *Henrys* family to the depot. *Kate* wept freely when she left us – & was very sorry she ever made up her mind to go away.

January 8 – Removing fence – I feel the necessity of being more industrious. I regret that I have so little time to read. I lost much, by not improving my time as I ought, in youth.

January 20 – My hired man *Isham* was disrespectful to my wife & I rebuked him very sharply. Just before breakfast, we discovered our barn on fire – just in time to save it. The damage was slight but the peril was great & the smoke of burning tobacco stalks made us quite sick for a time.

January 25 – After almost 48 hours of rain, we rejoice to see the Sunshine. I have a rheumatism in my right arm, which is a new affliction, having never suffered with it until a few days before Christmas, having it ever since. After dinner I chopped wood until almost exhausted.

February 5 – After a busy week making plant beds, getting wood, repairing fences &c. – I went to Allensville to Quarterly meeting. Quarterly conference advanced Petrees salary from 800 to 1000$. This is right & was necessary to equalize the proportion between his pay & the P[residing] E[lder]s which is estimated at $125. on this circuit. The Conference requested me to preach at each appointment on the support of the ministry. I do this the more cheerfully as I have no claim or share in the collections this year.

Robert received his long expected box of $1.00 goods from Parker & Co dollar store in Boston Mass. Some of the articles are very cheap, others not really worth the money, & dearer than they would cost at home. I ordered 3 Broad cloth caps for my boys & was amused to find them Yankee soldier caps! Roberts Stereoscope is cheap & interesting.

After much indecision & frequent consultation, I allowed my boys to get a checker board to play drafts. I was afraid of the influence, yet did not see any good cause for interdicting an innocent amusement. Dr Lee, Joshua Knowles, J. A. Lewis & other good men pronounced it a harmless amusement.

February 22 — Snowy & disagreeable. I was pained to learn that our neighbor, Dr. Tompkins, was going to sell whisky at Olmstead. This is the first move of the kind there & creates quite an indignation. We have been thankful & proud of our sober neighborhood & regret to see a bad change.

February 23 — I went over to see Dr Tompkins — talked very plainly — pointedly & kindly to him — remonstrated against his traffic — told him that I & others would do all in our power to break down his trade & discountenance & oppose him as a merchant — as a neighbor & a dentist if he persisted. I begged him to be advised. As I passed by in the evening he called to me & stated that he had considered what I had said to him & declaimed the idea of selling whisky. I told him I was highly gratified to hear it — & felt very much more like giving him a part of my trade & influence small as they are.

March 9 — Ground hard frozen. Dragging down corn stalks on wheat, with a log. Hansons team ran away & Rock fell down with him but did not hurt him. Aunt Betsy has a letter telling her that *Allen* is very ill with Pneumonia & anxious to see her. She is in great distress & would go if she could, but as she cannot I must go for her.

March 10 — I rather reluctantly went to see poor old *Allen* nearly 20 miles. I did not feel very well & kept thinking of many other sick people that I would like to visit — felt that I was going to accommodate aunt Betsy more than a sense of duty. I found him very ill, very uncomfortably situated in a dark, open cabin — insufficient clothing & scanty food. He was rejoiced to see me. I took him a few pounds of sugar & coffee — some light bread & biscuit for which he seemed grateful. I read some scripture, sang & prayed with him & found that he was trusting in Jesus & resigned to die.

March 11 — Aunt Betsy is very sad to hear of *Allens* destitution & is going to work liberally & energetically to supply his wants. She is very much attached to her family servants.

March 17 — I have been unwell since Tuesday & stay in doors. Aunt Betsy hired *Henry Bell* to go down & see *Allen* — take him some shirts — boots &c. — & a heavy blanket. He returned this evening with the sad news that poor *Allen* died last Tuesday. Aunt Betsy is greatly grieved & seems like a mother weeping for a son.

March 20 — I went to Sabbath School & to Ash Spring — then went to see old Bro Brake who is slowly dying with cancer. He was delighted at my visit. Said he did not feel the triumphs & overflowing love of God as he desired. While we talked together he was greatly blessed. He shouted & rejoiced until his strength was exhausted. I have not seen him so happy since the day he was converted, Oct 10th 1846.

March 22 — Very busy planting potatoes in a piece of new land. My dear wife & Hanson were both taken suddenly sick. Hanson remarked, as we were going out to work, that he felt strangely about the breast & was sick. I sent him to the house, & learned afterward that he reached home with great difficulty, lying down & vomiting several times. When I came to the house I found him & his mother both similarly affected — vomiting yellow bile in large quantities & occasionally a little blood, & some cramping. Lizzie would not agree to have the doctor called in & supposed it was only a bilious spell that would soon pass off. I inquired if they had eaten any thing. Hanson said "nothing but bread & gravy" but presently remembered that he & his mother had eaten an artichoke in the garden. I knew there were no artichokes there & was afraid they were poisoned. After the violent symptoms were arrested — I examined the artichoke & found that they had eaten a young & tender poke root, which has a sweetish taste but is an active poison. I feel thankful that they escaped with their lives. I suppose the emetic properties of the root saved them. It also produced purging & I doubt not would produce death if eaten in large quantities. Lizzie only swallowed a little of the juice, but Hanson ate a piece of the root.

April 6 — This day my Luther is nine years old & is a lively hearty lad, but I am ashamed that I have done so little toward his education. He can barely read in monosyllables & spell in dyssyllables. I hoped that Helen would teach him when she finished her own education.

April 16 — After two weeks of the most balmy beautiful April weather I ever saw, pushing on the grass — & unfolding the blooms, we were surprised this morning to see a heavy snow storm for a time covering green fields — trees & also the houses with a robe of white.

April 25 — For the first time in Kentucky negroes are allowed to vote[13] — they nearly all vote radical. I voted for Genl Lewis, democrat, to fill the place of Mr Golladay, resigned.

May 20 — To night at nine oclock a precious little daughter was born to us, our eighth child. I feel truly grateful to our Heavenly Father that the crisis is past & Lizzie is doing so well. Dr Hutchings & my mother were with us. The Lord is better than our fears. I call the child "Lizzie."

---

13. The Fifteenth Amendment, which guaranteed black suffrage, went into effect on March 30, 1870, despite having been resoundingly rejected by the Kentucky legislature on March 13, 1869. Coulter, *Civil War and Readjustment in Kentucky,* 422.

September 6 — We have had a most fruitful season, rain in abundance — crops in low lands drowned out. There was never a heavier crop of corn in the country, tobacco is unusually fine — grass plentiful & fruit abundant. For several weeks our dear Little Lizzie Warfield has been almost constantly at deaths door, caused by disease of the bowels & affection of the brain. She is now alive with but little prospect of her recovery. We try to give her up to God. Bro Petree baptized her on the 1st of this month.

[Over the past few months] I have preached occasionally, I trust with good effect. My own poor heart has often been sad & spiritually lean. I sorely lament my follies, sins & backslidings. Christ is all my hope. I fear I am not able to do itinerant work another year. I have worked almost as much as I am able on the farm. If I can get good prices for the crops, I can aid my father in paying his security debt.

September 8 — Circumstances have conspired to keep me away from meeting at Allensville. My dear little Lizzie continues in a state of almost hopeless prostration — she seems to be a victim of starvation. When she needed mothers milk she could not get it — & now that we have a nurse, the milk does not come.

September 17 — Sad day to our house! Our dear little Lizzie died this morning at break of day. She died calm & easy. God be praised for granting thus much of our prayer. Dear little sufferer — thy pains are over now. While thy natural eyes are glazed in death — thy spirit eyes behold "The king in his beauty & the land that is afar off." She had mild blue eyes slowly deepening into dark color, fair complexion — benignant — amiable countenance — beautiful form & regular features. Her expression was very sprightly & caused frequent remarks. She noticed more than any of our children of her age — up to the time of the fatal illness. Even when almost worn out with pain & fever she would force a smile in response to our coaxing. Dear one — sleep on till the resurrection of the just. May our sad bereavement drive us nearer to the cross of Christ.

We buried our precious babe near her little angel sister Ginnies grave. Home is dreary without her.

Volume V
1870–1877

*"Surely this is to all other Expositions what Niagara is
to all other cataracts."*

Editor's Note: In the years following little Lizzie's death, George Dick's life continued to revolve around the church and his family. The supernumerary status to which he had been assigned by the Louisville Conference of the Methodist Episcopal Church, South, in 1869 was renewed in 1870 and 1871. He was, nonetheless, requested to assist on the Allensville Circuit (1870–71) and at Auburn and Bibb's Chapel (1871–72) as much as his health allowed. By 1872 he was well enough to accept a full-time appointment to the Allensville Circuit, and for the next two years George Dick ministered faithfully on a rotating schedule to the following congregations: Allensville, Bethlehem, Ash Spring, and Keysburg. His journals reveal that during these two years he preached 148 sermons, conducted 24 funerals, performed 20 marriages, and made 421 pastoral visits, including 186 to those who were ill.

Although the journal entries relating to George Dick's experiences as a preacher on the Allensville Circuit are, for the most part, routine and undistinguished, several provide fascinating, and sometimes humorous, glimpses into the man and his times. On November 5, 1872, for example, he married Robert Campbell to Nannie Browder "with the Episcopal service & the ring – the first time I ever used the ring service." George admitted that he was "somewhat excited, but not embarrassed." On May 31, 1874, he attended a dedication service for the newly completed Trenton Methodist Church, "a model of neatness & taste." George Dick noted that as Dr. Wilson preached a dedicatory sermon on accountability to God, "his false teeth fell out of his mouth, onto the pulpit, but he readjusted them & did not seem the least embarrassed."

At least two pastoral calls during these years were also noteworthy. On February 2, 1873, George Dick stopped on his way home from Allensville "to converse & pray with Mr. Gregorys family. They are very poor & the old man very wicked. Mrs Gregorys mother had ten daughters & 6 sons – each daughter had 14 or 15 children – & the sons wives almost as many. She said that her mother had 200 children, grand children & great grand children before she died!" One of George Dick's most memorable visits occurred on August 7, 1873. On his return from Pleasant Grove, he called at Dr. Marion Bailey's to see Duncan Hines, a black preacher, whom he described as "very ill with consumption of the Bowels – & cannot live long." As George Dick remembered his visit:

> I asked him about his state – he said "Im bound to die – & it is right." I asked if he felt that he was standing on the Rock Christ Jesus. He said, "Yes, yes, there's not a cloud in my way" – said he had enjoyed himself more with me than any preacher he ever saw in his life & was anxious to see me while he could talk to tell me of his "ups & downs." Said he – "Ive had a jubilee!" Poor Duncan, I always thought he was a good man. He certainly had the most thrilling voice I ever heard & was strangely eloquent for an uneducated man. He was peculiarly gifted in prayer – & used to stir large congregations with his powerful appeals. When overly burdened in spirit & calling the Lord to help – he would repeat – & dwell upon – the interjection Oh! oh!! – with a rising cadence that was peculiar to himself & reached real sublimity that was actually thrilling – until he seemed to feel that he had gained the ear of the Lord –

when he would pour out such petitions as his soul desired. Once I heard him pray at Red Oak Camp Meeting a prayer that swayed the multitude as wind sways the standing corn. One petition that rung out above the rest was, "Oh thou good shepherd – when we come to the swellings of Jordan let us try the waters by thy staff." From present indication he is almost in the flood & passing through the valley, yet he fears no evil – he is trying the waters with the great shepherds staff.

I read the 12 of Hebrews & sung & prayed with him, for which he seemed grateful – although very weak & breathing heavily. He was much moved when I took leave of him & sent a grateful remembrance to "Miss Lizzie" (my wife). In his humility he always called me Master, as well now, as when he was a slave. He had a fine memory & quick perception – & although entirely uneducated – he used to make some exhortations & deliver some sermons that would have done credit to men of better advantages. He quoted texts & scriptures from memory & used to make some strange mistakes in his pronunication – but was generally correct in his scriptures texts. I once heard him announce a text from "The 1st ver[se] in the 12 chap[ter] of the Book of Esdras-Astes" "Remember now thy Creator" &c. I think in this sermon – in urging consistency in Christian life – he exclaimed – "I have no faith in that religion that serves God with one hand & pulls a chicken off the roost with the other." Duncan doubtless has had his faults & follies with the rest of our erring race – but he has had fewer faults than most of his kind. I had some words with him when he left the Southern church & joined the Zionites – & told him I doubted if he had acted wisely. He replied that he had gone through these regions a long time "feeding the sheep & now he was only marking a few of his lambs." In slave times he was the property of John Hines & was faithful to his master. One Autumn in 18 – I held a protracted meeting for the negroes – with great success & much of that success was due to Duncans earnest labor. He worked all day in his masters field – then walked four or five miles at night & preached – & sung & cheered the host on to battle & to victory until a late hour in the night – & this continued for a considerable time. I think more than 30 negroes professed conversion at that meeting & many of them continued steadfast in the faith as long as they remained in these parts – & some of them that still linger around this spot after the changes of war – are now the pillars of the colored Methodist church – South. May the gracious Lord grant Duncan a smooth passage to the grave & bring him in triumph to the home of the blest.

When Duncan died ten months later, George Dick preached his funeral sermon.

It was also during his tenure on the Allensville Circuit that George Dick's reputation as a fund raiser began to gather momentum. His first effort, entirely unanticipated, occurred under circumstances which immediately attracted the attention of the church leadership. The setting was a District Conference at Elkton on June 29, 1873, with Bishop H. H. Kavanaugh presiding. As George Dick described the occasion:

Gloomy morning, sprinkling rain. Methodists all discouraged about the prospect of a congregation & the paying of our heavy debt incurred in trying to repair our church. It is now beautiful. Greatly to our delight the sun came out – people came to church – house full. Bishop Kavanaugh preached an excellent sermon on the benefits of a house of worship & the spiritual blessings implied. Bro Morton was to have raised the collection, being skilled in that department. He could not be found. Sensation – suspense. What shall we do!

Bro J. A. Lewis the pastor called Bro Browder to raise the collection. I could not refuse to do what seemed duty – though I doubted my adaptation. I made a short appeal – told them who answered with 100$ & 50$ & 25$ &c as well as I could remember – told them that these good men were all gone & I hoped in Heaven & now a rededication demands a response from their children & the inheritors of their labors. I was never better equipped for work than I was in a few moments & then I called for help. I was humorous & kept the whole audience cheerful & quiet, & often laughing as I passed through them & raised 100s, 50s, 25s, 10s, 5s, 1s until we raised more than 1000, greatly to our relief & the apparent delight of the entire audience. I was greeted & congratulated on all sides by preachers & people, gentlemen & ladies – & some even dared to tell me that I had plucked Bro Mortons laurels off from him. Bishop Kavanaugh said "Browder do the people always give you money like they did today?" I said, "No sir I never tried to raise a large collection before." He said "Well, if you improve on your first effort, you will be successful." Said he had never in his life seen an audience kept so patient & cheerful & give so readily during the entire collection. Some of the Baptist friends said they wanted to "borrow me" at the dedication of their new house.

When the Louisville Annual Conference met at Russellville the following October, George Dick was pressed into taking offerings on successive evenings for Logan Female College, the Preacher's Aid Society, and Conference missions. Each effort was remarkably successful, but he was not unaware of the implications of his emerging role as a fund raiser, exclaiming: "I begin to fear that I will be too much mixed up in the money collections & lose part of my spiritual interest in looking after the temporal interest of the church."

He had reason to be concerned. When the next annual conference met at Princeton in October 1874, Bishop William M. Wightman removed him from the Allensville Circuit and appointed him as agent for Warren College and Logan Female College, a task which George Dick characterized as "a laborious field, without much promise at present." During the next two years he visited scores of potential patrons and wrote hundreds of letters ("I try to write heart letters"); he also continued to preach at every opportunity. Despite the hard times following the Panic of 1873, George Dick acquitted himself well. Although many contributors gave reluctantly, he rarely encountered the kind of response he received on a trip to Calhoun in June 1875. Shortly before sunset, at the close of a day with little success, he called at Joe Jeff Bennett's place where

a *large very large* woman barefooted came to the door. Said her husband was not in, would be back at night. I told her I was a Methodist Preacher & had been directed to her house as a place where I could spend a night – and asked permission to remain. With some apparent reluctance she said she supposed I could stay. I went in & she asked with scrutinizing look if I had business with Mr B. I told her no more than I had with all Methodists & friends of the church. She said "You aint after money are you?" I said yes, in part & told her my business. She said – "We've done too much of that already. A man by the name of Redford came here on that business & I hope he'll never come here again – he just talked & talked & pulled & hauled Mr Bennett to sign a whole lot of papers that he never ought to have signed," & much of such sentiment. I was very mild & pleasant in my replies – but I thought my presence was not very pleasant so I left & she kindly told me that "Mr Foster was a mighty nice

234

man & had gals & all to help & he'll let you stay there." She came to the door & said "You wont go off & tell now that I drove you off – will you?" "No madam," I said "I didn't understand that you were driving me away, but I thought I had better go farther."

As college agent George Dick attended a number of district conferences seeking their endorsements for his work. Although the one held at Bowling Green in May 1875 was not especially memorable for advancing the interests of the colleges, a rather extraordinary incident took place that had deep personal meaning for him. During a morning love feast, Dr. A. S. Walker gave the following testimony:

> When I was a school boy in Logan county, Ky, I went to spend a night with a neighbor & relative. As I drew near the house I heard the voice of song & saw through the open window a young mother, rocking a babe in the cradle & in soft & tender tones singing – "Attend young friends while I relate, The Dangers you are in. The evils that round you wait, While subject unto sin" &c. I listened & that song sent an arrow to my heart. I was awakened to a sense of my condition as a lost sinner. I went into the house & rocked the cradle & the good lady sang the remaining verses of the song. God sealed the sentiment upon my heart. I had no rest in my spirit, I sought Gods mercy. I have been happy a thousand times since & I am happy this morning in my Saviors love. No one need tell me that a little boy cannot enjoy religion. I was a boy when I was converted & my face is still toward the Heavenly City. Sisters, Oh Sisters sing the old songs, sing with spirit. God will send them into sinners hearts as he did mine. I must tell you that the little boy whose mother was rocking him in the cradle is now a minister & on this floor, & that sainted mother whose song led me to God was the mother of Rev Geo. R. Browder, & he was the infant in the cradle.

George Dick observed that "this episode created quite a sensation & many of us were melted to tears."

During these years in which George Dick's health enabled him to return to an active life as preacher and college agent, he continued to experience the strength and joy of enduring family relationships. Despite the hard times, these were, for the most part, happy years for the Browder family. The two most noteworthy exceptions involved close relatives. Lizzie's father, George H. Warfield, died on December 9, 1870, at the age of 66. His loss was aggravated by the unethical practices of the Warfield executors who not only delayed a settlement of the estate until June 1875, but whose speculation with Warfield's money resulted in a loss of nearly $25,000. Financial problems also cast a long shadow over Robert Browder as he continued to struggle with a $4000 debt owed to the creditors of D. B. Hutchings. The extent to which the entire Browder connection agonized over his plight is revealed in George Dick's anxious statement: "We are all in trouble about my dear old fathers burden with D. B. Hutchings security debts. I would rather be turned out of home myself than see my father impoverished in his old age, now nearly 70 years old."

As George Dick and Lizzie grappled with the lingering vexations of the Warfield estate and and security debts, they took considerable delight in the good health and progress of their children, three of whom had grown to adulthood by 1875. On December 7, 1871, Helen married Charles W. (Charley) Roach of Todd County, who took his bride back home with him to the Pinchem community, just northwest of Guthrie. On July 31, 1873, the first of their eight children, Anna Lizzie, was born at George Dick's home where Helen had gone to stay during her confinement. Helen's motherhood apparently served to intensify her desire to return to more familiar surroundings. Consequently, when she and Charley returned to Olmstead in October for Anna Lizzie's baptism, they announced their intention to buy the Wintersmith farm which was located on the Clarksville Road, just south of Richard Browder's place. When the Roaches moved to their new home in January 1874, Anna Lizzie spent the day at George Dick's to "coo & crow for her old grand pa & grand ma." A second daughter, Ruth Morrison, was born to Helen and Charley on April 16, 1875.

The early 1870s were eventful years for most of the Browder boys as well. This was particularly true of their spiritual development, a matter that lay close to their parents' hearts. One can well imagine the satisfaction with which George Dick recorded on September 5, 1872, that at the conclusion of a service at Bethlehem Church four persons came forward for prayers, "one of them my own dear Luther, 11 years old, the age at which I was converted & beyond which age, none of my children have as yet deferred the time of seeking the Lord." The next evening Luther again came forward as a mourner, this time accompanied by his fifteen-year-old brother George. His father noted that George had made a "profession of religion" six or seven years earlier, "& I hoped was converted, but I have all along had some fears about his understanding of the subject." George's spiritual condition continued to trouble his parents for a number of years.

Whatever doubts George Dick's two oldest sons, Robert and Hanson, may have entertained during these years had more to do with their life's work than their eternal destiny. When Robert turned twenty-one in 1874 his father noted: "I have tried to give him a good education & teach him industry & economy, but my chief concern has been to train him, & all my children 'in the nurture & admonition of the Lord.'" In the light of that heritage, Robert's decision to preach the gospel apparently came as naturally and as effortlessly as did his father's twenty-eight years earlier. On September 22, 1874, the Quarterly Conference of Russellville District at Allensville unanimously recommended Robert to the Louisville Conference of the Methodist Episcopal Church, South, "as a suitable person to be received into the travelling connexion." Three weeks earlier Robert had commenced a year of teaching at the Ash Spring School to earn enough money to continue his education. The following autumn he enrolled in a program of theological studies at the new Vanderbilt University in Nashville.

Hanson's career decision came less easily and only after he had suffered a major disappointment. On October 6, 1874, George Dick noted that his son, now nearly twenty years old, was reviewing for a competitive examination to determine whether he would receive an appointment to the United States Military Academy, a move which gave his father "a considerable anxiety." Four days later Hanson, after a gruelling eight hour written test in the study room of Warren College[1] in Bowling Green, easily outscored eight other boys and received the congratulations of the teachers and "some of the competitors." His departure for West Point eight months later on June 2, 1875, was traumatic not only for him and his family ("Hanson is gone & we are sad. We will miss him so much. Oh – so much") but for the small close-knit fellowship at Bethlehem Church as well ("Everybody seems loathe to give him up. The Sunday School was deeply affected & all present wept when he took leave."). As George Dick travelled to Calhoun the next day, his heart continued to ache for his son: "The road was sad & dreary to me, thinking every minute of my dear son far away for a long time. I felt such a sense of loneliness & felt so much for my dear wife that I came very nearly returning home."

The lengthy separation that George Dick so much dreaded did not materialize. On June 29 Hanson returned home "weary & troubled," having passed a fine entrance examination in everything but history "& withal not as well up on that branch as he ought to have been he failed & was rejected." Hanson was mortified. Nevertheless, two months later, his courage restored, he set out to accept the West Point challenge once more. Although his examination this time went well, Hanson's ardor for a military education rapidly diminished in the face of a growing conviction that he ought to preach the gospel. George Dick, in a characteristic spirit of resignation, accepted his decision on September 10 with the observation: "I, of course give my consent – but am sorry he did not decide the matter before he spent so much time – labor & money in getting into the Academy. Yet it may be that Gods hand ordered it all. He led Joseph to his usefulness through a dungeon – & Moses renounced Egypt & its glory for the reproach of Christ. I still trust God to guide my children in all their ways!"

George Dick provides only a few glimpses into the life of his youngest child during the early 1870s. When Wallace celebrated his seventh birthday on October 12, 1872, his father described him as "a sprightly promising boy, very industrious & has fine ideas of business, but has never been to school & does not seem fond of books." Two years later, however, Wallace's performance at school had elevated him from relative obscurity to a neighborhood celebrity. The occasion was the annual student oratory contest at Bethlehem Church on June 10 and 11. All of the Browder boys performed well, including Robert who won the ten-dollar gold medal offered to the best declaimer, but it was little Wallace who carried the day. A proud father recorded that when Wallace delivered his

---

1. Warren College was chartered in 1866 by the Louisville Conference of the Methodist Episcopal Church, South, for the purpose of educating young men. The College, with Dr. J. G. Wilson as President, opened in 1872 with eighty students. It lasted only four years. The two major reasons for its demise were: (1) threatened competition from a proposed Ogden College, which offered tuition-free education to all students in Warren County, and (2) the opening of Vanderbilt University in 1876, which provided the Louisville Conference with a satisfactory alternative for training young men for the ministry. Historical Society for the Centennial Session of the Louisville Annual Conference of the Methodist Church, *Century of Progress 1846–1946* (Hopkinsville, Kentucky, 1946), 37–38.

speech entitled "School Experience," he "was very much frightened at the crowd & could not help crying, but made the bravest, manliest effort that I ever saw a little boy make & in spite of his tears & agitation spoke every word so clearly & made his gestures so naturally that he won rounds of applause & many thought the crying was artificial & part of the performance. He was much compliment-ed." The following day, as the exhibition continued, Wallace was called on to repeat his speech at the conclusion of which an admiring lady presented him with a "Badge of Honor" inscribed to "The Little Hero of Yesterday, Master Wallace Browder."

Although George Dick was understandably pleased with the triumphs of his children during these years, he characteristically found little in himself about which he could boast. Each birthday was a time for quiet introspection as he lamented his failures and weaknesses. Unlike his earlier annual musings, however, George Dick's reflections as he entered his late forties indicate a growing concern about his physical condition. His entry for January 11, 1875, is typical:

> This day 48 years ago I was born. I ought not to be old but I am. I am sensibly failing in strength of mind & body. I am now called "old brother Browder." My head & beard are very gray. I am fleshy & need more rest – get about with more difficulty. It comes very natural to me to walk alittle slower & tire a little sooner. I find it desirable to get on a stump or step to mount into the saddle. I feel more inclined to stay at home & when I am away I am restless to get back. My teeth are bad & my hearing is not so good & I feel more pains. I know that *I am growing old.*

Despite these pessimistic premonitions of declining strength, George Dick's resolve to "endure hardness as a good soldier of Jesus Christ" sustained him during the last eleven years of his life and rarely permitted his frail body to keep him from his appointed rounds.

* * *

[Editor's Note: We return to George Dick's entries beginning with October 1875. At that time he was just concluding his first year as agent for Logan Female College (Russellville) and Warren College (Bowling Green). As we pick up the narrative he is accompanying his son Robert to Nashville, Tennessee, to enroll him in Vanderbilt University.]

October 1, 1875 – Robert and I left on the evening train for Nashville to attend the dedication exercises of Vanderbilt University. We stopped in Bowling Green and spent the night – & next morning visited Warren College. I did some work for college interest, then took train for Nashville. Stopped at Foulks boarding house and went at night to hear Governor Fowlers eulogy on Andrew Johnson – in honor of whom there was a grand street parade.

October 4 – We were most cordially welcomed at Dr Morgans and invited to remain during our stay. The crowd at the university was immense – the speeches were grand – the prayers were earnest and the music enchanting. Governor Porters address of welcome was beautifully appropriate and well-timed. Dr Deems dedication address was far beyond my expectation and Dr Lipsombs speech on the University Idea was all that could be expected. The services were enlivened by the reception of two dispatches from Cornelius Vanderbilt. The occasion has been very satisfactory, and my heart is touched with gratitude for the kindness My Dear Sister Morgan has shown by promising to take care of Robert and bring him to her house if he should be sick and inviting him whenever he felt lonely and wanted to see his mother, to come and spend a night with her boys. I settled with Treasurer, Board of Education, & took evening boat for Cloverport. Bishop Doggett and a crowd of preachers on board bound for Conference. We had a lively time but many of us slept on cots out in the cabin.

October 11 – Many of the preachers feverish about their appointments. I have hardly ever had any special anxiety about mine. Am resolved to do the work assigned me – or locate.

November 1 – For two weeks I have done almost nothing for the colleges – being afraid to leave home in my present condition, coughing & hoarse & lungs so tender & sensitive to cold as to make me fear Pneumonia.

November 5 – Aunt Betsy very unwell & threatened with loss of mind & strength.

November 9 – Aunt Betsy is too ill for me to leave home. I sat up with her & saw that she was failing.

November 11 – We did not go to bed. Aunt Betsy was dying. At 11 Oclock & 15 minutes – or near that time the weary wheels of life stood still. The poor old lady had suffered long & always dreaded the *pains* of death – though confident of her acceptance with God & hopeful of a home in Heaven. I had often tried to console her with the thought that she might suffer less than she had often suffered before. I felt relieved when the struggle was passed that she died with comparatively little apparent suffering – having fallen into a deep slumber from which she never awoke. My Sister Mary & Cousin Minerva kindly performed the service of draping the body for interment. We feel lonely without her & remember her kindly & affectionately, yet we cannot grieve at her release from sorrow & suffering. Almost 76 years she had lived, most of the time in poor health & the last two or three years, she was a constant sufferer both in body & mind without any hope of ever getting better. She was a true hearted & clear headed woman – with many excellent traits of character. She was one of the very best housekeepers & domestic managers that I ever knew & withal a superior gardener & farmer. She had few equals among men or women in general business sagacity. Never having had children, she had those views and feelings of saving everything for the necessities of old age, peculiar or rather common with childless people. She was a fine economist & very industrious. Her judgment was nearly always reliable on any matter of domestic economy. She prided herself in her hospitality & the elegance of her table fare & the general comforts of her house. As a Christian she was conscientious & willing to bear what she *believed to be her proportion* of church expenses — but did not allow others to judge for her. She was a sensible strongminded woman & had confidence in her ability to manage her own affairs. The same tact — energy & ambition in a man of reasonable opportunities would have made him wealthy. Thomas E. Browder came over this morning & we examined her will — being appointed her executors. She has made our wives her principal heirs. She has lived in my house about seven years and her absence now leaves a melancholy loneliness. Her room shall still be called "Aunt Betsys room." So often — oh so often, have Lizzie & I been roused up from sleep to go & rub & stimulate her in her attacks of paralysis. Sometimes she would say "Oh my children, you are so good to me I ought to give you all I am worth" — at other times she would feel differently & think we did not care for her. The nature of her disease affected her mind & depressed her spirits & at times made her very nervous & irritable but naturally she was very cheerful & amiable & when in health had an extraordinary exuberance of spirit. I am glad that we never neglected her, nor unnecessarily denied her any pleasure. The whole family was more or less under tribute to her & the best of *every thing* that we could command was given to her. If there was an extra nice apple or pear or peach or any other fruit or flower she was sure to get it. The children as well as Lizzie & I seeming to understand that she depended on us for society & attention. She was fond of company & we entertained a great deal of company for her & in a word did all that could be expected of us for her comfort. My dear wife is well nigh worn out with watching & anxiety & I really fear that her health is seriously impaired. I am anxious now for her to take some pleasure in visiting her relations & mine & be free from close confinement. Aunt Betsy was her fathers only full sister.

November 12 — I sent my son Hanson down to the old homestead to remove her husbands remains to my fathers to be buried in the same grave with her and I went to Russellville & selected a beautiful & elegant walnut burial casket worth sixty dollars, the best I could find in the town.

November 13 — To day at 3 ½ P.M. we buried our poor old aunt & the crumbling bones of her long dead husband in the same grave. Hanson says the form of the coffin, in uncle Water's grave was perfect, but crumbled at a touch. Nothing but decaying bones was found in the coffin, but the shape of the boots & even the tie of the cravat remained perfect — yet crumbled into nothing at a touch. He bought a new coffin & case & removed all that could be brought — so we have kept our promise.

November 22 — Tom Browder & I went to town & probated aunt Betsys will & qualified as Executors. There is *possible* room for some dissatisfaction about the settlement of aunt Betsys board. She agreed & promised to pay reasonable compensation for board for herself & servant – all the time she was here. This I prove by many living witnesses & her written statement. The neighbors, best acquainted with the trouble & expense of boarding & taking care of the dear old lady in the latter years of her life – all agree that her entire estate would not pay my wife for the service she has rendered. The *very lowest* estimate made is $350. pr year while good judges say $500.00 pr year is a moderate compensation. I think no one should complain, at allowing us $250 for the entire time – for each year = 1750.

November 27 – [Elkton] At work for the college. I dined with Bro Morton at William Harrisons. He told me about having to marry two couples last Tuesday in the rain – about 15 miles apart & the last bridegroom failed to get to the appointment. Said "It was so rainy he thought no body would go," but he came the next day & was married.

December 17 – [Olmstead] I went to see my dear old parents. Eliza Rutherford reported a poor old man cold & hungry in the kitchen. I went to look for him & he was gone. I followed & found him. A pitiable sight – head of enormous size – tremendous eyes – & a hideous look – very filthy & ragged – and a diseased leg – badly swollen & infected with a running sore. He was begging for work – was willing to work even for bread & meat, but said *no one would hire him.* I brought him back – & warmed him & mother gave him breakfast. He had slept out on the naked ground & was nearly perished with cold. I questioned him about his habits. He said he was perfectly sober & honest – was a Presbyterian & had always tried to do right, but was *unfortunate.* I talked *plainly* & *honestly* with him – told him that no one would like to hire a man that looked like him. I brought him home & got soap & water & made him scour his face and hands – then gave him socks – shirt – pants – vest & coat – a complete suit of good second hand clothes. The poor wretch looked at me with an expression of gratitude & surprise & hesitated – said the clothes were too good for him & he would never be able to pay me – & when I made him put them on – he said with emotion that I was the *first* man that ever showed him such pity. He begged me to let him cut up my wood – or shuck corn, or do something to show his gratitude. Wife gave him a warm dinner & also a days supply to take with him & away he went toward Memphis – leaving us the blessing of a poor tramp.

December 24 – Robert came home from the Vanderbilt University in apparent good health, glad to see us all again. I think he is studying faithfully. I went to Allensville on business, paid off my accounts – got some things for Christmas presents – amongst others, a nice fur cape as a surprise for my Dear Wife & a dress for Sister Biggs, our Pastors wife.

December 25 – Blessed Morning! Blessed Children! How they rejoice over toys, nuts, candys, tropical fruits, musical instruments, pocket knives &c. Surely money spent in making home happy is money well spent. Then this is a good time to tell children of the grace of our Lord Jesus Christ by whom all our blessings come.

December 28 – I rode to Russellville – paid for aunt Betsys casket $60.00. Wrote a labor contract for my hands.

December 29 – Went to depot – was surprised to find my account so large after all the cash payments of the past year. The youngsters are having a *pound* party at Charley Roach's. The weather is as warm as May & I fear the old adage, "A green Christmas makes a green graveyard" will be true. We have a moral community in the main, but the prospect is not hopeful – for the young men of the present – either for themselves or their wives. High living – fine dress – freedom from labor, seem to be the prevailing ideas. I have tried to guard my children from such follies.

December 31 – At home – reading – writing. This is the last day of the year. I spent some time reading Wesleys Journal – was particularly interested in Mrs Susannah Wesleys account of her family Discipline. She set her children to learning – next day after they were five years old. Kept them at their books, three hours in forenoon – & 3 P.M. – six hours per day. Sam. learned all alphabet large & small in a few hours – rest all in one day except Nancy & Molly who were a day & a half. Next day after learning alphabet – they were put to spelling & reading in the 1st Chap[ter] of Genesis, & kept at it until they could read – which they learned very early. Her children were not allowed to cry aloud after a year old. She had excellent ideas of government & raised noble children, but her rules would not work in this country. I think she was hard on the little dears – to keep them six hours a day at work – when they were five years old – & it seems strange to put a child to read Genesis as soon as it has learned the letters. At 9 Oclock we went to church to hold a Watch night meeting. A few only were present. We knelt down to consecrate ourselves afresh to God & rose up to sing – "Come let us anew, our journey pursue – roll round with the year and never stand still till the master appear."

January 1, 1876 – The weather continues as pleasant as May. Windows & doors open & no fire needed on the hearth. Wheat fields & grass lots green & flourishing. It looks like the beautiful South. Robert left us at dawn to return to Nashville. I am called to marry Am. Gregory – a sort of halfwitted man to a woman named McCormick. Hanson went with me at 4, to the marriage. There was a crowd of untidy looking people in a small shanty. The woman was said to be a widow – & had a babe, yet the license was issued in the name of *Miss* Mattie McCormick & her brother said that was her name – so I married them – he standing on the left side instead of the right side. I expected neither pay nor thanks & was not disappointed.

January 8 – Went through Trenton to Geo Thornhills, near Bells Chapel. Met Bro & Sister Gray returning from the burial of her oldest daughter – 14 years

242

old – a sweet good – sprightly girl – the third they have buried in 8 days. Surely the year 1876 opens to them in sorrow. God pity them.

January 10 – Went to Elkton – worked for college – got 6 or 7 $5.00 subscriptions. Work goes slow. Road home rougher than I want to drive over again.

January 11 – To day I enter my 50th year – 49 years ago to day I first saw the light – in half a mile of this house. I am very gray – beard white – hearing alittle impaired – eye sight good – only need glasses in dim light & bad print – flesh increases – weigh 175 lbs – am easily fatigued – memory not quite so reliable – less inclined to work & study – more inclined to stay at home – energy not so good – getting old.

January 12 – I went to Bowling Green at Dr Wilsons request to assist in a meeting. Stopped with my friend Henry Hines. I am sorry to learn that he was withdrawn from the church. The church was grieved that he continued in the liquor traffic & he could not see the way clear for him to change his business. I advised him in one of my conversations by all means to get out of a traffic that was certainly leading to great crimes & was under the ban of all the churches.

January 14 – I am looking around for the college & helping in the meeting.

January 15 – Went to prayermeeting – Cumberland & Methodist Pastors & Members present. I suggested that there be a *united* effort & all the Christians in the town be invited to take common interest in the meetings – now held by Cumberlands & Methodists. The proposition was gladly accepted & a mass meeting for prayer, appointed for Sunday 3 ½ P.M. at Cumberland Church.

January 16 – At 2 ½ Dr R. K. Smoot of Presbyterian Church delivered a lecture on Temperance – very sound & logical – putting it on its true ground as one of the graces & deprecating the idea of the ultra & extreme grounds that some people take in putting temperance societies above the church. Immediately after – the Mass meeting for prayer assembled & I was appointed to conduct the service – 9 different ministers of 5 different churches were present & *all* took *some* part in the delightful services. Surely the prospect is improving.

January 19 – I went to Russellville to the great revival.

January 20 – Bro Finley preached a good sermon. I exhorted. At the close of meeting old Wilson Mason the Marshall & Auctioneer came in from the street – shouting & praising God for the conversion of his soul after three years of penitence & seeking. It was thrilling & amusing to hear him talk. Long an auctioneer & in the habit of crying out "going" "going" "going" "gone" – he cried out in heavenly hopes – "Glory to God, I'm going to Heaven" – "going" "going" – but he did not say *"gone"* he said glory. Dr Grubbs an elderly sinner, who has been seeming serious and asking people to pray for him said to John Barclay – "John I'll be dogged if it aint in the very air." Surely Russellville has not been so moved for many years.

February 23 – Went to Trenton – spent night at Bro Grays. Poor Sister Gray looks very sad & sorrowful after the death of *all* five of her children with Diptheria.

March 4 – Papers are full of accounts of Genl Balknaps malfeasance in office. He is charged with high crimes and misdemeanors in *selling* the offices at his command and has been impeached in Congress.[2] His wife is a party to the disgrace. Alas for our country. Crime runs riot. Men in High Places are corrupt.

March 8 – Doing some work for college. Had a lot of circulars struck containing my appeal to 5000 persons for a centennial contribution of 1.00 each.

March 17 – The balmy spring weather is gone & March is roaring – howling – freezing – with fitful gleams of sunshine & gathering clouds. Very cold & my throat so sore, I fear to go out. Writing college letters & reading.

March 18 – Hanson and I went to Ash Spring to Quarterly meeting. The Quarterly Conference unanimously voted to recommend & License my Son Hanson and Capers Crumbaugh to preach "the gospel of the grace of God." I am sure that my boy is moved by heartfelt convictions of duty. I rejoice that two of my sons feel moved to labor for the good of souls.

March 29 – I called at T.E. Browders to settle aunt Betsys board account. After consulting with divers disinterested persons – all of whom estimated the value of the board higher than I claim – I made out the account & qualified to it at $5.00 pr week for herself and servant. It certainly seems that no fairminded person ought to object to this charge. *No amount* of money apart from filial duty & affection would induce my wife to endure again the watching, anxiety, weary confinement & restraint, that the dear old aunts infirmities demanded in the last four or five years of her life.

April 7 – Cousin D. B. Sydnor was taken dangerously ill yesterday with stricture of the bladder & could only be relieved by the aspirator – an instrument that pierces the bladder from within & by a pump removes the water. Truly a wonderful display of inventive genius. Without it his death would have been certain.

---

2. Scandals rocked the second administration of President Ulysses S. Grant. Five of them involved members of his own cabinet, including his Secretary of War William W. Belknap, who accepted quarterly bribes from Indian traders at Fort Sill, Oklahoma. Belknap was impeached by the House of Representatives and barely escaped conviction by the Senate. David Loth, *Public Plunder* (New York, 1938), 188–90.

April 8 – Went to see Cousin D. again. He is no better. I went to Russellville to try to find a catheter of better shape than the ones employed, but failed to get it.

April 12 – Cousin D. some better. I left for Franklin.

April 14 – At work for the college – with only moderate success. Franklin Methodists say they are poor and pressed and other people have their own schools &c to support.

April 18 – [Olmstead] Up early, had breakfast and off to Nashville to see Robert, found him at lecture in Dr Granberrys class. He was joyfully surprised to see me. I find him doing well & apparently very popular. We went through the building & through the grounds & I see the greatness of Mr Vanderbilts beneficence. The Museum is wonderful. Everything seems of the best class. I dined with Robert at Wesley Hall.

August 28 – A long skip in my journal. I was much away from home through Spring & Summer working for Logan Female College. I visited different towns and counties – speaking – seeking patronage – trying to find friends who would help us pay the debts – but with very limited success. I attended District Conferences – Protracted Meetings – Quarterly Meetings &c. I was at Trenton – at Woodburn, at Henderson & Bradfordsville Dist Conferences. I was at Bowling Green, Glasgow, Shepherdsville, Lebanon – Franklin, Woodburn – Rich Pond, Rockfield – Oakland, Smiths Grove – Glasgow Junction – Russellville, Allensville, Olmstead – Guthrie, Kaskys Station, Hopkinsville, Henderson, Cairo, Corydon – Smithsmills – Morganfield – Antioch – Uniontown – & divers other places. I went to the Mammoth Cave & surveyed its gloomy splendors. Mr Miller the Proprietor was very polite & courteous & the guide Nicholas was full of humor & entertainment. The *cave* is a grand *cave* – but a cave for all that. It is a great wonder – but "distance lends enchantment to the view." I preached a great deal through the season – some of the best preaching of my life, but I do not know with what result. I visited many sick & prayed in many families – talked to many people – old & young – seriously & personally about their obligations to God & the worth of their souls – but I always felt & still feel a painful sense of personal unworthiness. I have so failed to make the improvement I ought to have made that there is a constant sense of demerit. My weakness! My weakness! My leanness! My leanness! I trust that I am not all selfish. I do in many respects live for others.

The Board of Directors have been very reasonable & liberal with me. Were willing to allow me Ten hundred Dollars – and a month to go to the Centennial – but I settled at 900, & a months absence.

August 29 – *We started to Centennial.* Lizzie, Robert, George & I of my family. Tom Sydnor, Sister Mary & Annie – Tom Browder & Lizzie & Susie & Fannie Browder, Carrie Walker & Johnnie & Cousin Mary Hughes – David E. Sydnor & wife – & Miss Lutie Sullivan – Miss Mattie Muir & George Johnson – Mrs

Sue Heard & her sister Lucile Blakey – 21 in all composed our company. We were delayed & had to spend a night in Louisville. A little boy insisted on carrying my valise for a nickel – then *ran* about a *mile* keeping up with the street car to carry it for another nickel. I gave him a *dime.*

August 30 – At seven A.M. we all met at O & M Depot and rolled away to Cincinnati. We enjoyed the ride greatly – along the banks of the beautiful Ohio – & through fertile meads and thriving towns. I rode on the top of an Omnibus through Cincinnati & for the first time saw the great Metropolis of the Ohio. We made connections & soon went whirling rapidly over a fine country – interspersed with belts of poor land – over streams – through populous cities & in the night rolled into the grand Depot at Cleveland on Lake Erie. Here some of us were anxious to rest – & take the Lakeshore Route by Daylight, but the young bloods were anxious to press on & we yielded – sitting up & catching such snatches of sleep as we could in crowded – whirling coaches. Daylight brought us to Buffalo N York. After a hasty breakfast we hired hacks & drove down to the boat landing on Lake Erie. Went upon the observatory & had a splendid view of the beautiful fresh water sea & its multitude of sails. Went to see the splendid City Hall – drove through the principal streets of the city & got back in time to take the train for Niagara Falls – but not until we quarrelled with the villainous hackman who promised to take us down & return us for 25 cts each & then tried to compel us to pay 50 cts each & even threatened us with the policeman. Some of us paid the extortion rather than protract the dispute. These hackmen are notorious for their sharp practices and swindling. It seems to be their study.

We reached Niagara by 10 Oclock – dusty, tired & out of sorts – & stopped at the Spencer House. After much ado with soap and water we got into some clean clothes – hired some hacks & were off to see the greatest natural wonder on the Continent if not in the world. We drove to the Whirl Pool Rapids – paid 50 cts & were delighted with the wild sublimity of the foaming waves leaping 10 to 20 even 40 feet into the air & foaming & soaring as language cannot describe. We then went to the Whirl Pool and paid 50 cts more to see the grand Niagara River gathered into a narrow compass – in a deep unmeasured chasm – forcing its mighty volume of rushing torrents against the massive rock to find an outlet, then recoiling & eddying back in grand retreat to find an escape on the opposite side, whirling & plunging – rolling – tossing its foam crested billows as if a thousand demons were stirring its hidden depths – and leaping & charging against its hurrying, rushing current. Leaving this wild & weird scene, we drove across the lower bridge into Canada – and on the bridge got the *best* view of the rapids we have had anywhere. This was my first visit to a Foreign Land, but the wonders of Niagara were about us & we had but little time for reflection on the Queens Dominion. We drove past the Bridal Vail Falls – up in front of the Grand Cataract & alighted from the coverage with head uncovered. God of power! Here is thy handiwork! The flashing sunlight upon the broken waters – the golden beams permeating the moving spray – the prismatic colors – gathering upon the crested foam & arching in myriad numbers over troubled waters — all reveal the handiwork divine. There is but one Niagara & here we stand — awestricken & amazed — gazing upon its mighty waters — dashing onward in wild commotion — then seeming to apprehend the fearful plunge — look as if pausing & wishing to retreat — then — gathering their strength & fury & turning as green as the meadows of spring or the vernal robes of the forest — they pour themselves with tremendous shock 160 feet down the perpendicular crag. We see the changing colors & varied beauties & sublime displays of this great wonder. We feel our souls join in the eternal thunder hymn that swells up from those unfathomed depths. We look & wonder. Such sensations seldom possess our souls. We draw near — & look down the dizzy depth. We see the rainbows mingling in the mist. We stoop down & bathe our hands in the grand stream that rolls onward to its fearful leap. We gather pebbles from the stream as the mist falls upon us. We go up on the upper portico of the Cataract hotel & look upward at the surging — dashing — white capped & wildly leaping waves of the rapids above the falls. The splendid houses — the long trains — & the fiery charging iron steeds that draw them — the airy suspension bridge that spans the awful chasms — & bears the ponderous engines & coaches & crowds in safety over the furious river — the combination of electric wires that send the news on the lightnings fiery wing — all these grand attractions are there with scenic effect — but all are lost or overlooked amid the awful majesty of this great work of God.

We lingered & looked & looked & lingered & were loathe to leave the enchanted spot — but we could only see & think — so we hurried away to regret that we did not stay longer & see more. We paid 15.00 for three hacks & four hours — & 1.00 each for dinner & a room — besides the tolls at the bridge — & then away on the grand Four Track N York Central R.R. to Albany. The weather was warm & balmy — the country picturesque & highly improved, the cars were comfortable & the speed like the wind.

At a late hour in the night we rolled into Albany the capital of N.Y. & stopped at Stanwick Hall for a few hours sleep. We rested well until breakfast, got an unsatisfactory meal — more for want of attention than quality of food — crowded into & on top of an omnibus & drove to the landing where we boarded the splendid Steamer C. Vibbard — for a sail down the beautiful Hudson. The weather was delightful & the crowd was eager & expectant. It was ascertained that Mrs Heard had left her valise with her ticket & all her money at the hotel! She was greatly troubled & wanted to blame somebody. My dear boy Robert with true gallantry — leaped into a hack & hurried away to the hotel — got the valise all safe & got back in time to go with us down the river. He was much praised for the sacrifice he made, risking the loss of a trip that he had so greatly desired to make to accommodate a lady careless enough to leave her valise when she had no one else to look after it.

This days journey was worth all the expense of a trip from home. I had always imagined the Hudson about the size of the Cumberland. I found it a broad — deep beautiful stream larger than the Ohio — with scarce a current — rather an extension of New York Bay than a rapid river — its banks now gently sloping — now rising grandly into towering hills & then the bleak points of lofty mountain ranges – covered on the sides & summits with a peculiarly beautiful cone shaped ever green. Lighthouses stand on every turn & villages & towns & cities – & splendid mansions lie like pictures along the grassy slopes or crown the higher points. A Rail Road lies just on the bank – & often runs out into the river – & its long trains are often seen rolling past us. Newburg, Lansingburg, Troy, Hudson, Catskill, Poughkeepsie, West Point – are some of the places of interest we saw. But these beauties must be seen to be appreciated. No description is adequate. I had read much of the beauties of Hudson River scenery, but the half had never been told me. The highlands – the Mountains, the Palisades – the deep widening river – the thickening towns & cities – all intensified the interest. The boat was a splendid palace with three decks and had about Two Thousand souls on board this trip. We ran from Albany to N. Y. 145 miles in about 10 hours. The world seems to center here. The rush – the crowd – the jam – the pressure – the cry of hackmen – the presence of police – the wilderness of houses! My dear wife & George & Robert & the rest of us were all amazement. We stopped in the city at the grand St Nicholas Hotel & had everything in first class style. The charges are high 4.00 to 4.50 pr day but we get all we pay for – there is no cheat – no sham. We look out of the windows on the swarming throngs of people on Broadway & wonder where they are going & how they get along. The hum & tramp & bustle – the roll & rattle of hoof & wheels seem to continue through the night.

September 1 – We took street car & went to Central Park – hired carriage & drove through some of the principal drives – saw much to admire of natural and artificial beauty. Saw many splendid buildings & beautiful squares & pleasure grounds in the great City. Went on Broadway to A. T. Stewarts great Retail Store – the finest establishment of the kind, I suppose in the world. Thousands of men in his employment in his different houses. I went down to the Fulton Ferry – saw the shipping – the bridge – the prison – the shot tower – the city Hall – Brooklyn &c – found a cheaper place to board – but the company did not go to it.

September 2 – Sabbath. Robert & I went over to Brooklyn to see Mr Laurence Spalding 123 Lafayette Avenue – where we get good boarding at 1.75 pr day. Walked out to Fort Green where the battle was fought in 1776 – saw the ground where the soldiers were buried who were killed on the crowded ship.[3] At night we went to the great tabernacle & heard Rev T. Dewitt Talmage preach a forcible sermon on the value of Bible study. This is a fine house & the largest audience that I ever saw inside of walls & everything in perfect order & the

---

3. George Dick is referring to the Battle of Brooklyn Heights, August 27, 1776, in which the victorious British took nearly 1100 American prisoners. To house them and other prisoners from later engagements, the British used ships in the New York harbor. Overcrowding, poor sanitation, and inadequate food took a heavy toll. Reputable authorities estimate that as many as 11,500 prisoners died aboard these ships, most of which were anchored in the Wallabout Bay area. Mark M. Boatner, III, *Encyclopedia of the American Revolution* (New York, 1966), 894–95.

behavior most excellent. I was very tired & got to sleep. A nice young man at my side gave me a touch & raised me.

September 3 − Up and out with the ladies − to the beautiful scenes & historic ground of Fort Green. Mr Spalding went with us to Greenwood Cemetery. This far surpasses all that ever I have seen in a cemetery − such beautiful walks & grades & hills & monuments & lakes & streams. I climbed to the summit of a naked hill − no path − no grave − no monument marked it − just the naked hill, but there I saw the grandest view that my eyes have beheld in lifes journey. The world seemed before me. There was New York & Brooklyn & Williamsburg & Jersey City & Hoboken & East River − with the harbor & the sails. On my left was New York Bay & its wilderness of masts & sails & steamers. On the right was the Atlantic Ocean stretching away in its grandeur − & seeming like some vast plain covered over with molten silver & a world of sailboats and steamers floating on its bosom. We walked & looked & rested & walked again − wondering & admiring as we walked − until weary with travel − then in the cars and on to the Ocean! Who can tell the beauties of Coney Island. The clean white silvery sands − the pearly sea shells − & the rippling waves. But the Ocean! The Ocean! The *grand* Ocean − away it stretches & rises in the distance until you just see the mast head of the departing & approaching vessels. The beach is thronged with men & boys − girls & women in bathing dress − plunge in − to rise & sink & laugh & scream & jump & shout as the waves roll and dash. My boys went in with shout & glee − & an irresistible desire to feel the waves seemed to possess us all. Lizzie & I stripped off shoes & stockings & walked in the beautiful sands & splashing waves − ankle deep & more − gathering shells & following the receding tide. It was delightful sensation & we enjoyed it heartily. We felt cheered & exhilarated & I drank some of the sparkling brine. We waited & looked with regret that we had not another day to spare. How I longed to sail away to Rockaway Beach 13 miles − out of sight of land but my company were panting for Centennial scenes, so we donned our shoes & stockings, mounted our steamwinged train & soon landed amid the wilderness of walls & spires & the labyrinth of streets in Brooklyn − ate a hearty, hasty dinner with good Mrs Spalding − paid two cents fare at Fultons Ferry − threaded our way through the hurrying crowd − went through famous Wall Street, with its large & long blocks of Banks and Brokers − thought of its untold treasure & guilty intrigues − its mizers & its millionaires − its Jay Goulds & Tweeds & Fisks − its Vanderbilts & its moneyed kings − the fierce encounters of the "Bulls" & the "Bears" − the heart aches & the wrecks & ruins that have followed their "futures" & "margins" & other devices of gambling & speculation. Pressing & pushing through the surging sea of human travellers on foot & in coaches − along narrow busy streets − we at last found seats in the grand reception room of Jersey City Depot − with South river & New York behind us − & in due time were on the train − speeding onward to Philadelphia. Part of the company were ahead & had telegraphed us to meet them at Parkview Hotel. We changed cars at German Town & soon landed amid the din of voices & clamor of hackmen − hotel drummers − baggage packers − transportation agents &c − besides the crowd of strangers like ourselves not knowing where to go nor whom to follow. The Policemen are welcome assistants. We love the police. We asked them – what thousands of others have asked – & they tell us all they know about our routes. At last we found the Coachmen for Parkview Hotel – & rattling away along side of the Centennial Grounds & wonderful buildings – gazing upon the ceaseless lines of lamps & jets of flame – we halted at the Parkview and entered. The house was crowded & not sightly – away out from the heart of the city & our company gone thence to the Markoe house between 9th and 10th on Chestnut Streets – leaving a note for us to follow. Again entering the cars – crossing the famous Schuykill River & driving miles down the lighted streets – gay with banners – & thronged with people – we at last found the "Markoe" but found it crowded from cellar to garrett. By putting four in some rooms & six in another – & separating husbands & wives we got comfortable beds & as good fare as we could expect – but cooked entirely different from the fare at home – meats rare & unseasoned – bread cold & often hard.

September 4 – My Dear Lizzie was sick & worn out with travel – so she staid in & rested & I went to the Centennial. Wonder of wonders! Here is the world in miniature. Its babbling millions of population – its hundreds of nationalities – with their arts & sciences & productions & manufacturers – their books & houses – their implements of peace & war – the tools of the field & the utensils of the house & kitchen – their native stocks & manufactured goods – the people with their costumes & dialects all more or less represented here in this great Main Building – covering 21 acres of land & adorned & festooned with all the banners & ensigns – the pomp and paraphernalia of earths wisest & mightiest nations. Surely this is to all other Expositions what Niagara is to all other cataracts. The surging crowds that rush or roll or slowly tramp through in every direction – pushing against or running before – intercept – & separate companies so that it is impracticable for a number of persons to remain together. We agreed to take our own routes through the exposition & return to the hotel at each ones pleasure. Such crowds gathered around the restaurants & lunch stands that hundreds found it impracticable to get refreshments. "The Dairy" furnishes good bread & milk & butter for 25 cts – but most of the charges were extortionate. It is not easy to imagine the fatigue of a days tramp & excitement through these wonderful scenes. You feel as if you had met the world & all its children.

September 5 – Lizzie was up & anxious to be off to the grand exposition. We even forgot that this is the anniversary of our marriage. How industriously has she labored & how rigidly economized in all these years to keep my credit good & my home pleasant! She deserves perpetual praise – and yet this great day of excitement made us both forget it. There was to be a grand parade of firemen ten thousand strong. The original old "Independence Bell" whose solemn peals announced the signing of the declaration & multitudes of primitive fire engines followed by the modern improvements – the *old hand* workers – & the new and splendid *steam workers* – with the elegant hose carriages – hook & ladder companies with all the modern appliances for extinguishing fire & saving life & property — all these with brilliant decorations — ensigns & banners — were to pass along Chestnut Street under our window — so we staid to witness the pompous pageant. We went to old Independence Hall & saw the identical papers signed by the illustrious men who declared us "independent" — the table on which they wrote — the inkstand they used — the chairs they sat on — & the portraits of most of these grand history makers — together with the museum, the old cracked liberty bell — the swords & clothes &c worn by Genl Washington — the boots &c that did service in the terrible trials of the army at Valley Forge & many relics & memorials of the revolutionary war. It was a visit of vast interest & the old quakers in the long coats & short pants — with stockings & knee buckles & the cocked hats of ye olden time brought the stirring scenes of that momentous era visibly before us. I bought a copy of the *first* newspaper published on the continent & pictures of the first railroad cars ever used — facsimile. We went through the "mint" & we saw the preparation of metal bars — the wonderful force & stroke of the "die" — the glittering heaps of new coined money — & heard the "chink" & "clatter" as piles of coin were pushed out & removed — but the crowd was so dense & the air so suffocating from the throng & pressure that we were glad to get out alive.

We went to the Colosseum & were carried up its giddy heights in the groaning elevator — until far above the city — we looked down upon its domes & towers — its gilded spires & its world of homes — palaces & hovels — intersected & crossed by squares & angles — & hundreds of miles of streets — adorned with banners & devices of all nations. This is a grand view of the largest city in area on the continent & perhaps second only to London in extent of land. Added to the 800,000 resident population — the multiplied thousands more from all quarters of our own & foreign countries give this great place an air of thrift & throng that is seldom seen. The people too are taking pains & pride in making the Centennial a success — & creating good impressions for the future. We meet with courtesy & attention on all sides & the city was never so gay. The number of banners — flags & streamers of gay colors of all sizes & all countries that decorate & adorn the public & private houses — wave from the windows, swing across the streets — float from steeples & spires — liberty poles & masts of vessels — is truly amazing. Wonderful change between these rivers, Delaware & Schuykill, since good old William Penn settled here in 1682! The old city was two miles long & one mile wide — but the swelling tide of population, commerce & manufacture burst the boundaries & now I see before me one hundred & twenty nine square miles of city & suburb — 23 miles long & averaging 5 ½ miles wide — with one thousand miles of streets & roads, underneath which are six hundred miles of *gas* main & about the same length of *waterpipe*. Two hundred & fifty miles of street railway & two thousand cars furnish transportation to every part & the one hundred & thirty five thousand homes in which the vast population lives are nearly all accessible to each other. What memories crowd the mind as we gaze upon this "city of brotherly love."

Away out yonder stands Carpenters Hall where the First Continental Congress met — where the first public prayer was offered for American

Independence. There again you see Independence Hall — the birthplace of the nation. That plain old church yonder is Christ Church where George Washington, Benjamin Franklin, Robert Morris & others of those illustrious lives were to meet & worship God.

September 6 — Lizzie and I went to the Exposition — & over much of the ground I had traversed before. The foreign Departments. The French is a glitter from beginning to end. Splendid in all its departments — useful and ornamental — the finest cloths — textures — jewelry — implements, mechanisms — scientific appliances — art & elegancies — it would take a volume to describe them. The fine arts were perfectly splendid. A crucifixation scene represented Christ taken from the cross — the friends looking upon the pallid face — the ghastly side wound — the nail prints — the blood stains — the expression of countenance — the life size & look of the statuary — all seem perfectly marvelous.

Brazil makes a grand display — all aglow with tropical splendor — varied productions — splendid specimens of mechanical and manufacturing skill — fine arts & ornaments. Jewels made of her strange specimens of insect life — bouquets of butterflies of richest & rarest colors, & most ingenious workmanship — vast collections of woods — plants — grains — seeds — ores — metals — pelts — and fibers &c — both crude & manufactured — all in excellent taste & proving the grand resources & progressive development of that vast Empire. Mexico has precious stones — & beautiful marble & fine coffee & multitudes of different forest growths — immense blocks of Mahogany root — many feet in diameter — many samples of fine coffee displayed to advantage in glass pyramids — large glass cases of vanilla emitting pleasant odors — fine specimens of leather, saddles &c — & a solid block of silver weighing I think 4,000 lbs — worth $72,000.

Italy had some fine statuary & works of art — naked human figures — beautiful & well executed. This taste for nude men & women in painting & sculpture seems popular in all the foreign departments & is growing in our own country. I think it betokens a growing sensuality & demoralization — which ought to be discouraged. Austria — Spain, Portugal &c — were all interesting & showed themselves capable of great things. In Italy we saw splendid musical instruments & the finest Leghorn hats — bonnets &c that can be made in the world. But we were anxious to get into China & Japan, the celestial empires. How odd these women with almond shaped eyes & little feet — but I think I only saw one with the cramped feet. The men have "cues" & long dresses much like our women — but most of them have donned our American costume, much to the disappointment of those of us who preferred to see them all in native dress & hear them babble in native tongue. Tea caddies & pagodas — curious carvings & wonderful ingravings. They have no equal in the world. Pearl & Ivory & precious metals in minute pieces & variously disposed — cut into table tops & statuary — & furniture in a manner so perfect that the naked eye can scarce discern the joining. Some of these small tables must have required skilled workmen years to execute. One bedstead was so carved & inlaid that you require a magnifying glass to examine it to perfection. The cost is only $12,000!

In Switzerland we saw the most perfect maps & charts that we saw in any division. Norway & Sweden presented splendid furs & draped pelts & skins & heavy cloths. Holland had dikes & canals & towns & walks mapped out in wonderful distinctness on her lands reclaimed from the lake & sea. Belgium is there with her varied productions natural and artificial − Brussels with her wonderful carpets. We walk & wonder & grow weary − sit down to rest & gaze at the exhaustless variety of interesting sights that greets the sight wherever the eye can look. Splendor & glitter − evidences of skill & advancement & national power are all around us & the deep solemn peals of organs and the stirring sounds of music ring in full notes all through the spacious hall, parallelogram in form extending 1880 feet E. and W. & 464 feet N. and S. − the central facade rising to the height of 90 feet. This day I was worn out & sick − had a chill & a fever & did not enjoy the sights & sounds as much as I ought. We went hurriedly through some of the other departments & noted with interest the acres & acres of machines − of every conceivable sort in Machinery Hall − all moved & worked by one grand engine in the centre − with rods extending through the building connecting the power with whatever machinery it was proposed to put in motion. Estimated equal to 2500 horse power but nominally called 1500 horse power. The gear wheel, 30 feet in diameter, is the largest cut wheel ever made. Weighs 56 tons.

September 7 − Provided with lunch of our own we are off to the Centennial again. The Art Gallery on the most commanding position in Landsdowne Plateau is the point of interest now. The plateau is 116 feet above the level of Schuykill river. The grand pile, in the modern Renaissance style, is built on granite, glass & iron. No wood, thoroughly fireproof. It is 356 feet in length − 210 feet in width − 59 feet in height surmounted by a dome. The main entrance opens a hall 82 feet long − 60 feet wide − 53 feet high. Three doors − each 16 feet wide & 25 feet high − open out of this into the Centre Hall which is 83 feet square with the ceiling of the dome rising 80 feet above it. On the East and West side of this are galleries each 98 feet long, 48 feet wide − 35 feet high − making all together one grand hall 287 feet long − 85 feet wide capable of holding *eight thousand* people. Temporary divisions are here for the better display of paintings. We go through & wonder. Here is a grand statue of Washington. There is Lafayette − here are splendid paintings from the great masters − landscapes & cities − battles − fancy & real representations − historic & poetic fancies. Acres of canvass! forests of statuary! Italy − France − Spain − England & American vie in these splendid works of art − but the older countries are ahead of ours. I would like to enter a protest − against displaying life size & full grown − the nude statues of the most perfectly formed & featured & best developed of both sexes to the gaze of mixed companies. While beautiful & attractive in themselves & splendid as works of art − that male & female amateurs gaze upon with delight − yet I fear the effect upon public & private morals. Whatever detracts from the modesty of our girls or boys is demoralizing.

We were delighted in Agricultural hall & saw the most interesting proofs of the upward march of civilization & development − the old plows & implements of the past – & the splendid implements of the present age – the old windmills & the new models – samples of grains – fruits & fowls & birds & beasts & domestic animals preserved in the best style of taxydermic art. There were two White Chester hogs – grown by Hon Samuel Cooper of Corydon, N.H. that were wonderful to behold. I could hardly realize that swine could grow to such length & height & thickness. I did not measure – but I think 7 or eight feet in length – & 4 feet in height is not an exaggeration. One weighed at 21 months old – 1307 lbs – the other at 19 months old weighed 1253 pounds! Here too we saw Daniel Websters large plow made & used by himself at his Marshfield home – & of which he said – "When I hitch four good oxen to this plow & see it turn over the glebe & hear the roots crack – I feel that I am doing more for my country than I ever did at Washington." We went through Horticultural Hall – built in splendid style on Landsdowne Terrace – in the architecture of the 12th century – & is composed externally of glass & iron – to remain a permanent ornament to Fairmount Park. In it we saw rare & valuable trees – plants – & flowers – oranges – lemons – and figs &c growing on their native stem.

We could not see all. Setting out for the hotel we saw a dark dense smoke push out of a house door a few feet in front of us. We would have been just about the door had we not paused a moment to ask the way. Soon the alarm of fire sounded & the crowd came rushing in all directions. Lizzie was greatly excited & we ran across Elm Avenue – down toward Girard. The surrounding houses were soon covered with people & the fire alarms continued to sound – but the engines were a long ways down in the city & were slow coming. The wind drove the flames & the surging crowd rushed pell mell & confused some toward & others away from the fire. House after house of the wooden city that sprung in violation of city ordinance around the Centennial melted down before the flame – playing havoc with certain disreputable institutions that were doing business thereabouts – as the papers report. Shantytown was gone. At last, the engines came, the horses panting & blood gushing from their nostrils – & in a short time the fire was under control. After considerable delay we got a car & were safe in the Markoe house.

September 8 – Sabbath. We went to Arch St Methodist Church – found every seat taken – crowded into the gallery & heard most of Dr Hatfields sermon. He is a man of talent, but is known as a radical in politics. He seems to have a spite at the Southern people – could not finish his sermon without a fling at *slaveholders*. He had a vast audience composed largely of strangers – many to my knowledge – Southern people. We thought it very bad taste – knowing as little as he does of the workings of slavery – to be making cuts & slurs at Southern people – invited to the nations birthplace – this centennial year of our independence. I heard him again in the afternoon. He preached a good earnest gospel sermon & made no *cuts* except at sin. I thanked him for *that* sermon.

I attended the same church at night & heard Rev Mr Kelley of Spring-garden St Church. I do not care to hear him again. His sermon was *ostensibly* to do good of course but impressed all that spoke of it in my hearing that his *chief* aim was to display himself. He has some talent & some learning – but I do not want him for my pastor. The flock would starve. An intelligent gentleman just ahead of me on the street remarked to a lady − "I would not give a picayune, a thousand for such sermons." Turning to another gentleman he asked "What do you think of him?" "He's a humbug" was the reply. "Complete!" said the first − "a complete humbug."

September 9 − Out again to the Centennial. We peep again through the main building − surprised to find how much we missed before − what wonderful show cases of British Porcelain & Queensware with oysters & fish & lobsters &c all *raised* in the dishes − striking Chinese statuary − strange feathers & birds from Africa − old fashioned African plows with crooked stick − one handle & a little piece of iron attached. Looked through the carriage department in the Annex & admired greatly the heavy substantial coaches of Europe as well as the elegant & graceful private carriages − hundreds in number and of every conceivable style. We went to the R.R. cars & saw the elegance & splendor of the parlor & sleeping coaches that rival the splendor of fashionable parlors in houses. Went to the Bible house & saw between two & three hundred tongues & dialects represented in scripture.

We walked again through the grand machinery department & the womans pavilion & elsewhere − but the Government building & the Main building we liked best of all. The Government building is of vast interest − you see the earliest Indian implements & instruments known − their stone axes & spears & arrow heads & earthen pots & clothing of skins & native costume − their wigwams & bark canoes & their bows & arrows & quivers & samples of their artifice − then some of their progress & developments under teaching − their needlework & writing & signs of civilization. You see the ruder days of our own country − portrayed in primitive implements − & the proofs of progress.

We have great cause to rejoice in the prosperity & growth of our own country − & in the liberty of our people & Southern citizens must not mutter when they see the broad grin on Abraham Lincolns face as groups of joyful negroes dance around him − wild with joy − while he shows the emancipation proclamation. Let them dance and let the South be glad. The whites are freed from a grievous burden & a crushing responsibility for escape from which they will someday be thankful. It may not be amiss to have this picture in the Centennial show. You see too − that we may well dispense with our bluster & egotism. Other nations are yet our superiors in many things & we have much to learn & much to do to be equal in all things with the foremost. Even the heathen countries represented have a civilization & arts & sciences that may well excite our wonder.

We are weary & worn with walking & talking − telling & seeing − yet we have not "done" the city. The fine cemeteries must be left unseen. We have had no drives through Fairmount Park. We have not visited the Zoological gardens − nor passed over the principal streets of the city − but we are tired & must leave. We have been kindly treated & the hotel clerk calls us the "jolliest most cheerful best behaved − & easiest pleased crowd that has been in his house the whole season." So we paid our bill ready to leave in the morning.

September 10 – Out of the Baltimore & Washington Depot – some confusion about the right cars. Lizzie & I & Tom & his children were to stop in Baltimore & go out to visit our relatives in A[nne] A[rundel] County[4] – the rest were to go on to Washington. We passed over some fine country – but much of Maryland is poor – bleak – sandy – pine & gravel land. Baltimore was quiet – like a deserted village after the crowd & hurry of Phil[adelphia] & N. York. We got a polite hackman to drive us through the principal streets & to see the principal buildings. We went to the monuments that give Baltimore its title – Monumental City. Battle monument is a fine pile of white stone carved with suitable inscriptions commemorating the battle of North Point.

We drove out to Druid Hill Park & were charmed with the good taste in making it nature instead of art. The forest is well kept – but it is forest. The drives are beautiful. We saw a large number of deer grazing & sleeping – a beautiful lake one mile in circumference – a collection of monkeys & parrots – & some other curious animals. Looked over the city & bay from "prospect hill" but all is tame here compared to what we have seen. There is more nature in Druid Hill, Balt[imore] than in Central Park N.Y. but infinitely more art & nature combined in Central Park. We drove to the Boat Landing & saw some of the signs of life & commerce – then to the depot (Potomac) where we took the Popes Creek line to Collington in Prince George Co. Md. We passed over a poor dreary – desolate looking country – crops *very* poor – some fields verifying *literally* my jokes with cousin Julia Beard about gathering corn in baskets instead of wagons. We reached Collington – a mere rough box house to hold tobacco &c – & no accommodations. We locked up the trunk & packed our valises up the hill to a store where we found several men with the appearance of drinking & loafing around – the first men we have seen that had time to pitch horse shoes since we left Olmstead. We found a Mr Wells who agreed to take us out to aunt Rebeccas for 4.00 & we hurried him off to get his carriage & horses. He seemed clever & we were glad to get away from Collington. We reached aunt Rebeccas in the darkness & found no one expecting us – aunt R. & cousin Mollie both sick – cousin Julia barely able to be up – & no servant. We were tired and sleepy and glad to rest.

September 11 – We walked about the premises – gathered fruit – picked up pebbles white & clear out of the acres of sand that seem to form the soil of this region on the Patuxent river. This whole country since we left Kentucky seems to be full of fruit. Lizzie is in her *native* land but oh how changed. This family is wonderfully changed since uncle Beard died. The manner of growing – curing – housing & prizing tobacco is all different from ours. They let it bloom before they top it – want all the leaves they can get – prefer the plants with leaves nearest together – cut it off close at the ground – without "priming." Cure it without fire & assort it by colors instead of size & quality – & finally fill one hogshead full – then another with a *false* bottom is filled, the bottom taken out

---

4. George Dick is referring to Lizzie's side of the family. She was born in Anne Arundel County, Maryland, on January 26, 1830.

& both lain horizontal & the tobacco forced out of one into the other at one effort — they say here it saves time — but is very odd to us Kentuckians. Tom Beard came over & was glad to meet us, invited us to his house.

September 13 — Tom Beard came to pilot us over to his house. We like the looks of things much better there. It is above the sand beds — more like home. Tom has a beautiful place & ought to do well but I fear he is not a good farmer. His wife is a nice pleasant lady & we were very kindly treated & well entertained. Tommy took us out driving around Davidsonville where we saw some beautiful lands & fine crops & the highest evidence of thrift & prosperity we have seen in Maryland. This is indeed a garden spot, an oasis in the desert. We spend a pleasant night with Tom Beard & pray blessings on his head.

September 14 — Tom Beard kindly furnished us his carriage & team & went with us up to uncle Charles Waters's, the home & birth place of my wife's mother. We found him a very nice well informed old gentleman & aunt Margaret his wife a very pleasant lady. The daughter Mrs. Cooksey a polished & elegant lady with sprightly children. Julia is the married daughter. Maggie the single one. Jacob is the single son. Maggie is a genial pleasant girl & Jacob pleasant as well. A dreary rain set in. This is an old poor looking place.

September 15 — Such a rainy Sunday, when did I see! Rain blow — storm — no church today. We talk & sing & read & I try to be agreeable & to make good impressions — for the truth of God. Uncle Charles is not a church member but his wife & daughters are Methodists. The rain so flooded the creek that the mill was endangered & uncle Waters & the boys had to go down & open the flood gates — or move the embankments to save the house.

September 16 — We drove down to Annapolis — the capital of Maryland — a quiet staid old city. The capitol and governors residence are nice places but the chief attractions are the Naval Academy and its beautiful grounds — & the Navy Yard some miles below the city. We went to the River & boarded the U.S. Man of War Santee — a sail vessel with about 40 guns. It was in nice order & everything seemed kept clean & trim, yet they said it was out of sorts. The officers allowed us to look through every part of the vessel & explained what we did not understand. There was also a Monitor — a gun boat of peculiar shape lying at anchor in the river but we did not board it. We got an elegant stew of fresh oysters with good bread and butter & pickles enough for us all for 1.60 — 6 of us to eat. We had a very pleasant day at Annapolis & left well pleased with the plain old town & its sober people. Tomorrow we take leave & are off for home via Washington.

September 17 — Up & off in time — took leave of our dear friends in Maryland perhaps to see them no more. Mr Talbert was kind enough to go with us & take the trunk. We had often heard of Governors bridge & supposed it a place of some importance. This morning we saw it by Daylight — & under circumstances to remember. The Patuxent River was out of banks & almost up to the bridge – stretching away into the flats beyond. Mr Talbert was afraid to go forward. We met a colored man who had forded to the bridge & he thought we could get over. We gave him a dime to drive the cart & I followed driving the carriage. The current rolled & roared & the water came up in the carriage – we all got upon the seats – the horses stopped and we thought were in trouble – but they started again and we got across safely – thankful for the escape. A bridge was washed out on the Collington road & we turned to Mitchellville which we reached in time for the train.

We got safely to Washington & stopped at the Milliken Hotel. This is a grand city – broad – clean streets & avenues & palatial houses but the principal attractions are the public buildings. Take these away & Washington is a small affair. But the Government has spent money with a lavish hand & adorned & beautified her works until they are said to be the finest of the kind in the world. The Capitol is a marvel of magnificence and splendor. No other state house on earth is equal to it. The iron dome is itself a study. We went up – up – up – flight after flight – until we stood upon the last place of ascent. The streets radiate to & from the Capitol & the view is grand & the reflections historic. Yonder rolls the Potomac at flood height – yonder is Georgetown – there is Alexandria – yonder is Arlington heights & Va – back yonder you see Maryland – all around you is a vast and beautiful city – but the public buildings make Washington – Patent Office – Post Office – Treasury & State Departments – Executive Mansion or White House – Smithsonian Institute – Washingtons Monument yet incomplete – these with the inexpressibly beautiful grounds around them – gravel walks – fountains & flowers & groves – give the city its glory & its charm. We went through the Patent Office – & the White House – sat down in the presidents chairs – walked through his grounds – admired his flowers & fountains – walked around the Treasury & State buildings & through the beautiful grounds around the Smithsonian Institute & through the building. This Institute is a collection of natural history & curiosity & is a wonder to all who visit it. We saw many of its rare birds and beasts at the Centennial. It would take several days to see it to the best advantage.

At night Tom & I went to one of the public Halls to see & be present at a meeting for the relief of the yellow fever sufferers at Savannah Ga. The famous Dr Newton, ex chaplain of Congress & other distinguished men were to speak. About two dozen people were present & a few dollars only were raised. I was much inclined to make some remarks – when "any other gentleman" was invited to speak, but I held my peace.

September 18 – Breakfast over & bills paid we hurried to the Balt. & Ohio depot & remembering Mr Wintersmiths counsel to get seats on the *right* hand side of the car – we were soon whirling homeward. There is nothing of special interest until we touch the Potomac River. We trace its meanderings & keep near its bed to find a passage for the cars. We see its falls & rapids & watch the tops of the mountains rising in the distance. The beautiful river grows less in volume. At Harpers Ferry it cuts through the mountain & the scene is wild & ragged –

towering mountains – naked crags – & the roaring river rushing wrathfully through the narrow gorge. We look out for the armory where the notorious "Old John Brown" seized the U.S. Guns & swords & armed the negroes to slay the whites – which act of abolition fanaticism eventually culminated into a war between the North & South.

We roll on through Virginia with Maryland to the right. The soil is poor – but less sandy than Maryland. The country is away behind in signs of thrift & improvement. We eagerly eye the mountains, rising in majesty around us. We watch the train circling on the brink of yawning precipices on one side & lofty perpendicular cliffs on the other. The Potomac diminishes more & more as we ascend but is flushed & foaming – just from a grand overflow. The town of Piedmont was not yet dry – the houses having been invaded by the flood almost to the second story. Our train is long & the grade steep. Three powerful Engines puff & push & on we crawl like some huge reptile – hugging the hillsides & peeping curiously down the terrible precipice where we see the river foam & dash over rocks and down declivities – now we hide in a dark tunnel – then look out upon far reaching mountain chains – rising peak after peak – point above point – higher & higher until the clouds are beneath us & behind us & we feel the clear – pure air & see the flashing sun light of the upper Alleghanies. Grand – exhilirating – sublime!

Higher & higher still we rise & away – away – farther & farther still stretches this grand array of "everlasting hills." The Potomac is now a small creek coming down one gorge & a mountain branch coming down another. It winds its way in the tangled thicket – now lost to sight & again appearing – leaping down a shelving rock – turning around a curve – rushing madly on to the sea. The train halts. We look out & see immense crowds of laborers with picks & spades. We are told to be easy, take our time – walk down this hill – cross the South Fork of the Potomac on a plank – walk up the next hill – & the train beyond will meet us. There is a break in the road. A flood like a waterspout has gathered in the gorge & earth & bridge and train are washed away. Yonder lie the coal cars – scattered half a mile down the branch. How we dread this loss of time. We were anxious to see Deer Park & descend the mountains in daylight – but the sun went down on us & night shut out the vision. Such crowds of people! The cars are packed & jammed. We had great difficulty in getting seats & sleep was out of the question. I wanted to lie over & rest & go through on daylight – but Tom was anxious to get on. We were startled from a doze by the order to "change cars for Cincinnati!" So into darkness we hurried at Parkersburg – or some other place – & again crowded & uncomfortable we were rolling homeward.

September 19 – We lay over at Cincinnati – & after a cheap breakfast we walked through the city – saw some its splendid business houses & beautiful residences – bought some mementoes & took train for Louisville. The hills we thought so beautiful as we went out had lost their grandeur in the comparison – but still the dear old Kentucky shore was to us "the land of promise." At Eight Oclock we landed at Louisville & found lodging at Alexanders hotel – though that was crowded — & once we thought we could not get in. The *same* boy who carried my valise on our way to the Centennial met me at the street car & asked to carry the valise again — said he carried it before & had been to Sunday School every Sunday as he promised me. I was pleased with the boy and gave him another nickel.

September 20 — Off for home. Sweet home! Found the dear children waiting at the depot — & Helen home with everything in nice order to welcome father & mother back to the dearest spot on earth. The servants were in great glee & had done tolerably well with the work. They seemed glad too to see us & proud of the presents we brought. With grateful hearts we bowed around the family altar & worshipped God whose kind hand had brought us safely over all the dangers of the way & made the journey so delightful to us. My dear wife was charmed with the trip & her health much improved. This is the only trip we have taken far from home since we were married — and after years of industrious self denial & economy she richly deserves the recreation & the pleasure & I am delighted that we have made the visit — & do not atall regret the money it cost us. Glad too that we took George & Robert & sorry we could not take all the rest.

September 22 — Quarterly meeting at Bethlehem. Lovefeast was a success. A Holy unction rested upon the people. Bro Biggs called for penitents & my dear little Wallace & my nephew Frank came forward for prayers — both seemed greatly in earnest & both claimed a conscious peace with God & joined the church. I was greatly rejoiced & feel that God has been better to me than I deserve. Dear little Wallace has been serious for some time. He had a spell of Typhoid fever in the summer, very mild indeed — yet he was very ill & I often talked with him about trusting in the Lord Jesus & found him exercised upon the subject. He talks very clearly on his conversion & I earnestly trust that he is a subject of saving grace. How my poor unworthy heart rejoices — that now *all* my children are in the fold & of their *own* accord have trusted in the Savior.

September 29 — I went to Russellville to meet the Board of Directors of Logan Female College. They seemed pleased with my report & accepted my suggestion to request the Presiding Elder to act as Agent — & not ask the Conference for a *paid* agent for the next year. The Board have been very courteous & kind to me. I am sorry I have not done more for them.

October 1 — We were startled by a messenger telling us that Helen & Charley [Roach] & both children were sick & that Lizzie had had two spasms. Poor Helen was going with me to Conference — but is sick in bed.

October 7 — [Annual Conference in Louisville] I was chosen to speak at the Missionary Anniversary tonight & the Committee of Arrangements for S. School Mass meeting appointed me to address the Mass meeting tomorrow Sunday evening — & the Committee on Public Worship appointed me to preach at Broadway Bap[tist] Church at 11 A.M. & at Chestnut St. Meth. Church at 7 P.M. This seems over work for a hoarse man.

October 9 – The application of F. M. English for readmission caused a spirited discussion. Dr N. H. Lee advocating his claim – assisted by Dr Cottrell – Bros Bottomley – L. B. Davison – H. C. Settle opposing his admission. Cottrells speech was pronounced "damaging very damaging" by Dr Redford. During its delivery the hour of adjournment came & Cottrell claimed the floor tomorrow.

October 10 – Pending the discussion of Bro English's application I gave as a reason for not admitting him that he had been vacillating – that he had been three times in & out of the itinerancy & once out of the church – that his talk against our itinerant operations had discouraged some of the young preachers & that his age – & the crowded state of our Conference impressed me that I ought to vote against his admission. He was rejected 44 to 32 – but he was very irate & abused the Conference.

At three the appointments were read out & I was sent P[residing] E[lder] to the Bowling Green Dist[rict]. While I feel the weight of responsibility – I feel a fixed purpose to do my duty & leave results with God.

October 11 – I reached home – thankful to find all well. Several of the preachers in the Bowling Green Dist. have expressed great gratification at my appointment – so also have the laymen whom I have met.

October 13 – Bro Jordan Moore came in & I paid him 25. more for aunt Betsys tombstone than the work was worth – but am *not* satisfied with the equity of the transaction. I did it under force of circumstances – & not from the convictions of justice that generally characterize all my transactions.

I saw in the Courier Journal of 12th an article from Bro F. M. English – headed "Mr English replies – His vindication of his character against the aspersions of the Methodist Conference." He was caustic & bitter – ridiculing Bishops Wightman & Kavanaugh – & L. B. Davison – & attacking the motives of Rev Thos. Bottomley – J. W. Shelton & myself – but was particularly bitter towards me. It was very unjust & in bad taste – did him more harm than any one else. I wrote a dignified – clear – & positive reply to be published in the same paper.

October 14 – Showed my reply to Bro Biggs & Father & others who advised its publication. I sent it to the Courier Journal.

October 18 – My article not appearing I wrote to the editor to know why he would allow me to be assailed in his paper & decline to admit my defense. The reporter replied that if my article was ever received it was misplaced & could not be found & if I would rewrite he would publish.

October 21 – [Franklin] Small attendance at Quarterly meeting. The brethren seemed anxious to be just & liberal in providing for the preachers. I declined to take any part of this Quarters Collection – because Bro Lewis needed it worse. The Conference & he seemed to appreciate the spirit.

October 25 — Wrote a reply to Bro English, sent it to the paper — mild in spirit — true in fact.

November 5 — [Glasgow] Bro Shelton had an engagement in the country to aid in dedicating a new Union church so I had the Quarterly meeting alone. At 11 Oclock I preached on the Judgment Rev[elation] 20.12 — with more than ordinary liberty. At 3 we had a good lovefeast. At night my congregation was much larger than in the forenoon & consisted largely of the leading men of the town. Governor Leslie came & introduced himself & wife & expressed great gratification at my visit to Glasgow. He wept under the sermon. It was on the providence of God in afflictions Lam[entations] 3.33–5.

November 6 — I went to the college[5] — conducted the chapel service for Prof Fuqua & made a speech to his girls. Went to see old Judge McFerran — who seemed glad to see me & invited me to stop with him when I return. He is a zealous Baptist & a great Democrat — & paralyzed as he is — he intends to get to polls tomorrow to vote for Tilden and Hendricks.

November 7 — This is Presidential Election day & millions of freemen are greatly concerned as to the result. I pray God to direct to the right result. I came home to vote — but the car caught fire at Russellville & we were delayed until the polls closed — so I missed the vote I was anxious to cast for my friend John W. Caldwell for Congress — & Samuel J. Tilden for President. News will be received with lively interest.

November 8 — The news of Tildens election is flashing over the wires — & the country is alive with expectancy. Tildens majorities are immense in the states he has carried — but he may not carry the electoral college.[6]

November 9 — Everybody is talking about the election. Democrats are exultant & Republicans are down. — but the result is yet uncertain.

November 10 — Up early & off to find Halls chapel on Morgantown circuit. At Russellville the people are jubilant over recent dispatches that Tilden has carried *all* the southern states — besides Conn — N. York — N. Jersey — Del — & Md & Oregon & Ind — securing a large vote in the electoral college. I reached Wm

---

5. That is, Liberty College, a Baptist school for women, which opened in 1875 with James H. Fuqua as president. *Barren County Heritage* (Bowling Green, Kentucky, 1980), 198.

6. The Democratic candidate, Samuel J. Tilden, had 184 electoral votes for certain, only one short of a majority. Twenty electoral votes from four states were claimed by both Republicans and Democrats. Congress finally established a special electoral commission, including five justices of the U.S. Supreme Court, to resolve the crisis. Against a backdrop of political maneuvering between Republicans and Southern Democrats, the commission awarded all of the disputed votes to the Republican candidate, Rutherford B. Hayes. See C. Vann Woodward, *Reunion and Reaction* (Boston, 1951).

Subletts in Warren County at night & was cordially welcomed. I heard guns firing through the night in commemoration of the Democratic successes.

November 11 – Bro Sublett went with me 12 miles or more to Halls Chapel in time for meeting. I preached on the Invitation & Refusal – Lu[ke] 14.15–35 with considerable liberty & proceeded at once to hold Quarterly Conference. While we were at church – the heavy boom of cannon sounded – in attestation of the wild joy of the Warren County Democrats over the reported election Tilden & Hendricks. I hope they are not too soon.

November 13 – Set out for home. I drove over as rough road as a buggie can well travel but Prince behaved well & I got through. I rested a little at Auburn & got to Russellville at or before sundown & stopped with Wilbur Browder. Found the town full of *painful* suspense on account of late dispatches that Republicans claim Louisiana – S. C. & Fla & Oregon giving Hayes a majority of *one* in the electoral college – while the Democrats claim that Tilden is beyond doubt elected on fair count. The whole country is excited & leading men are flocking to N. Orleans – to see a fair count of the vote. One more vote will elect Tilden.

November 14 – After getting myself & my horse shod – I came home through a drizzling rain blowing full in my face – but my gum coat came in good place. I find my dear wife & children well – but perplexed about the presidential suspense.

November 17 – I went over to the depot. Saw F. M. English's "reply" to my article in the Courier-Journal. It is so full of bully & bluster – so unfair & unjust – & betrays such a wicked spirit that I shall pay no further attention to him. I am sorry that he persists in virtually calling Bros Bottomley, Settle – Davison & myself "liars" but that seems to be his spirit. Poor man – he has convinced most of those who voted *for* him that the conference made a happy escape – in rejecting him. Bro Biggs was for him – but says now that he does not think he could get "five votes."

November 20 – I was gratified to receive a letter from my old friend & Bro George D. Blakey – now of Bowling Green – giving me some very kind expressions of appreciation of my course in the "little unpleasantness" with Bro English – & suggesting that I had no occasion to write any more as English's last article shows that he was like the huntsmans deer that need not be shot – as he jumped so high he would kill himself.

November 26 – [Smith's Grove] We had Love Feast conducted by Dr [W. W.] Lambuth. At night I preached on Charity – very serious attention and appreciation. I raised the Quarterly Collection – which was omitted in the morning. I had instructed the stewards to pay the entire receipts of the Quarter to Bro Lambuth in view of his necessities which he appreciated & spoke of as an exceptional case in his history. I thought it was right.

November 27 – Up several times in the night to note the time. The whistle sounded before I was dressed – & the station was a hundred yards – or more. I got on the platform – after the train started & by running & pulling up by the irons I *barely* got on board & reached Bowling Green before day – stopped at Potter house & at 1 Oclock met Dist[rict] Stewards – was pleased with the expressions & spirit they showed & satisfied with the estimate of 1025.00 for my salary. I hope they may be able to pay 70 pr cent of the claim. The train was 3 hours late & I got home at 9 P.M. thankful to find all well.

December 1 – [Franklin] The change is sudden & severe. The ground is hidden in snow. The waters are stiff & freezing still. A piercing west wind is blowing furiously & Scottsville is 26 miles away over a "hill country." I am glad to have the buggie curtains between me & the wind. Well-wrapped – gloved & shod – & Prince hitched in, I rolled away over hills & hollows – across creeks & ice beds – along the snowy way – & reached Dr Walkers in about 6 hours. Found a hearty welcome – good fires – warm supper – cozy room – elegant bed – & felt thankful for such friends & comforts.

December 3 – Very cold. House crowded. Good love feast. I had good liberty preaching on Christian Charity to an audience composed largely of Northern Methodists – their pastor Bro Humphrey present. I learn that Bro Goring applied for the Baptist *School room* for me to preach in tonight – knowing that they did not allow their *church* to be *desecrated* by other denominations – and was refused the *school room*. The flue was down in our house & the appointment had been made for a school room – rather more remote than the Baptist house – but the jailer warmed & lighted up the *court house* – the largest room in town – & I found it a good place to preach. It was crowded – from centre to circumference – & I doubt if any man ever had a more respectful & attentive audience. Men not in the habit of attending church were there & seemed deeply interested. Mr Mulligan – one of the principal lawyers in the place – a wicked man – was deeply affected & spoke often of the sermon. Being pressed to make another appointment I did so. Stay at Dr Walkers. Wrote my wife. The weather is cold & it will require over 100 miles drive to go home and get back to Neurow next week – so I consented to remain here.

December 4 – Preached in the court house again – to a very large & increasingly serious congregation – by request – on Christian Charity. This discourse seemed to strike everybody. John Gatewood – another prominent lawyer – spoke of it as about the best sermon he ever heard! I hope it will do him & the town some good.

December 5 – I was invited to dine with Bro Gatewood – & to sup with Mr Mulligan. I learn that the latter is an unusual occurrence. Talked with Mr Mulligan about his soul. I think he is more affected than he is willing to allow. I had another large congregation – with deep seriousness. Even the prison was opened & the jail birds allowed to come. One old man Mr Shrum charged with killing his wife listened with almost breathless interest – while I preached on the Parable of the Virgins. He said he had never heard such preaching before in his life. I had been to prison & talked to him – urged him to make ready for that tribunal from which there was no appeal.

December 6 – Did not expect to preach tonight but Bro Slate [Preacher in Charge] & others insisted & I consented – tired & hoarse as I am. My subject was hope. My friend Mulligan was out again which I learn is unusual for him. There seemed to be much feeling & Mulligan wept – audibly. I leave Scottsville tomorrow – glad that I came here – & trust that some good was done. The jailer John Huntsman seemed anxious for me to stay & said he would light up the house as long as I wanted it.

December 10 – [Walker's Chapel on Neurow Circuit] House crowded. Lovefeast *late* – interrupted by people constantly coming in. I felt that a sermon on the evidences of Christianity would be useful – so I took John 10.37–8 as a text. Most of the people listened with very earnest interest. The subject was evidently new to them & many spoke of it. The number of communicants smaller than I expected. I think the church in this country has erred in licensing unqualified men to preach & exhort. There seems great need of more learning. They have zeal not according to knowledge. They rely much upon "getting up a stir."

December 11 – I found in Franklin that I had been announced to preach tonight – but I was too hoarse & tired and had only spent *one day* at home in about 3 weeks – so I drove 45 miles to day & reached home before 7 oclock – left Franklin 1 ½ oclock – 30 miles in little over 5 hours. Helen & Charley & my dear grand-children here.

December 12 – We killed hogs – 17 in number – average weight 211 lbs nett – average age less than 10 months. Good pigs. Poland China and Berkshire. I sold 7 – average gross weight 281 ½ – sold at 5 cts gross – 6 ½ nett.

December 13 – I worked busily – cutting up & salting down the pork – thankful to have plenty & to spare. I have just sent my Bro Frank [in Alabama] a barrel of flour & must send him some meat in the spring. I learned that his last & only horse was dead & I wrote to him last night – that I would send him a horse if he wished. Poor boy. He has had bad luck. I pity him & wish I could help him more. I was sent for to see Lucy Anderson. She married a man named Stevenson – who got possession of all her money – told her various falsehoods – then left on pretense of going to see a sister at the point of death – wrote back to her that he was in Cincinnati – & has not been heard from for six weeks. The poor woman is nearly heartbroken – & is reaping the bitter fruits of her folly in marrying a stranger. She wants me to try to find her absconded husband. I promised to write & inquire of the preacher at Paris Ky. whether there is such a man or family there.

December 15 – I went to Bristov – thence with Bro Bunton to Thos Mill's 8 miles through the cold. Slept in an open house – no plastering – nor ceiling – nor floor – just the weatherboard – but we had good fire & plenty of covering & hospitable fare & I was comfortable & happy.

December 16 – The congregation at Pine Grove was better than I expected & I preached with some liberty & held a harmonious session of the Quarterly Conference.

December 17 – I have seldom heard such hearty congregational singing as they have in these hills. The people are poor – but they seem to be good & very hospitable. I have not seen a negro in the county of Edmonson.

December 25 – [Bowling Green] Blessed Birthday of our Lord! I rose at 4 ½ to go home. Found some drinking boys at the depot – talking irreverently. I tried to so order the conversation as to give a gentle reproof. I thought one felt it – with another it seemed to be casting pearls before swine. Train was an hour late but got home at 9 & found the children lively and Robert at home – with Helen and my grandbabies.

December 28 – The snow still lies frozen on the ground & more is falling. Willie Woodward from Bowling Green has been spending Christmas with the boys & they have had a fine time hunting. Poor Hanson writes – date of 23d – that he was sick with a hard chill at Marianna [Arkansas] and had to ride horseback 9 miles home! I wish he was at home now. I fear it was a bad move to let him go to Ark. but I thought it was best at the time.

December 29 – The snow continued all night & was falling fast & thick as I went to the train this morning to go to Franklin Circuit Quarterly Meeting. The trains were all so delayed & the storm so continued that I came home. The storm continues until nearly night – making more than 24 hours of continuous snow fall. This is about 12 inches – some places 36 inches or more.

December 30 – Cold – trains all out of time. I cannot get to my Quarterly Meeting. Willie Woodward, Frank Browder, Tom Browders children and my own are having a gay time playing blindfold.

January 1, 1877 – I went with Lizzie, Luther & Wallace to spend the night with Helen. Little Ruth called Lizzie "Grammy" first time. Little Lizzie sat on my lap & begged me to tell tales about boys & girls. First time Lizzie & I have staid there together except when little Lizzie had the spasms.

January 2 – Our hired man *Scott* & his wife left us to go & live with Tom Page. I hired *Henry Coleman* for the farm – at $140. & *Mary Winston* for cook & house servant at $5 pr month – if she does all the work. *Scotts* wife had too much company at my expense. A change was desirable.

January 3 — Bitterly cold — clouds threaten more snow. Stay in & read & write. I received a letter from Dr Redford indicating that the Publishing House is in financial trouble & asking me to concur in the Bishops counsel to raise collections in all the churches in Feb. I am for saving the property to the church — but there are some things in the reports — I mean the Agents reports — that seem to me to be inconsistent with the present cry of distress. Oh the horrors of this financial pressure! It burdens preachers & people — church & state. I received a letter from Bro Bunton telling me of the gracious revival at Pine Grove — which began under my preaching.

January 8 — [Franklin] Winter! Winter! Another deep snow & chilling blasts sweeping the falling fleeces into great feathery piles. I waited in Franklin to meet the Stewards of Franklin Circuit — but the snow storm & the cold detained all but one.

January 9 — Mercy on me! how cold! Mercury 14 below Zero — snow deep — coldest weather for years. I slept under a burden of cover at Bro Joe Crows — & did not suffer. Got home at night.

January 11 — My fiftieth birthday! I did not expect to live so long. God has spared me & my dear wife has taken care of me. I am getting old now — half a century — I was never strong & vigorous — but I am still reasonably active — but too fleshy — weight 175 — possible more. My hair is nearly white. My hearing is alittle heavy in both ears — very dull in the left. Thank God for my eyesight. I can read very small print without glasses by daylight — but better with glasses. My teeth are defective — several gone. My voice is not so mellow & clear as formerly — often it seems to me to be cracked & rather screaking — & I have had occasional hoarseness a long time — but my congregations do not complain. My mind is not so active nor capable of continued effort as formerly — & I fear that I am not as much disposed to work & study. My *principles* seem to *strengthen* — but my *emotions* are not so lively. I feel that I do belong to God — & if there is any rebellion in my heart against his known & acknowledged will, I am not aware of it. I look back over my life to day & lament its barrenness of results. Most of it has been spent in the church — 39 ¾ years — if I have the dates right — & more than 30 years I have been preaching with more or less acceptability to men. Yet I have done but little — oh! so *little* & the time to work almost gone! The *law* condemns but *grace* covers me! "I the chief of sinners am. But Jesus died for me." My life *outwardly* has been moral. I do not know that I ever swore an oath — or told a wicked lie. I never was drunk. I never played cards nor staked anything on a bet. I never went into a gambling house — nor a drinking saloon — nor a brothel — if I knew it. I never used tobacco — except to smoke a few cigars — & I quit that in 1848, but I have had many vain & wicked worldly thoughts & temptations — & only the grace of God & the principles taught by his word through my parents have deterred me from flagrant — overt sin — not my *own* goodness. I have loved ease & made too little effort & sacrifice to do the good I might have done. I have not "*labored* in word & doctrine" as I ought — & much of my preaching has lacked that *realizing sense* of *truth* & *importance* that would have made it more effective. Fifty years of my life gone & almost nothing done!

January 12 – Went to Bowlinggreen. Bro Hardison, one of my preachers – met me at the depot & took me to his house – in the college – & his good wife gave me a dinner *just suited to my notion* – good coffee – excellent cornbread & beef & superior milk & butter. I do not often enjoy a dinner more.

January 13 – Small attendance at Quarterly Meeting. I preached Phil[ippians] 2.12 with less than usual liberty. Dined at Bro Robt Hines's – had a long & earnest talk with sister H. about her love & practice of dancing. "Love not the world."

January 15 – Rain – rain – rain. I declined my trip to Glasgow on account of the weather. I read & visited until time to come home – had a fatiguing, muddy walk from the depot – but the cheering welcome of my dear wife who did not expect me for a week or more – & a good supper soon made me forget the mud & the mire. I was glad to have cheerful letters from Robt & Hanson. Dr Summers had made Robt a present of a copy of his commentary on Johns Gospel – as a premium in his class. Hanson had escaped chills for *two weeks.*

The paper today confirms the reports that the Republican State government of Louisiana is about to break down & the Democrats are getting stronger in their position. It seems now that *all* the Southern States are Democratic & the prospect is that the People will be more harmonious & prosperous than for years – & it is to be hoped that the Presidential question will be settled without war. There has been much talk in the papers & in private circles about civil war – the Republicans declaring that Mr Tilden is not elected & Mr Hayes *shall* be inaugurated & the Democrats with equal earnestness asserting that Hayes is defeated & that Tilden shall be inaugurated. The condition of public affairs has been *very critical* & the popular mind so much excited & the proofs of fraud in the Returning Boards of La. S. C. & Fla. so glaring – that collisions were constantly expected & if once begun – no man could foresee the end. Gracious Lord save our country from war!

January 17 – I sent Frank Browder a *mule* instead of the horse at my fathers suggestion – & advanced the money to pre-pay the freight. I also sent him a fine sow shoat.

February 1 – I took my father to Russellville in my buggie. The roads are smooth & dry & the weather warm as May. I hesitated long – but at last paid the premium on my wifes life policy. I think the policy holders have been badly swindled. At home I spent some time wrapping my apple trees – which the sheep have barked – with cloths saturated with grafting wax – hoping to make an artificial bark that would allow the flow of sap & save my trees.

February 2 & 3 – I had no Quarterly meeting so I staid at home, feeling the need of rest – letters asking me to aid in meetings come – but I am not able to go.

February 4 – Very drizzly & rainy all day & *dark* at night, that we stayed at home & read the Bible & good books with our Children. This was a happy day.

February 6 – I rode over to Mr Cokes where my father is having the graves of my mother – Grand mother & aunt Fannie Gwynn – repaired & the stones reset & redressed. I ought to have attended to this myself – but my father insisted that it was his duty to do it.

I paid Mr James Huckel 1.00 for the work & my father furnished the material for making a foundation & resetting the stone at aunt Betsy Waters grave which had fallen down. He said the stone was not worth one cent over $50. & that it was a swindle to make me pay $100.00 for it. I thought so when I settled the bill.

February 15 – The ten oclock train that does not stop here sounded the "stop" signal & I sent George & Luther with the lantern to see if Hanson had come. They soon returned in company with my dear boy & his cousin Lizzie Warfield – came to go to school. We were of course delighted to see them & relieved of a most distressing suspense. The rumor had got afloat that Hanson was to be married – which step just *now* I feared would interrupt his plans & hopes for the future – & I am thankful to find the rumor false.

February 16 – This ought to be All Fools day with me. I started to Allen County to my Quarterly Meeting without consulting my memorandum of time & went ten miles beyond Russellville before I discovered that I was *a week ahead* of my appointment! I felt blank & cheap – I turned in to spend the night with my old friend & Bro. Thos H. Gilbert where I always find a hearty welcome. He insisted that I stay over Sabbath & preach at Pleasant Run to which I consented.

February 17 – The country is now excited over the news that the electoral commission of 8 Republicans & 7 Democrats – by a *strictly party vote* – have decided to rule out all the evidence of glaring fraud & swindle & have given the vote of Louisiana to Hayes & Wheeler. It is indeed humiliating to think that men occupying the honorable & responsible position of judges of the Supreme Court of the U. S. would consent to be cheats & party tricksters for political demagogues – as either the one or the other set of these men seem to have done. I fear for our country.

February 19 – I got home in the afternoon in time to see a villainous dog tearing to pieces one of my finest lambs. I got my gun & pursued him – but he ran away & was lost. I offered a reward for information & soon learned from a negro woman that old *George Allensworth* – a negro man had a dog & a pup answering the description. I went there & found the identical dog & the old man acted very gentlemanly & said he must be killed, so I shot the dog – but spared the puppy which though in bad company I thought had not killed the lamb. I am glad I caught the thief.

March 4 – [Oakland] Large – serious congregation. Preached Rev[elations] 20.1. Considerable liberty. Deep impressions. Bro Bunton immersed some persons in the creek – came back *hoarse,* sore throated.

March 6, 7, 8 – Meeting continued day & night. I did nearly all the preaching. Several bright conversions. Edmonson is a poor county. I have not seen any real fine farm land in it. It has minerals & mineral waters. The people are hospitable & kind, but live in poor houses – men & women & children & visitors frequently sleeping in the same room. I judge in time past the morals here have been bad. I was in two or three families that now seem to be respectable in which there are illegitimate children – & yet the women married afterward. I hope such things will not prevail in the county. I found at James Wingfields the only nice plastered & framed house I have seen in the county – off the rail road. No doubt there are others. Mammoth Cave is in this county.

March 15 – [Olmstead] On Flora McFlimsey [George Dick's horse] I set out to Hadley where I had agreed to be with T. D. Lewis & hear his sermon on Baptism tomorrow.

March 16 – The School House of Hadley was crowded. The Baptists had been making some inroads on us there & had preached on the subject of Baptism – using the old talk that they were the church – the *only* church & the rest of us only societies – no baptism but by immersion &c. For 2 ¼ hours Tom Lewis showed in beautiful style & kind spirit – by invincible logic & Scriptural argument, that the Scriptures *do* not, *cannot* teach that *immersion* is a necessity to baptism. I have seldom been so well pleased with a discourse on that subject. In showing what seemed to him the unreasonableness of making such ado about the *mode* of administering *one* sacrament – & the utter indifference to *mode* in the other – no one claiming to administer the sacrament of the Lords supper in the precise *mode* practiced by Apostles – he said he could not see the reason. Three Baptist ministers were present – taking notes – Gardner, Jenkins & Williams. Jenkins spoke out & said – to Bro Lewis – "You've got but one eye. You cant see." (Lewis has a defective eye) He replied, sharply, "Bro Jenkins that is a very unkind remark in you & I dont thank you for it. My mother taught me that it was bad manners to make remarks about the deformities of people in their presence. I did not make my eyes – they are just as God made them – & if you had a good heart in you, you would not have said it" – & much more of the same sort. I told him that I did not think the brother intended an offence – but only alittle pleasantry to parry the force of his argument. Jenkins then rose & explained that he did not mean to offend, but had spoken unguardedly. Lewis accepted the explanation & modified his reproof. Except this little episode the occasion was very pleasant & profitable. The Methodists are satisfied – delighted. The Baptists say they must have another sermon.

March 27 – Came through Russellville – paid for some peach trees which I fear are dead 5.20 – got home & found that Helen has another daughter born this morning.[7] Lizzie away from home.

March 28 – Went to see Lizzie & my grand babies – 3!

April 2 – [Franklin] After calling on some friends – & attending to some business, I took sister Drane in my buggie & started for home. The road was muddy but Prince travelled well & we made it in good time. Sister Drane was lively & cheerful & having been long cooped up in town she enjoyed the ride hugely as I did myself – but when we got home & I found Lizzie gone to see Helen – not expecting me until tomorrow – I was embarrassed just alittle. I was just going to take her up to my sisters – but Hanson came in & went back & brought Lizzie home. I am always glad to see Lizzie, but her coming now was particularly agreeable.

April 6 – Bennett Harris came to tell me that Mrs Davenport died last evening & they wanted me to preach her funeral sermon. In a little while George Biggs came to ask me to stay & preach George Youngs funeral. Alas! alas! My old schoolmates are dying – called the same day to bury two of them!

April 8 – [Bowling Green] Slept at Woodwards. The family distressed at the misfortune of Sister Woodwards niece – Fanny Smith, daughter of my old friend Geo. W. Smith of Russellville – who was seduced – gave birth to a child – & then married Charlie Smith – the father of the babe. The marriage of course was right under the circumstances. Fanny was a nice girl – had access to the best families. Her mother is greatly distressed & many friends. Quite a number of illegitimate births have been reported in our county recently. I am pained to hear it.

April 10 – Up at 5 & off for home. Brought Dr J. E. Breeding with me – who extracted 19 teeth & roots for my wife & two for me. She suffered greatly & was much exhausted but was delighted to have the teeth out. I had some fears – but am pleased with Breedings work.

April 11, 12 – At home reading, thinking, praying – making a sermon on Sacrament of Lords Supper. Information on subject is needed in Bowling Green District.

April 13 – A long horseback ride – 40 miles to Bro Subletts on my way to Hadley.

---

7. Helen's third baby was called Sallie McLean. She died six months later. Inexplicably, George Dick never mentioned her death.

April 15 — Good lovefeast. The congregation was so large that we moved into the new church — Lewis Chapel — so called in honor of T. D. Lewis — the organizer of the Hadley Society. The roof was not completed — but the weather was all we could ask. The house was full & I suppose ⅓ of the people outside. It was understood that I would preach on Communion — & people were anxious to hear. I had liberty & I think made the matter clear in 75 minutes.

April 16 — I got home at night — very tired. Found my poor wife still suffering greatly with lacerated gums. They bled so freely that Dr B. failed to get out all the cotton he had applied to stop the bleeding — & that has increased the soreness.

May 1 — Hanson & I went to Nashville in the buggie — stopped at Dr. Redfords, by special request.

May 2 — Went to the Publishing House & saw many of the preachers — thence to the Vanderbilt. Robert was well and well spoken of by teachers & pupils. Dr Summers seems fond of him. I introduced Hanson to him & he said — "Is this Roberts brother? He is no account — Robert is worth a dozen of him." I told him he might think differently at the end of two years. He said — "A bird in the hand is worth two in the bush."

May 19 — [Neurow Circuit] Large audience at Stony Point. I had unusual liberty preaching on Sauls conversion. There was an uproar of praise & thanksgiving — many wept aloud & some shouted — before the sermon was ended. These people seem wonderfully demonstrative in their religious emotions & cordial in their hospitality, but they have a poor idea of the obligation to support their pastor.

May 20 — Fine melting time in love feast. Dr Hoyte from Nashville a Presbyterian preacher — was present & I invited him to preach. He gave us an excellent sermon on Christ our Advocate — preached a real Arminian sermon — & told us he was Presbyterian. When I arose to administer the Sacrament I said "I was very much obliged to Dr Hoyte for his able & earnest sermon — that if he had not taken the pains to tell us he was a Presbyterian — the people would have gone home supposing they had heard the real old time Methodist gospel." He ran to me & hugged me & said "Brother the Methodists must have some good texts." I replied "Yes Dr. God bless you — the Bible is so full of good Methodist texts that you Presbyterians cant preach good sermons without using them."

May 27 — [Pleasant Hill] Excellent love feast. The house could not hold the crowd. I preached on Sacrament of Lords Supper. Before I closed the whole audience seemed convulsed with weeping & shouting. The pulpit was crowded with local preachers — some of whom seemed overcome — & some shouted Halleluiah — apparently at the top of their voices. It did seem that God was applying his word with wonderful power. I went to Scottsville to preach at night on Missions – had *light* – but not *heat*. I heard from home that my dear daughters youngest child was very ill – not expected to live.

May 28 – I thought I would try to ride home – but sundown found me worn down & I stopped at Thos Gilberts.

May 29 – Home by 10 Oclock – the dear babe improving – God be praised.

June 4 – [Franklin] I went with Bro Peters in his buggie out to the neighborhood Shiloh where I am to preach the funeral sermon of Rev & Hon Benj. P. Wilson.

June 5 – Early the crowds began to gather – & so did the clouds. We had a beautiful morning shower – which ceased before church time. The face of the earth around Shiloh seemed covered with wagons, carriages, horses & people of all sizes & sexes. It was estimated that 2000 people were present. The seats & stand were arranged in the grove – but a brisk gale was blowing – so that a voice three times as strong as mine could not have reached over half the people. The text was Matt[hew] 22.30 – "They neither marry nor are given in marriage" &c. People seemed anxious to hear & I was laying a good foundation for argument – when the storm of wind & rain broke upon us – scattering the people in all directions. The church & school house – & lodge room – & carriages & umbrellas sheltered most of the people – but many were exposed to the storm & got wet. So abruptly closed the services.

June 6 – Returned to Franklin – dined with T.D. Lewis & took him in my buggie out to Cedar Bluff College[8] where we witnessed part of the examination & a comic colloquy performed by a number of the pupils most admirably. Miss Odom from Texas stood a splendid examination in music & I have not seen in any school a better enacted play than that of the Borrowing Neighbors written by Mrs B. W. Vineyard of Cedar Bluff. She is a woman of decided talent & a beautiful writer as evinced by her address to the class who won distinctions. I was called on for an address – & made a short impromptu speech that elicited applause.

June 7 – A large crowd at the exhibition – performances good – essays excellent. I detect the style of Mrs V. who I doubt not did most of the polishing & mending. One young lady – Miss Alice Batsell of Franklin was so embarrassed that she could not read her graduating essay. Mrs V. read it for her & just as the curtains were about to close – I stepped to the front & addressed the audience about in these words. Ladies & gentleman, I wish to volunteer a remark & hope

---

8. Cedar Bluff Female College was a nonsectarian school in Warren County, southeast of Woodburn. It graduated its first class in 1869. Cedar Bluff's catalog for 1891–92 lists Hanson Browder as president and his wife Jennie as lady principal. The college burned on January 31, 1892. Jennie B. Cole, "Cedar Bluff College," typescript in Special Files, Kentucky Library, Western Kentucky University.

you excuse me. The essay just read is a beautiful production & does great credit to the head & heart of the young lady that wrote it & it is not to her discredit that timidity & embarrassment prevented her from reading it. When we remember that strong men frequently choke down − with confusion on their appearance before a public audience − it is not strange that a timid girl should be overcome with emotion. One of the greatest men England ever produced − the celebrated Robert Hall, the champion & defender of the Baptist faith − on his first & second appearances in public made a signal failure. He covered his face with his hands & cried out "All my ideas have left me" and sank back in his seat weeping like a child. Yet he made one of the grandest men of any age. It is rather a compliment than a discredit to Miss Batsell that her timid nature shrinks from a public reading of her well written essay. This speech brought down the house with applause & teachers & citizens expressed their gratification & approval. They said "Alice Batsell will love you as long as she lives." I went to Bowling Green & stopped with my old friend judge Hines, putting Flora in the lot at Warren College.

June 9 − I pressed on to Mt Nebo in Edmonson co[unty] to hold my Quarterly Meeting. Found Bunton & one other man at church. Two others came & we held Quarterly Conf[erence].

June 11 − Off for home. Hope there is some spiritual benefit in this visit. The people are doing very little to support their preachers. I left Flora in Bowling-green in Bro Hardisons lot & came home on the train − learned that Jimmy [Browder]s mare had become frightened at the cars & run away with the buggie throwing father & mother out − stunning & bruising them very badly − but breaking no bones. My son Hanson was also kicked on the leg by a mule & badly hurt − but not dangerously.

June 23 − I expected to do much reading this week − but have done almost none − harvest − hot weather − company & lethergy all in the way.

June 25 − Dr Breeding is here to make my wifes teeth.

July 7 − [Franklin] Held Quarterly Conf[erence] at night. Finances greatly in arrears. I tried to impress upon the Stewards the importance of action. I have published an earnest appeal in the Advocate − to all our people to try to save the preachers from want.

July 12 − [Olmstead] I helped prepare a granary for my wheat. There is a distressing drought in the land & corn is likely to be very scarce.

July 16 − [Bowling Green] A busy day in pastoral visitations − Will Porter − Dr McCormack, Bro Brewer − sister J. H. Linn − Porter Thomas − John Woodward − Judge Hines − Joe Hall − Bro Hardison − sister Wilson − Bro Higgins. At night held Quarterly Conference. Much the best financial report that has been made at one quarter in the District – 353.50 of which I received 39.25.

August 7 – I find that I have preached 133 times – besides divers lovefeasts – & S[unday] School & college lectures – & travelled about four thousand miles – & am now nearly half way on the fourth round – & have not yet received 400 for my work. I am troubled about the supply of the District for the next Conference year. Some of the preachers want to be changed & some of the people desire changes. I always dreaded the responsibilities of Presiding Eldership – now I feel it. But I shall try to do my duty. God help me.

May 10th 1862.

The beginning of a new volume of my journal is always, rather exciting to me. I can but wonder what painful or pleasant events I may be called to note — what changes in our domestic ties I may have to record — what losses, or trials or changes, for better or worse may befal us. I am glad I have kept a record of the past. yet I do not know that my children will ever read it to see the labor I have undergone, to leave them a history of my life & times, which I should esteem a great treasure, if coming from my own father to me.

It is well for us that we cannot foresee future events. we would be too much depressed by some, & too much elated by the prospect of others to do justice to the matters that demand our present attention.

I enter upon this volume, doubting whether I shall live to write the last page — or if I should, it is most uncertain, whether all, around me now, will be alive, & still with me, when these pages are all full. I will probably record here the time & place when & where great battles were fought & victories won in this second revolution, that now sweeps over the entire South & shakes the nation from center to circumference — I shall probably record the close of this desolating war, & the conquest of the Southern people, or possibly I may write in these pages the acknowledgment of Southern Independence — Some profound Bible Critics make 61, & 62, one of the prophetic periods, & it is not improbable that these very pages may unfold to the memory of my children some of the most startling events known in all the history of our sin-cursed world — It is certainly a day of darkness in our land — distress in the nation, & discouragement in the church & none can tell, whether I shall write here the

---

A facsimile of a page from George Dick's diary. In this opening entry to the Civil War volume of his diaries, George Dick reveals the apprehension with which Kentuckians awaited the course of events following the withdrawal of Confederate troops from the state three months earlier.

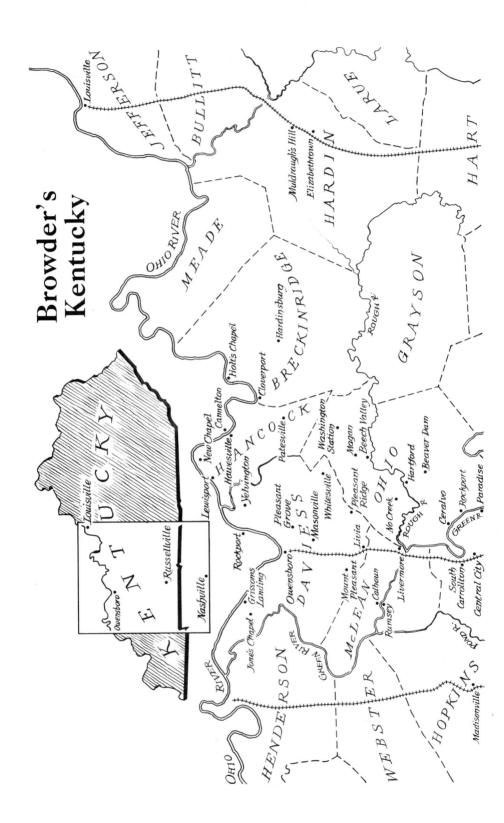

Browder's Kentucky

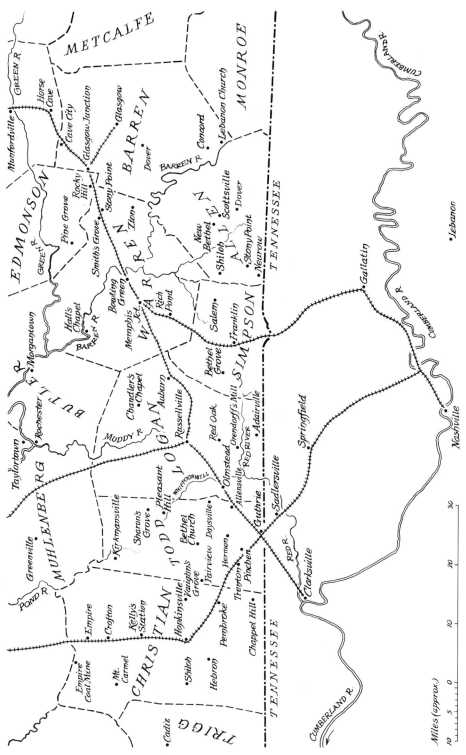

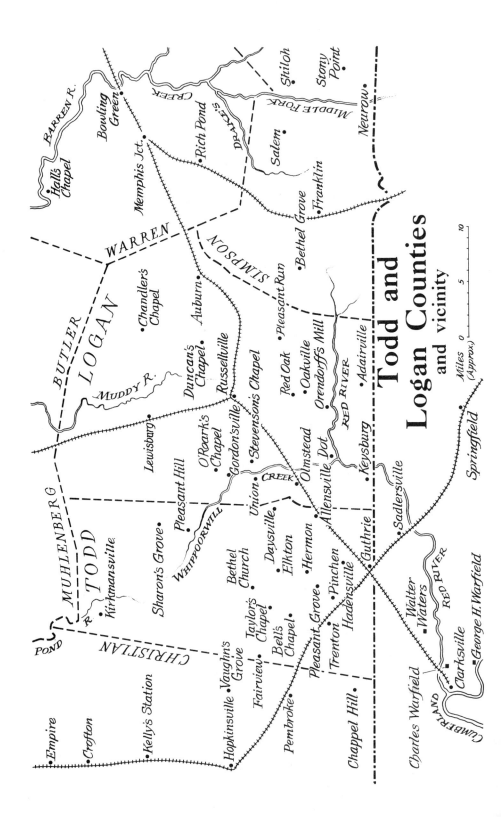

Todd and Logan Counties and vicinity

Miles 0 5 10 (Approx.)

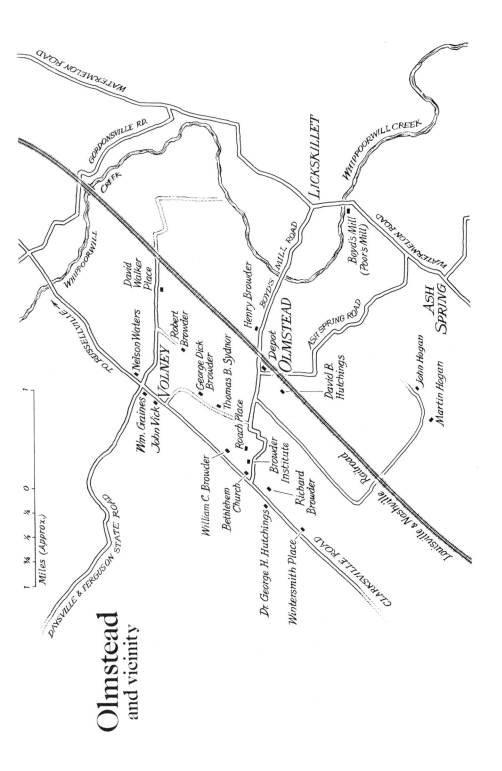

Olmstead
and vicinity

WATERMELON ROAD

GORDONSVILLE RD.

CREEK

WHIPPOORWILL CREEK

LICKSKILLET

WHIPPOORWILL CREEK

BOYD'S MILL ROAD

Boyd's Mill
(Poor's Mill)

WATERMELON ROAD

WHIPPOORWILL

David
Walker
Place

Henry Browder

Robert
Browder

ASH SPRING ROAD

ASH
SPRING

TO RUSSELLVILLE

Nelson Waters

VOLNEY

George Dick
Browder

Thomas B. Sydnor

Depot

OLMSTEAD

David B.
Hutchings

John Hogan

Martin Hogan

Wm. Gaines

John Vick

Roach Place

Railroad

William C. Browder

Bethlehem
Church

Browder
Institute

Richard
Browder

Miles (Approx.)

DAYSVILLE & FERGUSON STATE ROAD

Dr. George H. Hutchings

Wintersmith Place

CLARKSVILLE ROAD

Louisville & Nashville

All the Members of the 1st Quarterly Meeting Conference of Logan Circuit held at Stevenson Chapel Sept. 12th 1846 do hereby recommend to the Louisville Conference of the Methodist Episcopal Church South our Beloved Brother George Richard Bowden as a suitable person to be received into the traveling Connexion.

Signed in behalf of the Conference.

A. H. Lewis &

William F. Evans Secy

A copy of George Dick's local preacher's license. In applying for a local preacher's license in 1846, George Dick took the first step on his way to becoming a Methodist preacher. Local preacher's licenses were issued by the quarterly or district conferences of the Methodist church.

Know all Men by these Presents,

THAT I, *William Capers* one of the Bishops of the METHODIST EPISCOPAL CHURCH, SOUTH, under the protection of ALMIGHTY GOD, and with a single eye to his glory, by the imposition of my hands and prayer, have this day set apart *George R. Browder* for the office of a DEACON in the said METHODIST EPISCOPAL CHURCH, SOUTH, a man who, in the judgment of the *Louisville* Conference, is well qualified for that work: and he is hereby recommended to all whom it may concern, as a proper person to administer the Ordinance of BAPTISM, MARRIAGE, AND THE BURIAL OF THE DEAD, in the absence of an *Elder*, and to feed the flock of Christ, so far as his spirit and practice are such as become the GOSPEL OF CHRIST, and he continueth to hold fast the form of sound words, according to the established doctrines of the Gospel.

In Testimony Whereof, I have hereunto set my hand and Seal, this *Eighth* day of *October* in the year of our Lord One Thousand and *forty eight.*

Hardinsburg
Octr 8. 1848

W. Capers.

KNOW ALL MEN BY THESE PRESENTS,

THAT I, *James O. Andrew* one of the Bishops of the Methodist Episcopal Church, South, under the protection of ALMIGHTY GOD, and with a single eye to his glory, by the imposition of my hands and prayer, (being assisted by the Elders present,) have this day set apart *George R. Browder* for the office of an ELDER in the said Methodist Episcopal Church, South; a man who, in the judgment of the *Louisville* Conference, is well qualified for that work; and he is hereby recommended, to all whom it may concern, as a proper person to administer the sacraments and ordinances, and to feed the flock of Christ, so long as his spirit and practice are such as become the Gospel of Christ, and he continueth to hold fast the form of sound words, according to the established doctrines of the Gospel.

In Testimony whereof, I have hereunto set my hand and seal, this *22* day of *September*, in the year of our Lord, one thousand eight hundred and *fifty.*

Greensburg
Ky

Jas. O. Andrew

A copy of George Dick's deacon's and elder's orders. After receiving his local preacher's license and serving acceptably for two years on trial in the itinerant ministry, George Dick was eligible for the office of deacon and, two years later, for the office of elder.

The Roach place. When Helen Browder Roach and her husband, Charley, built this commodious Victorian house in 1884, George Dick observed that "it was too costly for a country house — and too fine for the neighborhood."

The storage shed on the Roach place. It was in the loft of this farm building that Walker Riley in the 1930s rescued the surviving volumes of George Dick's diaries.

The Robert Browder house. Robert Browder built this dwelling sometime during the 1830s. George Dick recalled that as young boy he helped make the brick in a kiln set up in the yard nearby.

Volume VI
1877–1878

"I think the Presiding Elder ought to be felt *in his District."*

December 11, 1877 – Since the 7th of Aug, I have made no entries in my diary. Then I was making the fourth round of the Bowling-green District – as Presiding Elder, and dreading the responsibilities of the coming Conference. I find in looking over my record of minutes that I filled all the appointments except one that occurred in the heavy snow storm, the last of December. I travelled about five thousand (5000) miles at my own expense & preached about 150 sermons – besides divers exhortations, school lectures – Sunday School speeches – & much pastoral work. My salary was estimated at 1025.00 of which I received about 600 – but surrendered some of my claims to the preachers who were poorer than I. The work was laborious – but except the absence from my family – I found it in the main pleasant. The people every where treated me kindly & eulogized me much more than I deserved. I was told every where that my return to the District was greatly desired.

I never felt the burden and care and responsibility of making the appointments as we did at the last Conference. I was burdened in spirit day & night – had very little rest but got my District, I think – well supplied. Some of the preachers felt that their interests demanded a change to other Districts, but every one expressed a desire to retain me as P.E. This of course was gratifying. I succeeded in securing the return of every preacher that was asked for – & in getting for each preacher that left my District a better place than he had in the District. I learned something too about the views and feelings of the preachers – that I did not know so well before. We hung in the Cabinet* 5 hours on the case of one man trying to do the best we could for him and the people. My idea is that other things being equal, it is better for one to suffer than many.

I had some painful solicitude in the case of Bro John W. Shelton of Glasgow. I had told him at his last Quarterly Meeting that there was some difficulty in the way of his return – which was unpleasant to me – discouraging to him – & painful to his wife. Some of his people demanded a single preacher – & his Walnut Hill people requested a return to the Smith's grove circuit. I wrote to them that they ought to talk candidly with Bro Shelton & let him ask for a removal, if it became necessary. I received in reply a letter signed by all the Stewards of the church in Glasgow, assuring me that a change was a necessity – & that they could not support a married preacher. Some of the principal paying members there had proposed to me to send them my son who expected to join Conference, but I told them he was too young & inexperienced, that they had better keep Bro Shelton. When I received this letter signed by the Stewards, asking for a single man I then wrote to Morgan Ashby who is Bro Sheltons earnest friend – and told him what had been said to me about Robert & asking if they would like to risk him – young & unordained as he was. They had already stated in a previous letter that they had informed Bro S. of their conclusion in the premises. They wrote to Dr Summers [Vanderbilt University] who gave Robert such an endorsement that they got up a petition of the principal members of the charge to which was appended a private note from Bro Ashby, requesting me to send Robert – as their pastor. I received three letters – to this effect, after I left home for Conference. I learned afterwards that Bro Shelton felt aggrieved at his removal, rather that his wife was greatly distressed and that they seemed to feel that I had removed them to make a place for my son. Never was a censure more unmerited. I would have preferred a good circuit for Robert – but Glasgow wanted a single man – & wanted *him*. I laid the matter before the Bishop & Presiding Elders & they advised the appointment. I wanted him in my District & was gratified that he was asked for – after it was known that Bro S. could not be sustained in Glasgow. Bro S. wrote to me after Conference requesting my consent to an exchange of appointments between him & Robert – to which I replied – giving him in full the facts bearing upon his case – and assuring him that I was ready & willing to make the change, if the petitioners for Robert – or the majority of the substantial members of the church, would consent to it. I think he was satisfied of the sincerity & propriety of my action in the case.

December 24 – Rainy – held a profitable prayermeeting with a few brethren. I pressed on home [from Bibb's Chapel]. The sky is dark & threatening & the roads muddy – but the air is warm & the fields are green. Lizzie & I staid alone – while the children all went to Charley Roach's to their sisters Christmas tree – but they came back proud of their presents. Dear Robert & Hanson too had come to spend Christmas with their parents. My own dear parents, & all their children – who are in reach – are to dine with us tomorrow. Only a few more such reunions – if *any* – await us in this world. Oh – may God gather us *all* together in Heaven! I am glad to have money enough to pay the servants what I owe them & to deal liberally with them.

December 25 – Cloudy & damp – but the little folks were up early – crying Christmas gift & looking after Santa claus's visit. Father & mother – Cousin D. B. Sydnor & Tommy, Mary, Bobbie & Robert Sydnor & Willie Morrison – Bro Wm & Sister Emma & Fletcher – Bro David & Sister Florence & Bailey & Anna – their children – Brother Jimmy – Sister Annie – Eliza Rutherford – Cousin Rebecca Robinson – & Susie Dortch of Clarksville & Frank Browder from father's – Tom Bs children, Lizzie, Susie & Nannie – & Helen & her sweet little Lizzie & Ruth & Miss Ellen Roach & my visiting sons – Robert & Hanson & Lizzie Warfield – 31 whites & several colored visitors, shared with us today, the elegant dinner my excellent wife had prepared. It was a pleasant reunion & right heartily did the children enjoy it. I regret that my dear boy, Hanson, was compelled to return tonight – the Christmas recess at Vanderbilt [University] being very short.

December 26 – Nearly all the company that was here yesterday & several others beside met at Charley Roach's to dinner. Helen is a woman of fine taste & displayed it to advantage in the management of her table. I have seldom seen a more elegant dinner – but I doubt the propriety of such trouble and expense.

December 31 – [Franklin] I reached the depot in time for train – went to Bowling Green – called to see quite a number of friends – & got home at night. My dear loving wife had sent Luther to meet me with a horse – & Bro Wm Beall of Franklin had given me a nice lantern, that I can carry in my valise – so I could get home through the dark.

This is the last day of the year 1877. Lizzie & the children are asleep. I am alone. I feel serious. I look back over the year – & see errors – short-comings – failures. I am sorry – I am ashamed – I am penitent – I wish I could recall every unguarded word – every wrong act – every wicked thought. Poor wretch that I am. Often I have resolved never more to do any thing wrong – & as often have I seen my weakness. I have pledged to work – read – pray – & preach more faithfully & to watch my heart & life more closely – yet I have failed – oh! so grievously failed. I could never go to Heaven on human merit. I am glad I have an Advocate with the Father – Jesus who pleads for me – covers my sin in his blood – "bore it in his own body on the tree." I will – I do accept Jesus as my Savior, my only trust. I will not presume to come before God in my own name. Jesus save me I pray.

January 1, 1878 – How the time flies! I shall not add many new years to my record. I have tried this day to watch myself & do right. I helped Luther & Wallace strip tobacco. Joe Harrison, the young man I hired to work on the farm – came up to day & begins well.

January 11 – My 51st Birthday! An old man. People call me "old Brother Browder" & I smile until I look in the mirror & see that they are right. Locks nearly white, form a little bent – but my face is still smooth – would not look older than I am if my hair was dark. When I was young, I thought if I lived to be fifty years old I would have so cultivated my heart & mind, that surely I would be good & wise but alas I am neither. I preach to the gratification of my people – they crowd out to hear me – they praise my efforts – & I try to preach the truth of God & desire to see the good seed take root & bring fruit. Yet I know that I am a poor weak creature.

January 16 – Started to Glasgow to help Robt in a meeting.

January 21 – Good morning meeting – large crowd at night. Interest manifestly increasing – Baptists & Presbyterians uniting & working with earnestness & zeal. We have tried to enlist the hearty cooperation of all the Christians & the response is cheering.

January 27 – At night we had an immense throng – more penitents & conversions. All through the week the meeting continues.

February 1 – Still the work goes on – 35 or more professions & many glad people. My Dear Robert is working like a hero & is greatly rejoiced at the success of the meeting.

February 4 – Considering my fatigue & the work before me – & that Bros Cottrell & Dempsey are expected this week – I decided to come home to day.

February 8 – Took train for Franklin – borrowed Bro McClannahans horse & saddle & pushed on my way to Neurow Quarterly Conference at Shiloh.

February 9 – We always have dinner at church at the Saturday meetings – on this & the Scottsville circuits – & on Bowlinggreen & Franklin. I find it a great relief. The Congregation stays & attends the Conference business with interest.

This is in the neighborhood of the late Snow tragedy. Jack Snow was horribly murdered in his bed – early in the night – his head cut to pieces & his throat. Nine or ten fearful gashes – either one of which it is said would have killed him – were cut in his head with a new sharp axe, which was left lying on the floor. Mrs Snow ran in her night clothes & barefooted, down to Walkers Chapel & alarmed the congregation, who were just dispersing. After the inquest & burial – suspicion was directed toward his wife as the perpetrator of the dreadful crime. Bloody clothes were found concealed in the house. Her night dress was untied behind by bloody hands – an unreasonable haste the night of the murder to wash her clothes – a singular want of real feeling on the occasion &c added to the fact of past disagreement & discord – led to her arrest & her conduct at & after the arrest confirmed all the people that I heard speak of the fearful affair, in the conviction that she was the murderer of her own husband. She is in prison in Scottsville. Several other dark & bloody tragedies have occurred in Allen county in the past year. A Mr Moore – a clever upright man was brutally murdered – & one of his sons – shot a ball into a man named Temple, while attacking his father. Temple & his sons who were charged with aiding in the murder, were arrested & lodged in jail – where I saw them – & talked with them – & urged them to prepare for a tribunal more solemn & more certain then earth affords. The old man was still suffering with his wound when I prayed for him in prison. A mob came to take them out & execute them but Mr. Huntsman the jailer prevented them. Last week – or very recently – the Temples escaped from the jail – but were rearrested – except the poor old man who was killed – the short time he was out. A man named Stark was charged with seducing & killing his sisterinlaw. The general conviction was that he was guilty. A mob took him out & hung him. A few months ago a man was killed in the night & dragged out & his hands & feet tied together & a rail put through them by which he was packed off some distance & thrown into a deep hole surrounded by briers & underbrush where he was found some days after the murder. These & other murders have occurred with Allen county people since I have been visiting the county.

February 14 – [Olmstead] Valentines day & the children are excited over the odd faces some of them get.

February 23 – [Glasgow Junction] Pleasant session of Quarterly Conf. Financial report tolerably good for Smiths grove circuit – 102.47.

February 24 – At the morning service I organized a new society at the Junction – beginning with nine members.

February 25 – Bro [Marshall] Dempsey preached an earnest & eloquent sermon on self-examination – by which I hope to profit. He is certainly an exceptionally fine preacher – wonderfully fluent – clear & logical. I have seldom heard a better preacher & yet he is down financially until he wears ragged clothes & looks like a tramp. The brethren here kindly gave him a new overcoat.

February 26 – My throat & voice need rest so badly that I came home. Dear little Wallace met me at the depot with a horse & told that George's fine pony was dead. I regret the loss of the pony. I never knew another that had all gaits in natural perfection as she had them. George is troubled about his colt – & also about his school report. It gives him a bad record for deportment. He says he always answered truthfully on the roll call of honor & confessed his deficiencies – while many others that talked as much as he would afterward answer "perfect" & so the truthful boys – though they deserve censure for talking – are still at a disadvantage in comparison with those who report falsely. I am mortified & troubled. I cannot justify a wrong even in my son. I know George is at fault, if his record is bad. I never had another child with a bad record at school. I am glad to find all well at home. We have sixteen lambs & 28 young pigs.

Bro Jesse Board of Morgantown circuit writes me that he has had 160 professions of religion since Conference. In one campbellite neighborhood he had a revival of 13 days. Forty professions & 35 accessions. We have had about 450 professions on the District.

February 27 – I went to see Mr Weeden about George's report – found the cause of complaint was talking in school. I shall stop this or stop him from school. I went to see about my tobacco bed & found that some "tramps" had lodged there & burned up my rails – so I had to haul more before I could make my bed. I got it on fire & about night the same or other tramps came to lodge at the fire – but I think they are to be pitied as well as blamed.

March 2 – Went to Quarterly Meeting at Mt Vernon in N. West of Warren [County]. Small congregation – preached with liberty & unction Mat[thew] 5.25. The church house is *very open* – no window sash or shutters – no door shutters – no ceiling – plastering – nor anything but the frame & weatherboards – wind blowing – could not keep lights nor have night meetings.

March 3 – Congregation much larger than I could have expected. Last year this church paid about 1.50 for the support of the ministry. Up to this second Quarter this year they have reported $1.00. I felt it my duty to preach on the *duty* of supporting the pastor who labors in word & doctrine. I dealt kindly & plainly – expounded the law & showed the sense & reasonableness – raised a collection – got 4.40 & some subscriptions – a large increase in percentum.

March 4 – My pay on this round was 1.00 & 4 pairs of woolen socks. My R.R. fare – about 2.00.

March 11 – [Rich Pond] I preached an earnest sermon on the unjust judge Lu[ke] 18, 1–8. Moses Potter – an *old* man whose heart has been all set on the world – has taken a deep interest in my preaching. He invited me home with him & I went. Had a *long earnest plain* talk with him about his soul. He said he would talk with me as he never had talked with any other man & unbosom himself to me in confidence – that he was very greatly concerned about his soul – lay awake many a night thinking of his condition – earnestly desired to do right & was seeking an evidence of peace with God – sometimes hoped that he was pardoned & accepted in Gods sight – but had not a knowledge of any great supernatural change. Said he had begun the world with nothing – his father was a day laborer without a dollar – & had ultimately made a fine estate – & that *he* (Moses) had worked day & night to prosper in this world – until at one time he owned more estate & paid more taxes than any other man in the county ever owned – sold annually 100 mules & sometimes 800 hogs – raised 400 acres of corn & 800 acres of oats &c – had 300 mules at one time & several large farms. His house stands in the centre of a tract of 2000 acres of splendid land, all of which he had bought & paid cash for – except 150 acres inherited by his wife. He has worn out his life making money – yet never loved *money* – wanted *estate* – wishes now he had freedom from his care & just enough to live on with comfort – *would give all he is worth to know exactly how to please God & save his soul.* He seemed greatly in earnest & often deeply affected while he talked. Of course I exhorted him to look to Jesus alone – throw himself unreservedly on the divine compassion – make a public profession of his faith in Christ by joining the church & setting an example to his children & neighbors. He got his family together & asked me to pray with them.

March 12 – There was a startling occurrence in Rich Pond this evening. The Mrs Richardson who professed conversion, or reclamation – night before last – was drawing water at the well – when she fell in & was drowned – but proper agencies restored the suspended respiration.

March 17 – My throat is very sore & needs rest badly. My wife is not well. I have been away 11 days & although the people beg me to stay, I feel that I ought to go home.

March 20 – [Olmstead] Hauling wheat. It weighs out well. The percentum of loss from shrinkage is less than I have been informed it was. We put up nearly 200 bushels – ground about 70 bu – sowed about 17 bushels – & yet the crop weighed out 595 bu – & brot 636.10, which is next to the largest sum I ever got for a crop of wheat.

March 26 – At Russellville I saw *Willie Woodward,* who left his father to follow & play in a troupe of negro minstrels. I urged him by all the arguments I could use to go back & submit himself to his father – but he seems incorrigible. I fear he will be a ruined boy unless he stops at once. I wrote to his father.

A letter from my dear boy Robert – tells me that he is in a revival at a school house near Glasgow which he has been conducting – 35 have professed & the work goes on. He has been successful. God be praised. Hanson is making a good record in his studies.

April 1 – This 1st of April finds Spring well advanced – pastures are green – wheat as forward as May – apples, peaches, pears, cherries &c in full bloom. The skies are bright & the weather warm. Many are planting corn. The prospect for renewed prosperity in our country is improving.

I have had to stop Luther from school to assist in making a crop. Honest labor is as important as study. To educate a boy's mind & not teach his hands to make a living is unjust to the boy & unrighteous in the father. How beautiful is the family circle where all, in harmony, act well their parts. If there is one place on all this green earth, brighter & purer than all the rest – on which Heaven's benediction falls with softest cadence – that happy spot is the home of a Christian family all consecrated to God & duty.

April 6 – Primary election. I do not like it. I had promised my vote to certain friends who insisted that I stay & vote for them. I wanted to see Bose Newman elected Clerk – because he was a good boy & worked for his mother & sisters in widowhood & poverty, and because he understands the duties of office & is faithful. I voted for George Hardy under an old promise given – because he too was the worthy son of a poor widow – working hard to make him self successful – & was well qualified – the others I voted for mostly on personal preference.

April 9 – Heavy rain most of the night & again this morning. I learned that Robt Murray is very ill – with Pneumonia – went to see him – talked with him some about his soul – did not have prayers – because he said he was suffering & dreaded fatigue. Saw Sister Blackford – said she was troubled because no one living could tell her whether she was ever baptized & in her long sickness she had lost all knowledge of it if she had been baptized – wanted me to administer the ordinance. I did so without hesitation – though the probabilities are that she has received it before.

April 11 – I went to Bowlinggreen to assist Bro Brewer in his meeting. I feel more & more inclined to stay at home – but duty calls & I must go. I think the Presiding Elder ought to be *felt* in his District & aid in the meetings as far as he can.

April 13 – I saw Bro J.R. Dempsey – more ragged & dirty than ever I saw the pastor of any church before. Shame that a man of his grand intellect & physical strength should be reduced to such destitution. I gave him a pair of pantaloons & kept him over to preach at night.

April 18 – [Olmstead] Bro Biggs came by & I went with him to see Bob Murray. His brother met me & said he was bound to die – was sinking fast. I saw that he was sinking – yet he knew me as soon as I called him. I said "Bob do you put your trust in Jesus?" "Yes I try." "Do you feel that you can rely upon him fully – trust your soul & body – & all your interest for time & eternity, to his hands?" He said – "Don't question me too fast – it confuses me." I said "Would you like for us to sing & pray?" He said "Yes?" I tried to sing, "Forever here my rest shall be" but could not sing. Bro Biggs sat down by him & in a low quiet voice said "Bob do you feel like you can trust Jesus?" He said "Yes sir." "Do you feel that you love God?" "Yes sir I love God." "Does God love you?" "Yes, God loves me." "Have you been praising to him?" "Not much." "Too feeble?" "Yes." "Do you feel that all will be well with you?" This question seemed to startle him – & he said "I hope it will all be well with me now & hereafter, but do you think there is no chance for me to get well?" Bro Biggs said "We hope you may get well, but you are very ill & the chances are against you." He called Dr Trabue who was near & asked him, "Dr do you think the chances are against me?" The Dr spoke very wisely & calmly. "Bob you are very weak – but I have seen others as low as you seem to be – by a miraculous effort of nature, react & revive – but not often. We do not know that you will not recover, but the chances are against you. Whether you get well or not – it will do you no harm to talk to these ministers & let them talk to you." He then said "Sing, I want you to sing." I asked – "What song would you like?" He began to hum the words & tune – "Jesus lover of my soul. Let me to thy bosom fly." He then said "Sing that" – and he raised the tune & sang ahead of us – nearly all the song – & repeated over & over the words – as loud as he could sing it "Hide me Oh my Savior hide – till the storm of life is past – Safe into the Haven guide, O receive my soul at last." He then said "Now I am ready to go. I have no fear. I am prepared to die. I am ready whenever he calls for me. I am happy. I am glorious. I will see Mother & sister in Heaven. I will be free from pain & suffering – all will be pleasure there. Oh just think of it! No chilling winds nor poisonous breath shall reach that beautiful shore. Sickness & sorrow – pain & death – are felt & feared no more. All oer those wide extended plains, Shines one eternal day. There God the Sun forever reigns & scatters night away." He repeated these words over & over – clapped his hands & shouted Glory to God – as loud as he could speak. He asked to be baptized. He said, "I don't know that water baptism is of any account to me – but it is a command & I want to obey it. I want to do every thing Jesus commands." Water was brought & I asked him – "Bob do you understand that in water baptism you express your faith in Christ as your Savior & that it represents that cleansing of the Holy Spirit by which we are prepared for Heaven?" "Yes sir I understand that." "And do you wish to be baptized in this faith?" "Yes I do." I baptized him & then he said "Sing again" – & he tried again & raised the tune Am I a Soldier of the Cross & sang as long as he could. Then he exulted & praised God. Resting a moment, he said – "I would have been glad to live & enjoy this world – but if it is Gods will I am ready to die – & one day in Heaven is worth more than one week on earth." He spoke of some debts he wanted paid. After some refreshment & a short sleep – he was asked how he then felt. He said "I feel like I want to go to Heaven. If I have to die, I would like to die now." There was a time of weeping.

April 19 – I learned that Bob Murray was dead. I rejoice that he died in peace. I went to Glasgow. Robt met me at Morgan Ashbys. A *large* audience met me at church – I preached 1st Cor[inthians] 12.7. A manifestation of the Spirit – &c. The celebrated Lincolns were to sing Temperance at the Hall after the sermon & I was alittle hurried – hardly had usual unction – baptized five or six & went to the Hall – was pleased with the singing. They seem to be earnest in the work – want some money out of it – ought to have it – 10 cts a head is reasonable for such songs.

April 22 – We held the Quarterly Conference. The reports were satisfactory. Robt had done good work – 100 professions – about 50 additions since last Quarter. He is immensely popular & they say they must have him again next year. It is important that he should be ordained a deacon* and as he is eligible I called up the Question of recommendation – in view of the possibility of a failure to hold the 4th Session of Quar[terly] Conf[erence]. There was a unanimous & cordial vote of recommendation & some of the members wanted to recommend him for Elder.* The finance was reasonably well sustained. Bro Ashby had given way to a weakness for liquor & made an humble confession which was accepted & forgiveness extended. We closed the session in time for me to take the 11.15 train for home. At Glasgow Junction I stopped with Judge York. Went over to the Hotel to see Mr & Mrs Charles Lincoln – the great singers, that have been at work in temperance cause. He gave me some items about the great Murphy movement[1] that I had not heard before. He says many of the men who have gone out to be temperance speakers are men of bad character – felons from the prison – the scum & filth of the towns & cities – many of them reform drunkards that he fears will not stay reformed & yet he thinks they are doing a great deal of good. I got home at night.

April 23 – It seems that some one has been borrowing our corn out of the stable without our leave & so we put it in the crib to lock it up.

May 7 – [Scottsville] Went to the prison & talked & prayed with two men (Temples) & one woman (Mrs Snow) confined under charge of murder. The old man Temple with whom I talked before was killed while the prisoners were out – the time they broke jail. The sons said their father often spoke of my visit & prayer & wished for my return. I talked to them earnestly & kindly & prayed for them. They seemed greatly affected & wept freely.

Mrs Snow – accused of a most brutal & inhuman murder of her husband – seems to be almost entirely devoid of sensibility. She is a stout – heavy set – well built & rather good looking woman – yet there is something forbidding in

---

1. After serving time for drunkenness in a Portland, Maine, jail in 1873, Francis Murphy spent the rest of his life holding meetings in which he encouraged his converts to take a pledge of abstinence and wear a blue ribbon in their lapels as a symbol of their commitment. Forty thousand in Pittsburgh and 50,000 in Philadelphia are reported to have taken the blue ribbon. J.S. Furnas, *The Life and Times of the Late Demon Rum* (London, 1965), 176–78.

her eyes. She sat close by the grate & talked to me as if nothing disturbed her. She said she was as contented & cheerful as any one could be in such a place. I urged her to prepare for the great day that would reveal all secrets. I told her of the certainty & exactness of that tribunal – the impossibility of escape to the guilty. I sang "Arise my soul arise – Shake off thy guilty fear" and then offered prayer for her soul. She looked me boldly & fully in the face all the time I talked with her – without the least embarrassment – but when I prayed she wept. She claimed that she was at peace with God & not afraid to die. She is a mystery. Mrs Huntsman, the jailers wife – has no confidence in her – says she swears. I fear she is awfully wicked & depraved.

May 9 – I received a letter from my dear wife – telling me that Mr Weeden had given Alick Warfield a very cruel whipping – on what the school children said was a very slight provocation – and Alick had gone home. There was great excitement & much indignation. I was greatly grieved & mortified. Alick has always been a good boy & I think Mr W. was under a wrong influence.

May 11 – Bro Slate took me in his buggy out to New Bethel – where I preached a successful sermon on the "Sower". One sinner gave me his hand for prayer & there was a general handshaking & weeping.

Quarterly Conference was as usual here on this circuit attended with some debate & some little cutting & slashing.

May 12 – Glorious lovefeast – one of the best. At 11 by request, preached on Sacrament to a crowded audience – & some out of doors. I "Swung clear" & the power of God seemed to rest on the people. Sometimes I could hardly be heard for the shouting.

May 13 – The weather is *cold*. Over coats & fires are comfortable. I took stage for Bowling green. Bro Bennett, the driver hurried up to make connections for me. We stopped at Mr Kirbys to see a pair of Texas Mule-eared rabbits. They are large – gray – with a stripe across the shoulder like a mule, with enormous ears – twice or thrice times as large as the ears of Ky rabbits. The old man & his wife & son were standing by & the old man asked my name. I said "Browder." The old lady threw up her hands & said – "Dear me I thought I had seen you – but I couldnt call your name. And this is brother Browder! Well, well! I've been hearing of you all around. Well I am proud to see you at my house. And now dinner is just ready. Come in – you & the stage driver both – & get a 'snack.' Ive got some coffee. I will be proud to have you to eat with me." I partook of a good comfortable dinner which she urged me to eat – heartily. "Here is a little tree molasses – pour it all out & dont leave any for manners sake" she insisted. "I will be proud to tell that Bro Browder has been here & ate with me. My son says I never heard such preaching as you do – he would rather hear you than any body he ever heard in his life" & on the dear old woman rattled greatly to my entertainment. After a song & prayer – we rolled on to Bowling green & at night I reached home – thankful to find my dear family all up – if not all well.

My home is very dear to me — but my poor wife is delicate & greatly troubled about Alick Warfields misfortune at school.

May 14 — I rode around alittle & made some inquiry in regard to the cause & extent of the whipping Mr Weeden inflicted upon Alick W. I think the fact — in all candor & in fear of the judgment — is about thus — that for a considerable time past Alick & *nearly all* the other scholars have been remiss in duty & careless of the rule forbidding talking in the school — and some of the *larger* boys had greatly provoked Mr Weeden & got him in a bad humor — & Mrs Weeden also nervous & irritated — at what she thought was bad behavior. About this time Alick missed a question in his Geography lesson which was passed to the next & answered, as the scholars say — just as Alick answered it. The next question that came to him he did not know & asked Mrs Weeden to excuse him — that he would study it at recess — and then turned himself half way round in the seat — his face away from Mrs W. who construed this into disrespect & sent him into Mr Weedens room. Nearly the whole school got into a conversation & Ida Vick began to talk to Alick & was called to order. Alick says he did not talk to her.

The next morning Friday — May 3d — Mr W. came to school in an ill humor — & having switches ready prepared — told the school — he wished Alick Warfield was there — he would show them how he would whip. The constant rain of that morning had detained Alick at home & when he got there — his class had recited. Mr Weeden spoke to him & said "Alick you look like you didnt rest well last night." Alick said "Yes sir, I rested very well." "Why didn't you get here sooner?" "I did come as soon as I got breakfast & the rain would let me come." "You staid out to miss your lesson again. Come up here sir. I want to talk to you" but instead of talking he began whipping him — first with a single switch — then stopped & twisted *two* together & whipped until he was fatigued & then stopped again & rested — & renewed the beating until Alick spoke & said "Mr Weeden that is enough." Mr W. said — "I suppose that is enough — now go to your seat & behave yourself." Alick asked to go home & Mr Weeden refused to let him go. At recess he came home complaining that his shoulder was badly bruised & very sore. My wife had it bathed with camphor & the soreness continuing the next day — she examined it & found it badly bruised & very purple. George, Luther & Joe Harrison — & my wife are the only persons that *saw* the bruise. The boys say his legs were also bruised & ridges or "whelks" raised on them. Ed Biggs & Wilson Riley say he got 150 lashes. Willie Morrison & Geo. Rutherford say 100. Carrie Jenkins & others say "a very severe whipping." I suppose that none of them counted the actual number of strokes. Alick told his sister Lizzie that he did not know how much — he supposed 40 lashes. Mr Weeden is reported to have said "he was so mad, he did not know whether he had given him 40, 50, or 75." I do not exonerate Alick from blame — a breach of rules by all the school but one does not justify that one — & a boy that is not too big to misbehave is not too big to be whipped — but from all I can learn — I feel confident that Alick did not deserve punishment more now than he has heretofore — nor *as much* as *many others* have on *divers occasions* — & while I think he may have deserved chastisement — I believe this one was inflicted in a spirit of anger & was excessive – & cruel – but I think it would have been *less* if Alick had manifested any sign of penitence or humility. I do not know it – but I believe his *unflinching* submission to the lash increased the anger that Mr Weeden brought with him to the school room. In excuse for that passion – I know how natural it is for a man to feel aggrieved & irritated when his wife tells him that she has been treated with contempt. There has been much talk against him that perhaps ought to be corrected & no one will contribute to that more than I – but I do think it is due to the character of Alick Warfield that Mr Weeden should say – at least as publicly as he punished him – that other scholars had behaved just as badly who had yet received no such castigation.

May 15 – Went in the afternoon to see Mr Weedens classes examined. A class of 20 in Anatomy gave very general satisfaction. I desired to talk with Mr Weeden about the Alick Warfield matter but he did not have time.

May 18 – [Grider's School House] Congregation very attentive. Quarterly Conf[erence] pleasant, but finances low. Poor Dempsey greatly troubled about his debts – would like for me to endorse his paper, but I cannot. It seems to me that I have all I can carry in that direction.

May 20 – A Bro Gleaves, living near by is reported to be guilty of cursing & profanity. I went to see him & talked of religion in the family – & parental influence & the responsibility of parents – in so skilful & earnest a manner as to get the *idea* into his mind without arousing prejudice. Mr Lay & his wife who went with me fearing his irritable nature – were surprised at the easy manner of meeting the case without giving offence to a man whose rash temper is his besetment.

May 29 – [Olmstead] I went down to see Mr Weeden about the cause of his whipping Alick Warfield. I was fully convinced of the correctness of my first information on the subject – that he had been for weeks annoyed by some disorderly conduct – & that he was exasperated by the report of Alicks not behaving right in his wifes room – & gave the poor boy a severe chastisement for less offenses than had been passed over in others. But he seems to think that he did right. I talked very plainly, but kindly in the presence of T.B. Sydnor & J.N. Morrow & told him what I thought of the case. I have so often erred, myself – that I ought not to judge others harshly.

June 3 – George finished prizing & hauling off tobacco – & found that we had raised about 10,000 lbs. Robt helped me get the reaper ready for wheat harvest – which has already commenced – mine being later than some on account of grazing it.

June 4 – Robert & I drove to Bro Frogges on our way to Morgantown Dist[rict] Conf[erence]. Crossing the R.R. beyond Russellville – we came near getting in the way of the cars – had just time to back off – jump out & hold the mare close to the track as the train flew by. Hanson saw us & waved from the window — coming home from the Vanderbilt.

June 6 — Conf[erence] opened with prayermeeting conducted by Bishop Kavanaugh. Robert Browder was elected Sec[retary] & did the work well — rather surprised me, by the clearness & readiness with which he got all the points in his minutes. He was appointed to preach this morning. The presence of the bishop & Conference embarrassed him less than might be expected. His sermon was clear & logical & delivered with an earnestness & animation that brought many of us to tears. Bishop K. & several of the other preachers spoke of it in terms of commendation. The Bishop expressed his personal gratification that I had so promising a son & said it gave him a good opinion of the Vanderbilt. In both his subsequent sermons he quoted from Roberts sermon & endorsed his positions on the atonement.

June 9 — Cloudy — threatening — raining. Yet the house was full & many extra seats occupied. Our love-feast was one of rare power & religious influence. Old Bro George Jones — 80 yrs old — Meth[odist] Prot[estant] preacher gave a good talk. At night the old ship of Zion rebuilt was sung by Bro Finley — being prefaced with some thrilling remarks in which he requested bishop K. to take a stand by his side & let all who hoped to meet him in Heaven come & shake hands with him. I invited the venerable "father Jones" to stand by the bishop & as old & young pressed forward to take leave of these veterans of the Lord — a spirit of weeping & praising came upon us & then there was an outcry & a time of power. The Bishop launched out into one of his exhortations & pictured the hopes of a pilgrim travelling to the city of God, in those true & glowing colors that the converted soul knows how to appreciate. Bro Finley & others also made some comforting & touching remarks — after which the new "Over There" was sung with thrilling effect. So closed one of the most religious & profitable District Conferences I have ever attended.

June 10 — Robt & I reached home 40 @ 45 min[utes] before Sunset — found all well and my dear Hanson in the field helping with the harvest. The wheat is very poor — yet we pay $2.00 pr day for common laborers & board them. A high price compared with other work.

June 18 — I reached home [from Russellville] at night, very tired. My dear Helen & her sweet little children had come home to spend the night with Papa & relieve his loneliness, because dear mother was gone [to Tennessee].

June 19 — My brother William has gone to Clarksville now to try to sell my tobacco because I thought he could do better with it than I could.

June 21 — Wm sold my tobacco. The crop badly handled & badly ordered — put up too damp & had soured. Price 6.19 pr 100 — 7 ½ pr 4 hogs [hea]ds good — 3 ½ pr 2 h[o]g [shea]ds lugs — 9995 lbs — after all the leakage — shrinkage &

short weighing. I am glad it did even so well – & am greatly obliged to my dear brother for his pains in selling it for me. Yet the low price leaves me with debts unpaid – & much to be done that I would like to do.

June 28 – I went to Russellville enroute to Chandlers Chapel. Had much talk with Col [John W.] Caldwell on his Congressional candidacy. Sorry he & my friend Mr Golladay are at variance.

June 29 – Heavy rain overtook me. Creeks up, fences washed out. Got to church & found Bros Frogge & Bowen both wet – no congregation – spent the night at John Chandlers. They are very poor & live in a miserable shanty – open & leaky but they were glad to see me – gave me the best they had & entertained me with good singing. We nearly all slept together in the same room & beds very near to each other.

June 30 – I spend the night with Rev James T. Chandler whose mother 87 years old walked a mile to church this morning – & back & this evening *rode* a *mule* – then came home able to cook the supper & set the table. A very remarkable old lady. Bro Chandler called me out to see a sight. A man, a girl & a calf all milking the same cow at the same time!

July 4 – This day once sacred in the annals of freedom, is celebrated in Louisville today by the big horse race – Mollie McCarthy from California & Tenbroeck of Ky – purse $10,000.[2] Hundreds of church members are going to see it. Shame on them. The negroes are having a big celebration at Allensville.

July 16 – Went security for my father & brother Wm on a note to Thos Jay Smith. This is one of the troubles my dear father has to bear by the misdoing of his nephew D. B. H[utchings].

July 17 – Went to see Mr Golladay – confined to his bed & very desponding. I read & prayed with him – & commended him to the mercy of God. He is greatly depressed by his sickness just at the highest of the excitement in his congressional canvass. Poor man, it may be a mercy. His overwhelming defeat is inevitable – & he would have lost his time & money and perhaps his life & soul.

July 19 – Went to Bowling green by invitation of my friend Dr Dick Thomas – & rode his horse out to Wm McGinnis's near Halls chapel – 8 miles from B[owling] G[reen]. Weather oppressively hot – mercury up to 98.

---

2. Thirty thousand people, many sitting on barn roofs and tree limbs, gathered to witness the four-mile match race between the "unbeaten heroine" of California and the "pride of Kentucky." Although Mollie McCarthy took an early lead, she was behind ten lengths at the end of the third mile and quit entirely in the last mile. Exulted the *Louisville Courier-Journal* for July 5, 1878: "Nice little girl, Mollie, nice little girl, but really, you oughn't to have tried to keep up with our boys, even if you are pretty fast, and did come from California."

July 20 – Bro Boards children are ill & he could not get to his Quarterly Meeting. Congregation not large – but *very* attentive. Text Gen[esis] 47.8. Got dinner at Geo. Cherrys. Quarterly Conf[erence] pleasant & harmonious. People all want Board & Browder back. Finances very low. I sent *all* to poor Bro Board – left myself barely enough to buy my dear wifes medicine & a R. R. ticket home. Poor Board needs it more than I do.

Cornelius Kelley & I went to Curren Hunters to spend the night. Curren was a poor orphan boy with *nothing* but his hands & head – not even an education – yet he has worked his way up to independence – owns a large tract of land – a new frame house – plenty of stock & many comforts. So much for energy – pluck & will. His father settled "Hunters Bluff" in Logan Co[unty] – now Butler on Green River – where the town of Suffolk was laid out but never built – ½ mile above the Mouth of Muddy River, where Rochester & Skylesberg now stand. Curren is a member of the church & takes great pleasure in having the preachers at his house. Says he never drank – never played cards – nor lost or won a bet – regrets all youthful follies & waste of time & when he sees young men of his acquaintance go into a saloon – he stands without & waits for them & pleads with tearful earnestness that they escape the fowlers snare & save their manhood – their money, their morals & their health – & spend their time & talent in useful pursuits. I was greatly interested in the man & his history. His was a rare family – of old German Lutherans. His grand father Joseph Hunter was the youngest of seven brothers & was born in Boons station in Fayette co[unty] Ky about 1758 – & died 97 years old. His was the shortest life of the seven. Charles was 100 more or less – Peter was 101 – John 102 – Isaac 122 & Jacob the oldest – 131 years.

July 23 – [Olmstead] Took Bro Biggs down to see Mr Golladay still in bed & very desponding. I did not think it was prudent to propose prayer again – & was not invited. He said he was not afraid to die – had lived a gentleman & trusted God. I fear he is self-righteous & does not see sin in its true light. Ambition has been his snare. His blasted prospects greatly depress him – sick & sore & weary of life. He seems to long for the quiet of the grave.

August 17 – [Scottsville] House crowded – from town & country. I preached with unction & power – Gen[esis] 47.8. I think many hearts felt it. John Gatewood – the leading lawyer in the town, wept as I never saw him weep before – & a hard young man stood crying on the street. There was more than ordinary talk in town about that text & sermon. The Quarterly Conference was large & lively as this one always is. There is nearly always some question on which Dr Walker & W. J. Crow cross swords. This time it was about dividing the circuit.

August 18 – Bro Lee held love feast. At 10 ½ I preached Matt 27.22 – What shall I do with Jesus. I had liberty & unction & the effect was powerful. Men & women – preachers & people, shouted aloud all over the house. I trust that God owned & applied his word. Some very extravagant compliments were passed. I shall not allow eulogies to affect me.

August 20 – [Olmstead] I went with George to talk with Dr Bailey about the study of medicine. George is anxious to be a Dr – & I think it is not a promising profession. I would greatly prefer that he should be a farmer.

August 29 – Hanson is preparing to go to the Vanderbilt to finish his course. It is painful to see him leave. I commend him to God.

The yellow fever reports are distressing. Grenada Miss[issippi] is almost wholly depopulated. All that take the fever die. Vicksburg, N. Orleans, Memphis & other towns are swept with the besom of destruction. I wrote to my cousin David Meade in Memphis to bring his family here – if they were unsafe where he is.

September 10 – A note from David Meade informs me of the death of his son Dr Wythe Meade of yellow fever. He claimed the peace of God on his deathbed. I sent 100 lbs of flour to Southern sufferers.

September 19 – Got home at night [from Franklin] in time to go to Bethlehem – weary as I was & preach for Bro Biggs – Acts 16.30 – with some clearness – was rejoiced in spirit to find my dear boy George penitent for his backsliding & weeping at the altar of prayer & when he claimed Gods pardoning grace & the joy of salvation restored – my soul rejoiced indeed.

September 25 – Helen sent for Lizzie last night at 3 Oclock. I went over this evening – saw another little grand daughter born this morning – fine large child.[3] Helen seems doing well. I am thankful that it is over. May Gods mercy spare her & Charley to raise their children right!

September 26 – Many letters to write – much thinking to do about my District.

September 30 – Getting ready for Conference – going in my buggie.

October 6 – [Cadiz] Business progressed smoothly – rapidly. Conference has been delightful. This morning we had a refreshing love feast. Bishop Pierce preached a wonderful sermon and ordained the deacons – my son Robert amongst the rest.

October 7 – We hurried business too fast to close tonight. I have never seen a fuller house than was our church in Cadiz when we met to read the appointments. I offered a resolution of thanks for hospitalities that no town ever surpassed. Some brethren were disappointed & troubled over their appointments & some changes were made after adjournment. I am grieved for some brethren in my District – but am not at fault in the matter. I am not without fears as to the future of our economy. Hitherto it has worked well but there is some friction.

---

3. The baby was named Sue Robert.

October 9 – I set out for home & found all well. Bethlehem is added to Allensville Station and T. D. Lewis is our pastor. I hope it will work well. I go to Bowling green District – S.R. Brewer, T.C. Peters, R.Y. Thomas, J.J. Tigert, Robt Browder, P.T. Hardison, A.G. Fraser, Jesse Board, J.W. Price, J.W. Bunton & B. F. Biggs are my preachers. God grant us success!

October 14 – There are fearful reports of the ravages of yellow fever in Bowling green – & people flying from the pestilence. I wrote Bro Brewer to publish the Quarterly Meeting for next Sat[urday] unless the panic made a deferment necessary.

October 16 – Bro Brewer writes that there is great confusion about the fever – sent me the statement of doctors reporting 13 cases of yellow fever – most of them fatal.

October 18 – Went to Bowling green – stopped with Judge Hines. Went to hear Dr McDonald preach at C[umberland] P[resbyterian] church. Very *small* audience.

October 19 – Several deaths & new cases of fever reported. Small congregation.

October 21 – Left Bowling green at 2 Oclock – got home at 7 by freight. Saw in Courier Journal name of Sarah A. Meade – dead at Memphis – fear this is the wife of my cousin David who was down with the fever. Sorry they did not come to my house when I invited them. Thank God I find my family well.

Volume VII

1878–1879

*"If God owns his word – & makes me useful –
I am thankful."*

October 28, 1878 – [Glasgow] At 3 I went to hear Mr Barnes the evangelist who is holding a meeting of several weeks continuance. He is an excellent talker – very interesting – apparently very earnest. Well read in O[ld] Tes[tament] Scrip[tures]. His theme was deliver us from evil (the devil). He drew a fearful picture of Satans power – malignity & influence & the necessity for prayer to God to deliver us from his power. He kept his eye on me nearly all the time he spoke. At the close he called all who could pray that prayer as they had *never prayed it before* to come up & be recognized or make some expression. I did not go. He looked at me intently & said "You may be in the way of others. You may be under the influence of Satan – he may have your ear" &c – continuing to look at me & speak. I said, "I do not understand myself to be included in your invitation. I have prayed that prayer with the same intent before. You asked those to come who could pray it as they had never done before." He said "I did not say that. I invited all who were willing to ask Gods blessing & protection." I said "I am always willing to do that," & went forward after which numbers of others also went forward. He had a sort of classmeeting asking what each one wished & repeating the answer. He sought an introduction to me & expressed gratification at my presence. I heard him at night again – was not so well pleased. I regard him unsafe as an expositor of Scripture & disorganizing in his procedure – connected with no church – responsible to no government – baptizing no convert – teaching that a simple *confession* of Christ is all that is needed – that "seeking the Lord" is a monstrosity – that prayer for pardon is wrong – &c. If all the ministers were to pursue his course the church would soon come to an end in its visible organization. I hear of many strange things said & done by him – some of which are probably exaggerations. It is said that the hundreds of converts he claims every where are seldom found after he is gone. Simply to go forward & give him the hand & *confess* Christ seems to be his idea of conversion. He seems to me to glorify himself to the disparagement of other ministers. I trust he is awakening thought in some hearts – but I fear he is doing much harm in lowering the standard of repentance & conversion.

November 3 – Jesse Board & Fayette Smith in one buggie & Sister Smith & I in mine set out [from Morgantown] for the Baptist meeting house at the Mouth of Gasper River. Buggies seldom ever go over rougher roads – stumps & steeps – gullies & hillsides – but Flora was trusty & at last as twilight was deepening into night we drove through a dense dark forest along the river bottom to the ferry landing & yelled & called in vain for the boatman. At length we all "halloed" in concert hoping to arouse someone. Two little boys came out & said the people were all gone to meeting & there was no one to take the boat over. There we were. Night on us – the river before us & no ferry man. At last some young men riding by on the farther shore heard the call & stopped to help. They found the canoe & crossed Gasper to get the ferry boat & brought it across Barren River to us. We drove both buggies down a *very* steep bank into the boat – & at last landed safely on the farther shore. Flora did grand work to pull us up the steep hill that winds along above the mouth of Gasper but at last we reached the church which was crowded to its full capacity – & Bro Jenkins was speaking zealously of "*eternal* salvation to all them that obey him." He was dwelling on *eternal* salvation as opposed to a salvation that might be enjoyed & then lost – & losing sight of the terms – *obedience*. Bro Board had been invited to help in the meeting & was called to exhort. He said "We all believe in eternal salvation & in order to [have] its enjoyment, there must be perpetual obedience." This short sentence set the matter right – since He is the author of eternal salvation to all them that obey him – that continue to obey him.

November 4 – I bought some chestnuts for Lizzie & the children & was glad to get home at night.

November 5 – Congressional election. I voted with a hearty good will for my old friend John W. Caldwell.

November 30 – Went to Pinegrove. Held Conference & went to Bro Henry Wells to stay. In most families I visit in Edmonson [County] I have to sleep in the same room with the family but it is the best they can do. They are kind & hospitable & seem to be religious.

December 2 – I preached to a small congregation in the morning – to a houseful at night. Text at night 1st Cor[inthians] 15.56,7 – fine effect – many backsliders – & many sinners came & asked for prayers. These Edmonson county people are much like Logan people were 40 years ago. They sing like them – worship like them – live in houses much like them – & walk to church – several miles – much as our people could do – & have week day services, as we did, before our people got wealthy & worldly. More than half the people that come to church come on foot.

December 11 – [Olmstead] Lizzie & I went over to assist Helen & Charley in moving their goods & chattels from their snug little home up to Dick Browders place which Charley has bought at about $15,000.[1] A fine farm – but a fine price.

December 19 – Lizzie & I went to see Helen in her new home – found her busy, putting down a carpet & arranging her furniture.

December 23 – Tom Sydnor came down & we went to the pond & swept off the snow, preparatory to getting ice tomorrow.

December 24 – Cold. Mercury zero in the air – ice thick. I dropped a large piece on my foot & bruised it very badly. Hanson got his ears frosted & Georgie thinks *his* feet were frosted. We got the ice house ⅔ full – & dismissed the hands for Christmas Eve.

---

1. The Dick (Richard C.) Browder farm originally belonged to William C. Browder, George Dick's uncle, who settled near Olmstead in 1828. The farm adjoined George Dick's to the southwest.

December 25 – Cold! Zero! Slept till 7 oclock. No children rattling around. Little negroes & Wallace had stockings hung up – got them full of toys & goodies. Not like the Christmas of the long ago when Helen & her brothers were small & our home was an Eden. Thank God it is still my Eden. My dear angel wife still lives & the blessed children come home. This snow storm kept Helen & her darling little daughters away – but Robert came – dear boy & brought his mother a nice present – a beautiful pitcher & slop bucket for the wash-stand.

December 26 – Another snow – several inches deep – ground slick – travel dangerous. I am lame with my foot – & with stock to look after, I can do but little reading. I have been entertained & to some extent profited yesterday & to day in examining the works of the distinguished Unitarian Divine, W.E. Channing. He teaches a very pure morality – & though not what we call orthodox – he is a charitable Christian.

December 27 – The young people have all gone to see Helen – quite a gathering & a grand dinner. The dear child is too proud & takes too much pains & expense in a fine table. Lizzie is poorly and I stay at home with her. She had no appetite & I broiled a piece of old ham on the coals to tempt her to eat, but she was *very* sick afterward.

December 31 – This last day of the year I have spent at home. It has been a very enjoyable day & my dear wife gave us an excellent & bounteous dinner. I trust that I appreciate & thank God for so many & so great blessings. Alas! alas! What sorrow & distress are in millions of homes! The cold & pinch of winter are driving thousands to beggary & thousands to shame & sin. In N. York alone 14,000 children are in the street, with no certain dwelling place & with no certain supplies. Here the snow has covered the ground for 10 days & many are barely supplied with necessaries.

The old year is passing out & thinking men are retrospecting the past & horoscoping the future. The coast is strewn with wrecks – morally – physically & financially. Bankruptcies have multiplied. Values have declined – property once worth thousands is now worth only hundreds. Debts contracted when money was plenty, now are due when money is scarce. Debts made when the price of one horse or one acre of land would have paid them, must now be paid with the value of *two* horses or two acres of land – & so there has been distress – & distress increases.

This year the farmers have made poor crops of tobacco wheat & corn & prices have been below the cost of production & farmers are discouraged. These Christmas holidays that used to be so joyous to the negroes have given them but little merriment. They seem not to comprehend the necessities of the farmers to reduce wages in proportion to the price of produce. They seem to forget that they can get more clothes, more provisions, more everything now with 125. than 150. would buy two years ago – & many of them seem moody & discontented, because farmers are not willing to pay former prices. I have hired *Plummer*

Warfield for the next year — a negro of good repute as a laborer. I board him & pay 125.00 & more if the average price of good hands in the neighborhood is higher.

The past year has been one of desolation & disaster to thousands of Southern homes. Yellow fever has claimed fourteen thousand reported victims — how many others — God only knows. Millions of property have been lost & great distress prevails. Our sufferings have been so light in comparison that we ought to be thankful. A great stream of charity in money — provisions, blankets — mattresses — fruits — nurses & physicians flowed from all parts of the land to the stricken regions. The asperities of the war were forgotten in the generous desire to relieve. So God brings good out of evil. Personally, during the past year I have labored much — preached a great deal & seen some excellent revivals — partly I trust through my instrumentality — yet looking back — the past year accuses me. I have not lived near to God, in all things & studied the word as diligently & faithfully as I ought to have. May God forgive the follies of the past & help me live a better life for the year to come!

January 1, 1879 — To day I have been very busy — reading, thinking — writing, preparing a sermon on the mode of Christian baptism. There are manifestly two sides to the argument, but my candid conviction is that the large preponderance of the testimony is in favor of affusion. I find *no reliable* proof of exclusive immersion.

January 4 — Mercury 9 below Zero. I read & wrote all day until 10 oclock at night — preparing a second sermon on the mode of baptism. Sent the boys to help father get ice.

January 6 — Still at home, reading & writing. Went over to see my father — read him part of my notes on baptism. He pronounced it clear & strong.

January 8 — Heavy snow storm — ground covered with ice. Train 4 hours late — went to Franklin. Snow still pours down — have not seen the like for years. It lies everywhere now 11 or 12 inches.

January 10 — [Franklin] Coldest morning of the winter. Mercury 16 below Zero. I walked out to the stable — fell down in the snow. I had just asked bro Ellis if any one had measured the depth of the snow — as I got up I said "I have."

January 11 — No service at church — town crowded with people — & candidates for state offices. I walked out alittle to see how Simpson county conventions are conducted — & was thoroughly disgusted. Oh the rabble — the cheating — the drinking — the whooping & yelling — civil men acting like lunatics — men aspiring to high offices treating to whisky & buying up votes — so said & I have no cause to doubt. John Underwood candidate for the high office of governor is reported to have bought up a large delegation with whisky & money to try to carry the convention. I was heartily glad he was beaten 4 or 5 to 1 when the vote was counted. I hope our county will conduct the convention in a more orderly manner. Dr Luke P. Blackburn, the yellow fever champion − seems to be the peoples favorite candidate for governor.

January 15 − [Olmstead] Tom & I went in the buggie to Russellville. Horses slipped & travelled badly on the ice & frozen snow. Had ice shoes put on & they did not slip atall as we returned.

January 17 − A *cold* cheerless steady rain − all day. I went on the cars to Bowling green − was glad to have a gossamer waterproof overcoat − large enough for full protection. I was gladly welcomed by the family of my friend Dr R. C. Thomas & most comfortably cared for. I called to see bro Brewer. I am pained to learn from him & others that a proposed change in the lesson papers of our Sunday School, substituting the publication of David C. Cook of Chicago for our own lesson paper published at Nashville, was likely to be a source of irritation & disaffection in the church. I went to work to promote harmony & conciliation.

January 18 − Small attendance at church. I preached with some unction 2nd Pet[er] 1.4 on the great & precious promises. Dined with bro Brewer in company with Dr McCormack & wife. I was invited around to Bro Peter Thomas's to see a beautiful patch work bed quilt made on the pattern called sunshine & shadow − with a beautiful blending of bright & somber colors − the center of the squares − velvet − the pieces of soft & well selected silk or woollen goods − & on the center piece was worked a large & beautifully embroidered letter "B." I was told that this beautiful & costly quilt had been made expressly for *me* − by my good Sister Peter Thomas & the following girls & single boy in her Sunday School class − Cornelia Hines, Annie Sumpter, Lillie Sumpter, Fannie Furman, Sallie Edmonds, Emma Potter, Elma Arnold, Minnie Porter, Jennie Porter and Herbert Drane.

It was a new occasion & I hardly knew how to manage it − but I wrote a note to Sister Thomas & the dear young people trying to tell how grateful I felt for such an expression of their appreciation & the interest I should take in their welfare. The stitches that these dear sisters made for me! Sewing & selecting & putting in their leisure hours − thinking how they would surprise & please their presiding Elder. Well they did surprise & please me. The kindly feeling indicated pleases me more than the valuable quilt, though that itself is a present to be prized & preserved & handed down as an heirloom. It is alittle remarkable that one woman, nine girls & a boy should keep this purpose on hand & persist in it until the work was done & the quilt presented & *not one of them* ever breathe a whisper to me about it. If either of my boys would marry either of those girls, the quilt must go to them.

Really I have met with expressions of kindness & appreciation in Bowling green that I had no right to expect − & I am at a loss to know how to do justice to such an occasion − but I know my dear wifes great big open heart & sound common sense will take in the situation & call it − *AN EPISODE* in the life of a presiding elder − and so it is.

January 20 – I sat up late last night comparing the Sunday School Scholars Quarterly published at Chicago with the S. School Magazine published at Nashville. I find the Magazine greatly preferable. I made a comparison to day between that & the *Teachers* Quarterly at Chicago. I find the comparison not unfavorable to our own Magazine. Ours is better in some respects – in other respects the Chicago publication has the advantage. I visited many friends today – find considerable feeling in some families arising mostly from a misconception of design about the attempted change in our S.S. literature. I hope all will work well. I held Quarterly Conference at night – had a long discussion of the Sunday School question – was pleased to find in the main a conciliatory Christian spirit and a satisfactory adjustment of the question of literature in the manner that I suggested – viz – use the lesson papers we have already bought for this quarter & then return to the use of our own.

January 21 – [Olmstead] Went to see Mrs N.H. Waters – whom I have not seen since her house was burned. I authorized her to buy a bedstead on my account from Mr Carter Harrison. After prayer & song I returned to spend the day with my father. I feel thankful that my dear father has been so long spared to us. I regret to see him growing infirm, pressing on to 75 years old – 23 years older than I am. His golden wedding – the fiftieth anniversary – passed unobserved Dec 23d.

February 4 – A long tedious ride to Bowling green [from Morgantown Circuit] Bro Brewer had a note for me – calling me home to the funeral of my dear Cousin R. C. Browder! Oh such a shock – such a grief. My dear Cousin. Shall I see him no more! There are no better men left behind. He was a true Christian – always faithful to duty – never away from church – prayermeeting – preaching – Sunday School – when he was able to attend. I think the best steward I ever saw – or as good as the best. I reached home at night – found my dear little Wallace waiting for me – neighbors all gloomy & sad hearted. I have not felt so bereaved in a long time.

February 5 – Lizzie & I went down to see Cousin Amanda – lately a loving happy wife – now a disconsolate widow. How my heart aches to think of it. I saw Mr Weeden this morning & settled the tuition of Dicks two little daughters Minnie & Helen. I presented the receipt to Cousin Amanda & she seemed really grateful. Lizzie had heard that she lacked a sufficiency of covering for her beds – & carried her a comfort & a blanket. Dick was industrious & economical but was ruined financially by endorsing for his brotherinlaw D.B. Hutchings. After prayer with the sorrowful family we called to see Helen & came home – sad & troubled.

February 6 – I found when I came back from Bowling green & beyond, that Mr Weeden had resigned the presidency of Browder Institute & the Trustees had elected my son Hanson as his successor. This is complimentary to Hanson – but no good seems unmixed with evil. Willie Hutchings was very anxious to have the school & was so chafed at his defeat that he went to work to get up an opposition school at Olmstead & will get the small children around the depot. I hope Hanson will behave well & prove himself worthy of a liberal patronage & I think he will get it – after a while. It is better to *deserve* success than to gain it.

February 9 – [Shiloh on Franklin Circuit] Immense crowd – house could not hold them – preached with liberty Psa[lm] 65.11th. Superior lovefeast. Bunton is a success in this work. Spent a pleasant time at Bro Bunton's studying up my *first* sermon on the mode of Christian baptism – announced for tomorrow.

February 10 – Good congregation – had some liberty – removed some doubts. A lady who had said she "wanted to be immersed until her head struck the sand" was the first to come & receive baptism by affusion & a gentlemen who had been long deciding came & was baptized. Others whose minds had been troubled on the subject were settled in their minds.

February 15 – Good congregation at Concord [Scottsville Circuit]. Quarterly Conference long – alittle stormy on question of salary. I was sorry for the difference between the views of preacher & stewards. Bro Biggs felt grieved that his salary was put as low as 500.00. I reduced my claim to a proportion with his. I fear he will not do as well as I hoped he would – but the people seem pleased with him.

February 20 – [Olmstead] Went to see my father. This is his 75th birthday. He seems feeble – had ridden out through a cold wind to do Mrs Hawkins a favor. I stayed & prayed with him.

March 1 – Pleasant day – good Saturday congregation [near Smiths Grove]. Pleasant Quarterly Conf[erence] except short finances – dont see how the preacher is to live. Bro Wm Archey a local preacher who has been baptized by immersion – is dissatisfied with the mode & wants me to baptize him by affusion. I advised him to wait & consider – that the *mode* of a thing was not *essential* to the thing *itself.* Went to Ben Wilsons to spend night. The custom here is for all to sleep in same room – men & women.

March 9 – [Salem on Franklin Circuit] Good lovefeast. *Large* congregation despite the threatened rain. As a matter of duty & conscience – I preached on duties of pastors & people – & tried to hew to the line. I had unction – liberty – words & utterance. I preached perhaps the longest sermon of my life 1-¾ hours. I shall not do that again. John Ellis said, "Bro Browder turned every pebble over & looked at the other side of it." A Baptist brother put a quarter dollar in the hat & said he would give a quarter anytime to hear such a sermon. I think the old hard shell Baptists that occupied this country first are responsible for much of the illiberality that prevails towards the ministry. They were good people, but they got the idea that a paid ministry were all mere *hirelings* – & false-shepherds – & hence they taught ministers ought not to be paid.

March 10 – I started early – stopped in Franklin – & got home at night very tired & hoarse – been going to meeting 17 nights out of 18. Did not feel like I ought to go tonight – after travelling 40 miles today. Sat up reading & writing until wife returned at 11 oclock.

March 12 – Packed up to go to Somerset – where I am appointed a fraternal messenger to the Kentucky Conference of the Methodist Episcopal Church (North). W.B. Harrison – my associate – writes urging me to go. I have not left home with more reluctance in a long while. My dear wife has been left alone until she feels it keenly & this morning was not able to suppress the tears that told her grief. I would have been glad of any good excuse to stay at home. Yet the Conference had selected me as their fraternal messenger & I felt that I ought to obey instructions.

March 14 – Somerset has greatly changed & improved in the 31 years, since I first saw it. It is now quite a town. Bro Harrison & I were directed to bro John Richardson's. I have not staid anywhere with a nicer, happier Christian family. They are Southern Methodists & received us gladly. Father Rankin – the oldest member of the Conference – Hartwell J. Perry – a veteran & one of "the loyal eighteen" that withdrew from the Ky Conf[erence] South to organize this (North) & bro Grinstead of the same Conf[erence] were at bro Richardsons & right well did we agree. Bro Harrison & I were introduced to the Conference & 10 ½ A.M. tomorrow fixed as the time to hear our message. Bishop Levi Scott presides – a genial old gentleman whose work is nearly done. I took a long walk this afternoon – climbed hills – overlooked the town – studied something to say tomorrow.

March 15 – At 11 A.M. Bro Harrison & I were presented to the Conference. I spoke first – perhaps 30 minutes – felt reasonably comfortable – alittle embarrassed – utterance reasonably clear – frequent demonstrations of applause – some weeping. Harrison followed with a message of melting love & Christian fellowship that was well received. Dr Walden of Cincinnati – offered a resolution reciprocating our fraternal spirit & requesting the appointment of a minister & layman to visit our Conference at Madisonville. I am pleased to learn that my address was highly appreciated – some of the eulogies were extravagant. Burr Harrison said he "never heard or read a speech better suited to such an occasion!" Zach Taylor said "he was proud of me." These things do not make me vain. I am past that point. If any good was done I am thankful.

At night there was a meeting to organize a Preachers Aid, or Mutual Relief Society. Amongst others I was called out to make a speech – very unexpectedly to me. I had been looking over the Conference roll & found quite a number of names that suggested punning – so I wove them into a sort of form & brought them out in a short speech which "brought down the house." I have seldom been greeted with such rounds of applause – or produced such real – spontaneous – unexpected laughter. Some little additions & alterations I now make, but in substance I said as follows –

Brethren – if your condition shall always continue as favorable as your conference minutes now indicate, you will have no need of a relief association – for I see that you all have *Holmes* of your own and I am sure that you live well and you have a supply of *Rice* & employ an experienced *Gardner*. You are prepared for housekeeping – for you keep two *Cooks* and a *double* supply of *Wood*. You can also have mutton & wool for I notice that you have a regular *Shepard*. I see that you all dress well & that is not strange since you have two *Taylors* at your own disposal and I notice that in color you are partial to *Green*, but as to race distinctions I see that you stick to the *Whiteman*. I do not accuse you of winebibbing – but you are certainly fond of good drink – for you keep a full stock of *Perry* & that of the *highest* quality. Your horses too must be in good trim – for I notice that you have plenty of *Barnes*. But you must like variety in travel as you also employ a practised *Boatman*. No wonder you are *Jolly*. I see by the minutes that you are 52 years old – yet you can put on your *Belt* & run up to your *Garrett* without any fear of the *Akin* in your body. You teach sound theology, for you contend for a *Newman* & in order to be saved you must continue *White* to the end. You are surely in Methodist succession for you have your own *Pleasant* Wesley – a natural son of *John* Wesley himself, so you can stand on your own *Hill* & feel yourselves *Rich* – and if adversity should ever come – you all have talent to *McAfee* (make a fee). What need have you of a relief association? I then gave some reasons why in coming times they would need help. Several persons asked me to write down the punning – & give it to them for their papers. I did so.

March 16 – Bro Slavens of the committee on public worship came to me to ask me to preach tomorrow. I told him I should leave on 10.45 train – but he begged me to stay as I could get home as soon – by taking the freight train in the afternoon. There were some reasons of conscience that induced me to stay & preach.

March 17 – I did not have full liberty, but I tried to be honest & earnest. The attention was good & there was much weeping. I think good impressions were made. A Scotchman, by the name of Rankin – from Wayne [County] had heard of me & came especially to see & hear me. He came up & introduced himself – said once when he was a boy going to the mill – a stranger overtook him on the road & finding that he was a Scotchman, told him about his countryman Robt Burns. He went to the church next day & saw the same stranger in the pulpit preaching & that man was myself.[2] He said "I am now a Methodist. I have a brotherinlaw named for you – Browder Gillespie. I heard of you & came to hear you & see you." He seemed delighted to meet me. Bro Harrison said my sermon was decidedly the best he had heard during Conference. If God owns his word – & makes me useful – I am thankful. I know that I am not indifferent to the

---

2. George Dick served the Wayne Charge during 1847–48, his second year in the ministry. *Minutes of the Annual Conference of the Methodist Episcopal Church, South, for the years 1845–1857* (n.p., n.d.), 110.

approval of my brethren — but I am sure that I value Gods approval infinitely beyond the eulogies & applause of all the world.

March 18 — Got home at night. Dear little Wallace met me at the depot with a horse. I sat up late reading & answering letters.

March 24 — Bro D.J. Starr, pastor of York St Meth[odist] Chur[ch], Cin[cinnati] — whom I met & admired at Somerset — sent me a copy of the Cincinnati Daily Gazette of Mar 18th, [18]79 containing his notice of my address to the Kentucky Conference — in which he does me honor over much — calling me "Dr" Browder & comparing me "in physiognomy & fervor of eloquence" to H[enry] W[ard] Beecher & making kindly allusions to the matter & manner as well as the spirit of my speech. I wrote him a kind letter correcting his mistake in giving me the "doctorate" & expressing my appreciation of his kind remembrance.

April 1 — I am here alone. Dear wife & George in Tenn. I read & write & think. I went to see my father & mother — visited Helen & the sweet little grand children — came home at night. Hanson, Luther, Wallace & I — but we miss Lizzie. She is the light of our home.

April 12 — [Glasgow Circuit] Robt & I went to Dover in a springwagon. We had a better congregation than usual — considering that Forepaughs great show was at Glasgow & we met crowds upon crowds of people, old & young — black & white — in wagons — on horses & on foot pressing into town to the show.

April 20 — [Morgantown] At 3 oclock I spoke to the Sunday School — plainly & earnestly plead with the young people & children to remember their creator in their youth. They were very serious & attentive & when I said, "I will now close as I do not wish to weary you" — little Alick Finley, a very small but a very bright son of Rev W. J. Finley spoke & said "We love to hear you talk" — an expression of interest I appreciated.

April 21 — At night I preached with great earnestness on the "Barren Figtree." A large number of penitents & 8 or 10 conversions. I think I have not heard such shouting in 20 years — as those converted boys & girls & their friends raised & *kept up* in that church. I could not be heard. Finley could not be heard — shouts of joy & hallelujahs! At last I dismissed the congregation & they went shouting to their homes. It was never seen in Morgantown after this sort.

April 22 — I went to the prison to talk & pray with the prisoners — several convicted of murder. I exhorted them & sung & prayed with them. At night I preached again with some unction & power — Mat[thew] 5.25 & again we had a crowd of penitents — several conversions & a time of rejoicing. Sorry I cannot stay longer, but the amount of work I have to do, forbids it. I am sorry for my friend Finley. His children give him trouble. He stayed in my room a long time

& told me how "the waves & billows had gone over him." Oh how children can bless or blight their parents lives!

May 3 – Out for Glasgow to preach the dedication sermon for Roberts new church – "Browders Chapel." Calculation is for a vast crowd. All horses & hacks &c at livery stable engaged & special train chartered – big dinner prepared in town & country & seats arranged in grove for 7 or 800 people.

May 4 – Rain! rain! Well the rain was needed – corn was drying up under the crust & oats needed watering – every garden needed rain & the Lord sent it. Blessed be the Lord. Hundreds of people were disappointed. New dresses & bonnets could not be displayed & many really anxious to hear the sermon could not go. Robt & I went out in a spring wagon – had the seats brought back to the church & wiped off. People kept coming – the house was full & I had fine liberty. Text Hab[bakuk] 1.4 & 7. The dedication was in good form & we had a splendid dinner – abundance of all manner of good things.

May 5 – Off to Smiths grove to preach a series of sermons on baptism & Lords Supper. Fine congregation – fine attention. Our people were pleased. Baptists & Campbellites say they like me – like my spirit, but cannot accept my positions.

May 6 – Spent day in reading & thinking – had more liberty than last night, made argument closer & clearer – kept same kind spirit. Methodists & Cumberlands grinning. Exclusive immersionists looking serious – say I mis-quoted Webster, but that I talk like a good man.

May 7 – Another fine audience. I opened Websters unabridged Dictionary & read definition of Baptism – then of immersion, showed they were essentially different – had fine liberty & a good religious spirit – drove the nail to the head – so to speak – clearest – closest – most convincing argument I have made. Methodists & Cumberlands jubilant – faces bright – smile before they speak to me. Candid immersionists say they never had the slightest idea of the strength of Paido Baptist positions – never heard but one side – see clearly that there are two sides – glad there is a man to bring out the points of difference in a true, candid Christian spirit. Prejudiced immersionists say the argument is "thin" – can be answered &c.

May 8 – Another large & most deeply attentive congregation. Subject – "Lord's Supper & right to partake." Close communion was at a discount. I think many went away feeling that to teach close communion in Smiths grove would be an ungrateful task. The argument that a necessary priority of baptism to the observance of religious duties – necessarily involved infant baptism – seemed to startle anabaptists. I maintained a perfectly good temper & kind candid Christian spirit all the time & whether my argument was weak or strong – it went to the mind & heart of *candid* unprejudiced people. I arrayed no prejudice against me. The most I hoped to do at Smiths grove was to show & make the truth patent, that there were *two sides* – while only *one* side had been presented there. I found oldish people who had *never heard* a sermon in vindication of baptism by affusion. No man had ever preached on the subject except immersionists whose harangues have been loud & frequent – boldly proclaiming that nothing is baptism but immersion – none baptized but immersed people – none in the church but baptized people. This is my *first* series of sermons on the subject – only *one* sermon before in my life on water baptism. I may have been neglectful on my duty on this subject – but there were so many other subjects more attractive to me – & so many other preachers who love to discuss these subjects that I have measurably ignored them – although I have read much in the mode & subjects of Christian baptism.

May 16 – After a few days at home, looking after my business – I set out for Smiths grove. Learned from several friends that Rev W. H. Williams, who spent several hours with me very pleasantly at two dinings & attended three out of my four sermons of the Sacraments at Smiths grove, & who himself had preached several sermons for several months in succession – on the subject – calling special attention to Methodism, undertook to answer my sermons last Sunday. Began by claiming sympathy – did not know that he was to be held to account for the few sermons he had preached. Baptists had always been persecuted – had been said here that Campbellites were killed & now Baptists would be – hoped they would not be buried alive &c. Said he was greatly pleased with elder Browders spirit – never saw a better spirit manifested – but his arguments were *"too thin."* Then I am told that he made a miserable failure at the attempted reply – much worse than in his original sermons – & left the impression that if my arguments could be met, he was not the man to do it & so misrepresented me that those who heard both saw the utter weakness of his defence – & our people think that his failure to meet the issue, left our position stronger than if he had not attempted a reply – and advise me to keep silent as far as he is concerned. Such an effort merits no notice. In reply to my inference that after three days of *fasting* & prayer & excitement – Saul was not supposed to be in a condition to march off to a creek or river in search of water for immersion & that the historian calls attention to the fact that after he had taken meat he was *strengthened* & this strengthening was *after* baptism – bro Williams reply was – "That is the first time I ever knew Paul was sick!" & that was in keeping with his other replies.

May 18 – [Zion, near Smiths Grove] Lovefeast not satisfactory – going in & out – members seem dead & listless. After dinner – as it had been announced through the paper, without my consent, that I would preach on the text "How old art thou?" I took that text & had considerable liberty. Wherever I have preached that sermon it has attracted attention – principally, I think by the plain appeal to husbands & wives – parents & children – masters & servants &c to do right by each other.

May 24 – [Rocky Hill, near Smiths Grove] Went to spend the night with Rev Elias Hawkins. I am to preach tomorrow the funeral of his father Rev John Hawkins – 93 yrs old when he died – a pioneer preacher in this land who took the gospel to his house – & afterward built a house for the lord on his own land. He was a man of great faith & religious joy – & had great power in prayer – read little else beside the Bible. It is supposed that he read that through at least fifty times in his life.

June 1 – [Bethel Grove on Franklin Circuit] No lovefeast – but good prayermeeting. I preached on "Wisdom justified of her children" had some liberty. Better behavior than common – people waited for the benediction before they left the house.

June 2 – Off for home – found the boys busy planting tobacco – finished the barn lot & part of Georges crop. He is raising a crop to help him through the medical college.

June 3 – Got returns for my wool crop at 25 cts pr lb in grease – fine price – great help – nearly paid for my new wagon.

June 11 – I went to see Alexander Saunders – from a conviction that 28 years ago I had lacked 1.68 cts of paying him for all his tobacco crop bot I think at 7 cts pr lb – & about 24 lbs or thereabouts by the scale, I had left unpaid. Thinking of it afterward, I thought I owed him the balance & always intended to pay it – but forgot it when I saw him or had the money. This morning I counted up the interest & made 4.48 total, so I paid him $5.00 to cover all contingencies. He said he knew nothing of the balance & seemed as much pleased as surprised. I am glad this long neglected matter is settled.

I also remember a balance of 1.07 on a bill of lumber due J.M. Hawkins at Nashville since 1868. I have neglected, forgotten – overlooked & then recollected that in some way I must write to see if he is still in Nashville.

June 17 – The boys finished cutting wheat – did better work – had less trouble with the reaper & the hands than usual. The farmers this year have generally hired hands at 1.50 pr day. Some hands have lost jobs by demanding 2.00 – the old price when everything was high. Labor ought to be well paid, but extortion is wrong in rich or poor.

July 1 – [Following a trip to Franklin] All has gone well at home – but the school trustees met – & elected Mr McQuilkin principal of Browder Institute – over Hanson. This by the failure of Thomas Browder to vote – fearing as he said, that it might be thought the Browders were trying to "run" the Institute although he preferred Hanson to McQuilkin. He first induced Hanson to apply for the place & voted for him & encouraged him to expect his support. To say the least of it – I think this is very strange & inconsistent conduct. I feel mortified & chagrined – but, pray God it all may work for the best. I am sure that if a daughter of his was in a school that she needed & that by my solicitation & had proven herself faithful, as I know Hanson has – no act of mine should turn her out & put a stranger in her place. But so the world goes. I hope it may be all for the best. I believe much in God's providence.

July 7 – George has not returned from Tenn. I feel troubled about that dear boy. I fear he has too much idea of running around. I learn that Mr McQuilkin has resigned the presidency of Browder Institute – claiming that he had applied for it under the idea that Hanson did not want it – & he having been elected to another school.

July 8 – Cool, refreshing breeze – welcome – so welcome after the intense heat of the last few days. Mercury in Bowling green Sunday was reported at 97. Just to think, that I preached over an hour – dressed in a cloth coat & vest. I planted cucumber seeds & looked over my crops, which are promising. I ought to be very thankful. In several counties of the state there has been almost no rain for six weeks – while we have been seasonable & our crops are flourishing – tobacco all planted & corn silking & tasseling – had our first new tomatoes 3d of July & Hanson had a small watermelon about ripe on the 4th. He has the finest melon patch I have seen for years.

July 9 – Mercury today 98 in shade at Tom Sydnors – 94 here. School trustees met again & all present. A majority of the board elected Hanson to the school & seemed anxious for him to have it. He will accept – & I trust it will all work well.

July 11 – Prof J.H. Fuqua staid with us last night – told us the sad news of reappearance of yellow fever in Memphis & the panic of the people. I went to the depot to take train for Glasgow. The cars were packed – crowded with refugees black & white – hardly standing room. I sat out on the steps until nearly to Glasgow Junction. People had left their homes & business all in great haste – fearing the fever & the quarantine. It was a pitiable sight.

July 12 – Hot – oh so hot – the air feels like the breath of a furnace. Mercury 98 early in the day – 102 in shade at noon. Was gratified at the earnest expressions of a desire for Roberts return next year. They say they must have him – married or single.

July 22 – [Olmstead] Lizzie & I drove down to see uncle Charles Warfield – in very feeble health & thinks his days are nearly numbered. He seemed cheerful.

July 25 – Showery. I went horseback to Franklin – stopped with bro R.Y. Thomas, came near being bitten by his ferocious dog – think I shall keep away from him on Josh Billing's idea, that "The feller thats bit twist bi the same dog, is better adapted to that sort of bizness than any other."

July 26 – Muddy ride to Stony Point [Allen County]. Congregation not so large as usual on account of rain. Good Quarterly Conference – asked for Buntons return – finances very low. Crops in Allen C[ounty] very poor – long burning drought – no tobacco season – no crop planted. Corn almost a failure – dont know what people are to do.

July 30 – Bro Martin Wilson preached this morning on Remembering the Creator. I followed him with an exhortation – ten or 12 seekers at the altar, others in the congregation – saints shouting. Oh! such shouting as these Stony Point people do – old men & old women – young & middle-aged. When they get happy they scream & jump & praise God just as loud as they can lift up their voices – dozens of them at a time.

August 4 – Hot air – fine breeze – late start [from Scottsville] – stopped in Franklin – had Flora shod – got home 9 Oclock P.M. 40 miles – very tired – thankful for home & rest.

August 5 – I found quite a lot of letters, several to be answered – did that first. The companies I insured my life in, for my wife & children, all broke & my money thrown away! I am sure there has been bad faith as well as mismanagement.

August 8 – Went to Smiths Grove – heard bro Creek of the Campbellite church preach in our church a sermon on "the knowledge of sins forgiven." From his stand point – the whole evidence rests on an act of the human mind – mans interpretation of what God says. Man believes Gods word – obeys God in Baptism and *knows* he is pardoned *because God says so.* This is the Campbellite theory. Then it all depends on *his own* interpretation of what God says. Most Bible students do not believe this construction of scripture. Suppose they are right & Campbellites wrong – then where is his knowledge of sins forgiven? Gods spirit testifying with mans spirit is the Bible idea.

August 10 – [Flat Rock, near Smiths Grove] Spend the night at Warren Grinsteads – a kind Christian family, whose cabin was the preachers home, when only one room was chamber, dining-room, parlor & kitchen. Now they are a little more comfortable, but still they love God & his church & entertain his ministers with a glad heart. The blessing of Heaven be upon Warren Grinstead & all his family.

August 12 – [Olmstead] The boys – Sam & Luther Warfield & my George went to a starlight picnic at Napoleon Rileys. The waste of time & money by the young people of this community is getting to be fearful. Poverty & want are in the future.

September 3 – The rain has greatly washed & the wind broken & beaten the tobacco. Still the prospect is for a good crop. My son Hanson has opened his school with reasonable prospects. My wifes uncle Charles Warfield died yesterday. I am glad we went to see him.

September 4 – My dear boy George R. left home this morning to attend the Medical Lectures in Louisville – going by Glasgow to spend a day or two with Robert. I do earnestly pray God to guide the boy aright & keep him from evil. I cannot see much hope for his success – the profession is *crowded* & I doubt if George has the tact & talent to push ahead of the crowd & get into a paying practice. I greatly desire that he should do good and be useful whether he makes money or not. I gave him 95.00 – all the money I had to spare.

September 15 – I got a note from George asking for more money. I sent him forty dollars – all I had.

September 26 – Considerable frost – no serious damage. Preparing pens for my tobacco – barns full from top to bottom – & ½ or ¼ of crop still uncut.

October 3 – [Annual Conference at Madisonville] Weather as hot as Aug[ust] – mercury up to 90. Preachers in new clothes suffer. I wear my summer clothes.

October 5 – Good lovefeast. Crowd in town immense – all the churches full & many left out. I requested to preach in the court house – did so with some liberty on a text that seems to suit more congregations than almost any other – one that I use & that suited the promiscuous gathering of religious & irreligious people that sat in & stood around the court house – viz – Gen[esis] 47.8. The audience was not large – perhaps 100 – but most of them were very attentive & many affected to weeping. Mr Ramsey – my host – told me that lawyers – doctors &c who heard regretted that the whole town could not have heard it.

Geo. Ramsey gave me his experience. He was the son of well-to-do Baptist parents – converted in his youth – joined the Baptist church – felt the need of a guiding hand in choosing a life-occupation & prayed daily to Almighty God to direct him into some business suited to his capacity & nature. One day while at prayer – an inward voice like an inspiration said – "Read law – read law" – and it continued with him. The next morning it was the same thing – & he borrowed a horse & set out for Madisonville to talk with a lawyer. Passing through an old field, the only lawyer of his acquaintance in the town met him – & he told his business. The man said he wanted just such a young man in his office – so he took him in hand – gave him the benefit of his books & counsel & got him ready for the bar in eight months. Judges Bowling and Grace certified to his qualifications and licensed him to practice. Business came & friends gathered around him. His early love was requited by a lovely wife & the road to prosperity lies before him. He continues his dependence upon God & recognized the obligations that blessings involve. He was mainly instrumental in building & paying for a neat Baptist church in the town of Madisonville.

October 7 – Last night was an eventful one with me. We worked & thought & prayed the whole night until 4 Oclock this morning. I have not seen such faith & patience as Bishop Doggett displayed. I hope I shall not see such an occasion for patience & forbearance as we have witnessed here. My intercourse with all our bishops has been very pleasant. Bishop Doggett has shown me especial respect – inviting to private conference – asking my opinion about important measures. I wish I was wise to give counsel, but alas! alas!! I feel and *know* that I am very weak.

We got our appointments by 12 Oclock & at 1.11 P.M. were off for home.[3] Got to Olmstead in a heavy rain. Robert – bro Wilson & I walked home through the mud & "slosh." I am happy to find my dear ones well – most of the tobacco cut & my dear boys at school. I came back to a happy home – a loving wife & dutiful children & an appreciative people – while many of my brethren go out not knowing whither they go or how they will be received. May Gods rich grace sustain me this Conference year and keep me humble – earnest & useful. My days will soon be past – and I have done very little for the Lord and the church. Oh for grace to do more & better. My old friend Dr Lee, for the first time in 41 years – is on the superannuated* list – but bears it bravely. Rev J.S. Scobee is at Allensville & Bethlehem. He & Murrell & myself are the sole survivors of the class of 1846.

*　　*　　*

[**Editor's Note:** George Dick's journal for October 8, 1879–November 8, 1880 is missing. During this period he completed his last year as presiding elder of the Bowling Green District; in October 1880 he became presiding elder of the Russellville District.]

---

3. George Dick was reappointed presiding elder of the Bowling Green District.

Volume VIII
1880–1882

"To pray for the poor & not help them when we ought does but little good."

November 9, 1880 – I had a long plain talk with our colored woman *Mary*. She with most of the negroes, seem of late to be dissatisfied with their wages and work. I pay *Mary* 5 per month and give her a house – food & fuel & board her – sum equals to one hundred & seventy five dollars if she had rent to pay & board for herself and son. I told her if her house was not desirable, she could look for another.

My dear little grand children – Lizzie, Ruth & Sue-Robert are here to day – cheerful happy little girls. I pray God that they may walk in right paths all the days of their lives. If they will be as good as their mother – or their grandmothers or either of their great-grandmothers – I shall be satisfied.

Soon after conference [at Glasgow where George Dick was named Presiding Elder for the Russellville District] I was informed that Rev T. B. Bosley who located – thought that I was his enemy. I wrote him, what I intended for and thought was a kind and brotherly letter, assuring him that I was his friend & would welcome him back to the conference, if he reconsidered his action – & explained to him the action of the Cabinet in his appointment. Today I received in reply a letter of 6 pages, of legal caps in which he accuses the Conference of "wrong," "fearful wrong" "insult" &c and thinks that I have unconsciously added to the prejudice against him. I wrote in reply, a kind gentle letter, hoping to relieve his mind of the idea he had of his brethren. I am now done with this matter.

November 11 – Went to prayer meeting. Luther led the service & we had a good meeting.

November 12 – Went to see Dr. Hutchings – very poorly, declining, does not expect to recover. Says he has strong *historical* faith.

November 18 – Another snow storm – last night, very cold this morning – Mercury 16. This is about the coldest November weather I ever saw. Mercury tonight down to 4 ½ above 0 out of doors.

November 19 – Bitterly cold – Mercury 4 below zero. I went to Elkton to meeting of District Stewards. They fixed my salary at 1000 – only four charges present.

November 22 – Last night was *cold* – again. People putting up ice 3 inches thick. I have suffered with rheumatism in my left arm. My man *Frank* seemed to be slow about getting wood & work generally & I rather complained of him. I learned afterward that he had sprained his ankle & I was sorry I complained – yet on general principles he deserves a lecture.

November 23 – Cold East wind, ground still covered with snow & likely to be for several days. I found Bro Griffin of Todd circuit without any overcoat, for this cold winter & bought him one until he can pay for it – & ordered shoes for his wife which he seemed to appreciate.

November 24 – To day the boys put up ice 3 ¼ to 3 ½ inches thick in our deep pond. It is thicker on shallow ponds. I suppose the oldest man has not seen winter so early, so severe & so continuous in Southern Kentucky. Snow still covers the ground.

November 26 – I got up early to start to Hopkinsville – rather to Hebron 6 miles beyond Hopkinsville, but found the road so covered with ice & the weather so threatening, that I came back to take the train tonight. Lizzie and I went to see my cousin Dr Hutchings. I fear he is steadily going down – starving to death in a land of plenty – good appetite – good digestion, but so terribly afflicted in his throat that he cannot swallow anything even milk or water without excruciating pain. He is a man of fine sense and large information – literary & scientific – a firm believer in the Bible, but is not a member of the visible church. He is confident that his mother, who died years ago, appeared to him recently as he lay on his bed. He reached out his hand to take hers & answered her call – says she called him as distinctly as she ever did & said she had come to stay with him. He takes it as an omen that his end is near. It is not impossible that God should allow such a visit. Thousands of dying people have asserted the visible presence of their departed ones – but I do not remember any case of one who recovered after seeing such a vision. The train was two hours late. The conductor told me I would have to lie over at Guthrie so I got him to stop & put me off – as I feared to sleep in a cold room, on a cold bed with my rheumatism. It was very dark & I fell in the cattle guard & skinned my leg.

November 27 – Up before day – got on the train and reached Hopkinsville at 12 – got Dr Hickmans buggy & horse & reached Hebron in time to hold Quarterly Conference. Spend the night with my old friends John A. & Sally Redford Browning – met my little pet Mattie Carr, that I used to nurse on my lap – kissed her as usual & then was surprised to learn that she was a married woman. How time flies! Her husband & sister laughed heartily at my surprise & mistake.

November 29 – Took train for home – fell in with Rev Stratton of the Christian Church – & we had a talk about dancing. He did not much oppose it except in some forms. I never saw dancing Christians that were noted for piety.

December 1 – [Olmstead] Up early to kill our hogs. Pleasant sunshine, glad & bright. The pigs 6 mos old weighed 144 1/5 nett. The hogs 12 mos old weigh 228 nett – very fine pork – 3000 lbs. We salted it down by dinner & I went to Depot – sent check to Peter C. Foster – for $50.40 for four barrels of sorghum syrup – one for Tom Sydnor, one for Charley Roach, one for Father & one for myself. I also sent a check for 17.50 to Ky Fertilizing Co. for 1000 lbs wheat fertilizer. Read, at night, part of Wesleys work on Original Sin in reply to Rev John Taylor of England, who taught that "temporal death *only* was the penalty of the law of Eden – that no *moral* taint descended from Adam – that Christ restored man what he lost in Adam & every man stands just as Adam stood." Mr Wesleys reply seems to me clear & satisfactory. Surely an evil nature descends in our very being — else the whole world would not go so far astray & sin be so universal in all our race.

December 4 — Rainy & muddy. Small attendance at Quarterly Meeting in Allensville. Only one woman, Mrs Adams, present but she brought dinner enough for all. By special request I went to spend the night with my old school mistress — Miss Susan Bibb, who always takes great interest in me & seems proud of me as if I were somebody and she had made me.

December 5 — Good congregation. I administered the sacrament of the Lord's supper with seven ministers around the table — *three* of them my own sons — Robert, Hanson & Luther. It was an occasion of deep interest to me & was the subject of remark. Such a scene is not often witnessed — a live father & three sons — all ministers — & the father less than 54 yrs old. I suffered with rheumatism — pain & weakness in my left arm. St Jacobs oil has not cured me.

December 13 — I reached home at night [from Auburn] and learned to my great sorrow that my dear Bro Wm's house was burned up last Saturday night, with nearly all the clothing & furniture. Poor Wm is already in debt, and this is a sad blow. I must try to help him all I can — but George's expenses at Louisville are very heavy & I cannot do much.

December 14 — I sent George a check for $25.00 and wrote him to economize.

December 22 — Our cook, *Mary,* has been in a fret for a day or two & will want another home, both for her own peace and ours. We have had her seven years — & in the main she has done as well or better than most of her poor unfortunate race — but she has become insolent & insulting & we must risk a change — although it may be worse. These annoyances come.

December 27 — My man *Frank* seems greatly surprised to find that he has been overpaid for his years work and has no money left. I made him a present of 5.00 & as *Foster* is out of money — I lent him 5.00 on next years wages. At night we had Bro Bunton & wife, Bro David & wife & two children, Dr DeWitt & two daughters, Charley & Helen & 3 children & Lucy Anderson — had to send some of the children away to lodge. We had 13 beside our own family sleep here — but all seem cheerful.

December 30 — Helped haul my fathers coal — not being able to hire hands. Our woman *Mary* left yesterday. She and the children cried & we felt sad to see the children leave. We have raised them almost from infancy. We hired a mulatto woman calling herself *Fannie Walker* & her daughter *Nannie*. They came in this evening & seem well disposed.

January 1, 1881 — Another New Year! I began well — visiting the sick and helping the needy. The weather had moderated some but the rheumatism in my arm indicates more snow.

January 3 – Was startled in the night by a call for some woman to help shroud our old neighbor Mrs Gaines. Lizzie was not able to go. I was sorry, but was not willing for Lizzie to risk her health any further. I went up this morning & arranged to dig the grave – then went to Whippoorwill and ordered the coffin.

January 4 – Sent my man *Foster* to haul a load of wood for F. M. Davenport who has been sometimes sick & not able to provide for himself. I am glad to help the poor when I can and have never lost anything by it.

January 11 – This is my fifty-fourth birthday. I begin to feel old – have less endurance & strength & more surplus flesh. I weigh 185 or 180 lbs and feel clumsy. Physical labor soon wearies me. My hair is almost white. The best of my years are past and my work time will soon be gone – and my suffering time may be near at hand. This birthday, I feel humiliated & ashamed of myself. I have spent my life & accomplished almost nothing. I am so ignorant, so inefficient – so worthless and so unworthy. There is so much natural meanness & selfishness and slothfulness in me, that I have cause to be ashamed & weep.

To day I attended the meeting of stockholders in Logan Co[unty] National Bank. [On my return] Hanson met me at the depot with his sleigh and team, and turned over & threw us both out three times before we got home. I set sleigh-riding down as a humbug! Fortunately we were dumped in the snow and not in the mud.

January 13 – Sent my friend Davenport a nice shoulder of salted pork.

January 15 – Quarterly Meeting in Russellville, house cold & congregation small. I walked out a mile to see Dr Lee – very feeble, in bed most of the time – asked me to come back Monday & write his will.

January 17 – Walked out to see Dr Lee – found him too feeble to dictate the will & his wife sick in bed. I gave sister Lee a little money for which she seemed very thankful, said they were often without a cent of money to buy medicine or anything else. I pity Dr Lee greatly. He has always been industrious, but he bought land at a high price & borrowed money at big interest – & now the land is low – produce does not pay & interest is eating them up – & he unable to earn 1 cent.

January 18 – [Olmstead] I went to see if T.B. Sydnor had sent Mr Davenport any flour – glad he has.

January 19 – We hung up our pork – 7 weeks in salt.

February 1 – Snow all gone after 42 days continuous stay. A messenger announced the death of F.M. Davenport. I went & assisted in shrouding the corpse of my neighbor & made arrangements for digging the grave.

February 2 — Preached the funeral of Bro Davenport. I believe that this is the 9th or 10th person connected with the Gaines family for whom I have been called upon to conduct funeral service.

February 4 — Mercy! How cold & cutting this E. wind! & I have to ride over the ice & roughest frozen roads imaginable to Frog Level [Sharon Grove] 12 miles beyond Gordonsville. Had a fearful ride — such lumps of mud tramped up & frozen. Flora fell with me twice but a kind Providence kept me from harm.

February 11 — I went to O'Roarks chapel [Logan County]. Raining much of the way. A fearful storm overtook me — almost blowing my horse out of the road — & drenching me with rain — but my waterproof overalls were a great protection. Bro Frogge was there ahead of me. The storm continued all night intermingled with snow & rain.

February 12 — Bitter cold — piercing wind blowing furiously — few at church — 10. Quarterly Conf[erence] finances *low* — *low* — 23.70 all told since Conference. I left it all with Bro Frogge — as he needs it more than I.

February 14 — Glad to be at home — this trip has been hard — mud, rain & storm going — cold, ice & rough frozen ground returning.

February 27 — My son George came home this morning — looking tolerably well & cheerful. He handed me his diploma saying "Here's your money." It has cost the poor boy much hard study, as well as me much money, but I am now satisfied that he has been faithful in the preparation and I think he will succeed. If he will be good & useful, I shall not regret the expense.

March 4 — The snow is falling almost as fast as at any time this winter and I have a long ride of near twenty miles before me — over muddy & rough road — but I propose to breast the storm & reach Fairview tonight. Thousands of people from thousands of miles will crowd into Washington City to day to see President Garfield inaugurated. No trifle should hinder the herald of the cross from bearing the glad tidings of a Saviors love to the children of sorrow & sin.

March 9 — [Olmstead] I had a visit from Hayes Moore M.D. telling me of a fine location for George to practice medicine at Sadlersville Tenn. which he is leaving on account of his connection with the arrest & punishment of the negroes who murdered Leonidas Lapraid. He represents the place as worth several thousands of dollars and is anxious for George to take it, but Lizzie & I are afraid that the moral influences are not good & many friends are soliciting George to settle here. I want him to do well — but pure morals are worth more than money.

March 14 — I went to see my father to advise with him and my brothers, as to the best way to dispose of his property and pay his debts, which have burdened him almost unto death. He has been kind hearted & by endorsing the paper of his friends, has well nigh ruined himself & put it out of his power to help to aid his children – and now he is old & feeble & the extortionate interest he has had to pay – & the ingratitude of those he has favored well nigh crushes him. David proposes to buy the land 280 acres at 45. pr acre – pay $6000.00 down & pay the balance on installments & take care of father & mother as long as they shall live for a reasonable compensation. This will pay the debts and leave father a competency & keep the old homestead in the family & give some rest to our dear parents in their old age. It is a great outrage that the result of their lifes labor & frugality should be wasted on ungrateful people who have betrayed their trust, but it was my fathers misfortune & not his fault. I do not censure him, nor reproach him. It was kindness of heart & a desire to befriend, that led him into security. He has spent principal & interest $14,000 or 15,000 dollars paying other peoples debts – enough to have given each of his children a comfortable home.

March 16 – At home – anxious about George – who has gone to Sadlersville to prospect for a situation in the practice of medicine. I greatly desire that he should settle here – but could not insist if he can do better there.

March 17 – Writing a sermon on Isa[iah] 25.6–8. I feel constantly anxious & concerned about George. Somehow I fear that there are immoral influences about Sadlersville – & then I feel personal disappointment, that my son has gone to another neighborhood when I wanted him here. I leave him in the hand of God.

March 24 – Spent some time burning grass off some corn land. My mothers negro cook professed religion and came out in the field, shouting and rejoicing in God. When I came home, *Dick Browder,* a colored man in Tom Sydnors employ, had just been converted after several days of deep & mournful penitence and came down to my house, rejoicing & praising God & embracing black & white shouting aloud the praises of God. "Oh Mars George" he said, "why didn't you tell me religion was so good? but you have been trying to tell me so long and I wouldn't believe it. Oh what a sinner I was & Jesus forgives me. Thankee Jesus – thankee Jesus – thankee Jesus." over & over and again. "Glory to God, thankee Jesus," he shouted until he was almost exhausted & went from house to house over the neighborhood telling white & colored people the good news of his conversion. I do not see how any one can doubt. He was a very wicked man of bad habits & low instincts. Whisky & women were his great besetments – & he made a mock of people shouting when they were converted. I shall note his walk with interest. About night two others – *Bill Medler* & *George Morrow,* on Tommys place, professed conversion and shouts of praise sounded through the neighborhood. This seems to be a wonderful work. The meeting is led by brother *Collins,* a colored preacher, who came to Olmstead and preached a few sermons.

March 25 – Started to Kirkmansville – dined at H.G. Petrees – found Ben Griffins wife packing up to leave and go to her brothers, because the Todd circuit is not paying them enough to live on, and she does not think it is right to go in debt & not pay. They seem distressed and do not know what is best to do & I cannot tell them – but I think they had better make any reasonable sacrifice than go into debt with no probability of paying. I advised Ben to wait until Quarterly Meeting – before he decides to leave the work. His wife seems full of faith & wanted him to stay & preach, pay or no pay – & she will come back to see him & travel with him in good weather. It is refreshing to see a wife with such faith & fortitude. Oh if all preachers had such wives!

March 26 – Got to Kirkmansville in good time. Less than a dozen people at church. A little boy insisted on sweeping the house "because strange preachers are coming and the house ought not to be so dirty when strange preachers come." I told him the strange preacher would not want the dust flying all over his head and over the house – & he had better leave it as it was, and let us make a fire, but he insisted on sweeping the house "before the strange preacher got in" – & so he pushed & brushed the dust about, while I kindled a fire – and when I began the service the little fellow looked quite surprised, to see the "strange preacher" already there.

April 1 – [Olmstead] Whoever saw such a day on the 1st of April! A driving snow storm from the North – ground frozen and covered with snow – as much like winter as the middle of January. Our stock of coal is now exhausted – and we hear of none for sale. Mercury 28. All day the snow lay on the ground, increased by occasional falls.

April 5 – Still cold, ground frozen. I helped Luther haul two loads of coal – and felt broken down.

April 7 – I received a note that Bro Fisk was at the point of death. I hastened to Russellville on the next train – found him steadily going down. I asked him if his faith & trust were steadfast in the Lamb of God that taketh away the sin of the world? His answer was characteristic – prompt & in his usual manner – "O I suppose so." He has expressed himself as perfectly ready & resigned – said he had served God from principle – & his life & conversation was his testimony, rather than the talk of his last hours. I sat up with him until 11 Oclock, then lay down until 3 A.M. & then sat by him until he breathed his last, about 5 A.M. I gave him the last drink of water he took, & pressed my fingers upon his sightless balls. Robt Fisk was a good man. The Louisville Conference will miss his wise counsels – 46 years he was a travelling preacher & was emphatically "a faithful man in the earth and feared God above many."

April 8 – Witnessed the calisthenic practice at Logan Female College & was greatly pleased. I never saw anything better done. It is a beautiful exercise & must be very strengthening to the system. It brings every muscle & sinew into motion.

April 11 – Had a long talk and prayed with Bro Higgins who is still sick & setting every day to die, when I persuaded him to defer it until July & attend my Quarterly Meeting.

May 2 – Went to see Helen – expecting everyday to be confined with her fifth child. May the gracious God bring her safely through the peril!

May 5 – Wrote a long earnest letter to my son George. Dear boy, how anxious I am about him. I fear he is losing his religious interest and I fear his surroundings are not the best. He goes to church regularly, but seems to lack interest.

May 11 – When I got home [from Russellville] – I found that Helen had a son – the first of her family of five.[1] Helen is quite sick & her mother is with her.

May 12 – Called to see my darling daughter – doing tolerably well – and my little grandson – big & promising – a ten pounder.

May 30 – I went to see my father – called on poor old *uncle Ned*. He is evidently sinking – says he has no fear – trusts all to Christ – has no ill will to any mortal – is very thankful for all the kindness he has received – wants to be buried plainly in his own clothes, *clean* and in a plain walnut coffin. I promised to see it done if I was on hand. He said but for being robbed, he would have been ready for buying his own burial casket. He has been a good servant & faithfully has my father cared for him in his old age.

June 1 – There was a large crowd this June 1, 1881, to see my sister Annie married to [Dr] Daniel Bailey. I performed the ceremony by request of both parties.

June 10 – I stopped in Russellville – walked out to see Dr. Lee – found him very feeble – evidently declining – yet spiritually full of hope and confidence – desired me to take charge of his funeral service – gave me a few salient points in his life, as the basis for a memorial service. I wish I was or could be such a student as Dr Lee has been. By nature he was irritable & peevish, but by grace he reads his title clear to mansions in the skies. I am not worthy to preach the funeral of such a man. I gave sister Lee some money for necessary expenses.

June 13 – "*Old Uncle Ned*" died this morning. He has been on the place, every year, but one, since 1826, and has been a most faithful servant. In his old age, he has had every needed comfort at my fathers expense and now a neat walnut coffin at his request for his burial. I attended his funeral with appropriate remarks and followed him to the grave, attended by all the members of my

---

1. George Dick's first grandson was named John Browder.

fathers family and my own who a̲ᵢ ˙ in the neighborhood. He was an honest man and hated evil works. When his strength was failing and he could only speak with effort, he said "I am so glad Im going clear away from the devil, I dont know what to do with myself." Poor old man – now rest in peace. He was disappointed, and often said so, in his estimate of negro emancipation. His race had not been benefited by the change as much as he desired.

June 14 – [Olmstead] Our barbed wire fence has been a most unprofitable & unsatisfactory investment. Our hogs squeeze through it – injure themselves and destroy the crops. My fine mare Flora is still lame & in danger from cutting her foot on the barb.

June 15 – I had just sat down to write a sketch of the life of Dr N.H. Lee when Robert Brown of Russellville came in & called me to go to town and preach Dr Lees funeral. He died yesterday evening. I hastened to town – went to Bro Browns & finished the sketch – about 9 pages & then got ready to preach – by 2 ½ P.M. I read the biographical sketch & preached the funeral with considerable liberty & unction on the text Psa[lm] 23.4. At the close Bro Lewis spoke of his last interview with our departed brother – & his counsel to his children – & then opened the doors of the church and four younger children who had not joined the church came forward weeping – to fill their places in the church of their father. It was a touching scene and brought tears to many eyes. We followed him to the grave where I read the burial service – & we left him to await the resurrection of the just. I feel that the ablest divine of the Louisville Conference has gone from us. George Bell took me with his fast trotting mare to the depot in time for the train.

June 16 – Have not felt well today. My boys are busy in Harvest and the merry lively clatter of the reapers, rattles all around us. The wheat is not fully ripe but in good condition to save & we fear it will fall.

June 23 – Early this morning Luther & I were on our way to Adairville – found a circus & Menagery on hand to divide the crowd with us. *All* the pastors of the District got in the 1st day. No Bishop present – I had to preside.

June 24 – Attendance increased – business progressed well & smoothly. Bro Tigert preached at night a very able sermon – full of thought & sense – clear, ringing argument – logic on fire – but his delivery was very objectionable – gesticulations violent – & awkward & incessant – voice screaming. I have not seen him so wild in his manner.

June 25 – Had a brotherly talk with Tigert – dealt faithfully with him in the counsel as to his delivery. He took it brotherly – said he would try to guard himself – that it was only occasionally that he got into that excited manner.

June 27 – We saw the Comet, in the N. West sky – its tail pointing S.E. It is large & awe-inspiring.[2]

June 28 – Mr Vick reports that he saw three *comets* at 3 Oclock A.M. this morning.

June 29 – I got up at 3, to see the comets – saw only one – but that a new one – N.E. instead of N.W. – tail pointing S.W. – just reverse of the one visible early in the night that seemed to be moving N.W. "Marvelous are thy works O Lord!"

July 2 – Horror! The telegraph reports the assassination of the President! Shot, just as he was going to enter the cars at Washington by a man name of Guiteau – or some French name – who had sought in vain to obtain a public office. The town is all excitement & sorrow. Mr Garfield has the heart of the great body of the American people – & was admitted to be a good & faithful man. His death is a national calamity – and will humiliate us in the eyes of the world. The act was that of a mad man. I pray God, the wounds may not be fatal.

July 4 – The reports from the president are not encouraging. I fear he will die.

July 20 – I wrote a long, earnest heart letter to my cousin Wilbur F. Browder – on the subject of his open avowal of infidelity. I did *not argue* the question – but gave some reasons why he should not make such sentiments public even though he held them. I do pray God to reach & save the son of sainted fathers & mothers prayers.

July 26 – The drought is now serious and alarming. The corn crop cannot yield half an average – the pastures are dried up and the young grasses are dying – gardens are failing & waters drying up. My cistern is dry for the first time since it was in use.

July 27 – I worked some time, cleaning out the cistern and getting it ready for rain. It is surprising, how much filth will gather in a cistern, protected by a charcoal filter as this has been.

August 1 – I had a long letter – 26 pages – from Wilbur Browder, in reply to my kind letter. He is respectful & kind to me, but fearfully blind & unbelieving in his idea of the Bible. His letter is inconsistent & vulnerable – like nearly every infidel book, but he claims to be & I suppose is honest in his convictions – & I trust God will lead him into the true light – but his utterances make me sad.

---

2. The *Louisville Courier-Journal* for June 27, 1881, reported that the comet was first sighted at Paris, France, on June 23. Professor Skinner of the U. S. Naval Observatory stated that it was the most brilliant to appear since 1843. The comet reportedly had a tail 4,000,000 miles in length.

August 2 – Went to see my father. He is very feeble and suffering – threatened with flux – troubled about his business. Tomorrow his land is to be surveyed and delivered to my brother David & his family and the proceeds mostly consumed in paying the penalty of trusting a man that he wished to befriend.

August 3 – I went to see my father – found him better – his home sold – & title given.

August 5 – This is the birthday of my dear daughter Helen. She has been a great comfort to her parents. Thirty years old this day. She has a young and beautiful face – but her head is grayer than her mothers.

August 8 – I paid T.J. Smith a check for 741.00 – balance of near four thousand dollars, that my poor old father has had to pay for D[avid] B. H[utchings] to this one man. It is hard – but unavoidable.

August 12 – Bro Bunton & I went together in my buggy as far as Elkton – through the hottest sunshine that ever I felt in my memory. Mercury 106 in the shade! The very moon beams seem hot and we get in the shade – out of the moonshine to get a cool breath. The wind that comes feels like it was blowing out of a furnace. The dust and drought still alarming.

August 22 – My father gave me a check for $1500. of the money I had lent him. I went to Russellville – & deposited the money with Logan Co[unty] Bank – & conditionally arranged to take ten shares of Logan Co. National Bank Stock at $100.00 pr share. I am very sorry to see my poor father sell his land – but I am thankful to be in a position to help him if he should need.

August 23 – We sold our hogs yesterday at 3¾ for light & 4 cts pr lb for large. We think it is a heavy loss to us, but it may all be best. The country was never so bare of corn – old & new – as it is now.

August 25 – I went with my father to Russellville on train & bought ten shares of Logan County National Bank stock for eleven hundred dollars – had four shares issued to myself – two shares to Helen, two to Robert & two to Hanson. I came home on 12 Oclock Freight train – am glad to see the rates of travel reduced – 30 cts to Russellville – instead of 40.

August 26 – I went to haul the 200 bushels of oats I bought from B.F. Turner at 50 cts pr bu. They are very heavy fine oats. I want to feed my horses on them & save my corn – to feed people who will otherwise suffer. The heat & drought have never been equalled in this country as a whole.

August 28 – Good love-feast. My daughter Helen was the only woman who spoke & she spoke well with good sense & good effect. Many at the sacrament. I baptized my little grandson John Browder Roach.

August 29 – The gathering clouds darkened the heavens – & the rain drops began to fall – but alas – it was only a sprinkle. The clouds passed away – & the blazing sun poured his fiery rays afresh upon the perishing crops.

September 1 – Bless the Lord O My Soul. The long prayed for rain is coming. The clouds are thick all around and the gentle showers are settling the furrows – and relief seems to be at hand. My sons Luther & Hanson left in the rain to go to Nashville. Hanson goes to give Luther a start in the Vanderbilt University. I feel sad & serious to see my children leave home. When we pack up their trunks and start them off to school – we have them at home but little more. If the Lord calls them to preach his word – I cheerfully give them up to him. The rain has been supremely satisfactory – watering the earth & filling the pools. Every body now will be thankful to exchange dust for mud – for a time.

September 4 – [Lewisburg] Blazing! Mercury above 100. Congregation jammed in & packed – all seats filled, many standing up – & many under the windows out of doors. I had fair liberty in preaching Hag[gai] 1.4–7 – 70 minutes delivering the sermon – one hour raising the collection & dedicating the house. Four hundred dollars to be raised – people poor – crops *all* short, corn less than half a crop – the outlook gloomy. I got 325.00 and the committee assumed the 75 – so we solemnly dedicated the house to the worship of Almighty God. I was fearfully weary & warm when we finished.

September 8 – [Olmstead] I went to see Dr Hutchings – just returned from Cincinnati – nearly out of heart of getting well. He evinced more feeling than I have seen in him before – shed tears while I talked with him about Christ & Heaven.

September 10 – Reached Chandlers [Chapel] in time – preached a feeling sermon on Lam[entations] 3.35–6. Held Quarterly Conference – pleasant session – finances starving to preachers.

September 12 – I preached at night to another crowded congregation. I had earnestness & liberty. Eight mourners at the altar – about 20 others came up to ask for prayer. Six girls & young women professed conversion & there was a time of great rejoicing. I felt as I always do just before such a display of spiritual power – an earnest, anxious, prayerful spirit & a sensation undefinable – that souls are about to be converted. I do not know that I have ever been disappointed when I have had just that sort of faith & feeling.

September 14 – [Olmstead] Went with Lizzie to see Helen. Her little daughters Lizzie & Ruth had just started to school & seemed proud to go.

September 20 – I left for home [from Red Oak] – met Dr Bibb on the way who told me of the death of president Garfield. Sad news for our country. I pray God to guide his successor in the paths of wisdom & true patriotism.

September 24 – [Kirkmansville] Very small congregation. Bunton & I held Quarterly Conference, harmoniously. Not one cent reported for preachers support.

September 25 – Small love-feast. Good congregation at 11. I preached with great plainness on the duty of pastors & people to each other. I raised a collection for Bunton, total amount – near 10.00 – 26.75 paid him by this people for a years work.

October 10 – Off early to Russellville [on the way to Annual Conference in Owensboro]. Mattie stood the trip finely – & is a valuable mare.

October 13 – I am pleased with Bishop Keener in the Cabinet – he seems candid & impartial but very firm & looks well into the work.

October 14 – Most of the day was taken up in electing delegates to the General Conference. Dr Messick & Dr Hayes were elected on the first ballot – then A.C. Morrison – then some ballots with no election. Then H.C. Settle D.D. – then some other ballots & no election – A.H. Redford & myself being the highest in the number. Then another ballot & no election – then another in which Redford received 54 & I 59 – & I was declared elected. Many of my friends were greatly delighted. I was very sorry the race was between my first colleague & myself. I never failed to vote for him – from my first opportunity until now – but this time I could not. I *cannot* be reconciled to his administration at the Publishing House – nor his attitude toward the Publishing interest.

October 15 – Conference business interesting, but tedious. The Bishop does not keep us up at night as Kavanaugh & Doggett did, but Presiding Elders have grave responsibilities.

October 18 – At a late hour Conference adjourned. I was reappointed to the Russellville District. Dr Redfords removal from the Columbia Dist[rict as presiding elder] – & appointment to Glasgow & Dover & Scottsville, caused more surprise, perhaps than any other. If the Bishop consulted any body about that appointment I do not know it. It was rather a surprise to me but I cannot condemn the Bishop. He has the right to select his own advisers.

October 19 – Off early for home. John McGhee met me at the depot – & accused me & [David] Morton of being the cause of Redfords removal & his own discontinuance from the Cabinet. I told him the charge was false – that I had nothing to do with the matter. I am sorry to be charged with doing what I had no hand in & blamed for *not* doing what I was powerless to do – but I shall not fret over it. I could not blame the bishop – for I think he acted conscientiously & on his own judgment. I had a talk with the Bishop on the train & am satisfied that he did what he thought was best.

November 2 — Beautiful Autumn! No frost to kill anything — not even tomato & sweet potato vines. Pastures luxuriant and my wheat completely covering & hiding the ground — cattle & sheep pasturing on it. The forest is yet in full foliage, but the leaves are assuming their grand autumnal tints. The vermillion & the gold greet the eye wherever it looks. I wrote to Luther, my son, to send him money for clothes. I sent him a 15.00 over coat from Allensville & a 10. check from Hopkinsville. I think he is doing well at his studies.

November 13 — [Bethesda in Todd County] — Good Congregation for preaching, but no love-feast. The congregation was very attentive with few exceptions. Some silly boys and girls laughed & talked. This neighborhood has had a hard name for bad men & lewd women. A brother told me that he had seen men and women both *fight* at church on Sunday.

November 14 — Men all gone to County Court & women at home. No meeting — went to Bro Salmons's [near Guthrie]. He showed me the spot where his daughterinlaw was attacked by the negro man — the spot where she was outraged & murdered & where she was lying when he got to her. He could not speak of it now without weeping. It was a fearful horror and it seems right that the mob took vengeance on the guilty wretch.

The congregation at night was not large & was much interrupted by some bad boys who I think had been drinking.

November 15 — Called to see my old play-fellow *David,* a negro man, that belonged to my father. He was not at home and his wife told me that I spoke to him Friday, & asked the route to Salmons — but neither of us knew the other. It is sad to think how the old family servants are scattered and the ties of the olden time will not be known by the rising generation. I got home to dinner and was glad to find the boys killing the hogs. The corn is too scarce to feed.

November 21 — I am very hoarse, almost speechless above a whisper — wrote to Luther — also Christian Advocate, Herald Enterprise, Weekly Messenger & Muhlenberg Echo — the last named being a spicy, piquant paper edited by R.Y. Thomas jr. He sends me a weekly copy — expecting, I suppose an occasional letter.

November 22 — George came up yesterday — seems well and cheerful. I continue hoarse and feeble. George gave me pills to stir the liver.

November 24 — This is the National Thanksgiving — but it is only observed in the towns. I am not well enough to go even to Allensville. The driving snow and piercing wind look much like winter. I stay in to read and write — thinking of a promise to send Charlie Nourse at Owensboro a copy of the puns I perpetrated on the names of the members of the last Louisville Conference. I wrote him this to day, viz —

The Louisville Conference of the Methodist Church, South that convened in Owensboro, in Oct, 1881, was a formidable body. A copy of their printed Minutes is before me – and if their names indicate their condition they are respectable, sensible and comfortable in their surroundings. There is not one member of the whole Conference destitute of a large *Merritt.* They seem to be cultivated gentlemen & can point with pride to their *Breeding.* They are intellectual for they keep a *Keene* man in the body and a *Keener* at the head of their Conference. They are well supplied also with help, for they have a *Mann* of their own – & beside him they keep a *Free*man at their beck and call. They are married people and have plenty of sons, some of them of very desirable quality – especially their *Good*-son and their *Hardi*-son. They also have names for their sons, a *John*-son – A *Davi*-son, a *Harri*-son – a *Morri*-son & a *Clark*-son. They are well supplied with provision – a large stock of the very best *Bacon.* If any should intimate that they *Need*-ham – they can show as a sample at least one *Big*-ham of superior quality. They take good care of their horses also, and keep quite a variety of *Hayes,* all of them of good quality, but if any should fear a lack of tons, they can show a *New*-ton, an *Over*-ton & yet a *Mor*-ton – and if still there be any lack – they can supply it, for they keep their own *Carter.* They can afford to dress well, for they keep their own *Taylor,* and as to color of cloth, they seem partial to *Brown.* They seem to be very sober people and pass strong temperance resolutions, yet they insist on keeping a very superior *Brewer* & a good supply of *Bowles* – notwithstanding their abundance of good *Waters.* They do not indulge much in flowers, yet they seem justly partial to the *Rose.* As to fowls they are not very particular, but they have a pair of excellent *Crows* & plenty of *Brents,* nor are they very fond of animals, having little more than one *Tiger*(t), one *Lyon* & a couple of *Campbells.* In the fish department, they prefer *Pike.* They must be fond of game, else why keep a *Hunter* and a *Bowman* always on duty? Their stock of grain must be ample, for they can always point with confidence to their *Stubblefield* and they ought to have peas enough, for they have a real *Pe*-tree. They are mostly travelling preachers – and sometimes go *Rushing* – and no wonder, for they have a very energetic *Spurrier.* As to roads, they like a *Lane* and as to crossing streams, they can have a choice between the old *Ford* & the *Red*-ford. Their government seems to be regal, for they have a *King,* and their exchequer is in good condition, for they keep an active *Cashman* and can always raise the *Means.* With all their pleasant surroundings, their *Bliss* is not perfect, for there is always some *Akin* in the body, although it does not *Pierce* deep. On the whole they are a happy family and have a double portion of *Love* amongst themselves. So may they ever *Settle* and have their *Slate* always ready for entries.

November 25 – Went over to Allensville to meet with District Stewards – only three present. They allowed me 1000 – & assessed 1025.00. Some thought it ought to be 1200. I like it as it is.

December 8 – Called to see my father and show him a letter from sister Alice informing me that my brother Frank had gone to Florida to take a contract, with five gentlemen to grade 5 miles for 4000. on the R.R. from Pensacola to Milton. She said for herself – that she was making 15. to 18. pr month on butter & 5. pr month on eggs & sewing enough beside, to pay her servant hire. Certainly she must be industrious and frugal. I do not feel well enough to be out at night. I still cough — am hoarse and throat sore.

December 20 — Cloud & rain. I am glad to be at home with Lizzie. Wallace at school, she would be alone. Christmas is coming — but it does not impress me as it did in youth. Age & responsibility wonderfully change our feelings. The poor negroes in the country do not enjoy Christmas as they did in the old time. Many of them are without homes or supplies and many are stealing and getting in jail.

December 21 — I rode over to see my father getting ready for his sale tomorrow — saw a letter from my Bro Frank — troubled about next years operations. Labor is so demoralized in the South, that he is afraid to rent land & hire hands again.

Wallace went to the depot and brought the box of Christmas goods, that Robert selected for us in Louisville — cheese, mincemeat, oranges, apples, prunes, nuts — candies, crackers &c — with a few packs of fresh Salmon — all cost money, but Christmas is a joyous occasion & deserves to be celebrated with good things — and we expected our dear children home, to eat together at mothers table again. I am sorry that Luther & Robert cannot be here.

December 22 — Clear & bright, good crowd at the sale — & the articles sold as well as could be expected, but my father looks serious to see his chattels sold & feel that he is no longer a house-keeper. I am sorry for him — sorry for the necessity. I brought corn at 4. & 4.05 cts pr bl — some brought 4.25. I got a stack of hay for 9. estimated at 50 @ 75 cts pr 100 lbs. The mules were old & sold low.

December 26 — George came up to day. Had a serious talk with him. I fear he is grievously back-slidden — yet I trust he will be restored. He goes to church and pays his dues & I do not know of any immoral habits. O for the full restoration of my dear son!

December 27 — To day I had my father & mother — Tom Sydnor & family, Bro Wm. & wife — Sister Florence — Eliza Rutherford — W.R. Browder — cousin David Sydnor — Francis Page — Bro E.R. Harrison & a lot of young boys — & my granddaughter Lizzie Roach to dinner with us & my good wife had a magnificent dinner — as good as any poor preacher is able to set before his friends — a fine, fat turkey gobler — nice old ham — fresh or new chives, several sorts of bread, good butter, celery, potatoes sweet & Irish, divers pickles & preserves, cheese & crackers, as good I ever tasted, pound cakes, fruit cakes — chest-cakes — mince pies & plenty of rich sweet milk — all served up in good style and eaten with zest by old and young. We may never be able to afford the like again.

December 31 — Up early to go to Russellville and to get our cook & family off to Nashville. Changing servants is troublesome, but sometimes a relief. We are glad to see these go.

January 1, 1882 – I am thankful to be alive another year. I think I have been rather a more uniformly consistent Christian the past year than the years gone by. I always see much to condemn in myself, but I think I see *less* this past year than usual. I lean upon Christ with a steady comfortable trust & have a fixed & steadfast purpose to press on & be faithful to the end.

January 9 – I called to see & pray with Harmon Bailey, dined with sister Annie – thankful to see her so comfortably set up for house-keeping.

January 11 – My 55th Birthday. It looks strange that I am an old man – 55 years old! I am slowly failing in strength of body & perhaps in quickness of mind & memory. I see that my endurance diminishes & my hearing is duller & sight not quite so keen – yet I can read ordinary print without glasses. I am very fleshy – & long riding wearies me. I do not sleep so soundly as formerly and have more trouble with my stomach, liver and kidneys – but I have had less rheumatism this winter than last. I feel that my days are passing.

January 13 – I went through the rain to Olmstead – took train to Kellys Station beyond Hopkinsville on the Crofton cir[cuit] in time to go to Jas M. Miles' to dinner. He met me with his horse Walter & showed me the way. He is a clever, plain man – in a poor country, with a large family. The similarity in the names of his children is singular – Nancy Ann, Nancy Jane, Anna, Sylvester & Sylvanus. I slept warm & well under plenty of cover in a hall between two rooms.

January 14 – Bro Miles & I reached Bethlehem [Church] in due time. The house was cold & the congregation moderate. Bro Drake, the preacher was not present. Quarterly Conference seemed harmonious, but alittle discouraged about the preachers failure to come. They paid me 7.25 cts. I preached again at night – to a congregation mostly of sinners and Universalists – Heb[rews] 6.20 – had some liberty.

January 15 – House full & some out of doors. I felt moved to preach Mat[thew] 5.25 – on account of the strong Universalist influence in this country – had some clearness & some unction. After dinner I returned with Bro Miles. The children all seemed glad to see me. I have taken pains this trip to give good instruction to the children.

January 16 – Back to Kellys Station by Bro Miles' kindness & the strength of his horses William & Walter – laid over several hours at Guthrie & came home through a hard rain. Hanson met me at the depot with a horse, but Dr Russells horse had broken loose and left him – so I lent mine to him & walked home through the dark – so dark.

January 17 – I received the Oxford Teachers Bible, that I ordered & am delighted with it – think it the best arranged Bible I ever saw – Tables, notes, maps, index, concordance, names – with meaning and pronunciation – marginal readings & references, birds, reptiles, rivers &c described – bound in heavy morocco – flexible back.

January 25 – I was suddenly called to see Wm Mills' daughter Lou reported dying. I found her patient – trustful – resigned & ready – had been expecting to join the church, ever since she was converted last Aug at Camp Meeting – but had not been at meeting when she could – wanted to be received & baptized. I prayed & talked with her & baptized her – then her sister Harriet, sick in another room, also a convert at a Methodist meeting, desired to be baptized & received into church – which service I performed. These children of a Baptist family wish to die in the Methodist church & being of age could act for themselves. These cases demonstrate the advantages of affusion over immersion, in the administration of water baptism.

January 31 – Went to see my father & also visited Mrs Hogan – a poor widow very ill with Pneumonia. Sent her a load of coal as she was entirely out – & the snow 5 in. deep. To pray for the poor & not help them when we ought does but little good.

February 8 – The N. bound train – Capt Lytle in command – halted at Olmstead – started before we got off & was stopped – started again before all the passengers could get on. Dave Hendricks was on the step coming in & was told by me & the brakeman to get down until the passengers got out. The train pushed off again before he could get aboard – he called to the conductor to stop the train or else he would sue the company. Rev R.R. Brown – chief of Russellville police was waiting to get on & did so, while the train was in motion. Hendricks still called aloud, "Bring that train back or I'll sue the Road. I'll sue the road." The Agent E.A. Vick told him to be quiet – that the train would come back for him. The train stopped just at the mail box – 30 or 40 steps from the end of the platform nearest it. Hendricks started but Vick the Agent said Dont do that. Stand just where you are, the train will come back to you. Mr Hendricks called out angrily "bring that train back here or Ill sue the company." He had a large valise – he said it weighed 50 lbs. The train stood still long enough for him to have *walked* to it, but it did not come to the platform. Vick the Agent waved his hat violently to the train & called on them to come back – but the train started off – & left Hendricks standing on the platform. He called immediately for paper & wrote down the names of divers persons who were present – & witnessed the occurrence – declaring that he would sue the Company & make them pay for leaving him. He took my name as a witness and I write this true statement to assist my memory if I should be compelled to testify.

Volume IX
1882–1883

"It will be sweeter to meet each other in Heaven when we have loved and sympathized with each other here."

February 9, 1882 – In Autumn 1846 – I began to keep a diary & with occasional interruptions, have kept it up. I am not certain that it has been of much value to me or will be to others, yet there is some pleasure in looking back & reading over the events of my unprofitable life.

February 10 – Lizzie & I went to see Helen. Came home and was looking at my ewe with three young lambs when Hanson exclaimed – "Oh! Uncle Williams barn is on fire." Sure enough it was. John Boyer & his boys had been stripping tobacco, built up a fire – & instead of getting water & putting it out – he undertook to *stamp* it out. I suppose coals or sparks fell in the surrounding trash. My brother, that very day had remonstrated with him for taking fire to the barn. This is a sad loss to Wm – just recovering from the burning of his dwelling last Dec. 12. He loses now, a good frame barn, almost new – his reaper and drill & plows &c and nearly all his crop of tobacco – a loss of $1000 to a man already in debt and hard pressed.

February 17 – Reading and writing alittle. A large company of young people from Russellville & this neighborhood came in to spend the evening – kept me up until 12 Oclock. Lillie Stark, Johnnie Butt, Albina Alexander, Rose Bailey, Lizzie Brown, Jessie Shaw – from the College – & Ella Vick & Fannie Porter – from Russellville, Ida Vick, Mattie & Helen Browder of Olmstead – also Ernest Vick, Bob Young, Rice Gill, Willie Brock Browder, & my bro Jimmy & nephew Fletcher, & our own boys with Wallace Sydnor, make a merry crowd.

February 28 – Up early & off for home [from Hopkinsville]. Went by Sadlersville to see George. He came in in time to go back with me to Guthrie where we talked over his plans. He has been imprudent about going in debt, but has done as much work as could be expected under the circumstances. He left on the train – but in a few moments was back on the freight train with a poor boy who had fallen from the engine, or "tender" in front of the train and had both legs cut off – the left just above the ankle, the right above the knee. George was taken on to assist in the case & the poor boy was taken off at Guthrie – the most fearful maiming that I ever saw. He·spoke of his mother as deprived of her only son – "Oh! my mother" he said. I asked his mothers residence & told him she should be called at once by telegraph. "Yes and she'll come" he said. "Four children and only 1 boy & here I am cut down. No more will I ever get about & do as I have done. Ill never be able to work any more." Then he cried – & said "oh how I suffer." I got down by him & tried to comfort him. "Possibly you may recover" I said but he answered "Oh no Ill never be taken out of this house alive." I said "My poor boy, I'm a minister. I want to point you to Jesus Christ who is able to save you even now. Trust your soul & body to him even in this hour of extremity," but he made no reply. The doctors gave him whiskey and morphine and prepared for the unavoidable amputation. The bones were ground to pieces like a finger nail for size – & there was no hope to save either leg. I have not seen such a sight before – hope I shall not again. That awful stump – the flesh cut & sewed up & the leg gone – it was too bad – but the poor fellow was chloroformed and unconscious of his agony. My train came. I could do no more & left him. George staid with him – his mother came – but there was no reaction – his prophecy was true – he was carried out dead, the next day – died that night. The young mans name was Pike, and lived at Earlington. I would like to know more of his history. He seemed brave & noble in remembering his mother. I was told he begged to be killed when he knew his condition.

March 2 – Gave Hanson some help, loading our little crop of tobacco, sold to John B. Hutchings at 5 cts pr lb loose. The yield was very small – hardly 500 lbs pr acre – 2793 lbs in all.

March 8 – Not very well. I wrote to W. H. Cato. Crofton Mission [Christian County] gives me trouble. People want preaching & the preacher fails to come. I send another & he fails.

March 9 – Most of the day, yesterday and all night last night up to this writing 9 A.M. a cold dreary rain from the East & S.E. has continued. Our cistern for the first time is level with the surface of the ground. The streams will be on a big boom again. Such continuous high waters have never been known as we have had this winter. Tennessee river, I suppose has never been so high & living people have never seen Cumberland in such a flood. The Ohio has seldom if ever caused such distress – 60 feet above low winter mark – and the Miss. & other southern rivers are now flooding the country – by thousands of square miles & tens of thousands of people are driven from their homes – many of them in destitution & suffering – stock drowned, crops destroyed, houses washed away, or water covered, to the very eaves. Boats cannot land – passengers describe many houses almost covered & people looking anxiously & sadly out of the upper windows. Those of us free from such calamities cannot realize their sufferings. We ought to be thankful for our exemption and willing to render all the assistance we can, with justice to those who depend on us.

March 12 – The afternoon was threatening and the night dark. I staid home and read the Bible. Of late there is a special charm to me in reading the Scriptures. I have read more Scripture in the past six weeks, than in six months previously.

March 13 – Last night Lizzie & I were here alone. It seems strange to have no children with us. Sent Robert 10.00 to pay for mackerel and herrings – best we have had for a long time. I find it well to sell alittle bacon & buy alittle fish for variety – it is economy & comfort.

March 18 – Fearful mud, not safe on horseback. Fine Saturday congregation at Duncans chapel [Logan County] – preached with utterance & power, on the parable of the talents. I dined with Bro Keaton, a poor man, but hospitable & kind. Jas King told me once that a rich man considers it a charity to feed his preacher, often, when a *poor* man feels it a *privilege.*

March 30 – George left us yesterday for Sadlersville, thence to Fairview, where he expects to locate. He seemed rather sad & I was sorry to see him leave. His books show good work but he cannot collect. His credit will suffer unless I help him which I will do as far as my ability and justice to my other children will allow. A little pressure may teach him a valuable lesson, as to the propriety of earning money before spending it.

Rev J. W. Bunton writes that he is going into an "invalid home & faith cure" at Louisville and wants his goods shipped there. I think Bunton is an excellent devoted man. I wish I could fully enjoy the peace that he seems to realize. I believe in prayer for Gods blessing, on all *means* employed, but I do not understand that the Scriptures teach us to expect *miraculous* body cures – any more than *miraculous* supplies of "daily bread." The prayer for both implies the use of means.

April 3 – [Hopkinsville] Dr Brown told me of some universalists who were greatly pleased with the morning sermon [at Hall's Chapel] & gave alittle money in the collection but were outraged at the idea of a hell, as brought out at night & wished they had their money back. (The *whole* collection was 55 cts!) I told him to tell them that I did not get any of the money or I would give it back to them.

April 11 – [Olmstead] The papers are full of accounts of the killing of Jesse James, the bandit & robber at St Joseph, Mo. by Robt Ford, a detective who had been in James's gang. Reports of robberies of over $20,000 are given & many robberies with no amounts stated. The band has been the terror of the country for 16 years – have killed perhaps 100 people. They robbed the Russellville Bank in 1868, and got the money I had deposited there for Helen. Woodson Hite a son of George Hite of this county was afterward induced to go with them and was recently killed by some of the company. A younger brother of his Clarence Browder Hite – named for me, also went in and is now in the Missouri penitentiary for 25 years. Ford is much censured for killing James as he did, shooting him behind his back, and is doubtless a very bad man – but James would never have been taken alive & was an outlaw no more entitled to life than a mad dog. He married Zarelda Mimms, who lived in this neighborhood, & has been at my house. The Mimms & Jameses are clever people. The outlaw's father Rev Robert James was a pious & popular Baptist minister.

April 13 – Have sore throat & think it not prudent to go to prayermeeting. Sorry I am getting to feel the necessity of taking more care of my outer man. Brethren at Hopkinsville want me to preach on baptism, Sunday week. I must study the subject more. Have read the Bible a great deal of late – am fully satisfied that infants ought to be baptized and trained & taught in the church – & that affusion is the primitive mode of baptising – but I am certain that Baptists are honest & sincere in their differences of opinion. I make no war on them.

April 20 – At home reading – working the garden alittle. Tomorrow I go to Hopkinsville – thence to Dist[rict] Conf[erence] & then to Genl. Conference – not much at home, for some time to come.

April 21 — Met David Morton at Guthrie, staid with him in Hopkinsville. We talked until two oclock. I preached at night to a moderate congregation — Heb[rews] 6.20 with no great liberty. Had been expecting to preach a sermon on the mode of baptism — but found the preachers Bottomley & Brewer desired me to preach on Infant Baptism, so I had to study up that subject — & was weary.

April 23 — Rainy. Congregation moderate — preached with more liberty & success than I expected the *first* regular sermon I ever preached on Infant Baptism — dealt kindly — lovingly with those who differ with us — made some good points — not as systematic as it might have been.

April 24 — I left after breakfast — got home before 9 A.M. Hurrah for Rail-Roads!

April 25 — Went to Allensville to find a suit of clothes, did not find them to fit.

April 26 — Hanson & I went to Hopkinsville. I looked over Elkton, Fairview & Hopkinsville, but did not find clothes to fit, that suited me. Saw George — heard that he is doing well.

April 27 — Came to Hebron this morning to Dist[rict] Conf[erence]. No Bishop — so I presided, as best I could.

April 30 — Bright sky — good roads, cool air & Hebron grove was crowded with horses, carriages & people. Excellent love-feast. At 11, I preached 77 minutes to a packed & jammed audience in the house & as many out of doors — on Sauls Conversion — Acts 9.17–18. Altogether this has been a delightful District Conference and Hebron hospitality has been equal to every demand. Everyday the table groaned beneath a load of luxuries — fatted fowl & lambs & hams — pickles, fruits — cakes — pies & bread of extra quality — all freely given to *all* who came. Not only our own people, but other denominations coming in with full baskets — & opening their doors to our guests. Well done Hebron! Hanson made an ingenious speech in favor of Bethlehem yesterday [as the site of the next District Conference] & beat Auburn & Trenton in the vote. We left after dinner & went to Fairview.

May 1 — This morning I gave George 10. beside the 10. I gave him Apr 26. Stopped in Elkton & found a nice hat to fit me — 3.00, got home to dinner — was sad to hear of the death of my friend & neighbor John Vick last Friday. I must see my father this evening as I leave for General Conference tomorrow morning.

May 2 — Lizzie & I found a number of friends on the train, going to Nashville. We paid the hack 1.00 & landed at Bro Tigerts door, most kindly received. I went to the city in the afternoon & bought a suit of clothes from Bolivar H. Cook & Co. for 26.50 — good clothes but not what I wanted. I am hard to fit.

May 3 – General Conference convened – most of the delegates answered to roll call. Our venerable Bishop Paine was in the chair. Dr Thos O. Summers, looking more dead than alive, was elected Secretary. I called to see him yesterday – found him very feeble, but full of spirit & resolved to work. He seems to expect to die at the Genl Conference – and go from the Genl Conf. to the one in glory! He was elected by a rising vote – & went home exhausted. In the afternoon we met & I was appointed on the Committee on Boundaries.

May 4 – Organization harmoniously completed. Committees called together & I was elected Chairman of my committee, much to my surprise, as we were all strangers to each other. Poor Dr Summers is failing. I helped him out of his carriage & assisted him to a seat – he seemed rather to fall than to sit in it.

May 5 – Dr Summers reported very ill. I went to see him. He was unconscious.

May 6 – Our good & great Dr Summers is dead! Our hearts are very sore & sad. He was such a friend to my sons – was so pure & so wise. Who can fill his places – Teacher of Systematic Theology in Vanderbilt University, Book editor – editor of Quarterly Review – Sec. of Genl Conf. &c. We are bereft indeed. The whole church mourns. The Genl. Conf. adjourned the morning session, in respect to his memory. He will rest beside the remains of McKendree & Soule, on the Vanderbilt Campus – buried by his brethren.

May 7 – I went to the penitentiary, by request & preached to the convicts. Mr Watkins, the colored chaplain, treated me most courteously. My text was Mat[thew] 11.19. Every eye seemed fixed upon me, and there was much weeping both amongst the white & colored prisoners. A number of small negro boys sat just before me. I made a personal appeal to them, to stop – & do wrong no more. I was deeply impressed with the importance of this work, and would have preferred this to any other appointment for the day. At 4 P.M. the largest crowd assembled at the Vanderbilt, that was ever on these grounds, to attend the burial of our lamented & beloved Dr Summers. Bishop Keener preached a plain, dull sermon – & the General Conference buried our distinguished brother.

May 8 – Our new Secretary, Dr J. S. Martin of Baltimore, does his work well – reads loud enough to be heard above the hum & buzz of the throng that crowds the Conference & the continual conversation that makes our body seem disorderly. General Conferences do not behave any better than Annual Conferences.

May 9, 10, 11 – Nothing of remarkable interest, except the report of Publishing Agent and Book Committee – which represents the Publishing House, as about being relieved of its embarrassment – with good hope of ultimate success. The details of settlement between the Book Committee and Rev A. H. Redford, Ex Agent puts the latter in so unenviable a light, that all the Louisville delegation united in asking the Genl Conference to allow him to explain – which was granted and for three hours – he read rapidly and impressively a most ingenious & artful presentation of his side of the question – not *denying* a single point in the Committees Report, but showing, that the figures though right, did not prove what the Committee claimed – & endeavoring also to show that Dr McFerrin had done what *he* (Redford) is censured for doing. There was much laughter & applause, as his keen thrusts seemed to put the Committee at a disadvantage & many thought his vindication complete – but I was sad & sore – & felt that he had failed to explain, to my satisfaction, transactions that my conscience condemns. Dr McFerrin & Judge Whitworth, feeling themselves assailed, asked & obtained leave to reply & their rejoinders made the transactions look worse than before. He, Redford, published books as an individual – & sold them to himself as Agent, at 156 pr cent profit, by whole editions – leaving the house to take the chance of sales & collections, while he made a profit of 17,000.00 dollars on his publications – while at the same time he was getting 5,000.00 pr year salary as Agent – & part of those books were turned over to his successor unsold. He was also owning & keeping a Book-store in Louisville, with which he dealt as Agent & charged the house in Nashville 10 pr ct advance on books bought for it from Eastern houses & shipped directly to Nashville having these books rebilled at Louisville – without ever stopping there. He claims that money was worth 10 pr cent – but 10 pr ct pr annum & 10 pr ct on an invoice of books between N.Y. & Nashville, which he bought as a paid Agent are different things. I shall send his defense to his friends and mine & hope that he did not *intend* to do any wrong, yet I am not satisfied. I cannot justify a wrong, if my best friend does it. He will never recover from this shock. He asked leave to reply again – but the Conference declined unanimously to spend any more time on the personal explanations. Charity hopeth all things – he still has many friends.

May 12, 13 – Crowds of visitors from the Southern church are coming in. The Conference is perfectly sandwiched with men & women who are not members. The question How many Bishops, excites large discussion & takes up much time. Six & four are the numbers contended for. I am for four.

May 15 – After much talk & much time we concluded to elect 5 Bishops & do it tomorrow.

May 16 – Immense crowd. Conference ordered, on Bishop McTyeires suggestion, that the chairman of each delegation collect the vote of that delegation & put it in the hat or box of the tellers. It was an admirable suggestion – the only one that, under the circumstances, could have secured absolute certainty. Dr A. W. Wilson was elected by *one vote* on the first ballot & Dr A. G. Haygood only lacked *two* votes of election. Afternoon session Linus Parker, A. G. Haygood & J. C. Granberry were elected on second ballot – Dr R. K. Hargrove only lacking *two* votes of election. Another ballot was ordered & he was elected overwhelmingly. The applause was wonderful and exciting – when ever the figures indicated an election. The result is marvellous. Gods hand must be in it. Such unanimity growing suddenly out of such uncertainty was startling. Was it an answer to prayer?

May 17 – Conference was surprised – amazed, by Dr Haygoods declining to accept the Episcopacy on the conviction that his duty called him to another field. He rises immensely in moral power, by this devotion to his conviction, but the Conference regrets his action. I think we ought not to elect another. The Episcopal bee has buzzed busily in many ears – now he will be silent a while.

May 18 – Conference agreed to organize a church extension society. I think I will advocate the election of David Morton as Sec[retary]. I was pleased with the action in declining to elect another bishop *vice* Dr Haygood. At 4 Oclock P.M. in the audience room of new McKendree church, Bishop Paine consecrated Alpheus W. Wilson, Linus Parker, John C. Granberry and Robert K. Hargrove as Bishops in the Methodist E. Church, South – in the presence of an immense throng – the first ordination of Bishops I ever witnessed and the last the dear old Bishop Paine will ever do. He is so frail & feeble, that he stood with difficulty. I doubt if he ever preaches another sermon or performs another ministerial service. The church seems satisfied with the selections for Episcopacy. I voted for all who were elected, except Dr. Haygood & if I had my work to do again, I should vote for him. He is a better, greater man than he has been represented to me.

May 19 – Much talk makes Conference business tedious.

May 20 – In accord with a resolution, the Conference went to call on Mrs Jas K. Polk widow of Ex-president Polk. We were cordially received, introduced by name & shook hands with the distinguished lady. She looks old, but graceful and elegant – said she appreciated the delicate compliment. I am appointed to preach at the Penitentiary tomorrow, by request of Chaplain and prisoners.

May 21 – When I got to the prison I found an order from the Physician forbidding any visitors to enter on account of small pox rumor. I went to West End church & was called upon to administer the Sacrament of the Lords Supper. I requested Bishop McTyeire but he declined. There were many preachers, ordained and unordained – and I felt embarrassment, officiating in the presence of the Bishop.

May 22 – Conference progresses slowly. We elected J. B. McFerrin – Book Agent, W. P. Harrison – Book editor, R. A. Young – Missionary Secretary, D. C. Kelley – Missionary Treasurer, David Morton – Secretary of Church Extension Society, O. P. Fitzgerald – Editor of Advocate, W. G. E. Cunnyngham – S. School Secretary & editor.

May 23 – An episode in Conference routine was the appearance of the "Jubilee Singers" – a group of African men & women – seemingly pure blood negroes –

giving an exhibition of their musical talent. They were well-dressed and educated. A young woman played splendidly on the organ and they sang several songs, in such symphony & beauty that many of us were melted to tears. They were loudly applauded, encored & praised. It was indeed a rare treat – which we hugely enjoyed.

May 25 – After a hard days work and an afternoon session – Conference adjourned at 6 Oclock P.M.

May 26 – Off to my sweet home! I found Luther at Olmstead with the buggy.

May 27 – I looked over the place alittle, then got dinner & rode 16 miles to Stuarts School [Logan County] house for tomorrows service – *very very* tired – worn out when I left Nashville.

May 28 – Bro Stuart & family give me the best their house affords & I am grateful for their humble hospitality. I get no financial pay this trip. They paid Bro Frogge less than 6.00 pr month this Quarter. Many of these people can barely live. Country poor – crops a failure.

June 2 – [Olmstead] I noted, carefully, Dr Redfords reply to the Book Committee & Dr McFerrin. Part of his reply is clear & vindicates him – part of it is neither ingenuous nor satisfactory. He makes McFerrin a villain & a persecuting knave – but does not give the proof. His very soul is bitter as the waters of Marah and he seems to live amid the storms of Mt Ebal. Poor man, I wish he could see his own faults as clearly as he thinks he sees the faults of others. The Womans missionary meeting is held at our house this evening. My wife is President. Wallace is President of the Juvenile Society, Luther is out trying to sell a religious book. George writes that he is doing some practice – has had an adventure helping to arrest the negro burglars that robbed Shaw & Vaughans store in Fairview. They caught six & put them in jail – have recovered most of the stolen goods. I learn today that W. R. Browders granary has been robbed of 20 bu. of wheat. I fear that theft will increase as the supply of provision diminishes.

June 4 – [Gordonsville] I called to see uncle Billy Washington. The poor old man is very frail. I paid 6.50 on his board. Dear old saint, his poverty will soon end in the riches of heaven.

June 6 – [Olmstead] George, my Dr boy came up to see us – seems to be doing well in his practice – but gets no money.

June 17 – I went to Wash Sydnors – talked with him about the trouble between him and Ed Hughes, tried to be wise as a serpent, and harmless as a dove – hope the difficulty will be reconciled. Wash seems ready to do right & confess his wrong.

June 18 — I spent the night pleasantly at Ed Hughes — talked over the trouble between him and the Sydnors. He seemed disposed to do right & I think he & Wash will be neighborly, if not *brotherly*. I had a pleasant visit — tried to be prudent and faithful.

June 19 — I called to see Wash again & found him pleased with the idea of reconciliation and grateful for my efforts. Cousin Ed [Hughes] gave me a beautiful 'Shepherd' puppy, which I brought home in my arms & in my saddlebags.

June 22 — Lizzie & I went to see Tom Sydnor, sick with flux — then out into the field to see Davids new self binder cut and bundle up the wheat.

June 23 — *Minor* came in & reported the two young mules Jack & Jerry, which Hanson had chained together — to be in a tangle & one choking the other to death. I ran out & found it even so. Jerry was down & Jack dragging him by the neck. All we could do could not save him. He was dead in a few minutes and we had to cut the chain with a chisel to save the other one. That is a costly lesson to us, to fasten stock with something that can be *cut* in case of accident. The mule was worth about 100.00. The tieing seemed a necessity, to keep them out of mischief.

June 26 — This is court day & many people in town. I heard Clarence M. McElroy & John Halsell, both of Bowling-green — candidates for Congress — address the people. McElroy is a sprightly, young man, but Halsell carried the crowd. There was a sale of buggies, carriages &c — at Auction. I bought a buggy & harness at 36.00 but the lot was afterward sold as a whole to one man & I did not get the buggy.

June 29 — Bro F. A. Yost spent the day with us. I bought from him a set of Springs for a bed at 5.00 which I hope will add to my wife's comfort although her economy opposes the purchase.

July 2 — [Pleasant Grove] Cloud — threatening — good love-feast — fine congregation at 11, considerable liberty preaching on Diversity of gifts — 1st Cor[inthians] 4.7. Good sacramental service. My Bro David came for me to preach the funeral of little Mattie, daughter of Jno. T. Young, who died last night, with Flux. I made a hard, muddy drive to reach Dr Baileys just after the body was laid in the grave — and there to a large concourse of sympathizing friends, I spoke the words of life in a short earnest discourse — then went to see John Young's family & spent the night at Dr Bailey's. All sad at their sore bereavement & the second grand child Dr B. has lost lately — little Daniel Bailey Sadler dying two weeks ago with flux.

July 3 — I called to see George Sadlers family — had some words of comfort & prayers, then got home about 10. A.M. Dave Hendricks came over & desired me to become his security for suit against the R.R. Co — in the matter referred to Feb 8th, 1882 — but I was not willing to go on the bond, and advised him against the suit. I have received the first number of the "Gladiator" the new paper, published by my old friend A. H. Redford D.D. There are some good things in it — but I am sorry he introduces into the first number, the quarrel he is waging against Dr. McFerrin & the Book Committee.

July 4 — This "Independence Day" seems to have gone into disuse as an occasion of big displays & speechmaking, in our country.

July 8 — A rough ride to Grissom's Chapel — a small congregation — an earnest sermon — a poor financial report — 7.50 for P[residing] E[lder] & P[reacher in] C[harge]. This is the second trip I have made to Crofton cir[cuit] & did not receive a cent for services.

July 12 — [Olmstead] The papers report war between Egypt and England, Alexandria bombarded yesterday & several of the forts destroyed. Wonderful telegraph, to tell in a few minutes what is done across the world.

July 25 — Threshing wheat — reaper not running well — but cleaning wheat well — gets on slowly. The boys finished threshing wheat and put it away in good dry condition — 675 bushels on 50 acres — two acres of which was badly drowned out. A good crop & we are thankful.

August 11 — My daughter and her sweet little children called to see us this evening. They are bright & pretty children but not taught as they ought to be. Helen is not strong, and her pleasant manners and warm hospitality keep her house full of company that she has but little time for her family. That is one of the objectionable features of our neighborhood. There is a constant influx of visitors — that diverts attention from business and from study. Comparatively few hours I have to devote to study and reflection. I have been trying to read some today, but have done but little.

August 14 — I learn that Harriet Mills died on Saturday & they sent for me to preach the funeral. My dear old school mate W. C. Mills has been sadly bereft — four grown daughters dead.

August 15 — Resting and reading at home — but reading does not seem to profit me. I fail to remember well — too much work and too little study.

August 16 — I called to see Dr Blakey & family, found him sick in bed. I slipped & fell as I got down from my horse, bruising my shoulder alittle & badly soiling my clothes, as cattle had been standing about the gate.

August 22 — I got home at night [from Bell's Chapel] worn out. I found as usual several letters to answer. My precious little grand-child Sue Robert was the first one to meet me – a bright, lively little chatterbox. Thank God for my home & family.

August 25 – [Parsons Grove camp meeting] At 11 I preached on the right of sinners to pray and be prayed for. I had some liberty & some unction – invited penitents but none came. I came home to entertain Bishop McTyeire & Dr J. B. McFerrin. The Bishop was detained alittle at Nashville. Luther waited at Olmstead until 1 Oclock A.M. & brought the Bishop over through the rain. We had a pleasant time – first Bishop I have entertained.

August 27 – Good love-feast at 9. Fine sermon by Bishop McT. at 11 on Sin. "He that saith he hath no sin deceiveth himself" &c – a clear, logical, sound, incisive sermon. I followed with an earnest exhortation, called penitents, one young lady came and was soon happily converted. There was an immense throng. I should say 2000. people – some said 3000. I never saw as many buggies at a camp-meeting & yet the behavior was admirable.

August 28 – Immense congregation for Monday. Sweet melting time at morning meeting. Bro. Tigert preached a superior sermon at 11. At 3, Bro Emerson preached one of his best and most earnest sermons and at night Bro S. R. Brewer preacher a sound sermon on the doom of the wicked. The sinners seem hard to move.

August 29 – Still the crowds come and listen with interest. Morning meeting a sweet time – at 11, Dr Hanner preached the finest sermon of the meeting & one seldom surpassed for beauty & thought by any man living or dead. I was surprised to hear such a sermon from a man 72 years old. I felt inclined & made him a present of 10.00 feeling the more tenderly toward him, because he had married me to my wife. The meeting as a revival does not measure up to former ones.

August 30 – Lizzie & I came home with our family. Luther is preparing to leave for Vanderbilt & I must take my cousin Courtenay Meade to Alex. Fulchers in Todd Co. where I hope to get her a school that will support her. Bro Tigert came home with us – we were talking of the camp-meeting and the grand preaching – the best as a whole I ever heard at a camp-meeting or any where else – & I was praising Dr Hanners sermons – when Lizzie Warfield said, "A young preacher said he had read part of that Sunday sermon in a book." I demanded the author of the statement and she gave my son Luther. I demanded Luthers authority and he went & brought a copy of "Sunday Magazine" & read out of Dr C. F. Deem's sermon on "Christ satisfied" &c – two columns & more, verbatim et liberatim of the beautiful thought and language of the sermon that so pleased us all. I had heard before that he borrowed largely, even the woof & web of a whole sermon – but had no positive detection until now. I suppose he has a conception of it that justifies. I would have thought much better of it – if he had given Dr Deems credit. The rest may be borrowed, as well. What we learn is all we know, but down-right plagiarism is mean in the eyes of most people.

August 31 – I go with Courtenay – reached Bro Alick Fulcher's [Pembroke] at 3 P.M. We are kindly received & after an excellent dinner, rode around to see the patrons. Fulcher has four or five children & will board the teacher, for their tuition and give her all the tuition of other scholars. I advise her to remain.

September 4 – [Olmstead] Annual Conference is nearly here, and I have most of my personal preparation to make – it seems impossible for me, to meet all the demands upon me, and also *study* & prepare sermons.

September 5 – Hail welcome day! Thirty two years ago I was married to my wife who in all these years has been the truest, best friend of my life. How I regret the needless pain that I have caused her to feel. My poor weak impulsive nature has often caused me to say or do things that I ought not. I have been blessed beyond deserving – especially in the wife and children that God has given me.

September 11 – I gave Wallace money to go to Louisville & get him a suit of clothes. He has been one of the best children in *every respect* that I ever knew – has worked faithfully all the season and deserves some recreation – and now that rates are $3.05 for a round trip it is not very expensive to let him make a visit to his brother – & to the Exposition – & the Fair. George wants to go also & see a Dr about his eyes – which have caused him trouble & Helen & Charley want to go & get some supplies. So the bait of cheap fare catches many people & makes them spend time and money foolishly. The cars were so crowded that there was barely standing room inside.

September 16 – [Chandler's Chapel] I preached to a fine Saturday congregation on Immortality of the Soul. Quarterly Conference was pleasant. People appreciate Gilliams service & success & want him back – are trying to pay him. I dined with the good Baptist Sister Patterson – the first woman or man that ever seriously called me *old* – when I was 35 years old or earlier than that. She is now 71 yrs old and still insisted that I let her take my horse & feed it! I wondered what sort of preachers she had seen – to think I could sit down & let her feed my horse, when I was able & strong to it myself. I stay with old mother Chandler in her 93d year – yet walks ¾ of a mile to and from church, both at morning and night service for a whole week.

September 17 – Gilliam laughs heartily at the expression of an Old Baptist sister – praising my preaching. She said – "I tell thats a splendid preacher" – then a pause & she repeated it – adding "The old thing reasons well." "The old thing" tickled Gilliam.

September 18 – I met the board of [Logan Female] college Directors at Russellville & we agreed to borrow money on the property, for the completion of several additional rooms, that are now in demand for scholars already in the house – & engaged to come in. I got home in the night very tired & found my dear little Lizzie Roach very ill with Scarlet fever & Ruth also not well. I helped nurse them through the night.

September 22 – Lizzie Roach seems better. Ruth looks pale & does not eat – hope she will not take the fever. I have not seen Wallace for nearly two weeks – must keep him at his sisters until danger of the dread fever is gone.

I called to see Sister Annie and her baby – a chubby, sweet little girl. I went over & spent the night with Dr J. R. Bailey, who was anxious to talk to me about his spiritual condition & did so with deep concern – such, he said, as he had not expressed to any one before in his life. He is a good upright man – does not *know* that he loves God only through man. I talked with him as well as I knew how.

September 26 – Very busy writing sermon on Prov[erbs] 11.30 "He that winneth souls is wise." I design it for my Conference sermon. Lizzie Roach has been restless – complaining of pain in her stomach & great nausea. Dr Peter came & feared inflammation of the stomach.

September 27 – Went to depot and got ice and rice for Lizzie Roach.

September 28 – My precious child is no better, rather worse. We called in Dr J. R. Bailey this evening. Lizzie has a fearful fever and is passing bloody water & mucous, from her bowels – with inward soreness.

September 29 – A sad anxious night of watching, to my dear wife & Helen. At 4 Oclock A.M. Hanson was called up to go to Russellville after more ice. He was back in about 3 hours from the time he started – 20 miles – and time to buy the ice. The Dr thinks there are indications of a favorable change.

September 30 – Lizzie symptoms so much more favorable that I went to Crofton – could neither hire nor borrow a horse – found a wagon going to the neighborhood of Concord – rode 9 miles on that – then walked a mile or more to Jas. R. Browns, got supper & rode in his wagon two miles over hills & rocks & gulleys, preached to a good congregation of most attentive listeners 1st Cor[inthians] 7.4 – & slept soundly at Bro W. H. Cato's – being cordially welcomed to his humble home. He said "the fare is rough, but there's plenty of it." I found it good enough for me.

October 1 – Love-feast late. House crowded at 11 & many out of doors. I had liberty preaching on soul winning Prov[erbs] 11.30. Waited for 9 ½ train and went to Guthrie – sat there until 1 A.M. & took train to Olmstead – got home – at 2 Oclock A.M. Very thankful to find my precious grand-daughter greatly improved. I am much worn with the hard trip – but glad I made it. If those people had been rich & prosperous I should not have gone to them.

October 5 – My old buggy is nearly worn out. I had a wheel mended, this morning, then drove down to R. L. Smith's to look at a buggy that Eugene proposed to sell me cheap. It is one of Baker & Bro's best 300. buggies – almost new – no sign of wear on tire spindle or any part, excellent patent wheels –

leather top & curtains — lock box under the seat — all perfect. I bought at $100 and brought it home. My wife and children seemed much pleased.

October 11 — Bishop McTyeire opened Conference. More absentees than usual.

October 12 — Many missing brethren have come in. I was to have preached the Conference sermon tonight, but the Bishop called the presiding elders — and an immense crowd, I learn, was disappointed. I was sorry, but was not at fault.

October 14 — After work all day I staid in at night to study my sermon.

October 15 — I was appointed to preach at 3 P.M. at the ordination of elders. I had considerable liberty. Many brethren expressed high appreciation — & Bishop McTyeire expressed great delight in hearing the sermon.

October 16 — Another day of anxious and exhausting work. The Bishop tells me that the solid men of Louisville earnestly ask my appointment to that District and he had decided to send me. I told him I was not the man, but he says I am and he will expect me to move my family to the city. I feel that it would be a hard work to me and many difficulties, as well as sacrifice to many home interests but I have surrendered myself to God and the church.

October 17 — The Bishop told me this morning, that he had considered the matter, over and over and while he still felt that I was fully equal to the work — he yet felt that it would be a great sacrifice & he had decided not to ask me to make it — much to my relief. I am *sure* that I am wanted on Russellville District — and it is near my home. The Conference by vote on resolution offered by P. T. Hardison and Silas Newton requested me to publish the sermon I preached — either in pamphlet form or in Christian Advocate.

We received our appointments at 11 O clock, and as usual, some brethren were greatly grieved and in much distress. I gave alittle money to two who were in trouble — and surrendered part of my interest in the Missionary claims, to two others.

Jas. A. Lewis was greatly afflicted at being appointed to Elizabeth-town District — & T. C. Peters at his appointment to Greensburg. My judgment was not consulted in either case — but I told the Bishop of the distress of the brethren & he sent Peters to Elizabeth-town District and Lewis back to Adairville. While the train was standing at Bowling-green, Brethren of that city came to the Bishop and protested against the appointment of Dr Redford to that station. I sympathize with both preacher and people. Dr. Redfords love of self & money have been greatly in his way — but he seems to desire to do right — he says he does — but he does not know the extent of opposition to him — I know that he looks upon me as his enemy, because and only because I condemn his course in the Publishing house matters and the controversy growing out of it. Yet I can recall *no* time nor place in which I failed to defend him, where I thought he was wrongly accused.

I found Hanson at the depot, with the buggy and was soon at home with my own dear wife and the only two children now with us. I am very tired and worn out with anxiety.

October 20 — I have the promise of a house for Bro Goodson our Pastor.

October 24 — The boys finished getting in our Irish potatoes — one half acre made nearly 100 bushels. I weighed ten that weighed 8 lbs.

October 26 — Busy at home — writing — thinking — reading.

October 27 — Forepaugh's great show, in Russellville, draws the schools and negroes. Wallace has gone. I went to depot at night to go to Russellville to meet the Directors of Logan Female College, but the train was late and I did not go. Afterwards I regretted it — heard that the Board waited for me. I went to see Tom Bailey's child, very sick — continuation of Scarlet fever.

October 30 — Went with Lizzie to see Tom Baileys sick child. She staid all night to help nurse it.

October 31 — I sat up until midnight to finish writing my Conference sermon — have had to do it by little at a time — 36 pages of letter paper.

November 1 — Went to Olmstead to meet Bro. Goodson's family. Goodson and I went to Allensville to look for a house. Hanson went last night, to set up, again, with Tom Bailey's little Grayson. I went tonight to set up with the corpse. The first death that has occurred in Dr Hutching's family, of children or grand children — and they are very sad. Grayson was the brightest of children.

November 4 — [Chappel Hill in Christian County] Moderate weather. Up early and off soon after sunrise to see Chiles Barker — very ill. A clever, courteous, intelligent gentleman who has a wide influence & is much beloved, but is not a church-member. He is vastly wealthy for this country, worth perhaps half a million dollars. He received me most cordially, inquired after my parents — spoke of his admiration for my father — and his approaching old age. I turned the conversation to that land where old age, disease and death will never come — told him about the comfort I have, in the faith of a meeting with friends, beyond the grave. I saw that he was deeply interested although he has been called skeptical. He said, "Mr Browder, that is a serious problem to me, which I have never been able to solve to my satisfaction." I replied that no living man has personal knowledge of the world beyond, but that I had a strong satisfactory faith in its reality. He said "For which you ought to be very thankful." I said "I trust I am" and then told him of the simplicity of faith in Christ — seeing that in man is no help — it is but reasonable to trust the plan which we believe God has revealed. He said "Mr Browder, I have tried to be a Christian without being a member of any church." I told him that while mere nominal church membership could not save – and while no one denomination of Christians was the church, yet, they were parts of the visible church, and every man ought to make some open confession of Christ and be identified in some way with those who claimed to be his followers and give his influence to His cause. He said *thoughtfully* and with some feeling "I know that is the general opinion but I have not done it." When about to leave, I said Mr Barker, for a long time I have been in the habit of praying with the families I visit, if there be no objection I would be glad to read a portion of scripture and pray with you, if you do not object. He said, "Indeed it would be a very great pleasure to me." He added "I have some peculiar ideas about prayer and yet I suppose few men pray oftener than I do." His wife got the Testament and called in the children. I read in the 4. & 5 chaps of James and knelt by his bed in prayer. There was much feeling and he as well as his family was deeply touched – and with tearful eyes he thanked me for the visit and most cordially invited me to come again. He asked me what I thought the soul is. "Is it that immortal breath of life that God breathed into man?" I said "I think so." He said, looking me earnestly in the face – "Mr Browder, I do not hear many men preach but I would like to hear *you* preach. I have heard a great deal of your preaching and would like to hear you. My wife claims to be greatly benefited by hearing you." I said "I am thankful if my preaching does any body any good."

I write particularly of this visit because it is a lesson to me. Here is a man with all that wealth can give him – yet no rest in his soul and there are thousands of rich men whose minds are uneasy & who need the gospel as much as the poor. I fear that I and my brethren have too often neglected the *very* rich and the *very* poor – though I have been ready, when the door was open to go to both.

November 7 – Bright, pleasant weather – no frost yet. Fields green. I went to Olmstead and voted for John E. Halsell for Congress against Dr Hunter – Republican. Old Mr O. R. Malory first voted and because he said orally who his ticket was for his vote was ruled out. I doubt if that is right. The law forbids the officers to *see* the ticket, but does not prohibit the voter from telling who he votes for.

November 8 – The election news is crushing to the Republicans, all the votes heard from, going Democratic – N. York – Pennsylvania, Indiana – Massachusetts &c.

November 9 – The Democrats are in a glee over the elections. N. York gives Gov[ernor] Cleveland 200,000 majority – so reported.

November 11 – [Hopkinsville] Quarterly Conference at night very pleasant. Brethren had fixed preachers salary at 850.00. Bro Bottomley is kindly received, but the people are very sore over the removal of Bro. Brewer and some of the sisters abuse me & bishop McTyeire but I hope all will work well in the end.

November 14 – [Olmstead] *Cold.* Big frost – first killing frost of the season – potato & bean & tomato vines green & growing up to this date. I have been reading a speech of Senator Vest of Mo. against the prohibitory liquor law proposed by the temperance people of Mo. While I am a temperance man – I think the text of the proposed law will defeat it as it does not allow a man to make his own grapes into wine for use on his own table – nor make or sell wine for the sacramental supper. Pity that we cannot have "zeal according to knowledge."

November 16 – Reading the papers. My bro William is still in Ala[bama] looking for land. I fear, he is making a great mistake. Kentucky is more prosperous than Alabama. Frank has worked hard there for ten years and I doubt if he is worth now the money that father has given him.

November 17 – Wrote to Bishop McTyeire and to several brethren to find a preacher for Crofton mission. Bro R. B. McCown writes me that he has been there and cannot fill the work. I was in hopes that after 12 or 13 years spent in his own interest, under the plea of supernumerary & supernumerate, he would now be in a frame to do good work, as he reported himself effective. I am sorry to have trouble with that mission again.

November 20 – Pressed on home [from Bethel] – got here to dinner and was sad to learn that my Bro Wm had bought land in Ala[bama] and was proposing to leave us, next Christmas – three brothers in Ala[bama], 3 brothers and 2 sisters in Ky. I am sorry for his choice. I fear it is not best for him. It is sad to lose our relations & neighbors from our midst.

November 21 – Lizzie and I went up to see my Bro Wm – not at home. We offered Eliza Rutherford a home at our house. She wept with gratitude & thanked us over and over again. She is so devoted to my father & mother and has been with them so long, that I do not wish to see her separated from them.

November 22 – Reading and writing. Nothing very profitable. *Kind* letter from Sister Brewer, with warm assurance of good will – and disclaiming "a shadow of a thought," that I was at fault about their removal from Hopkinsville. A letter from my brother T. C. Peters, surprises & grieves me. I could hardly have believed that he would feel hurt with me for the change in his appointment after the letter I wrote him – but he is. I wrote again, another heart letter, which I hope he will appreciate and which I hope will satisfy him. If not, I must wait and *endure,* until his own experience as a Presiding Elder shall teach him that he cannot always have done what he would like, nor prevent what he does not like. He is one of the purest, best men we have and has been one of my best friends – as I *am* and have been one of his – there can be no alienation between Tim Peters & me.

November 23 — Last night, I was restless & troubled. I do not rest kindly under censure that I do not deserve. I may err in judgment — doubtless I do — but I am conscious of the integrity of my purposes. I *know* that I have not been the cause of Bro. Peters' change. Hanson took one hand and team to help move Bro. Goodsons furniture to the house he has been so faithfully working to get in order. For three weeks Tom Sydnor & I have had him and his family and find them pleasant, good people.

November 24 — I went in the buggy to Allensville to meet the District Stewards. There was a good attendance and much harmony. They fixed my salary at 1025. and seemed willing to put it higher if I had asked it. A letter from Bro. Bunton tells me that he cannot take Crofton circuit.

November 27 — [Elkton] I called at the Bank, and got 25.00 raised at a concert, for poor old "uncle Billy" Washington. Hayes Petree gave me 5. more & John Street 1.10 & I will add enough to make the sum two month's board — so he does not go yet to the poor house. This concert was in answer to my appeal through the paper.

November 29 — [Olmstead] William is in trouble, his debts are more than he supposed and he is not in condition to meet his proposed payment in Ala[bama]. I wish I was in condition to help him.

December 4 — Reached home just at dark and found that Hanson had killed the hogs & cut them out — & Lizzie was drying up the lard, 12 hogs average 13 months old — weighed 3140 lbs nett — 260 average. Fine hogs, to have been brought up to feeding time with almost no corn — found several letters to answer, one from W. H. Cato abusing me and bishop McTyeire for sending R. B. McCown to Crofton. I have received 75 copies of Christian Advocate of Dec 2nd containing my Conference sermon and mailed several to friends. It is too long — 2 pages of paper & 2 columns on 3d page.

December 19 — Tuesday is generally a weary day with me and my good wife let me sleep late this morning. I wrote to H. G. Petree enclosing check for $90.00 interest on the money we borrowed for Frank. If taking some trouble and some risk enables my brother to secure a home for his family I shall always be glad. I am trying now to help my brother William in his distress. It seems to me it will be sweeter to meet each other in Heaven when we have loved and sympathized with each other here. "Behold! How good and how pleasant it is for brethren to dwell together in unity." This train of thought recalls an incident. On the night of Nov 24, after the family had retired I wrote the following — the substance of which Bro Goodson that night related to us.

An Incident

Rev J. P. Goodson and family have been spending a few days with us.

Tonight he told us this incident that occurred in his younger days. He was a ship-builder by trade and one winter, when work for the season was suspended he went with his brother-in-law down on the waters of the Wabash river in Ind. and built a lumber boat & got a cargo of lumber to freight to the Southern market. In the early Spring they floated out on the Wabash – into the Ohio. On one occasion when the night was clear they pushed out away before day and Goodson took charge of the oars while all the men beside himself retired below and were soon sound asleep. The scene was an inspiring one to the young boatman. The air was cool and bracing, the skies were clear and no cloud nor mist obscured their brightness. All the starry worlds were out in their grandeur each trying to outshine the rest – each in the majesty of silence proclaiming the Creators power and handiwork. The Ohio was clear & smooth and on its glassy bosom were mirrored in perfect outline the grandeurs of the over arching skies – worlds answering to worlds – stars above and stars beneath as if the boat were floating amid the spheres with glittering glories all around. The distant shores were draped in darkness and only the heavens above and heavens below were in reach of the young sailors eye. The stillness and the grandeur of the scene awakened deep thoughts of Gods wisdom and omnipotence, the skill of his hands, the vastitude of his dominions and the stability of his government – and so impressed the pious mind of young Goodson that he broke out in a full-souled song, his clarion voice rolling over the waters and echoing on the shore as if an hundred tongues were ringing on the morning air. Feeling a sense of security, as he thought of the waters bearing up his heavy boat – the song that rose into his heart & rolled out his lips was suggestive –

> How firm a foundation ye saints of the Lord
> Is laid for your faith in his excellent word –
> What more can he say than to you he has said,
> You who unto Jesus for refuge have fled.

At the end of the first stanza he paused and out of the darkness, away down the stream, he heard another voice as clear & strong as his own – catching up the same tune and singing with evident feeling the second verse –

> In every condition in sickness in health
> In povertys rule or abounding in wealth.
> At home or abroad, on the land on the sea –
> As thy days may demand, shall thy strength ever be.

Then calling out in the distance "Sing the next verse." Goodsons heart beat quick as he sang with deepening emotion –

> Fear not, I am with thee, O be not dismayed.
> I, I am thy God, and will still give thee aid.
> I'll strengthen thee help thee, and cause thee to stand
> Upheld by my righteous omnipotent hand.

Then the unseen stranger, with a melody that showed the feeling of the heart sang –

When thro the deep waters I call thee to go
The rivers of woe shall not thee overflow
For I will be with thee thy troubles to bless
And sanctify to thee thy deepest distress.

And then Goodson again in the true spirit of the song continued on the next verse —

When through fiery trials thy pathway shall lie,
My grace all-sufficient, shall be thy supply
The flame shall not hurt thee — I only design —
Thy dross to consume and thy gold to refine.

And the stranger still out of sight replied in the next verse —

Ev'n down to old age, all my people shall prove
My sovereign eternal unchangeable love.
And when hoary hairs shall their temples adorn
Like lambs they shall still in my bosom be borne.

And then the two united together in singing the last —

The soul that on Jesus still leans for repose
I will not, I will not desert to his foes.
That soul, though all hell should endeavor to shake
I'll *never* no *never* No Never forsake.

And now the stranger called out, "Where are you from?" and Goodson answered "From the waters of the Wabash in Indiana." "And I am from Green River in Ky," said the other. "Steer this way" "What is your name?" "My name is Goodson" "And my name is Purcell," said the unseen singer. "Steer this way" "What church do you belong to?" "I'm a Methodist," shouted Goodson. "I'm a Baptist," said the stranger. "Come nigher." Meantime young Goodson had been straining on his oars to overtake the unseen Christian fellow sailor — and by this time the boats were side by side and the Baptist brother seizing a rope jumped on to the Methodist boat & seizing his brother by his hand they embraced each other as friends of Jesus — and lashing their boats together, stem & stern — they sat together and enjoyed the communion of a true christian fellowship while all on board of both boats beside themselves were wrapped in unconscious slumber — and on they journeyed never far apart until both boats tied up at the landing in Memphis — where one cargo was sold — and the new made friends parted never perhaps to meet again until on Canaans sunlit shore — then sing once more together — "The soul that on Jesus still leans for repose. I will not, I will not desert to his foes."

This incident illustrates the spirit of unity that is slumbering in many Christian hearts and only wants the occasion to bring it into action. The Baptists and the Methodists and other Christian crafts float upon the same stream of divine love and are making for the same celestial harbor. For convenience or for conscience each may carry some freight that the other has not on board — but the bulk of each cargo is the same grace — and each keeps oil in the vessels — and although winds & waves may sometimes drive them alittle asunder — yet their signals are ever beckoning each other — the same songs are ringing and the same prayers are rising, and the same guiding star of Bethlehem is shining over all – and despite their differences their hearts are flowing together & each is shouting to the other with cheering questions and glad responses. "Where are you from." "From the city of Destruction." "Where are you going." "To the Heaven Zion." "Steer this way." "Who is your commander?" "Jesus is our captain." "And he is ours." "Come nigher." And when at last they drop the anchor & tie up on the coasts of Heaven – they will sing in grand concert –

> "Now safely moored, our perils oer
> We'll sing first in Nights diadem
> Forever kind forever more
> The star, the star of Bethlehem."

Another remarkable narrative was given to me in a recent letter from Rev David R. Lockert, a Cumberland Presbyterian preacher for whom I entertain much respect and on whose veracity I fully rely. He says "When I was a boy, there lived in the vicinity of my father two very old men. Mr H. & Mr F. Mr Hoskins was a pious exemplary man. Mr F. was 'a noted profane' who delighted in getting men to drink to excess and quarrel and fight. He said it did him good to see the boys knock. One morning when I was a grown young man riding on the highway, I met a friend, Mr Henry Rudolf & we stopped to talk under the shade of a large oak. I asked 'What news?' He said 'I am just from old Mr Hoskins's. He died an hour or two ago, the most triumphant death, I ever witnessed. Just before he died he spoke to me & said "Henry, I am going to leave you. I want you to read a chapter and pray before I die." I did so and then he called his son Josiah, who was a nice gentle man, but known to be a Deist – and did not believe in life beyond the grave, and said to him – "Josiah, my son, we have agreed together, that if you are with me, & I am in my right mind when I am dying, I shall tell you whether I realize then that I am fading out of existence or whether there is life beyond – and now I feel that I am just entering upon a glorious state of real life. I want you to come, my son and kneel by my bed that I may pray for you the last time." Josiah came, with deep emotion & knelt by his fathers dying bed, and the old man laid his hands on his head and prayed the most fervent prayer I ever heard, and then his face beaming with joy, he spoke to me & said "Henry can you see the angels?" I replied "No. I can't see any angels." He said "O Henry, they are all around you – by your chair & by my bed, thousands of beautiful angels are here!" & then he ceased to breathe – a halo of brightness still lingering on his face.'"

Bro Lockert continues – "Just three weeks from that day, I met Mr Robert D. at the same place & we halted under that same oak tree. He said he had not slept all night 'and a sad night it was to me.' I inquired the cause. He said 'Old Mr. F. was dying & I went to set up with him. Soon after dark he cried out to us – "Come and drive the black devils off me." We went to him and he said "Bring the light." There were five candles burning in the room and we had to split boards & keep a large torch light in the fire place, beside. All through the night he would cry out – "Will not my children and neighbors keep the black devils off me, till I quit breathing." Just before he died he screamed out in a fearful agony and ceased to breathe with the most terror stricken countenance that I ever beheld. O! may the good Lord keep me from ever spending another such night, or witnessing another such scene!'

"I said, 'Mr D. perhaps the old man was delirious.' He said, 'No, he was perfectly rational on every other subject. He told me the year he came from Carolina & where he settled and all through the night he seemed perfectly sane.' I asked, 'Did the rest of you see any thing strange?' He said, 'No, nothing atall.' These statements were made to me by two as truthful, pious & reliable men as I ever knew in my life, and on the same spot – just three weeks apart – describing the death scenes of two of the oldest men I had ever known up to that time – perhaps each more than 90 yrs old. I found myself saying, 'Look out young man, there is a God and there is a hereafter and here is a contrast in the end of the wicked and the righteous.' I will add that Josiah Hoskins left his fathers bedside, a convicted sinner and began to pray to his fathers God, and in six weeks time was converted & joined the church – lived a useful officer in it and died in peace. I also professed religion at the same meeting."

What a fearful comment is this narrative on the words of scripture "The wicked shall be driven away in his wickedness, but the righteous hath hope in his death." I sent this narrative to the 'Advocate' for publication, according to Bro Lockerts suggestion – hoping that it may be a warning to some and a comfort to others.

December 20 – I went to my brother William's sale. His goods sold for fine prices – more than I expected. I bought the remnant of his corn before the sale at 35 cts pr bushel – having but little land to put in corn next year – & corn being extra good this year. Lizzie & I went to Olmstead & bought a lot of Christmas presents for our children & friends – servants &c. I bought a pair of fine flannel shirts, as a present for my dear old father – & would have gotten some for mother, but she said she had a good supply.

December 21 – Did not go to prayermeeting tonight – staid to see *Bob Clark* & his prospective wife *Lizette,* who came to hire to us for next years work – and with whom we agreed – 125. for *Bob* – 60. for *Lizette* & we board them, furnish house, food & fuel.

December 22 – I went to see my father about buying Williams buggie horse. He needs the horse – but thinks he is not able to get him. So I gave Wm my Mike mule, worth 100 – for the horse and gave him to my father – to pay for him at his own convenience.

December 25 – My family dined with my brothers & sisters & their families with our dear old parents, at the old home, now owned by my Bro. David – perhaps the last time that so many of us will ever take Christmas dinner together again. Father & mother are getting very infirm. I never saw father's hand tremble, as it did to day, trying to write his name – it made me very sad. Wm is going to Ala. in a few days & we will not likely all be together any other Christmas. The young people have gone to the Christmas tree at the Institute & father, mother & Eliza are here with Lizzie and me, and we are thankful to have them. My dear wife treats my parents as gently and kindly as she could her own and they seem to love her as well as their other children.

This Christmas gives me joy as well as pain. I think through the past year I have maintained a more pious and conscientious frame of mind, and have less to repent of this year than almost any other year of my life.

December 26 – Letters to write – long letter to Robert – advising him against speculation, for which he seems to have a thirst and agreeing to raise $500 for him, if he insists on the venture.

December 28 – At home, reading some and nursing a troublesome tooth. Our hired help *Bob* & *Lizette* just married tonight came down to occupy their new quarters.

January 1, 1883 – I came home [from Allensville], and learned that my Bro Frank has lost his little daughter Alice 2 yrs old with measles.

The New Year opens with a chill air & a murky sky. Just as we were going to bed a stranger called for lodging. We took him in.

January 3 – A dreary, cloudy, chilly, sleeting morning. I have work in doors & no Quarterly Meeting this week. Robert wants me to help him a few days in Louisville.

January 5 – I bade adieu to my brother Wm & his wife, who leave next Monday for their new home in Alabama. The Nashville train was late and I waited an hour at Bowling green – reached Louisville at 4 P.M. – was gladly welcomed at Prof. S. T. Scotts – where Robert boards. I found Robert hard at work as usual. There was a small congregation at night. I preached on the talents with some liberty. I am glad to see the work that Robert has done & the estimation in which his people hold him. The new church [West Broadway] is fully as large as necessary and quite a beautiful house – especially within. After preaching, I was introduced to many of the membership who seem to love Robert very dearly. An old German woman – Sister Romeizer – patting him on the shoulder said to me, "Brudder Browder I glad to see you – brudder Browder's fader – but this is my faithful servant – this is mine faithful servant."

January 6 – I went through the city and was pleased to see the progress. J. S. Lithgow took us through his immense manufacturing establishment and showed us the works. It is on Main St. & occupies nearly a whole square. He took us in & showed us where they made the electric light, one of the marvels of this age.

January 9 – Did some shopping – went to H. C. Morrisons to dinner. He had invited quite a number of friends to meet me – & we had a delightful time and a splendid dinner – oysters & crackers – turkey & ham, hot rolls & butter &

cheese, Maccaroni – tomatoes, potatoes, pickles – then fruits & confections, bananas, oranges, apples & Strawberry ice cream, cakes &c – it seemed to me too much for a Methodist preachers table. At night our congregation was the largest I have seen any week night, since I came. I had considerable liberty preaching Acts 16.30.

January 10 – Snowing again. I decided to go home. I left at 1. P.M. The wind roared & the snow swirled & drifted as the train sped on. I walked home through the snow and was rejoiced to find all well. The sheep got to the tobacco and ate enough to kill several lambs. The papers give full accounts of the capture of Marshall T. Polk the absconding Treasurer of the state of Ten[nessee]. He is said to have stolen $400,000 of state funds – is a cousin of President Jas. K. Polk – ought to end his life with other thieves, in the penitentiary.

January 11 – My fifty sixth birthday! When I was young I did not expect to see 50 years. God has spared me in his mercy. I am now white headed, but not wise according to my years. Men think of me above my deserving. My family honor me and I am grateful, but I wish I had done more for them. They surprised me greatly by a splendid Christmas present – an elegant Walnut writing desk & book case with two large and two small drawers and two side cases, and a top with divers pigeon holes with all necessary locks & keys – bright and new in perfect repair – worth $30.00 – bought at 20. To day it stands in the place of the old one – with books, papers &c all in it when I came home – quite an improvement on the old one. On the shelves there is room for Clarkes Commentary & other books. I do most highly appreciate this tender expression of my childrens love and I do not know any more suitable selection they could have made and yet I think it is more than they were able to do – in view of the fact that they will have very little patrimony. I have spent considerable money in their education and hope they will improve their talent and do well for this world and the next. I am now past the age when I can expect to do much more for them. Robert is popular & gets good salaries for a young man. Hanson has done well in making, and saving, a thousand dollars. George has good business prospects and Luther is studying well – & Wallace also. My daughter Helen is all that a father could ask in a child and her husband is prospering & living comfortably – so that this 56th birthday finds me a grateful happy old man, at home with as true a wife as ever blessed any husbands life. The snow covers the ground and the wind is keen & chilling, but the coal fire roars on the grate and I thank God for all his mercies. I can still read without glasses – and retain my hearing better than thousands of others. For the first time in my life I am wearing beard all over my face – and do not look like myself. I am fleshy – weight 185 or 190.

January 12 – Up betimes and off to Crofton Mission – waited at Guthrie from 7:30 A.M. to 2:17 P.M. Bro Miles met me at Kellys & his big horse Walter carried me safe over, while he rode William. His children Sylvanus & Sylvester, Dora, Annie & Nannie were eager for my coming – expecting candy again and were not disappointed. I love to please and instruct the children.

January 13 – Raining, sleeting, freezing. I rode 7 or 8 miles to Bethlehem, found a few official members – held Conference. Bro. Drake was there, but the majority requested me to employ Rev Geo. W. Demoss – others objected that evil rumors touching his character were in circulation – but not well founded. Some objected to Drake that he was inefficient & incompetent though earnestly pious – so I was left in doubt & trouble. I spent the night with Alick Hammond and his young wife – sleeping in the same room with them – sharing their warm hospitality in their humble home. I sat up late & wrote & read, beside the old-fashioned log fire.

January 15 – Got home on freight train before night – glad to find all well and the ice house full of ice.

January 16 – A busy day! Wrote to Geo. & Luther – worked hard, nearly all day long & in the night looking over the papers of a life time to put my new desk in order.

Volume X

1883–1885

"All over this country the idea of ministerial support is humiliating."

January 18, 1883 – I sent a bag of meal & flour to bro Goodson – thankful that I am able to divide with him.

January 25 – Hanson starts to Ark. on a visit & to take our niece Lizzie Warfield home. She has been several months with her relation in Ky & Tenn. I felt sad to see him start away – yet did not want Lizzie to go alone. He is one of the best sons in the world and worthy of our fullest confidence.

January 31 – Heard that Hanson had reached his aunt Sarahs safely – speaks of going to N. Orleans before he returns.

February 1 – Of late it seems to me that I have almost no time for efficient study – mind and body seem to be wearied. I read and get sleepy or else read and forget. There is more or less tenderness in my lungs, nearly all the time. My dear wife also seems to be failing, but tries so faithfully to do all her duty.

February 6 – Snow, rain, cold – *heavy* sleet, biggest I have seen for a long time – fences, trees, houses – ground covered with ice & snow. I have not left the house unnecessarily all day. Have been looking over the diaries of the first & second year in my ministry. I see much that is weak and boyish, but much that was earnest heart work for Christ & his church – & it seems that I had more immediate results then than now. I note the same complaint of coldness & unfaithfulness and the same resolves on improvement & the failures that followed, that I still encounter. The breathing cry for a *pure* heart free from *all* sin or taint that rose up in my heart then still rises in it. I thank God I never forfeited my intention to serve him. I never yielded to wrong of any sort without being ashamed of it & sorry for it & I am as much resolved this day to serve God as I was 36 years ago on the Hopkinsville cir[cuit].

February 8 – One more bright day. Snow & ice rapidly melting in sunshine, but freezing in the shade. I have been afraid to ride today – the ground has been so full of ice and yet my dear old father nearly 79 yrs old rode over on horse-back from Daniel Baileys where he & mother have been spending nearly two weeks.

February 11 – [Bethesda in Todd County] Very few persons at church, but I preached a very earnest & plain sermon on Tit[us] 2.1. After a good dinner at Bro. Wyatts, consisting in part of some of the best rye hominy I ever ate, I went home with Bro. Paul H. Salmon & sat up until a late hour talking with him on religion subjects. He seems to be an excellent man & his wife is a great-niece of Thomas Jefferson 3d president of the United States – a plain, sensible housewife – said to be also a descendent of Pocahontas.

We were told today of a fearful tragedy in North Todd [County] that occurred yesterday a few miles from our meeting, at the sale of property at the residence of Elder Barrow. Mr Ed Lacey had a son, it seems, who seduced a daughter of Mr Romile Martin, a very clever, plain man – that was trying to do right & bring up his children respectably. He told young Lacey that he should marry his daughter or be killed, or else kill him, if he staid in this country, and young Lacey left. The older Lacey & Martin tried to prevent a collision between the young men, but at the sale yesterday Ike Martin, brother of the ruined girl, got into a fight with the father of the seducer and as they grappled & were cutting each other with knives, a younger son of Mr Lacey drew a pistol & shot Ike Martin three times. Then Romile Martin, the young mans father took a stone and knocked the oldest Lacey down, striking him on the head – whereupon the young Lacey shot Martin dead on the spot & then Lee Wilkins, the constable called upon the posse to arrest Lacey, but the young man, still armed said, "No interference here gentlemen, I don't want to hurt any of you," and deliberately walked away. The officer ordered him to halt, but he kept on & Wilkins fired at him – when young Lacey stopped and returned the fire & started towards Wilkins, who thought it prudent to get out of the way & Lacey made his escape. This was told me by two sons of Geo. W. Latham who were present and saw the painful occurrence. This is a painful warning to young men, disposed to trifle with the honor of young women & to girls who transcend the limits of prudence. Here are a brother & father hurried into eternity, & a daughter in disgrace in one family & one son a seducer & another a murderer, & the father badly wounded in another – all growing out of an imprudence, that both parties, ought to have been ashamed of. The danger of carrying pistols here finds another illustration – but for that most likely no life would have been lost. The Laceys are people in good circumstances and as respectable as any family in that section of country.

February 12 – [Elkton] I called to see Dr John O. McReynolds, who got a severe fall, on the slippery pavement and was badly hurt. He seemed glad to see me and as usual was ready for a joke – said he had been practicing some bad Methodist doctrine – falling from grace. I said "You are under a mistake Dr – *ice* is not *grace*. Campbellism did that – too much water." He saw the point and joined in the laugh. He is one of my best Campbellite friends. After getting new shoes put on Flora, I plodded homeward through the mud. I was very weary, and glad to get home, but sorry that Hanson has not arrived. I felt uneasy about floods, from the time he left & I now fear that he will have trouble and encounter danger, in getting back. The newspaper accounts of flood & disaster, N. & S. are distressing.

February 13 – At home, reading over my diaries & weeping afresh over the picture of my dear little Ginnie's death.

February 14 – I went to Russellville mainly to introduce Mr. S. W. Taliaferro to Mrs Mary Phelps, but she declined to receive any gentlemen that had matrimonial intentions. A messenger came for me to preach the funeral of Lena Edwards, youngest daughter of Peyton G. Edwards. She & her cousin Dumpie Lewis, were riding & the horses became frightened, & ran away. Lena was thrown against a stump & so stunned that she died at nine oclock Tuesday night. Dumpie Lewis was thrown and so hurt that for hours, she was unconscious.

February 16 – I went to Fairview. Papers report awful floods in the Ohio – largest ever known – higher by 9 inches than the big flood of 1832. Thousands of people in Louisville driven out of their homes – hundreds of houses washed away, many entirely under water. Beargrass backed up until it was running down Broadway street – ½ of N. Albany & Jeffersonville under water – Cincinnati & Frankfort & other cities in great distress. The Cin. Southern R. R. depot, situated on a big fill, sunk down in the flood carrying 75–100 people and a freight train ran in on them – all drowned. Tidings of distress come from many other places. How thankful ought we to be who are free from such calamities. My son George seems to be very busy in his practice – booking more than 100 pr month, but I think he will get very little pay for most of it.

February 19 – A miserable ride [from Fairview], over *deep* mud, just alittle frozen on top. Such a constant pull, through mud & slush, for nearly a whole day I have seldom had. I got home, alittle before sundown. I was glad & thankful to get home safe & find all well – and my dear boy Hanson returned from Arkansas. As I rode up to the gate and saw cedar posts set for more wire fence – I knew that Hanson had come. Robert arrived on the 7 P.M. train & we have a happy evening at home.

February 26 – A note from Luther asks for more money, but I have none on hand – must try to get it from those who owe me.

March 1 – I was busy helping Hanson sack his potatoes – Irish, sold at 60 cts pr bushel – so much more profitable than tobacco that he proposes to put his tobacco land in potatoes, this year. If he makes less money, he raises *food* instead of narcotics.

March 8 – Bro Campbell called to buy our Sept lambs at 3.00 each & I bought Bro Goodsons Durham cow Anna for 30. – 10 lambs for 1 cow – 4 yrs old – no calf. I got a letter from Bro John telling me of fathers safe arrival in Montgomery.

March 11 – [Adairville] Congregation good & I had some unction in preaching 1st Cor[inthians] 9.11. After dinner I went to see Clarence (Jeff) Hite – at W. Bowling Browders. Gov Crittenden [of Missouri] had pardoned him out of the penitentiary & he came home to die with consumption.[1]

March 12 – Jeff Hite died this morning – about the time I was praying for him at church. I felt sorry for the poor boy – decoyed into crime by older and worse men.

---

1. See entry for April 11, 1882.

March 13 — I attended the funeral for poor Jeff Hite, made some remarks that Bro Lewis & others called "touchingly tender and appropriate." If the dying thief found forgiveness who can limit the compassion of Christ. There was quite a company at the funeral & at the grave. The family was once highly respectable and the poor boys mother was a good woman. We should speak gently to the sorrowful.

> What are other's faults to me, Have I a vultures bill
> To peck at every flaw I see And make it wider still.
> Tis enough for me to know that I have faults my own.
> I'll on myself the care bestow And let my friends alone.

March 14 — I preached on prayer to a small congregation. There is small pox in the neighborhood and I had Dr Townsend to vaccinate me — although I have been several times vaccinated before — it having *taken* only once. I came home very weary.

March 28 — Tom Sydnor came last night to see me about repairs on our church, before Dist[rict] Conf[erence]. We will have the seats & necessary changes, if he and I alone have to pay for all. I ordered lumber for a suitable outhouse for women & children — a convenience that has long been needed. Hanson has rented some more corn land and we are likely to have more corn than we expected. Our crop prospects are encouraging & we trust God for success & we propose to be liberal, as God prospers us.

April 3 — Dr Hutchings tells me that some of the members think we are doing very wrong to spend any more money in repairing the old church and make an excuse for not giving by telling that a few of us want to carry everything our own way — and then have all the rest pay for it. I felt grieved — but simply said I thought the church needed repairs and was willing to be liberal to get it done — and thought all ought to help. Let patience have her perfect work.

April 6 — I was glad to meet Bro. Demoss, waiting for me at Empire [in Christian County] with a horse. I passed through the coaling — saw boys coming out from under the ground with mule loads of coal.

April 7 — Considerable walk over wet roads — divers branches — streams, fallen trees &c — brought us to Martin's chapel — a substantial log house — but like all the other churches here, unfinished & unseated. A moderate congregation listened with apparent interest, to a faithful sermon on the true nature of revivals. The people all through this country greatly need indoctrination. Their religion is largely in excitement — they have very low ideas of duty in gaining knowledge & supporting the church. What is done, is done by few. The Quarterly Conference licensed a man to preach who never read the Discipline — owns no Bible and does not pray in his family, yet seems to be very pious & talks with feeling about his religious experience. Only three persons in the whole charge of seven congregations gave *anything* to the support of the pastor. The stewards had not raised *one cent* – and yet all seem greatly pleased with the preacher. I resolved then to preach a *faithful* sermon on the duties of pastors and people. We got dinner with Rev Ranson Martin – one of the best of men. He lives in a poor, open house, and works hard to live – though old and infirm – yet he does more to build a house for the Lord than any other dozen people in this region – and helps to pay the pastors salary – but all over this country the idea of ministerial support is humiliating – hundreds of people claiming to be Christians will not give one cent in a year to support a pastor. I went home with John W. Martin, the newly licensed preacher. I talked plainly to him about improving himself so that he might preach to edification.

April 8 – House pretty well filled – good religious love-feast – several shouts in the camp. At 11. I preached to a *tolerably* attentive congregation a very plain, and faithful sermon on the duties of pastors and people – tried to show and *did* show that according to Gods law, common sense & common honesty, the workman should have his hire. If there is any fruit it will be in the future. People who are able to pay & admit that the preacher ought to be paid, will not because some others do not & make this their reason – just as if they had a right to cheat because others do. Dear old Bro Martin tried to get money enough to pay my R. R. fare but failed, and I declined to accept what he personally proposed to pay. My throat & lungs very sore. I sometimes think my work is nearly done.

April 9 – Up early – walked half a mile to hire a boy to take me to the R. R. At Empire, I went to see Mr Mason, the Supt of the Coaling company – in the interest of a church for these poor miners – but he gave no encouragement. It has rained steadily from 1 oclock P.M. until night & I had a muddy and dark walk home from Olmstead but felt thankful to get home. I had more than ordinary dread of this trip to Crofton and am glad it is over. A letter from Robert reports he has made some sort of investment, which he thinks is likely to be very profitable – and wants me to borrow $300.00 for him, but I do not know where to look for it. I fear Robert is too prone to speculate – but I will try to accommodate him.

April 10 – A letter of yesterday just received says he has bought an one half interest in some sort of gas-meter-test & new gas fixtures, or burners, that he thinks will pay him well. I wrote to R. L. Smith, H. G. Petree & D. K. Mason to see if I could get the money for him – pledging my crop of tobacco to Mason for the security.

April 12 – I got a letter each from Thos M. Smith & H. G. Petree offering to lend me the money for Robert – 300. Smith demands 8 pr ct – Petree simply says 'interest.' I take his offer – glad of the chance to help my boy.

April 13 – I wrote to Petree & Smith and also to Robert – got a letter from R. saying that he had bought an interest in a gas-meter test & Parson's automatic gas burner – that was already growing rapidly into popular favor & making fine profits on the investment – making 25 cts clear on each burner & orders ahead of supply – 600–800 now ordered for Galt House [in Louisville]. I hope it may be a means of some financial help – but all is not gold that glitters.

April 14 – Bro Goodson went with me to Russellville. At night I went with the College girls, to see the competitive drill between the "Broom Brigade" & the Logan guards – & the "Fan Drill" by the little girls. It was a very entertaining evening. I was really surprised to see how perfectly the girls performed their military evolutions & practiced the manual – with brooms as if they were muskets. I never saw the movements excelled – either by men or women. The "guards" under Capt Joe Barclay seemed almost *perfect* in their manual exercise & in all the tactics that could be displayed in the building. They seemed to excel the girls in some things & the girls excelled them in some – but the judges were gentlemen and the "Brooms" got the benefit of their gallantry & won the prize.

May 2 – Bro James Lewis came home with me – seems much pleased with the fine colt that Hanson bought from Geo. A. Wilgus – for 150.00. He is an extra fine colt, but that is a big price for a 3 yr old – a deep blood bay, clean bone & fine form – 15 or 15 ½ hands high – by West-wind out of a fine blooded mare – Lexington – a fine blooded – fine looking animal.

May 3 – The Herald-Enterprise reports & justifies the killing of Walter Davis by Hon Phil. Thompson (Congressman) on the impression that Davis took advantage of Mrs Thompson's love of strong drink, to get her intoxicated, in Cincinnati & then carried her to his room and defiled her chastity. Public sentiment may justify the killing, but in the sight of human & divine law it was murder & ought to be so regarded. Both Mr Davis & Mrs Thompson denied the charge & said Thompson had been misled. I regret that public journals seem to encourage man-slaughter. I wrote an earnest protest against the spirit of the paragraph asserting that it is a man's solemn duty to take the life of one who despoils his wife. It is, on the same grounds, the duty of the woman to kill the paramour of her husband. If a man who under great temptation commits adultery, is worthy of death, why is not the man who under great provocation commits murder, equally worthy of death? The same law that forbids adultery also forbids murder. I think law abiding men ought to discourage individuals or mobs from taking the law into their own hands.

May 5 – Spent most of the day in the study – bought a new saddle from C. B. Webb – spring seat – highly recommended by J. A. Lewis, Bro Emerson & others – my old one is not decent to ride.

May 14 – Got home by 1 oclock [from Bethesda] & went to see my dear father & mother – safe back from Ala. I hugged & kissed them both, thankful in my heart to see them alive & well, again in their Kentucky home.

May 27 – [Zion Church, north of Russellville] But little interest in love-feast, fine congregation at 11 – the old house & rickety benches, well filled & some out of doors. I preached a *very plain* & earnest sermon on 1st Cor 9.11. No one failed to see that the church ought to pay a faithful pastor. This church of about 60 members has paid about 8.00 *all told* for their pastor this year. I lodge with Bro. Hogard – a good earnest preacher. He seemed anxious to divide the quarterage with me, but I did not feel free to do it. He is not able to get good clothes for himself & family.

May 30 – [Olmstead] Floods of rain. I went to examination of pupils at Browder Institute. Nothing specially striking. I was pleasantly surprised on my return to find my son Luther at home, looking well and in good spirits. He has finished the English Theological course at Vanderbilt University and brings a Diploma with him.

May 31 – This had been a very enjoyable, if not a very profitably spent, day. Went to Bethlehem this morning to hear the speeches & compositions of the school children. Some of them did admirably – much better than I expected – notably Maimie Small, Willis & Robert Boyd, Bailey & Wallace Browder. My son Wallace & my nephew Bailey surprised me. I never saw a *little* fellow excel Bailey. At night, the school building was densely crowded – with people living near & far – eight or 10 miles. The porticoes & windows were packed & jammed to see the exhibition. I surrendered several seats to ladies – but finally was invited up to the stand to offer prayer & so I saw & heard most of the performances & was again well pleased. Willie Boyd, Wallace Sydnor, Marion Campbell, Mary Small, Minnie Morrow, Bailey & Wallace Browder, did exceptionally well. We got home & to bed about 2 Oclock A.M.

June 2 – [Bibb's Chapel] Good Saturday congregation – preached on "Satans devices." Young Russell told me that he was not satisfied in Cumberland church & expected to join the Methodist. I told him it was a serious matter to change churches, and advised him to consider well before he decided to leave his church.

June 3 – My old friend John A. Miller was at both services to day – did not take sacrament, nor take part in love-feast. I had a talk with him & found him backslidden. Too sad! Too sad! I talked plainly & earnestly with him. The number of backsliders in the land is alarming.

June 6 – Luther went with me to Russellville, to the commencement exercises of Logan Female College. Six graduates read essays. Taken as a whole, I think I never heard them surpassed at any school. Lillian Lewis surprised me & yet I was expecting something superior. She has a splendid dramatic talent & could make her mark on the stage. Her essay on awakening from a dream was the most brilliant of all, & she read it the best. Next was Jennie McGhee on Mardigras – a well considered – well expressed, well read paper on the disgusting festival &

the masquerading of our whole deceitful & sin cursed race. It is the best thing I ever heard or read on the subject & is worthy of publication. The parting between Dr Stark & his girls was very affecting. Many eyes were shedding tears as they saw him pale & feeble – stand up & tremble – too feeble to talk. A fine gold headed cane was presented by the graduating class, as a token of their esteem. By request Luther & I dined with the Dr & I went to attend the Director's Meeting. Several applicants that impress us favorably. We cannot afford to make a mistake in the selection of a successor to Dr Stark. Luther & I did not get home until dark. Hanson finished thinning corn. John Hardy, the deputy sheriff, says that ours is the finest field of oats in Logan County. I have not seen any equal to it in my district.

June 11 – Luther has gone to Louisville to work for Robert – at 45.00 pr month – selling gas meter-tests & burners. Robert thinks he will do well with it.

June 13 – Looking up material for a Missionary sermon. I got a letter from my cousin Geo. N. Moore asking for help to get his son through Dental College. I am sorry I am not able to help him with justice to my own children – but I have no great faith in the dental profession – good mechanics & farmers are much more independent than the average professional man.

June 15 – Reached Fairview at night – stopped with George at Bro. Shaw's. Started to the Post Office – but got into a saloon – soon discovered my mistake. Dont go into saloons.

June 16 – [Vaughn's Grove in Todd County] Sun fearfully hot. Small congregation – people sleepy – had some liberty preaching against the devil. Tom Shaw went with me to P.A. Cushman's. I was much interested in Mr Cushmans Shepherd dog – Nellie. He told her to go into the field & bring the sheep – & away she went. He would call to her to "go round them" or "bark at them" & she obeyed him & brought all the sheep to the house. He said that a gentleman staid at his house who had bought a flock of sheep – and at night they were talking in the presence of the dog, about getting up early & driving the sheep out of the fields into the lot to be separated – & when they went out to the lot early in the morning the dog had already brought up the sheep & had them in the lot & was lying at the gate (which had been left open) to prevent the sheep from going back to the field! Did the dog understand the talk?

June 22 – [Olmstead] A note from my father tells that my dear little niece Fannie Carson Bailey died in the night & will be buried at 3 oclock – & I am expected to preach the funeral. My poor sister Annie seems almost heart-broken & Daniel is greatly distressed. Quite a crowd gathered in the shade of the burying ground & I tried to talk to them as well as I could. I was compelled to hurry home [before the service was over] as I was called to a meeting of the Board of Directors of Logan Female College. There was a *full* meeting of the Board – every member present – & we talked long and earnestly and still left without any real light upon the subject of electing a successor to Dr Stark.

June 27 – I wrote an earnest letter to my cousin Geo. N. Moore, who I learn has quit going to church and is in a gloomy state of mind. I have had much care and anxiety about him in days gone by.

June 28 – At 3.15 I set out with Flora & the open buggie on my way to Fairview – enroute to Crofton Mission – got to Tom Shaws at night.

June 29 – Had a rough – long drive to Mt Carmel church – preached at night to more people than I expected. Bro. Demoss is not well. People much elated at getting glass windows and ceiling in their church – and a chandelier from the church in Hopkinsville. It is a sight to many of these people in the hills. I heard it called "a shandaleem" & some one is said to have remarked that "it would do no good there, for nobody would know how to play on it."

July 1 – Hot – so hot – house crowded & more out of doors than in the house. Spent the night with Bro. Shepherd. He is in good spirits over his success in raising *ten whole dollars* for the pay of pastor & presiding elder six months. I gave *all* the proceeds of this quarter $22.00 to Bro. Demoss – as I did also the last Quarter – because he needs it more than I do. I fear the gospel does not much affect this people – 300 members paying 7.00 pr month for the entire support of a pastor & the prorata of P.E.!

July 2 – Bro. Shepherd came to Hopkinsville with me in my buggie. I reached Fairview 1 ½. Fearfully hot – reached home at 8 ½ – 44 miles to day – over road partly very rough – partly muddy.

July 3 – Letters to answer as usual – one of four full pages – from my old School-master Wm A. Washington – over 80 years old in a smoother, neater, more perfect hand than one man in ten thousand of *any* age can write – & the style & diction equal to the penmanship. It is a rare letter – full of love & full of religion – a godly Campbellite Christian.

July 4 – National day! No observance of it here.

July 6 – Tom Sydnor has kindly lent us his self binding reaper to cut our oats. They are fine, but rather green – but it seems wise to save them before they fall down. At 1 P.M. a sudden shower relieved the heat & wet the oats. Hanson drove his colt Prince to Allensville to get repairs for the reaper. I think there is too much machinery in the self-binder. It gives trouble.

July 8 – [Russellville] I called to see Bishop Hargrove at W. F. Barclays. The town was startled by a horrible tragedy. Spencer Longs son Nimrod & his cousin Nimrod Briggs, 14 and 15 yrs old were playing Soldier & Indian – snapping empty guns at each other – when Longs gun discharged a heavy load of buckshot into the head of young Briggs – killing him instantly to the inexpressible grief of the boy & the crushing overwhelming sorrow of the wealthiest family in town &

the head and font of the Baptist church. A gloom rests upon the whole town. Nim Briggs was a bright, pleasant boy – a sort of general favorite & especially dear to the cousin, whose sad lot was to snap the fatal empty gun at his head. Spencer Long is a very worthy good man, and more cautious than most men – in *never* allowing a loaded gun in his house. The dogs had been killing his sheep in a lot close by & Stephen, his son had charged this old gun with 9 buckshot to kill the dog – & the younger son did not know it. The boy seems paralysed with grief & sorrow & sad results to him are feared. Mrs Briggs, mother of the dead boy & aunt of the even more unfortunate one, was in labor at the time & was delivered of another son in just 5 minutes after the death of the other.

July 9 – We held Quarterly Conference at night. Small financial report. Exulting over their brilliant success in raising means to pay off their church debt – they seem to overlook the necessities of their pastor. I called special attention to this point.

July 10 – Our fine potato crop is not likely to pay much profit – 25 cts pr bu. We will not sell at that just yet.

July 17 – Went last night to Russellville – met the Board of Directors of Logan Female College. After canvassing the claims we elected Prof H. Taylor of Vanceburg Ky. Pres. of College. He seems a rising young man, whose talent and methods betoken success.

July 25 – Daniel Bailey came for me to preach the funeral of his uncle, Dr J. M. Bailey who died last night. Lizzie, father & mother went with me. There was a very large attendance – white & colored. My text was Psa[lm] 23.4. I spoke out in the open air. Dr Bailey was a prominent man – and a great friend to our church. He was U.S. Consul to Glasgow, Scotland, under Mr Lincoln's administration – & was a Surgeon in the U.S. army – during the war. He was one of the best and most influential friends of our camp-meeting association.

August 3 – Luther has his clothes-ironing machine at work on the back porch and numbers of people – white and colored – are in to see it. It seems to save much labor for the wash-women.

August 7 – My dear boy Luther started out for Hopkinsville, Princeton, Paducah, Henderson &c to establish agencies for the sale of the Cottingham Ironing machine – for which he is Agent in Kentucky and Indiana. I do not feel very hopeful of his success nor satisfied that he is in the best place for himself. I would feel safer to have him go at once into his ministerial work. Today we have a house full of friends and kindred, Helen & family = 6, Sister Sarah Warfield & two children = 3, Fletcher & Lillie Browder = 2, Robert & Nannie Browder = 2, Miss Fannie Smith from Allensville & Mrs Henkle and daughter from Louisville – with her children = 3, my sister Annie and several colored persons besides – at least 20 in all. I am glad to be able to entertain the friends that come.

August 9 — Robt left for Louisville. His time has been so taken up with young people and company, that we have had but little pleasure in his visit. I am sorry that he put what little money he had in the ironing machine. It will divert his mind from his *best* ministerial work — & I fear result in the loss of all the capital he has saved or that I have given him.

August 12 — [Bell's Chapel] Congregation small. Dinner was on the ground and at 2.30 I preached a short sermon — Eph[esians] 3d 14–21. I had some pathos, but not much power — nor logic — but no body went to sleep — & people seemed to feel — went to Dr Russell's. He is a grand son of Genl William Russell of Revolutionary fame — & a kinsman of the world-renowned Henry Clay of Kentucky. He has been very wealthy — lost $60,000. worth of slaves by the war — is a member of the church — but does not enjoy a *conscious* peace with God — says a hasty temper is his besetment.

August 14 — [Olmstead] Campmeeting day. We loaded the wagon — packed in a full stock of provisions — beds — & varieties — got dressed & the buggy ready — when here came the thunder & the rain. We drove into the barn & let the wagon stand — but still the rain pours down and we are thankful to be at home — safe under a good shelter — with little worry besides unloading the wagon again.

August 15 — Off to campmeeting [at Ash-Spring]! Load too big — broke a wheel — sent back for another wagon — too narrow for our bed — looked up still another wagon — Buck Poor's, willingly loaned — loaded our goods again & got started when here came clouds & rain — paused alittle before a barn — drove on towards camp-ground — big rain overtook us, but we got into Francis Pages barn in time to save our beds &c from getting wet — got nearly to camp-ground — broke a trace chain — had to go on & get another wagon to divide our load — got in & beds spread & all dry. I was overcome with heat and exertion.

August 19 — [Returning from Chandler's Chapel] I reached the Camp-ground at 10 P.M. and was prepared, by the immense train of buggies & horsemen that I met — to believe the accounts given me of the largest crowd ever at the Camp-ground. I had a pain and weakness through my back and could hardly get up when I was down.

August 20 — Hardly able to move about — good melting time at morning meeting — several penitents and conversions. Old Bro Jimmy Pittman preached an excellent, earnest — old time Methodist sermon. Congregations immense — hundreds of people besides those encamped. Emerson preached an excellent sermon at 3 P.M. & R. F. Hayes at night. While Hayes was preaching — one of the oil lamps fell & set the straw on fire — causing considerable commotion for a little time — but doing no serious damage.

August 21 — A sweet growing day — hundreds of people consecrating themselves to Christ. Dr Hanner preached one of the finest sermons I ever heard – on Dives & Lazarus. The effect was electrical – and nearly everybody was weeping. The altar was thronged with penitents and Mrs Henry Sugg came forward – in her wealth and splendor & besought God for mercy & peace. In the afternoon she came again and was happily converted. Oh this was a sweet day to many souls.

August 22 – Another precious season at morning service. Bro Lewis proposed that the church members come forward & shake hands with Cousin D. B. Sydnor – my father & Bro Absolom Miller – the oldest members of the church in the circuit. There was a general move and a time of weeping. At 11 A.M. old Bro Thos Bottomley over 78 yrs of age preached a grand sermon on "serving the Lord." At 3 ½ P.M. I preached with considerable unction on "Wisdom justified of her children" – there was deep feeling – & many penitents and some conversions. Bro Goodson held the night service. There was a crowd of mourners. A young woman by the name of Whiting – who had been in great distress for days – shrieking and crying piteously while at the altar & not answering any questions – suddenly sprang to her feet and exclaimed, "I am happy, yes I am happy!" and rejoiced aloud & leaped & praised God. She was a backslider who went through a similar exercise two years ago at Pleasant Grove.

August 23 – A solemn closing service. I received 17 members into the church – mostly Sunday School children & baptized eight of them. We left two penitents at the altar and the church was in a good working frame.

August 24 – Off to Crofton – 5 hours in Guthrie – Bros Jas R. Brown & R. D. Wade were both waiting with mules at Crofton. Demoss was also there – troubled on account of some rumors affecting his character. Poor man! he has either been very unfortunate or very imprudent – possibly both.

August 25 – After a good rest at Bro Brown's we went to Concord. A fair attendance. Text Mat[thew] 11.19. In Quarterly Conf[erence] under Ques. 2. "Any Complaints?" W. H. Cato said grave complaints had been made of impropriety on the part of the P[reacher in] C[harge] Geo. W. Demoss, toward sister John Brown – wife of the steward of this church. Demoss rose to explain. The husband of the woman said he told "a lie" & I called him to order. Conf. requested me to appoint a Committee & we proceeded to business. Cato was *very friendly* and gracious with me & his manner seemed to imply regret for the letter he wrote me. Old Bro Ranson Martin preached at night, an earnest sermon – if sermon it be with no respect to the English Grammar. I went back with Demoss to Jas R. Browns. He disavows any evil intent but admits indiscretion & impropriety in his talk with Mrs Brown – who with her husband seems much offended. He (Demoss) insists that the matter be settled before I leave here & is willing to accept a reprimand.

August 26 – I talked with W. H. Shepherd – & Revs R. D. Wade & Ranson Martin – whom I appointed a committee – this morning on the Demoss case.

They exonerate him from *crime,* but thought the impropriety was of such a grade & is so publicly talked of, that there ought to be a public statement that the church did not tolerate such improprieties & that the preacher ought to be reproved − & the preacher himself approving the idea − painful as it was to me, I made the statement & the reproof − in the presence of a large congregation − the accused brother fully consenting. I tried to guard the interests of the church as well as I could and also the character of the preacher − but it was embarrassing & humiliating − & made necessary it seems because repeated rumors have followed the poor man − who yet seems to be trying to do right & says he is persecuted.

August 30 − [Olmstead] Read the Advocates until noon − went to see Buford Boyer very sick with flux − at Dr. Hutchings. I went to the cabin to see poor old *Samson* now nearly 100 years old, blind & helpless. He did not recognize me at first, but when I told him who I was he wept for joy − said he had long been wondering why I did not come. Said in a plaintive tone − "Im old & helpless now, when Im down I cant get up & when Im up I cant get down. I cant see anything and this poor old body suffers day and night − these poor old bones and all through my body − such pains that I just scream and scream − but I leave all in the hands of my heavenly Master. More than fifty years I have been trying to serve him and when he set me free he filled me with love to all Christians, white and colored all the same." He seemed grateful for all the mercies shown him − told me how he always loved me − and hoped to see me in Heaven − and a great many touching things he said − thought the difference in race and color was providential − and did not take it hard that he had been a slave. I repeated some precious Scriptures to him, then sang and prayed with him. He says he was a man grown & had a wife and children when my father, now in his 79th year, was a school boy. He said that in old times negroes had no means of keeping their ages − and were often represented younger than they were to increase their market value, just as some men now misrepresent the age of horses &c to get a better price. He spoke in high terms of the honorable dealing of *his* white folks. Dr Hutchings gives him a good house − good food and plenty of fuel & sees to his material wants.

September 5 − Thirty three years ago this day I was married. Thank God that my dear wife has been so long spared to bless and gladden my life! We are getting old now and strength failing − yet each year I see more and more the beauty of her life. She has borne with me and loved me through all my faults. There is no reasonable expectation that I shall be here long. My mothers family are not long lived − & I am mentally & physically much like them. They have heart disease − dropsy of the chest or some similar disease − symptoms of which I have had. Die when I may, I want my wife to feel that she has been at all times the true and trusted wife, the object of my love. We have not always understood each other − but in nearly everything we have seen eye to eye and face to face. If I have been of any service in the world, my wife has had much to do with it.

September 6 — [Russellville] I paid some accounts, went shopping with Lizzie, gave her money to buy a new bonnet and a nice silk dress — shoes — gloves &c. Spent above $30.

September 13 — [Olmstead] For some time I have been writing an occasional letter to the county paper. In the last I have an article on "Logan county preachers — their work and their pay" — trying to stir up the people to their duty. In the same issue I notice, copied from the Bowling-green Gazette — a very handsome compliment to my letters & to myself personally — some thing that I was not expecting.

September 19 — Lizzie went to Russellville to have her new dress made. I went to see the Allensville brethren about their church matters — was sorry to find that they are not satisfied with their pastor and want a change — and some of them censure me, for not returning Bro. Emerson. I am learning to bear unjust censure and criticism with more patience than formerly. At 8 P.M. I went in the wagon with my children & nieces to church. Bro Goodson gave us a plain earnest exhortation. He is a good and useful man — has been an eminent success in many places — and yet our Allensville people and some at Bethlehem and also at Keysburg and Ash-Spring are not satisfied and ask a change. It is to be a delicate and *painful* task to deal with the appointing of preachers. I try to take it to the Lord in prayer.

September 20 — Church at night — congregation small. Luther preached for us. His text — "All things work together for good to them that love God." His exposition was clear & his illustrations in the main, were suggestive. There was some lack of naturalness, some need of animation that experience will bring out. On the whole he did very well. May God go with him & give him success!

September 22 — Quarterly Conference [at Bethlehem] — much better up with the preachers pay than I expected. Some disagreement about the return of Bro Goodson. Allensville seems solid *against* his return — Keysburg solid *for* it. A large majority at Bethlehem willing to take him — some few prominent men much opposed. Ash-Spring divided & the leading men desiring a change and yet he has done more work & better work out of the pulpit than any man we have had here for many years. He is a good & true man. No body denies that. The only objection is that he is a poor preacher — blunders in his grammar — and tells too much about *himself* — what *he* has done — his *own* successes.

September 24 — My dear boy Luther started back to the Vanderbilt University — to finish his education. I felt sad to see him go, but suppose it is best. This age seems to demand an educated ministry & I wish to do all I can, for the success of my children — and at best can do but little. I lent Bro Hall 10. to pay a debt which presses him. Not entirely convenient to me — but in the spirit of "bearing one anothers burdens, fulfilling the law of Christ." Bro. Goodson came over & I had a serious candid talk with him about the favor & disfavor of his return.

September 25 – Lizzie and I leave for Conference. We stay with Lewis G. Wood & family at Hopkinsville – Robert being quartered at the same house.

September 26 – Bishop McTyeire opened Conference. Many preachers absent. Business goes smoothly when McTyeire presides.

September 28, 29 – The Cabinet has less than usual difficulty in providing for & adjusting the men to the work. There are more locations than usual. Some good men fall out of rank – not being able to live on the pay they receive. Our superannuated list grows on us. We send some of our promising young men to the West. Some we receive by transfer. There is considerable dissatisfaction with the transfer of old Dr. R. H. Rivers, to be stationed at Broadway. He has floated about from one Conference to another, seeking & getting the best appointments – & now in his superannuated old age – gets himself transferred to us & goes into one of our best appointments over the heads of other men equally as able and as good, who have been brought up with us & never left us. There is indignation and I cannot call it unjust. I told the Bishop that I did not heartily accept the action in that case.

October 1 – The Bishop was sick at night and he left the elders to station the preachers – leaving me in the chair. We made good speed – agreeing amongst ourselves as to most of the appointments & referring all to the Bishop.

October 2 – Bishop was up. He approved most of our work – *all* of it I believe. The Conference was opened by one of the preachers while we finished up the appointments, which were read & then announced & Conference closed. As a whole the appointments please me better than usual – but some distress me – yet I could give no relief. I part with Goodson & his family with much regret. His influence and example are good – but so many people complain of his lack of preaching talent that the Bishop & elders thought a change would be well for him & the work. He talks much of himself and his own achievements, & people call it pride. Enoch Crow calls it 'Sanctified vanity" but he does not feel vain or proud. It is an egotism that is not criminal. His removal is not of my will or my seeking. I trust that Bro Keen will be well received and very successful. No one, with a tender heart – who has not tried it, can tell the anxiety & agony of a Bishops or Presiding Elders work. As a whole our plan is excellent – but subject to abuses – like every thing that is human.

October 4 – I went to see Bro. Goodson, found him sad & laboring under the same impression that chafes my own heart, that injustice has been done him. I have never been as sorely troubled by an appointment since I have been a preacher. The opposition to Goodson on this circuit is most unfortunate. I find many people sad over the change.

October 9 – Wallace & I took train for Louisville – where I am to meet the Presiding Elders tomorrow, in the interest of our Centenary Collections next year. Bro Presley McGuiar, had asked for me to board a day or two with him at the Galt House — & he received me most cordially. Robert took Wallace to his boarding house at Prof. Scotts — as he goes back to fill his 3d year at W. Broadway. At night we went to see the Great Southern Exposition. It is indeed a grand affair — in some respects approximating the "Centennial" but of course on a small scale — like the small cataract compared with Niagara.

October 10 — From 9. to 12. A.M. & from 3 to 4. P.M. the Presiding elders — 7 of us — discussed matters connected with our Centenary year — made a Programme & recommended Logan Female College & our Conf[erence] Board of Education as the institutions for which we would ask help.

October 11 — I spent two hours or more at the Expo[sition] — then took train for home — running through without accident. Hanson went to Louisville to day — but we did not see him as the train passed. He seems to be making arrangements to change his manner of life — from a *single* to a *double* state.

October 12 — I go to day to Trenton cir[cuit] Quarterly Meeting at Chappel Hill — beginning of 1st round of my 4th year. This is Wallace's birthday — 18 yrs old! Lizzie & I will soon be old and lonely. Two men came here to buy my sheep — but Hanson was away & I could not separate them. They told me that two negro men, accused of killing Dick Winlock — last Wednesday, were taken out of jail last night and hung by a mob. Surely our country is making a bad reputation for lawlessness & bloodshed. Mob-law is dangerous — even if it punish those who *deserve* the penalty.

October 16 — [Olmstead] I went over to see Bro Goodson & his family. I gave Ed a pair of boots, Ida a pair of shoes — Fanny a pair of gloves & Joe 50 cts to buy something for himself. They all seem to love my family. I feel really bereft by the separation. Bro Keen moves into the same house. He is well received & we are glad to have him.

October 22 — Hanson was at Olmstead and I helped him get his new buggy set up & rode home in it. He goes as far as Hopkinsville tonight on his way to Greenville where he is to be married Wednesday morning to Jenny, only daughter of Dabney Martin and my old friend Lizzie Britt. We pronounce our blessings on the union and approve of his choice. She seems to be sensible, amiable and well-balanced. Her father once very wealthy is now poor — and she has the good sense to suit her wants to the circumstances.

October 24 — I came home [from Horse Cave] on 4 P.M. train — & in the crowd got the benefit of the civil rights bill by having a drunken negro thrust himself down in a seat by my side.[2] Wallace was waiting at Olmstead with wagon,

2. The Civil Rights Act of 1875 provided that all persons, regardless of race, were entitled to "the full and equal enjoyment of the accommodations, advantages, facilities

buggies & horse to receive Hanson & his wife & company. I met her at the gate with a kiss and a fathers welcome & Lizzie received her at the door with the same cordial greeting. Numerous handsome bridal presents were given – none surprised us all so much, as a handsome silver cake basket from Nannie Browder and her mother of Frankfort. Our present was a nice set of bedroom furniture – bedstead, bed & bedding – wash stand & dresser – carpet &c. Robert sent a set of chairs – Helen valuables for the table – Tom & Mary, pickle stands &c – Daniel Bailey & Annie – syrup stand – Dora Warfield – napkin ring – Pattie Hendrick – nice breast pin. My dear sister Mary & Sister Florence had prepared & brought over nice things in abundance & so we had a joyful time and a full supply, notwithstanding we had a housefull of company & had made but little preparation. We were delighted – heart-glad to see all who came, but in a family like ours we could not *begin* to *invite* because there would be no place to *stop* – so we invited none. Jennie seems happy and at home.

October 27 – [Pleasant Hill] Quarterly Conf[erence] pleasant. Bro. Ausburn Rudd was on hand again, expecting to be licensed to preach, but had not been recommended by his church. He seems to be ignorant of church law & Scripture – yet insists that he ought to preach. There has been a recent controversy in the Elkton Register, between some one signing himself "Rupert" said to be Jas Malone, and Thos H. Shaw – Malone affirming & Shaw denying that the ministers of North Todd were "more stupid & ignorant" than their congregations. The licensing of illiterate and ignorant men is generally a mistake – and in the end brings trouble – although classical education is not indispensable.

October 29 – I got an early start & reached home 8.30 A.M. I was surprised, this morning to find Luther at home – talking of going to Florida to take work in the next Conference. It is not easy for me to decide, but it seems to me that he ought to stay at school!

November 6 – I got a postal, this P.M. from Bro. B. F. Orr of Fairview, telling me of a revival at Fairview in which some had been converted and some backsliders reclaimed, amongst them my dear George, who had resumed the vows of the church and set out to discharge the duties of a Christian. I rejoice greatly over this intelligence.

November 12 – Came home at night [from Elkton] – found Mr Martin, Jenny's father, here – and Hanson about persuaded to go with him to Hopkinsville and begin the manufacture of tobacco – with the original Trade-Mark "Greenville Plug Tobacco" on which the old man made a fortune and prospered, until speculation in *leaf* tobacco & the war swept away everything and left him poor. He thinks it will be a bonanza for Hanson. I look upon the move with misgivings – yet am afraid to oppose it.

---

and privileges of inns, public conveyances on land or water, theatres and other places of public amusement." Alfred H. Kelly and Winfred A. Harbison, *The American Constitution: Its Origin and Development* (New York, 1970), 495.

November 13 – Letters to write – then off to Keysburg to help Bro Keen alittle – had a good meeting. Alick Watts – a wicked man – was powerfully converted – & went through the house praising the Lord. A. F. Young was freed from his burden, but was not satisfied fully because he could not shout.

November 16 – [Olmstead] Was writing up this diary when Tom Sydnor came in and startled me with the tidings that Dr Hutchings died about an hour ago. I am greatly shocked. Lizzie and I went to see the family and assist in preparing for the burial.

November 19 – Pressed on home [from Pleasant Run], well nigh worn out with work & the ride – found my wife gone to stay with Helen who has another son born Saturday & she and the "man child" are both doing well.[3] This greatly relieves my anxiety. I have prayed much for her safety in this trial.

November 20 – Jenny went with me to see Helen & my second grand-son – a fine nine pound fellow. Helen is doing finely. Looking over my accounts I see that I have given to my children, since they were of age – 3,618.85 – most of which was spent in their education.

The tobacco market in this country is excited and prices are high. Three factories proposing to operate at Olmstead – two *new* houses going up for that purpose – Thadd Young & Co. & Guthrie Coke & D. B. Hutchings. I regret now that I did not adhere to my own judgment last spring & plant tobacco. I shall greatly need some money for Hanson.

November 26 – [Adairville] Rain. Small congregation. Bro Lewis led meeting. I went home with Bro J. T. Hildebrand who seemed greatly concerned about his children – and was troubled because he had neglected their baptism – his wife being opposed to infant baptism. The children were now from 6 to 12 years old & he did not know what to do – wished me to talk with his wife and with the children. I advised that as the duty has been neglected so long & the children were now morally accountable – he should not require them to be baptized against their wish & I should not administer it. The wife (Olive Combs) was an intelligent C[umberland] P[resbyterian] woman educated in a Catholic school but still opposed to the baptism of infants. I conversed with her – weighed her objections – & she finally seemed rather anxious that the children should be baptized. I talked with the children and explained the nature and design and the three oldest – Henry, Combs, & Sally were greatly interested & much affected & requested to be baptized – the youngest, Carrie, a very bright, intelligent child – stoutly objected – so I baptized the three older, but declined to baptize Carrie.

---

3. Helen named her sixth child George Browder.

November 27 – Came home – found Lizzie still with Helen who is not doing so well – & the babe has fearfully sore eyes.

December 5 – Reached Hopkinsville in time to see the big fire. Henry Ballards coal oil ware house & his tin & stove house – Gwynns grocery – Webbs Saddlery & other houses on Main & Nashville streets soon went down under the flames – greatly damaging if not ruining, financially some of our best Methodist people. A poor drunken man named Cobb was run over by the Engine & was said to be fatally hurt – but the report was exaggerated. I had been to the druggist to get some medicine, & was returning with it when the first alarm sounded. The crowd that rushed to the fire, of all sexes, colors & conditions was immense.

December 10 – Up & off for home, while the stars were yet in the sky – expressed my saddlebags to Olmstead & reached Fairview by 11 ½ – rested until 1 then rested ½ hour at Elkton – and reached home 20 min to 6 – 36 miles – good travel for an old fat man & an old 14 year mare.

December 11 – Hanson had killed 12 hogs – average 215 lbs nett. Lizzie & Jenny worked at the lard & sausage & got all done by night – lots of sausage and hundreds of lbs of lard – meat all salted down – feet cleaned & "hogkilling" wound up – but I fear my poor wife has made herself sick. I went to see Helen – thankful to find her well & baby Georges eyes getting well.

December 12 – Tom Sydnor & I went to Russellville, in my buggy. I found that almost the entire 350.00 due me on 1st installment in my Bank-Stock has been overchecked – a large amount of it given away – and my debts still remain, unpaid. I am anxious to be liberal. I may, sometimes, go too far for my ability.

December 17 – On Saturday [in Allensville] I bought a coat & vest from John Adams – at 13.50. A nice fit except in front where no ready made coat fits me – without being too large elsewhere.

December 18 – I spent the forenoon in writing to Robert, George & Luther – fatherly letters. Hanson took our three young mules to Hite Small's sale and sold them for 91.00 121.00 & 150.00 – the last, the cheapest & the only sale that I regretted – though it may be best, as we needed the money.

December 19 – Winter! Mercury 21. Snow and hail two or three inches thick – covering the ground. Lizzie & Jenny are getting ready for Eliza [Rutherford]'s marriage here tomorrow.

December 20 – Quite a company came in to see the marriage. Eliza was beautifully dressed by the gifts of kind friends – as nicely as almost any girl who has married around us. I performed the ceremony with becoming solemnity. I do not know another girl whose path has been strewn with sharper thorns or overshadowed with darker clouds, with no fault of her own. She is a good woman and I am glad we gave her a home in our house. Mr Cheatham was her lover in the bloom of her early life and being rejected then he married another woman, who died leaving him three children – and now he returns to woo and win Eliza. I went to the train to see them off, as did my dear old father who has had her in his care from her childhood until his home was sold for the debts of others. We feel sad to part with her, yet we think it best.

December 25 – Christmas guns! sky rockets! noise! negroes! Once our own dear children arose in great glee to search stockings. This morning *William* & *Minor* our two little colored boys came down at 4 A.M. to find toys & sweetmeats in their stockings.

December 28 – Bright sunshine – ground frozen. Lizzie gave us a splendid dinner – oysters, Turkey, old ham, Chive sausage, pickles & jellies – light-bread – bakers-bread – corn-bread – biscuit, crackers – cheese – coffee – Irish & sweet potatoes, raisins, apples, oranges, coconut – fruit cake – pound cake – silver cake – etc – such a dinner as we poor Methodist preachers are not often able to set before our guests – once a year is enough for me.

January 2, 1884 – Mercury 4 above zero & wind blowing a steady gale. I shivered over the fire, reading the papers. Read a plain, sensible, fruitful sermon by Dr Eaton of the Baptist Church – in Louisville, preached to an immense congregation on the text – "Thou shalt not commit adultery." I have tried to warn my congregations against this as well as other sins – but never preached a sermon on it to a mixed audience of male & female. I did to a congregation of men only at Franklin Ky, by request of Quarterly Conference.

January 3 – Gathering ice over 2 inches thick. Lizzie is trying to teach *Minor* & *William*, two little negroes. *Dick Browder*, the reputed but *not* the real father of *Minor* came Monday to take him away – but the child was not willing to go and my wife would not give him up. The plea was that he wished *Minor* to go to school – but he has a better school here than he could find elsewhere. *Dick*, at last consented for him to stay.

January 4 – Not well atall – lungs and throat sore – bad cough & feverish. I packed my valise & went to Depot to take train for Trenton – train so late that there was little hope of getting away from Guthrie – so I came home through a blistering N.W. wind – & well I did come back, for I waked up in the night with a distressingly sore throat & tenderness increasing in my lungs – not far it seemed to me from Diphtheria & Pneumonia. A cold room and a cold bed at Guthrie would most likely have caused my death.

January 5 – Mercy! mercy! how cold. Mercury 12. below zero & ground covered with snow – cant take a full breath without pain & coughing.

January 7 – Mercury rising, 11 *above* 0. I slept warm & well nearly all night, but am still quite unwell. I gave our hired man *Bob,* a plain – *faithful* talk this morning, on the danger of intemperance to which I fear he is drifting.

January 8 – Snow 6 inches deep – mercury rising. I thank God that we are comfortable. I am improving alittle but not able to go out. I spend the time reading and writing. Our man *Bob* went hunting – brought in 6 rabbits & 4 quails. The number of rabbits & quails killed this season has been immense. I think quails were quoted in Louisville at 20 cts per dozen & rabbits at 30 cts pr dozen. This cold & snow will thin them out of the country. Papers report the coldest weather known in many years. Mercury in Dakotah 48 below zero – Chicago 27, St Louis 24, Nashville 10, Chattanooga 2, Cincinnati 20 below zero – all on Jan 5th.

January 11 – My Natal day! 57 years old – beginning to fail perceptibly – teeth getting bad – sight not so good – hearing heavier – more signs of physical decay & loss of manhoods vigor – dont sleep quite so soundly – more trouble with my stomach, kidneys, liver & bowels – appetite not so good – voice weakening – cant endure physical exertion – weary more quickly, rest more slowly – emotions & sensibilities duller – in a word I am getting old. My work is nearly done.

January 14 – Negroes are telling that *Foster Thompson,* the colored man who lived with me, was cut open by another negro, nearby Allensville and his bowels fell out. It is feared that he will die. Truly life is cheap in Logan county. Our present court has condemned one man to be hung for murder committed at Fergusons. That may check the killing.

January 15 – The dreariness of winter! Dismal – cold – white fields & snow covered houses. Not much relief to birds & beasts.

January 23 – I sent to Mr Addison Bush, to return the cow I had lent him – as I had sold her. He seemed offended, as though I had done him injustice to let him feed & milk the cow only a few weeks and then take her away – that he would not have taken her on such conditions. I reminded him kindly that it was *no* favor to me to take the cow from a calf that I was anxious to keep fat – that I told him at the time I might sell the cow – that I only let him have her to accommodate *him* – not me & told him to send her home anytime that it was not profitable to him to keep her, but I could not afford to miss the sale of my surplus cows – that if he had bought any food for the cow which was left over I would give him the money for it. He went away, apparently reconciled. I am sorry to disappoint him, but he seems not to appreciate a kindness – seems to feel that I am the beneficiary & not he. So it is with some people.

January 29 – Hanson is hanging up our meat – for smoking. George writes that he is busy day and night – great deal of Pneumonia – had lost one patient with it

– and two others with other diseases – one blood-poisoning. His books show over $10 a day since 6 of Jan – has a cough himself. Luther has improved some in health – was out of humor about a rough remark, that Dr Baskerville [of Vanderbilt University] made – about boys *lying* who told him that they were sick, just after Luther & another boy had told him they were sick. I am glad that he had sense & grace enough to suppress his temper and get the physicians certificate & present it to Baskerville at the next recitation. If the professor has the elements of a true Christian gentleman in him – he will apologize – if he is full of self importance & infallibility – he will say nothing – or more charitably, he may regret his remark and yet not think it best to say anything more about it. I wrote to Luther approving his conduct & sending him money for his next months board, books &c.

January 30 – [Trenton] Small attendance – fair financial report – good dinners with Bro McGuire & off for home – not feeling well enough for a night service. At Guthrie there were a number of ladies and gentlemen waiting for the train – & some little children. A young man in the R.R. employ passed in & out of the ladies private apartment – locking the door and taking the key out – ladies tried to get in & could not. I remonstrated with the young man & an old gentleman named Bell with his wife & daughter & her children requested him to leave the door unlocked but he would not. I told him that I would inquire into his right to keep that door locked. He said "Suppose you do" in rather a defiant – but not insulting manner. Several gentlemen present expressed decided approbation of my remark – & I shall certainly request the management to issue an order for the door to be kept open to ladies and children.

January 31 – Warm for the season – spring-like. I wrote to Mr Colecamp (Wm) at Memphis – Supt of this R.R. requesting him to give order for the greater comfort of passengers waiting at Guthrie. I do not know that the young lady, Nora Barker, who was in my charge – was incommoded, but I know that other ladies were.

February 4 – Sad! A messenger came from Allensville bringing a telegram for Jenny that her father was very ill at Hopkinsville. She and Hanson started immediately. I fear the old man will die.

February 7 – Papers give fearful accounts of flood in Ohio – eclipsing the unprecendented flood of last Feb. Mr Colecamp Supt. of Lou[isville] & Nash[ville] R. R. *thanks* me for calling his attention to irregularities at Guthrie & promises immediate correction.

February 11 – Sent the buggy for our daughter Jenny & her mother, Mrs Martin – returning sad-hearted from the burial of her father. Mr Martin died at Hopkinsville 2 ½ P.M. on Friday, Feb 8th of Pneumonia followed by paralysis. His wife will now be compelled to live with Hanson – & he will do a sons part for her – that is his duty.

February 12 — I fear I shall have to stop Luther from School after this term. He complains so much of headache and soreness in his lungs. The last news, from the flood in the Ohio, is more distressing — Cincinnati worse flooded than last year & additional rains — on Sunday extending as far up as Pittsburgh. Thousands of people are driven out of their homes — but the noble Christian response to the cry for help shows what the gospel is doing for us.

February 13 — *Mary Winston* (colored) came over & after full understanding, signed a paper putting *Minor* under my control & *William* under Hansons — as long as it suits us to keep them.

February 27 — [Crofton] I preached a very plain & practical sermon on Tit[us] 2.1. John Drake a Saloon man, met Bro Birchett & me at the Depot & took us to his house — gave us supper & pressed us to stay all night — occupying a bed in the room with him & his wife, which is a very usual practice all over this country.

February 29 — We got dinner with John Drake & I had a serious personal talk with him about selling whisky. He said it was a low down business this whisky selling & he felt ashamed of it — but it was a good profit — and made a living &c — but he did not justify it. Henry Durham had brought me a horse & Birchett & I had a pleasant night with his family, despite the howl of wintry winds & the additional fall of snow. We slept in the same room, with him & his wife. They are all just recovering from the itch & we dont know whether we catch it or not — it seems to prevail in many families here.

March 8 — Dreadful mud as Bro Keen & I plodded on to Keysburg. Found a joyous, spiritual congregation. Blue Young met us shouting the praise of God — & the fire soon kindled in other bosoms. Keen & I spend the night by special request with Henry Pace — a liberal-hearted Baptist. Keen has stirred up this country on entire sanctification and a higher life — and many criticisms have been made. Henry Pace told an amusing remark of a negro, *Alick Northington,* who was stripping tobacco with him, when Bro Keen passed by. *Alick* said seriously "Mr Pace is dat de sanctified preacher?" "Yes" said Mr Pace — "that is the man." *Alick* looked very thoughtful for several minutes — working in silence & then said in a very earnest manner — "Mr Pace when I gits a 'ligion I wants a common 'ligion." This story raised a rousing laugh from all present and none more than Keen himself.

March 9 — Good love-feast and fine congregation. I had considerable liberty in preaching a Centenary sermon — & think I showed our church to good advantage. I raised a collection for the American Bible Society 4.60. Went to dinner with Frank Bailey's family. Frank was glad to hear of "uncle Billy Washingtons" good luck — receiving 1000. in money & a suit of fine clothes from friends in the North — Genl Grant & Pres. [Rutherford B.] Hayes being contributors — through Mrs Blakemore of Philadelphia, who showed a letter she had received from the old man. I have been a helper to the dear old man for years. I thank God that he is now comfortable. At night Bro Keen preached an earnest sermon on universal charity. I was very tired & unfortunately went to sleep, and while I did not fall & break my neck like Eutychus, yet I snored loud enough to arrest attention and make myself very much ashamed.

March 10 – Thad Young surprised me by telling me that he and his brothers wished me to go to Tobin's Merchant Tailor in Elkton & have a fine coat made & charged to him! I have seldom been more surprised by a present. A few days ago I sent Robert 5.00 for flood sufferers – this morning I got the promise of a fine coat, so it goes. I give to the Lord & he pays me back.

March 14 – Tomorrow is my Quarterly meeting at Russellville and I am poorly prepared for my work. It seems that my studies are so interrupted that I learn but little.

March 15 – I was kindly invited to make my home with Dr Rizer Perry during this visit. Dr Perry's mother was one of the friends of my younger ministry & he always treats me with marked respect. He shows a kind heart in having Alick Finley to come down often & take a meal with him. Alick Finley is a brother of Rev W. J. Finley but is of very singular mental make up. He is a lawyer, but has no clients these days. He is a well informed, sensible man, utterly disregardful of dress or personal appearance – except that he wears a clean shirt – seldom ever wears a vest – is frequently ragged and I fear frequently hungry – has lived up a small patrimony & is now very poor. A friend gave him a suit of good clothes, but he does not wear them. In morals – he is irreproachable – never swears an oath, or drinks spirits – or keeps vile company or uses corrupt conversation. I never knew him to be absent from prayer meeting – preaching or Sunday school when able to be present – is a diligent faithful S.S. teacher & a Bible Student. Hardly any body dies without his presence and help at the burial & frequently he does the service of washing and dressing the dead. No body seems to suspect him of anything wrong. He was shot during the war – by a drunken man – Pres. Roberts – because he was a unionist – but he behaved like a hero and like a Christian and sought no revenge. He spent years in getting up material for a history of Logan County – based on reliable and authentic data – & printed a small volume – valuable to people locally interested – but attracting no notice from the outside world. He has now a theory by which he proposes to visit the moon & several of the stars & return again to earth. He will make an immense gun – 10 or 12 miles long – with a succession of inner guns of immense size that can be exploded at will and, he being in the gun – protected & prepared with water, air, food & fuel – will at the right moment as he flies through space – discharge another gun carrying him still further toward the moon – & getting in reach of the moons attraction will turn his gun & shoot himself the other way to break the force of gravity & let himself down with moderate ease – make a survey of the planet & with the remainder of the guns & supplies come back to earth or go to some other planet. He does not show *any sign* of insanity – and yet argues that idea with the earnestness & clearness of a philosopher. No body believes his theory — but he seems to think that it will ultimately be done and all that keeps him from starting is the lack of 100,000,000 of dollars to procure the outfit. We sat talking to a late hour.

March 16 — Bright, balmy, beautiful Sabbath. I held the love-feast — largest attendance I have seen there in a long time & many earnest speeches. After discussion a number of brethren & friends — pastors & others came in to consider the propriety of having the legislature prohibit the sale of intoxicating liquors within five miles of the colleges of Russellville. Committees to prepare business were appointed & a grand mass-meeting called for Wednesday night. I felt prostrate & lungs seemed collapsed after the labors of the day. I spent the night at Dr Perrys — but waked up in the night with difficulty of breathing.

March 18 — Up at 5 A.M. I got home weary to find a letter from George telling that he was very sick — thought he had measles, asking some of us to come to him. His mother was anxious to go — but I thought she was not able so Hanson went.

March 20 — Hanson writes that George is quite sick. Lizzie & I propose to go see him tomorrow. Tom Sydnor insists that Lizzie & I take his two horse buggy for our trip & use one of his horses — gentler than one of mine. Very kind.

March 21 — Lizzie & I reached Fairview at 2 P.M. — found George quite sick & very nervous — glad to see us. Mrs Lane is kind to him & received us kindly. I have seldom in a life-time driven over as bad roads as we travelled to day. One horse could not have pulled us. It was hard on two.

March 22 — George was very restless all through the night — severe inflammation in the rectum — bloody & *very* painful evacuations. Gave him Doves powder & got him quiet.

March 23 — Up nearly all night, with my poor restless, suffering son — dreadful ear-ache besides the torturing pain in the extremity of the lower bowel — suppose I was up & down 15 or 20 times. He insisted that I pour a few drops of chloroform into his ear. I put a very little into a few drops of laudanum & poured it in. He sprang up — screaming at the top of his voice — delirious with pain — startled nearly every body in the house. I allowed him to inhale alittle chloroform which seemed to relieve him temporarily. I lay in bed with him & nursed him until he got under the influence of a little morphine & Doves powder — then he slept well & seemed better this morning.

March 24 — George slept well — nearly all night — greatly relieved. I was up with him only one time. I fed him & he seemed to relish his breakfast. I think the crisis is past — so I left his mother with him and came home.

March 27 — I finished pruning my young trees & a grape-vine. Very seldom do I take any time for manual labor — but the season is so backward & there is so much to do, that I ought to do such little jobs as I can. The house seems lonesome to me when Lizzie is gone, but Jenny makes everything comfortable. She is a sweet good daughter & she & Hanson seem happy in their married life.

March 28 — Wallace & I got Tom Sydnors carriage & went to Fairview — for Lizzie & George. Roads greatly improved.

April 8 — [On returning from Hopkinsville] I found Robert at home, George improving & Hanson well-forward with his corn-planting. All this is well — but I get sad news that my dear sister Annie is suffering dangerously, with some unnatural growth in her throat of which she has been complaining for months — & the Dr is very uneasy.

April 9 — Robert, Lizzie, sister Mary & I went to see Annie. It is dreadful to see what a change is in her condition. I fear she is bound to die & that before many weeks or even days. Her throat is rapidly filling up with an awful growth that the Dr fears is cancer. She can now only swallow liquids & talks & breathes with difficulty. It is too bad — too bad, to see her lie suffering & sad and hopeless for this world — in prospect of being a mother again in a few months & yet not expecting at all to live to see the time. Her Christian faith is strong and her resignation well-nigh perfect. Converted when a small child — she has always been conscientious & good & now says the way is clear & she is not afraid to die. I read & prayed with her & sang "Take the name of Jesus with you" — a song which she used to sing with peculiar sweetness & fervor. I think she will soon be with her precious babe & loved ones gone before in the place which Jesus went to prepare. Her fatherinlaw Dr. J. R. Bailey says he thinks she is the best woman he ever knew.

May 5 — Corn & potatoes coming up — grass & wheat growing finely. Lizzie & I went to see Annie — found her sitting up and looking better, but I fear not really improved.

May 14 — Busy writing. I see the papers everywhere speaking of our Sec. of Board of Church Extension as *Dr* David Morton. The doctorate has never been conferred upon him & while modesty compels him to be silent I am sure the situation must be embarrassing — so I wrote to Bishop Keener — to Dr R. H. Rivers & to Dr Fitzgerald suggesting to them to use their influence with some respectable college to have a "D.D." conferred upon Bro Morton — his *prominence* entitling him to have in name, what the papers are forcing upon him in fact. "D.D." is not now a title of *great* learning & deep research in theological lore as in former days. It is given to men of note *pro honore* as much *pro merito* & as such Morton is entitled to it & ought to have it — hence my movement, unsolicited, unsuggested by any body.

May 19 — I learn, with sorrow, that my own dear mother is very unwell, has had two spells of fainting, & unconsciousness and that my sister Annie has been worse than ever. I much fear that serious trouble is just before us.

May 22 — I cut potatoes & did alittle work in the garden. Mary came by in great haste to take Lizzie to Annie who is reported to be in a critical condition. I have grave fears that she will not pass this ordeal.

This is the annual exhibition at Browder Institution. The crowd was not so large as usual & in the main, the behavior was good, but two or three boys were rude enough to hiss & whistle, in a disagreeable & insulting manner. The performances, in the main were creditable — some of them superior. I think Bailey Browder is the most natural and altogether the best declaimer of his age, that I ever heard — perfectly self-possessed, and his pieces perfectly memorized — his modulations — gestures & emphasis, are all remarkable, for a boy ten or 12 years old. Many experienced public speakers are not his equals. Some of the smaller boys and girls acted their parts admirably — & there was about the usual amount of forgetfulness. I always sympathize with a child who forgets part of his speech. That was my failure at my first public effort as with race-horse speed I hurried over the verses that I did remember in S. G. Goodrich's poem — "Columbus was a sailor brave — The first that crossed the Atlantic wave" &c. My son Wallace delivered the valedictory, in the main, original & reasonably well rendered. It was loudly applauded. We got home by midnight.

May 23 — Lizzie returned from Dr Bailey's. Annies baby died in 6 hours after its birth. She is doing well under the circumstances. Her throat is no better.

May 31 — Best Saturday congregation I have seen at Ash-Spring for many years. The Quarterly Conference was full of business. Before the session began Luther preached a short earnest sermon, that showed some thought. I think he will sometime make a preacher. He & I came home. A rare thing for me to be at home Sat. night.

June 8 — [Grissom's Chapel near Crofton] I was surprised to see so large a crowd — & such serious listening to so long a sermon. People here are compelled to take children, babes & all to church — & as the day was sultry, there was much crying of babes & as the seats were split logs, with pegs driven into auger holes & no backs, I doubt not that many people were weary. I preached a Centenary sermon of one hour & twenty minutes — & raised a collection to be applied to completing that house — got ⅕ of what it should have been — $30.00. These people have small ideas of giving.

June 12 — [Olmstead] Still cloudy, cool & threatening. Harvest is almost on us. Most of our wheat seems to be good. To day there is a trial of reapers — self-binders at Elias Riley's. I ordered one of Wood's binders two weeks ago at 170. & am now offered the Champion at 150. delivered at Olmstead. Wonderful change since when I was a boy, we cut our wheat with the handsickle! Truly the boys of this age have much to inspire gratitude.

June 13 – To day my heart has been tender. I have been working on a sermon on family training. Text Gen[esis] 18.19. "For I know him, (Abraham) that he will command his children and his household after him, and they shall keep the way of the Lord to do justice & judgment; that the Lord, may bring upon Abraham that which he hath spoken of him." My mind has turned often back to my own dear father, now 80 years old – & to my childhood home & happiness. I have lived again in the dear "old house" with a room below & one above. I have worn my *first* pants over again – and tramped about in my first boots – and set my snares and baited my traps – & fed my sheep – & brought up the calves with black *George* & *David* – & I have waded in the branch – and rolled in the snow, and rambled in the orchard – and played in the barn. Ive picked cotton at night around the log-fire and roasted potatoes at the barn, as my father fired tobacco at night. I have carried brick, on the yard – & set up at the brick-kiln – and helped carry brick to build the new house – and Ive risen up – before light to get away to the old horsemill at Smalls sometimes & sometimes at Hansboro's to get meal – in dry weather – & Ive been again, on horseback with a bag of corn or a bag of wheat, away down to Donley's on Elk-fork or to Orndorffs on Red river – and at both the Poor's mills on Whippoorwill. Ive turned the bolt, by hand to get alittle flour – & Ive hauled water, from Moores Spring, with the cart & oxen. Ive done my *first* plowing with old Fox & a wooden mould-board – and dropped corn and tobacco plants in the field. Mother has taught me the catechism, over again & I have been to my first school to uncle Hutchings at old Bethlehem & then to Mrs Collard & then to Mr Washington – & on and on, my life has come up before me – and the brightest of all its pictures is home – father & mother – dear little sister Helen & then Amelia – that died, in child-hood. Ah! how sadly I remember that sweet, beautiful little Helen cried to go with me & because she was too small to keep up, I would not let her go – & in a few days she took scarlet fever and died. I was a small boy, perhaps six or seven years old, but not since have I seen a child, that fills my ideal of excellence and beauty like my first, sweet sister Helen – named by my loving step-mother, for my own sainted mother, whose place she has tried so faithfully to fill – and in my childhood memories this day – my fathers morning & evening songs in his family worship ring on my ear & thrill in my heart – and the old time Methodist preachers come into the little old house & sleep up in the room over head – and I hear the rain patter on the shingle roof with no plastering between. I hear my father laugh & joke. I ride behind him to church, on old Fan, while mother rides old Jule with the baby in her arms – and growing alittle larger I ride a mule, by myself – with a sheepskin saddle and a blind bridle. I call up the old black dog "Nero" and I remember the deer that was killed & brought to the house & the wild turkies – and the evening visits father & mother used to make to the neighbors, to sit till bed time & talk & sing & pray, and the old camp-meeting at Bethlehem, when I was four years old – and the impression on my mind, when my father gave me a silver dollar to put in the missionary hat – & how one of the preachers laid his hand on my head & said "Lord bless the little boy and make him a missionary" and that blessing & that prayer rest on me this day. I remember, too, how sick my father was at Campground & they took him down to old uncle "Benny"

Browders — and once, how the oxen ran over the bluff into the creek with him, when he was going to mill with the cart — & he came up to uncle Moore's where I was staying with George Nick — faint & bleeding — bruised & nearly killed and how my dear aunt Nancy, turned pale when she saw him & cried out — "Why Robert! What in the world is the matter with you?" I see too, the old crooked trough, in the stable, that fell on me one day & would have crushed me to death but for the crook — a large — hollow gum log — & I see yet my father running to me as I screamed, & straining to raise the log off me — & mother following in to pull me out — alarmed and unnerved with the excitement — & I call up the day, when I was playing in the wheat up the new room stairs — and hearing my father coming I started down out of the window, on the sleet covered scaffold & half way down — I slipped off & fell with my back on a pile of broken bricks below — & screamed out, "Oh! Im dead Im dead," and my father, in great alarm came running down & took me in his arms & carried me to the bed — & examined to see if any bones were broken — and I remember when I jumped out of the old schoolhouse loft — with my bare feet, on a nail, in an upturned plank — that cut into my foot to the bone — & how the teacher let me go home, & mother bound up my foot in a bag of dry ashes from the fire place, which arrested the swelling & the pain & enabled me to walk to school the next day — and oh so well do I remember many of my early school days — & plays with the boys — & struggles with my lessons & trials with my teachers & occasional floggings & frequent stayings in at play time & much that enters into a school boys life. I see now much anxiety & uneasiness that father had about me & much care that mother had, that I would not have given them if I had known then what I know now. I go back to the day I was converted, when a small boy — certainly not older than 11 years — at a morning meeting at Ash-Spring. While old uncle John Moore was preaching, I was strangely moved — to weeping & sorrow & was led, by my mother to the altar — & in deep & solemn prayer I cried to God to save me. It seemed to me that I would sink into Hell — & deserved such a fate — & giving up in despair I looked to Jesus as the *only* hope — & trusting him I felt the thrill of a new creation — a life from the dead rushing through my young heart — & I was the first one to know & tell it. A young preacher, named McLoughlin, seeing my distress & earnestness, before this, had raised me up & said that God had blessed me — but I knew no relief & knelt down again, in the straw seemingly unconscious of all human surroundings, when God revealed his mercy & grace to my poor despairing soul. I knew it first & told it first — & went, after rejoicing a while, to look up my cousins, but to my amazement they were afraid of me and ran away from me. That night I received another blessing, fuller & sweeter than the one in the morning & I went to my father the next night at supper table, after his return from Hopkinsville, & told him of my joy in the Lord — and I remember well — his tears and his expression of gratitude. For weeks & months I was as happy a boy, I suppose as lived and have been in the main as happy a man as any other. I have much to be thankful for — & would be glad to make other homes happy — and for this I am preparing the sermon on Family government — with tender memories of home.

June 21 – [Hopkinsville] Busy all day till 5 Oclock – writing out my sermon on family government. Held Quarterly Conference – expressing my appreciation of the treatment the brethren had given me for four years & taking leave of them as their P[residing] E[lder]. Bro Bottomley replied that he but voiced the sentiment of the whole Conference when he said they had all been pleased with me and my work & regretted to part with me – & so said they all. Of course I was gratified.

June 24 – [Olmstead] Hanson is well pleased with Wood's Self-binder – it cuts low or high, straight or tangled, thick or thin wheat – ties it tight in a bow-knot, cuts off the thread & throws it down. Three good horses pull it with comparative ease – four would be better.

July 1 – Lizzie & I called to see Annie. She is alittle stronger, but I fear that the hateful tumor will do its fatal work.

July 2 – In the afternoon [at Bethlehem Church] I pursued the study of sanctification as taught in the Bible – without note or comment, & I am more & more convinced that the Scriptures do *not* distinguish between regenerate Christians & sanctified Christians – but does distinguish between regenerate & unregenerate people – & in the Christians, recognizes degrees of development – children, young men, fathers – "little faith" "great faith" – blade, stalk, full corn. The law seems to be of growth – "go on" "grow up" "grow." Regeneration is sanctification, perfect in its degree – as the infant child *as* a child, is as perfect as a man. There is nothing in nature that does not gain its fullest development by *growth* – perfect in its infancy – *developed* by its growth. Regenerate souls – *babes* in Christ – need to be fed with "milk" until they can use "meat." Christians are compared to "vines" & "trees" & "grain" – all under the law of growth. The spirit of God sanctifies – every day & always – when the soul is laid on God's altar – and while there *may* be instantaneous sanctification or cleansing, from all sin – yet the *rule* seems to be one of development. God regenerates – puts in the leaven & the leaven works. God works *in* us *to* will, not *the* will & we must "work out our own salvation" by improving the grace given.

July 3 – Hanson finished his wheat harvest to day – having lost some time in cutting a crop for our colored neighbor *John Warder,* who could not get any body else to save his wheat for him. Hanson can, I hope now, have time to go to church.

July 5 – [Sharon Grove] Immense congregation & patient listening to a sermon one hour & twenty minutes long, in one of the hottest days I ever felt. I preached on the Centenary & tried to raise a collection for a thank-offering but the people think they are poor. I am ashamed at many people in my District.

July 6 – Crowd at 11 very large in the house & out of doors – preached on family government again with considerable unction. Many people begged me to have the sermon published. A Baptist Brother James Agee seemed deeply concerned – & said he could raise the money to print a thousand copies. I got a fall this morning that came well nigh being serious. The stile block, at Bro Brakes's turned under my weight & threw me some distance forward on my face & catching with my hands – to save myself, I sprained my right wrist – & my nose was badly bruised & skinned – & bled for a considerable time. I am thankful that it was no worse.

July 7 – [Olmstead] I see marks of a storm – trees in my yard & orchard, badly broken – many wheat-shocks uncapped & many blown down. A large locust limb blew across the house & did some damage to the roof. I was quite surprised to find that I have been appointed a delegate to the Centenary Conference to meet at Baltimore Dec 9–17 1884. The Louisville Conference delegation stands Clerical – Geo. R. Browder & B. M. Messick. Lay – Presley McGuiar & H. G. Petree. I only wish that I were worthy of the compliment implied and able to represent, as I ought, my brethren of the Louisville Conference. If I had been allowed to choose my associates I could not be better pleased – but it seems to me that there would have been a propriety in sending the venerable Thomas Bottomley, whose first work in this country was in Maryland – if not in Baltimore, & I am sure he would have been a good representative.

July 8 – The meeting last night [at Bethlehem] was more interesting. Bro. Godbey's strong expressions & fearful denunciations of ritualism will offend some people – but *may* do good in the end. Some of his ways are peculiar, & seemingly extravagant – but he is evidently a man of God, & despite his eccentricities – he seems to be doing a great work. God forbid that I should hinder it. There is great need of a profound awakening in this community. I went to church at night. Godbeys manner is peculiar – & his look peculiar – his ideas seem sound & scriptural & he drives things to their conclusion – logical result – says plain – seemingly harsh words & offends some people. So did Jesus. I think his methods are singular – & could be improved – but I shall rejoice in all the good he does.

July 9 – It is rumored that a negro who killed a man in Todd Co. was taken from jail in Russellville & shot to death by a mob – on Sunday night. Such things in Kentucky are fearfully frequent. The uncertainty of law as to punishment of crime has much to do with it. Courts & juries seem to be corrupt & the people, in many places, feel driven to take the law into their own hands – seemingly forgetful that if they kill a man without authority of law, they are as guilty as the murderer himself – doing what he did – killing unlawfully. I would not encourage such a thing, whatever the crime of the guilty party.

Young Mysonhimer preached at night, rather exhorted – full of fire & zeal – led quite a number of boys to the altar of prayer. He runs all over the house – into the pulpit & down the aisles, frequently during his sermon – seems to be holy – claims to be sanctified. God grant to me such an experience – full sanctification – perfect purity of heart – but the mannerism I do not like.

The Trustees of Browder Institute held a meeting to day and elected Hanson as the teacher – I think a wise selection for them. He is certainly competent & faithful but I have some fears for his health. He has been quite unwell for two days – threatened with Flux.

July 10 – Bro. W. B. Godbey took leave of us last night – saying that he was "inwardly moved" to leave here and go to Adairville – but said "If the congregation protests against my leaving, I am not compelled to go *at once.*" Some understood this as a bid for an uprising in his favor – but Bro. Keen told him that we had been accustomed to regard the leading of the Spirit & if the Lord moved him to leave, we could not protest – & there was none. Some people seem to be relieved that he has gone. He is certainly a good man, but not entirely balanced.

We had a good meeting at 4, and again at night some professions. Mysonhimer seems earnest – but has much more zeal than knowledge. His talk is a rambling, sort of rant, that hardly amounts to a respectable exhortation – no elements of a sermon – yet it seems to take effect.

July 16 – Reading some, working in the garden – hoeing my cabbages – & sowing turnip seeds – but my sprained arm cannot stand much.

Daniel Bailey & my sister Mary took Annie to Nashville to day, to be examined, but the Drs do not offer any encouragement.

July 19 – [Gordonsville] Went in my buggie to Stuarts Chapel to Quarterly Meeting. The house was not roofed & the school house was too small – so the friends had built a nice brush arbor in the grove. Quarterly Conference interesting – but this people with all their kindness show a humiliating lack of interest in the support of their pastors. Bro Hogard pays 5.00 a month for a house & has received less than 140. for 10 months of ministerial work. This circuit has paid me six dollars – for all my travel & labor & 15 sermons.

July 23 – [Olmstead] Hanson & I went to town – on Summons to testify in suit of Dave Hendricks against the R.R. but the court business is several days behind and we were dismissed for the day. I do not feel comfortable over Dave Hendricks suit. I could neither go to Gilliam's District Conference nor Deering's camp-meeting, because I have to answer this summons – & many farmers and businessmen are called from home at a time when it ill suits them to go – to testify in a case of imaginary damage, in which they can have no interest. I tried to keep him from bringing the suit.

July 28 – Much sickness is reported. Flux especially. Our hired man *Bob* is down with it.

July 30 – After consultation with the brethren, I published the postponement of camp-meeting, until further notice, in view of the sickness & hindrances caused by rains.

July 31 – The long delayed suit came up again to day and the trial proceeded. I narrated the facts just as they occurred. Many other witnesses were called, some of whom saw things differently, but the court gave Hendricks a verdict $500.00 damages – $475.00 *more* than his own estimate of the value of a day's time. Wilbur Browder & Geo. Edwards made able speeches in his favor & W. W. Lyles & John Rhea ably & artfully defended the R.R. I think that prejudice against a corporation had much to do with the verdict. Ten per cent of his $5000. was much more than I expected him to get – & more than he justly deserved.

August 1 – I went over to see Robt Boyds family, several of whom have been down with flux & three now in bed – his wifes condition critical.

August 2 – Sickness made the congregation at Red Oak smaller than usual. Quarterly Conference small. Some unpleasant feelings, on bro Lewis's part – grew out of the postponement of the camp-meeting [at Ash Spring] – before he was consulted – characterizing my action as "precipitate" & charging the campers as ignoring him as their pastor – speaking with evident spirit & ill humor. I assured him that I acted on advice of campers – a majority of whom I learn could not camp now – & certainly did not intend to ignore or overlook him, but thought that the campers *only* were competent to settle the *time* when they could leave home & move to the camp-ground – that I expressed no opinion as a presiding elder, but only as a *camper*. The brethren disclaimed any intent to ignore him – & said they had sent for him to consult, but could not get him. I suppose this is the first time in my life that Jas. A. Lewis ever felt that I had done him injustice – and in this I am certainly innocent of any intentional wrong. I am sure that upon reflection he will feel & think differently.

August 4 – [Red Oak] Mrs [John A.] Miller died yesterday of flux. It was sister Millers request that I should preach her funeral. There was a *large* congregation at 9:30 A.M. & I preached with some unction & liberty Isa[iah] 25.6–8. The one thing that touched me most was the devotion of the Sunday School class to their dead teacher. They wept like they had lost their mother. Her dying request to the superintendent was "Put a godly woman in charge of my class."

August 5 – [Olmstead] Lizzie & I went to see sister Boyd. Before we got in we heard the weeping & wailing of her children. She was surely dying. Seven daughters & two sons & the poor old husband, with a number of kind neighbors, were present. Seldom have I witnessed such grief – so tenderly do those children love their mother – "O mother! Oh, mother" they cried. "Speak to us once more. Mother do you know your children – all around you? Mother – Mother – let us hear your voice once more. Oh mother, call my name – one more time – one more time." – & so they wept & groaned – as eagerly and tenderly they stood & pressed to catch her last word. It was sad & sweet to be there. I could but recall the words of the poet – "The chamber where the good man meets his fate, is privileged beyond the common walks of men, quite in the verge of Heaven." She lay some time this morning – gazing up as if she saw some thing above – in so much that Mrs Minerva Hutchings remarked that "she seems to see some body" when she sweetly said – "Jesus can make a dying bed feel soft as downy pillows are." We wept with them – then left them – other kind neighbors remaining to see the last & do the last service.

August 10 – I carried some nice apples, pears & lemons to my poor afflicted sister Annie. That dreadful tumor is growing, she can hardly talk intelligibly & swallows with great difficulty – yet seems patient and resigned.

August 13 – It is sad to see my poor sister dying by inches, as that fatal tumor grows into her throat closing up the space for swallowing & breathing. Her speech is so indistinct that we can hardly understand her. One of her eyes is forced into an unnatural position & she is a mere skeleton. She is remarkably cheerful & resigned, says she dreads the pangs of death but wishes it were all over with her.

August 23 – I have quite a sore-throat this morning – possibly from close cutting of my hair & beard yesterday, then sitting in the open air. Wallace wants to go with me to town to day. He is a good boy & I promised him 5.00, in addition to what he has, to get him a good silver watch. He has lately shown a spirit of filial obedience & thoughtfulness that pleases me much. I bought him a watch of Ben Settle for 13.50 – a stem winder & good works, heavy silver case – such as he sells for 17.00. Wallace was greatly pleased. I bought two large water melons for 25 each & came home.

August 25 – I feel much anxiety about campmeeting. The change in time disappoints the preachers who had promised to be with us, & I fear we will lack help.

August 26 – We all moved in, without accident – *all* the camps full & people cheerful & ready for the *first* service.

August 27 – Religious influence steadily increasing – behavior all that could be desired.

August 28 – Jas A. Lewis preached the best sermon of his life on "Beholding as in a glass the glory of the Lord." The church is awake, working & praying – & sinners beginning to tremble.

August 30 – The Quarterly Conference of Allensville circuit, met at the preachers tent at three oclock while bro Hooker preached. Every church reported full payment to pastor & presiding elder – & good reports on the other collections. My son Luther was recommended for deacon's orders & for admission on trial into the Annual Conference. I do not doubt his sincerity & I think he will make a preacher – if he can retain his health.

August 31 – Good morning meeting. Immense concourse at 11. estimated at from 3000 to 5000 people. I never saw so many buggies, carriages, wagons, horses & mules at meeting, before, that I remember – & no man ever saw so large a concourse keep more perfect order. Bro Emerson preached an excellent sermon on Christ & the atonement. Keen preached on Sanctification at 3. a bold, earnest, ingenious sermon – making some application of Scriptures, that caused talk & criticism. I think he misunderstands some of the Scriptures quoted – but he is laboring to bring up the church to a higher plane of living & experience. Spurrier preached a masterly sermon at night, on the worth of the soul. Interest steadily increasing – tide rising *all* the time.

September 2 – All the meetings delightful, morning – noon & night. The meeting *grows every day* – in interest – each day better than the preceding – no *ebbing* of the tide & in this it differs from any other meeting that I have attended. It is surely God working in us & through us.

September 3 – The best day of all – sweet – spiritual – powerful time. Oh such conversions! Oh! such rejoicings. I am sorry I have to leave for Crofton Mission. Vol P. Thomas came in just as I was leaving – and in the highest tide we have had. I feared a lack of preachers, but we have had plenty of help of the *best kind.* The preaching was the *right sort* for results – Bottomley, Emerson, Keen, Lewis, Spurrier, Hooker, Luther Browder, Chas Hall & myself – 31 conversions up to my leaving.

September 4 – Took train for Empire Coal mine where I preached tonight. There was a good congregation of miners & citizens at the Schoolhouse and I preached a very earnest, plain sermon on Luke 14. The invitation to & rejection of the gospel. I tried to suit myself & my subject to the audience before me & I could not ask better attention. The women brought their babies, but the children did not cry. The men came in their shirt sleeves & the women in plain – not to say scanty apparel – but all listened & I "made the vision plain." Quite a number gave me their hands in promise of repentance & reformation.

September 5 – I went down the shaft into the coal mines – away down – down – down 60 feet into the ground & then stopping & following Bro John David, the Supt. I went away – under the entries & saw the sooty miners, bending down & picking out the coal. I talked to some of them about keeping ready to die. Following my guide with a little glimmering light in this region of total darkness, is a good illustration of faith in Christ. Bro Birchett & I took noon train back to Crofton. The house was ready, new church – the chandeliers up & lamps filled with oil & everybody glad at the idea of a new church in Crofton, where for so long a time there has been no house of worship. I thought it well to preach the first sermon in it, on the nature & work of the Holy Spirit whose aid we invoke in all our work. This is the anniversary of my marriage & as I cannot be with Lizzie – I wrote to her this morning.

September 6 — Our congregation was good. All the churches were represented. Bro. Birchett has a strong hold on this people — all want him back — yet they have not paid him. He has worked like a hero to finish the church here and at Grissom's & has succeeded, and they make him & me pay for it, by withholding our small pay. Yet they have gone far beyond any other year of my knowledge.

September 7 — Hot! so hot! At 11. I preached the dedication sermon Mat[thew] 27.22 — to as attentive an audience as so hot a day & such a crowd could give anywhere. I *suffered* — my clothes were wet with perspiration. There was a debt of 36.80 due on the house, which I expected to raise without trouble — as there were several rich citizens in the congregation — but to my surprise we only got 16.00 — but Birchett assumed the balance & we dedicated the house to the worship of God. I administered the Sacrament at night after Birchett preached, then raised the remainder of the money for the church debt — greatly relieving Bro Birchett & greatly pleasing the people — who all seemed in a great glee, as if they had done a wonderfully handsome thing. Some Universalists & Campbellites proposed that if they could get a regular day in the house, they would help us pay it out & put in stoves, carpet &c. I stated publicly that Methodists had always been liberal & charitable in opening their houses of worship to other Christians — that as there was no other house of worship in the town, we would be glad for any Christian people, who accepted the Bible as the word of God & Christ as the only hope of salvation — to occupy the house, when we were not using it — that we would have given that liberty if they had never given a cent to the house — but that we could not give any right or claim to any day, except by courtesy & not as a *consideration* for the payment of any sum small or great — that I could raise the money elsewhere & relieve Birchett but I thought *they ought* to do it — & then they did & seemed happy over it. I raised, I think, $1200.00 in Elkton once, with less labor than it required here to raise 36.80.

September 8 — I took train for home, better pleased with Crofton after getting better acquainted with the people. A dollar to most of them is quite a sum.

September 9 — Went with Lizzie to see father & mother at Tom Sydnor's. Mother fell out of bed & was hurt — cannot walk. I felt very tired & worn out all day. I am sorry to go to Conference broken down, but there seems no help.

September 10 — I have had a trial yesterday & to day to keep in a good humor. Our cook *Lizette* was very insolent & insulting to my wife — & very unjustly. I never could tolerate that, but I kept calm & said nothing — intending to talk at the right time. Mother still suffering at Tommy's.

September 11 — More patience needed. My principal farm hand, *Bob Clark,* cook's husband — told me yesterday that he would not go to Russellville to the show to day — & on his word I had a considerable lot of tobacco cut down — to be taken up this morning — & this morning he & his wife and all the hands insist on going to the show and leaving the tobacco down on the ground. There is great danger of sun-burn. We fortunately found some other help & got the tobacco taken up. I am glad that I did right & kept calm.

September 16 — Off to Conference. Took in many preachers on the way — divided my lunch with several.

September 17 — [Louisville] Bishop Wilson is ill in Baltimore & Bishop McTyeire holds our Conference. The preachers are mostly present, *many* of them with their wives & part of their children, taking in the city and Exposition, at little expense.

September 19 — Luther was admitted on trial into the travelling connection — expects to transfer to Florida. If he can be more useful there than here, I ought not & do not object — though he goes far from home.

September 21 — A glorious love-feast. At 11. Bishop McTyeire preached an excellent funeral discourse, by request of Conference, on the death of Bishops Kavanaugh & Pierce. At the close eight men were ordained deacons. My son Luther one of them.

September 22 — At 11 A.M. in Conference room I received a telegram announcing the death of my dear sister Annie. It was too late for me to get to her burial. She was a sweet, loving sister & I was sad to know that I should see her no more. I wrote to my dear stricken parents, and staid to do my work at Conference. We received our appointments tonight. I was sent to Owensboro District & Robert to Elizabeth town Station. Owensboro asked for me & Bowling-green Dist[rict] also made an earnest effort to have me returned to them, but the bishop thought I ought to go to Owensboro. I was much grieved that he removed bro John S. Keen from Allensville to Portland. I think that we were too much hurried in getting ready to adjourn. Another day would have been better. I learn from many brethren that there is great dissatisfaction on the Bowling-green Dist[rict]. I am sorry for them, but glad that I am not responsible for the appointment. They told Dr Ford that they did not want him [as presiding elder]. I am surprised that a man would consent to be forced upon a people that were not willing to receive him. I would have been willing to go to Bowling-green — but can possibly do more good at Owensboro. The only serious trouble is the distance from my dear parents in their age and affliction.

September 23 — I would have staid another day, but I was sad & the dear ones at home were sad. So I took train for Olmstead, where I found Hanson waiting for me with the buggy. We stopped alittle at Tommy's to see my dear old father & mother in their grief. Annies death was peaceful & happy — so patient, so trusting. For months she had been saying that she was ready — & resigned to the will of God. No one knows how much she suffered with that fearful tumor growing more & more inside and out — and yet she said to Mary — "Sister I would not take this lump off my throat if I could unless I believed it was God's perfect will." When the last hour came, she said "I feel so strangely. Daniel (her husband) am I dying?" but poor Dr. was weeping so he could not reply. Mary said, "yes child you are dying." She replied – "If this is dying, it is not hard. I want you all to know that I am not afraid to die. Do you understand? I am not afraid to die." She said "Jesus" "Sweet Jesus" & then all was over, her sweet spirit was gone to heaven. She begged Daniel to be a good Christian & meet her in Heaven & he promised to try. So passed away a bright jewel to glitter in the Saviours crown.

September 24 – I went to see father & mother. My poor mother has not walked alone, since she fell out of bed two weeks ago. She seems sad and desponding & father takes it to heart that I am sent so far away from home.

October 2 – Bro W. C. Hayes our new pastor, reached the circuit & came to my house – went with us to prayermeeting. We gave him a cordial welcome & will try to make his work pleasant and successful.

October 3 – I left my dear wife & children, with more than average seriousness, to make my first round of Quarterly Meetings on Owensboro District. The trains were late & I was in the night getting to O[wensboro]. Bro G. W. Dennis came on the train & took me to his house, in the District parsonage, which he is occupying. The parsonage is a good house, mostly unpaid for & I am expected to raise the money to pay for it – & this in part is the cause of anxiety to get me on this district. I hope to do my whole duty, in this as in all other church work.

October 17 – [On board the *B.S. Rhea* between Cloverport and Lewisport] The B.S. Rhea is a comfortable, neat, but small boat. At Cannelton we transferred to the little Mattie Hayes – very small and almost no comforts. My old friend F. M. English came on board at Cannelton & went down with us. He was respectable & courteous to me – gave me his card – a candidate for Congress on the Green-back ticket. I thought I detected the odor of whisky on his breath & a spice of irreverence in his talk. At Lewisport I was kindly welcomed by the excellent & homelike family of Bro. J. Pell. They seem to have my ideas of family government.

October 20 – A slight swell in the river brought the B.S. Rhea down & I boarded for Owensboro. On board I wrote to sister A. H. Redford – having seen his death reported in yesterdays *Courier Journal*. He died on Friday [October 17]. His death is to me cause of serious reflection. He was the pastor of my childhood & my first colleague in the ministry. I tried to comfort his widow as much as I could. I wish Dr. R's sons would be better men.

October 28 – [Olmstead] I got home to breakfast – thankful to find all well. Lizzie & I went to see Helen – found her busy at the new house – preparing to move in. It is indeed an excellent house – in the main, well planned & well furnished – but too costly for a country house – & too fine for the neighborhood.

November 4 – [Owensboro] Drizzly & dreary. Town full of people – quiet [presidential] election.

November 6 – I took train for Hartford cir[cuit] – changed cars at Central City & got off at Beaver Dam – went home with bro Harber B. Taylor in his wagon. I find him like the rest of the democrats – jubilant over [Grover] Clevelands election although the republicans are still claiming the election of Mr [James G.] Blaine. The news is conflicting – but the Courier Journal is full of roosters crowing & guns are booming in the towns.

November 7 – A day to rest & read, without molestation. What a treat! I wish I had three such every week.

November 8 – [Liberty, near Beaver Dam] Was pleased to see a large Saturday Congregation. I had liberty and unction in preaching Mat[thew] 11.19. After dinner at John Taylors – I held Quarterly Conference – every church was represented & every one *paid something*. I gave the Stewards a plain, good talk & urged them to a liberal policy toward their preacher & they brought in an allowance of 700. & parsonage for the pastor & 200. for a local preacher – Rev Gabriel J. Bean to assist – far beyond the estimate for the last year. Pleasant A. Edwards the preacher was delighted – said "Bro Browder, I have had a number of Presiding Elders – all of them good & great men – but I have never in all my life heard a talk to a Board of Stewards that equalled that." A note from my dear wife tells me that my mother is very ill with Pneumonia & advises me to hurry home. No train till 1.45 Sunday.

November 10 – [Olmstead] Mother says she is better, but she looks badly & I am uneasy about her. Cousin D. B. Sydnor is very ill & the Dr. thinks he will die.

November 12 – Last night Lizzie & I sat up with my dear mother & cousin David – both surely, steadily going down. About midnight, he grew rapidly worse & his children thought he was dying, & called up those who were sleeping, but he seemed to revive & for a time was more quiet. He overexerted himself to get out of bed, & afterward had a severe chill. I was alternately with him & mother – as were the rest of us. It was a sad, solemn time to us all. My sister Mary is losing her mother & her husband his father, in the same house – & both seemingly nearing their end together, and I feel it almost as much as they. Mother has been all to me that she could have been to her own child & Cousin David, all my life, has been a true & loving friend. I never called on him for a favor of any kind, that he did not cheerfully & gladly grant if in his power. Thirty three years I have been his nearest neighbor & never had cause to mistrust his good-will. My family feel as if they were losing a father. I pity his children & I pity myself – but most of all do I pity my poor father. Fifty five years he & mother have walked lifes pathway together – & now the journey will be lonely to him. He & cousin David had been near neighbors & much together for about 50 years – and now when father is nearly 81 years old, he is to lose his wife and his friend & associate, so

406

near together! About 3. this morning I lay down & slept several hours. Last night while watching my dying mother & kinsman – I heard the noise, & saw the light of bonfires & rockets at the depot, as a lot of boys celebrated the election of Grover Cleveland to the presidency. The men of the neighborhood had intended a grand demonstration with cannon & torches, but declined it on account of the illness of Cousin David & my mother – a consideration that we appreciate – though delighted with the election.

November 13 – At early dawn I arose & went to see my precious mother and Cousin David – could not see much change except shorter breathing, gave her some milk toddy & wrote again to my brothers. In a short time Wm Browder came down to tell us that mother was nearly gone. I started at once, but she had breathed her last – calmly & peacefully as an infant going to sleep. No purer, lovelier, more unselfish, or confiding spirit ever went from earth to Heaven. My poor old father is almost heart-broken – the second time he has had such a grief – and dear Mary with neither mother nor sister left – feels lonely indeed. We have much to inspire gratitude in the midst of our sorrow. We have had our parents longer than most people and we have had better parents than almost any other children. I sent Luther to town to get a coffin. Cousin David is going down – cannot live through the day. I called after dinner & found him sinking, but thought he might live until I could go to see Elijah Barnes & return. Barnes has a fearful malady that Drs call gangrene in his foot and leg – amputation is said to be a necessity & I fear amputation will kill him. He was glad to see me. When I got back to Tommy's I found Cousin David dead & laid out – died in a few minutes after I left & he & my mother lie dead in the same room. She died only 7 hours before him. I have been long going to houses of mourning & the bedsides of the dying, but have never before, that I remember, witnessed a scene like this – two people 76 & 81 years old dead the same day in the same house. I have not expected my mother to live long since her fainting at Daniel Baileys. We lose her, but Annie and Robert & Amelia & Helen & Amelia & a little brother & sister not named will find their mother again. I look back to a multitude of kind deeds my mother has done & call up her counsels. She taught me my catechism & my prayers – & I remember little verses that she taught me when I was a child. She bore much with my waywardness – & has overvalued any little kindness I have shown her. When I have made her a present of any sort she has been afraid that I would disfurnish myself or family – & yet she would almost have given away her eyes to accommodate & relieve me or my family. If she has ever loved her own children more than me, she has not shown it in any conduct, to my disadvantage. She always treated me as the oldest son & taught her children to respect me as the elder brother. I am very thankful that, in the main, I have been obedient and dutiful to both my parents.

November 14 – The day was bright & balmy, but our hearts are sad. At 1 P.M. an immense concourse of people – from the villages & country around came to the funeral – the lower rooms & halls were full & the porches back & front – I think there were more people in the yard than in the house. Bro W.C. Hayes read the lessons – James A. Lewis made the opening prayer – H. C. Morrison read the biographical sketches & bro Bottomley preached a most excellent & appropriate sermon on "Precious in the sight of the Lord is the death of his saints." We then laid Cousin David away, by the side of his sainted wife – then went to mothers old home & buried her beside her children & her sister Mary to wait till Jesus comes.

December 4 – *All* our dear children & my precious old father were here together – a happy joyous gathering, by the grace of God.

December 5 – Lizzie & I took train for [the Centennial Conference of the Methodist Church in] Baltimore. We found Eliza Cheatham at the [Louisville] depot with conveyance to her house. I stopped on the way to consult with Dr Messick & Bro McGuiar & finally purchased tickets & berths on a sleeper over the Chesapeake & Ohio R.R. & reached Mr C[heatham]s just at dark. Eliza had an elegant supper & good fires for us – & seemed thankful that she could entertain us in her own home.

December 6 – Up before day – early breakfast & off to Mt Sterling where, by special invitation of bro McGuiar, we rest on sabbath. We reached Mt S. at 1 ½ P.M. & after an excellent dinner I went to the Court-house and heard part of Mr Pattersons withering speech against Corneilison, the lawyer who beat & cowhided judge Richard Reid – and which it is said caused the suicide of the judge. The sentiment is strong against Corneilison.

December 7 – We rested until 12 P.M. & went to the depot & waited for the train, which soon came & we got into a splendid sleeper & rolled away toward Baltimore.

December 8 – Morning found us amidst the mountains & we enjoyed the scenery hugely. This trip was of thrilling interest to me. The road brought me by the scene of my school days at Lagrange & by the State capital & public buildings at Frankfort & through the farfamed "blue grass" region, by the city of Lexington & some of the finest stock farms of the world, the Scotts, Alexanders &c – along the shores of the Kanawha, over the big Sandy River by Charleston W. Va. – by the Hawksnest & White Sulphur Springs – & Charlottesville & the University of Va & Staunton & its schools – & the world renowned Valley of Va or the Shenandoah Valley – along the Blue Ridge & through Manassas, near the battle ground & on to Washington City. At Washington we missed our train by just one minute or less – through the red-tape particularity of the management – but the delay was only 1 ¼ hours. Meantime we rested in the very room where President Garfield was assassinated & saw the silver star fixed in the floor where his head struck when he fell. I stood in the very niche, near the door from which the fatal shot was fired by Charles Guiteau. We landed in Balt. at 12.30 & by little past 1 A.M. were in a comfortable room – 119 I think – in the Eutaw Hotel, in the heart of this great & growing city.

December 9 — After half a nights rest, we got breakfast & went down Baltimore Street to Exeter & from Exeter to 61 Hillen St where we found uncle Charles Waters and his daughter Mrs Cooksy — in a small & crowded house. Since Mr Cooksys insanity & death, they have been hard pressed for means of support. I left Lizzie with them, & went to 353 Hollins St. to John E. McCahan's to whom I was assigned during the Conference. They said that if Dr J. B. Walker of N. Orleans did not come, they would be glad to have Lizzie stay with me. At 3 P.M. I attended the primary meeting of Southern delegates, to fill vacancies, perfect the roll &c — at night went to First Street, the outgrowth of the old Lovely Lane Meeting House where the Christmas Conference of 1784 was held & where the M[ethodist] E[piscopal] Church was organized — one hundred years ago. It was a grand occasion. Main audience room and galleries were crowded. White & colored delegates sat promiscuously through the house. Mr Hunt of Baltimore, a layman, presided over the meeting. Bishop E. G. Andrews of M.E. Church (North) made the address of welcome. It was unique, elegant, perfectly appropriate & in the best of taste. The reply by Dr J. B. McFerrin of Nashville was just the thing. It captured all hearts & was greeted with rounds of applause. Prof *J.C. Price* of Salisbury N. C. a full-blood Negro, made some excellent remarks & was duly applauded — but in some of his references, he was in bad taste and not historically correct. Bishop A. W. Wilson who had been long at deaths door, was able to be present & consecrate the elements for the Lord's supper. He & Bishop J. C. Granberry are the only Southern Bishops present. It was an occasion to be remembered — representatives of more than 4,000,000 of American Methodist Members & 56,900 local & travelling preachers, meeting with the descendants of the original church & near the very spot of ground in which the first General Conference of 63 preachers representing 85,000 members met one hundred years ago & organized the Societies into a church.

December 10 — The Centennial Conference assembled at 9:30 A.M. in Mt Vernon Place Church — the finest in this great city — & most likely the finest Methodist Church in the world. The music was grand beyond any thing I ever heard. The great organ & cornet & choir & cushioned & silver marked pews — and grand galleries & gas lights & parlors & lecture rooms, and all modern appliances, contrasted wonderfully with the first Conference of 100 years ago. The church seats 1600 people & the space was all needed & crowds were standing up in the galleries. Dr. John A. Martin of the Church South was elected Secretary & Bishop Granberry of the Church South was chosen to preside over the first session. The opening sermon by Bishop Randolph S. Foster who was chosen to supply the place of Bishop Pierce — dec'd, whose alternate, Bishop Simpson, had also died, was fully up to my highest conceptions of what such a sermon ought to be. I do not see how it could have been more appropriate. He said he was compelled to deviate from the habit of his life & *read* his address — that he had only read about 3 sermons in his long ministry, but this would not be a sermon. "You must bear with me," he said, "I am a poor reader. I am a miserable reader. I shall wear out your patience. I shall wound your feelings. I shall say things that you do not wish to hear. I shall disappoint your expectations. I shall read along time. My text is a *topic* – 2 Chron[icles] 32.2–3. And when Hezekiah saw that Sennacherib, King of Assyria, was come & that he was purposed to fight against Jerusalem, he took counsel with his princes & his mighty men. Psa[lm] 48.12–13 – Walk about Zion, and go round about her: tell the towers thereof. Mark ye well her bulwarks, consider her palaces; that ye may tell it to the generation following."

I shall not hear in a life-time anything to surpass that sermon. He read two hours & ten minutes & yet threw out a large part of the manuscript – but such reading! It was electrical – thrilling – grand. He seemed inspired – his soul & voice & brain & strength were in it & when he proposed to throw out some, the ring of a hundred voices cried "No no – read it – read it. We want it all." "We'll stay 'till night" one man said. The Hallelujah anthem by the choir at the close seemed akin to the music of celestial trumpeters & "harpers harping on their harps" & such voices! The afternoon service was interesting but my boarding place is so far away and our dinner so late that I missed part of the essays read. It was a noticeable fact that the Bible used by John Wesley in preparing his sermons & used at the great Ecumenical Conference in London, was also used at the opening of this Centennial Conference & Bishop Asbury's Bible was used for the daily readings.

December 11 – At Conference again. Crowd not so large as yesterday – no choir to peal its grand anthems. The essays & discussions were animating & eloquent. Each paper presented seemed to be the very best that could be prepared on that subject. I saw several points in which I should have been glad to put in a word, but so many seemed anxious to be heard & so many, perhaps a dozen, springing up at one time crying "Mr Chairman, Mr President" &c – that a modest man had but little encouragement to try. "Our brother in black" as Dr Haygood calls the negro, seemed especially anxious to be heard & in proportion to size of delegations, more of them than any others seemed to be seeking opportunities to speak. The Presidents seem impartial & perfectly courteous. Dr Edward G. Andrews, Bishop of M.E. Church, seems to be a general favorite. I have never seen a man more ready for every occasion. Dr J. B. McFerrin always captures the crowd.

December 12 – The paper by Dr J. D. Blackwell on Methodism & its outlook & the paper by H. B. Ridgaway on the Personnel of the Christmas Conference were thoughtful, eloquent and remarkably well put. After supper Lizzie & I went to hear Dr Granberry & another brother, but I was so tired & worn with walking and thinking & seeing and hearing, that I must reserve my judgment until I can read the addresses in the Centennial Daily.

December 13 – The papers read by J. H. Vincent on the possible dangers to Methodism & the one by Dr Chas J. Little on the pioneers of Methodism were amongst the best prepared & read that I have heard – & were received with rapturous & continued applause. Clapping of hands seems to be the order of manifesting approval. I have not seen much of this in Southern congregations. I stay in at night & rest for the Sabbath as I am appointed to preach tomorrow at the Associate Reform Church (Presbyterian), the Venerable Dr Leyburns church. Bro McCahan, supt. (assist) of Public Schools, says it is a compliment to be sent to preach to Dr Leyburns congregation – one of the most influential & reliable in the city.

December 14 – Chilly & disagreeable. Never before perhaps was Baltimore as full of Methodist preachers, as this day. Our own churches & most of the other Protestant churches are supplied by members of the Centenary Conference. I had a good congregation & considerable liberty in preaching on Sauls conversion. I have seldom had better attention from beginning to end. Old Dr. Leyburn & his assistant Dr Lefevre sat with me in the pulpit & listened with marked attention & at the close they both expressed great pleasure & profit by the sermon. "I have been edified. I shall not forget you. I hope to meet you in Heaven. If the people in Kentucky hear that sort of preaching, they ought to get to Heaven" & other such expressions, the old Dr made. Mr Lefevre was almost as much outspoken in offering thanks, & many of the "elders" and women crowded around to be introduced & to thank me for the sermon – & one old lady who could not come, sent one of the elders to "give her love to that brother." I do not know when I have been as much complimented & congratulated. I was rather surprised as I was alittle restricted in time and left out some of the best points in the sermon. We went to St Pauls at 3 to hear Dr Carlisle on S.S. Schools, but the house & galleries were so full that we had to stand up to hear.

December 15 – The Centennial Conference and the goodly city of Baltimore grow on me – over one hundred Methodist Churches in this one city – its grand streets & its fine houses & schools & churches – its beautifully paved streets – its magnificent system of street cars – & its orderly population. I have been here a week tonight and have spoken to many people on the cars and on the streets & everybody has been courteous. I have not yet heard an oath nor seen a drunken man. The cars seem all to be drawn by horses – many of them very fine & large. I see very few mules, but have seen more fine draft horses & coach horses than I remember to have seen in any other city.

The Centenary Conference is composed of men selected out of all the bodies they represent and are in the main representative men. It is an inspiration to see them & hear them. Blessed be God, that my eyes behold this assembly. These essays ought to be preserved in a "Centennial book" & it ought to have a large sale. I cannot describe the papers read. I must read them over & over. They show thought, research, & zeal for the Lord. They are wonderful productions. The occasion of the day, socially, was the reception given by the Methodist women of Baltimore to the Conference & visitors in the Academy of Music. The building is beautiful – one of the finest I was ever in. The music was grand. The speeches were excellent. Mayor Latrobe made the address of welcome in a very facetious & pleasant manner. The replies were all good, but as usual Dr McFerrin captured the crowd. Mayor Latrobe spoke of welcoming the representatives of so many different churches – recently the great Catholic convention & now the great Methodist Conference – so soon after the Conference of Catholics – said he had no power to pardon sins, but could remit fines & if any of us got into trouble & got fined & called on him at the City Hall, he would remit our fines! This joke, of course caused a hearty laugh. Dr McFerrin said – "You speak of the Methodists coming after the Catholics. That is not strange sir – the Methodists have been *after* the Catholics ever since they were organized. There was a time Sir, when the Mayor of a great city like Baltimore would not be found amongst the Methodists, but since we had that great ecumenical Conference in London & the mayor of London was a Methodist & gave a grand entertainment & could get happy & shout – the rest of you mayors can meet a Methodist Conference!" There was a grand outburst of merriment – clapping of hands &c. The table was filled with substantials and delicacies. Fried Oysters, large & luscious, in great abundance, steaming hot – chicken salad in immense dishes heaping full, coffee, tea & chocolate, hot & abundant, cakes &c – & the dishes were handed about over the house – none being invited to the table, no difference being made between white & colored delegates – in this displaying good taste on such an occasion. I had eaten a hearty dinner & did not taste any of these dainties, but my good wife enjoyed the occasion & indulged herself in these far-famed Baltimore Oysters. We took the remainder of the evening to look about the stores & get up a few things to take home. Lizzie went to day & bought a nice "Oxford Bible" for Hanson – at 6.05 including the lettering "Rev H. W. Browder, from his mother."

December 17 – A note from Hanson reports my dear father's case less encouraging & Jenny sick. We took sorrowful leave of the kind McCahans, who have entertained us so hospitably. They insisted on our staying a day longer to see more of the city, especially the son Harry, who has been unremitting in his polite attention. He went with me to Johns Hopkins University & the City College & the Peabody Institute & the Western Female High-school & other places of interest. The Hopkins & Peabody are conspicuous already & will be famous. Western Female High-school has about six hundred girls from 13–18 years of age – all looking neat & tidy & intelligent. I did not observe a really ugly one in the lot. They are likely to perpetuate the fame of Baltimore for beautiful women. I have seen but few women here of rare beauty – but *very* few really ugly. The drill & movement of these girls is really interesting, & Harry & his father have helped me in seeing these things.

The good sister had breakfast for us, the R.R. men came to the house & checked our trunk through to Louisville & Harry went with us to Calvert St Depot – seeming to part with us very reluctantly. Bro McGuiar & the girls failed to meet us at nine Oclock – but we steamed away to Washington & stopped over there to see the city & the Congress & my Senatorial Cousins James David Walker & Wilkinson Call. We went to the presidents house, into the East Room only – took a good look at the Washington monument, just completed 555 feet high – went through the museum of war relics – & saw the public buildings, took another look at the Capitol – went into the lobby & saw the Senate &

Lower House in session – heard part of the discussion on the R.R. bill – equalizing passage, freights &c – saw my friend John Halsell – was introduced to "Little Phil" Thompson, who killed Daviess about his wife, and took a good look at the great statesmen of the union – & my deliberate conviction is that they are not equal in looks, talent or behavior to the Conference we left in Baltimore. The lower House (House of Representatives) seemed disorderly – smoking, walking, talking & many on the floor at the same time, calling "Mr Speaker" "Mr Speaker" – & the speakers gavel – rapping – rapping. The Senate was more orderly, but a much smaller body. I could not send any message to them before 2 Oclock and I could not see any man that reminded me of my cousin & schoolmate David Walker. When the Senate went into "Executive Session" no one could send in, or even go into the gallery – & I feared that I should not see David atall – but the Executive Session ended & my card brought him out to the "Marble Room" to which I was invited. I saw several gentlemen passing about, but no David Walker. At a length a portly, tall gentleman stopped before me & said "Is this the Rev. Mr. Browder?" I said, "But this is not David Walker!" Neither of us recognized the other, but were glad to meet again. We brought Lizzie around to the "Marble Room" & sent in for Mr Call who seemed glad to see me & invited us to his house. David sent messages to his friends & as I was leaving, slipped one of his fine congressional knives into my hand, with a request that I accept it as a token of friendship – said he was sorry he did not have time to get something for Lizzie. He begged me to stay a day longer – that he would pair off with somebody & give me a whole day for sightseeing – but I was uneasy about my father & could not stay. It was singular & pleasant that we met at Washington almost all the company that went over with us, McGuiar & the girls – H.G. Petree & wife, & several other pleasant friends – & some of us got exactly the same berths on the sleeper. We left Washington at 5.10 & had a pleasant time all seemingly happy & improved in condition. The cold wave & snow storm struck us in the night.

December 18 – Passed over much of the Road in daylight, that we passed in the night going over – saw Catlettsburg – Charleston Va &c. At Lexington, our sleeping car ticket being out, we went into a forward car – but found it cold & uncomfortable – & I thought we had better have submitted to the extortion of an extra dollar. The wind cut like a razor when we got out at Louisville – & we walked two squares before we found a car. At the Arlington, corner of 12 & Main, we got a good supper, warm room, good bed & after a little spell of vomiting & nausea, I slept well.

December 19 – Very cold. I got shoes for Lizzie & myself – paid 3.25 hotel bill, got a few oranges for the children & took the train for home. Got reduction of rates, home –⅔ off – as we paid full fare going. We found dear Wallace & Luther waiting for us at Olmstead – had a *cold* walk home – the boys thought too cold to ride – heard that Father & Jenny were both better. We bowed in humble thanksgiving around our family altar to acknowledge the kind providence that defended us from the perils of the way & brought us together safe at home once more.

December 20 – Went to see Father – found him much improved – his face brightened when he saw us. The weather is cold. We are putting up ice. The negroes are drinking – and alittle insolent. Every body ought to work for the extermination of drunkenness – & the means that lead to it.

December 22 – The boys are hauling off our wheat – 65 cts pr bushel – lowest price we have had for years – sheep, hogs & wheat all low. No profit again, from the years labor – expenses too high for the price of crops. Costs too much to board & pay hands. Luther leaves for Florida tomorrow & we are all serious. I have too many letters to write.

December 23 – A sad morning with us. Luther left home for his work in Florida. We parted in tears with earnest prayer to God for blessing, guidance & protection. I went with him to the depot – got his trunk checked through to N. Orleans. His ticket to Gainesville was 26.75. I had written to J. P. Moore to get a boarding house for him in N. Orleans, while he sees the great Exposition. Poor boy! His heart will ache many a time to see his parents & his home, but I trust that the good hand of God will go with him & bless all his labor & sacrifice. He is sincere & acts on convictions of duty. It may be best that he go to a milder climate & a new field. Tonight I am writing up, from memory, this diary from Nov. 15th – the day after my mothers burial. What a crowd of business & care. Possibly a hundred letters & postals to write in these weeks – obituaries – letters to Herald-Enterprise &c. A letter from Geo. Nick Moore, after long silence, on his part, asking me to intercede with friends in the U. S. Senate – to get him appointed Post Master at Marion Ill[inois]. I wrote to him – giving some suggestions – also to Courtenay Meade who wants a Government appointment. I have requests to write obituaries for Mrs Fannie Green – & also my cousin Hannie Lewis who died in Texas while I was away in Baltimore. My friends are going – but they died in the faith of Jesus & hope of Heaven.

December 24 – Reading & writing. We got the ice-house filled – made arrangements with *Bob Clark* (colored) to raise tobacco on the shares next year. The man & woman Hanson hired have disappointed us. My neighbor J. N. Morrow – got in an ill humor & talked to Hanson about his school in a very insulting manner. In *some* men, I should consider it a serious offense. We spent some little time distributing gifts for Santaclaus.

December 25 – All slept late – no clatter of children. *Minor* & *William* were pleased to get some presents. We have had them since they were children – infants – now that they begin to be valuable, their mother proposes to take them away. A cold, dreary snowy day – less like Christmas than any Christmas I have seen for years. Not much serious meditation – not much merriment – not much time to read. For some time I have read but little – not even kept up with my newspapers – not much Bible-reading – except at church & family worship – busy – busy – busy & but little done. I called to see my dear father again – he seems to miss me so much when I am away – & I leave tomorrow for

Owensboro, Cloverport, Lewisport, & Hawesville. I have been nearly sick with cold.

December 26 – Got to Owensboro at night. Bro. Dennis met me at the train – had a warm fire & good supper for me. My cough & hoarseness are serious.

December 27 – Cold, sleet, rain. No body at church. Weather so bad & my cough so serious that I staid in the house.

December 28 – Went to Sunday School. Small attendance – still raining & cold. Small congregation at 11. I preached with difficulty – hoarse & coughing – Text Mat[thew] 11.30.

December 30 – Wind so high that I wait until tomorrow for a boat to Cloverport. The Ohio is high & rising.

December 31 – Got off on the Rain Bow – a beautiful boat – reached Cloverport about 9 P.M. I went to bro Wm Vests where I found most comfortable quarters. The wind is high & *very cold.* In the night I was startled by the ringing of bells. I jumped out of bed & ran out on the porch to see if there was a fire, but saw none – soon found that the boys were ringing in the new year & I felt thankful that God spared me to see *1885.*

January 2, 1885 – I am well received at Cloversport. Bro. & Sister Vest are solid, substantial, sensible people. They have a neighbor who has two sons in the penitentiary for horse-stealing – both young men. Sister V. told me of some of the anxiety & trouble she had to control her boys & keep them away from those children whose fathers set a bad example & whose influence on her own children she so much feared. I saw the point. It is better to offend the best friend· & nearest neighbor, if the necessity is forced upon us, than allow them to demoralize & ruin our own children.

January 5 – Quarterly Conference was well attended & the business pleasantly transacted. The Stewards insisted that as I received no pay the first quarter, I must allow them to pay me in full to date. I objected, until they promised to raise Cottrells pay to the same proportion – so they paid me 36.25 – which added to 3.75 before makes 40.00 – half my claim.

January 6 – I took supper with a bro Dyer – had the best beef steak & crout that I have seen for a long time. Steak was like my fathers cook, old *aunt Sukey* used to cook it. I went to Cloverport hotel, to be waked up in the morning for the boat to Hawesville.

January 7 – Was almost left – the boat had left the wharf, but came back & took me aboard. I got breakfast on the boat & soon found cordial welcome at the Carlton house in H[awesville]. I wrote an article for the Breckinridge News in answer to Mr Gruells advocacy of mob-law, in his paper of Jan 7th. I read it to a few friends at Hawesville, who highly approved it & urged me to send it to the editor which I did. I went out with Bro. Sam Hughes on his hay wagon & spent the night. I ate too much rich bread for supper & was sick in the night.

January 9 – Reading, writing, visiting &c. Not many people here that invite me to *stay* with them – some invite a call.

January 10 – Muddy & disagreeable – moderate congregation – some liberty & "plainness of speech" on bearing the yoke of Christ. Quarterly Conference poorly attended. Some friction between preacher & people on a change in Stewards and a financial plan. Report rather meager. Bro Campbell, pastor & bro Black one of the displaced stewards had a plain, open talk in my room – each saying something that chafed the other – but both agreeing to blot out the past & love each other. We concluded with prayer & I trust that things are in a better shape.

January 11 – This is my natal day – 58 yrs old, the working part of my life nearly gone and almost nothing done. It will be a great mercy if I get to Heaven.

January 13 – I got off on the Mountain boy at 6 A.M. & soon reached Lewisport – found a cordial welcome at Bro. Joe C. Pells – a good room, good fare, a fire & lamp & time to read – a privilege much to be desired.

January 14 – Wrote some verses – by request of Bro Pells Children. Carrie, 10 yrs old is a *bright*, good child – pious & conscientious – but sickly – suffers much with tonsilitis.
　　Playing upon the sound of her name, I kept it up –

> There was a girl named Carrie Pell
> Who learned to read & write & spell
> And always knew her lessons well
> And many pretty tales to tell.
> Sweet flowers she would raise to smell
> And nice things make to keep or sell
> And the love of friends compell
> No wonder she should be a belle
> That charming little Carrie Pell.
> As sweet as any Caramel
> I wish you could be fairly well
> Without a dose of calomel.

This raised a sensation, and then Ida, the grown daughter brought her album and requested a verse and an autograph – so I wrote for her – almost impromptu –

> There was a girl, whose name was Ida
> An active walker and a careful rider
> With just one loving beau beside her
> Who by every art had tried her.
> To see if he could but decide her

To be his own and let him hide her
Where his ardent fancy spied her.
But failing oft, would often chide her
And sometimes, too he would deride her
As if his smiles, he had denied her
But when alone, with tears he "cried" her
And then with saddened heart he sighed her.
Wishing that he could abide her
Where no ills should e'er betide her.
But to her fathers home she hied her
To eat her cakes & drink her cider
Merry as a dancing spider
Laughing 'till her mouth grew wider
Did that jolly hearted Ida
With her mama still beside her.

I write this from memory, but it is nearly the same. This brought Joe, with his album & as I was in a sort of accommoding mood, I wrote —

I knew a boy, they called him Joe
Who went wherever he had to go,
Whether he liked the trip or no
Whether on horse or on his toe.
And no one dared to call him slow
For if they had, 'twould not be so
Of boy as brisk as any crow
That flies as swift as wind can blow.
A useful boy was master Joe
To work with spade or plow or hoe
And make the corn & pumpkins grow
Down in the field so rich and low
Where he had toiled the seed to sow
When the plowed ground was free from snow.
Blessings on you, my good friend Joe
May your lifestream forever flow
Where sin and shame you shall not know
To dim and blight your hopes Rain-Bow.
But may your soul with joy o'er flow
Amid the ever bright'ning glow
Of glories which God shall bestow
In that pure world to which you go.

Then Ed must be remembered. Ed was younger than Joe. He did not have an album — but Ed had a calf & he wanted to sell the calf & buy a watch & that was his talk, to buy a watch — so I wrote for him —

I heard him talk that boy called Ed
A watch was working in his head.
He thought of it upon his bed.
"I want a watch, I want it 'bad'"
In firm & earnest tones, he said.
Ed had a calf which he had fed
To make it fat & sleek & red
So quickly to the field he sped
And with a rope the calf he led

417

To butcher who the people fed,
Who shot the calf with gun and lead
And soon as it had freely bled
And shown that it was truly dead
He laid it on his wagon bed,
And paid the price to eager Ed
Who bought a watch, as he had said,
But some how, had sort of dread,
To know the calf from him had fled
And he had only a watch instead.
Cheer up my boy, Cheer up my Ed
The watch may level up your head
And show you how your time has sped
Before you find the girl you'll wed.

These mere verses cannot be called poetry, but they made a pleasant impression on a pleasant family & may, in after years recall pleasant memories that will help the young people to a steady purpose to do that which is right. The continued use of *one* sound, in the final syllable or word is rather out of the usual order — a sort of rhyming that seems to come natural to me — though like much else that clings to me, of little value.

January 15 — I had made an appointment for preaching tonight, but a steady cold rain has been falling all day and continues till away in the night. The mud is deep in the streets & the night as dark as Egypt, so we sent word to the sexton not to ring the bell.

January 19 — Still cold — the swollen river chafing with its shore. I took leave of Lewisport & set out on the Cin[cinn]atti Steamer J. W. Gaff for Owensboro & home. Spent the night with Bro. R. F. Hayes in Russellville.

January 20 — Up early & off to depot. Train was on time & I got home to breakfast — thankful to find all well & my Father able to sit up. A large lot of letters was waiting for me. Luthers of course was most interesting, as he is far away & in a new world to him. I was pleased and surprised to find that he had been appointed jr preacher at Gainesville, the seat of the Conference — Rev R. Pasco, the P[reacher in] C[harge] being engaged in school that takes much of his time. The brethren received Luther with open arms. Some of them being my personal acquaintances sent messages of remembrance. I am thankful that my poor boy is so fortunate in his first appointment. I trust that he will prove himself worthy. He stopped at Montgomery to see my brothers. At N. Orleans he was gladly received by my cousin J. P. Moore & in Tallahassee by my uncle David S. Walker & my cousin D. W. Gwynn. Surely I have much to inspire gratitude. George writes me a statement of his years work. He lost considerable time with sickness, yet made accounts of more than two thousands dollars — over 1000 of which he is sure to get — has already gotten most of it. I hope he is doing well morally & religiously, though he does not write much on that subject.

January 22 – Bitterly cold. Mercury 3 below zero at Sunrise. I read & wrote – too cold for visiting. I shall not start to Hartford tomorrow, if Mercury is still so low. My lungs are too tender for a long ride through such weather. Bro Gabe J. Bean of Hartford writes me that on account of deep waters and bad roads, I will find it difficult to reach Beech Valley. He advises me not to try it in my present condition & I shall take his advice, though I dread to miss an appointment.

January 23 – Still cold – ground icy & travel dangerous. I am thankful to God for a home & home comforts. Our little grand daughter Sue Robert Roach has been with us several days – a bright joyous child. She often comes & says "Grand pa tell me some tales." She listened this morning with special interest to the story of Jesus healing the blind beggar – & curing the impotent man at Bethesda, & the ten lepers – & calming the storm on the lake of Genezareth. The children everywhere love for me to tell them stories & I frequently please them well. I miss my dog Roxie. She has been gone several weeks – killed or stolen I fear. My favorite mare Flora lost a fine mule colt, while I was away.

January 25 – Hanson & Jenny & Wallace getting ready to start to N. Orleans.

January 26 – Up at 5 A.M. & breakfast ready – the dear children off to N. Orleans to the great Exposition – at a cost 15. round trip – i.e. 21. now & a rebate of 6.00 on their return. I commend them to the care of God & hope to see them back improved physically & mentally. Hanson & Jennie have both been unwell & a spell of rest & recreation may be good for them & Wallace has been so industrious & obedient & so careful with his clothes that he *deserves* a pleasure trip & I am thankful to be able to give it to him. He will learn more than the money is worth. Luther, dear boy writes word to Wallace, that he will pay his way, rather than see him disappointed – very kind & brotherly – a real pleasure to me to see my children so devoted to each other. Hanson has been insisting on paying Wallaces way, but I prefer to do it myself.

Volume XI

1885–1886

"We have had so much sunshine that perhaps some trials may be best for us."

February 19, 1885 – I started to Livermore & Calhoun circuits – spent night in Russellville with Sister Fisk.

February 20 – Up early to reach train – found it an hour late. I went to Bevier House and got breakfast. Mr. Drake, the proprieter, said he never charged a preacher. I told him we did not go there as preachers, but as travellers & I expected to pay – but as he objected, I compromised by paying him half price – 25 cts each. He said he was like his father – that any preacher was welcome at his folks house – to preach in it. One day a stranger called & asked if he could make an appointment there for preaching? "Yes sir – if you are a preacher," said the old man, "any preacher can preach in my house." "I suppose" said the stranger, "that I ought to explain to you that I am a Mormon preacher." "Bill! Bill," the old man called his son – "Run quick & bring my shot-gun here, I'll kill this scoundrel" but the Mormon did not tarry for the gun, he made tracks in lively haste to parts unknown.

March 1 – [Calhoun] I preached at night to a crowded congregation, one of the plainest and most earnest sermons of my life, on the evil & sin of intemperance. Text Prov[erbs] 20.1 "Wine is a mocker – strong drink is raging – whosoever is deceived thereby is not wise." There was the most perfect listening & many liquor drinkers and liquor sellers were present. I did not abuse nor deride, but reasoned with them & showed the consequences, physical & moral, of intemperance. I felt constrained, as a matter of conscience, to preach to this people who patronize 5 saloons & several drug-stores & other places that sell whisky – & who seem to have decided that they will not *now* be religious.

March 2 – Mr Tanner got two good horses & a light carriage & despite the deep mud, got me to Livia in time for the train – so I got home at night – thankful to find my family well.

March 3 – Balmy as spring – bright & clear – the mud drying rapidly. Letters to read & answer. Geo. N. Moore fell on the slippery street in St. Louis & badly hurt his hip – has not been able to walk or sit up for over a week. I fear he is seriously hurt.

March 4 – This is the day of inauguration. Grover Cleveland of N. York takes his seat – a big day in Washington City. Went to the depot – got a note from Luther, speaking of the probability of his being removed from Gainesville to Levyville, where they have no preacher atall. I wrote quite a number of letters – one to Senator Wilkinson Call of Fla – now in Washington, asking his help in getting Geo. N. Moore appointed Post Master at Marion Ill[inois]. Geo N. is now at 709 Chestnut St – St. Louis.

March 5 – The sky is bright & clear – no March wind. I go to Russellville enroute to Yelvington on Owensboro circuit – invited to stop with Bro. Hayes.

March 6 – Train was late & I went to E.R. Rizers to breakfast. Just as we began to eat the train came & I had barely time to get on. At Owensboro I found that Bro Wright had brought his horse for me & I came out to Yelvington. The meeting was in progress & 75 or more persons had professed conversion. Bro Miller the Baptist pastor preached at night, a plain exhorting sermon – that produced much less effect than the exhortation of bro Stewart, a layman of the Baptist church, who volunteered a most excellent and earnest appeal – that roused & moved a number of persons to action who had not responded to the appeals of the preacher. I got a good opinion of the Bro. Stewart.

March 7 – My man Stewart the Baptist layman, made another rousing exhortation – with which I was well pleased & expressed my satisfaction to him. I thought he was perhaps a preacher rather than a layman.

March 8 – The house was full this morning. I felt constrained to preach on the sacrament of the Lords Supper – as we last night received 45 members into the church & they needed instruction. I was in good spirit & trust that I made the vision plain. At 3 we had a large attendance at love-feast, but very few spoke. I was surprised at this considering the great revival reported. I fear there is a lack of power & vitality. Perhaps this people need training. At night the congregation was large again & I had considerable liberty & some unction in preaching on sinners excuses Lu[ke] 14.18. When I gave the invitation to penitents none came. Friends went out & invited them but they did not come. Bro. Dennis made an earnest & effectual effort & several came forward. He called on Bro Stewart to pray – & he prayed about his persecutions & told the Lord that the people knew him & his manner of life – but that he was wrongly judged, & thanked God that Jesus also had enemies & prayed for grace to bear his trials & to do right always. I could not imagine the cause of his troubles & his peculiar prayer. When the congregation was dismissed, he called upon them to remain & hear him a little while. He repeated again that they all knew him & his manner of life – & God knew that he had tried to do good & came to church praying to do good – that all his work had been for good, but that he had been insulted, persecuted by name & publicly held up to scorn before this congregation – that his talk the night before had been by consent of the pastor – but if God could forgive him, he could never take such a liberty again from such a man – who had publicly called his name twice in the sermon & held him up to the scorn of the congregation. I then saw for the first time that he was offended at me & thought I had wronged him by alluding to him in my sermon. I had made the remark at the commencement for the benefit of some young people who talked in church, that I hoped I would be allowed to *do all* the talking until the time came for others to talk. I saw at one point that he seemed deeply interested, as I was commenting on Christs counsel at the Pharisees table & I called Bro Stewarts name, as I frequently do some member of my congregation, supposing that he approved my comment – & in my final appeal to the unconverted to cease their vain excuses – I said – "You offer those excuses to me & to Bro. Dennis & bro Miller – to Bro Stewart & to Bro. Joiner – but will not dare present them to

God. Does your own conscience approve then?" The dear old brother mistook my first remark to the young people as a rebuke to him for exhorting last night – & thought that I was exposing & persecuting him by name before the congregation. Never before in my life have I been the subject of such a charge – it was a surprise & a grief to me to know that I had been so utterly misunderstood by a man to whom I had become attached. As soon as I was confident of his meaning, I asked him publicly if he was referring to me as calling his name? He said he did. I said, "Then my dear Brother, I am greatly surprised & very sorry. I assure you that nothing could have been further from my intention. I never dreamed of you when I asked to do all the talking, & when I called your name it was because I thought you were interested & approved of what I was saying." He replied, excitedly not to say angrily, "You had as well sing Psalms to a dead horse as tell such stuff as that to me." I said I claim to be a gentleman & am trying to be a Christian and am entitled to my disclaimer. He said are you willing to leave it to this congregation. I said, No not until I explain the facts to the congregation & then I am. There was great confusion & much excitement during which he left the house. Bro. Dennis then requested the congregation to be seated & said that I had expressed to him deep & brotherly interest in Bro. Stewart & he considered my allusion to him by name as a compliment to his work. A Bro Taylor (Baptist) then asked to be heard. He said he was satisfied that no one present, except Bro Stewart himself understood bro Browder as he did. He said "I am a member of another church & never saw Bro Browder until now, but I know him through the press & by reputation as a man of eminent piety & of great influence in his church and I know he could not have intended any wrong to Bro Stewart. I am exceedingly sorry & pained at what has happened & I am sure that Bro Stewart who is a good man & a bosom friend is mistaken & will see it himself." Bro Allgood (Baptist) also asked to be heard. He said "I am certain that Bro Stewart misunderstood Bro Browder. I understood him just as he explains & I think all the congregation except Bro Stewart understood him just as I did." A number of others crowded up to tell me that I had committed no offence – had said nothing wrong & all the Baptists here feel that you have been misunderstood. Bro Taylor proposed that we now all pray & called on me to lead which I did as humbly and earnestly as I could. There was much feeling & some weeping. A good song was sung & a handshaking – a general expression of feeling in my behalf – by men & women – & so I trust no harm was done to the cause of Christ, but I felt sorely pained to think I had so innocently been the cause of grief to a good man. I told him that I would beg a hundred pardons if I had wronged him & would ask pardon of all if I had wronged any – but that I was innocent as an angel of wrong intent. I stated to the congregation that I had made it a life rule to confess my faults & ask pardon of any that I had wronged whether rich or poor – bond or free.

I came to my room at Bro Streets & was seriously meditating, when some one knocked on the front door. Bro Street went down & soon returned bringing Bro Stewart & his son & nephew. The dear old man came up extending his hand and said "Bro Browder forgive me, I have wronged you, I misunderstood you. I will get down on my knees to you if necessary. I am sorry. I hope you will forgive me." Oh how my heart warmed toward that good man that was so frank to confess his fault. I am glad that I had not indulged one single unkind feeling toward him. If I had, it would all have been gone in a moment, but there was none to forgive. I grasped his hand warmly & laid my arm around his neck and said "My dear Brother, it is all right. I was grieved but not angry — never had a grudge against you for a moment — and your Christian spirit in this thing has made me very happy." We all shed tears over it — & he explained how he got into the trouble and over and over asked me to forgive him, and to ask my church to forgive him — said he would be there tomorrow & ask them himself. He asked bro Street to forgive him & to ask his family to forgive — & in all possible ways showed the spirit of a true Christian that drew me nearer & yet nearer to him. This good man had gone to bed & when he was convinced that he had done me injustice, he dressed himself & came to hunt me up & ask my pardon. He made a mistake in his public speech — instead of asking an explanation privately, but he thought that he was justifiable. I shall love him & trust him.

This has been an eventful day to me. I hope to profit by its sad experience. I thank God for that grace that kept me *perfectly* calm & self-possessed & kept me from any evil temper or unguarded words.

March 9 — My man Stewart was at church, and begged to speak to the people, which, of course, I gladly allowed him to do. He tried to explain how he fell into the snare last night and then confessed his fault & publicly begged my forgiveness and the pardon of all who were present & requested all who would forgive him to come and give him their hand. I went first & I think all the rest followed while I tried to sing —

> Try us O God & search the ground
> Of every sinful heart — &c

There was much feeling & I commended the Christian spirit that the old man had shown. I began to expound the 32d Psalm, when the alarm of fire was raised & we all rushed out to try to save Bro. Henry Duncan's house, but the wind was high & blowing from the meat-house, which caught first, right through the dwelling — & that too soon went down. In trying to pull down a paling fence on fire I slightly burned my hand.

March 13 — [Oakford] I noticed from the Calhoun reporter a very complimentary notice of my sermon there on the evils of intemperance — calling it the "grandest temperance oratory that some of them ever heard" & stating that it made profound impressions & that a number of old topers had sworn off from strong drink.

March 16 — Bright & pleasant. I bought a Portfolio Scrap Book & took train for my own sweet home.

March 17 — Yesterday the sun w's partially eclipsed. A hazy mist gathered over the sky, as night came on, & the wind got cold. This morning the ground is covered with snow & the outlook is dreary. My dear old father & sister Mary, brother Jimmy & W.R. Browder & wife started for Montgomery & N. Orleans. I much fear that the trip is too much for my father as old & feeble as he is.

March 18 — Looking over my papers & getting pieces for my new Portfolio Scrap Book.

March 22 — [Owensboro] Ground & houses covered with snow & winter dominates the opening of Spring. Last night Mrs. Dr. Stirman called me, through the telephone to dine with her to day. The telephone system here is very complete & neighbors can stay at home and talk to each other & men do business with the towns around through the telephone. A wonderful age in which we live! I am glad that I live now rather than 100 years ago.

March 24 — I think I am gaining some on the Owensboro people. I hear of many kind things they say about me & they treat me with more consideration than they are accustomed to show a presiding elder.

April 2 — [Cloverport] Did not sleep well — paid 25 cts for my bed & came up to Dr [T. N.] Warfields for breakfast & wrote up my diary — waiting for the boat to Hawesville — boarded the James Guthrie about 10 A.M. — reached Hawesville at 11. Got dinner with "Miss Jennie" at the Carlton House — & walked down to see Bro. Campbell. He brought his horse out for me to ride down to bro. Sam Hughes's. The young mare became frightened as I tried to put my foot into the stirrup & wheeled round & round so violently & rapidly that I fell off in the street — bruising my hip & leg, and shaking up myself generally. I lay down and rested some time & was able to walk about without serious pain — but fear I shall not soon be free from it.

April 3 — I rested well and though I am bruised and sore, I can walk & feel comfortable and am thankful that it is no worse.

April 7 — I was a little too late for the Grey-eagle at Hawesville, but bro. Prescott, the ferryman took me across to Carrollton in a skiff & there I boarded the boat — & wrote to *Abram Warfield,* colored, enclosing him 1.00 in money & telling him to go to my house and get a suit of clothes & what else Lizzie could give him. The poor old negro writes to me to help him in distress. At Lewisport I was kindly received at Bro. Pells — and glad to find my little Carrie much improved in health. I stepped on to bro Pell's back porch to get a drink of water & aiming to go back through the hall. The cellar door, close by the hall door, had been left open & the hall door closed — so I walked into the cellar door & fell to the bottom, breaking one of the steps, overturning the milk bowl & bruising & skinning one of my knees & shin considerably. Sister Pell & the girls were greatly frightened & Carrie screamed out like her heart would break — thinking that I was killed. Joe ran off to the store for the men to come and bring me up & there was an extraordinary excitement. I soon got out alone – walked to church & preached a pointed, earnest sermon on Mat[thew] 25.14–30. I stay at bro Pells, my Lewisport home – where they all seem to love me as I love them.

April 8 – I patched up my bruises last night with Court-plaster & am comfortable this morning. I read the books of Exodus & Leviticus, in part, with more than usual interest in the forenoon. I spent considerable time in prayer but I seem to lack *feeling* – personal, vital contact and communion with God. Oh for a soul satisfying blessing to inspire my zeal & set me on fire for my work. Amen. I have a large upper room & good feather bed at bro Pells.

April 9 – Cloudy & cold. Some of the children asked me to put in verse the story of my fall into the cellar. So I *almost* impromptu wrote this –

> "Twas at the house of Joseph Pell
> The preacher tumbled down and fell
> And how it happened I will tell
> That you may know the story well.
> A merchant man is Joseph Pell
> Who keeps a stock of goods to sell –
> And entertains the preachers well
> And loudly rings his breakfast bell.
> He has a charming little daughter
> Who gives the preacher a drink of water –
> And always likes to be the first
> To see the preacher slake his thirst.
> This cloudly seventh April night
> In "Eighty-five" if I am right –
> This preacher asked the little daughter
> To lead him to the pail of water –
> And on returning, through the hall
> (As he supposed) he got his fall –
> He, walking through the open door –
> Stepped firmly on the level floor
> When lo! beneath his lifted feet –
> There was no other plank to meet.
> But treading on the vacant air
> Went whizzing down, he knew not where.
> A heavy man with heavy dash
> He heard the step beneath him crash –
> With feet behind and head before
> He landed on the cellar floor.
> The lumbering fall down in the cellar –
> Mid vessels of milk and butter yellow
> So frightened the children & sister Pell
> They raised a loud and frantic yell –
> And, Joe, in haste for some assistance fled
> And Carrie screamed, "O my brother Browder's dead.
> Mercy! on me! the cellar was open
> And I fear the poor mans neck is broken."
> But he was glad as glad could be

That a bloody shin & bruised knee
Was the only hurt that came to a fellow
Who went head-foremost down into the cellar.
The men and women were greatly alarmed
And feared that their preacher was badly harmed.
But when he came smiling with no bones broken −
They showed their delight, by every kind token.
And soft hands were plied to brush off the dust
And sweet lips expressed the hope & the trust −
That no other night, if it could be "holpen"
Any one should leave the cellar door open −
And now, if you wish, this tale you can tell
How the old preacher at Lewisport fell.
And if for the present, it cause you to smile
It may seem more serious after a while

All the family were much amused and Ida said she had asked me to write it & must have the paper as she was the girl who led me to the water.

April 10 − At night the congregation was larger than last night and an increase in interest. Some of the hardest sinners bowed − which was a new thing for them − but none came forward for prayers. There was considerable feeling & weeping in the congregation as I preached on Davids hope in Psa[lm] 23.4. Old Judge Patterson, a staunch Baptist had surprised many by attending promptly all the services & last night stated that while he had a hope worth more to him than all the world − he was still not satisfied with his experience & wished us to pray for him. Alas! that tens of thousands of professed Christians have no satisfactory experience of regenerating grace.

April 11 − March like weather, Mr Smith, called Professor Smith, a revenue officer lent me his fine sorrel mare & saddle & bridle to ride out to Asbury 8 or 10 miles. Bro Bowan & I reached the church in time − found the stove taken down & no fire. I preached to about 15 people on Lu[ke] 18th 1−8 with but little unction − held Quarterly Conference.

April 12 − Cold & clear. I was requested to preach on the Sacramental Supper − & did so a *long time* although there was no fire in the house. Bro Bowan & I went to Reuben Barkers to dinner & were well treated. Some one told the old lady that "Bro Browder wants 5.00 for the District parsonage." She replied, "Well he'll not get it here. Ive had to put up with one old house and one old man and one old churn − forty years & we cant help build a preachers house." I fear the parsonage will get but little help at Asbury as I only got one subscription. We came back to town through a chilling wind and rain. I have my room at bro Pells. Sister Pell had a mess of nice fresh fish & a cup of hot tea waiting for me. I am comfortable, but feel grieved sometimes to be so far away from my dear wife and children − and yet business men − for money, are making greater sacrifices.

April 16 − Warm & raining − with thunder & lightening. I arose at 4 A.M. to be ready for the boat. Mr Haden the Hotel man invited me to breakfast without charge & the Rain Bow took me to Cloverport at ⅓ reduction. We have a lively band of musicians on board – who play at every landing of the boat.

April 17 – Looking for a tobacco wagon or some other to take me to Patesville. William Baker, son of Sam Baker, was there with a buggy looking for me. Patesville is a small village out in the hills of Hancock Co. This is a county of hills, knolls & valleys – susceptible of wonderful improvement – picturesque & beautiful. Dairy & fruit & flock husbandry ought to make this land almost an Eden, but people are wearing it out with tobacco.

April 18 – Reading & writing, until 11 – preached to a small congregation on use of talents, got dinner with Bro. Baker, whose barn, stable & dwelling house were burned a few weeks ago by incendiaries. I had Conference at 4 P.M. & gave the stewards an earnest talk on their official duties. They are doing almost nothing for their preachers.

April 20 – [Hawesville] Up early & off on the "Grace Morris" to Owensboro – fare 50 cts. Mountain boy leaves same hour – for 1.00 – both small boats, both expected to be at O[wensboro] by train time. Mountain boy run against us at Tell City & broke two of her paddles – boatmen say "buckets." The Capt of this boat made me a present of a ticket to breakfast. At Owensboro I took train for home. Got to Russellville 10 ½ P.M.

April 21 – I got home to breakfast & found all well. I spent some time walking over the farm. Oats & grass seeds well up – wheat too thin, corn mostly planted – fruit trees blooming. Cattle poor – sheep & calves in the woods – provender being all consumed. My mare Mattie has a fine mule colt. I have quite a number of letters to write.

May 5 – Up early & home to breakfast [after a ten day trip]. Thankful to find all well. I had letters urging me to return to Lewisport – where the revival is assuming large proportions – between 20 to 30 conversions & 17 additions. Brethren think I can reach a certain class of people there – who will not be reached by others – but I labored there over a week & did not reach them – except to awaken seriousness – & besides my throat much needs some rest. Helen spends the day with us & George came this evening – so except dear Luther – we had all the children at home. Luther has been removed to Longwood Fla – a hard & unpromising field, where he cannot even get a boarding place – but says he will have to "camp" and do his own cooking & walk his circuit, as keeping a horse is expensive. I wrote to him proposing to help him.

May 7 – George Nick Moore writes me that he has not walked since his fall on the ice in St Louis eleven weeks ago. The Drs say he is crippled for life. I am very sorry for him. I wrote to Mrs Lewis E. Campbell to use her influence with Hon "Dick" Townsend to have him appointed Post master at Marion Ill[inois].

May 11 – I am quite hoarse & weary. Spent some time reading & resting – in need of both, sometimes I get discouraged about want of time to read – travel, talk, work, sleep, unavoidable, take up my time. Perhaps I write too many letters, but I would like to write many more. I use a pack of postal cards in a month and nearly a pack of stamped envelopes, 25 of each in a pack.

May 13 – Spent some time in reading Deuteronomy. All the scriptures quoted by Christ in repelling Satan were taken from this book. It is full of promises to the faithful & warning to the sinful.

May 18 – I brought father from Tommy Sydnors to my house – and at night rubbed his back & hips with liniment – to relieve his pains. He is very feeble, but stood his trip to the South very well.

May 20 – Luther writes of a pleasant surprise, that his people had prepared at church one evening – a reception – with ice cream, cake &c & a public demonstration to welcome him as their pastor – very gratifying to him, amidst the discouragements he has had. I went to Russellville on business. Wilbur Browder invited me home with him to dine. I hope that he is giving up his atheistic folly. He promised to read carefully Father L.A. Lamberts reply to Col. Ingersoll. Lambert is a Roman Catholic Priest of N. York state – & is a most invincible logician & refutes, with a masterly hand, every Atheistic assumption of this American copyist of Voltaire, Paine, &c.

May 21 – I saw in Russellville, yesterday, a pitiable object – A.C. Finley, a lawyer – an educated man – a strictly temperate & sober man – a regular & constant attendant at Church – a healthy, robust man – so ragged that his literal nakedness was not covered – so filthy that he ought not to go into company – & yet he seems unabashed in any presence – & will discuss questions in history, politics or religion, law or literature with any who will engage in talk with him. I inquired of several friends, if he would accept a suit of clothes & was told that he had clothes, but would not wear them.

June 9 – [Owensboro] Bro. Brewer & I went with the ladies of the Women's Christian Temperance Union to visit the prisoners. It was the first time in my life, that I had seen the fair hands of women, handing flowers & giving lemonade to rough, crime-stained men behind prison bars. I did the talking to the prisoners – & Bro. Brewer prayed in one cell & I in another. The prisoners seemed much affected – six of them & all that I saw wept. First I talked with Stroud the murderer in irons. He seemed to appreciate the interest in him – & wept several times. I asked about his training. He said that he had once been a member of the church – & promised to repent & seek the pardon of his sins. So every one promised, some of them weeping as I questioned each separately. I was sorry for a young woman who called herself Sallie Branstetter – 19 years old, charged with theft, but denying the charge. She wept freely & seemed much affected that ladies should give her flowers. She declined the lemonade. I asked if she had not kept bad company. She admitted that she had and promised to amend – said she could not read, but prayed every night & would try to do right hereafter, had never been to Sunday School nor had any religious culture. I was most affected to find Billy Gilbert, son of John Gilbert & Ann, in prison for stealing horses and a wagon. His grand-parents Billy Duncan & Silas Gilbert were amongst the wealthiest and best known people of Logan Co – the former a Methodist, the latter a Cumberland Presbyterian. This boys father was one of the best men in our country & his mother a Methodist. He and his brother John have given their mother great trouble, have been indicted for divers offences – charged with stealing, killing, house-burning, defying law &c. He seemed very glad to see me – reached his hand through the gate & called me "Brother Browder" and asked us all to come inside the cell – which Mrs. Lucas the Jailor also asked us to do. I talked very plainly & faithfully to the poor fellow & to all the rest – told them of our misery in the fall – our recovery in Christ – Gods forbearance & Gods mercy & his grace to any who would repent. He seemed much moved & wept – & promised to change his life. There was much feeling, both amongst the prisoners and the visitors – & we had several appropriate songs. Billy Gilbert sang with us – reminding me of the days, when his sainted sister Annie Lizzie – played & sang at the piano and these unfortunate brothers sang along & their parents looked on with fond hopes for their children.

June 11 – The morning Inquirer gives a complimentary account of my talk to the prisoners. I went to see poor old Mr Washington "uncle Billy" in his 86th year – feeble & failing, but strong in faith.

June 15 – Up early & off to Bowling green, thence to Olmstead. A letter from Luther leaves him well, just home from his Dist[rict] Conference – where he was complimented on his work. A letter from Bro. Chas. Fulwood, P[residing] E[lder] of Gainesville Dis[trict] assures me of Luthers fidelity & acceptability – another letter from Geo. N. Moore, asking for further help about getting the Marion Ill. Post Office – but I think I have done all that I can do. Sent Luther $5.00 – will send more, if necessary. The dear boy must not suffer.

June 16 – Rainy morning. I need rest – visiting – traveling, writing, reading & preaching 3 or four times a week, besides Love-feasts & Quarterly Conferences – takes all my time and all my strength. Hanson is busy planting tobacco – the plants were so tender & the season so light that few of them lived. I helped him drop plants a short time.

June 17 – I went to see Helen who has been quite unwell and is strongly threatened with paralysis of the optic nerve in her left eye. This is sad to me, & I devoutly pray God to avert the danger. I had some talk with gentlemen at the depot about the nomination of L.T. Brawner, a *Saloon keeper,* as candidate for the Legislature in Logan county – & I am glad to find that other democrats, besides myself, refuse to vote for him. I trust the Christian people of this county will refuse to endorse the action of any clique that in the interest of the whisky ring will nominate a whisky candidate for the legislature.

June 19 — My dear Father 81 years old went with me to Olmstead to drive the buggy back home. Bro Griffin met me at Owensboro & took me to his house, where I spend a pleasant night, notwithstanding my sore eyes & sore throat.

June 21 — A nice morning shower & a clear breezy day. I had much the largest congregation tonight that I ever had in this city, nearly twice as large as the day congregation, which was half as large again as any other day congregation that I have had here. The temperance sermon at night was very earnest, plain & pointed — a solemn faithful warning to this great city of distilleries & saloons — some of our Methodist members being large distillers & one of them rapidly going to ruin in health & morals by dissipation.

June 24 — I went to the prison again & had another serious talk with Bill Gilbert, who persists in his promise to lead a better life. Mrs. Lucas, the Jailer, told me that the first thing he does in the morning is to read the Bible to his fellow prisoners. I dined with Bro Duncan & boarded the Steamer Mountain-Boy for Hawesville. I made a short talk at prayermeeting.

June 27 — [Breckinridge County] Quarterly Meeting at Holts chapel. Weather warm & sultry. Bro Skillman lent us a horse & buggy & bro Vest a harness & Dr Cottrell & I reached the beautiful church in a lovely valley in due time. I have seldom ever seen a prettier country, rich alluvial lands — skirted with hills around on three sides & the Ohio River on the other — fine houses, overlooking the river & the fields, beautiful orchards & vineyards loaded with fruit, flower gardens & graded walks — fine horses, cattle & sheep & warm hospitality — a splendid country church, brick — with slate roof — walnut seats & cushions — organ, hymn books & all that is needful in a first class church — except *the church* itself. Eight or ten rich families own & occupy this valley of 2500 acres — and only a few very *few* of them are church members — while the poor tenants that work their lands seldom ever go to church. I preached to less than a dozen persons.

June 28 — The *rich* people of the valley were out to church — but not the poor — hence the congregation was small, but all paid excellent attention to a plain earnest sermon on Wisdom justified of her children. There were not above seven communicants at the Lords table — & they not all residents here — so small is the hold our church has taken in this beautiful valley. The fine house was built by Hon Joe Holt, Judge Advocate of the U. S. as a monument to his mother, who lived and died a member of the Methodist church in this valley — known as Holts Bottom.

June 29 — [Cloverport] I received postals from George & my dear wife. Helen was not well, but had gone to Elizabethtown to Womans Missionary Meeting & expected to go to Louisville to see an oculist about the poor eye that causes us trouble. Oh Lord — bless the remedies for my precious daughters recovery. As usual on Monday I wrote to Lizzie, Robt, George & Luther. I wish I could be more with them. I sit here to day, at Wm Bowmers beautiful home, overlooking the Ohio – and thinking of my dear loved ones.

June 30 – Our Quarterly Conference last night was well attended – seemed serious and thoughtful. The financial report was not up to time, but the brethren thought it would be. I presented the claims of the District parsonage, but not one seemed willing to aid in the purchase. I also called attention to the fact that I had assumed for the District 50.00 to secure the final payment of debt on our Conference college [Logan Female College] – believing that there were 50 people who would gladly give 1.00 each to its payment – and asking that all who were willing to help, should say so, but *not one* said so – hence I conclude that this people have no interest in these enterprises, or else that I am not the man through whom they will help. I find too that there is some restlessness about next years preacher. This church has had some of the ablest & best men of our Conference, both now & here to fore & yet the congregations go down. Several families have suggested that they would like to have me in this station, but I am certain that I should soon be as tame & unacceptable as some of my brethren have been. I fear this church is hard to please. I arose at 4 A.M. to be ready for the packet. I reached Lewisport on the fine Steamer Grey-Eagle – spent the night at Bro. Bowans in the newly purchased parsonage. He and I attended the Baptist church at night and heard elder Bruner discuss the baptismal question from the immersion stand-point. He claimed a kind spirit & freedom of speech to all but derided "baby sprinkling" and made some unnecessary thrusts at other people, but in the main showed a good spirit – with an occasional lack of candor & plenty of illogical deductions – yet, about as able a defense as I have heard one of his brethren make of their views for some time.

July 2 – I got a letter from my wife – dear woman, she is busy with Helens children, while Helen is away. I was interested in the progress of men, moving on wheels, bro Pells large frame Stone House, from Front Street to Fourth – on account of rapid washing in of banks on the river. The house is 60 ft long & 20 broad & is drawn by men with ropes & pulleys. At night I attended our prayermeeting & was glad to see a large attendance, over 50 & we had a good comforting meeting.

July 3 – Cool, clear, delightful weather for haying & harvesting. A note of yesterday from Robt. reports a revival in his church, at Elizabethtown – 20 conversions. I am thankful to learn that Dr Reynolds, the oculist in Louisville, reports that there is nothing wrong in the nerve of Helen's eye – as our Drs feared, but he says there is a *difference* in the two eyes, which require a separate glass for each & he will have them made. I had a letter yesterday from Lizzie – all well at home – good rains – harvest of wheat ended – yield very small. I preached tonight on Wisdoms children with good effect – opened the doors of the church & received 4 new members – baptized them and five children *in the house* just following Bro Bruners four sermons denouncing such things as sins for which we will be held to account.

July 4 – Bro Bowan carried me in his buggy to New Chapel [Hancock County] – passing some of the prettiest farms and vineyards that I ever saw. The church is neat & comfortable in the midst of a beautiful Beech Grove – but a shadow rests over the community. Just here is where poor Tom Fallin was accused of corrupting a mans wife – & suspended by a committee & was afterwards expelled by the Conference. The house in which the family lives is close to the church & there is a division of sentiment as to the guilt, some of our best people being on each side – hence there seems to be a weight & deadness on this church. Quarterly Conference was not well attended, & financial reports in arrears. Bro Fallin was present & spoke feelingly of his sorrows & trials – asserted his innocence & his character was passed & his license renewed.

July 5 – Good love-feast – but the talking was mostly by visitors. Fine congregation (for this place) at 11. I had considerable liberty preaching on Mat[thew] 27.22 & tried to arouse a spirit of work and effort in these people. After a good dinner at Joe Great House's – I preached again on Sunday schools & tried to stir the depths – in the interest of the children. There was a thoughtful, feeling listening & a general promising to rally to the Sunday School – but the Supt. elected *refused* to act & another & another *refused* to lead – & I was almost at my wits end – when I appealed to Wm Great House – who said with evident emotion that he would do the best he could – & I appointed next Sunday as the time – & advised an immediate collection for the purchase of lesson papers – &c. Bowan & I got a good supper with another Great House – & reached Lewisport after night.

July 6 – I was sick in the night – but up this morning & after a good breakfast at the parsonage, I boarded the little "Mountain Boy" for Owensboro – enroute to my own sweet home – & on the boat, now lying at Rockfort, Ind – I write up this record.

July 7 – Got home on morning train – found all well. Hanson was harvesting a good crop of oats – rains had been timely & I was pleased to see the growth in corn & tobacco & grasses. Wheat is worse than I expected. My dear old father is here, not well & Helen, Charley & the precious children came over. Little John is proud to be in pants, & was delighted to see the dog catch a rabbit in the oat field. Letters! letters! to read and answer.

July 8 – A note from Robert reporting 80 conversions in his meeting & still growing. He wants me to go to him next week. I wish I could go & help him a few days, but it seems impracticable. I am still hoarse & throat sore & still must go to my far-off appointments.

July 10 – Mr Jas Mosely met me in Owensboro – took me to his house – got there about 10 P.M. I had a serious plain talk with him on the road about his soul & warning him against the dangers of the whisky trade in which he was just engaging.

July 11 – Bro. W.K. Dempsy brought his horse for me. After a good rest & a good breakfast at Jas Moselys – all sleeping together in the same room – I walked to Bro. Ds – spent some time & rode his horse to church – Beech Valley [Ohio County]. Congregation was small – some of our own members had gone to a Roman Catholic Barbecue & dance, several miles distant. I preached an earnest faithful sermon – on Christs yoke – such a sermon as we needed. I made a very earnest appeal to the Quarterly Conference & showed them their duty – went to spend the night with bro Dempsy – a good man of good sense – with a plain, kind hearted wife. They have only one room for cook room, dining room, bed room and parlor, & old bro Burdette & a young lady Miss Lou Mercer were there also, yet we had a pleasant happy time & passed the night comfortably.

July 12 – A good attendance at Love-feast and several talks. At 11. the house would not seat the people & there were many babies that busied their mothers. I felt moved to preach on the proper use of life, and did so with great plainness of speech – for a long time – at least an hour. I rode Bro. Rev Wm Ford's horse to old bro Jack Wrights where I got a good dinner, & being much fatigued – I lay out in the yard & slept on my gumcoat – then went to the village of Magan at 4, & preached in a tobacco barn unfinished to a very large audience, most of whom listened, with deep interest – on the dangers & evils of intemperance – Prov[erbs] 20.1. Several whisky men, sellers and drinkers, were present & I labored to "make the vision plain." The principal saloon man – Mr Magan came up and asked me to spend the night with him – but I had promised to go to Wm Ralphs.

July 13 – Up at 4 A.M. The good old sister 70 yrs old, would get up & have early breakfast, so I could go 5 miles to Whitesville, in time for the 6 A.M. Stage. The stage was full – 10 of us, most of the way & I was glad to reach Owensboro in good time, at a cost of only .50 cts.

July 15 – I took 2.30 train for home – got here to supper – glad to see all well. Roberts note reports 45 additions to his church yesterday & 27 baptisms – 140 conversions reported in his meeting.

July 24 – My wife left for home [Clarksville, Tennessee] & I for Hartford. Poor Mrs John Gilbert was on the train going to Owensboro to attend Billy's trial. She thanked me, weeping, for the letter in Herald Enterprise describing "prison day" at Owensboro. Bro Edwards met me at Beaverdam.

July 25 – Mercy! mercy!! The sun is almost a ball of fire – so hot. I preached at No Creek [Ohio County] to a good Saturday congregation – on improving the talent. Mercury 99 in the shade.

July 26 – Good love-feast – a number of flaming speeches by godly women of the M.E. Church. The congregation at 11 was more than could be seated – the day was intensely hot & I labored & suffered in preaching a needed sermon on the duties of pastors & people. The steward had said that nothing more could be raised here for the pastor & yet 35.00 was lacking. I took a collection & raised over $20.00.

July 28 — Still hot. Bro Edwards & I called to see old bro Wash. Phipps — the richest man in Ohio Co & an old member of the church, whose whole life has been shadowed & clouded by the indiscretions of his younger years. Living, illicitly with a colored woman, who bore him children — he now lives with those children & provides for their support. The house is neat & comfortable — a piano & other signs of luxury. His grand children are nearly white & do not associate with negroes, nor white people with *them*. The old man is ill & the Dr did not allow company.

July 30 — Still hot. I had a vomiting spell in the night. Reading some this morning. A lively breeze relieved the intensity of the heat — hottest day of the year — mercury 104 in the shade — 125 in the sun.

August 2 — A delightful breeze & cloud. We had a good love-feast. I baptized one child & preached with liberty & unction on Sauls conversion. There was a time of weeping & one man broke out in a shout of joy. I administered the sacrament & rode with Bro Hunter in his wagon to his house — got dinner & a horse & reached the river at South Carrollton, just as the cars whistled so I lost the chance I was anxious to have of voting for a sober, godly republican against a whisky drinking & whisky selling democrat & for a temperance candidate for state treasurer.

August 3 — Got to Russellville in time to get home at night. I saw a poor sad woman on the train, trying to keep her husband from drinking. He was already drunk — & several others also. I was more than ever anxious to see whisky put down. I learn that this grand old democratic county of Logan has rebuked the whisky ring that manipulates her conventions by electing today Geo. T. Blakey, Republican, over Lou T. Brawner, a whisky democrat. Well done Logan county!

August 5 — Our dear daughter's birthday — 34 years old — a bright sunshiny, Christian woman. I trust that God will restore her health and spare her to us. Hanson is poorly & his hired man *Martin* suffering with symptoms of sun-stroke.

August 8 — A good Saturday congregation at Mt. Pleasant [Daviess County] & I had much liberty & unction in preaching.

August 9 — Very warm, again. A good love-feast. Congregation at 11. A.M. two or three times as large as our house would hold. Our Baptist brethren kindly invited us to occupy their larger house, which I did & still left a good congregation out of doors. I felt moved to preach on "How old art thou."

August 10 − Mr Tanner drove the stage & took me to Calhoun.

August 11 − Visiting a few friends & reading alittle − not feeling well − partly the effect of overwork.

August 12 − Still feeling puny − staid quiet, mostly.

August 13 − Walked out to Gibson Ayer's but laid on his cot most of the day − ate very little dinner & soon threw up what I ate − trouble also with my bowels − taking medicine. Mr Livers a Catholic man & saloon keeper who heard my sermon on Temperance − sent me an invitation to take tea & lodge with him & he would be sure to get me up in time for the boat to Paradise [Muhlenberg County]. I accepted − gladly, went to prayermeeting & attempted to talk a little but was taken sick & had to quit.

August 14 − I left Calhoun about 3 A.M. feeling better than I expected − resting quietly through the night & sleeping some time on the boat. My old friend Capt Everhart was very courteous & attentive to me. I reached Paradise − about 10 A.M. & was kindly received at Bro Jared Browns. My good friend Mrs. A.J. Ayer insisted on giving me a bottle of her home-made grape-wine & I used alittle of it only. The stopper came out & when I reached Paradise, my saddlebags had quite a vicious odor. I was very feeble all day & lay down most of the time − taking frequent doses of cholera medicine.

August 15 − I was sick in the night, but better to day. Since my Quarterly Meeting was published, our Baptist brethren changed the time of their meeting here, so that our appointments to day & tomorrow clash. Bro Maddox their pastor, recognizing the precedence of my appointment, courteously & kindly declined my invitation to preach to day & insisted that I proceed with my regular services. I preached half hour with some liberty on "wisdom and her children," but was feeble & fatigued. I find great relief to my stomach & bowels from sister Browns *black-berry wine*.

August 28 − [Owensboro, following a brief stay at home and appointments at Masonville and Pleasant Grove in Daviess County] I boarded the Steamer "Two States" for Grissoms Landing − thence to Jones's chapel. Quite a crowd had assembled there to attend a baptismal service. Bro Lucy was sick & could not be there, so I attended to the work, received three into the church, made a short talk on the design & mode of baptism − & baptized one man in the house − and went 3 miles to the Ohio River in Henderson Co and immersed 12 or 14 men & women, in about equal numbers. I think they were mostly people of little information − as I asked one to write her name & she could not do it. There seemed to me a lack of reverence & devoutness, both in the subjects & the crowd that came with them. Some of the women seemed frightened & shuddered much & some got strangled. I cannot believe that Jesus instituted this cumbersome rite as the invariable way of expressing the purifying of the Holy

Spirit. I came near failing to get clothes to change in & had to rip & tie up a suit loaned me by a man named Verble & then they were so tight on me that I was in dread of some unseemly accident. I put on my long linen duster on the outside to preserve a decent appearance. A bro Hathaway carried me in his wagon & brought me back to bro James Jones's where I spend the night. Bro Lucy had a fine meeting here & added 35 or 40 to the membership – some Baptists & some Catholics joining. I think now that 500 have professed conversion in this district since last Conference. There is a Mrs Waldon from Ind. & her daughter here. She thinks that she was called to preach & that women ought to preach, or do aught else that men do in business & professions.

August 29 – I do not feel any worse for going in the River yesterday & coming 2 miles in wet clothes, but I put on my water-proof outside & kept warm. This morning I spent some time repairing some damage to my clothes, and was glad I could sew alittle & had a place to sew in. Our Quarterly Conference was not well attended and the finances are much in arrears. People want Lucy back. He has taken in 75 members & improved the parsonage. I find that our people in this county have built two new churches on ground to which they have no title. They may yet have trouble. We dined at Bro Jones's whose dining room is in Henderson Co & half of his house in Daviess. He calls Daviess a poor county and says he has to go to Henderson everytime he gets anything to eat.

August 30 – Good attendance at Love-feast, but none of the young converts spoke. Large audience at 11 & fine attention. I preached with some liberty on Diversity of gifts 1st Cor[inthians] 4.7. The community today is excited over the killing of a negro *Nelson Moran* at Grissoms Landing, by Mr Shelby Hicks, who was watching the bonded warehouse into which negroes had broken several times lately & stolen quantities of whisky. He saw this negro coming to the warehouse at an unseasonable hour, & he says he halted him 3 times and the negro kept coming, so he shot & killed him dead. I had a full house again at night & with great plainness of speech, I expounded the second chap. of Titus. The attention was serious & I hope good will result, but this is a mixed population of Roman Catholics & Baptists, Presbyterians & Methodists, and there seems to be a lack of reverence, & a lower order of training than we see in some other places. The people are hospitable & friendly, but many of them are renters and not fixed residents.

August 31 – At Owensboro I went with bro. Brewer to see Mr Henry Perkins, an old and wealthy citizen, a member of our church – a leading *distiller of whisky* – & a constant *drinker*. He is now well nigh burnt out & is very ill with some alarming stomach trouble – another victim of the whisky fiend – a clever honorable man – ruined by his appetite. The church has tolerated him possibly to his injury – hoping to save him. He seemed glad to see us, and after some talk, I prayed for him, which he seemed to appreciate. At night I met the called session of Quarterly Conference & was glad to find the stewards in good hope of paying out our claim. The Brethren *all* expressed especial approbation of my work and said they would not be satisfied if I were not returned to the District – that they had never heard from anybody a word of disapproval, but many things in my praise – that the women of the church were *all* for me – old bro. Duncan said all the women and *three thirds* of the men.

September 1 – North-wind cool & dry. Came home and found the School Institute in session & our house full of company. Luther writes of great success in a meeting in Florida – 30 or 40 professions and many hard cases converted. I was greatly rejoiced to hear that my precious grand-children Lizzie & Ruth Roach had professed religion. May God keep them faithful to the end.

September 2 – Cool & very dry, yet I find that my corn is good and most of the tobacco very fine for the season. I do not see any larger or better. We have great cause to be thankful. I went to Bethlehem, to the School Institute – quite a large attendance of teachers and visitors. We are entertaining quite a number of them – but I do not and cannot feel reconciled to the unjustifiable opposition that Elias Riley & B.C. Jenkins worked up to defeat Hanson as the teacher of this school. Mr Riley has shown a stubborn prejudice against Hanson & took it on himself to ride around & talk to the other trustees, who had voted for Hanson to induce them not to vote for him at the next meeting. Mr Jenkins wanted the place for his brotherinlaw & failing in that – seemed mad because Hanson got it – and trying it again this time and failing – opposed Hanson in favor of Prof. Vick. I had no objection to Mr Vick – & consider him a gentleman – neither do I think less of those who, preferring him to Hanson, voted for him, but I do not feel resigned to Hanson's defeat by the means employed, but I am glad now that Hanson is out of the school. God will overrule it all for good – although we may feel –

> "How sharper than a serpent's tooth
> It is to have a thankless friend."

When John Hutching's mules died, Hanson lent him his, to haul his tobacco & plow his ground & yet he allowed Riley to persuade him to vote against Hanson. When Willie Jenkins needed a friend, to set him right, before the public & make a sentiment in his favor – in his claim against Dr Rist's estate, for nursing the Dr through Small-pox – I volunteered to write for the paper & received the thanks of Dr King & Mr Jenkins – but now Jenkins loses no chance to oppose my son. I will try to judge charitably, and act in a Christian manner. We have had so much sunshine that perhaps some trials may be best for us. Hanson has had much bad treatment – but he bears it bravely.

September 5 – Thirty five years ago this day I married my wife – the best days work for this world that I ever did. I owe to her love and energy & common sense more than I can tell. I thank God that we have lived together so long and our "honey moon" still lasts.

September 8 – We had a fine rain – for a little while in the night – for which God be praised. Other showers followed, until we had a good rain, greatly reviving the crops and relieving us from hauling water – the cistern being dry. I helped Hanson strip tobacco several hours – first work I have done for a long time.

September 10 – I had a sick spell of vomiting and purging in the night & have been feeble all day – reading & writing – by turns.

September 11 – I helped Hanson finish stripping last years crop of tobacco – the first time in my life that we had *old* tobacco to strip in Sept. We put it out in the dew last night – & found it soft enough this morning. We have some Michigan boys named Johnson, Bob & Walter, cutting corn. They are very uncouth & uncultured, but they seem willing to work – & put up 10 shocks each in a day – the oldest 15 yrs old.

September 13 – Clouds & rain – blessed rain – how it showered down & then stopped for the thirsty ground to drink and then showered again, until we got all we wanted – but we had no preaching. At 4 p.m. I baptized John and Charles Riley by immersion in the creek, just below Boyds Mill. The creek was rising rapidly and very muddy & the clouds were baptising with pure water – dropping from the skies, while I was plunging into muddy water below. I sang & prayed & got home before night. This service was made necessary by Bro W.C. Hayes first declining to immerse, and then proposing to do it – rather privately in a pond, near the house. If I believe the *mode* invalidated the ordinance, I should not immerse, but as it does not I accept our church view in good faith and give the candidate the benefit of his conscience.

September 14 – Bro. Hayes came & I paid him 10.00 on his collections. I was glad that our circuit paid bro. Hayes his *whole claim* – he says the first time in his life that he was ever paid in full. I was to have been at the meeting of [Logan Female] College Directors tonight, but felt too unwell to go – stomach and bowels both out of order.

September 15 – Very sick again in the night – feeble & a little dizzy this morning – but must start to Conference. The interest of the Owensboro District & at least 12 preachers is more or less involved in my representation. My dear wife will go with me, but is not very well herself. Going to Conference is a serious matter with me, very different from my youthful views. I go now thoughtfully, prayerfully, I might say fearfully. My own district is in good shape & I am not burdened to make changes, but many brethren will be changed & their families will be troubled. We reached Greenville [Muhlenberg County] in good time and met a hearty welcome at Thos. Jones's where they had asked for us.

September 16 – A good attendance at Conference & business progressing. Bishop Wilson advised us to talk with our preachers & presiding elders to day & be ready for work tomorrow – & a cabinet meeting tonight at the college.[1] It gives me ½ a mile to walk each way.

September 17 – Bishop Wilson pleases us all by his candor & impartiality. We get on well.

September 18 – Dr Settle had been requested by Mrs A. H. Redford to prepare a memoir of her husband, but the chairman Jas A. Lewis, had requested me to prepare a memoir & he liked my paper best – & we both objected to some expressions in Dr. Settles paper. I felt the delicacy of the situation – & advised a modification that would make Settles paper acceptable. Mine was sent to Mrs Redford & she approved it – so I rewrote the last page & put in some of Dr Redfords dying statements – assuring us of his peace with God.

September 19 – We elected B.M. Messick, David Morton, H.C. Morrison, Geo. H. Hayes & S.R. Brewer clerical delegates to the General Conference – every one of whom I put on my first ballot & four of whom were elected on first ballot – S.R. Brewer & myself were the next highest voted for – & on the next ballot Brewer was elected & my vote, I am glad to say, was cast for *him*. On the next ballot – for reserves – I was first choice – no other getting a majority of votes cast – & no more balloting today. J.G. Carter & W.B. Machen & J.R. Hindman were the only lay delegates elected after several ballots. Mrs. Redford requested an interview with the committee on memoirs & with decided spirit insisted, not to say *demanded,* an allusion to Dr Redfords Publishing House troubles & his testimony in his last illness that he was right in the matter. Lewis & I thought there should be no opening up of old wounds, that would possibly produce controversy in a memorial service – & Settle coincided – & I wrote the last page of the memoir as to be acceptable to all the committee.

September 21 – The cabinet work has less than usual friction. The Bishop & presiding elders and their wives were invited to supper at George Eaves's. It was a delightful occasion, but we had a very short time to enjoy it. We had set this night of the memorial service, but so many other things were crowded into it – that we were kept until a late hour. I think sister Redfords judgment was in error when she *selected nine* brethren to speak about Dr Redford – better left that to the spontaneous expression of those who knew and loved him, as Mrs. T. D. Lewis did about her husband & as others have *always* done – but she was anxious & fearful that something might be said that she would not like or something left out that she would like to hear, and the circumstances make

---

1. Greenville College was founded in 1850. Between 1858 and 1880 it was affiliated with the Cumberland Presbyterian Church. In 1883, three years after the school was sold to a Methodist named E. W. Hall, it was taken over by the Louisville Conference of the Methodist Episcopal Church, South. Otto Rothert, *A History of Muhlenberg County* (Louisville, 1913), 211 ff.

excuse for her solicitude. Jas A. Lewis read the memoir of T. D. Lewis & I read the memoir of Dr Redford — & then all the brethren, selected, spoke of brother Redford — & a number of others spoke out of the fulness of their own hearts of their love and sympathy for Thos D. Lewis, one of the purest & best men that we ever had in our Conference.

September 22 — We reconsidered the vote by which two brethren were admitted on trial and the application was withdrawn. This is the first case of the kind that I have known — but it was right. We have admitted many men not suited to itinerant work. After much business the Conference adjourned in time for most of the brethren to board the noon train. Lizzie & I reached home in good time.

September 23 — Letters to write to day as usual. Yesterday morning Mrs Redford sent for me & thanked me heartily for the memoir — said it was just what she desired & that she would always love me &c & several brethren spoke in terms of commendation. On Monday night the question of change of name was put and the proposition to change the name of our church from M[ethodist] E[piscopal] C[hurch] South — to M[ethodist] E[piscopal] C[hurch] in America was unanimously rejected. I see no good resulting from a change, but most likely trouble and dissension. Bishop Wilson called me to the chair to hold the memorial service & he retired. That was my first presiding over an *Annual* Conference & will likely be the last. This Conference was pleasant, & yet serious but it did not burden me as some sessions have done. There were comparatively few changes — only one in my District, & that because bro W.B. Lucy preferred to get to a higher region, fearing his health on the Oakford circuit. S.R. Brewer, J.B. Cottrell, L.E. Campbell, J.W. Bowan, J.C. Brandon, P.A. Edwards, J.T. Rushing, & T.V. Joiner — all return. Geo P. McGhee goes to Oakford & bro Kimbler to Patesville.

September 24 — At home — tired & sleepy.

September 25 — Wallace came home from Russellville reasonably well pleased with Bethel College.

September 27 — We had a fine rain tonight & Wallace insisted on returning to town to be in time for chapel service. After much thought I decided to send him to Bethel College — under care of his old tutor J.H. Fuqua. It is a Baptist College but the teachers are competent and he is near home — & boarding in an excellent family — F.M. Page's convenient to college. I think it is well to exchange courtesies & the Baptists are patronizing our female school in the same town.

October 1 — Cloudy & showery. We finish prizing our old tobacco this morning — and are firing the new crop in both barns. For several days rather weeks, I have been annoyed by an itching humor & little fleabite looking spots on the lower part of my bowels & upper part of my thighs. I thought it began from chigger bites at camp-ground. To day I showed it to Dr Peter & he gave me a prescription, which he said would relieve me. If it had been on the wrists or hands or about the joints, I should have thought it was the abominable "itch."

October 2 – I spent the day in Russellville looking after business and calling on friends – dined with F.M. Page, where Wallace is boarding – went to the bank & found that I had overpaid the heirs of aunt B[etsy] & had also overlooked a note which I gave some time back – so that I am harder pressed, than I supposed.

October 6 – [Owensboro] I have had a pleasant day in the line of duty. I called on my old teacher uncle Billy Washington, who seemed delighted to see me again – but said he expected to be in another world before winter is over & seems anxious to go home.

October 8 – I read & visited a few friends – & held prayermeeting at night. I am still much annoyed with an itching, burning humor of some sort of the lower part of my bowels & insides of my thighs, that does not readily yield to treatment. I have tried Cuticum, Red Precipitate & Huskells salve outwardly – & sulphur & cream of tartar inwardly with only partial relief. It is stubborn and distressing. I wish I could be at home.

October 12 – [Cloverport] Wrote to my wife & three absent sons. Luther reports his strength failing under the continuous labor & great heat that he has endured in Fla. I wrote to him to moderate his exertions.

October 13 – Too cold & damp to go to Hardinsburg. I visited several friends here. I find Cloverport people hospitable, courteous & agreeable in their manners, but if their wealth is not misrepresented & overrated, they have small ideas of financial obligation to the church. There is need here of faithful, loving instruction & a revival of deep, spiritual christianity. I have a comfortable room, and I trust a cordial welcome at Wm. Bowmers. The children seem to love me. I tell them Bible stories & urge them to be good.

October 20 – [Olmstead] Up early & off to see my brotherinlaw Dr Bailey, married to my cousin Fannie E. Browder, at 7:30 A.M. at her father W.R. Browder's home – Bro I.W. Emerson *reading* the ritual as laid down in the Discipline.

I walked over the farm, glad to find Hanson as well forward with his work as he is – tobacco all in & mostly cured up, nearly all the apples gathered, & two thirds of the wheat sown – rye coming up well & hogs improving – more young calves & other signs of a living.

October 21 – First killing frost of the season. Today is P.J. Bailey's sale. He inherited a good estate, married first a wife with some property & then a second wife, Florence Kimbrough, with considerable estate – & yet in spite of all, he is broke & hopelessly in debt not by speculation or gambling, but by living too fast & working too little, just as hundreds of others in this country are doing.

October 22 – Cool & clear – heavy frost. My cropper *Bob Clark,* is dissatisfied and wants to sell his interest in the tobacco. I wish to do him full justice, but not to injure myself. I think one hundred and fifty dollars is all that I will be safe in paying him. Much of the tobacco is badly spotted – & nearly or quite half of it will be lugs – & the price likely low. He had ten acres of land, but he allowed two of the richest bottoms to be drowned out – by neglecting to open a ditch as directed, & the plants under the trees did no good on account of drought. I suppose there will be 7500 lbs – but to take all the risk of loss & damage – & wait until Aug – for the sale, leaves me almost no margin after paying him 150. for his half of the prospective proceeds.

October 23 – Off early to Owensboro – found the "Frank Stein" going up & took passage on her – pd 50 cts to Hawesville. Bro. L. Campbell & all the children had gone to the River to meet me, but I missed them & got to his house first, where I always find a pleasant welcome. The children love me dearly & crowd around me to hear stories that amuse and instruct them.

October 25 – Another bright & delightful sabbath. I had unusual liberty & power in preaching on the great commission. Lewis Campbell & I took up a subscription of more than $40.00 for Foreign Missions – more than twice as much as the whole circuit gave last year. Campbell was greatly delighted – said he never heard a missionary sermon that pleased him better – thought he had never heard me preach so well about anything. There was profound attention. The Love-feast at three was more than usually interesting for this place, but the speech that affected me most was made by little Paul Campbell, eight years old, the boy I received into the church last summer. He said in a very earnest & tender tone, "Bro Browder, I love Jesus and Ill try to do his will." At night I preached on the use of time Gen[esis] 47.8 with considerably liberty & then administered the sacrament of the Lords Supper.

October 26 – I learn that the sermon last night has produced a profound impression on the town. Several lawyers & others declaring it to be the best & most practical sermon ever heard in Hawesville, & some people have already begun a better course of life. By request I went out to Hardins chapel, two miles from town and preached at night. I was surprised to find the house full of people, including a considerable number who had walked out from town – Mr Riley, editor of the paper & others in the number.

October 28 – Bro Campbell & I called to see Mrs Mason the lawyers wife whose husband seldom ever goes to church, but who was greatly impressed with the sermons of Sunday morning & Sunday night, so much that he proposed to his wife to go with him to hear me again tonight, despite the rain & mud – but I had no appointment. They called to see me at the Carlton House & insisted that hereafter I stop with them. I have been rather surprised to find so many doors open to me in this town, where it is said the presiding elders have had but few invitations. I am now in a cozy room in the Carlton, with a warm welcome & a good fire – waiting for the Mountain Boy at six in the morning.

October 30 – [Owensboro] District Stewards met & put my salary at 1000. Same as last year, & would have gone higher, if I had said so. I shall get on last year about 850.00 & 150. will perhaps pay actual travelling expenses. Owensboro showed a liberal spirit toward me.

October 31 – Up early & off to Washington Station S[chool] H[ouse] 18 miles distant [in Ohio County] – got in on time & preached with fine liberty on Lam[entations] 3.33–5 to a deeply interested audience. Young bro H.T. Kimbler, the new preacher was there. I hope he will succeed. The stewards allowed him 210. & paid him 11. I went home with George Crow – slept in same room with his family. I every now & then come across places of this sort. It does not seem to embarrass the family atall.

November 1 – I preached at 11 on Missions, made the vision plain, & urged the people to give liberally. I went home with Joe Miller – & at night preached with liberty & unction on the work of the Holy Spirit. We had a melting time and two old fashioned shouts. I stay at Rev Wm Fords, well received, but sleep in the family room again. Bro Kimbler was with me. This is his first year in Conference and I tried to give him fatherly counsel. He has the curliest hair I ever saw on a white mans head, his lips are thick and his foot thick & broad. He seems zealous.

November 9 – [Hartford, Ohio County] The repairs on the church, making it new, have just been completed & will be ready for reopening Wednesday evening & bro Edwards has announced that I will preach. I must prepare a suitable sermon.

November 11 – Studying & calling. At night there was a fine congregation – the house and furniture are beautiful & the announcement that just 146 years ago this night John Wesley, in the old Foundry, in London, preached the *first* sermon ever delivered in a Methodist church, caused a sensation. I was clear in historic statements – and my argument on the philosophy of the rapid growth of our church, attracted attention. I did not have extra liberty, but my people were pleased and the subscription was more than enough to pay the debt & some for sexton &c and every body seemed happy.

December 2 – [Olmstead] I wrote to Bishop Hargrove, & also to Rev. Chas. Fulwood of Fla, asking for Luther *no favor,* but only that he be sent where he could serve the church to the best advantage – whether in a hard or an easy place – & not where he will have to move before the end of the year.

December 3 – Bro. Pleas. A. Edwards of Hartford circuit writes me that Dr. J.S. Coleman, the Baptist champion, *denied* the accuracy of statistics given in my reopening sermon at Hartford – but did not call my name – only said he wanted the people to be *correctly* informed. Bro Edwards asks for the figures used & the *source* of my information & I took some time to put them in form & tell him that the Methodist Year Book of 1884 – Baptist Year Book of 1885 – U.S. Census of 1880 – & Minutes & Newspaper items of later date, had furnished me with the figures that give 1,343,282 more Methodists than Baptists & 9854 more Meth. than Baptist churches – & property worth more than $30,000,000 in excess of Baptist church property. I take Baptist numbers as given in Baptist Year Book of 1885 – & Methodist numbers as given in Meth. Year Book of 1884 – & Dr. Dorchesters paper on Statistics, read at the Centenary Conf[erence] in Balt – last Dec. How do Baptists know our numbers better than we do ourselves? If we take their statements, why should they "doctor" ours?

December 8 – [Owensboro] Staid at Dr. Hickman's – one of our stewards & a rich man. His name is published in the papers as one of the managers of the German dancing club. I talked with him freely and kindly about it – & was glad to find that he had never attended the dance & had nothing to do with the club nor had authorized the use of his name. Two other members of our church are published as managers and I told Bro. Brewer to talk kindly & brotherly to them.

December 16 – George P. McGhee came to take me to the country. We spent the night at Ashley Covey's near the C[umberland] Pres. Church, Pleasant Ridge [Daviess County]. We attended church at night & I was pressed into service & preached – rather under protest, as I was hoarse & not every well – but the word was effective & the first penitent during the meeting came up for prayer.

December 17 – After a pleasant nights rest, at Mr C's & some time in reading, I went to church again, not thinking that I would again be pressed to preach, but there seemed no evasion or escape, except by direct refusal – so I preached again – on God's providence in afflictions. Never, perhaps in my life, did I preach a sermon that so completely impressed & carried away a whole congregation, as this one carried away these Presbyterians. It just suited them and they were extravagant in some of the expressions that were afterwards reported to me. Some of them claim to be greatly benefited – if so I am thankful – if not, then all the eulogies they could give, amount to nothing.

December 20 – Beautiful clear, spring-like weather. Fine love-feast. At 11. the house was full & the behavior perfect. I had liberty & some unction, preaching on Pauls conversion. For more than an hour – everybody listened and at the close I took a collection for the District Parsonage – of over 30.00 – 22.63 cash in hand – much better than I expected – thanks to the help of my Cumberland brethren. They also helped buy an overcoat & a nice suit of clothes for Geo.

McGhee which generosity I highly appreciate. We closed our service to meet at night with the Cumberlands. I went to church feeling sure that I should hear a sermon, but hoarse and weary as I was – I allowed myself to be overpersuaded to preach. Bro. Barr came to me & said many in the congregation, sinners & backslidden, sent a special request that I should preach – that some men, deeply impressed were anxious to hear me again – so I preached a plain & earnest sermon on "Agree with thine adversary" Mat[thew] 5.25. I spent the night with my friends, the Coveys. So many – many people of our own & the other church beg me to stay that I really feel sorry to leave them, but I must go home – duty demands it.

December 22 – [Olmstead] I have been busy all day – writing most of the time. I sent 10. to Robt to pay for a nice pair of Blankets & set of knives & forks as a bridal present to my brother, Jim, who to day leads to the altar Miss Maggie Walker of Louisville – daughter of Hon John C. Walker – a girl of good reputation. A letter from Luther reports an extra meeting, under his care in a school house, near his cabin. The Catholic man who became offended at him for his sermon on Temperance – came up for prayers – & his wife and daughter also. They invited him home to their house & seemed very penitent. I hope the dear boy is doing well. I want to send him 5.00 for a Christmas present.

December 24 – I went with Lizzie to get some Christmas presents – for servants & children. I am thankful to have this Christmas at home – & dear Father with us. This Christmas eve is silent at our house. No little children to hang up stockings! Dear wife is busy, preparing for the grand children, & the little mulatto girl of Mrs Martins, that makes our fires. We bought a few things today for the Christmas tree.

December 25 – Christmas! Welcome bright day of Christs Nativity! We arose later than usual. No clatter of eager children. A few guns – & fire crackers arrested our attention. At breakfast we all found nice things around our plates – oranges, figs – dates, candies &c beside something of utility. My father was pleased with a pair of new gloves. I got a clothes-brush, & the rest something of equal worth. Dear Wallace is out from school & seems happy to be at home – once more. I wish our other dear children could be with us.

December 26 – Clear & colder. For the first time in a longwhile, I drove up the horses and fed them while Hanson milked the cows – the hired help being away. David comes back from Hopkinsville, well pleased with our new sister, Jimmy's wife. The children have a candy pulling tonight at my brother David's.

December 28 – We had a fine company and a splendid dinner with Jimmy & his bride at Tom Sydnors. A very enjoyable day. Two of my humorous propositions resulted in roars of laughter. 1st – if there is a married man who is not henpecked let him hold up his hand. There was no vote. 2nd – if there is a married woman here who has not an ugly husband let her raise a hand. Up went every hand, except my daughterinlaw Jenny's & a big laugh followed at Hanson's expense. Not often of late have I seen a more genial & humorous occasion.

December 29 – A dining at Davids. Dinner good enough for a royal festival – good company & good cheer – warm, pleasant sunshine – just like spring. My son George came tonight. Hanson thinks he will go to Ark[ansas] & buy land there & George speaks of going with him. I fear it is not best for either of them – but cant tell & cant interfere. I shall dread to see them go – but help Hanson all I can.

December 30 – Warm & cloudy – alittle rain in the night. We had quite a company to day, to meet Jim & his wife & share our nice dinner. Jenny's culinary and artistic skill does not suffer in comparison with the best I have seen. I never saw a nicer cake – nor better chicken salad, on any table – indeed I thought the salad was the best I ever saw & all else was in keeping – a splendid dinner, beautifully arranged – all enjoyed it – & it was a pleasant occasion – but too expensive & stylish for a poor man. I shall help Hanson pay for the purchased articles. Tom Browder's 3 older daughters came – Tom Sydnor & David Browder & their families – Charley Roach & family – Geo. Warfield & two daughters – Daniel Bailey & his wife & father – Sue Gardner – & one of Wallaces School-mates Seldin Trimble, Rosa Bailey – & above all my dear old father – and also W.R. Browder – 36 whites, beside my own family – & quite a number of negroes, such as generally manage to be around on such an occasion. The children seem to have had a big day – playing much in the yard – so mild is the air – mercury 56.

January 1, 1886 – New Year's day! How time flies! I am an old man – will enter my 60th year in ten days more – & I feel sensibly the diminishing of my physical powers. My voice especially is failing & my lungs are weaker & my general strength is less. I do not hear so well. I get weary with less exertion & go to sleep over my reading. My eye is not so clear nor my appetite so keen – nor my spirits so buoyant & vivacious. People call me "old bro Browder" & "Father Browder" and there is a reason for it. I am less a man, in many respects than once I was. I am on the downward grade and must go with accelerating speed. Children are all grown, & nearly all of them gone or preparing to leave – & wife & I will soon be "old folks at home" almost alone. I am trying to be ready, & bear with patience the ills that may be in store. I have had a happy life – more sunshine than shadow, more mercies than miseries, by a thousand fold – honored in my parentage, & in my marriage and greatly blessed in my children – in my kindred & in my home – with many other earthly joys – & a well-grounded hope of Heaven when I die. I can afford to be still & await my share of the woes of life. I cannot say that I am indifferent or without apprehension – but I shall not take the trouble before it comes. The kind hand that hath led me hither to – will lead me on to the end. I dedicate myself and all that I am anew to God & resolve afresh to do my duty to God & man & leave the rest all in the hands of an all wise, all gracious God – whose "mercy endureth forever." I have more blessings than I deserve. The weather is beautiful, balmy & bright. Lizzie & I went by to see Tom B. & family & Geo. Warfield – & read for them two good letters just received from Luther. He has had a good meeting & some happy conversions – & added 11 members to his church. The Catholic man, Mr Fortier, who was so enraged with him for preaching a temperance sermon – made a profession of religion & his wife also & both joined the Methodist church. His people will about pay his expenses – by his living hard & boarding himself – cooking his own meals & walking to his appointments. They say they want him again. The membership at Longwood has more than doubled under his administration – not large now – but the increase is encouraging.

January 2 – Weather delightful. Mercury 58–60 but a steady rain. Hanson has stripped about 400 lbs of tobacco of pretty good quality. Mr L.A. Freeman called to collect pay for wheat threshing. He is active for prohibition in the county & we are getting up a petition to the Legislature to order a vote upon the subject – next August.

January 3 – I was requested to preach at Bethlehem to day. I had prepared to preach on Temperance, but seeing several people who had been in distress I changed my plan & preached again on Gods providence in afflictions Lam[entations] 3.33–5. There was a deep feeling & I trust much good resolve was formed. I am sorry to see the congregation going down. Our church here seems to encounter discouragements.

January 4 – Colder – freezing alittle. Wallace went back to Russellville to school. At ten oclock A.M. the big snow flakes were coming down in wintry grandeur.

January 6 – A letter from Rev. S.R. Brewer [Owensboro] informs me of the dangerous illness of his son Theodore. This is sad news to me. I have seldom in a life time crossed such a boy as Theodore Brewer – so noble – manly – intelligent, trusting & pure. I join my humble prayer with those of his fond parents that God would spare him for a life of usefulness.

January 8 – Mercy on me! What a snow storm! Last night when prayermeeting closed at our house, I told Lizzie that the sky indicated snow & this morning it began & has shifted & drifted & piled up all day until dark – some places five or six feet deep – & 8 to 12 [inches] on the levels. Furious winds blew & rocked the train as the large, feathery fleeces beat in every open crack & the wind grew colder & colder until at night it settled down to Zero. Geo. Dennis met me [at Owensboro], & with difficulty I waded along the unbeaten path to the parsonage – almost falling under the weight of my saddlebags. We called at Bro. Brewers. Theodore is *very ill*. His condition is critical – one lung entirely hepatized and badly gangrened. Drs Stirman & Tyler speak very doubtfully of his recover.

January 9 – Winter! Oh! the winter. Mercury 8 below Zero & wind high. I pulled through the deep snow down to bro Brewers – facing a fierce wind that froze the tip of my nose. I spent the day waiting on Theodore & staid at night with Bro. T.H. Frayser, whose kind family seem to like me & to make me comfortable.

January 10 – Cold! so cold! Mercury 12 below 0. Went to church at 11. Small congregation. Sexton had the fire burning in good time but the mercury was Zero in the house. I sang & prayed and dismissed the people – not safe to stay there. I spent the day waiting on Theodore – hope he is improving alittle. The family greatly appreciate my help – & Theodore loves me dearly.

January 11 – My 60th birth day! 59 yrs old! It seems strange to me. I wrote to my family & several friends, then spent the day nursing Theodore. Bro. Brewer is sick. Mrs Brewer is worn out – & they have no help. I pack up the coal & water – go to the Grocer – Baker – Butcher & Apothecary & help nurse the dear boy & hope his life will be spared. I am glad I can help them. Our Quarterly Conference at night was not largely attended, but was very harmonious.

January 12 – Still colder – mercury sinking 22 below 0 at some cold points & some claim 26 below.

January 13 – Moderating – bright & clear. I work again with Theodore. He must be improving. We held our sacramental service tonight – small attendance. Brewer sick. I sat up all night with Theodore. Mrs Brewer was so worn out that I made her lie down & sleep, while I did all that was to do, giving medicines & attending to the dear boys wants until 5 ½ A.M. when Mrs B. awoke & refused to lie down again. I had a happy peaceful night – thankful in my heart that I could serve a godly family in distress. I slept from about 6. to 8. A.M.

January 14 – Helping with the sick boy until noon – then slept an hour or two – & after reading & writing some, I slept well until breakfast.

January 15 – Raining & freezing – streets solid ice. I walked with difficulty – got ready to leave for Cloverport & found that the boats had laid up on account of floating ice in the river. I took a train & came home, had a hard walk through snow drifts, mud & slush from Olmstead home – was very tired – but glad to see all my dear ones well & up. Hanson had put up ice & had taken good care of all the stock.

January 17 – Sick all night – lungs tender and great difficulty of breathing – was very uneasy & feared an attack of Pneumonia. I staid in & read. Just as Hanson was getting his horse to go to Sunday S. he found that his cow Maud had broken through the ice & was fast in the middle of the pond. It took considerable time to cut a way for her to get out, but he saved her at last.

January 18 — Cloudy again. I still suffer with this difficult breathing — but not so much. Poor old Mrs Coulter came in looking for work. We had no work for her, but *gave* her meat, lard & flour, for which she seemed grateful. I got a letter from W.H. McCarty — editor Herald-Enterprise — asking for a story written by me on "Hard-Times" & published in Herald in 1874 — which was then extensively read & praised. McCarty says, "A number of persons have requested its republication."

January 20 — I went with Hanson to look at the farm & houses on the Jesse Page place, owned by Dr Rist, with a view to buying it for Hanson. I found houses *very* inferior, old, & uncomfortable — fences *all* in bad condition — & a very insufficient supply of timber & fully one half of the land very poor — with say 75 acres of very fine land — but needing rest & clover. I am willing, if Hanson wants it, to help him buy it at $3000 for the 225 acres — but it is not worth more.

January 21 — I started to the train, but was too late — went with Hanson to look at the Dan Herndon place. I was agreeably surprised to find it as good a place as it is, the land being in better heart, and more level, than I supposed. The dwelling house has been burnt, but the buildings that are left on the place are worth more than those on the Page land — & a much larger proportion of the land available for crops. I authorized Hanson to buy it at 20. pr acre, or even more — if time could be had on the deferred payments. The dear boy is 31 years old this day — and needs a home. I have prayed God to overrule and direct and trust we may be wisely guided. I go to Russellville tonight, enroute to Hawesville.

January 22 — Train late. I got to Owensboro after 12. River still full of ice and no boats running. I was not well enough to go horseback to Hawesville — staid & nursed Theodore Brewer, who is still very ill — sat up all night with him. He seems more confident and quiet, when I am with him.

January 25 — Still with Theodore — hope he is a little better — sat up with him again until 4 ½ A.M.

January 26 — Spent the day watching the dear sick boy — whose condition is little better than hopeless — yet he is brave & cheerful and insists that he will get well — says he wishes to live to take care of his mother, but is not afraid to die — believes that he will go to immediate rest in Heaven. Surely the Christians hope is glorious. Infidelity offers no such comfort. I see more and more of the grandeur of this faith in Mrs Brewer & her noble boy. She is frail & feeble, yet has the nerve of a hero, the wisdom of a philosopher & the faith of a Christian. Brewer does all he can, but does not know how to nurse the sick. They greatly appreciate my help & I sit up more than I would, because Mrs B is so worn out & needs rest — & seems to trust me as she does no other nurse.

January 27 – With Theodore again – day & night – sitting up until after 6 A.M. Was then suffering with Asthma or some difficulty of breathing.

January 28 – Not well – soreness of chest and trouble to get breath. Nursed the sick boy part of the day & went to bro Fraysers at night but could not sleep – gasping for breath & suffering all night & like Paul, longing for the day.

January 29 – Cold & dreary – boat waiting at the wharf – but I was too unwell to go to Lewisport. I took train & came home – still breathing with difficulty – have never had an asthmatic trouble so severe – or so continuous.

January 30 – I prepared an inhaler & freely inhaled vapor of turpentine, which gave me some relief.

January 31 – Sunday at home – not able to preach – staid in nearly all day – walked up to see my father alittle while, and had another sick night – breathing short & with labor.

February 1 – Bright, clear and pleasant and I breathe with less difficulty – several letters to write – one to Dr Cottrell asking if he could go to Patesville for me, in the absence of Kimbler who has not returned to the work.

February 2 – I slept well – found a light snow on the ground – but it continued on until bed time without a moments intermission – covering houses – fields & trees with the deepest snow of the season.

February 3 – Mercy! Mercy!! The ceaseless snow was still falling at 11. last night – & this morning it is two feet deep on our porch – and nearly up to the tops of the fences. It seems to average about two feet over the yard. I think I never saw such a snow before. How thankful that I am at home & all my family & domestic animals in comfortable quarters, with plenty of provision – food, & fuel. How I pity the poor. Many of them thinly clad, scantily fed – badly sheltered & with little fuel. I am glad I have a heart to help them. Tenderness in my lungs continues and I still breathe with some difficulty. I shall not start out in such condition in such weather. I watched Hanson going to the barn to feed his sheep – the snow was nearly up to his waist – he says over two feet on level lands – it is up to the top of the gate near the stable & drifted up against the barn doors, so the cattle cannot get out on the South side. Many of the drifts are beautiful round mounds. I suppose the oldest man never saw such another snow in Kentucky.

February 4 – Mercury at Zero in the morning. Sun shining clear & bright. With considerable difficulty, I rode up to Tom's to see Father. The snow in places was as high as the fence – & in the roads, was nearly belly deep. A note from Robt left him suffering with his head. I do not like those attacks. He is overworking. He was at Campbellsville two weeks & preached two to 3 times a day, all the time with great success – 45 professions & over 30 additions.

February 5 — Coldest day of the winter. Mercury 18 below Zero. We kept warm by the dining room stove.

February 6 — A letter from Geo. Dennis tells me that Theodore Brewers case less hopeful.[2] Lewis Campbell writes telling how I was needed at Hawesville & how they missed me at Quarterly Meeting & what a fight he is making for a revival in the town & some of the members opposing him. J. W. Bowan writes of the great disappointment at Lewisport caused by my sickness & sends me resolutions adopted by Quarterly Conf[erence] expressing sympathy for my afflictions & approval of my course & promising prayer for my recovery. This was very grateful to me & filled my eyes with tears of joy.

February 7 — As beautiful a sabbath overhead as one could wish — & the warm sun melts & settles the deep snow. I went to see Helen & Charley & the dear grand-children & brought little John home with me. Sue Robert has been with us several weeks. They are cheerful happy children. Little George is a bright baby two years old nearly, but will not try to talk at all — has learned to make himself understood by signs.

February 8 — Colder again. Mercury 6 above 0 & the heaviest & prettiest frost work on all the trees — weeds & spires of grass, where any appear, that I remember to have seen — a full half inch in delicate & feathery sprays & spangles the frozen moisture spreads out around the scrolled twigs. The elm tree in our front yard seems almost unearthly in its beauty, and the crusted snow lies still a full foot deep & more over all the level ground. This will long be called the big snow of 1886 — the snow of 1835 being remembered by old people as next in depth to this one. The Louisiana Moss that hangs in frozen festoons from our locust trees is beautiful & glittering and the wire clothes-line & a cord suspended from it are marvels to behold, in the abundance & delicacy of the frost wreathes that stand out all around. The still, cold air is laden with frosty mist through which the rising sun is shooting his beams, kindling the fields and the forests with a splendor that no pencil can imitate, no tongue describe. Marvellous are thy works O Lord of Hosts. "He giveth snow like wool, he scattereth the hoar frost like ashes. He casteth forth his ice like morsels: who can stand before his cold?" Psa[lm] 147. 16–17.

February 10 — I had a hard night — up and down with a painful difficulty of breathing — sometimes like actual suffocation. I think sometimes that my days are nearly numbered. I am certainly not as strong as I have been, & my lungs have had a weary, worn out feeling, a long time. I have had so many mercies & blessings at the hand of the Lord, that I may expect my days of affliction. I must

---

2. Theodore Brewer survived his illness, and after completing bachelor's and master's degrees in English at Vanderbilt University, he eventually received an appointment as head of the English department at the University of Oklahoma, a position he held from 1908 until 1938. He died in Norman, Oklahoma, on September 19, 1940. *The Oklahoma Daily* (Norman, Oklahoma), September 20, 1940.

be patient & trust in the Lord. I tried last night to resign myself – soul & body to his keeping & to leave results all in his hand. If I can have reasonable health, I would like to live to see all my children married & settled – but if I am to be an invalid & burden to my family, I should prefer to depart & be with Christ which is far better.

I shall see the Dr. & try to get relief. He examined carefully & said there was no organic trouble – not the slightest indication of any lung trouble, respiratory murmur, clear & distinct in every part – & no indication of disease in the action of the heart. He advises rest – & some attention to diet – with a mixture of cream of tartar & epsom salts – teaspoonful doses. The weather is warm & snow rapidly melting.

February 11 – I raised my head higher last night and slept more comfortably. We had a slow, cold rain all night & with the melting snow, we may expect high-water. I hope to get off to Hartford.

February 12 – Felt much better this morning. Train two hours late. At night I heard B.A. Cundiff preach an earnest sermon full of illustrations. Several penitents at the altar – my unitarian friend Dr Cole, among them. He seems perfectly candid, inquiring for the truth. I emphasized to him the promise "They that hunger & thirst after righteousness, *shall* be filled." A universalist woman was by his side – both asking special prayer for them, that they might know the truth & "have a religion, that made them happy." I left Central [City] at 11:30 P.M. & got to Beaverdam at 2 A.M. very tired.

February 13 – Up at 7. R.D. Hocker hired a Baptist brother Tichenor to take me to Hartford – roads fearfully muddy, but we made good time. Our people had given me out & were much discouraged – rather disappointed. I have seldom been more warmly greeted. The congregation at 11. was unusually large for Hartford & the roads. Quarterly Conference well attended – 42 new members reported – financial returns full & every body cheerful. I raised the money & paid off the old parsonage debt that has annoyed us ever since I have been here.

February 14 – I still suffer with difficult breathing – start up in the night with a sense of suffocation. We had a good love-feast this morning – at the close of which James Thomas, a very substantial citizen, applied for membership, much to the pleasure of our people & the disappointment of some others. The house was filled to its capacity, the aisle being crowded with chairs, & some old skeptics out, who only come, I am told, when I am here. I had good liberty preaching on Isaiah 25.6–8 & the largest attendance at Communion ever seen in Hartford as reported by all who spoke of it. Bro Edwards & I dined at Harrison Taylors, the oldest & wisest skeptic in town. He is said to be very friendly to me & always comes to hear me. The S.S. was well attended & the night congregation so large that some left, not able to get seats. By request I preached on "How old art thou." People who have not been seen out for a long time were present & said to be deeply impressed. The attention was all I could ask — and many came up to give thanks and congratulations. Prof. Wayland Alexander — president of Hartford College — was extravagant in his eulogies. He grasped my hand & said "I never did before what I am going to do now. I tell you that was the best sermon that ever fell from the lips of man." Others, lawyers, doctors, merchants &c were profuse in their praises. My fear is that the serious effect produced will be diminished by the abundance of commendation. Satan is wiley & may take that device to break the force of truth.

February 17 — Edwards had an appointment for me at the college, yesterday morning — & an appointment at our church tonight. I was very tired & did not do justice to either occasion or to myself — dining & supping & calling & no time to study is not good for pulpit success. Difficult breathing again.

February 18 — Got dinner with Rev Gabriel Bean at the prison & took stage for Beaverdam enroute to Taylortown. John Septimus Brown met me with a horse, and I had a long weary ride of 16 miles over awful roads to his house, where welcome, rest & comfort awaited me.

February 19 — Went to Taylortown — had instructed my wife to write to me at T. town — & lo it is only a country school house in the woods — used also for a church — called Taylortown on account of the number of people named Taylor that live around, but it ought to be called Taylor-Brown as the Browns are almost as numerous as the Ts. It is estimated that 1500 Taylors & 1000 Browns live in Ohio Co. Eight or 10 persons out. I read & expounded Acts 10th.

February 20 — I was called to preach the funeral of Mrs Scott Taylor. Some liberty in preaching Psa[lm] 23.4. Went to Calvin Taylors to dinner & went by request to spend the night with Lewis W. Brown.

February 22 — Bro. John S. Brown lent me his horse & bro John Moore proffered to lead him back from Beaver-dam — so I set out for home — had a fatiguing ride through mud & slop. I took train for Central City & in getting off left my overcoat on the coach. Got John Taylor to telegraph for it. I got home at night & found Hanson very ill — had taken a dangerous relapse in Mumps & was suffering fearfully.

February 23 — I had a hard night of difficult breathing — a dreadful sensation of suffocating. Hanson seems better & the Dr. says is doing well.

February 24 — I am surprised to find how large are my unpaid accounts at Grocers & Merchants — one of the evils of credit system. I paid 40. on old accounts & owe twice that much more. We will be compelled to economize more rigidly. I have given away more money than most people of my means, but I hope to worthy objects. The Dr pronounces Hanson out of danger — for which I am thankful. I was going to see my dear old father & met him coming here. Another batch of letters to answer.

February 25 — I went to the depot & brought the new wagon — sent by Geo. Warfield — Stude Baker — 3 horse $62.50 — good wagon.

February 27 — [South Carrollton, Muhlenberg County] Small congregation. Bro Rushing reported 130 conversions — 95 additions — financial report small. No preaching at night — not well.

February 28 — Fine, large congregation at 11. & good liberty — on "feast of fat things." Old Mr Ross the universalist was there — & surprised everybody by contributing something to the hat collection for support of pastors — said to be the first time in 30 years. Love-feast was well-attended & my converted Unitarian friend Dr. Cole made an excellent talk. I stay at bro McCowns — breathing freer.

March 3 — [Greenville] I spent a hard night at Bro. Tom Jones. No people could be kinder, but I had a night of hard breathing.

March 4 — I rested better last night — made a talk to the male students at the college & preached at 11. with unction & liberty — a short sermon on "Gods providence in afflictions."

March 6 — [Calhoun] Good week day congregation — good liberty preaching on Holy Spirit. I spent night at R.E. Glovers — had another night of painfully difficult breathing — seems to be colic — or indigestion.

March 7 — Best love-feast we have had at Calhoun. At 11. congregation was so large that our house could not hold them. I accepted the invitation & preached at the Baptist church — with unusual liberty & power — after such a night of suffering.

March 8 — Up early & went to the church to get my discipline & Memorandum book — left there Saturday. Stage came before I got breakfast — but Mr Tanner waited for me. At Russellville I went to see Wallace & gave him 15.00 to pay his board. I found my dear wife suffering with Neuralgia.

March 9 — I wrote to Luther — went to see my father — have been rather poorly to day with bad cold — difficult breathing.

March 31 — I stay in-doors and suffer. This sense of sinking, suffocation, and prostration is distressing. I bear it patiently, but hope to get better. I have had so much to enjoy that I ought to endure with patience. My dear wife and children are so good to me, and my home so comfortable, and God's grace so sufficient, that I am happy even in affliction. I do not suffer much pain, but feel at times like dying away and breathing no more. I have no special fear on the subject, but would prefer to live, if I can be of any further use to my family or the Church.

Epilogue

George Dick's entry for March 31 was his last. Five months later, on September 3, 1886, at 12:20 A.M., he died at his home "of valvular heart disease." In the family record section of his Bible, Lizzie noted sadly that "he suffered long and patiently. Trustful and hopeful to the end. He left us without a struggle or a gasp." George Dick's wish to be buried near his beloved Ginnie went unfulfilled; instead, on the morning of September 4, his body was carried one last time along the familiar nine mile route northeastward on the Clarksville Road to its final resting place in Russellville's Maple Grove Cemetery.

Death soon claimed other members of his family. On February 25, 1889, Bright's Disease carried off his son George. Robert Browder, George Dick's father, died in his eighty-seventh year on August 17, 1890. Lizzie continued to live at her Olmstead home until shortly before her death on October 2, 1897; she spent her last days with Hanson in Clarksville, Tennessee, where he was teaching at the time. The years from 1915 to 1925 witnessed the death of all but one of the remaining members of George Dick's family. Hanson, who went on to become president of several colleges in Kentucky, Alabama, and Missouri, died while visiting relatives in Clarksville, Tennessee, on August 16, 1915; Robert, after a distinguished career as preacher, presiding elder, chairman of the Educational Board of the Louisville Conference, and trustee of Vanderbilt University, died in Russellville, Kentucky, on March 23, 1916; Helen, whose home became the meeting place for Browder family get-togethers after Lizzie's death, died of pneumonia on March 12, 1920; and Luther who preached in Florida, Colorado, and Kentucky for twenty-four years before moving on to Georgia in 1912, died while pastoring in Barnesville on June 4, 1925. Wallace far outdistanced his siblings in his length of days. After a career as county agent in Kentucky and as head of the Alabama Farm Bureau, he retired to Olmstead where he died in his eighty-fourth year on April 15, 1949.

Time has swept away not only the people who inhabited George Dick's world, but virtually all of the landmarks as well, including his house, which was destroyed by fire in 1926. As one travels north along US 79, past the prosperous farms and through the gently rolling countryside of southern Logan County, the only structure from the Browder era in the Olmstead neighborhood still visible from the highway is the two-story brick home built by his uncle William during the 1830s. Located just northeast of the intersection of state road 775 and US 79, the house is still occupied, though in a poor state of repair.

Two other buildings, also badly deteriorated, stand as reminders of an age long forgotten and as silent witnesses to the comings and goings of George Dick.

In visiting his father Robert's house, located less than a mile north of Olmstead and connected by a long lane to state road 1309, one remembers that as a boy during the 1830s George Dick helped to carry the brick used in building the structure. And in driving east on state road 775 between Olmstead and US 79, past a grove of mature silver maples shading the impressive white frame house built in 1884 by his daughter, Helen, and her husband, Charley Roach, one is reminded of George Dick's comment that it was "too costly for a country home – & too fine for the neighborhood." The latter dwelling yielded one treasure as I rummaged through its deserted rooms in 1976 in an unsuccessful search for the missing volumes of George Dick's diaries. In the downstairs bedroom I found his family Bible with its valuable genealogical records.

Sooner or later, after surveying these few remaining structures and becoming familiar with the landscape, the roads and lanes and waterways of Browder country, today's visitor will eventually discover the three cemeteries in which those who figured most prominently in George Dick's life are buried. One, located on the old David Walker place about a mile east of US 79 on state road 1309 contains the graves of his grandmother, Mary Barbour Walker; his mother; and his aunt, Fannie Walker Gwynn. A second burial ground lies about fifty yards to the east of his father's house and includes the ashes of his father and step-mother; his wife's aunt Betsy and uncle Waters; and his two precious infant daughters, Ginnie and Lizzie. The remaining graveyard, and the one evoking the greatest nostalgia, is situated nine miles to the northeast. Russellville's Maple Grove Cemetery became the final resting place for George Dick's wife Lizzie and all of his grown children except Luther who was buried in Georgia. Here also lie the remains of many whose lives were intertwined with that of George Dick: the Sydnors, the Perrys, the Rizers, the Blakeys, the Barclays, the Caldwells, the Ewings, the Mortons, and the Rheas. As you walk among the gravestones of varying size and style, pondering the often poignant inscriptions, you will eventually make your way to the northeast section of the cemetery and find an impressive shaft of gray marble on which is inscribed the following:

> Rev Geo R. Browder
> Born
> Jan 11, 1827
> Died Sept 3, 1886
> For 40 yrs a faithful
> Preacher in the Lou
> Conf. M E Church
> South
> They that be wise shall
> shine as the brightness
> of the Firmament & they
> that turn many to righteousness
> as the stars forever and
> ever   Dan XII

Glossary

Annual conference was composed of all itinerant preachers and selected lay delegates from each district in the conference. It met once each year with a bishop presiding and was considered the basic body of Methodism. Preachers had a special relationship to annual conference, belonging to it as a lay person belongs to the local church. Its duties were almost entirely ministerial, including: receiving on trial those preachers nominated by quarterly or district conferences; admitting into full standing those who have been approved in their studies, qualifications, and conduct; electing proper persons to deacons' and elders' orders; and examining the character of preachers. It also encouraged missions, church extension, Sunday schools, and education within the conference. At the conclusion of the conference, the preachers received their appointments for the ensuing year.

Bishops were the highest executive officers in Methodism. They were elected by the general conference. Among their duties were: presiding at the general and annual conferences, appointing presiding elders and preachers, consecrating bishops, ordaining elders and deacons, deciding all questions of law arising in the proceedings of the annual conferences, and overseeing the spiritual and temporal interests in the church. They were equal in authority and exercised joint jurisdiction in every part of the church. They usually met twice a year as a group to arrange for the times of annual conferences and to distribute the work among themselves.

Bulking tobacco refers to the practice of placing the leaves in piles, which were kept moist. After tobacco was cut it was hung in barns to dry. Because dried tobacco leaves were brittle and crumbled easily, farmers waited until humid weather conditions made the leaves soft and manageable. The tobacco was then taken down and bulked after which the farmer was ready to begin the stripping process.

Cabinet was a term used to designate the bishop and presiding elders when they met together at the Methodist annual conferences to arrange for the appointments of preachers for the ensuing year. In George Dick's day the cabinet was not mentioned in the church's *Discipline* and had no legal status.

Campbellites were followers of Alexander Campbell (1788–1866), the founder of the movement that became the Disciples of Christ. Among the most controversial positions held by the group was the belief that baptism was necessary for the remission of sins. They observed the Lord's Supper every Sunday, rejected any hint of organization above the level of the local church, and generally ignored the Old Testament in their emphasis on the New.

Circuit was a term that referred to the Methodist practice of assigning one preacher to a number of appointments in different localities, which he visited on a rotating basis. When individual churches on the circuit became strong enough to support their own pastor, they were dropped from the circuit and assumed the status of stations.

Class meetings grew out of the English Methodist practice of dividing the local church into groups with a class leader for the purpose of encouraging financial support for the church. In time it answered the need for better pastoral oversight as the class leaders not only collected money but inquired into the behavior of each member. Contributions were entered into a "class book" along with other information about the members that might be of help to the preacher when he came to the quarterly examination of their spiritual condition. Class leaders were virtually subpastors in the Methodist Church and acted chiefly under the advice and counsel of the preacher in charge who appointed them. They not only held the class meetings, but also gave religious counsel, advice, and encouragement, and reported on members needing or desiring a visit from the pastor.

Cumberland Presbyterians originated in a split in the Presbyterian Church in Kentucky over issues stemming from the Great Revival of 1800. Unlike most Kentucky Presbyterians, the Cumberland Presbyterians were strong proponents of camp-meeting revivalism. They were accused of improperly ordaining ministers by ignoring educational standards and not insisting on a strict adherence to the Westminster Confession of Faith.

Deacons in the Methodist Church were ministers in regular standing. To become a deacon one first had to become a local preacher, that is, receive a license to preach by vote of the quarterly or district conference. Local preachers who desired to devote their full time to the ministry were then recommended to the annual conferences, which voted to receive them on trial. Two years later, having passed satisfactory examinations and being approved as ministers, they were ordained by a bishop as deacons. Deacons were authorized to preach, administer baptism, and perform marriages. They could assist the elders in the communion service but they could not consecrate the elements. After two years as deacons they were eligible to become elders.

District conference was composed of all the itinerant and local preachers, exhorters, district stewards, and one Sunday school superintendent and one class leader from each pastoral charge within a presiding elder's district. It met once or twice a year at the discretion of the presiding elder who also chaired the meeting except when a bishop was present. The conference had general oversight of all temporal and spiritual affairs of the district and had the power to license local preachers, recommend local preachers for deacons' and elders' orders, and try any local preacher against whom charges were preferred. It was also concerned with benevolent collections, Sunday schools, and church extension within its bounds. Meetings of the conference usually included reports from the presiding elder and by each pastor, local preacher, exhorter, steward, superintendent, and class leader as to the work represented by each.

Elders exercised the full office of the ministry in the Methodist Church. After a preacher had been elected deacon and served acceptably for two years in the ministry, he was eligible for the office of elder. After being elected by an annual conference, he was ordained by the laying on of hands by the bishop and the elders assisting him. There was no higher office than elder in the Methodist Church; even the bishop was considered simply an elder set apart and consecrated for a special type of work.

Exhorters were lay officers in the Methodist Church whose primary task was to urge their hearers to the performance of some duty or to deter them from pursuing a course of wrong. They normally exercised their spiritual gifts at the conclusion of preaching services or at meetings specifically called for prayer and exhortation. Exhortation was not confined to this group, however. Frequently when two or more preachers were present at a meeting, one of those who had not preached would get up at the end of the service and exhort.

Firing tobacco referred to the practice of burning wood on the dirt floor of the barn in which tobacco had been hung to dry. It was normally done to a variety of tobacco known as "dark" tobacco. Firing not only caused the tobacco to dry faster by lowering the humidity, but also produced a desired coloration and a distinctive taste.

General conference was the supreme governing body of Methodism, dominating and directing the work of the church. It met quadrennially and was composed of ministers, elected by the annual conferences, and laymen, elected by electoral commissions that met at the same time and place as the annual conferences. This body elected the bishops as well as other officials of the denomination, including book agents, editors of church periodicals, and the corresponding secretaries of missions, church extension, and Sunday schools. Traditionally the final decision on all questions of law and administration were placed in the general conference, but in the Methodist Episcopal Church, South, the College of Bishops had the right to declare any act of the general conference unconstitutional.

Itinerant preachers in Methodism were those who were subject to the appointive power of the annual conferences. Itinerancy was a distinguishing feature of the Methodist system by which preachers were moved from church to church so that at all times every preacher had a church and every church had a preacher. In this sense, then, itinerancy referred not so much to the preacher's mobility within a particular appointment as it did to the fact that each preacher faced the possibility of being moved by the bishop to a new appointment each year.

Liberty was a term commonly used by preachers in referring to a sermon in which the Holy Spirit removed all obstacles to an effective ministry and gave them unusual freedom in imparting spiritual truths.

Local preachers were a class of ministers peculiar to Methodism. They were laymen who had received a license to preach upon the recommendation of their home church and the vote of the quarterly conference. Qualifying as a local preacher was the first step for those who desired ultimately to become itinerant preachers. Many local preachers preferred to continue their secular vocations, devoting what time they could to the regular ministry. They were called local preachers, not because they were lay preachers, but because they were not members of the annual conference and therefore not subject to its appointive power.

Located was a term used by the Methodists to indicate the status of a preacher who had left the itinerant ranks and was no longer under the appointive power of the annual conference. Location was normally voted by the annual conference when one of its members requested it, but a preacher could also be located against his will if the annual conference deemed it proper to terminate his membership in that body. After locating, one assumed the status of a local preacher whose membership was in the local church rather than in the annual conference.

Love feasts originated in Apostolic times when Christians observed a common meal known as Agape. After falling into disuse, the observance was revived by the Moravians in the eighteenth century, and as a result of Moravian influence on John Wesley, the custom was introduced into the Methodist movement. The love feast involved the singing of hymns, prayer, the distribution of bread and the circulation of a loving cup containing water, a collection for the poor, and spontaneous testimonies, prayers, and hymns. In America the love feast was usually connected with quarterly meeting services with the presiding elder in charge.

Mourners was a term applied in the Methodist Church to penitents, especially those who indicated by some public act their desire for salvation. Sometimes they were invited to kneel at the altar in front of the church or tabernacle, or to occupy the front seats where they became the objects of prayer by the preacher and the congregation.

Presiding elders were officers in the Methodist Church who supervised all the interests of the church within the bounds of the district to which they were appointed. They were selected from among the elders by the bishops who allowed them to preside in the same district for a term not to exceed four years. Acting under the direction of the bishops, presiding elders were expected to travel through their appointed districts; take charge of all elders and deacons, itinerant and local preachers, and exhorters in their districts; hold quarterly conferences and decide all questions of law, subject to appeal to the next annual conference; oversee the spiritual and temporal interests of the church; see to it that the rules for the instruction of children have been observed; report at the annual conferences on the character and standing of the preachers; and advise and counsel the bishops as to the appointments of preachers.

Prizing tobacco referred to the practice of packing tobacco in casks or barrels before shipping it to market.

Quarterly conference was the traditional governing body of the circuit or station in American Methodism. It met once every three months and was composed of the itinerant preacher, local preachers, stewards, class leaders, exhorters, trustees, and superintendents of Sunday schools. The presiding elder of the district chaired the conference, which had the power to: recommend local preachers for deacons' and elders' orders or for admission on trial into the itinerant ministry; elect stewards, trustees, and Sunday school superintendents; receive and try appeals from members of the church; and elect delegates to the annual and district conferences. Since all temporal and spiritual matters of the charge came under the supervision of the quarterly conference, it was expected to appoint committees to deal with matters ranging from missions and Sunday schools to parsonages, furniture, church music, and preachers' salaries. The meeting usually began on Friday evening or Saturday morning and continued until Monday morning. The presiding elder did the preaching on Sunday. A love feast was held on Sunday morning before the preaching service.

Station was a term used in Methodism signifying a single church supplied by a pastor in contrast to the circuit in which a preacher served a number of different appointments.

Stewards were local officials in the Methodist Church who received, accounted for, and disbursed the collections. The number in each church varied from three to nine. One, who made and preserved the records of the church, was designated recording steward; another, who represented the interests of his church at the district stewards' meeting, was called the district steward. All stewards were nominated by the preacher in charge and affirmed by the quarterly conference. They held office for one year, subject to reappointment. In addition to their financial responsibilities, stewards were also charged with "tell[ing] the preachers what they think wrong in them."

Stripping tobacco involved removing the leaves from the stalks after the curing process was completed. The leaves were then graded according to color and quality and tied into "hands," or bundles.

Superannuated preachers were Methodist pastors who through age, infirmity, or afflictions had become permanently disabled and as a consequence were forced to withdraw from the active ministry. They retained all their rights and privileges as members of the annual conference except being eligible for appointment.

Supernumerary preachers were Methodist pastors who by reason of impaired health were temporarily unable to continue in the itinerant ministry. At the same time they were available to the annual conference to do any work that their strength enabled them to perform.

Who's Who

The names of hundreds of people appear on the pages of George Dick's journals, over nine hundred in this edited portion alone. Of the latter number I have found enough information to write a brief biographical sketch on only two hundred twenty-three. The rest, except for isolated references in such sources as newspapers, deed books, will books, or census records, have simply fallen through the cracks of history. In gathering material for the who's who section of this volume, I have made extensive use of the following: biographical encyclopedias; the minutes of the annual and general conferences of the Methodist Episcopal Church and the Methodist Episcopal Church, South; obituaries found on the now faded and brittle pages of nineteenth-century newspapers; the genealogical resources of the Kentucky Library at Western Kentucky University and a number of county and municipal libraries scattered throughout Kentucky and Tennessee; and inscriptions on tombstones in both public and family cemeteries.

Alexander, William (1818–83) was born in Christian County, Kentucky, on July 23, 1818. After the death of his father, the young lad worked at the carpenter's trade by day and studied by night, going to school at such times as his means would allow. At about the age of sixteen he was converted at the Asbury camp meeting near Lafayette in Christian County; shortly thereafter he felt the call to preach. In the fall of 1844 he was received on trial into the Kentucky Conference of the Methodist Church. When the church divided in 1845 he adhered to the Methodist Episcopal Church, South, and joined the Louisville Conference. He was ordained deacon in 1846 and elder in 1848. During his forty years as an itinerant preacher he held the following appointments: Lafayette (1845–46), Wayne Circuit (1846–47), Empire Iron Works (1848–49), Twelfth Street (Louisville, 1849–50), superannuated (1850–52), New Haven (1852–53), superannuated (1853–55), Empire Iron Works (1855–56), Smithland (1856–57), Agent for Tract Society (1857–58), Lafayette (1858–60), superannuated (1860–62), Logan Circuit (1862–64), Mammoth Cave (1864–65), Glasgow (1865–66), Barren River Circuit (1866–67), Princeton and Eddyville (1867–68), Oakland (1868–69), Auburn and Bibb's Chapel (1869–70), Henryville Circuit (1870–72), Trenton Mission (1872–74), superannuated (1874–75), Trenton (1875–76), Todd (1876–79), superannuated (1879–80), Mannsville (1880–81), Olmstead (1881–82), and Agent for Logan Female College (1882–83). He died in Christian County on March 12, 1883. Alick, as he was affectionately called by George Dick, reportedly read the Bible through consecutively at least seventy times. "He was a good man, full of the Holy Ghost, and the memory of his life will linger, a benediction to us who remain."

Alexander, Wayland (1839–1911), son of Joseph W. and Caroline Wells Alexander, was born near Louisville, Kentucky, on June 26, 1839. His father emigrated from Virginia in 1833 and settled in Jefferson County where he engaged in farming. Wayland attended the common schools of his neighborhood until 1853 when, at the age of fourteen, he was admitted to the University of Greencastle, Indiana. In 1855 he left Greencastle for Shelbyville College, Shelbyville, Kentucky, where he studied under Dr. William I. Waller for two years. During his stay in Shelby County he also studied law in the office of Judge Joseph P. Force. His first love was teaching, however, and in 1858 he opened a school in Sacramento, McLean County, Kentucky. On September 4, 1866, he married Jennie Davis, daughter of Dr. Charles W. Davis, a Muhlenberg County physician; of their seven children only one survived infancy. In 1873 he established in Muhlenberg County the South Carrollton Male and Female Institute. Except for the years 1880–83, when he served as president of Hartford College in adjacent Ohio County, he headed the Institute (called West Kentucky Classical and Normal College, after 1886) until financial difficulties forced its closing in 1893. Alexander was a member of the Cumberland Presbyterian Church. He died in Hartford, Kentucky, on August 28, 1911.

Andrew, Bishop James Osgood (1794–1871) was born in Wilkes County, Georgia, on May 3, 1794. Much of his early education came from his father, John Andrew, who was a Methodist local preacher and a country school teacher. Young James joined the Methodist Church at the age of thirteen and eventually became an assistant class leader at Asbury Chapel on the Broad River Circuit in Elbert County, Georgia. In 1812, at the age of eighteen, he was licensed to preach; later the same year the South Carolina Conference admitted him on trial as an itinerant preacher. He was ordained deacon in 1814 and elder in 1816. During the years 1812–32, he held the following appointments: Saltketcher Circuit (1812–13), Bladen Circuit (1813–14), Warren Circuit (1814–15), Charleston (1815–16), Wilmington (1816–18), Augusta (1820–22), Savannah (1822–24), presiding elder Edisto District (1824–25), presiding elder Charleston District (1825–27), Charleston (1827–29), Athens and Greensboro (1829–30), Athens and Madison (1830–31), and Augusta (1831–32). In 1832 he was elected bishop, a position he held until the memorable General Conference of 1844. Shortly before the conference met, he married a woman from Georgia who also happened to be a slaveowner. Although the bishop had no financial interest in the slaves and could not free them had he wished to do so, the general conference, dominated by the northern majority, voted to depose him. In the ensuing division of the Methodist Church, he was recognized as bishop by the newly created Methodist Episcopal Church, South, and in that capacity he ordained George Dick as elder in 1850 at Greensburg, Kentucky. He continued as bishop until 1866, when, at his request, he was granted superannuated status. He died five years later on March 2, 1871, in Mobile, Alabama, at the home of his daughter. "He was warm and devoted in his friendships; liberal in his benefactions, sympathizing in his spirit, playful with children . . . ; and he was eminently condescending to men of low estate, especially the colored people, by whom he was greatly revered."

Andrews, Bishop Edward Gayer (1825–1907) was born in New Hartford, Oneida County, New York, on August 7, 1825. When he was ten years old he joined the Methodist Episcopal Church. After attending Cazenovia Seminary, Cazenovia, New York, he went on to Wesleyan University, Middletown, Connecticut, from which he graduated in 1847. The following year the Oneida Conference admitted him on trial into the itinerant ministry. Six years later his voice failed and he became a teacher at Cazenovia Seminary. Except for a brief period when he served as president of Mansfield Female College in Ohio, he remained at Cazenovia until 1864 when he returned to the pastorate. He served in Stamford, Connecticut, and in several churches in New York City before the

466

General Conference of 1872 elected him bishop. In 1876 the board of missions and the bishops asked him to undertake a trip to Europe and India during which he organized annual conferences in Sweden, Norway, and South India. He spent his last six years of active service in New York City where he retired in 1904. Three years later he crossed the continent to attend a meeting of bishops in Spokane, Washington; the trip overtaxed his strength. Shortly after his return he died in Brooklyn, New York, on December 31, 1907. He was buried in Syracuse, New York, near the grave of his brother, Charles, who was Chief Justice of the New York Court of Appeals.

Asbury, Bishop Francis (1745–1816), son of Joseph and Elizabeth Rogers Asbury, was born near the foot of Hamstead Bridge four miles from Birmingham, England, on August 21, 1745. His family was poor and he had very limited schooling. After his conversion at the age of fourteen, his mother, who had an interest in Methodism, sent him to the neighboring village of Wednesbury to hear the itinerant preachers. It was the beginning of a lifelong association with the Methodists. Before long he became a local preacher and at the age of twenty-one he went to London where he was admitted to the Wesleyan Conference. After five years as an itinerant preacher, he volunteered as a missionary to America, arriving in Philadelphia in 1771. The next year John Wesley appointed him superintendent of the work in America, which gave him the authority to carry out his own ideas of church discipline. A year later, however, he had to surrender his leadership to Thomas Rankin, newly arrived from England. Never a good subordinate, he fell out with Rankin who complained to Wesley. The latter ordered him home in 1775 but in the face of growing tension between England and her colonies, he decided to stay on. In the hostilities that ensued, Rankin fled the country and Asbury took refuge in Delaware, eventually becoming a citizen of that state. During these years he played a key role in effecting a reconciliation between northern and southern Methodists over the administration of the sacraments, emerging from the controversy in all but title as the head of the Methodist movement in America. The title came in December 1784 when he and Thomas Coke, whom Wesley had sent from England, were chosen as joint superintendents by the conference assembled in Baltimore. Theoretically he shared episcopal functions with Coke but the latter's frequent absences left the practical control of affairs in his hands. During the next twenty years, despite frequent complaints about his autocratic exercise of power, he directed the great effort that sent circuit riders not only to the remote areas of the seaboard states but across the mountains into the frontier regions as well. It was not until his health failed that he accepted Richard Whatcoat as an associate bishop in 1800 and William McKendree in 1806. Active to the end, he died in Virginia on March 31, 1816, as he was making his way to Baltimore to attend general conference.

Bailey, Ann (Annie) Elizabeth (Browder) (1853–84), the youngest daughter of Robert and Sarah Gilmer Browder and half-sister of George Dick, was born near Olmstead in Logan County, Kentucky, on June 23, 1853. As a child she was religiously inclined, having been "brought up around the family altar, in the class-meeting and the Sunday School." At the age of nine she made a public profession of faith and joined the Methodist Episcopal Church, South. She was educated at Browder Institute and Logan Female College. Gifted in both vocal and instrumental music, she was frequently asked to perform in the interest of education and charity. On June 1, 1881, she married Dr. Daniel Bailey; there were two children, both of whom died in infancy. On April 8, 1884, George Dick received word that she was suffering from a growth in her throat. She died five months later, on September 21, 1884.

Bailey, James Marion (1830–83), second son of Daniel Bailey and Elizabeth Rice Bailey, was born September 20, 1830, near the small town of Dot in Logan County, Kentucky. His mother died when he was seven and his father when he was sixteen. After attending the schools of Logan County, he studied law under the supervision of George W. Ewing of Russellville and F. M. Bristow and Hazel G. Petree of Elkton. He graduated from the University of Louisville Law School in 1851 and spent one year practicing law in Arkansas. Upon his return to Logan County in 1852 he entered the office of his brother, Dr. Jonathan R. Bailey, and devoted himself to the study of medicine. After his graduation from the University of Louisville Medical School in 1854 he practiced medicine for two years in Missouri and Arkansas. Once again he returned to Logan County where he married Margaret Rebecca Daniel on November 10, 1856, and settled down to practice medicine. When the Civil War broke out he espoused the Union cause, entered the volunteer service, and served three years as assistant and surgeon in the U.S. Army. Although his health was failing, President Lincoln appointed him Consul to Scotland in 1864. When he returned two years later, he briefly located in Louisville where he engaged in a prescription drug business before returning to Logan County to settle in Gordonsville where he resumed his medical practice. He soon removed to his old homestead near Dot where he continued his practice until his death on July 24, 1883. George Dick preached his funeral.

Belknap, William Worth (1829–90), the son of General William Goldsmith and Ann Clark Belknap, was born in Newburgh, New York, on September 22, 1829. He attended Princeton College and studied law at Georgetown University. After being admitted to the bar in 1851, he set up practice in Keokuk, Iowa. During 1857–58 he represented his district as a Democrat in the Iowa legislature. When the Civil War broke out, he received a commission as a major in the 15th Iowa Infantry and served with distinction at Shiloh, Corinth, and Vicksburg. He was promoted to brigadier general on July 30, 1864, and as commander of Sherman's 4th Division he participated in the campaigns through Georgia and the Carolinas. After the war he served as collector of internal revenue in Iowa until 1869 when President U.S. Grant made him his secretary of war. He held that position until 1876 when he resigned after the House of Representa-

tives voted unanimously to impeach him for allegedly receiving $24,450 during 1870–76 from an appointee to a post-tradership at Fort Sill, Oklahoma. After his resignation he lived for a number of years in Philadelphia before returning to Washington, D.C., to practice law. He married three times, first to Cora Le Roy of Vincennes, Indiana; then to Carrie Tomlinson of Kentucky who died in 1870; and finally to Mrs. John Bower, the sister of his second wife. He died in Washington on October 13, 1890.

Bell, Caleb (1788–1872), the son of Caleb and Susannah Cole Bell, was born in Beaufort, North Carolina, on June 5, 1788. He, his parents, and an older sister were among the first to join the Methodist Church in that region. Caleb was converted in June 1806 during a revival in Beaufort. In 1809 he yielded to the call to preach and joined the Virginia Conference. He was ordained deacon by Bishop Asbury in 1811 and elder by Bishop McKendree in 1813. During 1809–15 he held appointments to Tampico Circuit, Beaufort, Mattamuskeet Circuit, Terrel's Circuit, Bedford, and Amelia Circuit. Then his health failed. Seriously threatened with a hernia and weakness of the lungs, he asked to be located in February 1815. Three months later, on May 3, he married Judith H. Moore of Nottoway County who bore him three children before her death in 1819. On September 6, 1820, he married Jane Browder, George Dick's paternal aunt, of Dinwiddie County, Virginia. A year later, "Uncle Bell," as George Dick called him, and his bride left Virginia for Greene County, Kentucky, remaining there one year before pushing on to settle permanently near Elkton in Todd County, arriving in December 1822. There he not only engaged in farming, but actively promoted Methodism as well. In the autumn of 1823 he called his neighbors together and held a camp meeting, which resulted in many conversions. In the years that followed, preaching frequently took place in his house where he boarded the circuit preachers and their families. When his goods increased, he decided to build a church on his own land. "Bell's Chapel," as it was called, was erected in 1835, much of the work being done by his own hands. He lived to see a second "Bell's Chapel," a large brick structure, erected in the same beautiful grove. His second wife died on October 6, 1836; a year later, on October 13, 1837, he married Mrs. Mary Greenfield ("Aunt Polly") who died on May 9, 1868. Four years later he followed her to her grave.

Benham, Henry Washington (1813–84), son of Jared and Rebecca Hill Benham, was born in Quebec, Canada, on April 8, 1813. When he was quite young his father died and his mother married Liberty Perkins of Meriden, Connecticut, who attempted to thwart young Henry's efforts to acquire schooling. With his mother's help he obtained enough learning to enter Yale University in 1832. Shortly thereafter he won an appointment to West Point, graduating first in his class in 1837. Commissioned as a lieutenant of engineers, he spent the next ten years working on coastal defense. He also married Elizabeth Ann McNeil of New Hampshire on October 3, 1843; there were three children. During the Mexican War he took part in the battle of Buena Vista and was brevetted captain for his gallant conduct. In 1848 he was promoted to captain of engineers and during the next thirteen years, except for the period 1853–56 when he was in charge of the U.S. Coast Survey Office in Washington, D.C., he was engaged in several engineering projects in New York City, Boston, and Buffalo. When the Civil War broke out, he was appointed chief engineer of the Department of the Ohio. As a result of his role in the battle of Carrick's Ford, West Virginia, on July 13, 1861, he was commissioned brigadier general of volunteers and given a brigade in West Virginia. Then came bitter disappointment. In November 1861 General Rosecrans charged him with disregarding orders in failing to capture Confederates at Gauley Bridge, West Virginia. He soon moved on to South Carolina where General Hunter relieved him of his command in June 1862 for disobeying orders in the unsuccessful attack on Secessionville. In August 1862 his appointment as brigadier general of volunteers was revoked, but an appeal to President Lincoln resulted in his restoration on

February 6, 1863. He then rendered valuable service as commander of the engineer brigade of the Army of the Potomac. After the Civil War he was in charge of the construction of the defenses of Boston Harbor and New York Harbor until his retirement from active service on June 30, 1882. He died on June 1, 1884.

Biggs, Benjamin Franklin (1826–1902) was born three miles south of Greensburg, Green County, Kentucky, on June 6, 1826. He came of good Revolutionary stock, his grandfather having served under General Washington. His father, John, who came to Kentucky from Virginia, was a stonemason who reportedly built the courthouse at Greensburg. After his conversion at Old Lebanon Church about 1843, young Biggs served as a class leader until he was licensed to preach under the pastorate of Rev. Thomas G. Bosley. During his term as a local preacher he received from Governor Thomas E. Bramlette an appointment as Tobacco Inspector. On July 4, 1850, he married Elizabeth Frances Wheat, who bore him eight children, all but one of whom preceded him in death. On October 14, 1866, Biggs was ordained deacon by Bishop Doggett at Elizabethtown. Three years later, on September 21, 1869, he was ordained elder by Bishop McTyeire, at Louisville. He served faithfully as a preacher in the Louisville Conference of the Methodist Episcopal Church, South, for over thirty-five years. Among his appointments was one to Olmstead where he served for three years as pastor to George Dick and his family. His first wife died in February 1890. Two years later on February 22, 1892, he married Miss Emma Moss who survived him. Biggs was still preaching in his seventy-sixth year when he died at Munfordville, Kentucky, on July 28, 1902. He had a reputation as a good storyteller and mimic, and as one brought up in the grand old tradition of declaimers, it was said of him that he was "a fine specimen of the primitive Methodist preacher" whose sermons had "bones, body, and living breath in them."

Blackburn, Luke Pryor (1816–87), the son of Edward M. and Lavina Bell Blackburn, was born in Fayette County, Kentucky, on

June 16, 1816. After attending neighborhood schools he studied medicine at Transylvania University; upon his graduation in 1834 he began his practice in Lexington, Kentucky. A year later he married Ella Guest Boswell; she died in 1855. When a cholera epidemic broke out in nearby Versailles in 1835 and the doctors there either died or fled, he offered his services free of charge. At the insistence of a grateful citizenry he moved to Versailles where he supplemented his income by investing in the manufacture of rope and bagging, a venture that failed. Although not particularly interested in politics at this time, he did represent Woodford County in the legislature in 1843. Three years later he moved to Natchez, Mississippi, where he assumed control of the yellow fever epidemics that broke out in the lower Mississippi Valley in 1848 and 1854. At his own expense he set up a marine hospital for rivermen; he also convinced the Louisiana legislature to erect a quarantine station on the Mississippi River below New Orleans. In 1856, as he was visiting New York City, yellow fever broke out on Long Island; again he took control and refused any pay for his services. The following year he toured Europe, visiting the principal hospitals in Scotland, England, Germany, and France. In Paris he met Julia M. Churchill of Louisville, Kentucky, whom he married on his return. He lived in New Orleans until the Civil War when, as an ardent secessionist, he offered his support to the Confederacy and served as a surgeon to the staff of General Sterling Price. After the war he lived on a plantation in Arkansas until 1873 when he returned to Kentucky, making his home in Louisville. In 1875 he took charge of the yellow fever epidemic around Memphis, Tennessee; three years later he directed a similar effort at Hickman, Fulton County, Kentucky. In 1879 he realized a long held ambition when he was elected to the highest office in his native state. As governor he granted a large number of pardons in an effort to relieve deplorable prison conditions. He died in Frankfort, Kentucky, on September 14, 1887.

Blackwell, John Davenport (1822–87), the son of John and Rebecca Blackwell, was born in Fauquier County, Virginia, on June 17, 1822. His father was one of the first Methodists in Fauquier County and for many years filled the positions of class leader and steward. Responding to the example and teaching of his godly parents, young John was converted at the age of fourteen. Sometime after his graduation with honors from Dickinson College, he accepted the call to preach and in the fall of 1846 he joined the Virginia Conference of the Methodist Episcopal Church, South. During the next forty-one years he served in the following appointments: Bedford Circuit, Hampton, Farmville, chaplain of Randolph-Macon College, Fairfax Circuit, Washington City, Warrenton Circuit, Richmond, Nottoway Circuit, Norfolk, chaplain of the Eighteenth Virginia Regiment, Amherst Circuit, presiding elder Murfreesboro District, presiding elder Lynchburg District, presiding elder Charlottesville District, Petersburg, and Portsmouth. Although he was offered the presidency of several colleges, including Randolph-Macon, he felt constrained to keep to his preferred work of preaching the gospel. He served as an elected delegate to the General Conferences of 1872, 1876, 1880, and 1884, and as a representative to the Centennial Conference of 1884 where he delivered a paper, "Essay on the Mission of Methodism." He was twice married, first to Julia Anna Butts of Southampton, Virginia, who bore him four children, and then to Fanny G. Smith, Fauquier County, who bore him five children. He died in Portsmouth, Virginia, on June 26, 1887. "Little children greeted him lovingly on the streets, and fathers and mothers, rich and poor, welcomed him to their firesides."

Blakey, George D. (1809–86), the son of George and Margaret Whitsett Blakey, was born near Russellville, Logan County, Kentucky, on February 21, 1809. His father was a Revolutionary War soldier who moved from Virginia to Davidson County, Tennessee, in 1790; five years later he moved on to settle three miles west of Russellville where he built his home, "Rural Choice." Early an abolitionist, George D. attended the Kentucky Constitutional Convention of 1849 and ran for lieutenant governor in the same year on an abolitionist ticket headed by Cassius M. Clay. As an outspoken Union man, he was forced to flee his home when the Civil War began and seek refuge behind the federal lines at Greencastle, Indiana. After the Confederate forces withdrew from Kentucky in early 1862, he returned to find his wife, daughter, and grandchildren ousted and their comfortable home converted into a hospital. President Lincoln appointed him as one of three commissioners in Kentucky charged with awarding compensation to loyal slaveowners whose slaves had enlisted in the federal army. Blakey was a Republican presidential elector in 1864 and one of three sent to notify Lincoln of his second nomination. During 1879–80 he attracted considerable local attention as the author of sixty-two articles entitled, "Men Whom I Remember," which appeared serially in the *Russellville Herald*. He married first to Lucy Thomas on February 23, 1830. She bore him six children, three of whom survived to adulthood. After her death in 1870 he married Sarah Jane West Barner. In later life Blakey moved to Bowling Green where he died in 1886. It was said that his always too long white hair was often braided by his granddaughter into a short cue and tied with a black ribbon.

Blakey, George Thomas (1822–1904), second child of William M. and Susan C. H. Breathitt Blakey, was born three miles west of Russellville, Logan County, Kentucky, on February 5, 1822. His father died when he was two years old. After his mother's death six years later he went to live with his uncle, George D. Blakey, who resided at nearby "Rural Choice." He was educated at the Russellville Academy. On February 15, 1844, he married Sarah Ellen McLean of Logan County who bore him four children. He and his family belonged to the Cumberland Presbyterian Church. In addition to his farming activities, he served as sheriff of Logan County (1863–68) and as police judge of Auburn, Kentucky, for three terms. He also accepted an appointment as a commissioner of the Logan Turnpike Co. in 1867 and as government storekeeper in 1884. He was originally a Democrat, but when his party advocated secession he left it and became a leading spirit in the Logan County Republi-

can party. He attended a number of Republican National Conventions, including the one in 1880 when he joined with 305 other old guard Republicans who held out for a third term for Ulysses S. Grant. In August 1885 he was elected to the Kentucky legislature, overcoming a Democratic majority of 500 registered voters with a majority of 300 for himself. He died in March 1904.

Blakey, Thomas (1794–1856), son of George and Margaret Whitsett Blakey of Albermarle County, Virginia, was born on June 17, 1794. When he was one year old his parents emigrated to Logan County, Kentucky. On January 28, 1823, he married Ann Haden Whitsett, a distant cousin. In addition to operating his farm near Shakertown in Logan County, he engaged in the practice of medicine for many years. He was also active in public affairs and served as sheriff and as magistrate of Logan County. He died on April 30, 1856.

Board, Jesse (1837–81), the son of Robert and Lydia Board, was born in Breckinridge County, Kentucky, on November 21, 1837. Shortly after his conversion at the age of 12, his mother died and, lacking her counsel, he wandered from the faith. In January 1856 he married Eliza B. McGuffin, who greatly aided him in his decision in 1862 to return to a life of piety. He was licensed to preach by the Methodist Episcopal Church, South, on September 7, 1862. In 1875 he was admitted on trial into the Louisville Conference. He served the Caneyville Mission during 1876–78 and the Morgantown Circuit from 1878 until his death on August 21, 1881. As a preacher he "witnessed scores and hundreds of conversions and built up the church wherever he went."

Bottomley, Edmund W. (1837–1901), the son of Thomas and Hannah Wilson Bottomley, was born at Milchester, near Baltimore, Maryland, in 1837. He accompanied his parents when they removed to Kentucky in 1840. As the child of a Methodist itinerant preacher, he attended school in the towns to which his father was appointed, including Hopkinsville, Elkton, Russellville, and Bardstown. At the age of eighteen he began the study of pharmacy in the old University of Louisville. Three years later, in 1858, he graduated with an M.D. degree. He practiced medicine in Paducah, Kentucky, for one year, then moved on to South Gibson, Tennessee, where he formed a partnership with a Dr. Yarnell. He became unhappy under the conviction that he was called to preach and, after a little struggle, he gave up his chosen profession to pursue the ministry. In 1860 the Louisville Conference of the Methodist Episcopal Church, South, admitted him on trial into the itinerant ministry. He was elected deacon in 1862 and ordained elder by Bishop Kavanaugh in 1864. During the forty-one years of his active ministry he held the following appointments: Petersburg (1860–61), Brandenburg (1861–63), Bowling Green (1863–65), Portland (1865–66), Brandenburg (1866–67), Campbellsville (1867–68), Twelfth Street (Louisville, 1868–69), Hawesville (1869–71), Allensville (1871–72), Franklin (1872–74), Elkton (1874–78), Lebanon (1878–82), Hopkinsville (1882–86), Henderson (1886–90), Main Street (Louisville, 1890–93), Chestnut Street (Louisville, 1893–97), Lander Memorial (Louisville, 1897–1900), and Wilson Memorial (Louisville, 1900–01). He died in his last charge in 1901 after months of suffering. "Even in congregations of which he was pastor during the Civil War, when house was divided against house and father against son, the memory of his impartial, loving life abides."

Bottomley, Thomas (1805–94) was born in the West Riding of Yorkshire, England, on June 2, 1805. His parents were so destitute that an uncle and aunt, living in an adjacent village, assumed the care and expense of his rearing. When he was twelve years old, he joined the Wesleyan Methodist connection; three years later he was converted. He soon yielded to the call to preach and delivered his first sermon on December 24, 1822. As a young preacher he had the privilege of listening to such pulpiteers as Adam Clark, Richard Watson, Joseph Benson, and Robert Newton. During these years he also learned the trade of a stonemason. In 1824 at the age of nineteen he married Hannah Wilson. Four years later,

convinced he should enter the traveling ministry, a course closed to married men in England, he set sail for America leaving his wife and infant son behind. After a brief stay in New York City, he moved on to Paterson, New Jersey, where he was licensed to preach in the Methodist Church on February 18, 1829. Shortly thereafter he went to Richmond, Virginia, where he earned enough money preaching nearly every Sunday and working as a stonemason on the stone locks of the James River Canal to enable him to pay his family's passage to New York. They then settled at Ellicott's Mills (now Ellicott City) near Baltimore, Maryland, where Bottomley continued to preach and work as a stonemason, superintending some of the construction of stone and brick work on the Baltimore and Ohio, the first railroad built in the United States. On March 18, 1832, Bishop McKendree ordained him deacon. He continued to reside in Maryland, working at his trade, briefly experimenting in the drug business, and preaching until 1840 when he was admitted on trial into the itinerant ministry. Bishop Waugh ordained him elder and transferred him to the Arkansas Conference. On the way to his new appointment his wife fell ill and they were compelled to stop in Louisville for an extended period of recovery. As a result of their stay he became enamored of Kentucky and in 1840 he joined the Kentucky Conference. Six years later, when the conference divided, he became a member of the newly organized Louisville Conference of the Methodist Episcopal Church, South. His appointments included: Eighth Street (Louisville, 1840–42), Hopkinsville (1842–44), Elkton (1844–46), presiding elder Louisville District (1846–47), presiding elder Hopkinsville District (1847–51), Russellville (1851–53), Logan Circuit (1853–54), Bardstown (1854–55), Shelby Street (Louisville, 1855–57), Brook Street (Louisville, 1857–59), Eighth Street (Louisville, 1859–61), presiding elder Louisville District (1861–65), Walnut Street (Louisville, 1865–67), Bowling Green (1867–70), superannuated (1870–71), Hopkinsville (1871–74), Franklin (1875–76), superannuated (1876–80), Trenton (1880–81), and superannuated

(1881–94). After nearly ninety years of life, after seventy-two years as a Methodist preacher, while his brethren were assembled in annual conference at Hopkinsville, Kentucky, and after his name had been called for the fifty-fourth time, he died on September 27, 1894. "He never failed to attach to himself by the lasting ties of friendship the most prominent, as well as the humblest, in every place he dwelt."

Bragg, Braxton (1817–76), son of Thomas and Margaret Crossland Bragg, was born in Warrenton, North Carolina, on March 22, 1817. After graduating from West Point in 1837 he fought against the Seminole Indians in Florida and served with distinction in the Mexican War. He resigned his commission in 1856 to become a planter in Louisiana, the native state of his wife, Elisa Brooks Ellis, whom he had married in 1849. On March 7, 1861, he was appointed brigadier general in the Confederate army and placed in command of the Gulf Coast from Mobile to Pensacola. Six months later he was promoted to major general and ably led General Albert Sidney Johnston's 2nd Corps in the battle of Shiloh in April 1862. After Johnston's death in that battle, Bragg was made full general and soon replaced General P.G.T. Beauregard as commander of the Army of Tennessee, which he led in the unsuccessful invasion of Kentucky, August to October, 1862. In early January 1863 General William S. Rosecrans forced him to retreat once more after the battle of Murfreesboro in middle Tennessee. After his success against Rosecrans at the battle of Chickamauga in September 1863, he laid siege to Chattanooga. General Ulysses S. Grant broke the siege two months later and forced Bragg into Georgia where he surrendered his command to General Joseph E. Johnston on December 2, 1863. He then spent some time in Richmond, Virginia, as military advisor to President Jefferson Davis. After General Robert E. Lee was appointed general in chief of the Confederate army, he returned once more to the field to assist General Johnston in North Carolina. In May 1865 he accompanied President Davis in his flight to Georgia where he was captured and paroled. After the war he practiced civil engineering in Mobile, Alabama, and later in Galveston, Texas, where he moved shortly before his death on September 27, 1876.

Bramlette, Thomas Elliott (1817–75), the son of Colonel Ambrose S. and Sarah Bramlette, was born in Cumberland County, Kentucky, on January 3, 1817. After completing a common school education, he studied law and was admitted to the bar in 1837. In the same year he married Sallie Travis who bore him two children; two years after her death in 1874 he married Mrs. Mary E. Graham Adams. In 1841 he was elected to the state legislature where he served for one term and then returned to his legal practice. Governor John J. Crittenden named him commonwealth attorney in 1848, but two years later he resigned, moved his law practice to Columbia, Adair County, Kentucky, where in 1856 he was elected judge of the sixth judicial district. When the Civil War broke out in 1861 he espoused the Union cause, received a colonel's commission, and raised the Third Kentucky Volunteer Infantry. He resigned in 1862 to accept President Lincoln's appointment as U.S. district attorney for Kentucky and took up residence in Louisville. The following year he was commissioned major general and while he was engaged in organizing his division, he was nominated as the Union candidate for the governorship to which he was elected by a large majority. As governor he dealt firmly with guerrillas and rebel sympathizers, opposed the recruitment of black soldiers, protested Lincoln's suspension of the writ of *habeas corpus* in July 1864, supported the adoption of the Thirteenth Amendment, objected to the extension of the Freedmen's Bureau into Kentucky, and opposed the adoption of both the Fourteenth and Fifteenth amendments. In response to his leadership the legislature in 1865 voted to establish an Agricultural and Mechanical College in Lexington, the forerunner of the University of Kentucky. On his retirement from office in 1867, he resumed his law practice in Louisville where he died on January 12, 1875.

Brandon, James C. (1848–1937) was born on February 16, 1848. In 1871 the Louisville Conference of the Methodist Episcopal Church, South, admitted him on trial into the itinerant ministry. He was ordained deacon by Bishop Keener in 1873 and elder by Bishop Doggett in 1875. On October 11, 1876, he married Elloie Dyer of Elizabethtown, Kentucky, who bore him three sons. During his forty-eight years as a Methodist preacher he served the following charges: Empire Mission (1871–72), Fredonia Circuit (1872–73), Empire Circuit (1873–74), Boston Mission (1874–75), West Point Circuit (1875–76), Trenton (1876–77), New Roe (1877–78), Curdsville (1878–81), Cadiz Circuit (1881–82), Carrsville (1882–83), Rockport (1883–86), Sharon Grove (1886–87), Mannsville (1887–89), Robards (1889–90), Cloverport (1890–92), Robards (1892–93), Hawesville (1893–94), Ceralvo Circuit (1894–96), Slaughtersville (1896–97), Lewisport (1897–98), South Carrollton (1898–1901), Auburn (1901–03), Lewisburg (1903–05), Smith's Mills (1905–09), Mount Washington (1909–11), Canmer (1911–12), Poole Circuit (1912–16), superannuated (1916–17), and Shepherdsville Circuit (1917–19). He was superannuated from 1919 until his death in Louisville on July 25, 1937.

Brewer, Samuel Richardson (1839–89) was born on November 10, 1839, in Gibson County, Tennessee. Brought up on a farm, he worked during the crop season and attended school during the winter months. For a short time he was a student at Andrew College in Trenton, Tennessee. After his conversion he joined the Methodist Episcopal Church, South. In 1861 he enlisted in the Confederate army and served during the entire conflict except for the nine months he spent in a federal prison. After the war he completed the study of law and practiced for about three years in western Kentucky. Unable to resist the call to preach, he applied in 1868 for admission into the Memphis Conference, which assigned him to Columbus Station (1868–70). Upon the division of the Memphis Conference he fell into the North Mississippi Conference in which he held the following appointments: Oxford (1870–71), Aberdeen (1871–72), and Grenada (1872–74). In 1874 he transferred to the Louisville Conference and served the following charges: Lebanon

(1874–75), Allensville (1875–76), Bowling Green (1876–79), Hopkinsville (1879–82), Owensboro (1882–86), and presiding elder of the Louisville District from 1886 until his death on December 4, 1889. He was married on October 4, 1871 to Mary E. Sullivan who bore him six children. "His sermons were not only clothed in faultless language and permeated with a genuine spirituality, but were delivered with vigor and earnestness, and when the unction from on high was upon him they were in demonstration of the spirit and with power."

Broadnax, Judge Henry P. (1769–1857) was born in Dinwiddie County, Virginia, on March 15, 1769. At an early age he emigrated to Kentucky and settled in the southern part of the state. He practiced law until he was appointed judge of the circuit court, a position he held until old age forced him to resign. He retired to his farm, twelve miles from Russellville, Logan County, Kentucky, where he died on February 4, 1857. For many years he was a member of the Cumberland Presbyterian Church, but late in life he became a Presbyterian. He never married.

Browder, David (1818–71), paternal cousin of George Dick and son of Richard and Elizabeth Anderson Browder, was born on November 11, 1818, near Petersburg, Dinwiddie County, Virginia. In 1820 his family emigrated to Green County, Kentucky; five years later they moved on to the rich farmland of southern Logan County near Olmstead. He was educated at the Academy in nearby Russellville. As a young man he entered the tobacco business, concerned primarily with the export trade. In 1842 he moved across the state line to Clarksville, Tennessee, where he continued his tobacco interests and he also conducted a prosperous mercantile enterprise. Sixteen years later he moved to Montgomery, Alabama, where he engaged in merchandizing and cotton planting until his death on January 6, 1871. He was married twice, first on April 16, 1838, to Mary Evans of Logan County who died without issue in October 1839, and then on November 8, 1842, to Elizabeth E. Irvine of Robertson County, Tennessee, who bore him ten children including Wilbur Fish Browder who became a leading Russellville attorney.

Browder, David Parrish (1848–1913), fifth son of Robert and Sarah Gilmer Browder and half-brother to George Dick, was born near Olmstead, Logan County, Kentucky, on October 19, 1848. Raised in a devout Methodist home, he was converted and joined the Methodist Episcopal Church, South, in his youth. As a good student of the Scriptures he was in demand as a Bible teacher and his pleasing solo voice made him a popular figure at revivals. On October 11, 1871, he married Florence A. Bailey of Logan County who bore him three sons. The greater part of his life was spent in Logan County in agricultural pursuits, but to give his children the best educational opportunities, he moved in 1890 to Nashville, Tennessee, where all three sons took degrees at Vanderbilt University. He died on March 7, 1913, in Richmond, Virginia, at the home of his son, David Phillip Browder.

Browder, Francis (Frank) (1843–1927), fourth son of Robert and Sarah Gilmer Browder and half-brother of George Dick, was born near Olmstead, Logan County, Kentucky, on June 6, 1843. When the Civil War came he and a neighborhood friend left the state on August 12, 1862, headed for Montgomery, Alabama, where two of his paternal uncles lived. Ten days later he was in the Confederate army. By November 1862 he had joined John Hunt Morgan's cavalry and was among those captured during Morgan's daring raid into Indiana and Ohio in July 1863. Confined initially at Camp Chase in Columbus, Ohio, he was later transferred to Camp Douglas in Chicago where he remained until the end of the war, arriving home on July 5, 1865. He married Alice Barton on November 12, 1867. Two years later, on December 30, 1869, he removed to near Montgomery, Alabama, where he spent the rest of his life as a cotton planter and buyer. On October 20, 1927, as he was walking in his cotton field, an airplane flying at an extremely low altitude struck and killed him.

Browder, George Richard, Jr. (1857–89), the third son of George Dick and Lizzie Warfield Browder, was born near Olmstead, Logan County, Kentucky, on June 17, 1857. He attended neighborhood schools, including Browder Institute from which he graduated in 1878. The following year he entered the University of Louisville Medical School, completing his studies in 1881. After settling briefly in Sadlersville, Robertson County, Tennessee, he moved in 1882 to Fairview, Todd County, Kentucky, where he established his practice. He never married. Afflicted with Bright's disease, he spent his last days in his mother's care at the old family homestead near Olmstead, Kentucky, where he died on February 25, 1889.

Browder, Hanson Warfield (1855–1915), the second son of George Dick and Lizzie Warfield Browder, was born near Olmstead, Logan County, Kentucky, on January 21, 1855. He received his early education at nearby Browder Institute. In June 1875 he left for West Point, but two months later he decided to give up his plans for a military career and returned home to prepare for the ministry in the Methodist Episcopal Church, South. The Ash Spring Quarterly Conference licensed him to preach on March 18, 1876. He pursued a theological and literary course of studies at Vanderbilt University from which he graduated in December 1878. For some reason he never entered the itinerant ministry, but spent the rest of his life as a local preacher, teacher, farmer, and school administrator. Beginning in February 1879 he was for a time principal of the Browder Institute, after which he assisted George Dick in operating the family farm for several years. On October 24, 1883, he married Jennie Martin of Greenville, Muhlenberg County, Kentucky; one son, George Warfield, was born to this union. In 1884 he returned to academic life and over the next twenty-one years he held the following positions: teacher at Browder Institute, Olmstead, Kentucky; president of Cedar Bluff Female College, Woodburn, Kentucky; teacher at the Female Academy, Clarksburg, Tennessee; teacher at Athens College, Athens, Alabama; teacher at Logan Female College, Russellville, Kentucky; president of Franklin Female College, Franklin, Kentucky; and president of Marvin College, Fredericktown, Missouri. It was while serving in the latter position that he died, on August 16, 1915, in Clarksville, Tennessee, as he visited relatives there.

Browder, Jennie (Martin) (1860–1932), daughter of Dabney A. and Elizabeth B. Martin, was born in Greenville, Kentucky, on May 10, 1860. She married Hanson Warfield Browder on October 24, 1883; there was one child, George Warfield Browder. She accompanied her husband to his several teaching and administrative positions in Kentucky, Tennessee, Alabama, and Missouri. On at least one occasion, when her husband was president of Cedar Bluff Female College, Woodburn, Kentucky (1891–92), she held the position of "lady principal." After her husband's death in 1915, she and her son moved to Clinton, Hickman County, Kentucky where she served for a number of years as librarian of the Hickman County Library, sponsored by the Clinton Women's Club of which she was a member. As a faithful member of the Clinton Methodist Episcopal Church, South, she taught the "Jennie Browder" Sunday school class for women. She was active until shortly before her death on January 8, 1932. Her son preceded her in death on October 11, 1930.

Browder, Luther Wools (1861–1925), the fourth son of George Dick and Lizzie Warfield Browder, was born near Olmstead, Logan County, Kentucky on April 6, 1861. He attended neighborhood schools, including Browder Institute. Converted in 1872, he yielded to the call to preach as a teenager; in 1880 the Methodist Episcopal Church, South, licensed him to preach. The following year he entered Vanderbilt University to pursue the two-year program of theological studies. In 1884 he joined the Louisville Conference but transferred immediately to Florida where he preached at Gainesville (1884–85) and Longwood (1885–87). He then spent one year in Colorado, responding to an appeal from Bishop Eugene R. Hendrix for workers in that field. In 1888 he returned to the Louisville Conference and held the following appointments: Clifton (1888–90), Louisville Circuit (1890–92), Rochester (1892–93), Princeton and Rock Spring (1893–94), Lewisburg and Drakesboro (1894–96), Eddyville (1896–98), Cerulean Springs (1898–1900), Cannes (1900–03), Smith's Grove (1903–04), Woodburn (1904–06), Sebree (1906–08), Providence (1908–09), Adairville and Oakland (1909–10) and Auburn (1910–12). Seeking a warmer climate and better health, he transferred in 1912 to the North Georgia Conference where he held pastorates in Crawfordville, Culloden, Rome, Cornelia, Milledgeville, and Barnesville. It was while serving in the latter charge that he died at Wesley Memorial Hospital, Emory University, on June 4, 1925. He was buried in Barnesville and thus, with the exception of Ginnie and Lizzie who died in infancy, he became the only member of George Dick's family whose remains lie outside Russellville's Maplewood Cemetery. On December 20, 1892, he married Carrie B. Sullivan of Mississippi who bore him three boys and two girls. One daughter, Mrs. Helen English of Monroe, North Carolina, now in her eighties, remembers her father as "a kind, gentle, and generous man and very compassionate."

Browder, Richard Cliffe (1830–79), son of William C. and Sarah Browder and paternal cousin of George Dick, was born near Olmstead, Logan County, Kentucky, on November 7, 1830. Born of godly parents, converted at an early age, and trained in Sunday school and class meeting, he became a spiritual leader in the Bethlehem Methodist Episcopal Church, South. On October 19, 1854, he married Amanda Small who bore him eight children. He was a farmer by profession. In 1869 he was ruined financially by going security for his cousin David B. Hutchings. Ten years later, on February 3, 1879, he died from a violent attack of pneumonia while visiting at the home of his nephew, John M. Roach. George Dick, in an obituary written at the time of his death, declared that in his thirty-two years of itinerant ministry he had "never seen a better steward nor a truer man than my departed cousin."

Browder, Robert (1804–90), son of David and Mary Cousins Browder and father of George Dick, was born in Dinwiddie County, Virginia, on February 20, 1804. He received a classical education with an emphasis on Latin and mathematics in a school taught by John Hubbard, who later became governor of Maine. In 1820 he and his older brother Richard emigrated to Green County, Kentucky; five years later they moved on to the rich farmland of southern Logan County near Olmstead. He taught school for several years after coming to Kentucky before settling down as a farmer. On December 30, 1825, he married Helen Sarah Walker, daughter of David and Mary Barbour Walker, who died in August 1827, seven months after George Dick's birth. The following year, on December 28, 1828, he married Sarah L. Gilmer, daughter of a Methodist preacher, Nicholas M. Gilmore, from Christian County, Kentucky. Sarah bore him twelve children, nine of whom lived to maturity. He was elected on four occasions to represent Logan County in the lower house of the Kentucky legislature: 1837, 1838, 1841, and 1857. He was successful as a farmer, acquiring a large body of land and owning a number of slaves, some of whom clung to him for counsel and support long after gaining their freedom. In the struggle between the North and South, he was a southern sympathizer and attended the southern conference, which met in Russellville in October 1861 to discuss Kentucky's connection with the Union. But when the convention proposed to meet again for the purpose of considering outright secession, he opposed the move. When the Confederate army retreated from southern Kentucky in February 1862, he left the state to stay with relatives in Montgomery, Alabama, to avoid prosecution for his open support of the Confederate cause. He returned to his home on May 5, 1863. After the war, as president of Logan County Southern Relief Association, he played an active part in responding to pleas for corn and meat from southern states. He was a compassionate man whose larder and granary were always open to the poor and needy. Generous to a fault, his willingness to go security for his nephew, David B. Hutchings, ruined him financially in 1881 and his farm was sold to satisfy his creditors. His children cared for him in his old age until his death on August 17, 1890.

Browder, Robert Walter (1853–1916), the oldest son of George Dick and Lizzie Warfield Browder, was born near Olmstead, Logan County, Kentucky, on April 23, 1853. He attended neighborhood schools, including Browder Institute. Converted at an early age, he yielded to the call to preach in 1874. After teaching for a year at Ash Spring, he enrolled in the two-year program of theological studies in newly established Vanderbilt University in the fall of 1875. His teachers included Thomas O. Summers and future bishop John C. Granberry. After his graduation in 1877, he was admitted on trial into the Louisville Conference of the Methodist Episcopal Church, South, and over the next thirty-nine years his appointments included the following: Glasgow and Dover (1877–81), West Broadway (Louisville, 1881–84), Elizabethtown (1884–88), presiding elder Elizabethtown District (1888–92), Henderson (1897–98), Bowling Green (1898–99), presiding elder Bowling Green District (1900–04), presiding elder Russellville District (1904–06), and presiding elder Bowling Green District (1906–10). During these years he also spent a considerable amount of time in promoting the educational interests of the Louisville Conference. With appointments as educational secretary and as president of the educational board during the years 1892–1916, he bore considerable responsibility for the Vanderbilt Training School at Elkton and for Logan Female College in Russellville. In 1884 the conference also elected him to the board of trust of Vanderbilt University, a position he held for thirty years; he resigned in 1914 after a valiant but unsuccessful effort to save the university for the Church. He married twice, first to Sudie Williams of Elizabethtown on April 26, 1887; she died a year later after the birth of a daughter. On February 19, 1896, he married Lydia Sullivan of South Carrollton, Kentucky, who bore him two sons. He died in Russellville, Kentucky, on March 23, 1916, from a complication of diseases, including yellow jaundice.

Browder, Wallace Warfield (1865–1949), fifth son of George Dick and Lizzie Warfield Browder, was born near Olmstead, Logan County, Kentucky, on October 12, 1865. He attended neighborhood schools, including Browder Institute from which he graduated as valedictorian of his class in 1884. He then spent at least two years at Bethel College, a Baptist school for men in Russellville. After George Dick's death in 1886 he returned home to look after his mother and to manage the family farm. Sometime during the 1890s he, along with his brothers Robert and Luther, invested in the coal mining business in Muhlenberg County. Wallace lost heavily in the venture, went broke, and lost the family homestead as a result. On December 27, 1905, he married Mary J. Williams of Logan County. After her death on March 15, 1907, he served for a time as county agent of Muhlenberg County, Kentucky, and as the first county agent of neighboring Ohio County. He then moved to Alabama where he headed the Farm Bureau. About 1926 he returned to Olmstead to live out his remaining years with his brother-in-law, Charles W. Roach, and, after the latter's death in 1929, with his niece, Miss Mary Roach. He died at the Roach place on April 15, 1949.

Browder, Wilbur Fish (1848–1919), second cousin of George Dick and son of David and Elizabeth Irvine Browder, was born in Clarksville, Tennessee, on December 12, 1848. When he was nine years old his family removed to Montgomery, Alabama, where he attended public school and received tutoring in preparation for college from Rabbi Moses, who later became rabbi of Hebrew Temple in Louisville. After three years at the University of Virginia from which he graduated in 1868, he entered the law department at the University of Kentucky where he earned a law degree in 1869. He was admitted to the bar in 1869 and began a lifelong practice in Russellville, Kentucky. On January 18, 1872 he married Elizabeth B. Wills, a native of Logan County and a graduate of Mary Institute of St. Louis, Missouri; she bore him five sons. In 1874 he was appointed registrar in bankruptcy for the Third Congressional District of Kentucky

and served until the bankruptcy law was repealed in 1878. He was one of the founders of the Logan County National Bank in 1875 and served as its president for several years. In 1880 he became master commissioner of Logan County, but resigned the same year. He was devoted to the town of Russellville and served it as city attorney, member of the city council, and as mayor for three successive terms. In 1887 he was appointed district attorney for the Louisville and Nashville Railroad, a position he held for twenty years; other important corporations also retained him as attorney and counsel. He was a member of the Protestant Episcopal Church and served as a trustee of Bethel College, a Baptist school for men in Russellville. In politics he was a conservative Democrat; as a "gold bug" spectator he attended the Democratic National Convention in Chicago in 1896. He died in Russellville on December 13, 1919.

Brush, George Washington (1805–80) was licensed to preach by the Methodist Church in October 1828. The Kentucky Conference admitted him into the itinerant ministry in 1829 and appointed him to the following charges: Breckinridge (1829–31), Bowling Green (1831–32), Germantown (1832–33), Cynthiana (1833–34), Shelbyville (1834–36), Frankfort (1836–37), Maysville (1837–38), Brook Street (Louisville, 1838–39), and Lexington (1839–41). During 1841–42 he served as agent for the Preacher's Aid Society; he then returned to the itinerant ranks and over the next thirteen years he held some of the most important pastorates in the Kentucky Conference, beginning with Louisville Fourth Street and closing with the Simpsonville Circuit in 1854–55. During 1855–58 he accepted appointments as agent for the American Tract Society and as pastor on the LeGrange and Simpsonville circuits. In 1858 he transferred to the Louisville Conference where he labored for the last twenty years of his life in the following posts: Middletown (1858–59), Jefferson Female Academy (1859–61), Eighth Street (Louisville, 1861–63), Walnut Street (Louisville, 1863–65), Shelby Street (Louisville, 1865–66), Jeffersontown (1866–68), presiding elder Louisville

District (1868–71), Owensboro (1871–73), Henderson (1873–75), Lebanon (1875–77), Jeffersonville (1877–79), and agent for the Widows and Orphans Home (1879–80). One month after he accepted superannuated status he died on November 13, 1880. It was reported that on his first circuit, in a single year, there were 260 conversions, "a signal proof of the divine recognition of his ministry – such an evidence as heaven, almost year by year, gave him and the church throughout his life."

Buckner, Simon Bolivar (1823–1914), the son of Aylett Hartswell and Elizabeth Ann Moreland Buckner, was born nine miles east of Munfordville, Hart County, Kentucky, on April 1, 1823. He attended schools in Greenville and Hopkinsville before entering West Point from which he graduated in 1844. He then taught at West Point for one year before serving in the Mexican War. On May 2, 1850, he married Mary Jane Kingsbury, daughter of an army officer. In 1855 he resigned from the army and went to Chicago where he spent several years assisting his father-in-law in business. When the Civil War broke out he was adjutant general of Kentucky in command of the state guard, but his sympathies were with the South and in September 1861 he accepted an appointment as brigadier general in the Confederate army. He participated in the defense of Fort Donelson, and after its surrender in February 1862, he was left behind to deliver it into the hands of his friend, U.S. Grant. He spent several months as a prisoner but was exchanged in time to lead a division in Bragg's ill-fated invasion of Kentucky in the fall of 1862. His Civil War career thereafter consisted primarily of assisting in the fortification of Mobile, commanding the Department of East Tennessee and directing a corps at Chickamauga, and serving as chief of staff to Kirby Smith in the Trans-Mississippi theater. After the war he lived in New Orleans for three years before returning to Kentucky to become editor of the Louisville *Daily Courier*. His wife died in 1874, and in 1885 he married twenty-eight-year-old Delia Claiborne of Richmond, Virginia. In 1887 he was elected governor of Kentucky, and

in the national campaign of 1896 he was nominated for vice-president by the "Gold Democrats." He died at his "Glen Lily" estate near Munfordville, Kentucky, on January 8, 1914, the last surviving Confederate general of lieutenant general rank.

Buell, Don Carlos (1818–98), son of Salmon D. and Eliza Buell, was born near Marietta, Ohio, on March 23, 1818. After his graduation from West Point in 1841 he fought against the Seminole Indians in Florida and in the Mexican War in which he was severely wounded at the battle of Churumbusco. Before the Civil War he served in a number of military departments on the frontier and in the East as a lieutenant colonel in the adjutant general's office. He was commissioned brigadier general of volunteers in the Union army on May 17, 1861. After helping to organize and train the Army of the Potomac, he was selected by General George B. McClellan to lead a force from Kentucky into east Tennessee. Despite objections from both McClellan and President Lincoln, he chose instead to advance on Nashville, a decision that may have contributed to the success of General Ulysses S. Grant at Forts Henry and Donelson. After taking Nashville he moved south to Shiloh where he arrived just in time to prevent a Confederate victory. After serving in the Corinth campaign, he was promoted to major general of volunteers on March 22, 1862. In September he moved into Kentucky to resist a Confederate invasion led by Generals Braxton Bragg and Kirby Smith. After occupying Louisville he engaged Bragg's army in the bloody but indecisive battle of Perryville on October 8, 1862. His failure to pursue Bragg led Washington authorities to relieve him of his command on October 24. After an official investigation he resigned his commission on June 1, 1864. After the war he settled in Kentucky where he operated an iron works and a coal mine. During 1885–89 he also served as a government pension agent in Louisville. He died at his home in the now abandoned village of Airdrie, near Rockport, Kentucky, on November 19, 1898.

Bunton, James W. (d. 1892) was born in Livingston County, Kentucky. After his conversion he joined the Methodist Church, married Sallie Durham, and settled down to the life of a small farmer in his native county. Soon he felt the call to preach and in 1873 the Louisville Conference of the Methodist Episcopal Church, South, admitted him into the traveling connection. During the next eight years he filled the following appointments: Jamestown Circuit (1873–74), Fredonia (1874–75), Brownsville Mission (1875–76), Brownsville (1876–78), New Roe (1878–80), and Kirkmansville Mission (1880–81). In 1881 he was located at his own request. Five years later he returned to the itinerant ranks and held the following charges: Falls of Rough (1886–88), Patesville (1888–90), and Fordsville (1890–91). He spent the last year of his life as superannuated and died in 1892. "According to his measure of capacity he made full proof of his ministry."

Burbridge, Stephen Gano (1831–94) was born in Scott County, Kentucky, August 19, 1831. After attending Georgetown College and Kentucky Military Institute, he settled down to practicing law and farming. When the Civil War broke out he volunteered for the Union army and was commissioned colonel of the 26th Kentucky Infantry. After his participation in the battle of Shiloh and the Vicksburg campaign, he was promoted to brigadier general to rank from June 9, 1862. Early in 1864 he succeeded General Jeremiah T. Boyle as commander of the District of Kentucky. The great majority of Kentuckians detested him for his arbitrary exercise of civil and military power. Among other things he arrested persons suspected of opposing Lincoln's reelection, he regulated commodity prices to force farmers to sell to the federal government at prices below the Cincinnati market, and he established a system of reprisals against civilians in an effort to suppress guerrilla activities. He was removed from his command in January 1865 and resigned from the army the following December. After the Civil War he and his family were socially and financially ostracized, and in 1867 he confessed that he was not "able to live in safety or do business in Kentucky." He was a frequent but unsuccessful applicant for federal offices. He died on December 2, 1894, in Brooklyn, New York.

Caldwell, John William (1837–1903), son of Austin and Eliza Harrison Caldwell, was born in Russellville, Logan County, Kentucky, on January 15, 1837. At the age of thirteen he accompanied an uncle to Texas where he worked on a farm and as a clerk and surveyor. Five years later he returned to Kentucky, studied law at the University of Louisville, and set up practice in Russellville. When the Civil War came he volunteered as a private in the Confederate army and was immediately elected captain of the "Logan Grays," a company of the 9th Kentucky Infantry. He saw action at Shiloh and at Chickamauga, sustaining wounds in both engagements. After the war he resumed his law practice in Russellville. In 1866 he was elected to the first of two consecutive four-year terms as county judge of Logan County. He then won election to three terms in the U.S. House of Representatives, serving from 1877 to 1883, declining reelection to become president of Logan County Bank. He died in Russellville on July 4, 1903.

Calhoun, John Caldwell (1782–1850), the son of Patrick and Martha Caldwell Calhoun, was born near Calhoun Mills, Abbeville District, South Carolina, on March 18, 1782. After graduating from Yale College in 1804, he studied law at Tapping Reeve's school in Litchfield, Connecticut, and then returned to Abbeville in 1807 to establish his practice. His marriage in January 1811 to Floride Calhoun, daughter of his cousin, John Ewing Calhoun, brought him a modest fortune. By adding to his landholdings he was able in 1825 to establish a commodious plantation homestead named "Fort Hill" in his native district. He was one of the outstanding leaders of the United States in the years before the Civil War. After a term in the state legislature (1808–09), he served in the following positions: member of Congress (1811–17), secretary of war under James Monroe (1817–25), vice-president of the United States under John Quincy Adams (1825–29), vice-president of the United States under Andrew

Jackson (1829–32), U.S. senator (1832–43), secretary of state under John Tyler (1844–45), and U.S. senator (1845–50). In his "South Carolina Exposition," written in opposition to the Tarriff of 1828, he set forth his views on states' rights and nullification. During his years in the U.S. Senate he became an unyielding defender of southern rights. In his last letter written in the heat of the debate over the Compromise of 1850, which he opposed, he declared that he found it "difficult to see how two people so different and hostile can exist together in one common Union." He died in Washington, D.C., on March 31, 1850.

Call, Richard Keith (1792–1862), son of William and Helen Mead Walker Call, was born near Petersburg, Prince County, Virginia, on October 24, 1792. When he was still a boy his father died and his mother moved to Logan County, Kentucky. He had little schooling but after his mother's death in August 1810 he attended Mt. Pleasant Academy just across the Tennessee line in Montgomery County. In 1814 he joined the U.S. Army as first lieutenant and served as a special aide to Major Andrew Jackson in the battle of New Orleans; he was promoted to captain in 1818. Four years later he resigned from the army and settled in Florida Territory where he studied law and commenced practice in Pensacola. He became a member of the Territorial Council in 1822 and brigadier general of the West Florida militia in 1823. He was elected as a Democrat to the U.S. Congress in 1822 and served one term. During 1836–39 and 1841–44 he served as governor of the Florida Territory, but in 1845 he was unsuccessful as a Whig candidate for governor of the new state. He devoted the rest of his life to defending the Union against the growing sentiment for secession. He died in Tallahassee on September 14, 1862.

Call, Wilkinson (1834–1910) was born in Russellville, Logan County, Kentucky, on January 9, 1834. He attended the common schools of his neighborhood and as a young man moved on to Jacksonville, Florida, where he studied law and established his practice. During the Civil War he served as an adjutant general in the Confederate army. He was elected to the U.S. Senate in December 1865 but that body refused to let him take his seat. As a prominent Florida Democrat he was selected by his party as a presidential elector in 1872 and again in 1876. In 1879 he was elected to the first of three consecutive terms in the U.S. Senate. After his retirement in 1897 he resided in Washington, D.C., until his death on August 24, 1910.

Campbell, Lewis Edwin (1844–1909), son of John and Mary Anna Torbitt Campbell, was born in Greenville, Kentucky, on July 6, 1844. He was converted at the age of eight in the hayloft of a barn while his pious Methodist father prayed with him. In his early twenties, some time after completing the course of study at Greenville College, he announced his call to preach, and in September 1869 the Louisville Conference of the Methodist Episcopal Church, South, admitted him on trial into the itinerant ministry. During his first year as junior preacher of the Greenville Circuit, under the watchful care of R. Y. Thomas, he reported seven hundred conversions. He was ordained deacon by Bishop Wightman in 1871 and elder by Bishop Keener in 1873. Over a period of forty years he held the following appointments from the Louisville Conference: Auburn Circuit (1870–71), Glasgow (1871–74), Bardstown (1874–76), Springfield (1876–80), Uniontown (1880–82), Hawesville (1882–86), Hartford (1886–89), Calhoun (1889–90), Cadiz (1890–91), Hardinsburg (1891–93), Woodburn Circuit (1893–95), Horse Cave (1895–96), Cerulean (1896–97), agent of the Preachers' Aid Society (1897–1903), financial agent of the board of education (1903–04), Bowling Green Circuit (1904–05), supernumerary (1905–06), agent for the Anti-Saloon League (1906–08), and supernumerary (1908–09). On October 5, 1875, he married Margaret Finn of Shawneetown, Illinois, who bore him six children. In 1893 he moved to Bowling Green, Kentucky, where by rigid economy he succeeded in educating his four sons in Ogden College and his two daughters in Potter College. For a number of years he played an active role in the cause of temperance and prohibition. It is said that wherever he pastored as long as two years, he put the local saloon out of business. He died of Bright's disease in Bowling Green on July 11, 1909.

Capers, Bishop William (1790–1855), son of William and Mary Singletary Capers, was born on his father's plantation at Bull Head Swamp in St. Thomas Parish, South Carolina, on January 26, 1790. His father, who was of Huguenot descent and a devout Methodist, served as one of General Francis Marion's trusted captains in the American Revolution. After attending Dr. Robert's academy at Statesburg, young Capers entered the sophomore class of South Carolina in 1805. Failing health forced his withdrawal before graduation in 1808. He then began the study of law under Judge John S. Richardson, but during the summer of 1808 he was converted, joined the Methodist Church, yielded to the call to preach, and by November found himself a licensed Methodist preacher. He was admitted into the South Carolina Conference in December 1810. On January 13, 1813, he married Anna White of Georgetown District who died in childbirth on December 30, 1815; the following year, on October 31, 1816, he married Susan McGill of Kershaw District. In addition to serving on several circuits, he was also stationed in such important cities as Wilmington, North Carolina; Georgetown, Charleston, and Columbia, South Carolina; and Milledgeville, Oxford, and Savannah, Georgia. He was recognized as the most popular Methodist preacher in the South. In 1821 he was appointed missionary to the Creek Indians and superintended the work until 1825 when he moved to Charleston to edit the *Wesleyan Journal.* In 1827 he began a four-year appointment as presiding elder of the Charleston District and it was during those years that he began the work of which he was most proud — the organization of missions to the slaves on the plantations of South Carolina. Within a few years the system he developed was adopted by evangelical denominations in all the southern states. In 1836 the general conference elected him editor of a new paper called the *Southern Christian Advocate,* a position he held until 1840 when he

began a four-year term as secretary of the Southern Missionary District. When the slavery question threatened the unity of the Methodist Church, he was a tactful exponent of the southern position. In the division of the church that occurred in 1844 he adhered to the Methodist Episcopal Church, South, which at its first general conference in 1846 elected him bishop. In that office he ordained George Dick as deacon in 1848. He died of heart disease near Anderson Court House, South Carolina, on January 29, 1855.

Carlisle, James Henry (1825–1909) was born in Winnsboro, North Carolina, on May 24, 1825. In 1853 the South Carolina Conference of the Methodist Episcopal Church, South, appointed him to teach at newly established Wofford College located at Spartanburg. He served as a faculty member from 1854 to 1875 and as president of the college from 1875 to 1902. For fifty years he gave himself to "the making of men; the development of immature youths into capable, honest, high-minded, patriotic citizens and Christians." A firm believer in cultivating personal relationships with students, he made a point of spending at least one hour with each student during the college term. He was also an active churchman, serving as an elected delegate to numerous general conferences of the Methodist Episcopal Church, South, and as a fraternal delegate to the general conferences of other denominations. A man of unusual gifts, he was one of the most influential leaders in South Carolina in his day. He died on the campus of his beloved Wofford College on October 21, 1909.

Channing, William Ellery (1780–1842), son of William and Lucy Ellery Channing, was born in Newport, Rhode Island, on April 7, 1780. After his graduation from Harvard in 1798 he spent a year and a half in Richmond, Virginia, as a tutor in the family of David Meade Randolph. During his southern residence his health failed and he was a semi-invalid for the rest of his life. When he returned to Newport he applied himself to the study of theology and in 1803 he was ordained and installed as pastor of Boston's Federal Street Church, a position he held for the rest of his life. His liberal theology touched off the "Unitarian Controversy." As the chief spokesman for those Congregationalists and others who were dissatisfied with Calvinist doctrine, especially its emphasis on human depravity, he preached the gospel of goodness and love, the dignity and perfectability of man, the validity of reason, and freedom of will and moral responsibility. At the same time he still clung to the supernatural element of the Christian tradition. A sermon he preached in Baltimore in 1819 at the ordination of Jared Sparks became the accepted Unitarian creed. The following year he organized the Berry Street Conference of liberal ministers; at one of its meetings in 1825 the American Unitarian Association was founded. After 1825 his influence spread beyond religious circles as a result of his speeches and essays on such subjects as education, literature, slavery, temperance, and war. He died in Bennington, Vermont, on October 2, 1842.

Chase, Salmon Portland (1808–73), the eighth of eleven children of Ithamar and Janette Ralston Chase, was born in Cornish, New Hampshire, on January 13, 1808. In his childhood his family moved to Keene, New Hampshire, where he was educated at the Keene district school followed by further training in a private school in Windsor, Vermont. When his father died in 1817 he was sent to Ohio to live with his uncle, Philander Chase, who was a bishop in the Protestant Episcopal Church. In 1823, after briefly attending Cincinnati College, he entered Dartmouth College, graduating in 1826. He then taught a school for boys in Washington, D.C., before deciding upon a career in law. He was admitted to the bar in December 1829 and established his practice in Cincinnati in 1830. He married three times, first to Katherine Jane Garniss (March 4, 1834), who died December 1, 1835; then to Eliza Ann Smith (September 26, 1839) who died September 29, 1845; and finally to Sarah Bella Dunlop Ludlow (November 6, 1846) who died on January 13, 1852. Six daughters were born to him, only two of whom lived to maturity. In addition to his legal duties he soon became a leader of the antislavery movement, defending fugitive

slaves, and playing an important part as an organizer of the Liberty party in 1841 and as a founder of the Free-Soil party in 1848. In 1849 he launched a distinguished career of public service, including: U.S. senator (1849–55), Republican governor of Ohio (1855–60), secretary of the treasury under Abraham Lincoln (1861–64), and chief justice of the Supreme Court (1864–73). As chief justice he presided over the trial of Jefferson Davis, in which he favored quashing the indictment, as well as over the Senate impeachment proceedings against Andrew Johnson. He stood with the majority of the Court in decisions upholding the Republican policy of Reconstruction. On May 7, 1873, he died of a paralytic stroke in New York City.

Cherry, George Washington (1822–1911) was the son of Captain William and Frances Taylor Cherry. His father, a native of Edgecombe County, North Carolina, and a veteran of the American Revolutionary War, migrated to the Green River section of Warren County, Kentucky, where George was born in 1822. The latter married Martha Frances Stahl of Simpson County, Kentucky, on April 29, 1850; there were nine sons, including Henry Hardin who was a leader in the movement to establish state normal schools in Kentucky and the founder of Western Kentucky State Teachers College (now Western Kentucky University) in 1906. George belonged to the Methodist Episcopal Church, South, in which he served as a steward for many years. He lived out his life on his farm located at the mouth of Gasper Road near Hall's Chapel, about two miles from the confluence of the Gasper and Barren rivers. There he died on May 29, 1911.

Cleveland, Stephen Grover (1837–1908), the fifth child of Richard Falley, a Presbyterian minister, and Ann Neal Cleveland, was born in Caldwell, New Jersey, on March 18, 1837. He attended neighborhood schools in Caldwell and in Fayetteville and Clinton, New York, where his father also held pastorates. When his father died in 1853, he had to undertake his own support. After working for a time at the New York Institution for the Blind, where he was acquainted with hymn writer Fanny Crosby, he moved west to live with his mother's uncle at Black Rock, near Buffalo. He undertook the study of law and in 1859 he was admitted to the bar. For the next twenty-two years he quietly practiced law, supported the Democratic party, and held such minor offices as assistant district attorney and sheriff of Erie County. Then his political career ignited. In 1881 he was elected mayor of Buffalo. His reputation as a reformer carried him not only to the governorship of New York in 1882 but to the presidency in 1884. On June 2, 1886, he was married in the White House to Frances Folsom who bore him five children. His conciliatory attitude toward the South, his vetoes of numerous private pension bills, and his advocacy of tariff reduction contributed to his defeat by William Henry Harrison in 1888. Four years later he won the presidency once more and thus became the only president to serve two nonconsecutive terms. His second administration was clouded by the Panic of 1893, which struck shortly after his inauguration. As a "hard money" advocate he responded to the financial crisis by pushing through Congress a repeal of the Sherman Silver Purchase Act. Equally controversial was his decision to send federal troops to Illinois to break the Pullman strike. In foreign affairs he intervened in the boundary dispute between Great Britain and Venezuela, and, as an anti-imperialist, he withdrew from the Senate a treaty that would have annexed Hawaii. When his second term expired in 1897 he retired to a modest home in Princeton, New Jersey, where he died on June 24, 1908.

Cottrell, Joseph Benson (1829–95), the son of a local preacher was born in Mt. Ariel (now Cokesbury), South Carolina, on May 6, 1829. At the age of twelve he was converted in Sylvestria, Mississippi. In 1851 he graduated from the Citadel Military Academy in Charleston, South Carolina. In that same year he married Margaret L. Jennings of Union District, South Carolina. They soon moved to Alabama where he was licensed to preach at Tuskegee in 1852. Shortly thereafter his wife died, leaving an infant son. In December 1852 he was admitted on trial into the Alabama Conference of the Methodist Church. He was married a second time on January 12, 1854, to Mrs. M. Caroline Duncan. In 1855 he was appointed to a chaplaincy in the U.S. Army, but returned to the itinerant ministry the following year. He filled circuits, stations, and districts in the Alabama and Montgomery Conferences until 1870, when he was transferred to the Mississippi Conference and stationed at Columbus. In 1874 he was transferred to the Louisville Conference and served the following charges: Owensboro (1874–77), Russellville (1877–79), Bowling Green (1879–82), Jefferson (Louisville, 1888–83), supernumerary (1883–84), Cloverport (1884–86), Cadiz (1886–88), Franklin (1888–91), Greenville (1891–92), and superannuated (1892–95). He died while fishing in Lake Dora, Florida, on March 6, 1895. "His mind was like a complicated machine, propelled by turbine action, whose wheels run in all conceivable directions, each, apparently, intent on discharging its function independently of all the rest."

Crittenden, Thomas Theodore (1832–1909), the son of Henry and Anna Maria Allen Crittenden, was born near Shelbyville, Shelby County, Kentucky, on January 1, 1832. After attending school in Cloverport, Kentucky, he enrolled in Centre College at Danville, graduating in 1855. He then went to Frankfort, Kentucky, where he studied law in the office of his uncle and U.S. Senator John J. Crittenden. During his stay in Frankfort he married Carrie W. Jackson on November 13, 1856; there were three sons. In 1857 he moved to Lexington, Missouri, where he practiced law in partnership with John A. S. Tutt. When the Civil War broke out, he volunteered for the Union army and was appointed major (later promoted to lieutenant colonel) of the 7th Regiment of the Missouri State Militia, a cavalry unit that saw action in Missouri and Arkansas. After the war he resumed his legal practice at Warrensburg, Missouri, in partnership with former Confederate General Francis M. Cockrell, a relationship that lasted until 1872 when he won election as a Democrat to the United States Congress. Although failing renomination in 1874, he was elected overwhelmingly once more two years later. In 1880 he won the governorship of Missouri. As governor he was successful in improving education and in ridding Missouri of the notorious Jesse James and his gang of train robbers. When his term expired in 1885, he moved to Kansas City where he practiced law until 1893 when President Grover Cleveland appointed him consul-general to Mexico. When he died in Kansas City on May 29, 1909, he was referee in bankruptcy for the United States district court.

Crowe, Enoch Martin (1829–1908), son of John W. and Nancy Martin Crowe, was born near Scottsville in Allen County, Kentucky, on October 15, 1829. He was one of eleven children. At the age of thirteen he was converted at a camp meeting and joined the Methodist Church. In 1855 he was licensed to preach and in 1856 he joined the Louisville Conference of the Methodist Episcopal Church, South. He was ordained deacon by Bishop Kavanaugh in 1858 and elder by Bishop Early in 1860. During his forty-four years as an itinerant preacher he accepted the following appointments: Leitchfield Mission (1856–57), Yelvington (1857–58), Hawesville (1858–59), Hartford (1859–61), Russellville (1861–62), Madisonville (1862–64), Henderson Circuit (1864–66), Hardinsburg Circuit (1866–67), Hartford (1867–69), Fairview (1869–71), presiding elder Bowling Green District (1871–75), presiding elder Owensboro District (1875–76), presiding elder Lebanon District (1876–79), presiding elder Henderson District (1879–80), presiding elder Princeton District (1880–84), presiding elder Gosport District (1884–86), Livermore (1886–87), Scottsville (1887–89), Hartford (1889–91), Jeffersontown (1891–93), Shepherdsville (1893–94), Greensburg Circuit (1894–96), Conference Missionary Secretary (1896–99), and Pleasant Ridge (1899–1900). On May 7, 1856, he married Frances Elizabeth Moore, daughter of Aaron Moore, who was also a preacher in the Louisville Conference. Their marriage produced thirteen children, six of whom died in infancy. Crowe lived in Hartford, Kentucky, during the first six years of his retirement. He then moved to

Scottsville where he died, nearly blind, on April 8, 1908. "He knew the deep joy and rapture of conscious communion with God, and often with mingled tears and praise gave testimony to the richness and fulness of his experience of perfect love."

Cundiff, Bryant A. (1830–1907) was born on January 25, 1830, in Hardin County, Kentucky. In August 1851 he was "powerfully" converted in a meeting at Pleasant Grove Church. A year later he was licensed to preach, and in 1854 the Louisville Conference of the Methodist Episcopal Church, South, admitted him on trial into the itinerant ministry. He was ordained deacon by Bishop Early in 1856 and elder by Bishop Kavanaugh in 1858. In his fifty-three years of preaching, "he never broke down." It is said that he preached more sermons and had more conversions than any other preacher in the conference. He was known as an enthusiastic advocate of the doctrine of entire sanctification or perfect love and some remarkable things happened in the revivals he conducted. Men and women, convicted under his preaching, would fall as if dead and after remaining in that condition for hours would arise shouting praises to God. In one of his early revivals in Crittenden County he prayed: "O God, strike down that scoffing in the back of the room," and immediately a man fell as if shot and remained unconscious for hours; he was then happily converted. Cundiff was known as a man "mighty in the Scriptures." One witness remembered his preaching a sermon in which he made "more than a hundred quotations from the Bible, giving book, chapter, and verse without ever once turning to the open page." He was married on March 10, 1858, to M. M. Rouseau of Wayne County, Kentucky, who bore him eight children, three of whom survived him. During his long association with the Louisville Conference he held the following appointments: Salem Circuit (1854–55), Smithland Circuit (1855–56), Wayne Circuit (1856–58), Scottsville Circuit (1858–59), Albany Circuit (1859–60), Wayne Circuit (1860–62), Glasgow Circuit (1862–63), Greenville Circuit (1863–65), Hardinsville Circuit (1865–66), Columbia Circuit (1866–67), Burksville

(1867–68), presiding elder Greensburg District (1868–70), Lafayette Circuit (1870–72), Hodgenville Circuit (1872–74), Hartford Circuit (1874–75), Brandenburg Circuit (1875–76), Marion Circuit (1876–80), Long Grove (1880–81), Big Springs Circuit (1881–83), Franklin Circuit (1883–85), Corydon (1885–89), Caseyville Circuit (1889–90), Owensboro Circuit (1890–92), McDaniels Circuit (1892–94), Leitchfield (1894–95), Falls of Rough Circuit (1895–97), Stephensport (1897–98), Marion (1898–99), Tolu Circuit (1899–1902), Mt. Washington Circuit (1902–04), Mannsville Circuit (1904–06), and Bowling Green Circuit (1906–07). Two months after he was superannuated he died at Corydon, Kentucky, on November 10, 1907. "The word of God was truly the sword of the Spirit in his hands."

Cunnyngham, William G. E. (1820–1900), the son of the Rev. Jesse and Mary Etter Cunnyngham, was born in Knox County, Tennessee, on December 3, 1820. In his early years he worked on a farm and attended neighborhood schools as he had opportunity. Converted in his youth, he eventually yielded to the call to preach and in 1843 he joined the Holston Conference of the Methodist Episcopal Church. During the next ten years he accepted the following appointments: Estillville, Chattanooga, Athens, and Knoxville in Tennessee, and Tazewell and Abingdon in Virginia. While serving in the Abingdon charge in 1852 he married Bettie Litchfield of that city. Shortly after his marriage he was appointed a missionary to China. For nine years he preached on the streets and in the chapels until the failing health of his wife compelled him to return in 1861 to the United States. The disruptions associated with the Civil War prevented his going home to Abingdon, Virginia, so Bishop Kavanaugh transferred him to the Kentucky Conference and stationed him at Shelbyville where he also taught classes in the Science Hill Academy. When the war was over in 1865 he returned to Abingdon where he spent the next eight years preaching at the Methodist Church and teaching at Martha Washington College. In 1873 he accepted an appointment to Church Street Station in Knoxville where he preached until 1875

when he was elected Sunday school editor of the Methodist Episcopal Church, South. He served in the latter position until his retirement in 1894. He spent his last years in Nashville, Tennessee, where he died on March 31, 1900. "From his youth on up he maintained an unbroken record of consecration."

Davis, Jefferson (1808–89), the tenth child of Samuel and Jane Cook Davis, was born in Fairview, Todd County, Kentucky, on June 3, 1808. When he was still a small child his family moved on to Mississippi where they settled on a small plantation near Woodville, Wilkinson County. Although his parents were Baptists, his early education included two years at a Roman Catholic Seminary in Washington County, Kentucky (1815–17); he also attended Transylvania University in Lexington, Kentucky (1821–24), before entering West Point from which he graduated in 1828. In 1835 he resigned from the army, married Sarah Knox Taylor, daughter of future president Zachary Taylor, and became a Mississippi planter. Less than three months after his marriage, his wife died of malarial fever; ten years later on February 26, 1845, he married Varina Howell, member of the local aristocracy. In 1845 he went to Congress as a Democrat, but he resigned the following year to command the Mississippi Rifles in the Mexican War and was wounded at Buena Vista. After the war he played an increasingly important role in national affairs, serving in the following offices: U.S. senator (1847–51), secretary of war under Franklin Pierce, U.S. senator (1857–61), and president of the Confederacy (1861–65). As president his autocratic methods and interference in military affairs aroused hostility among Confederate leaders. When Richmond, Virginia, fell on April 2, 1865, he was a fugitive until his capture at Irwinville, Georgia, by federal cavalry on May 10. He spent the next two years imprisoned at Fort Monroe, Virginia. Although indicted for treason, he was never brought to trial. His fortune ruined by the war, he spent his last years at "Beauvoir," a home provided for him on the Gulf of Mexico, where he wrote *The Rise and Fall of the Confederate Government.* He died in New Orleans on December 6, 1889.

Davison, Learner B. (1813–98) was born in Grayson County, Kentucky, on May 13, 1813. He was converted in 1831 and joined the Methodist Church in Hawesville. In 1842 the Kentucky Conference admitted him on trial into the itinerant ministry. He was ordained deacon by Bishop Soule in 1844 and elder by Bishop Andrew in 1846. During his years in the active ministry he held the following charges without interruption: Hopkinsville Circuit (1845–46), Lafayette (1846–47), Asbury Chapel (Louisville, 1847–48), Russellville (1848–50), Elkton (1850–51), Scottsville (1851–53), Lebanon (1853–54), Eighth Street (Louisville, 1854–55), Glasgow (1855–56), Logan Circuit (1856–58), Hopkinsville Circuit (1858–60), Madisonville (1860–62), Franklin (1862–63), City Mission (Louisville, 1863–65), Hawesville Circuit (1865–66), Cadiz (1866–67), Cave City (1867–68), Russellville Circuit (1868–69), presiding elder Hopkinsville District (1869–70), presiding elder Princeton District (1870–73), presiding elder Elizabethtown District (1873–77), Owensboro Circuit (1877–78), Greensburg (1878–79), Burksville Circuit (1879–81), Shepherdsville (1881–83), Lewisport (1883–84), Campbellsville (1884–85), Columbia (1885–87), Smith's Grove (1887–88), Owensboro Circuit (1888–89), Rochester (1889–90), Sharon Grove (1890–91), Morgantown (1891–92), Smithland (1892–93), Livermore (1893–95), and Asbury Chapel (Louisville, 1895–98). He was known as the greatest bookseller in the Louisville Conference, "sowing Methodist literature all over our great Conference field." As one who believed in working with his hands as well as his brains, he had the best of gardens and kept a fat horse and a good cow. He died in 1898. "He was a holy man, a sanctified man in the exact scriptural sense, a saint of God but not a rider of hobbies."

Dempsey, James Rufus (1825–98) was born in Rockingham County, North Carolina, on December 13, 1825. Shortly after his birth his family moved to Virginia where he grew to manhood. He then moved to Kentucky where he began to prepare for a career in medicine. Those plans were set aside when, about 1847, he was converted and yielded to the call to preach the gospel. In 1848 he was admitted on trial into the Louisville Conference of the Methodist Episcopal Church, South, where his membership remained for the rest of his life. He was ordained deacon in 1850 and elder in 1852. His first marriage was to Melcinia Coleman of Warren County, Kentucky, who bore him four children, one of whom survived him. His second marriage to Mary E. Linebaugh of Russellville, Kentucky, produced ten children, nine of whom grew to maturity. During his fifty years in the Louisville Conference, he held the following appointments: Salem (1848–49), Princeton (1849–50), Bowling Green Circuit (1850–51), Lafayette (1851–52), Greensburg (1852–54), Columbia Circuit (1854–56), Eighth Street (Louisville, 1856–58), Smithland (1858–59), Shelby Street (Louisville, 1859–60), Big Spring (1860–62), Hardinsburg Circuit (1862–64), Big Spring (1864–65), presiding elder Hardinsburg District (1865–67), presiding elder Henderson District (1867–69), Owensboro Circuit (1869–70), presiding elder Owensboro District (1870–72), Hartford Circuit (1872–74), supernumerary (1874–75), Auburn Circuit (1875–77), Mt. Holly Mission (1877–79), Big Spring (1879–81), Harrodsburg (1881–82), Hardinsburg (1882–83), Dixon (1883–85), and superannuated (1885–1898). He died on April 22, 1898, in Franklin, Missouri.

Dennis, George W. (1847–1924) was born in Greenville, Kentucky, on October 25, 1847. He joined the Louisville Conference of the Methodist Episcopal Church, South, in 1881 and accepted the following appointments: Calhoun (1881–83), Owensboro Circuit (1883–86), Cloverport (1886–89), and West Broadway (Louisville, 1889–92). He is reported to have witnessed 1070 conversions and 1136 additions to the church during his eleven years in the active ministry. He was superannuated in 1892 after he had the misfortune of being run over by a train, losing both legs and one hand. A little over a year later, his miraculous recovery enabled him to accept a job as a bookkeeper in the Revenue Service, a position he held for more than twenty-eight years. He died of a stroke on November 10, 1924. "He had a tender feeling for the unfortunate, denying himself to give them help."

Dewitt, Alanson C. (1809–92) was born in Redford County, Virginia, on February 23, 1809. He was converted on September 1, 1824; in the same month he joined the Methodist Church. On July 28, 1828, he married Julia Ann Markham; three years later he moved to Cumberland County, Kentucky. He was licensed to preach in 1833. In 1836 the Kentucky Conference of the Methodist Church admitted him on trial into the itinerant ministry. He was ordained deacon by Bishop Roberts in 1837 and elder by Bishop Soule in 1839. During his ten years in the Kentucky Conference he held the following charges: Elizabeth Circuit (1836–37), Glasgow Circuit (1837–38), Scottsville Circuit (1838–39), Brandenburg Circuit (1839–40), Owensboro (1841–42), Hartford (1842–43), and Columbia Circuit (1845–46). When the Methodist Church divided in 1845, he joined the Louisville Conference of the Methodist Episcopal Church, South, and received the following appointments: Campbellsville Circuit (1846–47), Madisonville (1847–49), Greenville Circuit (1849–51), Logan Circuit (1851–52), superannuated (1852–54), Franklin Circuit (1854–56), superannuated (1856–57), Rochester Mission (1857–58), superannuated (1858–67), Russellville Circuit (1867–68), Elkton (1868–69), Russellville Circuit (1869–70), Morganfield (1870–71), superannuated (1871–73), and Todd Circuit (1873–75). He was elected secretary of the Louisville Annual Conference fifteen times during 1846–1871. During the last seventeen years of his life he was completely blind. Death came on December 10, 1892. "He was a modest, sweet-spirited, gentle, faithful, old-time Methodist preacher, a class rapidly passing away, but who in their day wrought wonderfully for God in this new territory."

Doggett, Bishop David Seth (1810–80) was born in Lancaster County, Virginia, on January 26, 1810. He was a descendant of John Doggett, an Anglican minister, who immigrated to Virginia about 1650. His father, a lawyer and devout Methodist, sent him to the University of Virginia to prepare for a career in law. In 1829 he yielded to the call to preach, joined the Virginia Conference of the Methodist Episcopal Church, and became an itinerant preacher on the Roanoke Circuit in North Carolina. Rising rapidly in his conference, he subsequently served churches in Petersburg, Richmond, Lynchburg, and Norfolk in Virginia; and in Charlottesville, North Carolina. When his church divided in 1845 he adhered to the Methodist Episcopal Church, South. Five years later, when he became editor of his denomination's *Quarterly Review*, he moved to Richmond, Virginia, where he lived through the Civil War. During the conflict he traveled and preached throughout the South and in 1864 published *The War and Its Close*. Two years later, just as he was about to become a professor at Randolph-Macon College, the general conference elected him bishop. His discharged that office until his death fourteen years later on October 27, 1880, in Richmond, Virginia.

Early, Jubal Anderson (1816–94), son of Joab and Ruth Hairston Early, was born in Franklin County, Virginia, on November 3, 1816. After graduating from West Point in 1837 he participated in the Seminole War. In 1838 he resigned from the army to study law and from 1840 to 1861, with occasional interruptions, he practiced his profession in Rocky Mount, Virginia. During these years he also represented Franklin County in the state house of delegates (1841–42) and served as major of the 1st Regiment Virginia Infantry in the Mexican War (1847–48). Although he voted against secession in the Virginia Convention of 1861 he promptly entered the Confederate army as colonel of the 24th Virginia Infantry, which he led at the first battle of Bull Run. On July 21, 1861, he was promoted to brigadier general and took part in all the engagements of the Army of Northern Virginia during 1862–64. He was subsequently elevated to major general in 1863 and lieutenant general in 1864. From June 1864 until the end of the war he held an independent command in the Shenandoah Valley of Virginia where he obstructed Union communications and threatened

Pennsylvania and Maryland. He was relieved of command in March 1865 when his army was nearly annihilated by General George A. Custer at Waynesboro. After the war he settled down to practice law in Lynchburg, Virginia, and to pursue his interest in history, becoming the first president of the Southern Historical Society. He spent his last years in supervising the drawings of the Louisiana lottery and in an effort to discredit the military reputation of Confederate General James Longstreet. He died in Lynchburg on March 2, 1894.

Edwards, George B. (1854–1929), the son of George T. Edwards who was county judge of Logan County from 1851 to 1855, was born in Russellville, Kentucky, in 1854. He studied law at Yale University where his roommate was future president William Howard Taft. After his graduation in 1878 he returned to Russellville to practice law but he soon turned to banking and was for many years president of the Southern Deposit Bank. He died in 1929.

Edwards, Judge George T. (1818–95), son of Presley Edwards, a distinguished lawyer of Logan County, and Hester Pope Edwards, was born in Russellville, Kentucky, on July 30, 1818. His father died when he was young, leaving him an only child. He was educated in the schools of Russellville. In 1838, after studying law for two years, he was admitted to the bar and set up practice in Russellville. In March 1839 he married Margaret W. Connelly who bore him five children. After her death twenty-two years later, he married Mrs. Maria L. Allison, daughter of Swift Emett of Russellville. For a brief time during the 1850s he entered politics. He was elected judge of Logan County in 1851 and state senator in 1855, serving for only one term in both positions. In 1870 he retired from his substantial legal practice. He died in Russellville on May 3, 1895.

Emerson, Isaac William (1827–1909), son of Walter and Albina Casson Emerson, was born in Wayne County, Kentucky, on July 14, 1827. Although both of his parents were devout Methodists, his mother was especially remembered for her "ardent piety and burning zeal for the Church." In

later life Emerson recalled that his father's house "was always a preacher's home, and from my childhood a regular preaching place." When a church was built in the community, his father gave the lot and was the most liberal supporter of the enterprise. Early in his boyhood Emerson was converted at home and received into membership at Salem Church. He attended both public and private schools in his neighborhood. Although hesitating for some time, he finally yielded to the call to preach. He was licensed by the quarterly conference of the Wayne Circuit on July 6, 1850. Several months later he was admitted on trial into the Louisville Conference of the Methodist Episcopal Church, South. He was ordained deacon by Bishop Andrew in 1852 and elder by Bishop Paine in 1854. During this time, on April 28, 1853, he also married Sallie M. Parker of Somerset, Kentucky, who bore him eight children. For fifty years, including his service as chaplain in the U.S. Army during the Civil War, he traveled in the itinerant ranks of the Louisville Conference in which he held the following appointments: Big Spring (1850–51), Mt. Washington (1851–52), Asbury Mission (Louisville, 1852–53), Empire Iron Works (1853–54), Wayne Circuit (1854–55), Lebanon Circuit (1855–56), Bradfordsville (1856–57), Elizabethtown and Hodgenville (1857–59), Columbia (1859–61), supernumerary (1861–63), Wayne (1863–64), Campbellsville (1864–65), supernumerary (1865–66), Bradfordsville Circuit (1866–67), presiding elder Glasgow District (1867–68), presiding elder Bowling Green District (1868–71), Fairview Circuit (1871–75), Adairville Circuit (1875–77), presiding elder Russellville District (1878–80), Allensville and Bethlehem (1880–82), Fairview (1882–83), Portland (1883–84), supernumerary (1884–85), Franklin Circuit (1885–86), Elkton (1886–90), Adairville (1890–94), Allensville (1894–98), Hawesville (1898–99), and Morganfield (1899–1900). He requested superannuate status in the fall of 1900 and lived for several years in Olmstead, Kentucky; in 1907 he moved to Russellville, Kentucky, where he died on January 9, 1909. He lies buried in Maple Grove Cemetery, "a stone's throw" from

George Dick's final resting place. "He was generous, brave, and sincere; affectionate without dissimulation, modest without timidity, and courageous without rudeness."

Ewell, Richard Stoddert (1817–72), son of Dr. Thomas and Elizabeth Stoddert Ewell, was born in Georgetown, D.C., on February 8, 1817. He graduated from West Point in 1840 and spent his entire antebellum career in the Southwest where he received a brevet for gallantry in the Mexican War (1846–48) and won further distinction against the Apaches in New Mexico in 1857. Although a strong Union man, he resigned his commission on May 7, 1861, and offered his services to Virginia. He accepted an appointment as brigadier general in the Confederate army on June 17, 1861; he became a major general on January 24, 1862. He led a division under "Stonewall" Jackson in the Shenandoah Valley campaign and was prominent in the Seven Days' battles before Richmond and in the operations around Manassas Junction. In the second Manassas campaign he lost a leg in the battle of Groveton and thereafter had to be lifted into the saddle and strapped there. He returned to duty May 1863 with the rank of lieutenant general and became commander of the 2nd Corps. At Gettysburg his hesitation to exceed orders on the first day of battle cost the Confederates Cemetery Hill, possession of which might have turned the Union withdrawal toward that position into a rout. His corps also saw heavy fighting the following year around Spotsylvania Court House, Virginia. During this action his horse was shot from under him and the fall compelled him to retire temporarily from active field duty. He subsequently was placed in command of the defense of Richmond. When the city was evacuated, he and his decimated corps were surrounded and captured at Sayler's Creek on April 6, 1865. He spent four months in prison at Fort Warren. After the war he married his widowed cousin and childhood playmate, Leczinska Campbell Brown, daughter of Judge Campbell of Tennessee and one time minister of Russia. They moved to a farm near Spring Hill, Tennessee, where he died of pneumonia on January 25, 1872.

Ewing, George Washington (1808–88), tenth and youngest child of General Robert Ewing who migrated from Virginia to settle near Adairville in Logan County, Kentucky, in 1792, was born on November 29, 1808. He was reared on the farm and educated at the Russellville Academy and Princeton College. At the age of twenty-one he commenced the study of law with his brother, Judge Ephraim M. Ewing, and practiced in Russellville until the Civil War. He served in the Kentucky legislature during 1842–44 and 1859–61. When the Confederate Provisional Government of Kentucky was set up in 1861 and he was chosen a member of the Provisional Congress, he was expelled from the Kentucky legislature on December 21, 1861. He then served as a member of the permanent Confederate Congress from 1862 to 1865. After the war he moved to his farm of 400 acres near Adairville on the Red River. He was twice married, first in 1835 to Susan Moss who died in 1840, and then in 1846 to Nannie L. Williams. He died on May 20, 1888.

Ewing, Hugh Boyle (1826–1905), the fourth child of Thomas and Maria Wills Boyle Ewing, was born in Lancaster, Ohio, on October 31, 1826. Private tutors directed his early education; he also attended, but did not graduate from, West Point. The lure of gold attracted him to California in 1849. While he was there he joined an expedition sent out by his father, then secretary of the interior under President Zachary Taylor, to assist in the rescue of immigrants trapped in the High Sierras by heavy snows. When he returned to the East in 1852, he studied law and in 1854 began his practice in St. Louis, Missouri. Two years later he removed to Fort Leavenworth, Kansas, where he continued his practice in association with William Tecumseh Sherman and others. In 1858 he married Henrietta Young, the daughter of George W. Young of Washington, D.C. In that same year he returned to his native Ohio to take charge of his father's salt works and land in Athens County. When the Civil War broke out, he was appointed brigade-inspector of Ohio Volunteers and served under Generals McClellan and Rosecrans in their West Virginia cam-

490

paigns; in August 1861 he became colonel of the 30th Ohio Infantry. His performance in the battles of South Mountain and Antietam in September 1862 resulted in his promotion to brigadier general two months later. In that capacity he served under General Sherman at both Vicksburg and Chattanooga; in the latter battle his division sustained heavy losses in carrying Missionary Ridge on November 25, 1863. After the war President Johnson appointed him minister to Holland where he served from 1866 to 1870. Upon his return from Europe he practiced law for four years in Washington, D.C., and then bought a small estate near Lancaster, Ohio, where he resided until his death on June 30, 1905.

Fairleigh, Robert M. (1840–88) was born in Brandenburg, Meade County, Kentucky, on January 17, 1840. His father was a prominent citizen of Meade County and served as county and circuit clerk. After attending neighborhood schools, Robert began the study of medicine in 1859 under Dr. H. K. Pusey of nearby Garnettsville. During the winters of 1858 and 1859 he attended lectures in Jefferson Medical College, Philadelphia, from which he graduated in 1860. He returned to Brandenburg to begin his medical practice. When the Civil War broke out, he became assistant surgeon of the Third Kentucky Cavalry (federal); in June 1861 he was made surgeon of that regiment. He participated in all the engagements of the army of the West, from the battle of Pittsburg Landing to the start of Sherman's "March to the Sea." During the last year of the war he was surgeon of Eli H. Murray's Brigade of Kilpatrick's Division Cavalry. In May 1865 he married Anna Slaughter of Hodgenville, Kentucky, who bore him four children. After the war he established a large medical practice in Hopkinsville, Kentucky. He served as a member of the board of medical examiners for the Second Judicial District and in 1873 was elected vice-president of the Kentucky Medical Society. He was also active in local politics. From 1869 to 1879 he was a member of the Hopkinsville Board of Councilmen and in 1880 he led the movement for public schools. He died in Hopkinsville in 1888.

Finley, Alexander C. (183?–191?) was born in Russellville, Logan County, Kentucky, sometime during the 1830s. His father was a tailor who also served as postmaster of Russellville for a number of years. Alex learned the tailor's trade but early in life his love of books led him to take up printing as well. During his years as a printer he worked on the *Louisville Supply Journal,* edited by George D. Prentice, as well as the *Frankfort Yeoman* and *Danville Advocate.* He then turned to the study of law and was admitted to the bar, after which he practiced law in Russellville. For a brief period he was active politically, but politics soon lost their appeal and he was proud of being a "no voter." It was while serving as a clerk in the Logan County courthouse that he conceived of the idea of writing a history of Logan County, a project on which he labored for many years. He set the type and printed the three volume work himself. Early in life attracted attention for his eccentricities. He owned a whole town block a short distance from Main Street on which he grew a veritable jungle of trees and shrubs; a narrow path led from the street to his small one-room log house located in the center of the lot. In the topmost branches of a tall tree west of town he constructed a lookout from which he made his astronomical observations. He also built at the forks of the Bowling Green and Gallatin roads a huge furnace of brick and stone containing a block of steel with a hole bored to the center into which he packed base metals and chemicals. Under intense heating the block exploded hurling debris in all directions; several bystanders barely escaped with their lives. In his old age, unable to make a living for himself, he lived off of his friends scattered across the county, never staying two nights consecutively in the same place. He died in Russellville sometime during the 1910s.

Fisk, John Flavel (1815–1902), son of Dr. David and Abigail Fisk, was born in Genesee County, New York, on December 14, 1815. He was educated in neighborhood schools and at Freeman Carey Institute in Hamilton County, Ohio, from which he graduated in 1840. On October 14, 1842, he married Elizabeth S. Johnson of Cincinnati who bore him seven children. He eventually became principal of the Maysville Academy in Mason County, Kentucky, where he also began the study of law; he finished his legal studies at the Law School of Covington, Kentucky, under Governor James T. Morehead and James Pryor. He decided to remain in Covington where he practiced law and became recognized as one of Kentucky's leading lawyers. He was also active in community affairs holding directorships in several companies, including First National Bank of Covington, Covington and Cincinnati Bridge Company, Covington Gas-Light Company, Highland Cemetery Company, and Kenton Insurance Company. In addition he played a prominent role in local and state politics and served in the following offices: member of the Covington school board, attorney for the city of Covington, attorney for Kenton County, and state senator (1857–65). In 1861, in the absence of a lieutenant governor, he was chosen by the Senate as its speaker, and therefore next in line to the governorship. Because he was a Republican and a staunch Union man, he was unacceptable to Governor Beriah Magoffin, a pro-Southern Democrat, who wished to resign. In an ingenious series of maneuvers, Fisk resigned as speaker, James F. Robinson was elected speaker, Magoffin announced his resignation, Robinson became governor, and Fisk was once more elected speaker. When he left the Senate in 1865, he resumed his law practice in Covington. In 1868, he and his son, Charles H., formed a partnership that lasted until 1890 when he retired from active life. He died in Covington on February 21, 1902.

Fisk, Robert (1811–81), the son of Henry and Martha Fisk, was born in Monroe County, Virginia, on November 30, 1811. In his childhood his family moved to Montgomery County, Kentucky, where he grew up under the watchful care of pious Methodist parents. He joined the Methodist Church as a seeker a few days before his conversion at the age of sixteen. Shortly thereafter he felt the call to preach and in 1835 the Kentucky Conference admitted him on trial into the traveling ministry. He was ordained deacon in 1836 and elder in

1838. During his years in the Kentucky Conference he held the following appointments: Port William (1835–36), Georgetown (1836–37), New Castle (1837–38), Burksville (1838–40), Scottsville (1840–41), Lawrenceburg (1841–42), Princeton (1842–43), Franklin (1843–44), Logan (1844–45), and Cadiz (1845–46). When the church divided he adhered to the Methodist Episcopal Church, South, and for the next thirty years he accepted the following charges from the Louisville Conference: Owensboro (1846–47), Hartford (1847–48), Glasgow (1848–49), Elkton (1849–50), supernumerary (1850–51), Empire Iron Works (1851–53), Greenville (1853–54), presiding elder Glasgow District (1854–58), presiding elder Elizabethtown District (1858–60), Franklin (1860–62), Russellville Circuit (1862–63), Louisville Circuit (1863–65), Elkton (1865–66), Henderson Circuit (1866–67), superannuated (1867–70), Logan Circuit (1870–71), supernumerary (1871–72), Cave Spring Circuit (1872–73), Auburn Circuit (1873–74), and Henryville Circuit (1874–77). George Dick was at his side when he died in Russellville, Kentucky, on April 8, 1881. "Like the pure gold, the more he was tried the truer he was found."

Fitzgerald, Bishop Oscar Penn (1829–1911) was born in Caswell County, North Carolina, on August 24, 1829. At the age of fourteen, having been educated in neighborhood schools, he went to Lynchburg, Virginia, where he worked for seven years in the newspaper office of the *Weekly Republican.* In 1850 he returned to North Carolina where he taught for a year at a private school in Rockingham County before accepting another newspaper job, this time with the *Richmond* (Va.) *Examiner.* Two years later he moved on to Macon, Georgia, to work on the *Telegraph,* an influential states' rights newspaper. Shortly after reaching Macon he was stricken with typhoid fever, and upon recovering, yielded to the conviction that he ought to preach the gospel. In 1854 the Georgia Conference of Methodist Episcopal Church, South, admitted him on trial into the itinerant ministry and assigned him as junior preacher to Trinity Church, Savannah. The following year, in response to an appeal from Bishop Andrew, he transferred to the Pacific Conference. Shortly before his departure in 1855 he married Sarah Banks of Georgia. During the next three years he preached in the mining camps and elsewhere along the Pacific coast. In 1858 he was unexpectedly chosen as editor of the *Pacific Methodist,* a position he held until 1867 when he was elected state superintendent of public instruction for California on the Democratic ticket. Failing of reelection in 1871 he returned to the pastorate and filled the important stations of Stockton and Santa Rosa. In 1878, one year after he had undertaken the publication of his own *Fitzgerald's Home Newspaper,* the general conference of the Methodist Episcopal Church, South, elected him editor of the *Christian Advocate,* the official organ of the denomination. He served as editor until 1890 when the general conference elected him bishop, a position he actively filled until 1902 when he requested superannuation. He died at Monteagle, Tennessee, on August 5, 1911. "Often times he got over a difficulty by the free use of his never-failing humor; and in great emergencies he did not hesitate to fall back on prayer and song."

Ford, Henry Melville (1824–97) was the son of a medical doctor, Robert C. Ford, who practiced in Halifax County, Virginia. During a visit of Dr. Ford's wife, Margarita Smith, to relatives in Illinois, Henry was born on December 18, 1824. Several years after his father's death in 1826 his mother removed to Simpson County, Kentucky. Since there was no Methodist Church in the neighborhood in which they settled, they joined the Cumberland Presbyterian Church. Young Henry attended school in Princeton, Kentucky, finishing his studies in 1849. In the same year he married Jane Elizabeth Smith of Warren County, Kentucky. In response to a call to preach he entered the ministry of the Cumberland Presbyterian Church, filling some of their best charges. After several years of painful struggle, he became convinced that the Arminian theology as taught by the Methodist Church was more in harmony with the Scriptures than the Calvinistic views of his own church. Accordingly, in 1860, he joined the Louisville Conference of the

Methodist Episcopal Church, South. It was generally recognized that he had few, if any, equals as an expounder of the Scriptures. In recognition of his scholarship, Trinity College (North Carolina) conferred the Doctor of Divinity degree on him. During his thirty-four years in the Louisville Conference he held the following appointments: Owensboro (1860–61), Lafayette (1861–62), Bowling Green Circuit (1862–63), Henderson (1863–65), Owensboro (1865–67), Lebanon and Springfield (1867–68), Logan (1868–69), presiding elder Russellville District (1869–73), presiding elder Princeton District (1873–74), Franklin (1874–75), Henderson (1875–76), Shelby Street (Louisville, 1876–77), Elizabethtown (1877–79), presiding elder Lebanon District (1879–82), presiding elder Bowling Green District (1882–86), presiding elder Owensboro District (1882–86), Fairview (1889–90), and superannuated (1890–97). He also served for a number of years as a member of the Louisville Conference Board of Education and as a trustee of Logan Female College. He died at the home of his son, William S. Ford, in Corbin, Kentucky, on July 14, 1897. "In his most intimate friendships he opened his heart fully and therein was to be found the background of a humane and manly character."

Forrest, Nathan Bedford (1821–77), eldest son of William and Marian Beck Forrest, was born in Bedford (now Marshall) County, Tennessee, on July 13, 1821. When he was thirteen years old his father removed to Mississippi, where, after his father's death in 1837, he assumed responsibility for a large family. Despite the lack of a formal education he nonetheless acquired a substantial fortune as a slave dealer and in cotton plantations in Mississippi and Arkansas. In 1845 he married Mary Ann Montgomery and four years later he settled in Memphis. When the Civil War came he enlisted as a private in the 7th Tennessee Cavalry and raised and equipped at his own expense a battalion of troops that elected him lieutenant colonel in October 1861. After he captured a Union garrison at Murfreesboro, Tennessee, in July 1862, he was promoted to brigadier general and began the series of raids against Union communications that established his fame as a cavalry leader. Many military critics consider him the foremost cavalry officer ever produced in America. He was promoted to major general after the battle of Chickamauga in 1863 and to lieutenant general in February 1865. Superior forces finally overwhelmed him at Selma, Alabama, in April 1865. After the war he returned to the life of a planter and was for some years president of the Selma, Marion, and Memphis Railroad. He died in Memphis on October 29, 1877.

Foster, Bishop Randolph Sinks (1820–1903), the son of Israel and Polly Kain Foster, was born in Williamsburg, Clermont County, Ohio, on February 22, 1820. In his youth his family moved to Kentucky where he attended Augusta College in Bracken County, but on the advice of some friends who considered him a gifted boy preacher he withdrew in his sophomore year and in September 1837 he joined the Ohio Conference of the Methodist Episcopal Church. He soon acquired an enviable reputation as a preacher, but it was during his pastorate at Wesley Chapel in Cincinnati (1848–50) where he ably defended the doctrine of Arminian Methodism against the attack of N. L. Rice, a noted Presbyterian preacher, that he became famous. In 1850 he transferred to Mulberry Street Church, New York, and except for three years (1857–60) as president of Northwestern University, he spent the next eighteen years in and about New York in such appointments as Greene Street, Eighteenth Street, Washington Square, Trinity, Sing Sing, and Pacific Street. In 1868 he became professor of systematic theology at Drew Theological Seminary and served as its president during 1870–72. He found training young men for the ministry highly gratifying and it was with considerable reluctance that he accepted his election as bishop by the General Conference of 1872. During his twenty-four years in that office he was at times accused of harshness and arbitrariness in the exercise of episcopal power. He was a voluminous writer. Among his books were: *The Nature and Blessedness of Christian Purity* (1851), *Philosophy of*

Christian Experience (1890), and *Studies in Theology* (six volumes, 1889–99). He died in Newton Center, Massachusetts, on May 1, 1903.

Fraser, Alexander G. (1843–1924) was born on September 18, 1843. He was converted under the ministry of James C. Petree (who at that time held an appointment to Hopkinsville and Elkton, Kentucky) on June 30, 1864, at night on horseback as he was returning home from church. He received a call to preach on January 22, 1865, but he was not licensed until June 1869. Three months later the Louisville Conference of the Methodist Episcopal Church, South, admitted him on trial. He was ordained deacon by Bishop Marvin in 1872 and elder by Bishop Wightman in 1874. On November 1, 1876, he married Josie Hodges who bore him three children. During his thirty-seven years of active ministry he served the following charges: Cave City (1869–70), Shepherdsville (1870–71), Hudsonville Circuit (1871–72), Todd Circuit (1872–73), Brownsville Mission (1873–75), Belmont Circuit (1875–76), Shepherdsville (1876–77), Long Grove (1877–78), Brownsville (1878–79), Rockport (1879–81), Spottsville (1881–82), Hardin Springs (1882–84), Constantine (1884–85), Green Hill (1885–86), Morgantown (1886–88), Bonnieville (1888–90), Constantine (1890–92), Cerulean Springs (1892–93), Greenville Circuit (1893–94), Bowling Green Circuit (1894–96), Upton (1896–98), Munfordville (1898–99), Morgantown (1899–1901), Franklin Circuit (1901–03), and Canmer (1903–06). After eighteen years as superannuate he died in Bowling Green, Kentucky, on August 7, 1924. During his ministry he is reported to have witnessed 2000 conversions and 1900 additions to the church. It is said that he read the Bible through 37 times and the New Testament 110 times. "He spent much time in prayer and fasting."

Fremont, John Charles (1813–90), son of Jean Charles Fremon, a French emigre schoolteacher, and Ann Beverly Whiting, estranged wife of John Pryor, was born in Savannah, Georgia, on January 21, 1813.

(He later altered the spelling of his name to Fremont.) After his father's death in 1818, his mother moved to Charleston, South Carolina, where he attended the College of Charleston from 1829 until his expulsion in 1831. After spending some time as a teacher of mathematics aboard the sloop of war, *Natchez,* he received in 1838 an appointment as an army topographical engineer and accompanied an expedition conducted by J. N. Nicollet for exploring the region between the upper Mississippi and Missouri rivers. He then went to Washington where on October 19, 1841, he married sixteen-year-old Jessie Benton, despite the objections of her father, Thomas Hart Benton, U.S. senator from Missouri. During 1842–46 he led three important expeditions through the American West and played a leading part in the conquest of California. In 1850 he was elected to a one-year term as U.S. senator from California. As a result of his activities, "the Pathfinder" became a national hero and in 1856 he became the presidential candidate of the newly formed Republican Party. After his defeat by James Buchanan he returned to California where he engaged in mining until the outbreak of the Civil War when President Lincoln appointed him major general in the regular army. From then until his resignation on June 4, 1864, he was a controversial figure, shunted from command to command. On May 31, 1864, he was nominated for president by radical Republicans opposed to Lincoln, but he withdrew on September 22. By the autumn of 1864 he had lost his California holdings and for the rest of his life he was to some extent dependent on the literary endeavors of his wife. He served as territorial governor of Arizona from 1878–87 after which he settled in California. During a visit to New York City he died on July 13, 1890.

Frogge, Timothy Carpenter (1821–99), the son of Cornelius and Deborah Carpenter Frogge, and a grandson of the Rev. Timothy Carpenter, one of the pioneer preachers who helped to plant Methodism in Kentucky and Tennessee, was born on April 21, 1821, on Wolf River in Fentress County, Tennessee. He was converted in August 1837 at a camp meeting conducted

by the Cumberland Presbyterians at Popular Cove, eight miles from his home. A few days later he felt the call to preach and on September 18, 1837, he joined the Methodist Church. The quarterly conference of the Albany Circuit licensed him to preach in August 1840. Three years later the Kentucky Conference admitted him on trial. He was ordained deacon by Bishop Andrew in 1845 and elder by Bishop Paine in 1847. During his brief affiliation with the Kentucky Conference he preached in Columbia (1843–44), Greensburg (1844–45), and Wayne (1845–46). When the Methodist Church divided in 1845, he cast his lot with the Methodist Episcopal Church, South, and accepted the following appointments from the Louisville Conference after its formation in 1846: Albany (1846–47), Nealsville Mission (1847–48), Bowling Green (1848–49), Scottsville (1849–51), Franklin (1851–53), Hartford (1853–55), Greenville Circuit (1855–57), Bowling Green Circuit (1857–59), Russellville Circuit (1859–61), Bowling Green (1861–62), presiding elder Bowling Green District (1862–65), presiding elder Hopkinsville District (1865–69), presiding elder Henderson District (1869–73), presiding elder Columbia District (1873–77), Auburn (1877–78), Lewisburg (1878–82), Bowling Green Circuit (1882–83), Rich Pond (1883–86), Smith's Grove (1886–87), Lewisburg (1887–91), Sharon Grove (1891–93), and Gold City Circuit (1893–94). Five years later he died at his son's home on the old homestead on Muddy River, three miles east of Russellville, Kentucky, on November 28, 1899. He married twice, first in January 1847 to Harriet C. Wilson of Albany, Kentucky, who died at Hartford, Kentucky, in 1855. She bore him four children, two of whom died in infancy. On May 8, 1857, he married Mrs. Sarah Duncan Pillow by whom he had two children, one dying in infancy. She preceded him in death by one year. Though apparently an able preacher, Frogge was not popular with the masses. In response to the complaint that he preached too short and spoke too low, he replied: "I preach short that I may preach long; I preach slow that I may preach fast; I preach low that I may preach loud."

Fuqua, James H. (1836–1920) was born in Logan County, Kentucky, on September 27, 1836. His father, James Monroe Fuqua, a native of Buckingham County, Virginia, and one of twenty-four children, spent most of his adult life in agricultural pursuits. His mother, Lucy A. Williams Fuqua, whose ancestors also came from Virginia, was born in Franklin County, Kentucky. When he was but three years old his family moved to Tennessee where he received his early educational training. At the age of eighteen he attended Bethel College, a Baptist school for men, in Russellville, Kentucky. Immediately after his graduation with honors in 1858, he became principal of the preparatory department of the college. On July 8, 1859, he married Martha Ann Walker, daughter of the eminent physician, Algernon Sidney Walker of Scottsville, Kentucky. She bore him three children. In 1863, shortly after he was elected to the chair of mathematics in Bethel College, military authorities took over the school and made it into a hospital. He immediately took his family to Olmstead, Kentucky, and established the celebrated Browder Institute on land donated by George Dick's uncle, Richard. He continued as principal for twelve years and played an important role in educating more than six hundred boys and girls. In 1875 he was elected president of Liberty Female College at Glasgow, Kentucky. Five years later he returned to Bethel College to occupy the chair of Latin and Greek. When the president of Bethel College, Leslie Waggoner, resigned to accept a position at the University of Texas, Fuqua was the unanimous choice to succeed him. He was an immensely popular teacher and administrator; to his boys he was always known as "Skippy." In 1903 he was elected to a four-year term as state superintendent of public instruction, after which he returned to Bethel College once more as professor of mathematics. He died in Russellville on February 18, 1920.

Garfield, James Abram (1831–81), son of Abram and Eliza Ballou Garfield, was born in Cuyohoga County, Ohio, on November 19, 1831. When his father died two years later, it fell to his mother to provide a livelihood for him and three older siblings.

He attended Western Reserve Eclectic Institute (later Hiram College), joined the Disciples of Christ Church, and worked his way through Williams College, graduating in 1856. He then returned to Ohio as teacher and principal of the Institute at Hiram (1857–61). On November 11, 1858, he married Lucretia Rudolph, his childhood sweetheart, who bore him five children. In 1859 he was elected to the Ohio Senate as a Republican. During the Civil War he served with distinction in engagements at Middle Creek (Kentucky), Shiloh, and Chickamauga. His military successes made him a popular political figure in northeastern Ohio and in December 1863 he took his seat in the Thirty-Eighth Congress. He was reelected eight times. In 1880, despite the charge of corruption in connection with the Credit Mobile scandal, the Ohio legislature elected him to the U.S. Senate for the term beginning in 1881. As it turned out, politics at the national level preempted his senatorial career. When a deadlock over the presidential nomination developed at the Republican Convention of 1880, the delegates on the thirty-sixth ballot finally settled on Garfield as their candidate; in the presidential contest that followed he narrowly defeated the Democratic nominee, Winfield Scott Hancock. After a brief presidency in which much of his time was taken up with political battles over appointments and patronage, he was shot in the Washington railroad station on July 2, 1881, by a disappointed office-seeker. After lingering for nearly two months, he died on September 19.

Gatewood, John J. (1830–1907), son of Fletcher and Mary Calvert Gatewood, was born in Allen County, Kentucky, on November 8, 1830. He was educated in neighborhood schools and attended college in Scottsville, Kentucky. Immediately after leaving school he was appointed deputy sheriff of Allen County, resigning in 1853 to study law. In 1855 he was admitted to the bar. Later that year, on November 13, he married Fannie Burton of Allen County who bore him seven children. He soon entered politics. In 1858 he began a four-year term as county attorney. He then spent four years in the lower house of the

Kentucky legislature. In 1871 he was elected to the first of two terms in the state senate where he introduced an amendment to abolish the whipping post in Kentucky. After leaving the senate in 1875, he returned to his law practice in Allen County where he died on July 13, 1907.

Gilliam, John Davis (1842–1926), son of James and Eliza Gilliam, was born in Allen County, Kentucky, on August 3, 1842. His education was limited to the neighborhood schools of his day. On February 16, 1859, when not yet seventeen years of age, he married Eliza A. Russell who bore him two children, one of whom, John H. Gilliam, achieved notoriety as a judge and prominent jurist in Kentucky. On June 5, 1900, he married a second time to Olivia Pearl Griggs who survived him. When the Civil War broke out he enlisted in the Union army as a private. Four years later he was mustered out as a captain of the Fifty-second Kentucky Mounted Infantry. After the war he gave considerable attention to civic and political affairs. He served two full terms as the elected sheriff of Allen County, after which he served one term as county judge. Despite his political successes he could not resist the call to the full-time ministry, a call he had experienced soon after his conversion in his early manhood. Accordingly in 1880 he joined the Louisville Conference of the Methodist Episcopal Church, South, and received his first appointment as an itinerant preacher. For the next thirty years he served the following charges: Gradyville (1880–81), Auburn (1881–83), presiding elder Gosport District (1883–84), Burkesville (1884–85), presiding elder Columbia District (1885–87), presiding elder Gosport District (1887–88), New Roe (1888–90), Woodburn (1890–91), presiding elder Columbia District (1891–93), Scottsville (1893–94), Conference Colporteur (1894–98), Scottsville (1898–99), Fountain Run (1899–1900), Canmer (1900–01), Glasgow (1901–05), Canmer (1905–07), South Scottsville (1907–09), and Smith's Grove (1909–11). He lived out the last fifteen years of his life in Scottsville where he died on December 23, 1926. "No man has labored among us who was held in higher esteem by his brethren in the ministry, or who was more ardently loved in the homes to which he had ministered during the days of his active labors."

Golladay, Jacob Shall (1819–87) was born on January 19, 1819, in Lebanon, Wilson County, Tennessee, where his father, Isaac, was a merchant of Huguenot descent. At the age of nineteen he entered the wholesale store of Saunders and Martin in Nashville, Tennessee. He worked there until 1845 when he moved to Logan County, Kentucky, and made a living as a farmer and merchant. He married Elizabeth Cheatham of Nashville in 1848; she bore him five children. In 1851 he was elected as a Whig to the lower house of the Kentucky legislature and in 1853 to the state senate. He was elected in 1867 as a Democrat to the U.S. House of Representatives from Kentucky's Third District to fill a vacancy caused by the death of Elijah Hise of Russellville. In 1868 he was re-elected, but resigned on February 28, 1870, after the Military Committee of the House acquitted him of the charge of having sold a cadetship. He sought election to Congress once more in 1872 but was defeated when his district went Republican for the first time in history. He then retired from public life and practiced law in Allensville and Russellville until his death near Russellville on May 20, 1887.

Goodson, Jacob Peck (1822–95), the son of Joseph and Ann Peck Goodson, and a cousin of Walter Q. Gresham who became U.S. secretary of state, was born on February 4, 1822, in Washington County, Indiana. He was converted at the age of ten. In his youth he moved to Louisville where he worked at steamboat building. During these years he also served as a local preacher and in house-to-house visitation among the sick and needy. In 1846 he enlisted in the army as a volunteer soldier in the Mexican War, winning distinction in several battles, especially in holding, along with only eight companions, an important mountain pass against a large detachment of Mexicans. He was admitted into the Louisville Conference of the Methodist Episcopal Church, South, in 1851, and became one of its most successful circuit preachers. Under his ministry thousands were converted and added to the church. He also put his mechanical skills to good use. Wherever he served he improved or repaired the church buildings and parsonages, and with his own hands, with little assistance from others, he built one of the important churches in the city of Louisville. He was twice married, first to Ellen Deering who lived only a few years, and then to Rebecca Morrison who bore him five children. During his forty-four years in the Louisville Conference he held the following appointments: Tompkinsville (1851–53), Albany (1853–55), Scottsville Circuit (1855–1857), Columbia (1857–1859), Portland (1859–61), City Mission (Louisville, 1861–63), Middletown Circuit (1863–64), Jeffersontown (1864–66), Glasgow Circuit (1866–67), Logan (1867–68), Jeffersontown (1868–71), Portland (1871–73), Jefferson Street (Louisville, 1873–75), Louisville Circuit (1876–77), Shelby Street (Louisville, 1877–79), Caverna (1879–80), East Louisville Mission (1880–82), Allensville (1882–83), Hardinsburg (1883–87), Slaughtersville (1887–90), Hawesville (1890–92), and Louisville Circuit (1892–95). Though feeble during his last years, he continued in the itinerant ranks and on the effective list to the end. He preached twice on the day he died, July 28, 1895. "His preaching was plain, but sound and vigorous, and accompanied with an unction that was always persuasive, and sometimes overwhelming."

Granberry, Bishop John Cowper (1829–1907), the son of Richard A. and Ann Leslie Granberry, was born in Norfolk, Virginia, on December 5, 1829. Converted at the age of fifteen and called to preach shortly thereafter, he attended Randolph-Macon College from which he graduated in 1848. In the same year he joined the Virginia Conference of the Methodist Episcopal Church, South, and for the next twelve years he accepted the following appointments: Eastville (1848–49), Farmville (1849–50), Lynchburg (1850–52), supernumerary (1852–53), Loudon (1853–54), Randolph-Macon and Boydton (1854–56), Charlottesville (1856–57), supernumerary (1857–58), Washington,

D.C. (1858–59), and chaplain, University of Virginia (1859–61). When the Civil War came he served in the Confederate army as chaplain, 11th Regiment, Virginia Volunteers (1861–63), missionary to the Army Corps in northern Virginia (1863–64), and as superintendent of missionaries in the Army of Northern Virginia (1864–65). During the course of the conflict he was severely wounded and lost an eye. After the war he returned to preaching and held the following charges: Market Street (Petersburg, 1865–68), Centenary (Richmond, 1868–72), and Broad Street (Richmond, 1872–75). He spent the next seven years teaching at Vanderbilt University where he was affectionately known as "Old Granny." George Dick's sons, Robert and Hanson, were among his students. The General Conference of 1882 elected him bishop and for the next twenty years, until his retirement in 1902, he worked diligently to advance the missionary program of his church. He also published several books, including *Bible Dictionary* (1885) and *Experience: the Crowning Evidence of the Christian Religion* (1900). He spent his last years in Ashland, Virginia, where he died on April 1, 1907.

Grant, Ulysses Simpson (1822–85), son of Jesse Root and Hannah Simpson Grant, was born in Point Pleasant, Ohio, on April 22, 1822. He was baptized as Hiram Ulysses, but when he received an appointment to West Point in 1839, the congressman who nominated him reported his name as Ulysses Simpson. He graduated in 1843, 21st in a class of 39, and rendered distinguished service during the Mexican War. He then served for seven years in the Pacific Northwest where alcohol became a problem for him. After a warning from his company commander he resigned from the army on July 31, 1854, and spent the next six years unsuccessfully as a farmer, real estate salesman, customhouse clerk, and clerk in a leather store owned by his two brothers in Galena, Illinois. With the coming of the Civil War his career started upward. Few army officers in American history have achieved such rapid advancement from relative obscurity. On June 17, 1861, he was appointed colonel of the 21st Illinois regiment. Two months later he was promoted to brigadier general of volunteers and placed in command at Cairo, Illinois, from which he launched his assault on Forts Henry and Donelson. Their surrender in February 1862 won for him vast stretches of Confederate territory, the acclaim of the nation, the sobriquet "Unconditional Surrender," and promotion to major general of volunteers. After his victories at Shiloh (1862) and Vicksburg (1863), he was appointed major general in the regular army. Late in 1863 he was given a gold medal, the thanks of Congress, and supreme command of the armies of the United States with revived rank of lieutenant general for driving the Confederates from Missionary Ridge and raising the siege of Chattanooga. He then moved east to face General Robert E. Lee. In a campaign of attrition (Wilderness, Spotsylvania, and Cold Harbor) during May 5– June 3, 1864, he wore down Lee's resistance and, finally, by capturing Petersburg forced Lee's surrender at Appomattox, Virginia, on April 9, 1865. After the war Congress revived the rank of full general, unused since the days of Washington, and conferred it on him. He had little difficulty winning the presidency in 1868. Reelected in 1872, his second administration was scandal-ridden. After leaving the presidency he toured Europe for two years with his family and returned home to a life saddened by want, financial misfortune, and agonizing illness. In his last months he wrote his memoirs, which were published by Mark Twain and earned nearly $450,000 for his family. Racked by throat cancer, he died in Mount McGregor, New York, on July 23, 1885, and was buried in a granite mausoleum in New York City.

Grubbs, Thomas Henry (1820–77) was born in Russellville, Kentucky, on July 1, 1820. His father, Colonel Thomas H. Grubbs, moved from Hanover County, Virginia, to Kentucky in 1808 and by 1812 had settled in Russellville where he became a prominent builder and contractor. After his graduation from Russellville Academy in 1840, young Thomas chose a career in medicine. He studied under Drs. Withers and Wilson, attended a course of lectures at the University of Louisville in 1841, and then returned to Russellville to establish his practice. It was said of him that "he did not sit down and wait a year or two for a beginning, but began at once." He married Martha Duncan of Logan County in 1848; she bore him four children. In 1856 he took a course of lectures at the University of Nashville from which he received his diploma. He was admitted to the American Medical Society in 1858. During the Civil War he served as post surgeon of the U.S. General Hospital at Russellville. He died on June 22, 1877, at his home in Russellville of rheumatism of the heart, after two hours confinement to his bed.

Hall, Edwin Walter (1838–89) was born in Jefferson County, New York, on March 1, 1838. After his conversion in Fulton, New York, at the age of twenty, he entered Genesee and Wyoming Seminary at Alexander, New York. Shortly after his graduation in 1863, he married Sarah T. Trowbridge of Lima, New York, who bore him two children. He also accepted the position of principal and teacher of the high school at Watertown, New York, during 1863– 64. Over the next twenty-five years he compiled a distinguished record as president of a number of colleges, including: Greenville College, Greenville, Kentucky (1864–69); Macon College, Macon, Missouri (1869–72), Chaddock College, Quincy, Illinois (1872–78); Cazenovia Seminary, Cazenovia, New York (1878– 80); and Greenville College again (1880– 89). During his last appointment he joined the Louisville Conference of the Methodist Episcopal Church, South. After a brief illness, he died of pneumonia at his home in Greenville on February 27, 1889.

Halsell, John Edward (1826–99), the son of William and Mary Garland Halsell, was born at Rich Pond near Bowling Green, Warren County, Kentucky, on September 11, 1826. He attended neighborhood schools and Cumberland University, Lebanon, Tennessee. He then studied law in the office of Garland J. Blewitt of Bowling Green and returned to Cumberland University to complete his legal studies; in 1856 he was admitted to the bar and set up his practice. Shortly thereafter he became active in local politics and held the following elective offices: prosecuting attorney for Bowling Green (1856–60), trustee of Bowling Green (1866–70), and circuit judge of Kentucky's fourth judicial district during the 1870s. In 1883 he was elected to the first of two terms as a member of the U.S. House of Representatives. Unsuccessful in his bid for renomination in 1887, he returned to Bowling Green to resume his legal practice. After serving as mayor from 1888 to 1899, he moved to Ft. Worth, Texas, where he died on December 26, 1899. In 1849 he married Sarah A. Smith of Warren County, Kentucky. After her death he married in 1872 Mrs. Mary A. Gossom, daughter of Monroe Tucker, a wealthy farmer of Warren County; she died on July 4, 1874. For over thirty years he was a member of the Cumberland Presbyterian Church.

Hanner, John Wesley (1810–95) was born in North Carolina in 1810. He was converted in early boyhood and joined the Methodist Church. In 1828 he was licensed to preach; the following year the Tennessee Conference admitted him on trial in the itinerant ministry. During the next fifteen years he rose rapidly in the conference and filled the pulpits of some of the largest and most influential churches, including those in Huntsville, Alabama, and Clarksville and Nashville, Tennessee. Most of his remaining active years were spent as presiding elder of the following districts: Nashville (1844–48), Clarksville (1848–52), Franklin (1852–56), Clarksville (1856–59), Lebanon (1861–67), Nashville (1869–73), and Murfreesboro (1873–75). It was during his first term as presiding elder of the Clarksville District that he performed the marriage of George Dick to Ann Elizabeth Warfield on September 5, 1850. In 1875 he suffered a blow from which he apparently never recovered. For some unexplained reason the minutes of the Tennessee Annual Conference for 1875 record the following painful entries: "Question 20. Are all the preachers blameless in life and administration? Their names were called over, one by one, and their characters examined and passed, except that of J. W. Hanner, Sr., who was suspended from the office of the Christian ministry in the Methodist Episcopal Church, South." He was listed as

supernumerary from 1875 to 1882, and as superannuated from 1882 until his death in Clarksville, Tennessee, on October 20, 1895. "His great soul was a thousand leagues above all personal and petty strife. When he was reviled he reviled not again."

Hardison, Philip T. (1834–1904), son of John and Mary Browning Hardison, was born near Madisonville in Hopkins County, Kentucky, on December 19, 1834. As a young man he experienced a conversion that "was clear and bright, as was common among the Methodists in those days." When he was grown, his parents moved to Todd County, Kentucky. He married Mary McCown on December 7, 1858. In 1860 he joined the Louisville Conference of the Methodist Episcopal Church, South, and for the next thirty-nine years he held the following appointments: Cliftry Mission (1860–61), Albany (1861–62), Scottsville (1862–63), Princeton (1863–64), Marion (1864–66), Calhoun Circuit (1866–68), Madisonville (1868–70), Cadiz (1870–74), Bowling Green Circuit (1874–77), Princeton and Mt. Zion (1877–78), Smith's Grove (1878–79), Greenville Circuit (1879–80), Franklin Circuit (1880–82), Caverna (1882–84), Elkton (1884–86), Allensville (1886–88), presiding elder Gosport District (1888–90), Glasgow (1890–92), Leitchfield (1892–94), Cadiz (1894–96), Marion (1896–97), and Hodgenville (1898–99) after which he was superannuated until his death at his home in Hodgenville on November 14, 1904. "More than most men he craved confidence and affection . . . especially from his brethren of the Conference, and any apparent lack was distinctly and painfully disappointing."

Hargrove, Bishop Robert Kennon (1829–1905), the son of Daniel J. and Laodicea Hargrove, was born on a cotton plantation in Pickens County, Alabama, on September 17, 1829. After attending a neighborhood school and receiving college preparatory training at an academy in nearby Franconia, he entered the University of Alabama from which he graduated in 1852. He spent the next five years teaching mathematics at his alma mater. In 1857 he accepted the call to preach, joined the

Alabama Conference of the Methodist Episcopal Church, South, and spent the next ten years on the circuit and on stations, as chaplain in the Confederate army, and as president of Centenary Institute, Summerfield, Alabama. He then moved on to Tennessee where he spent seven years as president of a female college in Franklin and eight years as pastor and presiding elder. In 1882 the general conference of his church elected him bishop. In that office he played important roles in rescuing the publishing house from financial ruin, promoting foreign missions, and fostering improved relations with the Methodist Episcopal Church, North. When Bishop Holland N. McTyeire died in 1889, he succeeded him as president of Vanderbilt University. In 1852 he married Harriet C. Scott, who died in 1894; a year later, on June 30, 1895, he married Mrs. Ruth E. Scarritt. He died in Nashville on August 4, 1905.

Harrison, William Pope (1830–95) was born in Savannah, Georgia, on September 3, 1830. His formal schooling was meager, but he took advantage of every opportunity for acquiring knowledge. In 1850 the Georgia Conference of the Methodist Episcopal Church, South, admitted him on trial into the itinerant ministry. Two years later he transferred to the Alabama Conference; among his assignments in the years before the Civil War was a two-year hitch as principal of Auburn Female College. He returned to Georgia to preach in Columbus (1863–65) and in Atlanta (1865–77). He was chaplain of the U.S. House of Representatives for one year (1878) after which he held pastorates in Baltimore, Maryland, Washington, D.C., and Winchester, Virginia. He devoted his last years to editorial work and writing, having prepared himself over the years by reading widely and studying deeply in such fields as theology, history, science, and foreign languages. He served as editor of the *New Monthly Magazine* during its brief existence in 1871. In 1882 the general conference of his church elected him book editor, a position he held until 1894. After 1886 he also edited the *Quarterly Review*. Among his books were: *The Living Christ* (1883), *The High-Churchman Disarmed* (1886), and

Methodist Union (1892). He died at Columbus, Georgia, on February 7, 1895.

Hayes, George H. (1831–1912), the son of William and Sarah Hayes, was born near Richmond, Virginia, on May 26, 1831. When he was three years old his parents moved to Kentucky and settled near Brandenburg where he was raised. At the age of twenty he joined the Louisville Conference of the Methodist Episcopal Church, South. He was ordained deacon by Bishop Capers in 1853 and elder by Bishop Paine in 1855. On September 6, 1855, he married Hannah T. Kinchloe of Hardinsburg, Kentucky, a marriage that lasted for fifty-seven years. During his fifty years of active ministry he held the following appointments: Leitchfield (1851–53), Henderson (1853–55), Smithland (1855–56), Glasgow (1856–57), Bowling Green (1857–58), superannuated (1858–61), Morganfield (1861–62), Yelvington (1862–64), Hartford (1864–66), Hawesville Circuit (1866–67), Bradfordsville (1867–69), presiding elder Bardstown District (1869–71), presiding elder Elizabethtown District (1871–73), presiding elder Lebanon District (1873–75), presiding elder Henderson District (1875–79), presiding elder Owensboro District (1879–80), presiding elder Henderson District (1880–81), Owensboro (1881–82), Cloverport (1882–83), presiding elder Henderson District (1883–87), presiding elder Russellville District (1887–91), presiding elder Henderson District (1891–95), presiding elder Owensboro District (1895–97), and presiding elder Henderson District (1897–1901). His thirty years as presiding elder was a record unmatched in the history of the Louisville Conference. Early in his ministry he established a reputation as an effective defender of Methodist doctrines and his services were in demand beyond the borders of his own conference. He spent the last eleven years of his life in Henderson, Kentucky, where he died on March 24, 1912. "Into a section naturally hostile to Methodism he went with battle-axe and sword and not only silenced the shouts of her enemies but conquered a peace which abides to this day."

Hayes, Rutherford Birchard (1822–93), son of Rutherford and Sophia Birchard Hayes, was born on October 4, 1822, at Delaware, Ohio. His father died before he was born; consequently his uncle, Sardis Birchard, looked after him and helped pay for his education. He attended an academy at Norwalk, Ohio, and the private school of Isaac Webb at Middleton, Connecticut, after which he enrolled in Kenyon College, Gambier, Ohio, graduating in 1842. After a year and a half at Harvard Law School he returned to Ohio where he was admitted to the bar and began his legal practice at Fremont, near Sandusky, in 1845, removing to Cincinnati in 1850. By 1852 he had saved enough money to marry his childhood sweetheart, Lucy Webb, who bore him eight children. Entering the local politics of Cincinnati he was elected city solicitor in 1858, but the Civil War temporarily interrupted his ambitions. He served during the entire war, rising from the rank of major in the Ohio volunteers to major general of volunteers in the U.S. Army. After the conflict he resumed his public career. He won election to the U.S. House of Representatives (1865–67) and to three terms as governor of Ohio (1867, 1869, 1875). In 1876 the Republicans nominated him for the presidency. Although the Democratic candidate, Samuel J. Tilden, received a larger popular vote, a special electoral commission awarded all of the electoral votes of four disputed states to Hayes, thereby giving him the victory by one electoral vote. His administration was notable for ending military reconstruction in the South, initiating modest efforts at civil service reform, and for pursuing conservative labor and monetary policies. His refusal to serve alcoholic beverages in the White House earned for his wife the sobriquet, "Lemonade Lucy." Upon leaving the presidency he returned to Ohio where he devoted a great deal of time to his extensive library and to humanitarian causes such as the National Prison Association, the Peabody Education Fund, and the Slater Fund. He died on January 17, 1893.

Hayes, William Cook (1850–1917), son of Jesse Henry and Sarah Cook Hayes, was born near Union Star, Breckinridge County, Kentucky, on April 15, 1850. His father died in 1853; consequently it fell to his mother to provide for the family and to encourage their attendance in the neighborhood public schools. William completed two years of high school before he was fifteen. He was converted at the age of twenty and joined the Baptist Church; four months later he was licensed to preach. After a course of reading in matters of church doctrine, he concluded that his views were more in harmony with the Methodists. In March 1871 the quarterly conference of the Hudsonville Circuit received him as a local preacher in the Methodist Episcopal Church, South. The following October he was admitted on trial into the Louisville Conference and sent to the Buffalo Circuit where he enjoyed a remarkably successful year. He held a meeting at Little Mount in which there were thirty-four conversions. One of the converts, Mary E. Muir of LaRue County, became his wife on January 1, 1874. He was ordained a deacon by Bishop Keener in 1873 and an elder by Bishop Doggett in 1875. After his Buffalo appointment he preached at Jefferson Street (Louisville) and Portland (1872–73), Greensburg Circuit (1873–74), and Springfield (1874–75) before requesting a transfer to the Kentucky Conference. After serving a year each on the Bryantsville and Somerset circuits, he returned to the Louisville Conference and during the next thirty-four years he accepted the following appointments: Sacramento (1877–78), Slaughtersville (1878–82), Princeton (1882–83), Hartford (1883–84), Allensville (1884–86), Madisonville and Nebo (1886–89), Hodgenville (1889–91), Brandenburg (1891–92), Hawesville (1892–93), Bardstown (1893–95), Robards (1895–96), Owensboro Circuit (1896–97), Greenville (1897–99), Cadiz and Bethel (1899–1901), Hanson (1901–03), LaFayette (1903–04), Smithland (1904–06), Leitchfield (1906–07), Rome (1907–08), South Carrollton (1908–09), Lewisburg (1909–10), and Breckinridge St. (Louisville 1910–11). In 1911 he gave up the itinerant ministry and spent his last years in Greenville, Muhlenberg County, where he died on June 3, 1917. "He had wonderfully fine ideas of sermon building; a delicately sensitive conscience, broad knowledge of the Truth and an unrelaxing hold on God and eternal things."

Haygood, Bishop Atticus Greene (1839–96) was born in Watkinsville, Georgia, on November 19, 1839. His parents, Greene B. and Martha Askew Haygood, were devout Methodists and Atticus was a Christian from childhood. In 1852 his family moved to Atlanta where he attended old Trinity Methodist Church and with his own labor helped to build the new Trinity Church. He enrolled in Emory College in 1855; during his student days he was licensed to preach and regularly held services in the churches around Oxford, Georgia. Just before his graduation in 1859 he married Mollie Yarbrough who bore him four children. In 1860 the Georgia Conference of the Methodist Episcopal Church, South, admitted him on trial into the itinerant ministry and over the next ten years appointed him to the following charges: Columbus (1860–61), Sparta (1861–62), Watkinsville (1862–63), Newman (1863–64), Rome (1864–65), Trinity Church (Atlanta, 1865–67), presiding elder Rome District (1867–68), and presiding elder Atlanta District. In 1870 the general conference elected him Sunday school secretary, a position he held until 1875 when he resigned to become president of Emory College. During his presidency he also edited the *Wesleyan Christian Advocate*. When the general conference elected him bishop in 1882, he declined, preferring to continue as president of Emory. In 1885 he resigned his position to accept the agency of the Slater Fund, which was established to assist needy blacks. During these years he was an articulate advocate of temperance reform in Georgia and the South; during the great campaign for prohibition in Texas in 1888 he engaged in an extensive speaking tour of the state. The general conference elected him bishop once more in 1890. This time he accepted and carried out the duties of his office until he suffered a series of strokes and died on January 19, 1896. He was buried in the little town of Oxford, Georgia, where he began his preaching career. "He struck with manly blows the evils of the times, and struck to destroy."

Hendricks, Thomas Andrew (1819–85), son of John and Jane Thomson Hendricks, was born near Zanesville, Ohio, on September 7, 1819. In 1820 his family moved to Madison, Indiana, and two years later to Shelby County where young Thomas grew up, helping on his father's farm and attending Shelby County Seminary and Greensburg Academy before enrolling in Hanover College. After his graduation in 1841 he read law for a year before entering law school in Chambersburg, Pennsylvania, where an uncle, Judge Thomson, took him under his tutelage. He returned to Shelbyville, Indiana, where he became a very successful lawyer. On September 26, 1845, he married Eliza C. Morgan of Northland, Ohio; their only child, a son, died at the age of three. He soon became active in politics and as a Democrat held the following offices before the Civil War: member of Indiana legislature (1848–51), member of U.S. House of Representatives (1852–54), commissioner of general land office (1855–59), and U.S. senator (1863–69). A staunch conservative, he opposed emancipation, the Thirteenth Amendment, the Freedmen's Bureau Bill, the Civil Rights Act, and the Fourteenth and Fifteenth amendments. After retiring from the Senate he continued active in politics, winning the governorship of Indiana in 1872, running unsuccessfully as the vice-presidential running mate of Samuel J. Tilden in 1876, and winning the vice-presidency under Grover Cleveland in 1884. Nine months after his inauguration he died suddenly at his home in Indianapolis on November 25, 1885.

Hines, Thomas Hunt (1838–98), the son of Warren Walker and Sarah Carson Hines, was born at Woodbury in Butler County, Kentucky, on October 9, 1838. He attended neighborhood schools and also pursued an independent course of studies that prepared him to accept a teaching position at Masonic University in La Grange, Oldham County, in 1859. When the Civil War broke out he joined the Confederate army and eventually became a captain under John Hunt Morgan's command. He achieved fame for his part in planning and leading Morgan and five other officers in their escape from the Ohio

State Prison at Columbus in 1863 and for his role in the abortive attempt to free Confederate prisoners from Camp Douglas in Chicago later in the war. On November 16, 1864, he married Nancy Sproule of Cincinnati who bore him two children. After the war he sought asylum in Canada where he began to study law. He returned to the United States in February 1866, living for a short time in Memphis where he worked on the Memphis *Appeal* and completed his law studies under General Albert Pike. He was admitted to the bar in July 1866. In October 1867 he returned to his native Kentucky and settled in Bowling Green where he briefly edited the Bowling Green *Gazette* and then resigned to devote full time to his legal practice. He entered politics in 1870 when he won election as county judge of Warren County. In 1878, after his election as judge of the Kentucky Court of Appeals, he moved with his family to Frankfort where he lived for the rest of his life. He served on the court of appeals for eight years, the last two as chief justice. After leaving the bench he practiced law in Frankfort until shortly before his death on January 23, 1898.

Hogard, John P. (1830–1912) was born on the Asher Farm, five miles east of Marion in Crittenden County, Kentucky, on January 9, 1830. He was converted early in manhood and joined the Methodist Episcopal Church, South. In 1868 he received a license to preach, and in 1875 the Louisville Conference admitted him on trial into the itinerant ministry. For the next twenty-one years he held the following appointments: Smithland Circuit (1875–76), Princeton Circuit (1876–77), Parkersville (1877–78), Kuttawa (1878–80), Carrsville (1880–81), Shady Grove (1881–82), Lewisburg (1882–84), Richardsville (1884–85), New Roe (1885–86), Monticello (1886–87), Greenville Circuit (1887–88), Hibbardsville (1888–89), Dixon (1889–92), Bradfordsville (1892–93), Beech Grove (1893–95), and Fordsville (1895–97). He was superannuated from 1907 until his death at his home near Marion, Kentucky, on May 24, 1912. His only child, W. F. Hogard, was also a preacher in the Louisville Conference.

Holt, Joseph (1807–94), the oldest of six children of John and Eleanor Stephens Holt, was born in Breckinridge County, Kentucky, on January 6, 1807. He was educated at St. Joseph's and Centre colleges. In 1828 he opened a law office in Elizabethtown where he practiced for four years before moving on to Louisville where he worked as assistant editor of the *Louisville Advertiser* for a year and commonwealth's attorney for two. He then moved to Mississippi where he enjoyed such notable success as a lawyer that he was able to retire at the age of thirty-five and move back to Louisville to recuperate from tuberculosis, which had taken the life of his first wife, Mary Harrison. For the next fourteen years, except for his marriage to Margaret Wickliffe, his life was uneventful. In the presidential race of 1856, however, he campaigned actively for the Democrats and for his efforts President Buchanan appointed him commissioner of patents in 1857; two years later he became postmaster general and, in 1861, secretary of war. During these years of sectional crisis his attitude changed from one of opposition to coercion of a state by the federal government to an inflexible belief in the righteousness of the Union cause. Consequently, after Lincoln's inauguration he traveled extensively in the border states, Massachusetts, and New York City in an effort to rally people to support the federal armies. In 1862 he was named by Lincoln to the newly created position of judge-advocate general of the army. In that office, which he held until 1875, he rose to national prominence for his role in securing the convictions and executions of those who were involved in the plot to assassinate Lincoln and other high government officials. Not long after the trial, as national passions abated, he was accused of having suppressed important information favorable to the defendants. He spent a considerable amount of time then and in later years in an effort to vindicate himself. He died in Washington, D.C., on August 1, 1894.

Hood, John Bell (1831–79), fifth child of Dr. John W. and Theodoria French Hood, was born in Owingsville, Bath County, Kentucky, on June 1, 1831. After his graduation from West Point in 1853 he served with the 4th Infantry in California and with the 2nd Cavalry in Texas. On April 17, 1861, he resigned his commission in the U.S. Army and thereafter distinguished himself as regimental, brigade, and division commander in the Confederate Army of Northern Virginia. He enjoyed perhaps the most spectacular advance in rank of any officer in the Confederate service. He was promoted to brigadier general on March 3, 1862, and fought brilliantly in the Peninsular campaign and at Second Manassas. On October 10, 1862, he became major general and commanded the first division of General Longstreet's corps at Sharpsburg and Fredericksburg. After sustaining a severe wound in the arm at Gettysburg and losing a leg at Chickamauga, he spent the winter of 1863–64 in northwest Georgia under General Joseph E. Johnston. He was appointed lieutenant general on February 1, 1864. When he replaced Johnston before Atlanta on July 18, 1864, he was promoted to full general. After General William T. Sherman repulsed him in several battles in Georgia, he marched his army into Tennessee in pursuit of General J. M. Schofield who eventually crippled Hood's army in a bloody engagement at Franklin on November 30. He then pressed on to Nashville where his army was shattered by General George H. Thomas. Accepting full responsibility for his failure, he asked to be relieved of his command on January 23, 1865, and reverted to his permanent rank of lieutenant general. Four months later he surrendered himself at Natchez, Mississippi. After the war he resided in New Orleans where he engaged unsuccessfully in the cotton business. In 1868 he married Anna Maria Hennen who died of yellow fever on August 24, 1879. When the same disease took his life six days later, he left behind ten children, the oldest of which was nine years of age.

Hooker, Joseph (1814–79), the son of Joseph and Mary Seymour Hooker, was born in Hadley, Massachusetts, on November 13, 1814. He was educated at Hopkins Academy in Hadley and at West Point from which he graduated in 1837. After service in Florida, along the Canadian border, and as adjutant at West Point, he distinguished himself in the Mexican War, in which he won brevets of all the grades through lieutenant colonel, a record unsurpassed by any first lieutenant. In 1853 he resigned from the army and for the next eight years eked out a living in California and Oregon. When the Civil War broke out he was appointed brigadier general of volunteers on May 17, 1861, and aided in the defense of Washington. The following spring he was promoted to major general of volunteers for his role in the fighting at Williamsburg in the Peninsula campaign in which he inspired his men and directed the fire of his artillery even after he had fallen in the mud with his dying horse. A press wire reading, "Fighting—Joe Hooker" appeared throughout the North as "Fighting Joe Hooker," a sobriquet he disliked because it smacked of the buccaneer. He also exhibited daring and skill in ensuing engagements at the Seven Days, Second Manassas, and at Antietam where he was wounded in the foot and carried from the field. He was promoted to brigadier general in the regular army on September 20, 1862. Although out-generaled by Robert E. Lee at Chancellorsville, Virginia, in May 1863, he demonstrated effective leadership at Lookout Mountain near Chattanooga the following November and won promotion to major general. Then came bitter disappointment. When General William T. Sherman promoted his subordinate, Oliver O. Howard, to command the Army of the Tennessee, Hooker's field service came to an end when he asked to be relieved from duty in "an army in which rank and service are ignored." In September 1864 he became commander of the Northern Department at Cincinnati where in 1865 he married Olivia Groesbeck. She died in 1868, the same year he retired from the army on account of paralysis. His death occurred on October 31, 1879, in Garden City, New York.

Hunter, David (1802–86), son of Rev. Andrew and Mary Stockton Hunter, was born in Washington, D.C., on July 21, 1802. He entered West Point in 1818, graduated four years later, and served in the 5th Infantry until 1833 when he became a captain in the 1st Dragoons. Sometime between 1828 and 1831, during his stay at Fort Dearborn, Chicago, he married Maria Indiana Kinzie. In 1836 he resigned from the army and settled in Chicago to engage in business with his brother-in-law. Six years later he rejoined the army and served as paymaster with the rank of major under General Zachary Taylor in the Mexican War. In 1861, shortly after Lincoln's inauguration, he was given command of one hundred "gentlemen volunteers" to protect the White House. When the Civil War broke out he was appointed brigadier general of volunteers and as commander of the 2nd Division of General Irvin McDowell's army, he participated in the first battle of Bull Run in which he was seriously wounded. In November 1861 he replaced General Fremont as commander of the Western Department of the Union army, and the following March he assumed command of the Department of the South. When Fort Pulaski, Georgia, fell to his troops on April 11, 1862, he issued an order freeing the slaves that had fallen into Union hands; a second order on May 9 liberated all slaves in his department. When the latter move created uneasiness in the border states and excitement in Congress, President Lincoln annulled the order ten days later on the grounds that Hunter had exceeded his authority. The general also sanctioned the raising of a black regiment, an action that was upheld in Congress. After his defeat in the battle of Secessionville (South Carolina) on June 16, he spent the rest of the war on court-martial duty and, after May 1864, in command of the Shenandoah Valley sector where he was successful in weakening Lee's army at a critical hour. After the war he served as president of the military commission that tried the Lincoln conspirators. He retired from active service in 1866 and resided in Washington, D.C., until his death on February 2, 1886.

Ingersoll, Robert Green (1833–99), the son of John and Mary Livingston Ingersoll, was born in Dresden, New York, on August 11, 1833. His father was a preacher in both the Congregational and Presbyterian churches. During his boyhood his family moved to Ohio, then to Wisconsin, and finally to Illinois where he studied law and was admitted to the bar in Shawneetown in 1854. Three years later he moved on to Peoria where he became a distinguished trial lawyer. On February 13, 1862, he married Eva Amelia Parker; two daughters were born to this union. During the Civil War he became colonel of the 11th Illinois volunteer cavalry regiment and saw duty in Tennessee where on December 18, 1862, he along with hundreds of his men were captured by General Nathan B. Forrest. He was shortly paroled and took his discharge from the army on June 30, 1863. By this time he was already marked as one who questioned the Christian religion. While continuing his legal practice he also began to attract large audiences to his lectures on agnosticism, which eventually included such titles as: "Some Mistakes of Moses," "About the Bible," and "Why I Am an Agnostic." He used his oratorical skills in the political arena also. Initially a Democrat, he came out of the Civil War a staunch Republican and his nominating speech in support of James G. Blaine (to whom he referred as the "plumed knight") at the Republican convention of 1876 brought him recognition as one of America's greatest orators. In 1879 he moved to the east coast, first to Washington, D.C., and then in 1885 to New York City, where he continued his lucrative legal practice and his lectures. During the presidential campaign of 1896 his health broke as he stumped for the gold standard; three years later, on July 21, 1899, he died in Dobbs Ferry, New York.

Jackson, Thomas Jonathan "Stonewall" (1824–63), third child of Jonathan and Julia Beckwith Neale Jackson, was born in Clarksburg, (West) Virginia on January 21, 1824. He graduated from West Point in 1846 and served with distinction in the Mexican War. In 1852 he resigned his commission to become professor of military tactics and natural philosophy at Virginia Military Institute. He married twice, first, to Eleanor Junkin in 1853 and, after her death, to Mary Anna Morrison in 1857; both were daughters of Presbyterian ministers. When the Civil War broke out he was appointed colonel in the Virginia militia; on June 7, 1861, he was promoted to brigadier general. He earned the sobriquet "Stonewall" at First Manassas where his resistance to the Union attack inspired the retreating Confederate General Barnard E. Bee to exclaim: "There stands Jackson like a stone wall!" He was promoted to major general on October 7, 1861, and assumed command in the Shenandoah Valley where his magnificent campaign the following year against three Union armies has been called the most brilliant display of military tactics in American history. His fame spread throughout the South where his strict observance of the Sabbath and frequent resort to prayer also became legendary. On October 10, 1862 he was promoted to lieutenant general. The following spring, on May 2, 1863, he distinguished himself in his famous flank march at Chancellorsville, Virginia, where his assault on the Union right forced a federal retreat. Later the same evening, as he was returning to camp from making a reconnaissance, he was inadvertently wounded by his own men. He died at Guiney's Station, south of Fredericksburg, on May 10 from pneumonia, which developed after the amputation of his left arm. General Lee wrote: "He has lost his left arm; but I have lost my right arm."

James, Jesse Woodson (1847–82), son of Robert and Zerelda Cole James, was born near Kearney, Clay County, Missouri, on September 5, 1847. His mother was a Catholic and his father a Baptist minister who supported his family chiefly by farming. He and his brother Alexander Franklin (Frank) received little education but were trained in religious doctrine and were generally regarded as good boys. When Jesse was about four years old his father went to California where he died shortly after his arrival. His mother then remarried, divorced, and remarried a second time. Because Jesse's family was openly southern in their sympathies, their home in Missouri was raided on two occasions by federal militia during the Civil War. Jesse and Frank became Confederate guerrillas under the leadership of William Clarke Quantrill. After the war he, along with Frank, Coleman Younger, and others formed a band of brigands that for more than fifteen years carried out bank and train robberies from Missouri and Ken-

tucky to Minnesota. On March 20, 1868, the James Gang reportedly robbed the Nimrod Long Bank in Russellville, but it is not known whether Jesse accompanied them at the time. In 1870, while waiting for a posse to lose his trail, Jesse tried to commit suicide at the farm house belonging to his uncle, Major George B. Hite, located two miles northwest of Adairville. His sister Susan had announced her intentions to marry Allan Palmer, a Civil War guerrilla with whom Jesse had served under "Bloody Bill" Anderson. Jesse was strongly opposed, grew despondent when she did, and took sixteen grains of morphine. Dr. D. G. Simmons was called and he and Frank kept Jesse on his feet and moving all night until the drug wore off. In 1880 the gang encountered the relentless efforts of William H. Wallace, prosecuting attorney of Jackson County, Missouri, to bring them to justice. Three members were arrested and convicted, another gave himself up, and another was killed by Jesse on suspicion of disloyalty. On April 3, 1882, in St. Joseph, Missouri, Jesse himself was shot in the back of the head and killed by Robert Ford, a member of his gang. Six months later Frank surrendered and although brought to trial on two occasions, he was never convicted and spent the rest of his life as an honorable citizen. Jesse was married on April 24, 1874, to his cousin, Zerelda Mimms, who bore him a son and a daughter. He joined the Baptist Church in 1868 and to the end of his life maintained that he was a devout believer in the Christian religion.

Johnson, Andrew (1808–75), the younger son of Jacob and Mary McDonough Johnson, was born on July 31, 1808, in Raleigh, North Carolina. His father died in 1811 leaving the family in abject poverty, a condition unrelieved by his mother's second marriage. In 1826 his family moved to eastern Tennessee, eventually settling at Greenville where he became a tailor. At the age of eighteen, on May 17, 1827, he married Eliza McCardle who helped him improve his skills in reading and writing; she also bore him five children. By his thrift in managing his tailor shop, he accumulated a small estate. He professed sympathy with the Christian faith, but he

did not associate with any church. He soon
entered politics where he championed the
cause of the working man and, later, a
more equitable land policy. He served as
alderman (1828–30), mayor (1830–33),
state representative (1835–37 and 1839–
41), state senator (1841–43), congressman
(1843–53), governor of Tennessee
(1853–57), and as a Democratic member
of the U.S. Senate in which he distinguished himself as the only southern senator to support the Union during the Civil
War. Lincoln appointed him military governor of Tennessee in March 1862 with the
rank of brigadier general. Two years later
he was elected vice-president on Lincoln's
Union-Republican ticket; when Lincoln
was assassinated in April 1865 he became
president. His attempt to carry out Lincoln's conciliatory reconstruction policy
brought him into conflict with the Radical
Republicans who overrode his vetoes and
pushed through their own harsh reconstruction program. When he violated the
Tenure of Office Act by dismissing Secretary of War Edwin M. Stanton on February
21, 1868, the House of Representatives
voted to impeach him. In his trial before
the Senate, the effort to convict him of the
charge of high misdemeanor that would
have removed him from office fell one vote
short. When his term of office expired he
went back to Tennessee where he reentered politics and won election to the U.S.
Senate in 1874. During an adjourned
session of the Senate he died of a paralytic
attack on July 31, 1875, while visiting his
daughter near Carter Station, Tennessee.

Johnston, Albert Sidney (1803–62), son of
Dr. John and Abigail Harris Johnston, was
born in Washington, Mason County, Kentucky, on February 2, 1803. He was educated at Transylvania University, where he
excelled in mathematics and Latin, and at
West Point from which he graduated in
1826. He saw action in the Black Hawk
War before resigning from the army in
1834. After farming for two years he went
to Texas where he was appointed adjutant
general of the Texas revolutionary army on
August 5, 1836, and senior brigadier general on January 31, 1837. A year later he
became secretary of war for the Republic
of Texas and served until 1840. During the

Mexican War he was appointed colonel of
the 1st Regiment Texas Rifle Volunteers
and fought at Monterrey. In 1849 he was
reappointed to the U.S. Army, served on
the Texas frontier, became colonel of the
2nd Cavalry in 1855, and, as commander of
the Department of Texas from 1856 to
1858, led the Utah expedition against the
Mormons in 1857. He commanded the
Department of Utah from 1858 to 1860.
When Texas seceded from the Union he
again resigned his commission on April 10,
1861; on August 31 he was appointed full
general in the Confederate army and
placed in control of all troops west of the
Alleghenies. When he was driven from
Forts Henry and Donelson by General
Ulysses S. Grant in early 1862, his critics
urged that he be replaced, but President
Jefferson Davis responded: "If Sidney
Johnston is not a general, I have none."
Regrouping at Corinth, Mississippi, Johnston successfully attacked Grant at Shiloh,
but in his moment of victory he was
mortally wounded in the leg and bled to
death on the battlefield, April 6, 1862.

Joiner, Thomas Vance (1854–1913), son of
Nathan and Nancy Joiner, was born in
Trigg County, Kentucky, on September
26, 1854. He was converted as a young
man and joined the Methodist Episcopal
Church, South. The quarterly conference
of the Wallonia Circuit, which met at Cave
Spring Church, licensed him to preach on
March 12, 1881. Later that year the Louisville Conference admitted him on trial into
the traveling ministry. He was ordained
deacon by Bishop McTyeire in 1883 and
elder by Bishop Wilson in 1885. He served
the following charges during his thirty-two
years in the ministry: Empire (1881–82),
Shady Grove (1882–84), Livermore
(1884–86), Calhoun (1886–89),
Springfield (1889–90), Morganfield Circuit (1890–93), Corydon (1893–95),
Hopkinsville Circuit (1895–97), Cloverport (1897–1900), Marion (1900–04),
Russellville (1904–06), Franklin (1906–
10), Clifton (1910–11), and Hartford
(1911–13). On September 1, 1886, he
married Eufala A. Harris who bore seven
children, all of whom survived him. During
his last year at Hartford he suffered a
stroke and died on January 22, 1913. "He

had a heart to love a friend and forgive an enemy."

Kavanaugh, Bishop Hubbard Hindle (1802–84), son of William and Hannah Hubbard Hindle Kavanaugh, was born near Winchester in Clark County, Kentucky, on January 4, 1802. When he was five years old his father, an itinerant preacher, died, leaving his mother with six small children and little means of support. At the age of thirteen he was placed in the family of John Lyle, a Presbyterian minister, at Paris in Bourbon County to learn the printing business. In 1817, in the middle of a November night marked by considerable spiritual struggle, he was converted. Not daring to shout lest he startle Lyle, with whom he was sleeping, but at the same time unable to contain his joy, he turned to "hugging and kissing the old gentleman until he wanted to know what in the world was the matter. They then both rejoiced in God, and held, abed in the dark, all to themselves, an old-time Methodist lovefeast." After his conversion he joined the Methodist Church. In 1823 the Kentucky Conference admitted him on trial into the itinerant ministry and assigned him to the Little Sandy Circuit, a charge of twenty-four preaching places in ten mountain counties of southeastern Kentucky. As part of his equipment, he carried a marking iron to mark trees along the trail so he could find his way to his appointments. On July 24, 1828, he married Mrs. Margaret C. Green, daughter of Charles Railey, of Woodford County. Two years after her death in 1863, he married Mrs. Martha D. P. Lewis, daughter of Capt. Robert D. Richardson of the U.S. Army. In 1839 Governor James Clark appointed him superintendent of public instruction for the state of Kentucky; during 1839 and 1840 he also served as agent for Augusta College, a Methodist school located at Augusta, Bracken County, Kentucky. Neither of these assignments took him out of the regular itinerant life. In 1854 the general conference of the Methodist Episcopal Church, South, elected him bishop and he continued in that office until his death at Ocean Springs, Mississippi, on March 19, 1884. "While he was always inclined to give respectful consideration to all sugges-

tions, was ever ready to yield to the counsel of others in matters of which they knew best, yet when his mind had once been made up and his decision announced, he was the most inflexible of the entire College of Bishops."

Keener, Bishop John Christian (1819–1906) was born in Baltimore, Maryland, on February 7, 1819. He was tutored in the home of Wilbur Fisk, then a private tutor in Baltimore. When Fisk became the first president of Wesleyan University in Middleton, Connecticut, in 1831, young Keener followed him and was a member of the first graduating class in 1835. Returning to Baltimore he entered the wholesale drug business. Sometime after his conversion in 1838 he moved to Alabama where he yielded to the call to preach and in 1843 joined the Alabama Conference of the Methodist Episcopal Church. Five years later he transferred to New Orleans where he pastored several churches and served as presiding elder of the New Orleans District. During the Civil War he entered the Confederate service as a chaplain and eventually became superintendent of army chaplains west of the Mississippi River. In 1866 he was named editor of the *New Orleans Christian Advocate,* a position he held until 1870 when the general conference of the Methodist Episcopal Church, South, elected him bishop. During his twenty-eight years in that office, he reportedly typified the arbitrary attitude that often marked the bishops of his day. He requested superannuation in 1898 and died eight years later in New Orleans on January 19, 1906. "If he sometimes narrowed the range and power of his ecclesiastical leadership by a too rigid conservatism, it was, when not so fettered, superb and thrilling."

Kelley, David Campbell (1833–1909), the son of the Rev. John and Lavinia Margaret Campbell Kelley was born in Wilson County, Tennessee, on Christmas day, 1833. He was converted at an early age and after his graduation from Cumberland College in 1851, he accepted the call to preach and joined the Tennessee Conference of the Methodist Episcopal Church, South, the following year. He and his wife, Mannie, were immediately sent as missionaries to China where they remained until 1855 when her failing health compelled them to return. He spent the next five years preaching in Tennessee Conference. On the great moral and political questions of the day he was an abolitionist and a Unionist, but when the Civil War came, his loyalty to his native state overrode all other considerations and for four years, rising from private to colonel, "he drew in the cause of the Southern Confederacy one of the keenest sabers that ever flashed in Scotch-Irish hands"; he reputedly fought "side by side" with General Nathan Bedford Forrest. After the war he served the Tennessee Conference and his church in the following appointments: Lebanon Station, presiding elder Lebanon District, and president of Corona Institute, a college for girls and young women (1866–70); Tulip Street (Nashville, 1870–72); McKendree (Nashville, 1872–74); presiding elder Nashville District (1874–76); McKendree Church (1876–80); treasurer of the board of missions (1880–88); Gallatin (1888–90); Springfield (1890–92); Elm Street (Nashville, 1892–94); Bellbuckle (1892–96); Columbia (1896–98); and presiding elder Nashville District (1898–1901). During these busy years he also found time to run unsuccessfully in 1890 for governor on the Prohibitionist ticket, serve as president of the board of trustees of Nashville College for Young Ladies and as the first secretary of Vanderbilt University's board of trust, edit a magazine called *The Round Table,* and lent support to the Society for the Prevention of Cruelty to Animals. In his seventy-sixth year, upon learning that no one could be found to supply Bon Air and Clifty Mission, he offered himself for the work. He died of pneumonia two months later in Nashville, Tennessee, on May 15, 1909, at the home of his son-in-law, Dr. Walter R. Lambuth, noted missionary and future bishop.

Lambuth, James William (1830–92), son of John Russell and Nancy Kirkpatrick Lambuth, was born in Greene County, Alabama, on March 2, 1830. His grandfather, William Lambuth, had been sent by Bishop Asbury as a missionary to the Indians in Tennessee, and his father had volunteered to work among the Indians in Louisiana. In 1830, his father, without any explanation, left a camp meeting he was holding in Greene County and returned with the following announcement: "I was called home by the birth of a baby boy. In heartfelt gratitude to God I dedicated the child to the Lord as a foreign missionary, and I now add a bale of cotton to send him with." Shortly after James' birth his family moved to Madison County, Mississippi, where he grew up. He enrolled in the University of Mississippi, where during a revival in 1851 he was "powerfully" converted. Shortly thereafter he was called to preach, and after his graduation in 1851 he spent the next two years preaching, chiefly to blacks. He married Mary L. McClellan in 1852. The following year he joined the Mississippi Conference of the Methodist Episcopal Church, South, and immediately accepted an appointment from Bishop Andrew to assist in establishing a church mission in China. Arriving in Shanghai on September 17, 1854, he learned the language and began preaching on the streets of Shanghai and along the canals and creeks of the surrounding area. At the same time his wife organized a ministry for the women and children of Shanghai. When the New Testament was translated into Chinese, he was a member of the translation committee. Except for the years 1861–64 when complications growing out of the American Civil War compelled him and his family to return home, he labored faithfully among the Chinese until 1885 when he visited Japan with the view of opening a mission there. The following year he and his son, Dr. Walter R. Lambuth, accepted a commission to establish Southern Methodist missions in Japan. Under their leadership the work prospered in the industrial cities of Kobe and Osaka and in the inland sea area between the islands of Honshu and Shikoku. The elder Lambuth's travels by boat in this area earned him the title "Father of the Inland Sea Mission." Among his last words when he died at Kobe, Japan, on April 28, 1892, were: "I fall at my post. We have a great work to do. Tell them to send more men."

Latrobe, Ferdinand Claiborne (1833–1911) was born into a prominent Baltimore,

Maryland, family on October 14, 1833. In 1860 he married the daughter of Governor Thomas Swann. After passing the Maryland bar he chose a career in politics. He won election to the House of Delegates in 1867 and an appointment as judge advocate general by Governor Swann. In 1869 he was reelected to the state legislature and served that term as speaker of the House. He then sought to become mayor of Baltimore. He failed to win in 1873, but two years later, with the backing of the regular Democratic boss, I. Freeman Rasin, he won the city's highest office. It was the first of seven victories for him and Rasin and ushered in twenty years of "boss rule" in Baltimore. He served as mayor during 1875–77, 1878–81, 1883–84, 1887–89, and 1891–95. During his administrations he achieved considerable progress in the general efficiency of city government and in the expansion of city services in such areas as street paving, storm sewers, schools, and harbors. He also succeeded, after a ten year campaign, in convincing Baltimore's suburban residents to annex themselves to the city in 1888. During these years he was often criticized as a "spendthrift mayor," but despite continual charges of graft and corruption there apparently was little misuse of public funds. As a campaigner he was a formidable opponent. His aristocratic background appealed to a large segment of the upper and middle classes, and his frequent appearance at German beer-fests, Polish picnics, Irish balls, Italian festivals, and labor union outings made him popular with the ethnic and working class voters as well. Nevertheless, as the most visible member of the Rasin machine, he became the target of reformers seeking to end "boss rule." In the face of mounting opposition, he never ran again after the completion of his seventh term in 1895. He died in Baltimore on January 13, 1911.

Lee, Nathaniel H. (1816–81), the son of Andrew and Elizabeth Lee, was born in Campbell County, Virginia, on April 29, 1816. Six years later his family moved to Kentucky and settled in Monroe County where he attended the common neighborhood schools. The young man had a great thirst for learning, and since his father had

been ruined in finances by security debts, he arranged with the Rev. Henry Woods, president of Urania College in Glasgow, Kentucky, to give him the benefit of tuition and allow him to pay the charges when he could earn the money. Young Lee's dream was to follow his mother's family in the study of law and politics, but in his twentieth year he attended a meeting at Old Zion Methodist Church in Barren County where he was converted under the ministry of J. C. C. Thompson. He soon yielded to the conviction that he ought to preach the gospel. In 1838 the quarterly conference licensed him to preach and recommended him for admission on trial into the Kentucky Conference of the Methodist Church. His first appointments were to the Hopkinsville Circuit (1838–39) and Mt. Pleasant Mission (1839–41) in the mountains of eastern Kentucky. He was ordained deacon by Bishop Thomas A. Morris in 1840, and elder by Bishop Beverly Waugh in 1842. During these years his faithful ministry and his diligent study in Latin and Greek created a demand for his services. From 1841 to 1879 he held the following appointments from the Kentucky Conference of the Methodist Church and, after 1845, from the Louisville Conference of the Methodist Episcopal Church, South: Bardstown Station (1841–43), Owensboro Circuit (1843–45), presiding elder Morganfield District (1845–46), presiding elder Smithland District (1846–47), Louisville Eighth Street (1847–48), Hardinsburg (1848–50), presiding elder Bowling Green District (1850–51), presiding elder Hopkinsville District (1851–55), presiding elder Henderson District (1855–56), presiding elder Hardinsburg District (1856–58), Agent of the American Bible Society (1858–60), presiding elder Louisville District (1860–61), supernumerary (1861–63), Mammoth Cave (1863–64), Glasgow Station (1864–65), Logan Circuit (1865–66), presiding elder Bardstown District (1866–1869), president of Logan Female College in Russellville (1869–1873), presiding elder Henderson District (1873–75), and presiding elder Louisville District (1875–79). He spent the last two years of his life as superannuated. He was first married in 1846 to Fannie Evans, daughter of the Rev.

Thomas Evans, an English Methodist preacher; she died in 1859. He married his second wife, Sophie McDaniel, in 1860. In that same year he was thrown from a buggy by a frightened horse and suffered a fracture of the hip joint that lamed him for the rest of his life. His disability prevented him from riding a man's saddle; consequently on these occasions when travel by buggy was not possible, he had to ride on a sidesaddle. He died on June 14, 1881, at his home near Russellville, Kentucky. "With an eagle eye he watched the interests of the church, and sounded the alarm when he saw danger approaching."

Lee, Robert Edward (1807–70), fifth child of Henry ("Light-Horse Harry Lee") of Revolutionary War fame, and his second wife, Anne Hill Carter, was born at Stratford, Westmoreland County, Virginia, on January 19, 1807. After receiving his early education in Alexandria schools, he attended West Point where he graduated second in his class in 1829. Two years later, on June 30, 1831, he married Mary Ann Randolph Custis, only child of George Washington Parke Custis, a grandson of Martha Washington by her first marriage. The Custis estate of "Arlington" on the Virginia shore of the Potomac opposite Washington, D.C., thus became Lee's home after the death of his father-in-law in 1857. In the years before the Mexican War he served as an army engineer in such assignments as Fort Pulaski (Georgia), Fort Monroe (Virginia), St. Louis, and Fort Hamilton (New York). For gallantry and distinguished service during the Mexican War his regular rank was augmented by three brevets to that of colonel. After directing the construction of Fort Carroll in Baltimore Harbor (1848–52) and serving as superintendent of West Point (1852–55), he was commissioned lieutenant colonel in the 2nd Cavalry and spent two years (1855–57) in west Texas. Because of his wife's serious arthritic condition, he was on extended leave at Arlington House at the time of John Brown's raid on Harpers Ferry and led the detachment of marines that captured Brown and his followers in October 1859. He was strongly attached to the Union and the Constitution but when it became apparent that his native Virginia would secede and that he would be expected to aid the federal government in "suppressing insurrection," he resigned his commission in the U.S. Army on April 20, 1861, and was promptly made commander in chief of the military and naval forces of Virginia. When the Virginia troops were transferred to Confederate service, he was appointed brigadier general in the Confederate army (then the highest rank provided by law) and subsequently general to rank from June 14, 1861. During November 1861–March 1862 he was in Charleston, South Carolina, and Savannah, Georgia, organizing the defenses of the south Atlantic seaboard. On June 1, 1862, he succeeded Joseph E. Johnston as commander of the Army of Northern Virginia and for the next thirty-four months he displayed his military prowess in such battles as Second Manassas, Sharpsburg, Fredericksburg, Chancellorsville, Gettysburg, Spotsylvania, Cold Harbor, Petersburg, and Appomattox. He finally surrendered to Ulysses S. Grant at Appomattox Courthouse on April 9, 1865. After the war he refused a number of offers that would have brought financial security to him and his family. Instead, he became president of Washington College (now Washington and Lee University) at Lexington, Virginia, where he died on October 12, 1870.

Leslie, Preston Hopkins (1819–1907), the second son of Vachel and Sally Hopkins Leslie, was born in Clinton County, Kentucky, on March 8, 1819. He received a limited education but was always fond of books. Orphaned at the age of thirteen, he worked to support himself at various jobs: cart driver, woodchopper, ferryman, cook, and clerk in a dry goods store. He then studied law under General Rice Maxey and was admitted to the bar in 1840. In 1841 he moved to Tompkinsville in Monroe County where he practiced law and farmed. In that same year he married Louisa Black of Monroe County who bore him seven children; when she died in 1858 he married Mrs. Mary Kuykendall of Boone County, Missouri, who bore him three children. During these years he played an increasingly active role in politics. He was elected county attorney in

1842, and, as a Whig, he won a seat in the state legislature in 1844. Defeated in his bid for the state senate in 1846 by one vote, he was victorious in.1850 and served in that body until 1855. After Henry Clay's death in 1852 he became a Democrat. As the nation moved toward civil war he opposed secession and advocated negotiation, but when the war came he sympathized with the South. He refused military service, preferring to spend the war years practicing law in Glasgow in Barren County where he had moved in 1859. After the war he reentered politics and in 1867 won election to the state senate where he was chosen president in 1869. From that position he succeeded to the governorship in February 1871 when Governor John W. Stevenson was elected to the United States Senate. Later that year he was elected to a four-year term as governor. As a result of his administration state violence was suppressed, black testimony was admitted in the courts, the state's mental, deaf, and blind institutions were improved, education for blacks was inaugurated, the Southern Railroad opened up central Kentucky to northern and southern markets, and a geological survey uncovered a wealth of natural resources. When he left office in 1875 he returned to Glasgow to resume his legal practice. Public life still beckoned, however. In 1881 he became circuit judge in his district and in 1887 President Grover Cleveland appointed him territorial governor of Montana. When President Benjamin Harrison removed him in 1889, he stayed on in Helena and opened a law office. Except for the years 1894–98 when he served as United States district attorney for Montana, he practiced law in Helena until shortly before his death from pneumonia on February 7, 1907.

Lewis, James Andrew (1836–1911), the son of Napoleon B. and Margaret Barnett Lewis, was born near Mt. Vernon, Kentucky, on November 29, 1836. His father, a preacher in the Louisville Conference of the Methodist Episcopal Church, South, died on October 11, 1847, leaving a widow and three children, including John W. who joined his brother James in giving his life to the Methodist ministry. James was converted early in life at Ash Spring Camp-

ground in Logan County and became a member of the congregation at Keysburg. He attended school for a time at Stanford, Kentucky, studying under S. S. McRoberts, a Presbyterian preacher. He also spent two years at Elizabethtown, Kentucky, in the academy of Prof. Fayette Hewitt. He was called to preach at the age of seventeen but his heart was set on the legal profession; after four years of struggle he finally yielded to the call. In 1858 the Logan Circuit Quarterly Conference licensed him to preach and in the fall of that year the Louisville Conference admitted him on trial into the itinerant ministry. He was ordained deacon by Bishop Early in 1860 and elder by Bishop Kavanaugh in 1864. The two-year delay in his ordination as elder resulted from the disruptions associated with the Civil War that prevented bishops from attending the two preceding sessions of the Louisville Conference. During 1858–61 he preached at Salem, Brandenburg, and Scottsville. He was then appointed to Eddyville (1861–62) and Princeton (1862–63), but the turmoil of the war prevented his serving either. After two years on the Russellville Circuit (1863–65), and one year as supernumerary (1865–66), he transferred to the Kentucky Conference where he served one year at Lawrenceburg. He then transferred back to the Louisville Conference and for the next forty years accepted appointments to the following charges: Fairview (1867–69), Russellville (1869–70), Elkton Circuit (1870–74), presiding elder Princeton District (1874–75), Morganfield Circuit (1875–76), Cadiz and Bethel (1876–79), Fairview Circuit (1879–81), Adairville (1881–85), Madisonville (1885–86), presiding elder Elizabethtown District (1886–89), Bowling Green (1889–91), presiding elder Russellville District (1891–95), Russellville (1895–98), Henderson (1898–99), Adairville (1899–1901), Lebanon (1901–05), Hartford (1905–07), and Lewisburg (1907–08). He was superannuated in 1908 and spent his last years in Olmstead, Kentucky, where he died on February 16, 1911. He lies buried in the family cemetery on a hill above the picturesque winding creek at Keysburg, his boyhood home. "He was in some respects the last of the Cavaliers on horseback — that knightly band of heroes, who traversed the vast landscapes of Kentucky and preached the gospel to our fathers."

Lewis, John W. (1846–1918), son of Napoleon B. Lewis and Margaret Barnett Lewis, was born in Keysburg, Logan County, Kentucky, on April 10, 1846. He descended from pioneer stock; his great-grandfather, Colonel Aaron Lewis, an officer in the Revolutionary army, came to Kentucky with Richard Henderson and Daniel Boone, and lived for a time at Boonesboro. John's father, a Methodist preacher, died in 1847, leaving three children, one of whom was John's older brother, James A. Lewis, who also became a Methodist preacher in the Louisville Conference. Young Lewis grew to manhood in Keysburg, attending the village school, which was then taught by Professor Howlett Hunter. When the Civil War broke out and Keysburg was occupied alternately by Confederate and Union forces, he saw stores looted and men killed. More than once his own life was threatened. At the age of sixteen he left home to attend a school taught by a Rev. Campbell at the headwaters of Muddy River. For two years he boarded at the home of Rev. Timothy C. Frogge, a Methodist preacher. In 1864 he secured a teaching position in a district school at Lewisburg, Kentucky. About this time, while spending a day with George Dick at Olmstead, as they were walking across a field, his host turned to him and said, "John Lewis, has not the Lord called you to preach?" On receiving an affirmative answer, George Dick added, "I thought so." Lewis soon entered Kentucky Wesleyan College, then located in Millersburg, to prepare for the ministry. In the summer of 1869 he was licensed to preach. That same summer it was he who filled the Allensville appointment when George Dick's throat trouble forced him to withdraw temporarily from the active ministry. During these months Lewis made his home at Olmstead with the Browder family. In the fall of 1869 he was admitted on trial into the Louisville Conference of the Methodist Episcopal Church, South. He was ordained deacon by Bishop Wightman in 1871 and elder by Bishop Keener in 1873. During

the years 1869–1901 he held the following appointments: Franklin Circuit (1869–70), Glasgow (1870–71), Lebanon (1871–72), Elizabethtown (1872–74), Olmstead (1874–75), Hopkinsville (1875–79), Jefferson Street (Louisville, 1879–80), Henderson (1880–83), Middletown (1883–84), Chestnut Street (Louisville, 1884–86), Hopkinsville (1886–90), Bowling Green (1890–94), Walnut Street (Louisville, 1894–96), presiding elder Louisville District (1896–1900), and presiding elder Lebanon District (1900–01). In 1871 he married Lucy Donaldson of Bowling Green who bore him seven children. He decided to transfer south in 1901 and accepted an appointment as pastor of Central Church, Meridian, Mississippi (1901–03). He spent 1903–04 as presiding elder of the Jackson (Mississippi) District, and 1904–05 as presiding elder of the Nashville District, Tennessee Conference. A year later he transferred back to his beloved Louisville Conference in which, during the next twelve years, he accepted the following charges: presiding elder Owensboro District (1905–06), presiding elder Hopkinsville District (1906–10), presiding elder Bowling Green District (1910–14), Portland Avenue (Louisville, 1914–16), and Woodburn Avenue (Louisville, 1916–18). Death came during his fiftieth year in the ministry on April 10, 1918. "He was a loyal son of the Church . . . and had no patience with any lack of loyalty on the part of those in her ranks."

Lewis, Joseph Horace (1824–1904) was born near Glasgow, Barren County, Kentucky, on October 29, 1824. After his graduation from Centre College in 1843, he studied law, was admitted to the bar in 1845, and set up practice in Glasgow. He also entered politics and was elected three times to the Kentucky legislature; on two occasions he ran unsuccessfully for Congress. When the Civil War broke out he cast his lot with the Confederacy and became a colonel in the 6th Kentucky Infantry. He took part in the battles of Shiloh, Murfreesboro, and Chickamauga. Upon the death of Ben Hardin Helm in 1863, he succeeded to the command of the famous Kentucky Orphan Brigade and was promoted to brigadier general. When Atlanta fell, the brigade was mounted and attached to General Joseph Wheeler's cavalry in an unsuccessful effort to halt Sherman's "March to the Sea." Lewis finally surrendered as a part of Jefferson Davis' escort and was paroled at Washington, Georgia, on May 9, 1865. He returned to Glasgow, Kentucky, where he resumed his legal practice and his political aspirations. He was elected to the state legislature once more in 1868, and to the first of three consecutive terms in Congress in 1870. In 1880 he was elected to the Kentucky bench where he spent eighteen years, the last four as chief justice of the court of appeals. At the end of his third elected term, he retired to his farm in Scott County where he died on July 6, 1904.

Lewis, Thomas D. (1833–85), the youngest of eight children, was born in Christian County, Kentucky, on March 25, 1833. His father died a short time before his birth. When he was about three years old, his mother remarried and the family moved to Caldwell County, near Eddyville, where he remained until his nineteenth year. During these years he made the best of the meager educational opportunities afforded him by the common schools of that time. None of his family was religious and he only occasionally enjoyed the privilege of hearing the gospel preached; nevertheless he had a strong desire to be a Christian. After much Bible reading and prayer he was converted in the fall of 1849 and joined the United Baptist Church. Within a year his whole family made a public profession of faith in Christ. The young man soon felt the call to preach and in the course of preparing for the ministry he concluded that he was not in accord with the Baptist system of doctrine and church government. Consequently, he joined the Methodist Church at Reed's Campground, Eddyville Circuit, in 1853. The following year he was licensed to preach by the Eddyville Quarterly Conference. In 1855 at Greenville, Kentucky, he was received on trial into the Louisville Conference of the Methodist Episcopal Church, South. He was ordained deacon by Bishop George F. Pierce in 1857; two years later he was ordained elder by Bishop James O. Andrew. On May 30, 1858, he married M. E. Chambers of McLean County; she died on April 19, 1859. Two years later he married Margaret J. Smith of Warren County, Kentucky. During his seventeen years in the Louisville Conference, he filled the following appointments: North Christian Mission (1855–56), Dycusburg Circuit (1856–57), Calhoun Circuit (1857–59), New Haven (1859–60), Bowling Green Circuit (1860–61), Salem (1861–62), Eddyville (1862–64), Princeton Circuit (1864–65), Scottsville (1865–67), Bowling Green Circuit (1867–71), and Hartford Circuit (1871–72). Then his health failed and during 1872–73 he had a nominal appointment to the Bowling Green Mission and as a tutor in Warren College, Bowling Green, Kentucky. For the next three years he accepted a superannuated status. In 1876 he resumed regular work once more and for the next six years he served the following charges: Franklin Station (1876–77), Allensville Station (1877–78), Russellville Station (1879–80), and Henderson District (1881–82). In 1882 ill-health compelled him to become supernumerary, a status he held until his death on April 29, 1885. "He has poured consolation into a thousand hearts, and has communicated the cheerfulness of his own spirit to the many homes he has visited."

Linn, John H. (1812–76) was born in Lewisburg, Greenbrier County, Virginia, in 1812. He was raised in extreme poverty but the kindness of friends enabled him to acquire a superior education including a background in Latin and Greek. In his younger years he attended the Presbyterian Church, but after his conversion as a young man he united with the Methodists. Although he was impressed from childhood that he should preach the gospel, he did not yield to the call until 1835 when the Baltimore Conference of the Methodist Church admitted him into the itinerant ministry. Over the next forty-one years he held appointments in the following conferences of the Methodist Church and Methodist Episcopal Church, South: Baltimore Conference: Franklin Circuit (1836–37), and Lexington Circuit (1837–38); Kentucky Conference: Georgetown Circuit (1838–39), Maysville (1839–40), Louisville Fourth Street (1840–41), and Harrodsburg and Danville (1841–42); Missouri Conference: St. Louis Centenary (1842–44), agent for St. Charles College (1844–45), and Hannibal (1845–46); St. Louis Conference: Jefferson City (1846–47), and St. Louis Fourth Street (1847–49); Louisville Conference: Louisville Fourth Street (1849–51); Kentucky Conference: Cincinnati Soule Chapel (1851–53), Frankfort (1853–55), Danville (1855–56), Lexington (1856–58), and Shelbyville (1858–60); Louisville Conference: Louisville Walnut Street (1860–61), Louisville Brook Street (1861–63), Louisville Eighth Street (1863–64), Louisville Chestnut Street (1864–65), Louisville Brook Street (1865–67), and Louisville Broadway (1867–69); Baltimore Conference: Baltimore Central (1869–71); St. Louis Conference: St. Louis Centenary (1871–74); and Louisville Conference: Louisville Chestnut Street (1874–76); and presiding elder Louisville District (1876). Shortly before his last return to Kentucky, he had a slight attack of paralysis from which he never fully recovered. He had served only two months in his last appointment when he died on December 7, 1876. "His discourses were often a combination of the overwhelmingly sublime and of the transcendently beautiful."

Lipscomb, Andrew Adgate (1816–90), the son of William Corrie and Phoebe Adgate Lipscomb, was born in Georgetown, D.C., on September 16, 1816. At the age of eighteen he became a minister in the Methodist Protestant Church, as his father had been, and served in Baltimore, Washington, and Alexandria, Virginia. About 1839 he married Henrietta Blanche Richardson of Baltimore and shortly thereafter moved to Montgomery, Alabama, where he was ordained as a Methodist Episcopal minister. His first love was teaching, however, and he soon resigned his pastorate to found a school called the Metropolitan Institute for Young Ladies. About 1855 he left Montgomery to become president of the Female College at Tuskegee. His wife died soon after his move and he subsequently married Susan Dowdell, a former student. In 1860 he became chancellor of the University of Georgia, at Athens, a position he held until 1874 when he resigned after the death of his son. Shortly thereafter he left for Nashville, Tennessee, where he taught esthetics at Vanderbilt University, but after a few years he returned to Athens where he lived until his death on November 23, 1890.

Lithgow, James S. (1812–1902), son of Walter and Frances Stevenson Lithgow, was born in Pittsburgh, Pennsylvania, on November 29, 1812. His father, a planemaker, died within a year after his birth. At the age of fourteen he was apprenticed to learn copper and tin smithing. Six years later he moved to Louisville, Kentucky, where, after working several years for the firm of Bland and Coleman, he decided to enter business for himself. In 1836, with Allen S. Wallace as his partner, he began a copper, tin, and sheet-iron business on Market Street. Their venture prospered and by 1844 they built a stone foundry and warehouse on Second Street. In 1857 the buildings were destroyed by fire, but soon afterward they rebuilt at the corner of Main and Clay and specialized in iron hollowware, mantels, and grates. Their company soon became the largest establishment of its kind in the South. After Wallace's death in 1861, Lithgow formed another partnership in 1862 under the name of J. S. Lithgow and Co. Again, he prospered and was in the process of further expansion when the Panic of 1873 struck and drove him into bankruptcy. Undaunted, he established the firm of Lithgow Manufacturing Company and rebuilt his fortune by resuming the manufacture of stoves. He was also a public-spirited individual. In 1834 he served as president and chief director of the Merchants' Fire Company, a volunteer organization. For a time he was one of the directors of the Louisville and Frankfort Railroad and of the Elizabethtown and Paducah Railroad. In 1865 he was elected to the presidency of the Northern Bank of Kentucky. He served several terms as city councilman and alderman, and in 1866 he was elected mayor of Louisville to fill the unexpired term of his predecessor. He was also active in the Methodist Church, which he joined in 1843 under the ministry of future bishop, H. H. Kavanaugh. In 1870 he was a delegate to the general conference, which elected him a member of the board of church extension; he later served as president of the board for eight years. In 1837 he married Hannah Cragg, a native of England, who bore him eight children. He died in Louisville on March 29, 1902.

Little, Charles Joseph (1840–1911), the son of Thomas Rowell and Ann Zimmerman Little, was born in Philadelphia, Pennsylvania, on September 21, 1840. Though frail in health he spent his boyhood days in manual labor and his nights studying by lamp and candle light. Gifted as a linguist, he mastered Greek, Latin, Italian, and French. He graduated from the University of Pennsylvania in 1861 and shortly thereafter yielded to the call to preach. The following year the Philadelphia Conference of the Methodist Episcopal Church admitted him on trial and from 1862 to 1867 he pastored churches in the Philadelphia area. During these years his exceptional abilities were recognized and in 1867 he was called to teach mathematics at Dickinson College. Two years later he traveled to Europe where he spent three years at the University of Berlin. At the conclusion of his stay, on December 3, 1872, he married Anna Marina Elizabeth Bahn, daughter of Dr. Carl Bahn; three daughters and a son were born to this union. Upon his return to the United States, he spent two years as pastor of Christ Church, Philadelphia, and then joined the Dickinson College faculty once more as professor of philosophy and history. In 1885 he moved on to Syracuse University to teach logic and history, a position he held until 1891 when he was elected to the chair of church history in Garrett Biblical Institute, Evanston, Illinois. Four years later he became president of the school and served in the dual role of administrator and teacher until the day of his death. During these years when the church was involved in controversies over evolution and higher criticism, he held fast to old truths and believed in a thoroughgoing theological education in the old-time essentials. He died in Evanston on March 11, 1911.

Long, Spencer Curd (1835–99), son of Nimrod and Elizabeth Curd Long, was born in Russellville, Kentucky, on March 3, 1835. His grandfather, John S. Long, was one of the first settlers of Logan County. His father was for a number of years engaged in the banking business in Russellville and was wounded by members of the Jesse James gang when they robbed his bank in 1868. After attending Russellville schools he entered Georgetown College, Georgetown, Kentucky, from which he graduated with honors in 1854. He married Cornelia Gano, daughter of Dr. S. F. Gano, one of the leading physicians of Georgetown; she bore him three sons and three daughters. For a short time he managed his farm near Russellville, but in 1860 he sold it and entered into the commercial life of Louisville, Kentucky, where he became a partner in the firm of Hall and Long, provision dealers. Six years later he withdrew and became one of the leading tobacco dealers in Louisville until 1878 when he returned to Russellville to take charge of his father's bank. During his years in Russellville he served as mayor (1884–88) and as treasurer of Bethel College, a Baptist school for men. When his father died in 1887, he organized the Deposit Bank of Louisville and served as its president until 1891 when he resigned and removed to near Georgetown, Kentucky, where he engaged in farming and various business ventures in that city. He died in March 1899.

Lucy, William Bascom (1851–1914) was born in Clinton County, Kentucky, on October 23, 1851. Both of his parents were devout Christians. He attended neighborhood public schools as well as Albany Academy in Albany, the county seat of Clinton County. Early in life he was converted and joined the Methodist Episcopal Church, South. As a young man he was called to preach but the fear of making a mistake caused him to hesitate and for several years he taught school in Clinton County. In 1879 he finally yielded to the call and received his license to preach. A year later the Louisville Conference admitted him on trial into the itinerant ministry. He was ordained deacon by Bishop McTyeire in 1883 and elder by Bishop Wilson in 1885. Lucy received the following appointments from the Louisville Conference during his years in the active ministry: Peytonsburg (1880–81), Mt. Lebanon (1881–84), Oakford (1884–85), Constantine (1885–86), Wayne (1886–87), Breeding's (1887–89), Bradfordsville (1889–92), Mannsville (1892–94), superannuated (1894–95), Monticello (1895–96), Buffalo (1896–98), Upton (1898–99), Canmer (1899–1900), supernumerary (1900–02), Grand Rivers (1902–03), Hanson (1903–07), Mt. Washington (1907–09), and Long Grove (1909–10). When his health failed in 1910 he moved to El Paso, Arkansas, where he died on February 21, 1914. "He was a weeping prophet."

Lyon, Hylan Benton (1836–1907) was born at "River View," Caldwell (now Lyon) County, Kentucky, on February 22, 1836. Both of his parents had died by the time he reached the age of eight. After attending several schools in Kentucky he received an appointment to West Point in 1852, graduating four years later as a second lieutenant of artillery. When the Civil War broke out, he resigned his commission and entered the Confederate army as a battery captain in the 8th Kentucky Infantry; on February 3, 1862, he was elected lieutenant colonel. Shortly thereafter he was captured at Fort Donelson, Tennessee, and spent seven months as a prisoner on Johnson's Island, Ohio. After his exchange he joined General Lloyd Tilghman's division of the Army of West Tennessee and served at Holly Springs and Vicksburg. He was promoted to brigadier general on June 14, 1864, and commanded a brigade of four Kentucky cavalry regiments in General Nathan Bedford Forrest's corps. Toward the end of hostilities he became commander of the District of West Kentucky and led a raid from Paris, Tennessee, to Hopkinsville, Kentucky, during December 1864–January 1865. When the war was over he spent a brief time in Mexico before returning to Kentucky and settling on a farm near Eddyville in his home county. He later served as one of the lessees of the state penitentiary and as a commissioner to build a branch penitentiary at Eddyville. He died on his farm on April 25, 1907.

McClellan, George Brinton (1826–85), son of Dr. George B. and Elizabeth Brinton McClellan, was born in Philadelphia, Pennsylvania, on December 3, 1826. After attending local preparatory schools and, for a time the University of Pennsylvania, he received an appointment to West Point from which he graduated in 1846, ranking second in a class of fifty-nine. After serving with distinction in the Mexican War as a builder of roads and bridges, his activities during the next ten years included three years as instructor at West Point, an expedition to explore the sources of the Red River, various surveys of possible transcontinental railroad routes, and a trip abroad to study the armies of Europe. In 1857 he resigned from the army to become chief engineer of the Illinois Central Railroad. Four years later, when the Civil War broke out, he was president of the Ohio and Mississippi Railroad. On April 23, 1861, he was appointed major general of Ohio Volunteers; three weeks later President Lincoln made him major general in the regular army and placed him in command of the Department of Ohio. After the Union defeat at First Manassas in July 1861, he assumed command of the Army of the Potomac. Although his efficiency in organization and personal magnetism restored order, discipline, and morale to the army, his military record was largely one of lost opportunities and frustration. After a disappointing Virginia Peninsula campaign during the spring of 1862 in which he marched almost to the gates of Richmond only to be driven back, and a drawn battle at Antietam Creek the following September, President Lincoln relieved him of his command on November 7, 1862; he never again saw duty in the field. In 1864 he was the Democratic nominee for president, running against Lincoln on a "peace at any price" platform. He carried only three states. In the years after the Civil War his most noteworthy accomplishment was the three years (1878–81) he served as governor of New Jersey. He died in Orange, New Jersey, on October 29, 1885, survived by his wife, Ellen Mary Marcy, whom he married in 1860.

McCook, Edward Moody (1833–1909) was born in Steubenville, Ohio, on June 15, 1833. He was educated in neighborhood schools. At the age of sixteen he went to

Colorado (then Kansas Territory) where he became a lawyer; in 1859 he represented the Pike's Peak region in the Kansas legislature. When the Civil War broke out he became one of the fourteen "Fighting McCook's" who served in the Union army. Appointed lieutenant of cavalry in the regular army, by April 1862 he had risen to the rank of colonel and commanded a regiment in the 2nd Indiana Cavalry. He led a brigade of cavalry at the battle of Perryville (Kentucky) in October 1862 and a division of cavalry at the battle of Chickamauga (Georgia) in September 1863. He was promoted to brigadier general of volunteers on April 27, 1864. During the Georgia campaign his troops succeeded in cutting the Macon railroad south of Atlanta at Lovejoy's Station, but 950 of his men were captured in attempting to rejoin the main army. In October 1864 he accompanied General George H. Thomas northward to Tennessee in an effort to thwart a Confederate advance on Nashville. Just before the battle of Nashville (December 15–16), McCook led his troops into Kentucky where they skirmished successfully with Confederates under General Hylan B. Lyon who threatened Hopkinsville. In the closing weeks of the war he saw action in Alabama and Georgia. He resigned from the army in 1866 and served for three years as U. S. minister to Hawaii. In 1869 he returned to become territorial governor of Colorado, serving intermittently until 1875 when he retired from public life to take care of his considerable financial interests, which at one time made him the largest taxpayer in Colorado. He died in Chicago on September 9, 1909.

McCormack, Joseph Nathaniel (1847–1922) was born near Howard's Mill in Nelson County, Kentucky, on November 9, 1847. His father Thomas, a farmer and merchant, had emigrated from Ireland in 1836 and settled in New York before moving on to Kentucky where he married Elizabeth Brown of Hardin Country. Joseph was the fifth of sixteen children. He attended the public schools of Nelson County until the age of twelve when he dropped out to assist his father on the farm. He continued his education at home and through his own efforts mastered Latin and mathematics. In

1866, shortly after he began to study medicine, he left home for Cincinnati to become the private pupil of Dr. John A. Murphy and to attend lectures at Miami Medical College from which he graduated in 1870 as valedictorian of his class. Turning down an internship at Cincinnati Hospital, he returned to Nelson County to practice medicine. A year later he married Corrine Crenshaw of Glasgow, Kentucky. In 1876 the University of Louisville School of Medicine granted him a M.D. degree, and shortly thereafter he moved to Bowling Green where he formed a partnership with Dr. L.C. Porter. During the yellow fever epidemic of 1878, he worked closely with Dr. Luke P. Blackburn, later governor of Kentucky, in combating the disease in the Bowling Green area. When the Kentucky State Board of Health was created in 1879 to control cholera and yellow fever, Governor Blackburn appointed him a member. From that date until 1910, the board of health was in reality located in his office in Bowling Green. In 1881 he was elected president of the state medical association, the youngest man ever to hold the office at that time. The following year he went to Europe to continue his studies. Upon his return in 1883 he was appointed state health officer, a position he held until 1912 when he was succeeded by his son, Dr. A. T. McCormack. In that office he wrote and secured the passage of Kentucky's first medical practice act in 1888. When another cholera epidemic threatened the United States in 1888, he organized the Conference of State and Provisional Health Offices of North America; for his efforts he received the thanks of President Grover Cleveland. He served the Conference as secretary for six years and as president for eight years. During these years he appeared before the legislature of practically every state in the Union in his efforts to promote public health and medical education legislation. And in cooperation with Dr. George H. Summers of Chicago and Dr. P. M. Foshay of Cleveland, he rewrote the constitution and by-laws of virtually every state and county medical association in the country. In 1912 he was elected to the state legislature from Bowling Green and served for one term. He died on May 4, 1922, in Louisville where he had lived for three years before his death.

McFerran, William R. (1786–1871) was born in Virginia in 1786. At the age of fourteen his family moved to Kentucky and settled on a farm in Barren County. His father, John, was one of the early pioneers of Barren County and served for a time as high sheriff. William engaged in mercantile interests for about ten years during his early adulthood; at the same time he pursued the study of law under Judge Joseph Underwood. He was admitted to the bar in 1835. During the course of his legal career he served as commonwealth's attorney for eighteen years and as county judge for two terms. He continued to practice law until his death in May 1871.

McFerrin, John B. (1807–87), was born of Scotch-Irish parents in Rutherford County, Tennessee, on June 15, 1807. His grandfather fought in the American Revolution and his father in the War of 1812. Young John was converted at a Methodist prayer meeting on August 20, 1820; two weeks later he joined the church. In 1825 he was licensed to preach and joined the Tennessee Conference of the Methodist Episcopal Church. During the next sixty-one years he served the church in the following appointments: on the circuit (1825–28), missionary to the Indians (1828–30), on stations (1830–36), presiding elder (1836–39), editor of the *Christian Advocate* (1839–57), Book Agent and chaplain to the Confederate army (1857–65), Secretary of Domestic Missions (1865–69), Secretary of Foreign Missions (1869–77), and Book Agent (1877–1887). In the latter office he "ceased at once to work and live." In personal appearance he was commanding, standing six feet high and weighing two hundred pounds, "with health gushing from a thousand springs." In addition to his outstanding record as a churchman, he was also an active citizen: he owned real estate, held political opinions, voted on all election days, owned bank stock, made temperance speeches, was once president of a street railroad, and gave cheerfully to the poor. With the exception of those who were elevated to the episcopacy, he was the best known and most influential man in southern Methodism. He died in Nashville, on May 10, 1887. "In a great crisis he could travel so rapidly and toil so terribly that every obstacle seemed to be in a hurry to get out of his way."

Mackall, John J. (1790–1867) was born in Prince George County, Maryland, on February 3, 1790, and reared in Rockingham County, Virginia. About 1807 he emigrated to Logan County, Kentucky, and settled in Olmstead. The first society of Methodists in that neighborhood met in his home and eventually built old Bethlehem Church where George Dick worshiped as a youth. Mackall also filled a number of county offices "with credit and fidelity" before his death on June 10, 1867.

McReynolds, John Oliver (1827–1905), son of James C. and Mary B. McReynolds, was born in Appomattox County, Virginia, on November 30, 1827. When he was six years old his family emigrated to Trigg County, Kentucky, where his mother died in 1837 and his father in 1844. In 1846 he moved on to Elkton in Todd County where he studied medicine under Dr. James A. McReynolds. The following year he entered Jefferson Medical College of Philadelphia. Upon his graduation in 1849 he returned to Elkton to establish his practice. He married Julia P. Gorin in 1853; she died the same year. Six years later he married Ellen Reeves who bore him four children, one of whom, James Clark McReynolds, served as associate justice of the United States Supreme Court from 1914 to 1941. After practicing medicine in Elkton for half a century, he died in 1905.

McTyeire, Bishop Holland Nimmons (1824–89), son of John and Elizabeth Amanda Nimmons McTyeire, was born in Barnwell County, South Carolina, on July 28, 1824. After his conversion at the age of twelve, he spent his youth in farming and in attending Cokesbury Academy, Abbeville County, South Carolina. At the age of twenty he graduated from Randolph-Macon College, Virginia, remaining there one more year as a tutor in mathematics. Yielding to the call to preach, he joined the Virginia Conference of the Methodist Church in 1845 and accepted an appointment to Williamsburg. The following year he transferred to the Alabama Conference where for the next three and a half years he served at Mobile, Demopolis, and Columbus. On November 9, 1847, he married Amelia Townsend, daughter of Major John Townsend, founder and editor of the *Mobile Register*. In 1849 he moved on to the Louisiana Conference where he pastored the Felicity Street Church (New Orleans) and also preached regularly to a large black congregation. In 1851 he founded the *New Orleans Christian Advocate*, which he edited until 1858 when the general conference elected him editor of the *Christian Advocate*, the official periodical of the Methodist Episcopal Church, South, published at Nashville, Tennessee. He held the position until 1862 when the federal army took over the Methodist Publishing House for use as an arsenal and hospital. For the next four years he pastored the Methodist Church in Montgomery, Alabama. In the General Conference of 1866 he distinguished himself as a "fighting elder" in winning approval for a measure calling for lay representation in both the annual and general conferences of the church. The same general conference also elected him bishop. During his twenty-three years in the episcopacy he not only played an important part in the formation of the Colored Methodist Episcopal Church and in promoting the missionary enterprises of the church, but he was also the chief agent in the founding of Vanderbilt University. Cornelius Vanderbilt was so impressed with McTyeire's plans for the university that he made his selection as president a condition of his initial gift of $500,000 (later increased to $1,000,000). Their wives were first cousins. McTyeire continued as bishop and as president of Vanderbilt University's board of trust until his death in Nashville on February 15, 1889. He lies buried along with Bishops William McKendree and Joshua Soule on the campus of Vanderbilt University. It was he who wrote George Dick's memorial for the Louisville Annual Conference of 1886. He "always impressed one as being much greater than anything he did."

Magoffin, Beriah (1815–85), son of Beriah and Jane McAfee Magoffin, was born in Harrodsburg, Mercer County, Kentucky, on April 18, 1815. He attended the neighborhood schools and Centre College at nearby Danville, Kentucky, from which he graduated in 1835. He then studied law privately before entering Transylvania College in Lexington where he completed the law course in 1838. After practicing law for nearly a year in Jackson, Mississippi, he returned to Kentucky in 1839 to continue his legal career in his home town. On April 21, 1840, he married Anna Nelson Shelby, grand-daughter of Kentucky's first governor, Isaac Shelby; she bore him five sons and five daughters. He entered public life in 1840 when Governor Robert P. Letcher appointed him police judge for Harrodsburg. Ten years later he was elected as a Democrat to the state Senate and in 1855 he ran unsuccessfully as a candidate for lieutenant governor. In 1859 he won election as governor and soon entered upon an administration dominated by the secession crisis and the Civil War. Aware of Kentucky's vulnerable position, he tried desperately to persuade the southern states to pursue a course of reconciliation with the North. By January 1861, with his hopes of preventing secession fading, he sought to call a state convention to determine Kentucky's course of action, but the Unionist-dominated state legislature, fearing that the secessionists might gain control, rejected his request. Although he refused calls for troops from both Lincoln and Davis in April 1861, he secretly allowed Confederate agents to recruit in the state. In an effort to stem further division within the state, he participated actively in the formulation of Kentucky's neutrality proclamation, which he issued on May 20, 1861. During the months that followed, his position steadily deteriorated as the legislature overrode his vetoes and stripped him of his constitutional powers. Realizing the hopelessness of his situation and threatened with assassination, he resigned on August 18, 1862, after he was assured his successor, although a Unionist, would be "a conservative, just man." He returned to his ancestral estate and to his legal practice in nearby Harrodsburg. He did not reenter politics except to serve one term (1867–69) in the Kentucky legislature. After the war he lost the friendship of many Democrats when he advocated ratification of the Thirteenth Amendment and civil rights for blacks. He died at his home on February 28, 1885.

Martin, John S. (1815–88) was born in Alexandria, Virginia, on September 7, 1815. As a student in Benjamin Hallowell's school he obtained an education that served him well throughout his life. Converted at the age of sixteen and licensed to preach at nineteen, he joined the Baltimore Conference of the Methodist Episcopal Church in 1835. When the Church divided in 1845, he adhered to the Methodist Episcopal Church, South, and after 1866, he was a commanding figure at every general conference, winning election as secretary in 1882 and 1886. He also served as secretary of the Centennial Conference held in Baltimore in 1884. In the fall of 1887, at the age of seventy-two, he was appointed to his last charge at St. Paul's in Baltimore. He died the following year on July 8, 1888.

Marvin, Bishop Enoch M. (1823–77) was born in Warren County, Missouri, on June 12, 1823. Two years after his conversion in 1839 at a camp meeting in St. Charles County, he accepted the call to preach and joined the Missouri Conference of the Methodist Church. He rose rapidly in the esteem of his colleagues and within a few years he was agent for St. Charles College and also pastor of the Centenary and First churches in St. Louis. During the Civil War he served for two years as a chaplain in the Confederate army under General Sterling Price. The General Conference of 1866 elected him bishop. As bishop he not only traveled extensively throughout the conferences but made a yearlong missionary tour around the world during 1876–77. About three months after completing his trip he was attacked with symptoms of pleurisy and died of pneumonia on November 26, 1877. Among his published works were *Christ's Atonement* and *To the East by Way of the West.*

Mason, Michael A. (1853–95), one of the twelve children of James and Nancy Blincoe Mason, was born in Hawesville, Hancock County, Kentucky, on January 15, 1853. He married Sallie Taylor of Louisville, Kentucky, who bore him three children. After practicing law in Hawesville for a number of years, he moved to Atlanta, Georgia, where he died on September 21, 1895.

Meade, George Gordon (1815–72), son of Richard Worsam and Margaret Coats Butler Meade, was born on December 31, 1815, in Cadiz, Spain, where his father was United States naval agent. Two years after his graduation from West Point in 1835 he resigned his commission and engaged in railroad construction in the South. On December 31, 1840, he married Margaretta Sergeant, daughter of John Sergeant; she bore him six children. On May 19, 1842, he returned to the army as second lieutenant of topographical engineers and from that time until 1861, with an interlude of service in the Mexican War, he was continuously employed as a military engineer, advancing to the rank of captain on May 17, 1856. Soon after the start of the Civil War, on August 31, 1861, he was made brigadier general of Pennsylvania volunteers and spent the following winter working on Washington's defenses. He then joined forces with George B. McClellan in the Peninsular Campaign and participated in the Seven Days battles. At Glendale he suffered a wound from which he never fully recovered. After distinguishing himself at Second Manassas, Sharpsburg, Fredericksburg, and Chancellorsville, he took command of the Army of the Potomac on June 28, 1863, and immediately confronted a major Confederate advance into Pennsylvania. Although his victory over Robert E. Lee at Gettysburg in July 1863 won him the thanks of Congress, he was widely criticized for allowing the retreating Confederates to escape capture. Nevertheless, he was promoted to brigadier general in the regular army on January 28, 1864. After fighting through the Wilderness, Spotsylvania, Cold Harbor, and the long months of siege before Petersburg, he was promoted to major general. He remained in the army after the war, commanding successively the Military Division of the Atlantic, the Department of the East, and the third military district of the Department of the South. During these years he also served as commissioner of Fairmount Park in Philadelphia where he died of pneumonia on November 6, 1872.

Messick, Brinkley Morris (1837–1912) was born in Lexington, Kentucky, on February 3, 1837. His parents, Charlton and Martha Messick, were devout members of the Methodist Church and nurtured him in the Christian faith. He had unusually good educational opportunities, first at Centre College in Danville, Kentucky, where he was deeply influenced by Dr. Robert J. Breckinridge, and later at Transylvania University from which he graduated as valedictorian of his class. After receiving the call to preach he joined the Kentucky Conference of the Methodist Church, South, in 1857. He was ordained deacon by Bishop Early in 1860 and elected elder in 1862, but the absence of a bishop due to the disruptions caused by the Civil War prevented his ordination until Bishop Kavanaugh performed it in 1863. He accepted the following appointments from the Kentucky Conference: Oxford (1858–59), Richmond and Providence (1859–60), Lancaster and Stanford (1860–62), Danville (1862–63), Danville, Stanford, and Lancaster (1863–64), Maysville (1864–66), and Lexington (1866–67). He then transferred to the Louisville Conference and over the next nineteen years he held the following assignments, all in the city of Louisville: Twelfth Street (1867–68), Chestnut Street (1868–72), Broadway (1872–76), Chestnut Street (1876–78), Walnut Street (1878–80), Broadway (1880–83), and Walnut Street (1883–86). In 1886 he transferred to the St. Louis Conference; among his appointments were the following: St. John's (1886–?), Cook Avenue (1893–94), presiding elder St. Louis District (1894–97), St. John's (1897–98), superannuated (1898–99), and Cabanne (1899–1900). He then returned to Louisville where he served in the following charges: presiding elder Louisville District (1900–02), Fourth Avenue (1902–06), and presiding elder Louisville District (1906–10). He was superannuated from 1910 until his death in Louisville on September 30, 1912. "And yet eloquent and thoughtful as he was in the pulpit it is not too much to say that his daily life was his greatest sermon."

Moore, Thomas Jefferson (1824–67), son of John L. and Frances Moore, was born in Franklin, Simpson County, Kentucky on March 2, 1824. In 1836 his godly father died; three years later at the age of fifteen he went to Bowling Green to learn the art of printing. During the third year of his apprenticeship in 1841, he was converted at a Methodist revival. He soon became a class leader in the Bowling Green church. As his zeal increased he sought a larger field of service and yielded to the call of God upon him. Accordingly, he was licensed to preach and recommended to the Kentucky Conference of the Methodist Church by the Quarterly Conference of Bowling Green in 1843. He spent his first year on the Owensboro Circuit. In 1845 Bishop Soule ordained him deacon; two years later Bishop Paine ordained him elder. After serving on the Salem, Lafayette, and Hopkinsville circuits, his health failed and he spent 1850–51 as superannuated. He then returned to the itinerant ministry and received the following appointments from the Louisville Conference of the Methodist Episcopal Church, South: Lebanon Circuit (1851–53), Jefferson Circuit (1853–54), Logan Circuit (1854–56), Tract Agent (1856–57), Franklin Circuit (1857–58), Glasgow Circuit (1858–59), presiding elder Glasgow District (1859–62), Franklin (1862–63), Fairview (1864–66), and Logan Circuit (1866–67). In 1846 he married Emarine Bruce who bore him a daughter and two sons. He died of typhoid fever at Olmstead, Kentucky, on September 14, 1867, with George Dick at his bedside. "He was a man of genial spirit and warm heart, earnest in his friendships, and positive in his dislikes."

Morgan, Thomas Hunt (1825–64), son of Calvin Cogswell and Henrietta Hunt Morgan, was born in Huntsville, Alabama, on June 1, 1825. At the age of four he removed with his parents to a farm near Lexington, Kentucky, his mother's home town. After serving in the Mexican War, he returned to Lexington where he engaged in the manufacture of hemp and in the general merchandise business left him by his grandfather Hunt. On November 21, 1848, he married Rebecca Bruce who died on July 21, 1861, after spending many years as an invalid. On September 20, 1861, he entered Confederate service by leading his own company, the Lexington Rifles, which he had organized in 1857, to Bowling Green where he joined the forces of Simon Bolivar Buckner. Shortly thereafter he was elected captain of a cavalry company and early in 1862 he began the series of raids behind federal lines that made him famous and earned him the sobriquet, "The Thunderbolt of the Confederacy." He was promoted to colonel of the 2nd Kentucky Cavalry on April 4, 1862, and brigadier general the following December 11. On December 14, 1862, he married Martha Ready, daughter of Charles Ready, of Murfreesboro, Tennessee. His most famous raid through Indiana and Ohio in July 1863 resulted in his capture near New Lisbon, Ohio, and his imprisonment in the Ohio State Penitentiary. He escaped on November 26, 1863, made his way south, and in April 1864 was placed in command of the Department of Southwest Virginia. Early on the morning of September 4, 1864, as he bivouacked in Greenville, Tennessee, he was killed in a surprise attack by Union cavalry.

Morrison, Bishop Henry Clay (1842–1921) was born near Clarksville, Montgomery County, Tennessee, on May 30, 1842. Although frail in health during his boyhood, he secured an excellent classical education under a private tutor. He continued his studies at Alabama Agricultural and Mechanical College from which in later years he received the honorary Doctor of Divinity degree. After teaching school for several years he was licensed to preach in 1863 by the Methodist Episcopal Church, South. Two years later the Louisville Conference admitted him on trial into the itinerant ministry. He was ordained deacon by Bishop Paine in 1867 and elder by Bishop McTyeire in 1869. In 1868 he married Mrs. M. E. Ray who bore him two sons. During his twenty years in the Louisville Conference he received the following appointments: Millerstown (1865–66), Bardstown and Stover's (1866–67), Elizabethtown (1867–69), Middletown Circuit (1869–72), Shelby Street (Louisville, 1872–76), Broadway (Louisville, 1876–80), Chestnut Street (Louisville, 1880–

84), and Russellville (1884–87). He then transferred to the North Georgia Conference and pastored First Church, Atlanta, for three years. In 1890 the General Conference of the Methodist Episcopal Church, South, elected him one of the three missionary secretaries; he was re-elected four years later. His success in reducing the mission board's great financial burden attracted considerable attention and contributed to his election as bishop in 1898 at the age of forty-six. He discharged his episcopal duties until his death at his son's home in Leesburg, Florida, on December 21, 1921. "His religion was of the mystic kind, and he had a spiritual experience which gave him large views of the possibilities of grace working inwardly into human nature through the power of the Holy Ghost."

Morrison, William H. (1823–73) was born in Fayette County, Pennsylvania, on February 25, 1823. At the age of ten he was converted and joined the Methodist Church. On February 16, 1847, the Quarterly Conference of the Greenville (Kentucky) Circuit licensed him to preach. He was ordained deacon in 1849 and elder in 1851. During his first eleven years in the ministry, the Louisville Conference of the Methodist Episcopal Church, South, gave him the following appointments: Morgantown Mission (1847–48), Barren (1848–49), Cadiz (1849–51), Owensboro Circuit (1851–52), Big Spring (1852–53), Middletown Circuit (1853–54), supernumerary (1854–55), Elkton Circuit (1855–57), and Hardinsburg Circuit (1857–58). During the next eleven years he served as presiding elder of the following districts of the Louisville Conference: Bardstown (1858–1861), Hopkinsville (1861–1865), and Russellville (1865–1869). Declining health forced him to accept supernumerary and superannuated status during the last four years of his life. He died at his home near Casky's Station in Christian County, Kentucky, on March 4, 1873. Possessed of a "clear, well-defined religious experience, his piety, while not whimsical, was sufficiently emotional to impart a pleasant glow to his enjoyments, and in the process of time ripened into the most implicit confidence in God."

Morrow, Thomas Scott (c. 1821–?), son of James and Mary Scott Morrow, was born near Old Volney in Logan County, Kentucky, about 1821. He attended Old Volney School at the time George Dick was also a student there. About 1840 he married Elizabeth LaRue of Tennessee who bore him six children. When the Civil War broke out he enlisted in the Confederate army as a private in Company D, 2nd Kentucky Cavalry. He served until early 1863 when the company payroll for February 28 listed him as "absent without leave." According to family tradition he joined rebel guerrillas under William C. Quantrill and was especially adroit at using himself as a decoy to lure Union patrols into a trap. After the war he apparently did not return to his family in Kentucky, but lived elsewhere and raised another family.

Morton, David (1833–98), the son of Marmaduke Beckwith and Nancy Caldwell Morton, was born in Russellville, Kentucky, on June 4, 1833. His father was a farmer, banker, and county court clerk; he was an official of the Nimrod Banking Co. when it was robbed by the Jesse James gang in 1868. David received a classical education at the Russellville Academy where he studied under William Wines, a Vermont Yankee, and John P. French, a Virginia Cavalier. Reared in a devout Methodist home, he was converted when still a boy. As a teenager he clerked in a Russellville store, worked in his father's county court clerk's office, and served for a short time as deputy sheriff. He was called to preach in 1851, licensed in 1852, and admitted on trial into the Louisville Conference of the Methodist Episcopal Church, South, in 1853. The following year, on August 8, 1854, he married Hannah Wilson Bottomley, daughter of Thomas Bottomley, also a Methodist preacher in the Louisville Conference; she bore him nine children, four of whom died in infancy. He was ordained deacon by Bishop Paine in 1855, and elder by Bishop Pierce in 1857. Between 1853 and 1864 he accepted the following charges: Mammoth Cave (1853–54), Campbellsville (1854–56), Russellville (1856–57), Bardstown (1857–58), Owensboro (1858–60), agent for Southern Kentucky College (1860–61), Elkton (1861–63), and Hopkinsville Circuit (1863–64). From 1864 to 1868 he served as president of Southern Kentucky Female Collegiate Institute in Russellville, Kentucky, founded eight years before. In 1867 he drew up a new charter in which he changed the name to Logan Female College. In all, he was connected with the college for twenty-eight years as president, agent, and director. As agent (1868–74) he raised $35,000 for the school and was the driving force behind the erection of a new building in 1872. During 1874–76 he was presiding elder of the Russellville District. He spent the following year in the Denver Conference at Helena City (1876–77). Returning to the Louisville Conference, he held the following appointments: educational agent (1877–78), Elkton (1878–79), and educational agent (1879–82). At the general conference of the Methodist Episcopal Church, South, in 1882, he was elected the first secretary of the board of church extension, a position he held for sixteen years until his death. In 1883 Centenary College of Jackson, Louisiana, conferred the Doctor of Divinity degree on him. Keenly interested in the history of Methodism, he founded the historical society of the Louisville Conference. He died on March 9, 1898, in Louisville from blood poisoning caused by a splinter of wood stuck in his finger.

Mulligan, Rory O. (1860–1926), only son of Gilbert M. and Lucy Douglas Tate Mulligan, was born in Scottsville, Allen County, Kentucky, on June 15, 1860. His father was a lawyer who commanded an extensive practice in Warren and Allen counties. By the time he was seventeen years old, young Rory had achieved proficiency in the English classics, higher mathematics, and Latin. At the age of nineteen he decided to pursue a career in law. He attended Vanderbilt University for five months and completed his formal training at Cumberland University, Lebanon, Tennessee, from which he graduated in 1881. He then returned to Scottsville where he practiced law until his death on February 5, 1926.

Murrell, Schuyler L. (1815–90) was born in Adair County, Kentucky, on October 27,

1815. Two days after his conversion on January 3, 1837, he joined the Methodist Church. A year later, on April 26, 1838, he married Lockie S. Montgomery. On July 28, 1841, he was licensed to exhort, and on November 20 of the same year he was licensed to preach. When the Louisville Conference of the Methodist Episcopal Church, South, was organized in 1846, he and George Dick were among those admitted on trial into the itinerant ministry in that year. He was ordained deacon in 1848 and elder in 1850. Included among his appointments during his forty-four years in the Louisville Conference were the following: Barren (1846–47), Scottsville (1847–48), Burksville (1848–49), Franklin (1849–51), Greenville (1851–52), Logan (1852–53), Big Spring (1853–55), Elizabethtown (1855–57), Hartford (1857–59), Madisonville (1859–60), Hopkinsville Circuit (1860–61), Elizabethtown Circuit (1861–63), presiding elder Glasgow District (1863–67), Franklin (1867–69), Morganfield (1869–71), Jeffersontown Circuit (1871–73), Morganfield Circuit (1873–75), Greensburg Circuit (1875–76), Munfordville (1876–77), Caverna (1877–79), Smith's Grove (1880–81), superannuated (1881–83), Hodgenville (1883–84), superannuated (1884–85), and Mt. Lebanon (1885–86), after which he continued as superannuated until his death at Horse Cave, Kentucky, on September 3, 1890. "He was an earnestly religious man, quite emotional at times, with a bright personal experience that made him a happy, cheerful Christian."

Needham, George (1839–1903), the son of Parkman Smith and Rebecca Sandusky South Needham, was born January 22, 1839, on Linder's Creek, near Pleasant Grove Church, Hardin County, Kentucky. He was converted in 1860 at Millerstown while alone in the woods near Nolin River and received into the Methodist Episcopal Church, South, at Mount Carmel in Hardin County. He had only twenty-two months of formal education, but his wide reading provided him with a storehouse of general information. In 1860 he was licensed to preach by the Hudsonville Quarterly Conference, which met at his father's house. On July 9, 1861, he married Lizzie South

of Muhlenberg County, Kentucky. He was admitted on trial into the Louisville Conference of the Methodist Episcopal Church, South, in 1873. He was ordained deacon at the same conference by Bishop Keener; in 1877 Bishop Kavanaugh ordained him elder. He filled Munfordville Circuit (1873–75), Leitchfield (1875–76), West Point Circuit (1876–77), and Spottsville (1877–81). He then moved west and for the next twelve years preached in the following appointments: Denver Mission (1881–82), Pueblo (1882–83), presiding elder New Mexico District (1883–87), presiding elder Trinidad District (1887–91), Mission and Pueblo Collegiate Institute (1891–92), and Farmington Circuit and Mission (1892–93). He then transferred back to the Louisville Conference and served the following charges: presiding elder Columbia District (1893–97), Louisville Mission (1897–98), Louisville Circuit (1898–99), Bradfordsville Circuit (1899–1901), and Dixon Circuit (1901–02). Then his health failed. After spending a year at his brother's in Los Angeles, California, where he was treated for dropsy, he returned to Kentucky where he died in 1903 at his son's home in Hardin County. "Notwithstanding all his merit, his faith never seemed robust; it never seemed to penetrate through the mist and sorrows of this life and appropriate the great promises of God."

Nelson, William (1824–62), youngest son of Dr. Thomas W. and Frances Doniphan Nelson, was born near Maysville, Kentucky, on September 27, 1824. He attended Norwich Academy in Vermont from 1837 to 1839. On January 28, 1840, he was appointed midshipman in the United States navy; he became passed midshipman on July 11, 1846. During the Mexican War he served in the fleet that supported Winfield Scott's landing at Vera Cruz during March 9–29, 1847. Later he served with the Mediterranean Squadron. He was promoted to master in September 1854 and lieutenant on April 18, 1855. In early 1861 he made several visits to Kentucky to survey political sentiment, reporting his observations directly to President Lincoln. When the president sent him back to his native state to recruit for the Union and to arm loyalists, he distributed thousands of guns to the Kentucky Home Guard, the Unionist military organization of the state. In August he established Camp Dick Robinson in Garrard County, which became an important recruiting station and a rallying place for loyal Kentuckians. On September 16, 1861, he was commissioned brigadier general of volunteers and later went to eastern Kentucky to supervise recruiting camps. He soon joined Don Carlos Buell's Army of the Ohio and took command of the 4th Division. His troops played an important part in the Union victory at Shiloh in April 1862. Shortly after his promotion to major general of volunteers on July 17, 1862, he marched into Kentucky to oppose the invading Confederates under Braxton Bragg and E. Kirby Smith. The latter's army overwhelmed him at Richmond on August 30. Shortly thereafter, as he was engaged in organizing the defense of Louisville, he had occasion to reprimand Brigadier General Jefferson C. Davis for alleged negligence. A few days after the incident, on September 29, 1862, he encountered Davis in the lobby of the Galt House in Louisville. In the argument that ensued, Davis shot and killed him. He was the only naval officer, Confederate or Union, to become a full-rank Civil War major general.

Newton, Silas (1836–1907), son of Artemas and Polly Newton, was born in Wayne County, Pennsylvania, on December 10, 1836. After his conversion at the age of twenty, he joined the Methodist Church, the church of his parents. He took advantage of some excellent educational opportunities, attending the New York Conference Seminary for four years and Harvard University where he took his master's degree. At first he resisted the call to preach, choosing instead to emigrate to Kentucky in 1857 where he taught school at Shepherdsville one year and Hodgenville for two years. Finally, in the fall of 1860 he joined the Louisville Conference of the Methodist Episcopal Church, South. During the next forty-three years he was sent to the following charges: Smithland (1860–61), New Haven Circuit (1861–62), Taylor Circuit (1862–64), Calhoun

(1864–65), Logan (1865–66), Shepherdsville Circuit (1866–67), Asbury and Rose Lane (Louisville, 1867–68), Trenton Mission (1868–69), Lebanon and Springfield (1869–70), Cave City (1870–71), Kavanaugh and 13th Street (Louisville, 1871–72), Yelvington Circuit (1872–75), Cromwell Circuit (1875–77), Jeffersontown (1877–80), Hodgenville (1880–81), Franklin (1881–82), Scottsville (1882–83), Brandenburg (1883–86), Yelvington (1886–88), Smithland (1888–91), Cadiz (1891–94), Yelvington (1894–95), Calhoun (1895–97), Hartford (1897–99), Caseyville and Sturgis (1899–1901), Robards (1901–02), and Dawson (1902–03). He was a strong southern sympathizer during the Civil War and on two occasions federal authorities arrested him. He was released the first time through the influence of a northern officer who was an old schoolmate. On the second occasion he simply mounted his horse and rode away "without asking leave of absence." He was married on November 19, 1868, in Louisville, Kentucky, to S. Kate Brush, daughter of George W. Brush, who bore him five children. He devoted considerable time to caring for his children after his wife's death in 1885. Three of them survived his death on Thanksgiving Day, November 28, 1907. "His heart was as tender as a child's and his gentleness as that of the disciple whom Jesus loved."

Paine, Bishop Robert (1799–1882), son of James and May Alexander Williams Paine was born in Person County, North Carolina, on November 12, 1799. His great-grandfather, James Paine, was born in London, England, where he practiced medicine, and his grandfather, Robert Paine, served as an officer in the rebel army during the American Revolution. In 1814 his father, who had attended the University of North Carolina and was a man "of large means for those early days," emigrated with his family to Giles County in south-central Tennessee. There young Robert, who had earlier attended school near Leasburg, North Carolina, resumed his education with two classical teachers: Rev. D. C. Weir and Prof. Alexander whose school was located near Linnville in Giles County. His parents were Baptists but while at school he boarded for a time with a Methodist landlady and attended a Methodist camp meeting at Mt. Pisgah where he was converted on October 9, 1817. Shortly thereafter he was licensed to preach and in 1818 the Tennessee Conference of the Methodist Episcopal Church admitted him on trial into the traveling ministry. After two years on the circuit he volunteered as a missionary to the newly settled country beyond the Black Warrior Mountains in southern Alabama where he spent a year creating a new circuit. During the next nine years the Tennessee Conference appointed him to the following charges: Murfreesboro (1821–22), Shelbyville (1822–23), Franklin (1823–24), Lebanon (1823–25), presiding elder Jackson's Purchase District (1825–26), Nashville (1826–27), and presiding elder Nashville District (1827–29). In 1829 he was elected president of newly established La Grange College, a Methodist school in La Grange, Alabama, a position he held for the next seventeen years. Toward the end of his presidency he played an active role in the events surrounding the division of the Methodist Church. He was a member of the committee of nine that formed the Plan of Separation at the General Conference of 1844 and a member of the Louisville Convention of 1845 where the Methodist Episcopal Church, South, was born. At the first general conference of the newly formed church in 1846, he was elected bishop and for thirty-six years he continued in that office until shortly before his death on October 19, 1882. Bishop Paine married three times, first in early manhood to Susanna Beck, granddaughter of General James Robertson, pioneer of Middle Tennessee; second to Amanda Shaw, daughter of a Presbyterian minister of Columbia, Tennessee who died soon after her marriage; and lastly to Miss Millwater of Alabama who survived him. "Such was his modesty and diffidence that he always shrank from prominent positions, and was only induced to accept from a sense of duty and the urgent persuasions of his brethren."

Palmer, John McAuley (1817–1900), the son of Louis D. and Ann Hansford Palmer, was born in Scott County, Kentucky, on September 13, 1817. When he was fourteen his father, who held antislavery views, moved the family to the free state of Illinois, settling near Alton. Young Palmer attended Shurtleff College in Alton for two years; then he peddled clocks and taught in a country school before moving to Carlinville in 1839 where he read law and was admitted to the bar. On December 20, 1842, he married Malinda Ann Neely of Carlinville who died in 1885; she bore him ten children. In the years before the Civil War he was elected as a Democrat to the state senate where he was an outspoken opponent of slavery expansion. He played an important part in the formation of the Republican party in Illinois, serving as president of the Bloomington convention in May 1856; he was also a delegate to the Chicago Republican National Convention, which nominated Abraham Lincoln in 1860. He began his Civil War career on May 25, 1861, as colonel of the 14th Illinois Infantry. On December 20, 1861, after participating in engagements at New Madrid (Missouri) and Island No. 10 (Tennessee), he was promoted to brigadier general of volunteers. In 1862 he was made commander of the 1st Division in the Army of the Mississippi and, after serving gallantly in Tennessee at Stone River and Chickamauga, he was awarded the rank of major general on March 16, 1863. In August 1864 he asked to be relieved of his command as a result of a quibble over relative rank. Late in the war, when he was given command of the Department of Kentucky, he achieved notoriety by freely issuing his famous "Palmer's passes," which guaranteed safe passage to slaves who sought freedom across the Ohio River. He lived an active political life after the Civil War. In 1868 he was elected governor of Illinois on the Republican ticket. During the 1870s he returned to the Democratic party and ran unsuccessfully for governor in 1888, but in 1891 he was elected to a term in the U.S. Senate. In 1896 he and former Confederate Lieutenant General Simon B. Bucker joined hands as the nominees of the Gold Democrats who rejected the free-silver doctrine of William Jennings Bryan. Palmer polled only 130,000 votes. He died in Springfield, Illinois, on September 25, 1900.

Parker, Bishop Linus (1829–85) was born in Rome, New York, on April 23, 1829. At the age of sixteen he moved to New Orleans where he worked as a clerk in a dry-goods store. Shortly after his arrival he was converted in a revival at the Polydras Street Methodist Church. In 1846 he volunteered for the U.S. Army and spent some time fighting in Mexico during the Mexican War. Upon his return he felt the call to preach and in 1849 the Louisiana Conference of the Methodist Episcopal Church, South, admitted him on trial. He was ordained deacon in 1851 and elected elder in 1853. During his years as an itinerant preacher, he held the following appointments: Lake Providence (1849–50), Shreveport (1850–53), Elijah Steel Chapel (New Orleans, 1853–54), Felicity (New Orleans, 1854–56), Carondolet Street (New Orleans, 1856–58), presiding elder New Orleans District (1858–59), Felicity Street (1859–71), presiding elder New Orleans District (1871–75), Louisiana Avenue (New Orleans, 1875–76), and presiding elder New Orleans District (1876–80). In 1870 he was elected editor of the *New Orleans Christian Advocate*, a position he held until his election as bishop by the general conference of the Methodist Episcopal Church, South, in 1882. He died after a brief episcopacy on March 6, 1885, in New Orleans.

Parsons, Charles Booth (1805–71), the oldest of four children, was born in Enfield, Connecticut, on July 23, 1805. His mother was unable to provide for the family after his father died of yellow fever, so at the age of fifteen he set out for New York City where he found a job in a store. Most of his associates were members of a neighborhood thespian society and he soon joined them. On one occasion, after he had played the part of Sir Edward Mortimer in the "Iron chest," one of the city newspapers compared him favorably with the elder Keen, who was then considered great in that role. Filled with visions of fame, at the age of eighteen he joined a theatrical company preparing for a tour through the South. He rose rapidly in his profession and soon achieved recognition as one of the premiere actors of his day. On December 7, 1830, he married Emily C. Oldham of Louisville who bore him seven children. Sometime during the 1830s after reading a book entitled, *History of the Bible*, he was converted and yielded to the call to preach. In 1839 he gave up his acting career, joined the Methodist Church, and began to study for the ministry. Two years later the Kentucky Conference admitted him on trial as an itinerant preacher and assigned him to the Jefferson Circuit. He was ordained deacon in 1843 and elder by Bishop Soule in 1845. In 1845 he transferred to the St. Louis Conference where he spent the next twelve years preaching in St. Louis and other Missouri churches of the Methodist Episcopal Church, South. He then returned to Kentucky where he held the following appointments, all in the city of Louisville: Shelby Street (1858–59), Brook Street (1859–61), Walnut Street (1861–63), and Twelfth Street (1863–65). In 1865, after the Louisville Conference threatened to investigate him for "gross impropriety," he withdrew and joined the Methodist Episcopal Church, North. Three years later, as he landed at the Louisville wharf after a trip to Pittsburgh to dedicate a church, he was stricken with paralysis in his lower limbs. After a lingering illness, he died in Portland, a suburb of Louisville, on December 8, 1871.

Peak, Joel (1800–74), son of Hezekiah and Elizabeth Peak, was born in Mason County, Kentucky, on November 7, 1800. Soon after his birth his parents moved to Scott County where he grew up. He was converted at the age of fourteen and joined the Methodist Episcopal Church at Georgetown, Kentucky. On December 30, 1820, he married Cassandra Peak who bore him six children. Thirteen years later, on March 16, 1833, the quarterly conference of the Lexington Circuit licensed him to preach and in 1837 the Kentucky Conference admitted him on trial into the itinerant ministry. He was ordained deacon by Bishop Roberts in 1839 and elder by Bishop Soule in 1841. He continued in the Kentucky Conference until it was divided in October 1847. He then became a member of the Louisville Conference of the Methodist Episcopal Church, South, in which he held the following appointments:

Burksville (1847–48), Scottsville (1848–49), Albany (1849–50), supernumerary (1850–51), Mammoth Cave (1851–53), Franklin (1853–54), superannuated (1854–58), Rochester Mission (1858–59), Bowling Green Circuit (1859–60), superannuated (1860–62), Rochester Mission (1862–63), Franklin Circuit (1863–65), Gordonsville (1865–66), and New Roe Circuit (1866–67). Seven years later, on December 19, 1874, after four months of intense suffering, he died at Auburn in Logan County, Kentucky. "He labored faithfully as a 'field hand' throughout his active ministry."

Pell, Joseph Curtis (1822–96), son of Samuel B. and Elizabeth Curtis Pell, was born in Bracken County, Kentucky, on June 5, 1822. His father served as sheriff of Hancock County for fourteen years and as a member of the state legislature in 1855 and 1856; he died in 1864 while holding the office of sheriff. Joseph was the third of a family of nine children. After completing his education in Trimble County, he turned to boating on the Ohio River for ten years. On June 6, 1848, he married Ann Caroline Blincoe who bore him ten children, four of whom died in infancy. After his marriage he became a prosperous merchant in Lewisport, Hancock County, where he also acquired a farm of about 200 acres. As a devout Methodist his home was always open to traveling preachers, including George Dick. He died in Lewisport on July 9, 1896.

Penick, Thomas M. (1814–85) was born in Jessamine County, Kentucky, on May 30, 1814. He was converted early in life and joined the Methodist Church. As a young man he set out for Texas to seek his fortune. There he joined the Texans in fighting Indians and Mexicans. He also married Eliza Moore with whom he returned to Kentucky. She soon died and he afterward married Mary J. Barnes of Princeton, Kentucky, who also died a few months later. Meanwhile he yielded to the conviction that he ought to preach the gospel and in 1851 he was received on trial into the Louisville Conference of the Methodist Episcopal Church, South. He was ordained deacon in 1853 and elder in

1855. During these years he accepted the following appointments: Adairville Mission (1851–52), Lafayette (1852–53), Princeton (1853–54), and Hardinsburg Circuit (1854–55). In 1855 he transferred to the Louisiana Conference where he served on the Caddo Circuit for several years. There he married a third time to Mrs. Josephine E. Thompson, daughter of the Rev. Jesse Birch, a local Methodist preacher. When the Civil War broke out he took up the southern cause and enlisted in the Confederate army as a private. He participated in a number of battles, managing to avoid injury or capture. After the war he moved back to Kentucky once more and in 1872 was readmitted into the itinerant ranks of the Louisville Conference. During the next several years he held the following charges: Sharon Mission (1872–73), Morgantown Mission (1873–74), Brandenburg (1874–75), superannuated (1875–76), and Nortonville (1876–77). Although he was superannuated during the last eight years of his life, he continued to distribute Bibles and to hold meetings until he was stricken with a fatal paralysis in July 1883. He lingered for two years until his death on September 24, 1885, at South Carrollton, Kentucky. "He had some trials, and passed through deep waters, but God's grace was sufficient."

Peters, Timothy Carpenter (1831–1914) was born in eastern Tennessee on December 1, 1831. Brought up in a religious home, he was converted in his father's house at the age of nine. Rev. Timothy Carpenter, who baptized him in his infancy, received him into the Methodist Church. He felt the call to preach the gospel when he was eighteen. After completing his formal education, he taught school for three years; at the same time he was active as a local preacher, frequently holding revivals. On July 28, 1861, he married Rebecca Bosley Frogge, a sister of Rev. Timothy Carpenter Frogge. Three months after his marriage the Louisville Conference of the Methodist Episcopal Church, South, admitted him on trial into the itinerant ministry. He was elected deacon in 1863 and ordained elder by Bishop Kavanaugh in 1865. During the forty-six years of his active ministry he filled the following charges: Tompkinsville

(1861–62), Burksville (1862–63), Scottsville (1863–65), Greenville (1865–67), Cadiz (1867–70), Madisonville (1870–72), Slaughtersville (1872–73), Corydon Circuit (1873–75), Franklin Circuit (1875–77), Adairville (1877–78), Bowling Green Circuit (1878–80), Cadiz (1880–81), Fairview (1881–82), presiding elder Elizabethtown District (1882–86), presiding elder Lebanon District (1886–87), Big Spring (1887–88), Lafayette (1888–89), Horse Cave (1889–91), Woodburn (1891–92), Madisonville (1892–95), Elizabethtown (1895–98), Glasgow and Dover (1898–99), Greenville (1899–1903), Eddyville (1903–04), Leitchfield (1904–06), and Bardstown (1906–07). Near the end of his year at Bardstown he was stricken with paralysis and never fully recovered. Death came in 1914. "He gloried in the privileges of being an itinerant Methodist preacher."

Petree, Hazel G. (1820–1900), a descendant of one of the pioneer families of Kentucky, was born near Elkton in Todd County on July 5, 1820. As preparation for his life's work, he studied law in the office of F. M. Bristow of Elkton. He later married Bristow's daughter, Mary M., who bore him two children. After his admission to the bar, he entered into partnership with his father-in-law, which continued until Bristow's death in 1864. He was one of the founders of the Bank of Elkton and its president for twenty years. In 1891 he represented Todd County at the state constitutional convention. Four year later, he was elected state senator on the Republican ticket and represented his district for four years. He also served as a trustee of the Vanderbilt Training School in Elkton, to which he contributed substantial amounts of money. In like manner, he gave generous support toward the construction of a new Methodist Church in Elkton, which was named Petree Memorial in his honor. He died in 1900.

Petree, James Columbus (1831–1918), son of Hazel G. and Paulina S. Petree, was born near Elkton in Todd County, Kentucky, on July 8, 1831. He descended from some of the earliest settlers in Todd County and his parents' home was the preaching place for

Peter Cartwright, James Axley, and other pioneer preachers who laid the foundations of Methodism in south-central Kentucky. He attended the common schools in his neighborhood and spent one year at Cumberland University in Lebanon, Tennessee. At the age of sixteen he was converted at a camp meeting held at Hermon, near Elkton, and shortly thereafter joined the Methodist Episcopal Church, South. Six years later, on August 20, 1853, the quarterly conference admitted him on trial into the traveling ministry. He was ordained deacon by Bishop Paine in 1855 and elder by Bishop Pierce in 1857. During his fifty years of active work he filled the following appointments: Lafayette and Cadiz (1853–54), West Point (1854–55), Eighth Street (Louisville, 1855–56), Lafayette Circuit (1856–57), Smithland (1857–58), Bowling Green, (1858–59), Smithland (1859–60), Middletown (1860–61), Cadiz Circuit (1861–63), Hopkinsville and Elkton (1863–64), Lafayette (1864–66), Fairview (1866–67), Hopkinsville (1867–69), Allensville (1869–71), Adairville (1871–75), Corydon (1875–79), Elkton Circuit (1879–83), Morganfield Circuit (1883–87), Hardinsburg (1887–1891), Henderson (1891–92), Trenton Circuit (1892–96), Corydon (1896–98), Elkton Circuit (1898–99), and Hartford Circuit (1899–1903). He married twice, first to Annie Wilson of Smithland, Kentucky, on November 22, 1858. Two years after her death he married Amanda Walton on September 15, 1903. At the end of his fiftieth year in the itinerant ministry he requested to be made superannuate, a status he held until his death on March 16, 1918. "He was pre-eminently a man of prayer.... Those who heard his public prayers marvelled at the altitudes to which his enraptured soul would mount in his moments of highest inspiration."

Pierce, Bishop George Foster (1811–84), son of Lovick and Ann Foster Pierce, was born in Greene County, Georgia, on February 3, 1811. At the time of his birth his father was presiding elder of the Oconee District, South Carolina Conference, Methodist Episcopal Church. Few Methodist preachers could afford to send their sons to college in those days, but young George graduated from Franklin College, Athens, Georgia, and set out to pursue a legal career. The call to preach rested heavily upon him, however, and soon "the light of the future died out of Blackstone's pages, whilst a holy radiance issued from the leaves of the Bible." In 1831 the Georgia Conference admitted him on trial into the itinerant ministry. During the next nine years he filled a number of appointments in Georgia and South Carolina, including Augusta, Oglethorpe, Savannah, and Charleston. In 1840 he was elected president of Georgia Female College at Macon, the first chartered female college in the United States. During these years he also played an important part in the events that led to the division of the Methodist Church in 1844 and the creation of the Methodist Episcopal Church, South, in 1845. In 1848 he became president of Emory College, a position he held until his election as bishop in 1854. Among his published works was *Incidents of Western Travel*. He died on September 3, 1884. "He was deaf to the remonstrances of his friends, and not always obedient to the requirements of his physician, for it was meat and drink for him to preach the gospel."

Potter, Moses (1808–1902), son of Frederick and Elizabeth Kirby Potter, was born at the old Potter homestead in the Three Springs neighborhood near Bowling Green, Warren County, Kentucky, on February 27, 1808. His father was a native of South Carolina and his mother a native of Virginia. Moses was the eldest of thirteen children. He was educated in neighborhood schools and then devoted his life to farming, becoming one of the largest landowners in Warren County. He was one of the greatest tobacco traders in south-central Kentucky and also dealt extensively in horses and mules. On February 28, 1828, he married Elenor Eliza Butte of Culpeper County, Virginia, who bore him six children. After her death on May 10, 1879, he married Mrs. Tabitha Jordan Tully of Russellville, Kentucky, in March 1883. He died at the age of ninety-four on September 4, 1902.

Potter, Pleasant J. (1820–1915), son of Frederick and Elizabeth Kirby Potter and

younger brother of Moses Potter, was born in the Three Springs neighborhood near Bowling Green, Warren County, Kentucky, on March 29, 1820. He was educated in neighborhood schools and at Southern College in Bowling Green. In early life he devoted himself almost exclusively to agricultural pursuits, occasionally teaching school and working as a surveyor in Warren and other counties in southern Kentucky. On January 25, 1844, he married Julia R. Hill, daughter of W. Hill, a prosperous Warren County farmer; she bore him ten children. As a young man he also took an interest in politics. He was elected sheriff of Warren County in 1858 and won reelection two years later. In 1865 he was elected to the state legislature. Then he withdrew from public life to pursue his interest in banking. In October 1869 he engaged in general banking in partnership with J. H. Vivian who retired in 1875 for reasons of health. Nine years later he took his three sons, James Erasmus, Hubert P., and William J., into business with him and created the banking firm of P. J. Potter and Company. For a number of years he also served on the board of directors of the Louisville and Nashville Railroad. He soon became one of the largest property holders in Warren County and contributed generously to the Methodist Episcopal Church, South, and other philanthropic causes. For his large contribution in 1890 to a woman's college in Bowling Green, it was named "Pleasant J. Potter College for Young Ladies" in his honor. When the Potter Bank suffered reverses in 1905 he lost his holdings. He died on July 1, 1915, in Bowling Green.

Powell, Lazarus Whitehead (1812–67), the third son of Lazarus and Ann McMahon Powell, was born in Henderson County, Kentucky, on October 6, 1812. He attended neighborhood schools before enrolling in St. Joseph's College in Bardstown, Kentucky, from which he graduated in 1833. He then began the study of law in Bardstown under John Rowan, completing his training at Transylvania University in Lexington. After his admission to the bar in 1835 he formed in Henderson, Kentucky, a law partnership with Archibald Dixon. Politics was his first love, however, and in

1836 he won election as a Democrat to the lower house of the state legislature. On November 8, 1837, he married Harriet Ann Jennings who bore him three sons; she died in 1846. In 1848 he won the Democratic nomination for governor but failed of election. Three years later, running against his former law partner, Archibald Dixon, he was victorious. In 1858 he won election to the U.S. Senate and served from 1859 to 1865. Reflecting the majority sentiment in Kentucky, he strongly supported the neutrality of his state and desperately sought to bring about a compromise between North and South. And as a man of decidedly southern sympathies, he opposed the government's policy of political arrests and military interference in elections. He carried on in 1861 despite a call from the Kentucky legislature for his resignation and resolutions for his expulsion introduced by his Kentucky colleague, Senator Garret Davis. Not many years later both his state and his colleague admitted they were wrong. When his Senate term expired he returned to his home in Kentucky to practice law. In 1867 he was again a strong contender for the U.S. Senate, but the Kentucky legislature finally settled on Garret Davis. Six months after his defeat, he died of apoplexy at his home near Henderson on July 3, 1867.

Prentice, George Dennison (1802–70), the son of Rufus and Sarah Stanton Prentice, was born in Preston, Connecticut, on December 18, 1802. At the age of fifteen he entered Brown University, Providence, Rhode Island. Blessed with a remarkable memory, he is said to have recited, at a single lesson, the twelfth book of Xenophon's *Aeneid*. After his graduation in 1823 he turned his attention to the study of the law but soon gave it up in favor of pursuing a career in newspapers. He spent two years as an editor of the *Connecticut Mirror* and for a time was connected with John Greenleaf Whittier in publishing the *New England Weekly Review*. During the presidential contest of 1828 he traveled to Kentucky and, after writing the life of Henry Clay, settled in Louisville. On November 24, 1830, he issued the first number of the *Louisville Daily Journal*. When the *Journal* merged with the *Louisville Courier* in 1868,

he continued as one of the editors. From 1830 to 1861 his influence was perhaps as great as any political writer in the United States and his paper acquired distinction throughout the country and in Europe as well. When the Civil War broke out, he championed the Union cause and used his pen with great power against the rebellion; at the same time he was known as one who performed many acts of individual kindness to those who opposed him. In 1835 he married Henrietta Benham, daughter of the distinguished Kentucky lawyer, Joseph Benham. The couple had two sons, both of whom ironically became Confederate soldiers; one died while leading his company in the battle of Augusta, Kentucky, on September 27, 1862. Henrietta Prentice died in 1868, followed by her husband on January 22, 1870. "He was not, strictly speaking quarrelsome, but brave and aggressive; was ready, at any time, to support his doctrines by muscular strength, as well as by his pen, and was seldom or never worsted."

Price, John William (1842–1920), son of Thomas and Elizabeth Baker Price, was born in La Grange, Missouri, on December 30, 1842. While he was still an infant, his parents moved to Russellville, Kentucky, where he grew to manhood. He attended Southern College in nearby Bowling Green. In 1869 he married Mary E. Valentine who bore him six children. Though he was licensed to preach as a teenager, his heart was set on the study and practice of medicine, which he pursued for several years. Finally in the fall of 1864 he put his medical career aside and joined the itinerant ranks of the Louisville Conference of the Methodist Episcopal Church, South. He was ordained deacon by Bishop Doggett in 1866 and elder by Bishop McTyeire in 1868. During these years he accepted the following appointments: Woodburn Circuit (1864–65), Mammoth Cave (1865–66), Auburn and Woodburn (1866–67), Smithland (1867–69), Hopkinsville (1869–71), Henderson (1871–73), and supernumerary (1873–74). In 1874 he transferred to the Illinois Conference. After serving one year as presiding elder of Pana District he returned to the Louisville Conference to pastor at Lafayette (1875–77), Henryville (1877–78), and Auburn (1878–79). In 1879 he transferred to the North Mississippi Conference where his appointments included the following: Deer Creek (1879–80), Lake Lee and Leota (1880–82), presiding elder Greenville District (1882–84), Water Valley (1884–86), Columbus (1886–?), Water Valley (1893–95), Greenwood (1895–97), McNutt (1897–98), Holly Springs (1898–1900), Cleveland (1900–03), Areola and Hollandale (1903–04), Rosedale (1904–06), Lula and Lyon (1906–09), Tutwiler (1909–?), and Lambert (1915–17). He was superannuated until his death at the home of his daughter in Somerville, Tennessee, on June 22, 1920. "His pastorates were notably evangelistic, gracious revivals attending his ministry of the Word."

Price, Joseph Charles (1854–93), whose father was a slave and whose mother was free born, was born in Elizabeth City, North Carolina, on February 10, 1854. He was educated in freedmen's schools, after which he attended Shaw University in Raleigh, North Carolina, where he was converted during a revival. Yielding to the call to preach, he was licensed by the African Methodist Episcopal Zion Church in 1875 and entered Lincoln University in Pennsylvania to prepare for the ministry. He graduated in 1879 with a major in classics and then stayed on to complete a two-year theological course of studies. In 1881 he went abroad to attend the Ecumemical Methodist Conference in London. During his stay he toured Great Britain in an effort to raise funds for Zion Wesley Institute in Salisbury, North Carolina. With pledges totaling nearly $10,000, he returned to become president of the school, which was renamed Livingstone College after the famous African missionary and explorer. During the next decade he attracted national attention for his leadership in black education, which, he insisted, should include liberal arts as well as industrial training. As a famous preacher and a skilled orator, he used his talents to promote causes that lay close to his heart, namely, prohibition and racial justice. In 1890 a black civil rights organization, the Afro-American National League, named

him its first president. Three years later, at the height of his career, he was afflicted with Bright's disease and died in Salisbury, North Carolina, on October 25, 1893.

Redford, Albert Henry (1818–84), son of Woodson and Elizabeth Bent Redford was born in St. Louis, Missouri, on November 18, 1818. In early childhood he suffered an accident that crippled his right arm for life. His misfortune excited the sympathy of his uncle, S. W. Topping, who determined to give him the benefit of a classical education and prepare him for a lucrative profession. It was not to be. As a result of attending a Methodist church he was converted and shortly thereafter felt impressed to preach the gospel, much to the mortification of his uncle. In the fall of 1837 the Kentucky Conference of the Methodist Church received him on trial into the traveling ministry. When the church split in 1845, he cast his lot with the Methodist Episcopal Church, South, and held the following appointments from the Louisville Conference: Shannon (1845–46), Hopkinsville (1846–47), presiding elder Southland District (1847–50), presiding elder West Louisville District (1850–54), Shelby Street (Louisville, 1854–55), presiding elder Bardstown District (1855–58), and agent for Louisville Conference Book and Tract Depository (1858–66). His success as book agent for the Louisville Conference led to his election as book agent of the entire denomination at the General Conference of 1866. For twelve years he battled with the varying fortunes of the publishing house in Nashville, Tennessee, but he also found time to publish his three volume *Methodism in Kentucky* (1868–70). Unfortunately, some of his financial practices as book agent clouded his departure from the position when the General Conference of 1878 elected someone to replace him. Broken in health he was given supernumerary status for the next two years, during which he established in Louisville a religious newspaper called the *Southern Methodist.* In 1880 he returned to the itinerant ranks of the Louisville Conference and held the following appointments: presiding elder Bowling Green District (1880–81), Glasgow and Scottsville (1881–82), and Bowling Green

(1882–84). During his last months in Bowling Green he was stricken with a fever from which he never recovered. He died at his home in Nashville on October 17, 1884. "He had a rare talent for business and a keen eye to judicious investments, and was one of the few itinerant preachers who rose from poverty to comparative wealth."

Redford, Joseph F. (1827–1915), son of Woodson and Elizabeth Bent Redford, was born on February 26, 1827, in Shelbyville, Kentucky. He was the brother of the more famous A. H. Redford, historian of Kentucky Methodism and book agent for the Methodist Episcopal Church, South. Joseph grew up in Shelbyville where he was educated by private teachers and at Shelby College. In September 1850 the Louisville Conference of the Methodist Episcopal Church, South, admitted him on trial. He was ordained deacon by Bishop Andrew in 1852 and elder by Bishop Paine in 1854. In 1855 he married Hattie J. Briggs, daughter of Col. James T. Briggs, of Warren County. During the sixty-four years of his active ministry he held the following appointments: Empire Iron Works (1850–51), Wayne (1851–52), Elkton (1853–53), Mt. Washington and Shepherdsville (1853–54), Poplar Street (Louisville, 1854–55), Hawesville (1855–57), Morganfield (1857–59), Glasgow Circuit (1859–60), Calhoun (1860–61), Hopkinsville Circuit (1861–63), Cadiz (1863–65), Franklin Circuit (1865–67), New Haven (1867–68), agent for board of education (1868–74), City Mission (Louisville, 1874–76), Fairview (1876–77), Lafayette (1877–80), Princeton (1880–82), Smith's Grove (1882–84), Greenhill (1884–85), Bowling Green Circuit (1885–86), Franklin Circuit (1886–88), Barry Street (Bowling Green, 1888–90), Smith's Grove (1890–91), Conference Colporteur (1891–94), Barry Street, (1894–96), Woodburn Circuit (1896–97), presiding elder Bowling Green District (1897–1901), and State Street (Bowling Green, 1901–04). During the six years he spent as agent of the conference board of education, he raised over $30,000 for the purpose of educational endowment, and an additional $12,000 to purchase the grounds and building for Warren College, located in Bowling Green. In the early 1880s he purchased a modest home (later remodeled into a "commodious residence") on State Street in Bowling Green where he spent the last thirty years of his life. When he died on April 14, 1915, a prominent Bowling Green resident summed up the general feeling of the community by remarking, "If heaven is too crowded when Brother Redford gets there, somebody will have to go out and let that good man in."

Reid, Judge Richard (1838–84) was born near Mt. Sterling, Montgomery County, Kentucky, on October 3, 1838. After receiving his early education at home, he completed his studies at Georgetown College, Georgetown, Kentucky. He then studied law in the office of Judge Alvin Duvall in Frankfort and continued in the office of Governor Thomas P. Porter in Versailles, becoming the latter's partner for two years. He then returned to Mt. Sterling where he practiced law until his election in 1882 to the court of appeals of Kentucky. Among the cases coming before the court at that time was one involving a fellow attorney and townsman, John C. Corneilison. When the decision of the court went against Corneilison, he accused Reid of conspiring against him and on April 16, 1884, he caned and cowhided the judge, chasing him down the main street of Mt. Sterling. The code of honor at the time required that Reid, once attacked, retaliate to defend his honor, but he was a gentle, sensitive man who had no desire to engage in further violence. Humiliated by the attack and disgraced in the eyes of many citizens who insisted that he strike back, he shot himself to death on May 15, 1884.

Ridgaway, Henry Bascom (1830–95) was born in Talbot County, Maryland, on September 7, 1830. He was converted at the age of thirteen and accepted the call to preach four years later. Shortly after his graduation from Dickinson College in 1849 he joined the Baltimore Conference of the Methodist Episcopal Church. In 1855 he married Rosamond Caldwell, daughter of a Dickinson College professor. He rose rapidly in his profession and during his thirty years in the active ministry he pastored the leading churches of Baltimore, Portland (Maine), New York City, and Cincinnati. In 1882 he was elected to the chair of historical theology in Garrett Biblical Institute, Evanston, Illinois. Two years later, upon the elevation of President William X. Ninde to the episcopacy, he became president and professor of pastoral theology, a position he held until his death. He represented his church as fraternal delegate to the Methodist Episcopal Church, South, in 1882, attended the Centennial Conference in Baltimore in 1884, and served as a delegate to the General Conferences of 1872 and 1892. He wrote three books and was a frequent contributor to his church periodicals. Years of overwork took a heavy toll and despite a trip around the world in 1892 for the purpose of renewing his strength, his last years were marked by nagging illness. He died in Evanston, Illinois, on March 30, 1895. "The passion of his life was the love of Christ."

Rivers, Richard Henderson (1814–94) was born in Montgomery County, Tennessee, on September 11, 1814. He was converted in 1830 during a protracted meeting in Hardemann County. The following year he was licensed to preach and admitted on trial into the Tennessee Conference of the Methodist Church. Bishop McKendree ordained him deacon in 1833. He then relocated in order to pursue a two year course of study under Bishop Paine at La Grange College, Alabama. In 1836, when he was only twenty-one years old, his alma mater elected him to the chair of ancient languages, a position he held until 1843. In that year he accepted the presidency of the Tennessee Conference Female Institute at Athens, Alabama, where he remained until 1848. He then became president of Centenary College in Jackson, Louisiana. When his wife's paralysis compelled him to leave Louisiana in 1854, he accepted the presidency of La Grange College, which was moved to Florence during that year. When the Civil War broke up the college, he took charge of Centenary College for girls at Summerfield, Alabama. At the close of the war he left Centenary College for western Tennessee to look after his aged

mother at which time he accepted the presidency of Somerville Institute for girls, a position he held until 1868 when he resigned to become president of Logan Female College in Russellville, Kentucky. A year later he accepted an appointment as pastor of Broadway Church, Louisville, in the Louisville Conference of the Methodist Episcopal Church, South. Three years later he accepted the pastorate of the Chestnut Street Church in the same city. In 1874 he was transferred to the Tennessee Conference and appointed to the presidency of Martin Female College at Pulaski. Although the college prospered under his direction, his heart desired a return to the pastorate. He transferred to the Alabama Conference where he held appointments at Auburn, Eufala, and Greenville. In 1885 he retransferred to the Louisville Conference to pastor Broadway Church once again, a position he held for four years. A one year appointment to Shelby Street Church, Louisville, was his last. He was superannuated in 1890 and died on June 21, 1894. On June 9, 1836, he married Martha B. C. Jones. She and two of their seven children survived him. "His broad shoulders and big heart always bore heavy burdens, for the multitude were drawn to him with their sorrows as to a friend and father."

Rizer, Edwin Richard (1823–89), the son of Mathias and Catherine Rizer, was born in Franklin, Simpson County, Kentucky, on January 31, 1823. On March 4, 1845, he married Mary Ann Barkley Harrison of Elkton, Todd County, Kentucky, who bore him one son and ten daughters. He and his wife were devout Methodists. At about the time of his marriage he moved to Russellville, Logan County, Kentucky, where he made saddles and operated a leather shop. He later opened a shoe store, which he operated until his death on July 29, 1889, in Russellville.

Roach, Charles W. (1846–1929) was born at Hadensville, Todd County, Kentucky, on July 24, 1846. On December 7, 1871, he married Helen Susan Browder, daughter of George Dick, who bore him eight children. They lived for three years near Pinchem in Todd County before moving to the Olmstead community where they spent the rest of their lives. Although Charley, as George Dick called him, devoted most of his life to farming, he also spent some time in the mercantile business. In the January 4, 1877, issue of the *Russellville Weekly Herald,* he advertised as a "Dealer in Staple and Fancy Groceries, Hardware, Confectionaries, and Glassware." As a young man he united with the Presbyterian church and throughout his life he was a devoted member. After an illness of three weeks, he died in the Bowling Green hospital on September 28, 1929, nine years after his beloved Helen.

Roach, Helen Susan Browder (1851–1920), the first child and only surviving daughter of George Dick and Lizzie Warfield Browder, was born near Clarksville, Tennessee, on August 5, 1851. She was educated in neighborhood schools, including Browder Institute, after which she enrolled in Logan Female College in the fall of 1868; she withdrew after a brief attendance on account of illness. On December 7, 1871, she married Charles W. (Charley) Roach of Todd County; there were eight children, seven of whom reached maturity. After living for three years near Pinchem in Todd County, she and Charley purchased the Wintersmith place on the Clarksville Road near Olmstead; in December 1878 they bought the old William C. Browder place; six years later they built a new house close by which, according to George Dick, was "too costly for a country house – and too fine for the neighborhood." After her mother Lizzie moved from Olmstead to Clarksville, Tennessee, in the early 1890s to spend her last days with Hanson, it was Helen's house that became the gathering place for the Browder family. One of Luther Browder's daughters, Mrs. Helen English of Monroe, North Carolina, remembers her Aunt Helen as a "caring person, always helpful and doing things for other people," and as one who "always had huge amounts of ginger cookies, provided play things and a place to play" for the children who loved to visit her home. In 1918 her health began to fail; she died of pneumonia on March 12, 1920, after a two-week illness, and lies buried not far from the graves of George Dick and Lizzie in Russellville's Maple Grove cemetery.

Robinson, James F. (1800–82), the son of Jonathan and Jane Black Robinson, was born on October 4, 1800. He was educated at Forest Hill Academy and at Transylvania University from which he graduated in 1818. He then read law, passed the bar, and established his practice in Georgetown, Scott County, Kentucky. In 1851, as a Whig, he won election to one four-year term in the Kentucky Senate. When the Civil War came he returned to politics as a Democrat and in 1861 recaptured his senate seat. A year later on August 18, 1862, he succeeded to the governorship when Beriah Magoffin resigned. As governor he struggled with problems resulting from divided loyalties, guerrilla activities, a Confederate invasion, federal violations of civil and property rights, and the U.S. Army's policy of protecting runaway slaves. He was an outspoken opponent of emancipation. After leaving office in 1863 he returned to "Cardome," his 300 acre farm in Scott County, and continued to practice law in nearby Georgetown. During these years he also served as president of the Farmers' Bank of Georgetown and as chairman of the Georgetown College Board of Trustees. He died at his home on October 31, 1882.

Rodes, Robert (1824–1913) was born near Lancaster in Garrard County, Kentucky, on September 28, 1824. His father, Clifton, was a prominent banker in Danville, Kentucky, and his mother, Amanda Owsley, was the daughter of William Owsley, twice judge of the court of appeals of Kentucky and later (1844–48) governor of the state. In his early youth Robert's family removed to near Richmond in Madison County; fifteen years later they moved on to Danville where he spent the next five years. He was educated in the schools of Richmond and at Centre College in Danville from which he graduated in 1843. He then went to Frankfort, Kentucky, to prepare for a career in law, studying under Judge Victor Monroe who later became judge of the district court in Washington, D.C. In 1849 he married Mary Grider, daughter of Col. Henry Grider, who bore him six children. Later in the same year he moved to Bowling Green, Warren County, Kentucky, where he practiced law in partnership with his father-in-law. On two occasions he held public office. He was elected to the state legislature in 1853 and as a delegate to the Constitutional Convention of 1891. Throughout his life he was warmly attached to Presbyterian polity and doctrine and served the Bowling Green church as deacon during 1849–52 and as ruling elder from 1852 until his death on September 24, 1913.

Rosecrans, William Starke (1819–98), eldest son of Crandall and Jemina Hopkins Rosecrans, was born in Kingston Township, Delaware County, Ohio, on September 6, 1819. With little formal education he went to work at the age of fourteen. In 1838 he secured an appointment to West Point and graduated four years later. On August 24, 1843, he married Ann Eliza Hegeman of New York City. After an unexceptional career as an army engineer, he resigned his commission on April 1, 1854, and moved to Cincinnati, Ohio, where he tried his hand as engineer, architect, and head of an unsuccessful kerosene refinery. When the Civil War broke out he volunteered as aide-de-camp to General McClellan who at that time commanded the Department of Ohio. In June 1861 he was appointed brigadier general in the regular army and during the next year participated in campaigns in western Virginia and Mississippi. He was promoted to major general of volunteers on September 17, 1862, and given command of the Army of the Cumberland. In early January 1863 he repulsed Braxton Bragg's Army of the Tennessee in a bloody battle at Murfreesboro. Eight months later, after a series of brilliant maneuvers in which he pushed the Confederates toward Chattanooga, he was through his own error soundly defeated by Bragg in the battle of Chickamauga, forced back to Chattanooga, and besieged. Ulysses S. Grant replaced him on October 19, 1863. He commanded the Department of Missouri during 1864. He resigned his commission in the regular army on March 28, 1867. President Andrew Johnson appointed him U.S. minister to Mexico in 1868; President Grant removed him in 1869. Except for the years he spent in Congress (1881–85) and as registrar of the treasury (1885–93), he lived the rest of his

life on his ranch near Redondo Beach, California, where he died on March 11, 1898.

Rushing, James Thomas (1855–1941) was born near Bellbuckle in Bedford County, Tennessee, on March 20, 1855. By his own testimony he was converted at his mother's knee at the age of eight. On March 11, 1877, he married Emily Fulton Thurmond of Crittenden County, Kentucky, who bore him seven children. She died after fifty years of marriage. He then married Mrs. Mattie F. Rouse of Louisville on October 30, 1928. In 1877 the Louisville Conference of the Methodist Episcopal Church, South, admitted him on trial into the itinerant ministry. He was ordained deacon by Bishop Kavanaugh in 1880 and elder by Bishop Keener in 1881. During his fifty-three years of uninterrupted service to the Louisville Conference he held the following appointments: Princeton Mission (1877–78), Buffalo (1878–79), Falls of Rough (1879–81), Leitchfield (1881–83), South Carrollton (1883–86), Owensboro Circuit (1886–90), Elkton (1890–94), Greenville (1894–97), Portland (1897–99), presiding elder Lebanon District (1899–1901), presiding elder Owensboro District (1901–05), Henderson (1905–09), Virginia Avenue (Louisville, 1909–11), presiding elder Elizabethtown District (1911–15), presiding elder Owensboro District (1915–17), Messick Memorial (Louisville, 1917–23), Providence (1923–25), Princeton (1925–27), and Bardstown (1927–30). He received 1316 members into the church. In his years at South Carrollton he also attended West Kentucky College from which he graduated in 1885. Despite his meager salary, which ranged from $106.10 to $2165, he managed to "educate his family, assist others in obtaining an education, dress neatly, and entertain graciously." He spent the last eleven years of his life in Louisville where he died on August 28, 1941. "He was thoughtful and cautious, yet unafraid when it became necessary to defend a principle or stand for a righteous cause."

Scobee, Joseph S. (1818–1909), son of Christopher and Hannah McKee Scobee, was born on Stone River, four miles from

Winchester in Clark County, Kentucky, on January 9, 1818. At the age of eight his parents removed to Shelby County, seven miles northeast of Shelbyville. Reared in a devout Methodist home, he was converted at the age of ten while kneeling at his mother's knee. He attended neighborhood schools and later entered Transylvania University, then under the control of the Methodist Church, where he came under the influence of its president, Henry B. Bascom, a renowned orator and future Methodist bishop. After receiving a license to preach, he spent three or four years as a local preacher. When the Methodist Church divided in 1845, he preferred the Methodist Episcopal Church, South, and, along with George Dick, joined the Louisville Conference at its first session held at Hopkinsville in 1846. He was ordained deacon by Bishop Capers in 1848 and elder by Bishop Andrew in 1850. In the latter year he also married Fannie Covington of Warren County, Kentucky; she died in 1859. Seventeen years later, on December 12, 1876, he married Mrs. Julia Smith who bore him three children. During his early years in the ministry, the young itinerant was described as "a remarkably handsome man, tall and strong, erect of figure, with dark, expressive eyes and coal-black hair and beard." Between 1846 and 1862 he held the following appointments: Millville (1846–47), Mt. Washington (1847–48), Bowling Green (1848–49), Asbury and PeeDee (Louisville, 1849–50), located (1850–54), readmitted and assigned to Glasgow Circuit (1854–55), Bowling Green Circuit (1855–57), and located (1857–58). The following year he was readmitted and assigned as presiding elder of the Owensboro District (1858–62). In 1862 he located once more to raise the Tenth Kentucky Cavalry, a Confederate unit, which he led as both major and chaplain until the close of the Civil War. On the morning of September 19, 1862, as he, with his command of 385 men, advanced with other Confederates on Owensboro, where he had only recently served as presiding elder, he was recognized by a Methodist woman who cried out, "Thank God, my savior has come." After the war the Louisville Conference readmitted him and during the next forty years he served

in the following charges: Woodburn Circuit (1865–66), Bowling Green Circuit (1866–67), Bardstown and Stoner's Chapel (1867–68), Lebanon and Springfield (1868–69), Twelfth Street (Louisville, 1869–71), Princeton and Eddyville (1871–73), Bascom (Louisville, 1873–74), Cloverport (1874–76), Elizabethtown (1876–77), Lebanon (1877–78), Bethel and West Broadway (Louisville, 1878–79), Allensville and Bethlehem (1879–80), presiding elder Owensboro District (1880–84), presiding elder Princeton District (1884–87), presiding elder Lebanon District (1887–91), Jeffersonville (1891–92), Portland (1892–93), Jeffersontown (1893–95), West Point (1895–96), Anchorage (1896–97), Bardstown Junction (1897–98), Asbury (1898–1902), Brooks and Mt. Eden (1902–04), and Walnut Street (Louisville, 1904–05). He was superannuated from 1905 until his death on July 8, 1909. "A man of iron frame, gifted in song, well educated, a strong preacher rising at times to great power, imbued with the revival spirit, he went like a Paladin of old into the spiritual battle."

Scott, Bishop Levi (1802–82) was born near Cantwell's Bridge, near Odessa, Delaware, on October 11, 1802. His father, a class leader and a local preacher in the Methodist Episcopal Church, died two years later. Young Levi worked on a farm until his late teens and had little formal education. He was converted in 1822, accepted the call to preach, and in 1826, after serving one year as a local preacher, joined the Philadelphia Conference of the Methodist Episcopal Church. Over the next fourteen years he served as a preacher and presiding elder in the Philadelphia area. In 1840 he became principal of Dickinson Grammar School, Carlisle, Pennsylvania; three years later he returned to the pastorate. In 1848 the general conference of his church elected him assistant book agent at New York, a position he held until 1852 when the general conference elected him bishop. At the time of his death at Odessa, Delaware, on July 13, 1882, he was the senior bishop of the Methodist Episcopal Church.

Sehon, Edmund Waggoner (1808–76), son of Major John L. and Fannie W. Sehon, was born in Moorefield, Hardin County, Virginia, on April 14, 1808. When he was about four years old his family moved to Clarksburg after his father's appointment as chancery clerk of the western judicial district of Virginia. There Edmund grew up enjoying the advantages of a superior education. At the age of fourteen he entered Ohio University at Athens where he graduated with highest distinction four years later. During his college days, on September 20, 1825, just before returning to school for his junior year, he was converted at a Methodist camp meeting near Clarksburg. Shortly thereafter he accepted the call to preach the gospel, a decision his aristocratic father found difficult to accept. He was licensed to exhort on June 26, 1826; the Clarksburg Quarterly Conference licensed him to preach on October 10, 1827. Two years later the Pittsburgh Conference of the Methodist Church received him on trial into the itinerant ministry and appointed him to the Youngstown Circuit (1829–30) and the Monongahela Circuit (1830–31). In 1831 he transferred to the Ohio Conference where he was stationed at Cincinnati (1831–33) and served as agent for the American Colonization Society (1833–34). He then transferred to the Missouri Conference and served one year on the St. Louis charge before returning to the Ohio Conference to accept the following appointments: Columbus (1835–37), Western (Cincinnati, 1837–38), agent for Augusta College (1838–39), Eastern (Cincinnati, 1839–41), and general agent of the American Bible Society for the West (1841–46). When the Methodist Church divided in 1845, he adhered to the Methodist Episcopal Church, South, and became a member of the Tennessee Conference. A year later he transferred to the Kentucky Conference and spent one year at Soule Chapel, Cincinnati. In 1847 he transferred to the Louisville Conference and remained a member for the rest of his life. During the next three years he served two charges in the city of Louisville: Fourth Street (1847–49), and Third Street (1849–50). In 1850 the general conference elected him missionary secretary, a position he held for eighteen years. He resigned in 1868 to return to full time preaching in the following appointments: Shelby Street (Louisville, 1868–71), presiding elder Louisville District (1871–75), and presiding elder Bowling Green District from 1875 until his death on June 7, 1876. "While he possessed the true Catholic spirit in an eminent degree, he was a *Methodist,* believing Methodist doctrines, and embracing Methodist polity and usages with all his heart."

Settle, Henry Clay (1836–1903), the youngest child of Cooper and Sarah A. Cornell Settle, was born in Louisville, Kentucky, on May 26, 1836. His father was for many years the publisher of the *Louisville Journal* and a personal friend of the editor, George D. Prentice, and of the Kentucky statesman, Henry Clay, for whom he was named. After attending private schools he entered St. Aloysius College, a noted Catholic institution in Louisville, graduating in 1854 at the head of his class. While studying for a career in law, his health failed and he undertook a sea voyage to California. Settling in San Francisco he first took a position with a newspaper, then turned his attention once more to the study of law, but his religious inclinations, dating back to his Sunday school days at the Eighth Street Methodist Church, Louisville, moved him inexorably toward the ministry. In February 1855 he was admitted on trial into the Pacific Conference of the Methodist Episcopal Church, South, and during the next four years held the following appointments: Gilroy Circuit (1855–56), Grass Valley and Nevada (1856–58), and San Jose and Santa Clara (1858–59). During his years in California he also married Isabelle A. Kerr of Merced, who bore him ten children. Yielding to a longing to return to his native state, in 1860 he transferred to the Louisville Conference where for the next forty years he filled the following appointments: Bardstown (1860–61), Russellville (1862–63), Logan Circuit (1863–65), Cadiz (1865–66), Big Spring (1866–67), Owensboro (1867–70), Walnut Street (Louisville, 1870–74), Russellville (1874–77), Owensboro (1877–81), Jefferson Street (Louisville, 1881–82), presiding elder Louisville District (1882–86), Chestnut Street (Louisville, 1886–89), Walnut Street (Louisville, 1889–93), Hopkinsville (1893–97), Bowling Green (1897–98), Russellville (1898–99), and superannuated (1899–1903). From 1882 to 1894 he served as a charter member of the board of church extension. He died in Louisville on January 11, 1903. "For years to come his shadow will lie tenderly across the threshold of many Kentucky homes, and quite a number of men and women will recall that refined spirit and loving heart which pointed the way to Christ and led them there."

Seward, William H. (1801–72), son of Dr. Samuel S. and Mary Jennings Seward, was born in Florida, Orange County, New York, on May 16, 1801. After attending neighborhood schools he was sent to Union College, Schenectady, from which he graduated in 1820. He then read law, passed the bar, and established his practice in Auburn, New York. On October 20, 1829, he married Frances Miller, the daughter of his law partner, who bore him three sons and two daughters. He soon became actively involved in state politics, first as an Anti-Mason and by the early 1830s as a Whig. With the support of the powerful Thurlow Weed, with whom he developed a lasting friendship, he won election to the state senate in 1830. He failed of reelection in 1833, but by 1838 the changing political tides resulted in his election as governor. Four years later he retired to private life to recoup his finances, but not before he had attracted attention from a growing number of anti-slavery advocates. In 1848 he was elected to the U.S. Senate and reelected in 1854. As an outspoken opponent of slavery expansion, he opposed both the Compromise of 1850 and the Kansas-Nebraska Bill (1854). In a speech at Rochester, New York, in 1858, he referred to the slavery struggle as "an irrepressible conflict" between North and South. When the Whig party disintegrated in 1854, he rose rapidly in the new Republican party. He was an unsuccessful candidate for president in 1856 and again in 1860. President Lincoln selected him as his secretary of state in 1861, a position he held for the next nine years. Among his most notable achievements were: negotiating with the British over the *Trent* affair and the *Alabama* claims, forcing the French out of Mexico, and acquiring Alaska. At the time of Lincoln's assassination he was wounded by Lewis Powell, a co-conspirator with John Wilkes Booth, as he lay in bed recovering from serious injuries sustained in a carriage accident during the spring of 1865. Upon leaving Washington, he took a trip around the world before returning to his home in Auburn, New York, where he died on October 10, 1872.

Shackelford, James Murrell (1827–1909) was born on a farm in Lincoln County, Kentucky, on July 7, 1827. He attended schools in nearby Springfield and Stanford. In 1847 he enlisted in Company I, 4th Kentucky Volunteers, and was soon elected first lieutenant of his company. Mustered out a year later, he studied law and practiced in Louisville from 1853 until the outbreak of the Civil War. A staunch Unionist, he recruited the 25th Kentucky Infantry and was commissioned its colonel on January 1, 1862; his troops saw action at the Battle of Fort Donelson, Tennessee. He resigned his commission in April 1862 only to raise the 8th Kentucky Cavalry four months later; he was made its colonel in September 1862, and on March 17, 1863, he was promoted to brigadier general of volunteers. His greatest moment came in July 1863 when he pursued and captured the celebrated Confederate raider John Hunt Morgan after a chase through three states. He subsequently participated in the capture of Cumberland Gap, Kentucky, where he commanded a cavalry division. In January 1864 he resigned from the army and returned to Louisville where he resumed his law practice. In 1889 he was appointed federal judge for the Indian Territory; after 1893 he practiced law in Muskogee (now Oklahoma) where he represented the Choctaw nation. He died on September 7, 1909, at his summer home in Port Huron, Michigan.

Simpson, Bishop Matthew (1811–84), son of James and Sarah Tingley Simpson was born in Cadiz, Ohio, on June 2, 1811. His father died when he was one year old leaving his devout Methodist mother with the responsibility of raising him and his two older siblings. Although he had little schooling, he mastered the ordinary school subjects, as well as German and Latin, through his own efforts and acquired some knowledge of Greek during a summer at a Cadiz academy. At the age of nineteen he began a three-year study of medicine under Dr. James McBean of Cadiz. In the meantime he had become active in religious work and in 1833 he decided to become a preacher. The following year he joined the Pittsburgh Conference of the Methodist Episcopal Church, the first step in a career that would culminate in his achieving distinction as the most prominent Methodist of his day. In 1837, after filling appointments to Cadiz Circuit, Pittsburgh, and Williamsport, he was elected professor of natural science in Allegheny College. Two years later he was elected president of Indiana Asbury University (later Depauw) in Greencastle where he remained for nine years. During these years he also rose rapidly in the councils of the Methodist Church. As a member of the General Conference of 1844, which resulted in the formation of the Methodist Episcopal Church, South, he was an outspoken opponent of slavery. Four years later the general conference elected him editor of the *Western Christian Advocate* and through its columns his views on public questions, especially slavery, attracted considerable attention. His notoriety undoubtedly contributed to his election as bishop in 1852. When the Civil War broke out he used his influence as a friend of President Lincoln to secure the appointments of Methodists to national offices. He also persuaded Secretary of War Edwin M. Stanton, without Lincoln's knowledge, to place at his disposal all Methodist Episcopal Church, South, buildings in areas occupied by Union troops. He thus seized a number of churches in Tennessee, Louisiana, and elsewhere. When Lincoln was assassinated he preached his funeral at the White House and also at the burial site in Springfield, Illinois. His relations with Lincoln's successor, Andrew Johnson, were considerably less friendly. The latter disapproved of his church seizures and demanded that he return McKendree Church in Nashville,

Tennessee, to its owners. Understandably, the bishop applauded the Johnson impeachment proceedings. Busy with many things, he nevertheless found time to write *A Hundred Years of Methodism,* (1876) and to edit *Cyclopedia of Methodism* (1878). He died in Philadelphia on June 18, 1884.

Slate, William Cannon (1842–87) was born in Gilmore County, Georgia, on April 20, 1842. He was converted at the age of sixteen and joined the Methodist Episcopal Church, South. After his marriage to Mary J. Jones on August 25, 1861, he entered the Confederate army and served until 1865. After the Civil War he moved to Kentucky and settled near Smith's Grove in Warren County. He was licensed to preach in 1868 and as a local preacher he supplied the Brownsville Mission for four years. Bishop Marvin ordained him deacon on October 6, 1872. The following year he was admitted on trial into the Louisville Conference of the Methodist Episcopal Church, South, and assigned to the Scottsville Circuit (1873–74). His career as an itinerant preacher included the following appointments: Scottsville (1874–76), Burkeville (1876–77), and Scottsville (1877–78). Though brief, his ministry was fruitful. In his four years in the Scottsville area he reportedly witnessed the conversion of three hundred thirty souls and received into the Church two hundred seventy members. During his last year as a traveling preacher he suffered from severe hemorrhaging of the lungs; consequently he was superannuated until his death nine years later on August 17, 1887. His wife and eleven children survived him. "He realized that he had a message from God to the people, which he delivered with such earnestness, unction and power that sinners were brought by the hundreds to the mercy seat."

Smith, Edmund Kirby (1824–93), son of Joseph Lee and Frances Marvin Smith, was born in St. Augustine, Florida, on May 16, 1824. His father, a native of Connecticut, was a distinguished lawyer and judge. Young Smith attended Benjamin Hallowell's preparatory school in Alexandria, Virginia, and graduated from West Point in 1845. After serving in the Mexican War he was assistant professor of mathematics at West Point from 1849 to 1852. He then served in the Indian campaigns on the Texas frontier, winning promotion to captain in 1855 and major in 1860. When his native Florida seceded from the Union on April 6, 1861, he resigned his commission and entered the Confederate service as a lieutenant colonel of cavalry. On June 17, 1861, he was promoted to brigadier general. One month later he was severely wounded at First Manassas. While he was recuperating he married Cassie Selden, daughter of Samuel S. Selden on September 24, 1861; she bore him five sons and six daughters. After his promotion to major general on October 11, 1861, he was given command of the Department of East Tennessee. In June 1862 he took part in Braxton Bragg's invasion of Kentucky and, after soundly defeating William Nelson at Richmond on August 30, he occupied Lexington and threatened Cincinnati. Two months later he was promoted to lieutenant general and from 1862 to 1865 served as commander of the Trans-Mississippi Department. On February 19, 1864, he received the permanent rank of general in the provisional army. He was perhaps the last Confederate general in the field, surrendering to E. R. S. Canby on May 26, 1865. After the war he briefly served as president of the Atlantic and Pacific Telegraph Company. As a devout Episcopalian he longed to enter the ministry, but decided he was too old. Consequently he turned to education; he spent five years as president of the University of Nashville (1870–75) and eighteen years as a professor of mathematics at the University of the South, Sewanee, Tennessee. He died there on March 28, 1893, the last surviving general of either army.

Soule, Bishop Joshua (1781–1867) was born in Bristol, Maine, on August 1, 1781. At the age of seventeen he was licensed to preach by the Methodist Church; a year later he was admitted on trial into the itinerant ministry. In 1804 he was appointed presiding elder of the Maine district. As a member of the General Conference of 1808 his plan for a delegated general conference won acceptance. In 1816 he was elected to a four year term

as book agent. During his tenure he initiated the publication of the *Methodist Magazine* and served as its editor. The General Conference of 1820 elected him bishop, but he declined because he believed that the plan the conference had adopted for electing presiding elders was unconstitutional. During the next four years he held preaching appointments in New York and Baltimore. In 1824 the general conference again elected him bishop; this time he accepted. When the Methodist Church split in 1845, he adhered to the Methodist Episcopal Church, South, and made Nashville, Tennessee, his home for the rest of his life. For several years before his death he suffered from poor health. He died in Nashville on March 6, 1867. He was characterized as "a useful, popular, and sometimes an overwhelming preacher."

Stark, Anthony Butler (1832– ?), son of Terry W. and Mary Smith Stark, was born in Robertson County, Tennessee, on July 13, 1832. When he was three months old his family moved to Logan County, Kentucky, where he attended the neighborhood schools. At the age of twenty he enrolled in Cumberland College in Princeton, Kentucky, completing his studies in 1854 after only two and half years. Upon graduation he went to Elkton, Kentucky, where he taught for five months in the Male High School. He then bought the *Green River Whig* newspaper, changed the name to *Elkton Banner,* and for the next two years made it into an effective voice for the American or Know-Nothing party in south-central Kentucky. During these years he also married Ada Nelson of Elkton who bore him two children. In 1856 he gave up his newspaper and moved to Tennessee where he taught one term at Washington Institute near Nashville. He returned to Elkton to teach briefly at Male High School and then in 1856 accepted an appointment in McGee College, Missouri, as professor of language, a position he held for four years. During this time he thoroughly mastered Latin and Greek and began to write extensively for various Methodist periodicals, including a series for the *Southern Methodist Quarterly Review* with such titles as: "Wordsworth," "English Philology," and "The Moral and Religious

Teachings of Shakespeare." When the Civil War broke out, he sympathized with the South, left Missouri, and accepted the presidency of the Collegiate Institute at Port Gibson, Mississippi, where he remained until the fall of Vicksburg in 1863. He then taught for two years in the Female College at Tuscaloosa, Alabama. In 1866 he moved to Nashville, Tennessee, where, in partnership with the Rev. Felix Hill, he published the *Home Monthly* magazine. Four years later he became president of Corona Institute in Lebanon, Tennessee. In 1874 he moved on to Russellville, Kentucky, where he closed out his professional career as president of Logan Female College, a position he held until his retirement in 1883. The place and date of his death is not known.

Stevenson, Edward (1797–1864) was the son of Thomas and Mary Stevenson who were numbered among the early Methodists of America, having joined the church in Maryland in 1768 when there were scarcely two hundred Methodists in the country. They emigrated to Kentucky in 1786 and settled in Mason County. In that same year the first society of Methodists established in the wilderness of Kentucky was organized in their home, and for more than forty years their house was a regular place of preaching. There Edward was born on October 3, 1797. He was converted in his youth, and as a young man decided to enter the ministry. On the occasion of his first sermon, preached in his father's house, seven persons were converted. He entered the Kentucky Conference in 1820. When the Methodist Church split in 1844, he withdrew to spend the rest of his life in the Louisville Conference of the Methodist Episcopal Church, South. He served the Church in most of the large towns and cities of the state: Mount Sterling, Harrodsburg, Danville, Hopkinsville, Russellville on two occasions (1822–23 and 1840–41), Bowling Green, Shelbyville, Frankfort, Maysville, Lexington, and Louisville. He also spent four years as presiding elder of the Hopkinsville District. Stevenson was a member of the convention that met in Louisville in 1845 to organize the Methodist Episcopal Church, South. He was also a member of the first general

conference that met in 1846 in Petersburg, Virginia, and of every general conference after that until his death. At the first general conference he was elected missionary secretary and assistant book agent of the church. Eight years later the general conference elected him chief agent of the publishing house located in Nashville, Tennessee. In 1858 he accepted the presidency of Russellville Female Collegiate Institute, the forerunner of Logan Female College, a position he held for six years until his death on July 6, 1864.

Stirman, William Doswell (1820–93), son of James H. and Elizabeth Doswell Stirman, was born in Washington County, Kentucky, in December 1820. His father was a captain in the War of 1812 and received three gunshot wounds at the battle of the Thames. In his childhood William's family moved to Hopkinsville, Kentucky, then on to Memphis where his father died, and then back to Washington County. His mother finally located at Calhoun, McLean County, where he grew to manhood. After graduating in 1844 from St. Louis University where he studied medicine, he practiced briefly in Calhoun before returning to his alma mater as assistant professor of anatomy. He held that position until 1849 when he married Rachel Wall; shortly thereafter he moved to Owensboro, Kentucky, where he established a successful practice and built one of the finest residences in the city. George Dick was always a welcome visitor in his home during his visits to the Owensboro District. Stirman remained in Owensboro for the rest of his life, except for the four years (1857–61) he spent as professor of anatomy at the University of Louisville School of Medicine. One of his sons, Wilbur Fitzalban, later joined him as a partner in his Owensboro practice. He died on May 9, 1893.

Summers, Thomas Osmond (1812–82) was born in Dorsetshire, England, on October 11, 1812. When he was very young his parents died and he was brought up by near relatives who were Dissenters. At the age of eighteen he emigrated to the United States. In 1832 he joined the Methodist Church on probation; a year later he was "powerfully and happily" converted and in a short time began to preach. He apparently was a young man of great promise for without his application he was licensed to preach, and in 1835 the Baltimore Conference of the Methodist Episcopal Church admitted him on trial into the itinerant ministry. After two years traveling Maryland circuits and three years stationed in the city of Baltimore, he went as a missionary to the Republic of Texas and was one of nine preachers who constituted the first Texas Conference. In 1843 he transferred to the Alabama Conference where he preached at Tuscaloosa (1843–44), Livingston (1844–45), and St. Francis (Mobile, 1845–46). When southern delegates met in 1845 in Louisville to organize the Methodist Episcopal Church, South, he was made secretary of the convention, a position he also held at the first general conference held at Petersburg, Virginia, in 1846 and all succeeding general conferences until his death. The 1846 General Conference elected him assistant editor of the *Southern Christian Advocate* located in Charleston, South Carolina. From 1846 until his death he was connected with the publishing interests of the church. In this regard he served as general book editor of the publishing house of the M.E. Church, South, and chaired the committee that compiled the denominational hymn book. In 1855 he moved to Nashville, Tennessee, where he edited *The Quarterly Review* until 1862 when he returned to Alabama to accept pastorates in Tuscaloosa and Greensborough. Four years later he was elected editor of the *Sunday-School Visitor* as well as editor of the *Christian Advocate,* the official organ of the church. In 1876 he was elected professor of systematic theology in Vanderbilt University and also served as dean of the theological faculty, both of which positions he held until his death on May 6, 1882 in Nashville. "Positive in his convictions, and earnest in the expression of them, sometimes almost to roughness, he was as tender as a woman, abounding with the most heavenly charity."

Thomas, Robert Young (1825–1905), the son of Jonathan and Ellen Garrettson Thomas, was born in Warren County, Kentucky, on December 18, 1825, and educated in the common schools in his neighborhood. As a teenager he was converted at Elrod's Church and received into the Methodist Church on July 6, 1844. He served as a class leader at King's Chapel until March 29, 1845, when he received a license to exhort. On September 18, 1847, at a quarterly conference meeting at Old Zion Church in Barren County, he was licensed to preach. In the fall of 1848 he joined the Louisville Conference of the Methodist Episcopal Church, South. He was ordained deacon in 1850 and elder in 1852. During his fifty-four years in the ministry, he held the following appointments: Big Spring (1848–49), Leitchfield (1849–50), Mount Washington Circuit (1850–51), Salem (1851–52), Greenville (1852–53), Owensboro (1853–54), superannuated (1854–57), Russellville Circuit (1857–59), Logan Circuit (1859–60), Elkton (1860–61), Bradfordville Circuit (1861–63), Gordonsville Circuit (1863–65), supernumerary (1865–68), Greenville (1868–71), Bowling Green Circuit (1871–72), Franklin Circuit (1872–75), Greenville (1875–77), Franklin Circuit (1877–80), Greenville (1880–82), Marion (1882–86), Scottsville (1886–87), Caseyville (1887–89), Hibbardsville (1889–92), Calhoun (1892–95), South Carrollton (1895–98), supernumerary (1898–99), and Fredonia Circuit (1899–1900). He was superannuated from 1900 until his death on January 9, 1905. Thomas was a man of outspoken Unionist sentiments and, despite his appointments to circuit work during the Civil War, he managed to serve a term as chaplain in the federal army and received a pension from the government until his death. Clad in his federal uniform he stood before Bishop George F. Pierce at the Annual Conference of 1867 at Franklin, Kentucky, and defended his fidelity and fitness as a Southern Methodist preacher. He married twice, first to Mary Cox of Bardstown, Kentucky, and second, to Mary E. Briggs of Logan County, Kentucky, who, along with her one son and three daughters, survived him. "He labored among us with almost uniform success for more than half a century, and gathered many sheaves into the eternal garner."

Thomas, Robert Young, Jr. (1855–1925), son of Robert Y. and Mary E. Briggs Thomas, was born in Logan County, Kentucky, on July 13, 1855. His father was a preacher in the Louisville Conference of the Methodist Episcopal Church, South. He received his early education in the common schools in the several communities where his father preached. After graduating from Bethel College, Russellville, Kentucky, in 1878, he decided to pursue a career in law. He was admitted to the bar in 1881 and settled down to practice law in Central City, Muhlenberg County, Kentucky. Journalism also immediately attracted his attention. For a time he was editor of the *Muhlenberg Echo,* a newspaper published in nearby Greenville. He sent a copy of the *Echo* to George Dick in 1881. In 1884 he founded the *Argus,* the first newspaper ever published in Central City; he sold it the same year to T. Coleman duPont. Five years later he established the *Central City Herald.* During these years he also entered the political arena and held the following offices: member of the Kentucky legislature (1885–87), commonwealth attorney for the seventh judicial district of Kentucky (1903–09), and member of the U.S. House of Representatives (1909–25). He died at Red Boiling Springs, Macon County, Tennessee, on September 3, 1925.

Thomas, Val Peyton (1843–1908), son of Peter and Fannie Thomas, was born in Hartford, Kentucky, on July 23, 1843. A few years after his birth his family moved to Bowling Green, Kentucky, where he grew up. On June 5, 1867, he married Susan A. Valentine of Bowling Green. After his conversion at the age of fourteen, he joined the Methodist Episcopal Church, South. Shortly thereafter he felt the call to preach but resisted until 1868 when he was licensed to preach and received on trial into the Louisville Conference. He was ordained deacon by Bishop Paine in 1870 and elder by Bishop Marvin in 1872. During his thirty-eight years as an itinerant preacher he served in the following appointments: Campbellsville (1868–69), Brownsville Mission (1869–70), Leitchfield (1870–72), Smith's Grove Circuit (1872–73), Gosport (1873–75),

Smithland (1875–76), Caverna (1876–77), Rockport (1877–78), Cloverport (1879–80), Hawesville (1880–82), Trenton (1882–84), Louisville Circuit (1884–85), Shepherdsville (1885–86), Bowling Green Circuit (1886–88), Auburn (1888–90), Lafayette (1890–91), supernumerary (1891–93), superannuated (1893–94), Richardsville (1894–95), W. Scottsville (1895–96), Bowling Green Circuit (1896–97), Greensburg Circuit (1897–98), Morgantown (1898–99), Glasgow Junction (1899–1901), Buffalo (1901–02), Campbellsville Circuit (1902–03), superannuated (1903–05), and Salem (1905–06). He died on January 14, 1908. "His name lingers in the different fields where he traveled as 'ointment poured forth.' "

Thompson, Philip Burton, Jr. (1845–1909) was born in Harrodsburg, Mercer County, Kentucky, on October 15, 1845. He was educated in neighborhood schools and the University of Kentucky in Lexington. When the Civil War broke out he joined the Confederate army and served throughout the conflict. After the war he studied law and in 1866 established his practice in Harrodsburg. In 1867 he became city attorney for Harrodsburg and held that position until 1869 when he was appointed commonwealth attorney for the thirteenth judicial district of Kentucky. He was subsequently elected twice to that position and served until 1878 when he resigned, having been elected as a Democrat to the United States House of Representatives. After the completion of his third term in Congress in 1889, he moved to New York City to resume his legal practice. He died in Washington, D.C., on December 15, 1909.

Tigert, Bishop John J. (1856–1906) was born in Louisville, Kentucky, on November 25, 1856. His father, John James Tigert, was for many years a Methodist class leader in the Broadway Church. Young Tigert attended the public schools of Louisville advancing as far as the freshman class in high school. Sometime between 1872 and 1874 he was converted and in 1875 he entered Vanderbilt University to prepare for the ministry. He and

George Dick's son, Robert, were members of Vanderbilt's first class. Two years later, after completing his studies, he joined the Louisville Conference of the Methodist Episcopal Church, South, and received an appointment to Bethel in the Louisville District. On August 28, 1878, he married Amelia McTyeire, daughter of H. N. McTyeire, Methodist bishop and Vanderbilt University president, a marriage that apparently was not popular with the bride's father. After preaching for the next three years in Franklin, Kentucky, he was elected tutor in moral philosophy in Vanderbilt University. During these years he gathered materials for his *Handbook of Logic,* which was published in 1885 and became one of the textbooks for the Louisville Conference course of study for preachers. In 1890 he resigned his professorship to accept an appointment as pastor of the Walnut Street Church in Kansas City, Missouri, a position he held for four years. It was during his stay in Kansas City that he published his most important work, *The Constitutional History of American Episcopal Methodism,* on which he had researched for years. In 1894 the general conference that met at Memphis elected him editor of *The Methodist Review,* the most powerful journalistic organ of the church. As editor of the *Review* he wrote most of the book reviews and a great many articles as well. Several of the latter were collected and published in book form, including: *The Making of Methodism* (1898), *Theism* (1901), and *The Christianity of Christ and his Apostles* (1905). His influence as editor prepared the way for his election as bishop by the general conference assembled at Birmingham, Alabama, in May 1906. He enjoyed but a brief tenure. Six months later, during a trip to Oklahoma (then Indian Territory) he accidentally swallowed a small bone that lodged in his throat. Blood poisoning developed and he died at Tulsa on November 21, 1906.

Tilden, Samuel Jones (1814–86), fifth child of Elam and Polly Younglove Jones Tilden, was born in New Lebanon, New York, on February 9, 1814. Because of ill-health his early education consisted primarily of private tutoring at home. He entered Yale University in June 1834 but left after one term. The following year he moved to New York City where he intermittently attended the University of the City of New York. In 1838 he entered the University Law School and managed to complete the three-year course after which he was admitted to the bar and set up practice at 11 Pine Street in New York City. He rose rapidly in his profession. Although he initially attracted attention as a result of his role in cases involving fraud and murder, his real genius lay in litigation pertaining to the reorganization of railroads. He once observed that at one time or another more than half of the railroads north of the Ohio and between the Missouri and Hudson rivers were his clients. During these years he also played an active role in state politics but it was not until after 1866 when he was elected chairman of the Democratic state committee that he attracted considerable attention for his role in smashing the notorious "Tweed Ring" in New York City and in reforming and purifying the state judiciary. His accomplishments won for him the governorship of New York in 1874 and the Democratic nomination for president in 1876. Although he received a larger popular vote than his Republican opponent, Rutherford B. Hayes, a partisan electoral commission awarded all of the disputed electoral votes from four states to Hayes who thus won the election by one electoral vote. After the election, he spent most of his remaining years at "Greystone," a magnificent estate at Yonkers where he died a bachelor on August 4, 1886. At his death he possessed one of the largest fortunes in America, a considerable portion of which was used to fulfill his cherished dream of establishing a free library for New York City.

Trabue, Benjamin McDowell (1827–1909), son of Dr. William and Elizabeth McDowell Trabue, was born in Columbia, Adair County, Kentucky, on June 3, 1827. He was educated in neighborhood schools and at schools in Frankfort and Lexington, Kentucky. In 1846 he returned to his home town to practice medicine. With the exception of one year (1848–49) when he attended medical lectures at Transylvania University in Lexington, he continued to practice in Columbia until 1853 when he moved to Allensville in Todd County. In the latter year he also married Fannie Sale, daughter of Dr. F. E. Sale, who bore him three sons and six daughters. After nearly sixty three years of medical practice, he died in Allensville on April 15, 1909.

Vallandigham, Clement Laird (1820–71), son of Clement and Rebecca Laird Vallandigham, was born in New Lisbon, Ohio, on July 29, 1820. His father was a Presbyterian minister. He attended New Lisbon Academy before enrolling in 1837 in Jefferson College, Canonsburg, Pennsylvania, only to leave three years later without graduating after a heated argument with the president over a question of constitutional law. After reading law for two years, he was admitted to the Ohio bar and embarked upon a successful practice. During the 1840s he entered politics and won election to the Ohio legislature; for a brief period he was also part owner and editor of the *Dayton Empire.* On August 27, 1846, he married Louisa A. McMahon who bore him two children. He was defeated for Congress in 1852 and again in 1854, but two years later he was elected as a Democrat to the first of two terms in the House of Representatives where he denounced both sectionalism and extremism. When the Civil War came he strongly advocated peace on any terms; as a result he became one of the most unpopular figures in the North where many accused him of treasonable intent. When he failed of reelection to Congress in 1862 he emerged as the leader of the Peace Democrats or "Copperheads" in the Old Northwest. On May 5, 1863, after making two speeches defying the military, he was arrested for violating General Ambrose E. Burnside's General Order Number 38, which attempted to deal with expressed or implied treason. A military commission condemned him to confinement in Fort Warren, but President Lincoln banished him to the Confederacy instead. From there he made his way to Bermuda and eventually to Canada; by June 1864 he was back in Ohio where Lincoln ignored his antiwar activities. After the war he continued to be a prominent figure in both state and national politics. In the meantime he was also occupied with his legal practice and it was while serving as counsel for a defendant in a murder case that he lost his life. As he was showing a friend how the victim had been shot, he mortally wounded himself on June 17, 1871.

Vanderbilt, Cornelius (1794–1877), son of Cornelius and Phebe Hand Vanderbilt, was born in Port Richmond, Staten Island, New York, on May 27, 1794. His father was a poor farmer with a large family who also did some boating and lightering around New York harbor. Young Cornelius had little opportunity or inclination for education and did not spend a day in school after the age of eleven. Instead, he helped his father, and at the age of sixteen, with a $100 loan from his parents he bought a small sailing vessel and began a freight and passenger service between Staten Island and New York City. At the age of nineteen, on December 19, 1813, he married his cousin, Sophia Johnson, who bore him thirteen children. After her death in 1868, he married Frank Armstrong Crawford of Mobile, Alabama, on August 21, 1869. The War of 1812 brought increased opportunities and at its close he had several boats under his command. In 1829, after having accumulated a considerable fortune, he turned his attention to steamboating. His first ventures were on the Hudson River where as a result of rate wars he drove his competitors to the wall. The gold rush provided still another outlet for his energies. By working out an arrangement with Nicaragua for transporting passengers, his route to California was two days shorter than that via Panama; consequently he soon controlled most of the traffic. During the middle 1850s he entered into competition for the Atlantic trade between the United States and Europe, but it proved to be an unprofitable venture and with the coming of the Civil War he gave it up. As he neared the age of seventy he turned from shipping to railroads. Starting with the New York and Harlem Railroad in 1862, by 1867 he controlled the Hudson River and New York Central lines as well. By 1873 he had extended his rail system to Chicago and at his death he had created one of the great systems of transportation in America. Late in life he gave some attention to philanthropic causes. His gift of $1,000,000 for the founding of Vanderbilt University was his most famous bequest. At his death on January 4, 1877, he left $90,000,000 of his fortune of more than $100,000,000 to his son William.

Van Dorn, Earl (1820–63), son of Peter Aaron and Sophia Donelson Caffery Van Dorn, was born near Port Gibson, Mississippi, on September 17, 1820. His father was a lawyer and judge of the probate court; his mother was a niece of Rachel Donelson, wife of President Andrew Jackson. He graduated from West Point in 1842, fifty-second in a class of fifty-six. He served in the Mexican War (1846–48) and the Seminole War (1849–50), and by January 1861 had achieved the rank of major in the celebrated 2nd Cavalry. He resigned his commission on January 31, 1861, to become a colonel in the Confederate service. He was appointed brigadier general of Mississippi state troops on June 5, 1861, and major general in the regular army on September 19, 1861. Early in 1862 he was placed in command of the Department of the Trans-Mississippi and suffered a defeat in the battle of Pea Ridge, Arkansas (March 1862). Later, operating in defense of Vicksburg, he was defeated in the battle of Corinth (October 1862). He was then relieved of his command and placed in charge of cavalry. In December 1862 his troops succeeded in destroying Ulysses S. Grant's supply depots at Holly Springs, Mississippi, thereby temporarily disrupting Union operations against Vicksburg. He met a tragic end on May 7, 1863, when he was assassinated at his headquarters at Spring Hill, Tennessee, by a Dr. Peters who alleged that Van Dorn had "violated the sanctity of his home."

Vest, George Graham (1830–1904), the son of John Jay and Harriet Graham Vest, was born in Frankfort, Kentucky, on December 6, 1830. He attended neighborhood schools and then went on to graduate from Centre College, Danville, Kentucky, in 1848, and from the law department of Transylvania University, Lexington, Kentucky, in 1853. In 1854 he married Sallie E. Sneed of Danville, Kentucky. He then moved on to Missouri and eventually settled down to practice law in Boonville, Cooper County. In 1860 he was elected to the Missouri legislature. He is believed to be the author of the "Ordinance of Secession" adopted by the southern wing of the Missouri legislature in 1861; the same body elected him to the Confederate Congress where he served until January 1865 when he resigned to accept a seat in the Confederate Senate. After the war he returned to Missouri to resume his law practice, first in Sedalia, then in Boonville, and, after 1877, in Kansas City. In 1879 the Missouri legislature elected him as a Democrat to the U.S. Senate where he served until 1903. During his long tenure he attracted attention for his strong opposition to (1) the high protective tariff measures of his day and (2) the annexation of Puerto Rico and the Philippines. In 1900 the *Chicago Journal* referred to him as "that great big little fellow . . . with a tremendous intellect in a body so small and emaciated," and asserted that he alone was "still half the brains of the Democratic side of the Senate." As a trial lawyer he had few equals; his jury oration entitled "Tribute to a Dog" not only won the case in which it was used but was considered a masterpiece of its kind. He died in Sweet Springs, Missouri, on August 9, 1904.

Vincent, Bishop John Heyl (1832–1920), son of John Himrod and Mary Raser Vincent, was born in Tuscaloosa, Alabama, on February 23, 1832. When he was five years old his family moved north to the vicinity of Lewisburg, Pennsylvania, where he was educated in neighborhood schools and at Wesleyan Institute, Newark, New Jersey. At the age of eighteen he yielded to the call to preach, was licensed as a Methodist Episcopal local preacher, and from time to time studied Greek, Hebrew, French and physical science under special tutors. In 1857 he transferred to the Rock River (Illinois) Conference and preached at Joliet, Mt. Morris, Galena, Rockford, and Trinity Church, Chicago. Ulysses S. Grant attended his church in Galena and they became lifelong friends. Early in his ministry he saw the need for trained teachers in the church and beginning in 1855 he organized a class at his various preaching appointments for the preparation of Sunday school teachers. The idea spread beyond the limits of his own parish and in 1861 he held the first Sunday School Teachers Institute in America. He also published the first of a large quantity of Sunday school literature for teachers. In 1866 he was appointed general agent of the Methodist Sunday School Union in New York City; two years later he became corresponding secretary of the Sunday School Union and Trust Society and in that capacity he was also editor of all Methodist Sunday school publications. During these years he established the *Northwestern Sunday School Quarterly* and the *Sunday School Teacher,* introducing the system of Sunday school lessons with lesson leaves. All of these efforts culminated in 1874 when he and Lewis Miller of Akron, Ohio, jointly founded the Chautauqua Sunday-School Teachers Assembly, which initially met for two weeks at Chautauqua, New York, and eventually came to include a complete summer school with classes, lectures, concerts and entertainment. He founded the Chautauqua Literary and Scientific Circle in 1878, which marked the beginning of guided home study and correspondence courses. In 1888 the Methodist Episcopal Church elected him bishop. Before his retirement in 1904 he was stationed in Buffalo, New York; Topeka, Kansas; and Zurich, Switzerland. He was married to Elizabeth Dusenberry of Portville, New York, on November 10, 1858; there was one son, George Edgar, who became president of the University of Minnesota (1911–17) and president of the Rockefeller Foundation (1917–29). Bishop Vincent died in Chicago on May 9, 1920.

Walker, Algernon S. (1811–84), son of William and Sallie Holcomb Walker of Albemarle County, Virginia, was born in Jessamine County, Kentucky, on January 4, 1811. After his graduation from Transylvania Medical School in 1832, he located in Allen County where he practiced medicine for the rest of his life. In 1832 he also married Melvina Reynolds who bore him twelve children. His death occurred suddenly on January 28, 1884, as he ministered at the bedside of a patient.

Walker, David Shelby (1815–91), son of David and Mary Barbour Walker, was born near Olmstead, Logan County, Kentucky, on May 2, 1815. When he was but six days old his mother died and he was raised by his oldest sister, Frances (Fannie) Walker Gwynn, who lived in LaGrange, Oldham County; he was educated in private schools. In 1837 he moved to Tallahassee, Florida Territory, where he joined his brother George and his cousin Governor Richard Keith Call. He studied law in his brother's law office, gained admission to the bar, and established his practice in Tallahassee. On May 22, 1842, he married Philoclea Alston who bore him three sons and a daughter; upon her death in 1868 he married his second cousin, Elizabeth Duncan, who bore him a daughter. With Governor Call's support he entered politics and as a Whig he held the following offices: state senator (1845–48), mayor of Tallahassee (1848), state representative (1848–49), and register of public lands (1850–59). In the latter office he was *ex officio* superintendent of schools and because of his influence in securing the passage of the basic law of 1853, he is considered the founder of the public school system of Florida. When the Whig party collapsed he joined the American party and ran unsuccessfully as its candidate for governor in 1856. Three years later he was chosen associate justice of the Florida supreme court, a position he held until 1865 when he was elected governor as a Democrat without opposition under President Johnson's reconstruction program. When the Radical Republicans captured control of Congress in 1867, they brought his administration to an end; though his tenure was brief he is generally regarded as one of Florida's best governors. He resumed his law practice in Tallahassee until 1879 when he was chosen judge of the second judicial district, a position he held until his death on July 20, 1891. He died comparatively poor because of his lavish charity.

Walker, James David (1830–1906), son of James Volney and Susan Howard McLean Walker, was born near Olmstead, Logan County, Kentucky, on December 13, 1830. He attended neighborhood schools as well as Ozark Institute and Arkansas

College, Fayetteville, Arkansas. He also studied law under his second-cousin, Judge David Walker, whose daughter Mary became his wife in 1856. In 1850 he was admitted to the bar and established a legal practice in Fayetteville. In these years before the Civil War he also became judge of the circuit court, fourth judicial district in Arkansas. During the Civil War he served in the Confederate army as colonel of the first regiment of Arkansas infantry; he was captured at Oak Hills, Missouri, in 1861 and held prisoner for two years. After the war he resumed his practice in Fayetteville and served for some time as solicitor general for the state of Arkansas. In 1878 the Arkansas legislature elected him to the United States Senate where he served from March 4, 1879, to March 3, 1885. He declined to be a candidate for reelection, preferring to return to his law practice in Fayetteville where he died on October 17, 1906.

Warfield, George Hanson (1804–70), son of James H. and Ann Gassaway Warfield, was born in Anne Arundel County, Maryland, on May 9, 1804. He received a "plain English education" in neighborhood schools and on reaching maturity entered into mercantile business, having charge of a number of vessels on the Chesapeake Bay belonging to a wealthy relative. In 1826 he married Susan Waters of Anne Arundel County; she bore him seven children including Ann Elizabeth who became the wife of George Dick. About 1835 he emigrated with his family to Tennessee and settled near Clarksville in Montgomery County where he bought a large tract of land, which he cleared and improved. Four years after his wife's death in 1844, he married Elizabeth Johnson of Clarksville, Tennessee, who bore him nine children. For many years he was a stockholder and director in the Planters Bank at Clarksville. He also served on one occasion as president of the Montgomery County Agricultural and Mechanical Association. By economy and industry he amassed a considerable fortune. He died at his home on December 9, 1870. "His example was good, and his tithes were not withheld from the treasury of the Lord."

Warfield, George Waters (1843–1914), the youngest child of George H. and Susan Waters Warfield, and brother of George Dick's wife, Lizzie, was born near Clarksville in Montgomery County, Tennessee, on December 21, 1843. He was educated at neighborhood schools and at Stewart College in Clarksville. In 1861, at the age of seventeen, he enlisted in Company E, Fiftieth Tennessee Volunteers. Shortly after entering the Confederate army he was captured at Fort Donelson and spent seven months as a prisoner in Camp Douglas, Chicago, Illinois. After his release he saw action at the Battle of Chickamauga, where he was wounded. At the time of Lee's surrender he was on patrol duty at Petersburg, Virginia. He returned home to become one of the most prosperous farmers in Montgomery County, accumulating nearly five hundred and fifty acres of choice land. On October 20, 1869, he married Dora Pollard, who bore him six children. In 1886 he removed to nearby Clarksville where he died on April 7, 1914.

Washington, Fairfax (1778–1861), son of Colonel Warner Washington and a distant cousin of George Washington, was born in Virginia on June 28, 1778. He married Sarah Armstead who bore him nine children, including William A. ("Billy") who was among George Dick's teachers at Volney Institute. Sometime before 1810 Fairfax moved to Logan County, Kentucky, settling first on Whippoorwill Creek near the Tennessee border and later on Red River in the Dot community, six miles from Adairville. There he died on February 5, 1861.

Washington, William Armstead (1800–88), oldest child of Fairfax and Sarah Armstead Washington, was born in Virginia in 1800. Sometime before 1810 his family moved to Logan County, Kentucky, where he attended Volney Institute, near Olmstead. He later taught at Volney Institute as well as other early schools in Logan and neighboring Todd counties. George Dick, who always referred to him as "Billy," was among his pupils. Washington was also a poet and in 1860 published a small volume entitled, *Rural Minstrelsy and Fancy Pencillings.* He was noted for his "inimitable and faultless" penmanship. By 1873 he was living in Gordonsville, Logan County, with his two sisters. In his declining years he was in considerable financial need, having spent his life's earnings providing for an infirm father and mother and his two dependent sisters. George Dick contributed two months board in 1882 to keep him from the poor house. In 1883 he went to Owensboro to live with his niece, Mrs. Nourse. When Miss Mary Bailey of Logan County bequeathed him a sum of money in her will, he wrote a letter of thanks to her executor, Mr. Blakemore, in Philadelphia who was a cashier in the bank of George H. Stewart. The latter, upon learning of Washington's plight, initiated a campaign in his behalf, which resulted in contributions from President Chester A. Arthur and former presidents Ulysses S. Grant and Rutherford B. Hayes. A cash gift of one thousand dollars in addition to "a full and fine suit, over-wear, under-wear, hat, shoes, hose, and all, made to order, and just to fit the tall and dignified octogenarian" were presented to him on Christmas eve 1883. Before his death in 1888 he had the distinction of being the closest living relative of George Washington.

Webster, Daniel (1782–1852), son of Ebenezer and Abigail Eastman Webster, was born in Salisbury, New Hampshire, on January 18, 1782. He attended neighborhood schools, Philips Exeter Academy, and Dartmouth College from which he graduated in 1801. He then studied law and in 1805 began to practice in Boscawen, New Hampshire, transferring his work to Portsmouth in 1807. To his new home he brought his bride, Grace Fletcher, daughter of a New Hampshire clergyman, whom he married on May 29, 1808; after her death he married Caroline LeRoy in 1829. During his Portsmouth years he entered politics and served as a Federalist in Congress from 1813 to 1817. In 1816 he removed to Boston and in the following years he devoted himself to his law practice, appearing before the Supreme Court in such celebrated cases as *Dartmouth College v. Woodward, McCulloch v. Maryland,* and *Gibbons v. Ogden.* In 1823 he returned to the political arena and during the next twenty-nine years he emerged as

one of the most outstanding leaders in the United States before the Civil War, holding the following positions: congressman from Massachusetts (1823–27), U.S. Senator (1827–41), secretary of state under William Henry Harrison and John Tyler (1841–45), U.S. Senator (1845–50), and secretary of state under Millard Fillmore (1850–52). In 1836 and 1840 he unsuccessfully sought the Whig nomination for president. To the conservatives of New England he was known as "the godlike Daniel." Throughout his long public career he championed national unity, distinguishing himself in the famous Webster-Hayne debate (1830) with these words: "Liberty *and* Union, now and forever, one and inseparable." He died in Marshfield, Massachusetts, on October 24, 1852.

Wightman, Bishop William May (1808–82) was born in Charleston, South Carolina, on January 8, 1808. His father, William, was a native of Charleston; his mother, Matilda May Williams, of Portland, England. It is said that as a child she "had often been dandled on John Wesley's knee." Young William was converted during his student days at Charleston College at the age of sixteen under a sermon preached by future bishop James Osgood Andrew at a camp meeting held at Point Pleasant near Charleston. In 1828, a year after his graduation from college, the South Carolina Conference of the Methodist Episcopal Church admitted him into the itinerant ministry. During the next six years he preached on the Pedee, Orangeburg, Sumter, and Abbeville circuits and in the Charleston and Camden stations. He then became an agent for Randolph-Macon College, a position he held until 1837 when he accepted the chair of English literature in the same institution. Two years later he returned to the work of the regular ministry and served as presiding elder of the Cokesbury District. In 1840 the general conference elected him editor of the *Southern Christian Advocate.* After directing the publication for fourteen years, he became president of Wofford College at Spartanburg, South Carolina, at its opening in 1854. Five years later he was elected president of newly established Southern University in Greensboro, Alabama. In

1866 the general conference elected him bishop, a position he held until his death in the city of his birth on February 15, 1882. As bishop he had a reputation for rooting men of loose morals or erroneous doctrine out of the ministry as soon as possible. "There was a volcano in his breast . . . but with what power of sanctified will he quenched the rising flame, smothered his wrath, and the lion became a lamb."

Wilson, Bishop Alpheus Waters (1834–1916), son of Norval and Cornelia Howland Wilson, was born in Baltimore, Maryland, on February 5, 1834. He was educated at George Washington University, graduating at the age of eighteen. Later he studied law. In 1853 the Baltimore Conference of the Methodist Episcopal Church admitted him on trial and over the next nine years he accepted appointments in Virginia, West Virginia, and Maryland. Because his sympathies were with the South during the Civil War, he and sixty-five other preachers, as a protest against the chapter on slavery placed in the Methodist Episcopal Church *Discipline* in 1860, refused to attend the session of the Baltimore Conference that met at Light Street Church, Baltimore, in March 1862. As a result he and his fellow protesters were dropped from the Conference rolls. Between 1862 and 1870 he resorted to the practice of law in Baltimore to meet his financial obligations. In the meantime, in 1866, he joined the Baltimore Conference of the Methodist Episcopal Church, South. Carried on the roll as a superannuate the first year and as a supernumerary the next three, he returned to the itinerant ranks in 1870 and for the next eight years he preached in Washington, D.C. (1870–73), Mount Vernon Place (1873–77), and Calvary (Baltimore, 1877–78). In 1878 the General Conference elected him Missionary Secretary and during the next four years he attracted attention for his part in stirring the Southern Church to action on behalf of missions. He was elected bishop in 1882 and continued in that office for thirty-two years. As bishop he visited the church's missions in Brazil twice and those in the Orient six times, helping to organize the mission in Japan on one of his trips. He was a close student of the Bible and during the last thirteen years of his life he reportedly read his Greek New Testament through seventy-five times. He was superannuated in 1914 and died two years later in Baltimore on November 21, 1916.

Woolls, James Selby (1812–78) was born in Smyrna, Delaware, on September 22, 1812. He was converted in his youth and at the age of eighteen he was licensed to exhort by the Methodist Church. In 1836 he moved to Louisville, Kentucky; the following year he married Ann Sydnor Gwathmey who bore him one child, T. G. Woolls, who also became a Methodist preacher. After his wife died in 1850 he married Nancy A. Bottorff who bore him three children, two of whom died in infancy and one who died as a young man just two months before Woolls' own death. In 1840 the Kentucky Conference of the Methodist Episcopal Church admitted him on trial into the itinerant ministry and during the next six years he served in the following appointments: Jefferson (Louisville, 1840–41), LaGrange (1841–42), Winchester (1842–44), LaGrange (1844–45), and Logan (1845–46). When the Methodist Church divided in 1846 he joined the Louisville Conference of the Methodist Episcopal Church, South, in which he accepted the following charges: Middletown (1846–48), Hopkinsville (1848–49), Jeffersontown (1849–50), Brook Street (Louisville, 1850–51), Elizabethtown (1851–52), Hopkinsville (1852–53), Bardstown and New Haven (1853–54), Lebanon (1854–55), presiding elder Russellville District (1855–56), presiding elder Hopkinsville District (1856–59), Elkton (1859–60), Logan Circuit (1860–62), presiding elder Bardstown District (1862–66), Twelfth Street (Louisville, 1866–67), City Mission (Louisville, 1867–70), and Henderson (1870–71). In October 1871 the Louisville Conference took serious action against Woolls. In response to question 20 in the conference minutes – "Are all the preachers blameless in their life and official administration?" – one finds this response: "their character all passed, except James S. Woolls, expelled." He was readmitted in 1872 and assigned to Gosport and New Albany (1872–73) and Lebanon (1873–74). He transferred to the

West Texas Conference in the winter of 1875 and preached at the San Antonio City Mission until his death on July 22, 1878. "Whatever misfortunes may have befallen him, he retained the confidence and love of those who knew him best."

Young, Robert A. (1824–1902) was born in Knox County, Tennessee, on January 23, 1824. His father, Captain John Young, graduated from North Carolina University, after which he became a captain in the U.S. Army and fought under Andrew Jackson during the War of 1812. Young Robert spent his early years in farm work and in studying at a district school nearby. He left home at the age of sixteen. Two years later, in 1842, he was converted; in the same year he entered Washington College. After his graduation in 1844 he studied medicine with Dr. Brabson of Rheatown, Tennessee. About this time an impression from childhood that he ought to preach deepened into a positive conviction and he joined the Holston Conference of the Methodist Episcopal Church, South, in September 1845. A year later he transferred to the Tennessee Conference. Over the next six years he held appointments at Cumberland Iron Works (1846–48), Columbia (1848–50), Huntsville (Alabama, 1850–52), and Lebanon (1852–53). In 1853 he transferred to the St. Louis Conference where he accepted the following appointments: First Church (St. Louis, 1853–55), presiding elder St. Louis District (1855–57), and presiding elder Lexington District (1857–60). During his years in St. Louis he also wrote a series of articles for the *Home Circle Magazine,* published in Nashville, Tennes-

see, entitled, "Characters I Have Taken a Pen To." On the eve of the Civil War he transferred back to the Tennessee Conference, preached for a year in Lebanon, and then in 1861 accepted the presidency of Wesleyan College (Florence, Alabama), an institution having a larger enrollment at that time than any other in the South, except the University of Virginia. Three years later he returned to the pastorate and during 1864–74 he preached at Columbia (1864–65), and the following Nashville churches: Tulip Street (1865–66), McKendree (1866–70), and Elm Street (1870–74). In 1874 the Board of Trust of Vanderbilt University elected him financial secretary, a position he held until 1882 when the general conference of the Methodist Episcopal Church, South, elected him secretary of the board of missions; he held the latter office for four years. After spending 1886–87 traveling abroad he accepted the following appointments from the Tennessee Conference: presiding elder Nashville District (1887–90), superannuated (1890–91), Carroll Street (Nashville, 1891–93), superannuated (1893–94), Carroll Street (1894–96), and superannuated (1896–1902). He served for twenty consecutive sessions (1862–81) as secretary of the Tennessee Conference and for twenty-eight years as secretary of the board of trust of Vanderbilt University. Several years before his death he was named a regent of Belmont College in Nashville. He married twice, first in June 1847 to Mary A. Kennon who died in 1879, and then to Mrs. Ann Green Hunter. He died in Nashville in 1902.

Index

This Judith Markham Book is set in Garamond,
which is based on a type designed
by 17th-century printer Jean Jannon.
This type was chosen for its dignity and grace
as well as its antique feel.
The book was typeset on a Mergenthaler Linotron 202/N
by the Photocomposition Department
of Zondervan Publishing House,
Judy Schafer, compositor.
Maps were rendered by Hugh Claycombe.
Printed by Donnelley of Crawfordsville, Indiana.